HARVARD STUDIES
IN COMPARATIVE LITERATURE

HARVARD STUDIES
IN COMPARATIVE LITERATURE

FOUNDED BY

WILLIAM HENRY SCHOFIELD

XVIII

A BIBLIOGRAPHY OF THE

THEOPHRASTAN CHARACTER

IN ENGLISH

WITH

SEVERAL PORTRAIT CHARACTERS

LONDON : GEOFFREY CUMBERLEGE

OXFORD UNIVERSITY PRESS

A BIBLIOGRAPHY OF THE
THEOPHRASTAN CHARACTER
IN ENGLISH
WITH
SEVERAL PORTRAIT CHARACTERS

BY

CHESTER NOYES GREENOUGH

Prepared for Publication by

J. MILTON FRENCH

CAMBRIDGE

HARVARD · UNIVERSITY · PRESS

1947

PRINTED AT THE HARVARD UNIVERSITY PRINTING OFFICE

CAMBRIDGE, MASSACHUSETTS, U.S.A.

CONTENTS

INTRODUCTION

I

HISTORY AND PLAN OF THIS BIBLIOGRAPHY

THIS book attempts to present an adequate bibliography of the English contributions to the type of literature known as the character. It includes both separately published characters and character books, and both Theophrastan and Clarendon (or portrait) types.

The book was planned and the material was largely gathered by the late Chester Noyes Greenough of Harvard University, who died before he had time to put it into final form. Thus the general outline and the selection of titles, with a very few exceptions, are his. The immense amount of research which he was doing on it, like that involved in his elaborate study of the history of English prose fiction, was cut short before he could bring it to its intended conclusion. But it is hoped that the present volume will to some extent fulfill the expectations which he had for it.[1]

Professor Greenough originally planned a history of the character, to which this bibliography was to be attached as an appendix. The history, which was only outlined, is being written by Professor Benjamin Boyce. This will deal principally with characters of the Theophrastan type, whereas in the bibliography Mr. Greenough seems to have decided to include not only all the indubitable characters but also many sketches that lie somewhere on the border line between the character and other literary forms. It is therefore not to be expected that both the bibliography and the history will contain exactly the same items.

Before Mr. Greenough died, he had prepared notes for practically all the titles given in this book. Many of these notes were nearly or entirely complete; but there were many other books which he had not seen. The complete list is so much more extensive than any previous one that it probably offers whatever information is needed for a study of the character. Even before publication it had achieved wide recognition, and Mr. Greenough's preëminent mastery was acknowledged by everyone who knew of his researches.

But the very extent of his findings meant that a great amount of labor was still needed to prepare them for the press. After his death, therefore, and at the invitation of Mrs. Greenough, who had worked devotedly with him, I undertook the preparation of the material for publication. My work has largely consisted of verifying as many of his cards as I could, as he himself would have done, of supplying other editions of works in his list, of selecting the contents when he had not already done so, of searching for titles which he had jotted down but not seen, and of accepting or rejecting them in accordance with the principles on which he had worked, of supplying such bibliographical details as were necessary, of preparing the notes for publication, and of seeing the manuscript through the press. Though I have admitted an occasional title not found in his notes, when it came to my attention and when it seemed unquestionably to satisfy the specifications of the type, I have not considered it my function to enlarge his collection. This book is presented in a form which follows as faithfully as possible his plan.

II

SCOPE

Though Mr. Greenough never expected or even desired absolute completeness, which would be impossible in any case, the number of titles which he and I have personally consulted runs into the thousands. The entire range of titles extends from those which Mr. Greenough saw, and which

---

[1] For more details about his interest in this subject and his work on it, which lasted from the time of his doctoral dissertation to the last years of his life, the reader is referred to Mr. Greenough's *Collected Studies* (Cambridge: 1940) and to Ruth Hornblower Greenough's *Chester Noyes Greenough An Account of his Life as Teacher, Dean, Master & Scholar* (Cambridge: 1940), especially Chapter VI, "Scholar."

are carefully described in Miss Murphy's bibliography, to those of which Mr. Greenough merely caught fleeting glimpses through a bookseller's catalogue. The reader can probably distinguish without much difficulty what their status is according to the amount and detail of information given. There still remain, however, a good many incomplete entries. Those which neither I nor my assistants have seen and checked personally are marked by an asterisk. These are not necessarily in question, though some of them may be. Some are undoubtedly inaccurate and may prove on further examination to be either other titles under garbled forms, parts of other titles, or books which despite their titles have no right to be admitted here at all. When no information beyond the mere title appeared in Mr. Greenough's card file, tracing it was often impossible.

The editor submits these incomplete entries with some trepidation and regret. But there are several legitimate reasons for the lacunae. One is that the war has made it impossible to work in England, where alone many of the books can be found. Similarly, many American libraries have been stored away during the war. Again, when one or more editions of a work have been consulted and when the others presumably contain similar texts, it seemed wasteful to devote undue effort to tracking down comparatively inaccessible copies. Some titles, moreover, taken from secondary sources like the Stationers' Registers, from sale catalogues, or from chance mentions in other books, and therefore of uncertain dependability, could not be located at all. Numerous mimeographed lists of unlocated titles were sent out to a number of libraries by both Mr. Greenough and me in an effort to trace them, and a fair number have been found; others defy search. Finally, when only one number of a periodical appears here, it is a fair guess that other characters would be found if a thorough search of the complete files were made. On the other hand, years of laborious plowing through the dusty volumes of hundreds of forgotten magazines would be necessary for any measure of completeness; and the harvest would be doubtful.

Completeness, in a word, can never be attained. It therefore seems more desirable to issue the work in a reasonable state of achievement rather than to wait for an indefinite period. A live mouse is better than a dead horse; a bibliography in print, which scholars can consult, is worth more than a growingly exhaustive one which is inaccessible. Despite its omissions this book includes an immense amount of material. It is hoped that it may serve as a useful source book and guide to students, especially of English history, literature, economics, and sociology.

III

ARRANGEMENT

The entries in this book are arranged in one continuous chronological list ranging from the earliest in 1495 to the latest in 1941. Approximate dates have been treated, for convenience, as if they were definitely of the year of entry, but a note indicates their status. The entries of the last few years are admittedly sketchy, being limited to a few interesting items which caught the notice of the editor. Within each year the order is alphabetical by authors, and by titles under each author when there are two or more for any one year. Anonymous publications are grouped at the beginning of the year alphabetically under the first important word of their titles. At the end are two additional sections: (1) undated titles, arranged in one alphabetical list, and (2) titles consulted but rejected as not belonging in this book. Last come three indexes: by authors, by titles, and by individual subjects.

The typical entry consists of several parts, though not all of them necessarily appear with every title. These include (1) author, (2) title, (3) brief bibliographical description, (4) contents, if more than one character is present, (5) opening words, if the whole work is a single character, (6) references to other bibliographies when necessary, (7) notes. The original plan was also to give locations of copies of each title, but the need for saving space forced the removal of this section. A few words may be said about each of these parts.

1. *Author*. Wherever possible, even when there is some doubt, works have been ascribed to authors. For this purpose in cases of doubt the editor has depended on the *Cambridge Bibliography of English Literature*, the *Short Title Catalogue*, Halkett and Laing's *Dictionary of Anonymous*

and Pseudonymous English Literature, and ascriptions by catalogues of the British Museum, the Harvard College Library, and the Huntington Library. When the name of the author does not appear on the title page, the notes usually state what authority is followed in making the ascription, and the author's name is enclosed in square brackets. When the names of editors of magazines could be found, they have been given.

2. *Titles*. Titles as given here include only the words which are likely to be of value in this bibliography. The omission of large sections of long titles has saved much space — an urgent factor in a book of this size. But whenever any part has been deleted from the titles, except at the end, the omission is indicated by a row of dots. Without attempting to reproduce the kinds of type used in the title pages, the editor has kept the punctuation of the originals and their use of initial capitals or small letters.

3. *Bibliographical description*. Further to save space, the editor has reduced the bibliographical information to a minimum. The only facts given are the size of the book, the number of pages of text (omitting preface, introduction, index, and the like), the number of volumes or parts, the use of prose or verse, and, in a few instances, peculiarities such as erroneous numbering of pages, use of black letter, and the like. The terms fo, 4°, 8°, etc., indicate, not the size of the page, but the number of leaves in each gathering. The chief purpose of these descriptions is to aid the reader in distinguishing one issue or edition from another.

4. *Contents*. The individual characters contained in the works are listed in the order in which they occur, followed by the page, signature, chapter, or other reference on which each opens. When the same contents are repeated in later editions, the reader is referred back to an earlier edition.

5. *Opening words*. When the work is, as frequently happens, a single character in itself, the first few opening words are quoted as a means of identification.

6. *References*. A few abbreviated references to other bibliographies are given when available. These include the following:

BSC. *Catalogue of the Second & Remaining Portion of the . . . Library formed by the late Rev. Philip Bliss* (London: 1858).
CBEL. *Cambridge Bibliography of English Literature*, 4 vols., ed. F. W. Bateson (Cambridge: 1928).
Murphy. Gwendolen Murphy, *A Bibliography of English Character-Books 1608–1700* (Oxford: 1925).
Pforzheimer. Emma Unger and William A. Jackson, *The Carl H. Pforzheimer Library English Literature, 1475–1700*, 3 vols. (New York: 1940).
STC. A. W. Pollard and G. R. Redgrave, *A Short Title Catalogue* (London: 1926).
Thos. G. K. Fortescue, *Catalogue of the Pamphlets . . . Collected by George Thomason*, 2 vols. (London: 1908).
Watt. Robert Watt, *Bibliotheca Britannica*, 4 vols. (Edinburgh: 1824).

I regret that Donald Wing's new *Short-Title Catalogue . . . 1641–1700* appeared too late to be used for this volume.

7. *Notes*. The notes have been kept at a minimum to conserve space. The few that are used give cross references, offer authority for ascriptions to authors and dates, and mention certain other details. The phrase "Reprinted from 1707" or the like does not mean literally that the printer set up the edition from that of 1707, but that the material included is the same as that in the former edition.

IV

ACKNOWLEDGMENTS

If Professor Greenough had been able to complete his work, he would undoubtedly have wished to thank a number of people publicly for their assistance. It is now impossible to know who they were. It is obvious, however, that such a compilation as this must owe a good deal to the co-operation of many friends and acquaintances. I hope that they will take this anonymous expression of thanks as being the nearest possible substitute.

The present editor wishes to extend his gratitude to the following persons for their kindness in answering queries, checking lists, giving advice, and assisting in research: Professors Douglas Bush, William A. Jackson, Hyder E. Rollins, and George Sherburn, Mr. Roger Scaife, and Mr. David P. French of Harvard University; Mrs. Sidney Gleason of Cambridge, Massachusetts; Dr. Joseph Quincy Adams of the Folger Shakespeare Library; Mr. Leslie E. Bliss of the Henry E. Huntington Library; Dr. John T. Windle and Mr. Stanley Gwynn of the Newberry Library; Mr. David C. Mearns and Mr. Peter V. Weeks of the Library of Congress; Miss Honor McCusker of the Boston Public Library; Dr. Donald Wing and Miss Anne S. Pratt of the Yale University Library; Mrs. Ruth Reed of Pasadena, California; Professor Lambert Ennis of Northwestern University; and Miss Mabel Seymour of New Haven, Connecticut. I am also grateful to Harvard University for a grant in aid of publication from the William H. Schofield Fund.

Above all, I am sure that Mr. Greenough would have wished to single out Mrs. Greenough for particularly heartfelt gratitude for her constant devotion to the end for which he worked and for her unceasing efforts to make available to scholars the valuable results of his many years of research. I should like to be allowed to add my own deep appreciation of her unfailing help and graciousness to me.

J. MILTON FRENCH

Rutgers University
March 7, 1946

A BIBLIOGRAPHY OF THE

THEOPHRASTAN CHARACTER

IN ENGLISH

WITH

SEVERAL PORTRAIT CHARACTERS

BIBLIOGRAPHY OF THE CHARACTER

1495

Bartholomaeus, Anglicus.

De Proprietatibus Rerum. Westminster, W. de Worde, 1495.*

4°.

(1) Of an evil servant (Book VI, chap. 17), (2) The conditions of a good servant (VI, 18), (3) Of a good lord (VI, 19), (4) Of an evil lord or lordship (VI, 20).

Later reprinted. See also Stephen Bateman, 1582.

1510

[Lydgate, John?]

Here begynneth a treatyse of a galaūt. . . . [colophon] Here endeth this treatyse made of a galaunt. Enprynted at London . . . by Wynkyn de Worde.

4°, text sigs. A–A4v. In verse.

Begins: "Ryght as small flodes encrease to Waters fell."

Attributed by the STC to [Lydgate, John?].

1523

Mancinus, Dominicus.

Here begynnyth a treatyse intitulyd the myrrour of good maners conteynynge the .iiii. vertues callyd cardynall compyled in latyn by Domynike Mancyn: And translate into englysshe at the desyre of syr Gyles Alyngton knyght by Alexander Bercley preste and monke of Ely. . . . [colophon] Thus endyth the ryght frutefull matter of the fower Vertues cardynall Impryntyd by me Rychard Pynson prynter vnto the kynges noble grace with his gracyous pryuylege the whiche boke I haue pryntyd at the instāce & request of the ryght noble Rychard yerle Of Kēt.

6°, text sigs. A5v–H7v.

(1) Prudence, (2) Iustice, (3) Magnanamitie, (4) Temperaunce.

Dated [1523?] by the STC.

1533

Plutarch.

Howe one may take profite of his enmyes, translated out of Plutarche. . . . [colophon] Thus endethe the maner to chose and cherysshe a frende, Jmprinted at London in Fletestrete by Thomas Berthelet, printer to the Kynges most noble grace. Cum priuilegio.

8°, text ff. 2–16.

(1) The maner to chose and cherysshe a frende (f. 13v).

Dated [1533?] by the STC. Probably translated by Sir Thomas Elyot.

1547

Baldwin, William.

A treatise of morall phylosophie.*

See [1635?].

1550

Crowley, Robert.

One and thyrtye Epigrams. . . . Compiled and Imprinted by Robert Crowley . . . 1550.

8°, text sigs. A5–E4v.

(1) Brawlers (p. 17).

1560

Palingenius, Marcellus.

The Zodiake of Lyfe. Three Books. 1560.*

See 1588.

1561

Palingenius, Marcellus.

The Zodiake of Lyfe. Six Books. 1561.*

See 1588.

1563

Morice, Ralph.

A Declaration concerning . . . Thomas Cranmer, late archbisshop of Canterbury.*

Manuscript.

(1) Cranmer (fol. 405).

Corpus Christi College, Cambridge (MS. 128).

1565

[Awdeley, John.]

The Fraternity of Vagabonds. . . . London, Printed for J. Awdely . . . 1565.*

See 1575.

A unique copy, consisting of a fragment of the title page only, is in the Bodleian.

Lemnius, Levinus.

The Touchstone of Complexions. London, Printed by T. Marsh, 1565.*

See 1581.

Palingenius, Marcellus.

The Zodiake of Lyfe. 1565.*

See 1588.

1567

Harman, Thomas.

A Caueat or Warening for commen cvrsetors, vvlgarely called Vagabones, set forth by Thomas Harman. Esquiere. for the vtilite and proffyt of his naturall Cuntrey. Augmented and enlarged by the fyrst author here of. . . . Imprinted at London . . . by Wylliam Gryffith . . . 1567.

4°, text sigs. B2–H3v.

(1) A ruffler (sig. B2), (2) A upright man (sig. B2v), (3) A hoker or angglear (sig. B4v), (4) A roge (sig. C1), (5) A wylde roge (sig. C3), (6) A prygger of prauncers (sig. C3v), (7) A pallyard (sig. C4), (8) A frater (sig. C4v), (9) A abraham man (sig. D4), (10) A freshe water mariner or whipiacke (sig. D2), (11) A counterfet cranke (sig. D3), (12) A dommerar (sig. E1), (13) A dronken tinckar (sig. E4), (14) A swadder or pedler (sig. E2), (15) A jacke man, and a patrico (sig. E2), (16) A demaunder for glymmar (sig. E2v), (17) A bawdy basket (sig. E4), (18) A autem mort (sig. F), (19) A walking mort (sig. F), (20) A doxe (sig. F4v), (21) A dell (sig. F4v), (22) A kynchin morte (sig. F4v), (23) A kynchin co (sig. F4v), (24) Their vsage in the night (sig. F4v).

BSC 2126. Pforzheimer, II, 445.

This is the second edition. The first, issued also in 1567, is substantially identical. Many of the characters are taken with little change from Awdeley's Fraternitye of Vacabondes, 1565.

Lemnius, Levinus.

The Touchstone of Complexions. London, Printed by T. Marsh, 1567.*

See 1581.

1569

Agrippa, Henry Cornelius.

Henrie Cornelius Agrippa, of the Vanitie and vncertaintie of Artes and Sciences, Englished by Ja. San. Gent. . . . Imprinted at London, by Henry Wykes . . . 1569.

4°, text ff. 1–187v. In black letter.

(1) Of the magistrates of the churche (f. 87v), (2) Of the sectes of monkes (f. 90v), (3) Of kingly or courtly government (f. 110v), (4) Of the nobles of the courte (f. 112), (5) Of the common meane courtiers (f. 113v), (6) Of the women of the courte (f. 115v), (7) Of marchaundise (f. 117), (8) Of treasourership (f. 119), (9) Of nobilitie (f. 127).

1570

Ascham, Roger.

The Scholemaster Or plaine and perfite way of teachyng children . . . the Latin tong . . .
By Roger Ascham. An. 1570. At London, Printed by Iohn Daye.

4°, text ff. 1–67.

(1) Εὐφυής, apte to learning (f. 7v), (2) Μνήμων, good of memorie (f. 8), (3) Φιλομαθής, giuen to loue learning (f. 8v), (4) Φιλόπονος, that hath a lust to labor (f. 8v), (5) Φιλήκοος, that is glad to heare and learne (f. 9), (6) Ζητητικός, that is naturallie bolde to aske any question (f. 9), (7) Φιλέπαινος, that loueth to be praised for well doing (f. 9).

Pforzheimer No. 15.

Mancinus, Dominicus.

The Mirrour of Good Maners Conteining The Foure Cardinal Vertues. Compiled In Latin By Dominike Mancin, And Translated Into English By Alexander Barclay. . . . An. Do. 1570.*

See Mancinus's Here begynnyth . . . the myrrour [1523?].

1571

Ascham, Roger.

The Scholemaster . . . By Roger Ascham. ¶An. 1571. ¶At London. Printed by Iohn Daye.

4°, text ff. 1–67 (misprinted 66).

(1–7) as in 1570.

There were three editions of this year (STC 833–4–5). The Pforzheimer Catalogue (No. 15), however, calls No. 833 a "made-up copy of No. 832."

Chelidonius, Tigurinus.

A most excellent Hystorie, Of the Institution and firste beginning of Christian Princes, and the Originall of Kingdomes: Wherunto is annexed a treatise of Peace and Warre, and another of the dignitie of Mariage. . . . First written in Latin by Chelidonius Tigurinus, after translated into French by Peter Bouaisteau of Naunts in Brittaine, and now englished by Iames Chillester, Londoner. . . . At London, Printed by H. Bynneman . . . 1571.

4°, text pp. 15–199.

(1) Peace (p. 156).

Poor example of character.

1573

Harman, Thomas.

A Caueat of Warening for Common Cursetors, vulgarely called Vagabones, set forth by Thomas Harman, esquier, for the vtilitie and profit of his naturall Country. Augmented and enlarged by the first Author hereof. Whereunto is added the tale of the second taking of the counterfet Crank . . . Newly

Imprinted. Anno 1573. . . . [colophon] Jmprinted at London by Henry Middleton . . . An. 1573.

4°, text sigs. Bv–H3.

(1–24) as in 1567.

The title page of the Huntington copy, the only one listed in the STC, is mutilated.

Tusser, Thomas.

Five hundred pointes of good husbandrie. 1573.*

See 1580.

There were three editions in 1573 (STC 24375–6–7), and numerous later reprints, of which only that of 1580 is included, as being representative of the others, in this volume.

1574

Guevara, Antonio de.

The Familiar Epistles of Sir Antony of Guevara. Translated out of the Spanish toung by E. Hellows. London, Printed by H. Middleton for R. Newbery, 1574.*

See [1575?].

1575

Agrippa, Henry Cornelius.

Henrie Cornelius Agrippa, of the Vanitie and vncertaintie of Artes and Sciences: Englished by Ia. San. Gent. . . . Imprinted at London, by Henrie Bynneman . . . Anno. 1575.

4°, text ff. 1–187v.

(1–9) as in 1569.

Awdeley, John.

The Fraternitye of Vacabondes . . . Whereunto also is adioyned the .xxv. Orders of Knaues . . . Imprinted at London by Iohn Awdeley . . . 1575.*

4°, text ff. 2–9v.

(1) An abraham man (f. 2), (2) A ruffeler (f. 2), (3) A prygman (f. 2), (4) A whipiacke (f. 2), (5) A frater (f. 2), (6) A quire bird (f. 2), (7) An upright man (f. 2v), (8) A curtall (f. 2v), (9) A palliard (f. 2v), (10) An Irishe toyle (f. 2v), (11) A jack man (f. 3), (12) A swygman (f. 3), (13) A washman (f. 3), (14) A tinkard (f. 3), (15) A wylde roge (f. 3), (16) A kitchen co (f. 3), (17) A kitchen mortes (f. 3), (18) Doxies (f. 3), (19) A patriarke co (f. 3), (20) A curtesy man (f. 3v), (21) A cheatour or fingerer (f. 4v), (22) A ring faller (f. 6).

For lack of access to the original edition, the above information is taken from the 1869 reprint. First published in 1565.

Fenton, Sir Geoffrey.

Golden Epistles, Contayning varietie of discourse both Morall, Philosophicall, and Diuine . . . By Geffray Fenton . . . Imprinted at London by Henry Middleton, for Rafe Newbery . . . 1575.

8°, text ff. 1–200.

(1–10) as in Guevara's Familiar Epistles [1775?].

Guevara, Antonio de.

The Familiar Epistles of Sir Antony of Gueuara . . . Translated out of the Spanish toung, by Edward Hellows . . . Printed at London for Raufe Newberg. [1575?]

4°, text pp. 1–513. Black letter.

(1) A furious man, (2) Old men, (3) A friend, (4) True love, (5) A true lover, (6) Queen Zenobia, (7) An old man, (8) An envious man, (9) The couetous man, (10) An angry man.

Dated [1575?] by the STC. Much of the material is reproduced in Geoffrey Fenton's Golden Epistles, 1575.

1576

[Fulwell, Ulpian.]

The First Parte of the Eyghth liberall Science entituled Ars Adulandi. . . . London, Printed by W. Hoskins, 1576.*

4°.

See 1579.

The only copy listed in the STC is in the British Museum.

[Innocent III, Pope.]

The Mirror of Mans lyfe. Plainely describing, VVhat weake moulde we are made of: what miseries we are subiect vnto: howe vncertaine this life is: and what shal be our ende. Englished by H.K. . . . Imprinted at London, by Henry Bynneman. 1576.

8°, text sigs. B–K7.

(1) The Ladie Compton (sig. ¶8v), (2) A couetous man (sig. Fv), (3) The ambitious man (sig. F8), (4) A proud man (sig. G3), (5) Arrogante men (sig. G8).

Ascribed to Pope Innocent III and the translation to Henry Kerton (or Kirton), by the STC. There was another edition in the same year (STC 14093).

La Place, Pierre de.

A Treatise of the Excellencie of a Christian Man, and How he may be Knowne. London, C. Barker. 1576.*

See 1589.

Palingenius, Marcellus.

The Zodiake of Lyfe. 1576.*

See 1588.

[Rogers, Thomas.]

A philosophicall discourse, Entituled, The Anatomie of the minde. Nevvlie made and

set forth by T.R. Imprinted at London by
I.C. for Andrew Maunsell . . . 1576.

8°, text ff. 1–206.

(1) Of Ilwyll (f. 4v), (2) Of prodigalitie (f. 9v),
(3) Of lust (f. 11v), (4) Wicked or lustful love
(f. 21v), (5) Longing (f. 24v), (6) Of dreade
(f. 31v), (7) Of feerefulnesse (f. 35v), (8) Of
enuie (f. 44v), (9) Of molestation and affliction
(f. 60v), (10) Of the goodes of fortune (f. 64v),
(11) Of contemplation (f. 82), (12) Of reason
(f. 89), (13) Temperate man (f. 110v), (14) Of
magnanimitie (f. 140), (15) Celestiall justice
(f. 161v), (16) Naturall justice (f. 162), (17)
Judiciall justice (f. 165), (18) Of innocencie (f.
166), (19) Notes of unfained frendship (f. 177,
misprinted 179).

The dedication is signed Tho. Rogers.

1577

Anonymous.

The Pourtraiture of a trusty servaunt. 1577.*

Arber, Stationers' Registers, II, 309.
Licensed to Henry Bamford, March 4, 1576/7,
and sold to him by William Hoskins; later assigned to Richard Jones on March 3, 1577/8.

Fenton, Sir Geoffrey.

Golden Epistles, Conteyning varietie of discourse, both Morall, Philosophicall, and
Diuine: gathered, as well out of the remayn-
der of Gueuaraes woorkes, as other Authours,
Latine, French, and Italian. By Geffrey Fenton. Newly corrected and amended. . . . Imprinted at London for Raph Newberie . . .
1577.

8°, text ff. 1–185.

(1–10) as in 1575.

Grange, John.

The Golden Aphroditis . . . by John Grange
. . . At London Anno. 1577. . . . [colophon]
Imprinted at London by Henry Bynneman.

4°, text sigs. C–S4v.

(1) The paynting of a curtizan (sig. O4v).

Guevara, Antonio de.

The Familiar Epistles . . . London, Printed
for R. Newberrie . . . 1577.*

See [1575?].

[Innocent III, Pope.]

The Mirror of Mans Lyfe. 1577.*

See 1576.

The only copy listed in the STC is in the Bodleian.

La Place, Pierre de.

A Treatise of the Excellencie of a Christian

Man, and How he may be Known. London,
Printed by C. Barker, 1577.*

See 1589.

1579

Ascham, Roger.

The Scholemaster.*

See 1570.

Not in STC. Pforzheimer Catalogue No. 15. Book Prices
Current, 1909, 1910.

[Cheeke, Henry.]

The Forrest of Fancy. Wherein Is Conteined
Very prety Apothegmes, . . . VVith sundry
other deuises . . . Imprinted at London by
Thomas Purfoote . . . 1579.

4°, text sigs. Bv–U4v.

(1) Perfecte friendship (sig. C2v), (2) Pacience
(sig. F4v).

Signed (sig. U4v) H.C. Attributed to Henry Cheeke by
the CBEL. There were two editions in 1579 (STC 4271
and 4271a), of which the present is the second.

Fulwell, Ulpian.

The First Parte, Of The Eyghth liberall Science: Entituled, Ars adulandi, The Arte of
Flatterie . . . deuised and compiled, by Vl-
pian Fulwell. Newly corrected and augmented. . . . Imprinted at London, by Rich-
arde Jones . . . 1579.

4°, text sigs. Bv–Kv. In black letter.

(1) Ihon the Baptist (sig. D4v), (2) Pierce Pickthanke, a religious dissembler (sigs. Fv and F2),
(3) Drunken Dickon, a roisterer (sigs. Fv and
F2), (4) A faithful friend, Edmund Harmon
(sig. G2, in verse, the name spelled acrostically).

There are two characters of Pierce Pickthanke, one by
Drunken Dickon and the other by the author; and, similarly, two of Drunken Dickon, one by Pierce Pickthanke,
and the other by the author.

[Hake, Edward.]

Newes out of Powles Churchyarde. . . .
Otherwise entituled, syr Nummus. VVritten
in English Satyrs. . . . Compyled by E.H.
Gent. . . . [colophon] Imprinted at London
by John Charlewood, and Richard Ihones.

8°, text sigs. B–H8.

(1) The clergie (sig. B2v), (2) Men of lawe (sig.
B4v), (3) Judges (sig. B5), (4) Practisers at the
law (sig. B6v), (5) Attorneys (sig. B8), (6)
Phisitians (sig. C2v), (7) Apothecaries and Sur-
geons (sig. C7v), (8) Marchaunt men (sig. C8),
(9) Banckrowtes (sig. D7), (10) Fooles and roy-
sters (sig. D8v), (11) Gentlemen (sig. E7v), (12)
Userers (sig. Fv), (13) Bawdes (sig. F8).

The Dedication is signed Edw. Hake.

1580

[Cheeke, Henry.]

The Forest of Fancy; Wherein is contained very pretty apothegms and pleasant histories, both in meeter and prose . . . By H.C. London, 1580.*

4°.

Not in STC.

Taken from Halkett and Laing. If correct, this title must be a reprint of 1579.

Fulwell, Ulpian.

The first part of the eyghth liberalle science. Newly corrected. London, Printed by R. Jones.*

See 1579.

Dated [1580?] by the STC. The only copy listed is in the British Museum.

[Lupton, Thomas.]

Sivqila. Too good, to be true . . . Herein is shewed by waye of Dialogue, the wonderful maners of the people of Mauqsun . . . Printed at London by H. Bynneman . . . 1580.

4°, text pp. 1–178.

(1) Drunkennesse (p. 55), (2) Diceplay (p. 96, erroneously numbered 70), (3) Usurie (p. 146).

The dedication is signed Thomas Lvpton.

The only copy listed by the STC is at Huntington.

Tusser, Thomas.

Fiue hundred pointes of good Husbandrie . . . newly augmented to a fourth part more . . . by Thomas Tusser . . . London, Printed by Henrie Denham . . . 1580.

4°, text fols. 7–89.

(1) An enuious and naughtie neighbour (f. 61).

1581

Lemnius, Levinus.

The Touchstone of Complexions . . . Contayning Most easy rules . . . whereby every one may . . . knowe . . . the inclinations, affections, motions, and desires of his Mynde inwardly. Fyrst wrytten in Latine, by Leuine Lemnie, and now Englished by Thomas Newton . . . London . . . by Thomas Marsh. Anno 1581.

8°, text ff. 1–156.

(1) A sanguyne man (f. 87), (2) Persons phlegmatick (f. 111), (3) A cholerick person (f. 127), (4) A melancholique person (f. 135).

[Thimelthorpe, C.]

A Short Inuentory of a certayne Idle Inuentions The fruites of a close and secret Garden of great ease, and litle pleasure. By C.T. Imprinted At London . . . by Thomas Marsh. 1581.

8°, text fols. 2v–68.

(1) The kinge (f. 62), (2) The byshop (f. 62v), (3) The husbandman (f. 63), (4) The phisition (f. 63v), (5) The light woman (f. 64).

Attributed to Thimelthorpe by the Huntington Library Catalogue.

Not in STC. Huntington Supplement, No. 23952+. The Huntington copy is the only one known.

1582

Bateman, Stephen.

Batman vppon Bartholome, His Booke De Proprietatibus Rerum, Newly corrected, enlarged and amended. . . . 1582. . . . London Imprinted by Thomas East. . . .

6°, text ff. 1–426v.

(1) An euill seruant (Book VI, chap. 17 [misnumbered 16]), (2) A good seruant (VI, 18), (3) A good lord (VI, 19), (4) An euill lord or lordship (VI, 20).

See Bartholomaeus, Anglicus, 1495.

Fenton, Sir Geoffrey.

Golden Epistles . . . By Geffray Fenton. Newly Corrected . . . Imprinted at London by Ralph Newberie . . . 15 Octobris 1582.

8°, text pp. 1–347. Black letter.

(1–10) as in 1575.

1584

Anonymous.

The mirrour of friendship: both hovv to knovve a Perfect friend, and hovv to choose him. . . . Translated out of Italian into English by Thomas Breme Gentleman. Imprinted at London by Abel Ieffes . . . 1584.

8°, text sigs. B1–D4v.

(1) A perfect friend (sig. Biii, marginal gloss).

Not in STC. Huntington Supplement, 17978+. The Huntington copy is the only one known.

Guevara, Antonio de.

The Familiar Epistles of sir Antonio of Gueuara . . . Translated out of the Spanish tongue, by Edward Hellowes . . . At London, Printed by Ralph Newberie anno salutis, 1584.

8°, text pp. 1–347.

(1–10) as in [1575?].

The colophon is dated 1582.

[Lupton, Thomas.]

Sivqvila. Too Good to be True. 1584.*

See 1580.

The only copy listed by the STC is in the Bodleian.

1585

La Place, Pierre de.

A treatise of the excellencie of a Christian man, and how he may be knowne: written in French by M. Peter de la Place. 1585.*

See 1589.

There is some doubt about the existence of this edition, which is not mentioned in the STC.

1586

[Innocent III, Pope.]

The Mirror of Mans Lyfe. 1586.*

See 1576.

The Harmsworth copy is the only one mentioned by the STC.

1587

Anonymous.

A Picture of a Younge Man and a Nurse. 1587.*

Arber, Stationers' Registers, II, 475.

Apparently two titles, that of a nurse being distinct from that of a young man. They are entered as printed by John Wolf on September 11, 1587.

[Lupton, Thomas.]

Sivqila. Too good, to be true . . . Herein is shewed by way of Dialogue, the wonderfull maners of the people of Mauqsun . . . Imprinted at London by Abel Ieffe . . . 1587.

4°, text pp. 1–175. Black letter.

(1–3) as in 1580.

Rankins, William.

A Mirrovr of Monsters: Wherein is plainely described the manifold vices, & spotted enormities, that are caused by the infectious sight of Playes, with the description of the subtile slights of Sathan, making them his instruments. Compiled by Wil. Rankins. . . . At London Printed by I.C. for T.H. in Anno. Do. 1587.

4°, text ff. 1–24v.

(1) Queen Elizabeth (f. 1v), (2) Monsters [players] (f. 2), (3) Flatterie (f. 10v), (4) Ingratitude (f. 14), (5) Dissention (f. 18).

1588

Palingenius, Marcellus [P. A. Manzolli].

The Zodiake of life, written by . . . Marcellus Palingenius Stellatus . . . Translated out of Latine into English, by Barnabie Googe and by him newly recognised . . . Imprinted at London by Robert Robinson . . . 1588.

8°, text pp. 1–242. In verse.

(1) A true Christian (p. 7), (2) A rich man (p. 12), (3) A good wife (p. 73), (4) A comparison between a wife and a harlot (p. 74), (5) A gentleman (p. 90), (6) A man in infancy, youth, and manhood (p. 100), (7) A man guided by reason (p. 144), (8) A covetous man (p. 153), (9) Machivels or worldlings (p. 170), (10) Fooles (p. 170), (11) Mad men (p. 172).

The STC records nine editions in Latin.

1589

Ascham, Roger.

The Schoolemaster. Or, Playne and perfite way of teaching Children . . . the Latin toong . . . By Roger Ascham. At London, Printed by Abell Ieffes, Anno. 1589.

4°, text ff. 1–63 (misprinted 60).

(1–7) as in 1570.

[Dorke, Walter.]

A Tipe Or Figure of Friendship. Wherein is liuelie, and compendiouslie expressed, the right nature and propertie of a perfect and true friend. Also a conclusion at the end in the praise of Friendship. Written by W.D. . . . Imprinted at London by Thomas Orwin and Henry Kirkham, 1589.

4°, text sigs. A3–B2v.

(1) Friendship (sig. Bv).

The Dedication is signed Walter Dorke.
Not in the STC. Huntington Supplement, No. 7060+.
The only known copy is at Huntington.

Greene, Robert.

The Spanish Masqverado. . . . By Robert Greene, in Artibvs Magister. . . . Printed at London, by Roger Ward, for Thomas Cadman, 1589.*

4°.

(1) The Pope, (2) Philip, king of Spaine, (3) The cardinals of Rome, (4) The cleargie of Spaine, (5) The rest of the rascal rabble of the Romish church, (6) The nobilitie of Spaine, (7) The Duke of Medina, (8) Don Martines de Ricaldo, (9) Don Pedro de Valdes, (10) The princes, noble men, and other men of name, (11) The vice-gerentes of his Indies, (12) The common souldiours.

Border-line examples of character. The above description is taken from Grosart's edition of Greene, 1881–83.

La Place, Pierre de.

A Treatise of the Excellencie of a Christian man, and how he may be knowen. Written in French by Maister Peter de La Place . . . Whereunto is adioyned a briefe description of the life and death of the said Author . . . Translated into English by L. Tomson. . . .

Imprinted at London by Thomas Dawson for Christopher Barker ... Anno. 1589.

8°, text sigs. B7v–I3v.

(1) A Christian (sig. G6).

Not in STC. Huntington Supplement 15232+. The only known copy is at Huntington.

1590

Anonymous.

The Cobler of Cannterburie. London: Printed for R. Robinson, 1590.*

(1) Eight orders of cuckolds, (2) The gentleman, in verse, (3) The scholar, in verse, (4) The old woman, (5) The summoner.

The only copy listed by the STC is in the Bodleian.
A reprint of 1630 bears the title The Tincker of Turvey.

1591

Breton, Nicholas.

Brittons Bowre Of Delights. Contayning Many, most delectable and fine deuices, of rare Epitaphes, pleasant poems, Pastorals and Sonets By N.B. Gent. ... Imprinted at London by Richard Ihones ... 1591.

4°, text sigs. A–G4.

(1) S[ir]. P[hilip]. S[idney]. (sig. A), (2) A noble gentleman (sig. C3).

The only copy listed by the STC is at Huntington.

Spenser, Edmund.

Complaints Containing Sundrie Small Poemes Of The Worlds Vanitie ... By Ed. Sp. ... London Imprinted For VVilliam Ponsonbie ... 1591.

4°, text sigs. B–Z3v. In verse.

(1) A brave courtier (sig. O2).

Pforzheimer No. 968.

The courtier was probably Sir Philip Sidney.

1592

[Greene, Robert.]

Greenes Vision: Written at the instant of his death. Conteyning a penitent passion for the folly of his Pen. ... Imprinted at London for Thomas Newman ... [1592.]

4°, text sigs. B–H4.

(1) Sir Geffery Chawcer (sig. C, in verse), (2) Iohn Gower (sig. C), (3) Alexanders sentences in his Lunacie, against beautie (sig. F2v), (4) The ould mans description of iealousie (sig. F3v), (5) Salomon (sig. H2, in verse).

Attributed to Greene by the STC.

[Harman, Thomas.]

The Groundworke of Conny-catching; the manner of their Pedlers-French, and the meanes to vnderstand the same, with the cunning slights of the Counterfeit Cranke. ... Done by a Justice of Peace of great authoritie, who hath had the examinuig of diuers of them. ... Printed at London by Iohn Danter for William Barley ... 1592.

8°, text sigs. B–F4v.

(1–24) as in A Caveat, 1567, (25) The visiter (sig. A4), (26) A shifter (sig. Av).

Pforzheimer, II, 444.

The Huntington copy bears no imprint. Attributed to Harman by the STC.

Nash, Thomas.

Pierce Penilesse his Supplication to the Diuell. Describing the ouer-spreading of Vice and suppression of Vertue. ... Written by Thomas Nash Gentleman. ... London, Imprinted by Richard Ihones ... 1592.

4°, text ff. 1–40v. Black letter.

(1) The nature of an upstart (f. 6v), (2) The counterfeit polititian (f. 7), (3) The prodigall yoong master (f. 7v), (4) The pride of the learned (f. 8), (5) The pride of the marchants wiues [Mistress Minx] (f. 8v), (6) The pride of the peasants (f. 8v), (7) The pride of the Spaniard (f. 10), (8) The pride of the Italian (f. 10), (9) The pride of the Frenchman (f. 10v), (10) The pride of the Dane (f. 10v).

There were two other editions of the same year: (1) STC 18372, printed by A. Jeffes for J. Busbie; (2) STC 18373, printed by A. Jeffes for J. B.

Tymme, Thomas.

A Plaine Discouerie of ten English Lepers, verie noisome and hurtfull to the Church and common wealth: Setting before our eies the iniquitie of these latter dayes ... Published by Thomas Timme Minister. London Printed by Peter Short ... 1592.

4°, text sigs. A4–M4v.

(1) The proud or ambitious man (sig. F).

1593

Harvey, Gabriel.

Pierces Supererogation Or A New Prayse Of The Old Asse. ... Gabriell Haruey ... London, Imprinted by Iohn VVolfe. 1593.

4°, text pp. 1–220 (misprinted 120).

(1) Andrew Perne (p. 194).

Pforzheimer No. 452.

Nash, Thomas.

Pierce Penilesse his Supplication to the Diuell. London, Printed by A. Jeffes for J. B. 1593.*

See 1592.

The only copy listed by the STC is at the British Museum.

1594

Anonymous.

The Good Shepherd and the Bad.*

Arber, Term Catalogues, II, 651.

Willobie His Avisa. Or The true Picture of
a modest Maid, and of a chast and constant
wife. . . . Imprinted at London by Iohn Windet. 1594.*

4°, text ff. 1–65.

(1) Avisa (p. 4).

Pforzheimer No. 1068.

The prefatory sections are signed Hadrian Dorrell. A poor
example of character.

Huarte Navarro, Juan de Dios.

Examen de Ingenios. The Examination of
mens Wits. . . . By John Huarte. . . . Englished . . . by R.C. Esquire. . . . London,
Printed by Adam Islip, for C. Hunt of Exces-
ter. 1594.

8°, text pp. 1–333.

(1) Jesus Christ, by Publius Lentulus (p. 258).

The STC records two other editions of the same year:
(1) 13890, printed by Adam Islip for R. Watkins; (2)
13891, printed by Adam Islip for T. Man. The translator
is said by the CBEL to have been Richard Carew. Publius
Lentulus was probably an imaginary person, and the
character is probably a forgery of the fifteenth century.

La Marche, Olivier de.

The Resolved Gentleman. Translated out of
Spanishe into Englyshe, by Lewes Lewkenor
Esquier. . . . Imprinted at London, by Rich-
ard Watkins. 1594.

4°, text ff. 1–53.

(1) The vertuous Austrian prince (f. 36v), (2)
Ferdinand of Spain (f. 37v), (3) Maximilian of
Austria (f. 38), (4) Henry VIII (f. 41).

Attributed to La Marche by the STC.

Lipsius, Justus.

Sixe Bookes Of Politickes Or Civil Doctrine,
Written In Latine by Iustus Lipsius: which
doe especially concerne Principalitie. Done
into English by William Iones Gentleman.
. . . At London, Printed by Richard Field for
William Ponsonby. 1594.

4°, text pp. 1–207 (erroneously numbered 107).

(1) Humane prudence (p. 66), (2) The common
people (p. 68).

Nash, Thomas.

The Vnfortvnate Traveller. Or, The Life of
Iacke Wilton. . . . Tho. Nashe. London,
Printed by T. Scarlet for C. Burby . . . 1594.

4°, text sigs. B–O4.

(1) A magnifico's wife (sig. G3v), (2) Petro
Aretino (sig. H).

Reprinted again the same year and several times later.

1595

[Lodge, Thomas.]

A fig for Momus: Containing Pleasant Varietie, included in Satyres, Eclogues, and Epistles,
by T.L. of Lincolnes Inne Gent. . . . At London Printed for Clement Knight . . . 1595.

4°, text sigs. B–I3v.

(1) A covetous man (sig. E3).

Pforzheimer No. 617.

The dedication is signed (sig. A2v) Thomas Lodge.

Nash, Thomas.

Pierce Penilesse his Supplication to the Diuell.
London, Printed by T.C. for N. Ling. 1595.*

See 1592.

**Ovid [Publius Ovidius Naso], [Marlowe, Chris-
topher, and Davies, Sir John].**

All Ovids Elegies: 3. Bookes. By C.M. Epigrams by J.D. . . . At Middlebovrgh.

8°, text sigs. A2–F8v.

(1) Of a gull (sig. F), (2) Rvfus the courtier
(sig. F), (3) Qvintus the dancer (sig. Fv), (4)
Faustus, who always rides (sig. Fv), (5) Liber
the rake (sig. F2), (6) Medon a rich ass (sig. F2),
(7) Severus the Puritan (sig. F2v), (8) Cosmus
whose thoughts outrun his words (sig. F3), (9)
Dogged Cineas (sig. F3), (10) Geron of the un-
usual memory (sig. F3v), (11) Ciprius the new-
fangled (sig. F4), (12) Gallus the boaster (sig.
F4), (13) Gella a filthy wench (sig. F4v), (14)
Silla the cowardly lecher (sig. F5), (15) Dacus
the wretched poetaster (sig. F5), (16) Crassus
the liar (sig. F6v), (17) Philo the doctor (sig.
F6v), (18) Fvscus the playboy (sig. F7), (19)
Pvblius the law student (sig. F7v), (20) A gull
(sig. F8).

Pforzheimer No. 641.

The poems given above are the work of Sir John Davies.
There were several editions of this work between about
1595 and about 1640. The bibliography is so confused
that they are here all grouped under one heading. The
STC lists the following:

1. 6350. Epigrammes and elegies by J.D. and C.M.
(Certaine of Ovids elegies.) 2 pts. 12°. Middleborough.
[1590?]. British Museum, Bodleian (part 1 only), Huntington.

2. [18930a, not numbered]. Certaine of Ouids elegies.
[1595?, 1598?]. 8°. (part 2 of the preceding; two editions.) British Museum, Huntington.

3. 18931. Ouids elegies. [n.d.] 8°. Bodleian.

4. 18931a. All Ouids elegies. [n.d.] 8°. Bodleian (2
issues), Huntington.

5. 18932. All Ouids elegies. [1635?]. 8°. British
Museum.

6. 18933. All Ouids elegies. [1640?]. 8°. British
Museum, Bodleian, Emmanuel College Cambridge, Huntington, Clawson.

7. 18938. Ovid de Ponto. Containing four books of elegies. Trans. by W.S. 1639. 8°. British Museum, Bodleian, Emmanuel College Cambridge, Huntington.

8. 18939. Ovid de Ponto. Second edition, 8°. 1640. British Museum, Bodleian, Cambridge, Huntington.

9. 18981. P. Ovid de tristibus. Tr. Z. Catlin, etc. 1639. 8°. British Museum, Bodleian, Cambridge, Huntington, Newberry.

The Pforzheimer Catalogue mentions five editions dated 1639 or 1640.

The CBEL mentions four editions of All Ovids Elegies [1595?–1640], two of Certaine Elegies [1595?–1640], and one of Epigrammes and Elegies [n.d.]. All contain the same characters, though the paging differs somewhat.

1596

Huarte Navarro, Juan de Dios.

Examen de Ingenios. The Examination of mens Wits. . . . By John Huarte. . . . Englished . . . by R.C. Esquire. . . . London, Printed by Adam Islip. 1596.

8°, text pp. 1–333.
(1) as in 1594.

[Lodge, Thomas.]

VVits Miserie, and the VVorlds Madnesse: Discouering the Deuils Incarnat of this Age. . . . London, Printed by Adam Islip, and are to be sold by Cutbert Burby . . . 1596.

4°, text pp. 1–111.
(1) Vainglory (p. 3), (2) Ambition (p. 5), (3) Boasting (p. 8), (4) Curiosity (p. 11), (5) Fashion (p. 14), (6) Ingratitude (p. 15), (7) Scandal and Detraction (p. 17), (8) Adulation (p. 20), (9) Contempt (p. 23), (10) Usury (p. 26), (11) The broker (p. 32), (12) A lie-monger, or lying traveller (p. 35), (13) A bawd (p. 37), (14) A dishonest gamester (p. 40), (15) The covetous man (p. 43), (16) A lecherous man (p. 46), (17) An adulterer (p. 49), (18) A detractor (p. 53), (19) An envious man (p. 55), (20) A brawler (p. 62), (21) A blasphemer (p. 65), (22) A seditious man (p. 67), (23) An impatient man (p. 72), (24) A drunkard (p. 78), (25) A jester (p. 84), (26) An intelligencer (p. 85), (27) Desperation (p. 88), (28) A solven (p. 88).
Pforzheimer No. 623.

The dedication and the address to the reader are signed T.L. Some copies (e.g., one in the Bodleian) read Wils Miserie.

1597

Breton, Nicholas.

Brittons Bowre Of Delights. . . . By N.B. Gent. . . . Imprinted at London by Richard Ihones . . . 1597.*

4°, text sigs. A–F4.
(1) as in 1591.

The above information has been taken from Hyder E. Rollins's edition of 1933, which reproduces the title page. Apparently the second character in the edition of 1591 is not repeated here.

Breton, Nicholas.

The Wil Of Wit . . . Containing fiue discourses . . . Compiled by Nicholas Breton . . . London, Printed by Thomas Creede, 1597.

4°, text ff. 1–76.
(1) Beautie (f. 21v), (2) Riches (f. 22), (3) Honour (f. 22v), (4) Vertue (f. 23), (5) Friendship (f. 23v), (6) Loue (f. 23v), (7) Time (f. 24), (8) Nemo (f. 24).

[Hall, Joseph.]

Virgidemiarvm, Sixe Bookes. First three Bookes, Of Tooth-lesse Satyrs. . . . London Printed by Thomas Creede, for Robert Dexter, 1597.

8°, text pp. 1–67. In verse.
(1) Lawyers (p. 33), (2) Physicians (p. 36), (3) Tutors (p. 41).
Pforzheimer, II, 437.

Attributed to Hall by the CBEL and included in his Works, 1625 ff. There were two slightly variant editions in 1597. No copy dated 1597 and containing six books is known.

1598

Bastard, Thomas.

Chrestoleros. Seuen bookes of Epigrames written by T.B. . . . Imprinted at London by Richard Bradocke for I.B. . . . 1598.

8°, text pp. 1–184. In verse.
(1) Matho the wisher (p. 10), (2) Fortune (p. 47), (3) Melus the dull scholar (p. 96), (4) Dacus a miser (p. 119), (5) Cophus, careless of life (p. 121), (6) Lotus, of poor memory (p. 123), (7) Merus, a materialist (p. 127), (8) Robert Williams, a true friend (p. 144), (9) Matho the lover (p. 158, misprinted 185), (10) Misus the covetous (p. 166).

The dedication is signed Thomas Bastard.

Greenham, Richard.

The Description of a Righteous Man, upon Genesis 8. 1598.*

Arber, Stationers' Registers, III, 108.

[Guilpin, Edward.]

Skialetheia. Or, A shadowe of Truth, in certaine Epigrams and Satyres. . . . At London, Printed by I.R. for Nicholas Ling . . . 1598.

8°, text sigs. A3–E3v.
(1) A gull (sig. A6v), (2) A fine fellow (sig. Bv), (3) A malcontent (sig. B4), (4) Don Fashion (sig. D6v), (5) Opinion (sig. D8v).
Attributed to Guilpin by the STC.

[Hall, Joseph.]

Virgidemiarvm. The three last Bookes. Of

byting Satyres. Imprinted at London by Richard Bradocke for Robert Dexter . . . 1598.

8°, text pp. 3–105. In verse.
(1) The occupations of a young gallant (p. 28).

[Hall, Joseph.]

Virgidemiarvm, Six Bookes. . . . Corrected and amended. . . . Imprinted at London by Richard Bradocke, for Robert Dexter. 1598.

8°, in 2 parts, text pp. 1–67, 3–105. In verse.
(1–3) as in 1597, (4) as (1) in 1598.
Pforzheimer, II, 437.

Rankins, William.

Seauen Satyres Applyed to the weeke, including the worlds ridiculous follyes. . . . Whereunto is annexed the wandring Satyre. By W. Rankins, Gent. Imprinted at London by Edw. Allde for William Ferbrand . . . 1598.

8°, text pp. 1–49.
(1) Contra Martialistam, or a boastful soldier (p. 4), (2) Contra Venereum, or a lover (p. 13), (3) Satyrus peregrinans, or a foolish gallant (p. 27).

The only copy listed by the STC is at Huntington.

1599

Anonymous.

A Pageant of Spanishe humours wherin are naturally described and lywely pourtraied the Kyndes and qualities of a signor of Spayne. Translated out of Dutche. London: Printed for J. Wolfe. 1599.*

The only copy listed by the STC is in the British Museum.

Breton, Nicholas.

The Wil of Wit . . . Containing fiue discourses . . . Compiled by Nicholas Breton . . . London, Printed by T. Creede, 1599.*

See 1597.

[Hall, Joseph.]

Virgidemiarum. Part II. London, Printed for R. Dexter, 1599.*

See 1597.

1600

Anonymous.

The Real Character of a Clergyman of the Church of England.*

Listed in McLeish's Sale Catalogue 56, where it is dated [16--?].

[Breton, Nicholas.]

Pasqvils Mad-Cap. And Mad-cappes Message. London Printed by V.S. for Thomas Bushell . . . 1600.

4°, text pp. 1–43.
(1) The wealthy rascal (p. 2), (2) A poor man (p. 3), (3) An asse (p. 5), (4) A souldiour (p. 6), (5) A vicar (p. 8), (6) A lawyer (p. 10), (7) An unworthy rich man (p. 12).

Attributed to Breton by the STC.

[Breton, Nicholas.]

Pasqvils Mistresse: Or The Worthie and vnworthie woman. With his description and passion of that Furie, Iealousie. . . . Imprinted at London, for Thomas Fisher . . . 1600.

4°, text sigs. B–Gv.
(1) A fair but shallow woman (sig. B2), (2) A worthy woman (sig. B3), (3) A repulsive woman (sig. C3v), (4) Pasquil's mistress (sig. F), (5) Jealousy (sig. F3v).

Attributed to Breton by the CBEL.

[Garzoni, Tommaso.]

The Hospitall Of Incvrable Fooles: Erected in English, as neer the first Italian modell . . . Printed by Edm. Bollifant, for Edward Blount. 1600.

4°, text pp. 1–158.
(1) General fools (p. 1), (2) Frantic and doting (p. 8), (3) Solitary and melancholy (p. 15), (4) Idle and careless (p. 22), (5) Drunken (p. 26), (6) Hare-brained and forgetful (p. 31), (7) Stupid, forlorn, and ecstatical (p. 35), (8) Notted, gross, and of light carriage (p. 38), (9) Dottrels and shallow-pated (p. 41), (10) Senseless and giddy-headed (p. 44), (11) Plain lourdish and naturall (p. 49), (12) Vicious (p. 53), (13) Malicious and despiteful (p. 56), (14) Ridiculous (p. 60), (15) Ostenting and vain-glorious (p. 64), (16) Parasiticall or scoffing (p. 72), (17) Lunatical and by season (p. 77), (18) Carpet and amorous (p. 81), (19) Desperate (p. 87), (20) Heteroclite, reverse, thwart, and headstrong (p. 91), (21) Scoffing (p. 95), (22) Jovial, recreative, facete, and friendly (p. 99), (23) Testy and fustian (p. 103), (24) Outrageous, fell, and Bedlam (p. 108), (25) Gross and 3-elbowed (p. 113), (26) Obstinate (p. 117), (27) Pildpated and odious (p. 121), (28) Irregular and unbridled (p. 125), (29) Extravagant, extreme, and right (p. 129), (30) Mischievous or diabolical (p. 116), (31) Female fools (p. 140).

Attributed to Garzoni by the CBEL.

[Jonson, Ben.]

The comicall Satyre of Every Man Ovt Of His Hvmor. As it was first composed by the Author B.I. Containing more then hath been publikely spoken or acted. With the severall Character of euery person . . . London, Printed for Nicholas Linge, 1600.

4°, text sigs. A3v–Q4v.
(1) Brief characters of the persons in the play, in the *dramatis personae*.

There were three editions in the same year, and there have been many reprints since.

[Rowlands, Samuel.]

The Letting Of Humovrs Blood In The Head-Vaine. . . . At London, Printed by W. White for W.F. 1600.

8°, text sigs. A4–F3.
(1) Monsieur Domingo, a skilful drinker (Epigram 1), (2) Sir Lancelot, a braggart (ep. 2), (3) Thraso, a braggart (ep. 3), (4) Delfridue (ep. 5), (5) Sir Reuell (ep. 7), (6) Sir Gall-iade (ep. 8), (7) Drudo (ep. 9), (8) Polletique Peeter (ep. 11), (9) Fine Phillip (ep. 12), (10) Signieur Fantasticke (ep. 13), (11) Amorous Austin (ep. 15), (12) Caualero Rake-hell, a swearer (ep. 17), (13) Cacus, a crafty thief or sponger (ep. 19), (14) Soto, a hard drinker (ep. 21), (15) Signeur Sacke and Suger (ep. 22), (16) Humors, a humourous man (ep. 27), (17) A gallant (ep. 32), (18) A henpecked husband (ep. 33), (19) Seuerus, a gallant (ep. 35), (20) A lying gallant (Satire 1), (21) A usurer (sat. 2), (22) A dancing-school usher (sat. 3), (23) A gallant country gentleman (sat. 4), (24) Contempt (sat. 5), (25) A heavy drinker and smoker (sat. 6), (26) Covetousness (sat. 7).

Attributed to Rowlands by the STC. The epistle is signed S.R.

Thynne, Francis.

Emblems and Epigrams.*
Manuscript.

In the printed edition of 1876 the date is estimated as about 1600.

Vaughan, William.

The Golden-groue, moralized in three Bookes . . . Made by W. Vaughan . . . Printed at London by Simon Stafford . . . 1600.

8°, text sigs. C–Cc6v.
(1) A fearfull man (sig. G3), (2) A covetous man (sig. H6), (3) A flatterer (sig. L), (4) The properties of a gentleman (sig. S6v), (5) A good tutour (sig. X4v).

1601

[Breton, Nicholas.]

The Passion of a Discontented Minde. . . . London Printed by V.S. for Iohn Baily . . . 1601.

4°, text sigs. [A4v]–[D2v]. In verse.
(1) Use, or custom (sig. Bi), (2) Ill company (sig. Ciii).

Not in STC. This entry is made from the copy at Har-

vard. The STC, however, attributes the authorship to Breton, though under different years.

Johnson, Robert.

Essaies, Or Rather Imperfect Offers, By Rob. Iohnson Gent. Seene and allowed. London Printed by Iohn Windet, for Iohn Barnes. 1601.

8°, text sigs. B–H7v.
(1) Little mindes (sig. B3v), (2) Men of slowe capacitie (sig. B4v), (3) A too sharpe wit (sig. B5v), (4) Men of good reason (sig. B7v), (5) Education (sig. B8), (6) Historie (sig. C8v), (7) Discretion (sig. F2), (8) Men who rise into favor by putting others into disgrace (sig. H7v). Pforzheimer No. 535.

Jonson, Ben.

The Fovntaine Of Selfe-Loue. Or Cynthias Revels. As it hath been sundry times priuately acted. . . . Written by Ben: Iohnson . . . Imprinted at London for Walter Burre . . . 1601.

4°, text sigs. Bv–M2v.
(1) Hedon, a gallant (Act II, scene i), (2) Philautia, or self-love (II, i), (3) Anaides, an impudent gallant (II, ii), (4) Types of faces (II, iii), (5) Amorphus, a deformed traveller (II, iii), (6) Asotus, a prodigal (II, iii), (7) Crites, of perfect temper (II, iii), (8) Argurion, or money (II, iii), (9) Madame Moria, or folly (II, iv), Crites' acquaintances (III, iv).

[Powell, Thomas.]

The Passionate Poet, With a Description of the Thracian Ismarus. By T.P. . . . London Printed by Valentine Simmes . . . 1601.

4°, text sigs. A4–G2. In verse.
(1) Atheist (sig. B3), (2) Precisianisme (sig. B3v).

The only copy listed in the STC is at Huntington. The dedication is signed: Tho. Powell.

[Rowlands, Samuel.]

Humors Ordinarie. London, Printed for W. Firebrand. [1601–02?]*

A reprint of The Letting of Humours Blood, 1600. Dated [before 1603] by the STC.

1602

[Breton, Nicholas.]

The Passion Of A Discontented Minde. . . . London Printed by T.C. for Iohn Bailey . . . 1602.

4°, text sigs. A2–C4v. In verse.
(1–2) as in 1601.

Breton, Nicholas.

A Trve Description of vnthankfulnesse. Or

an enemie to Ingratitude. Compiled by Nicholas Breton Gent. At London: Printed by Thomas Este. 1602.

4°, text sigs. A3 (mis-numbered Biij)–B4.
(1) Ingratitude (sig. B3).

The only copy listed in the STC is at the Bodleian.

[Hall, Joseph.]

Virgidemiarum. Part I. London, Printed by J. Harrison for R. Dexter. 1602.*
See 1597.

Obendoerffer, Johann.

The Anatomyes of the True Physition and Counterfeit Mounte-banke. wherein both of them, are graphically described, and set out in their Right and Orient Colours. Published in Latin by John Oberndorff, a Learned German: & Translated into English by F. H[erring]. Fellow of the Coll. of Physitions in London. London, Printed for Arthur Johnson, 1602.*
4°.
(1) A true physition, (2) A mounte-banke.

The only copy listed in the STC is in the British Museum, which has also an undated manuscript of the same work.

1603

Crosse, Henry.

Vertves Common-wealth: Or The High-Way to Honovr. Wherin is discouered, that although by the disguised craft of this age, vice and hypocrisie may be concealed: yet by Tyme (the triall of truth) it is most plainly reuealed. . . . By Henry Crosse. London Printed for Iohn Newbery . . . 1603.

4°, text sigs. B–V4.
(1) Prudence (sig. B2v), (2) Iustice (sig. B3), (3) Fortitude (sig. B3v), (4) Temperance (sig. C2), (5) Liberalitie (sig. I4), (6) Pride (sig. K3), (7) A beautiful strumpet (sig. Lv), (8) Idlenesse (sig. Q4).

The Huntington copy is called the second issue of the first edition.

Reprinted 1605 as The Schoole of Pollicie.

Plutarch.

The Philosophie, commonlie called, The Morals Written By . . . Plutarch of Chæronea. Translated . . . by Philemon Holland. . . . At London, Printed by Arnold Hatfield. 1603.

6°, text pp. 1–1363.
(1) A false friend, or flatterer (p. 83).

1604

Dekker, Thomas.

The Honest Whore, With, The Humours of the Patient Man, and the Longing Wife. Tho: Dekker. London Printed by V.S. for Iohn Hodgets . . . 1604.

4°, text sigs. A2–K4v.
(1) A happy man (Part II, Act I, scene ii).

There have been many editions since.

Huarte Navarro, Juan de Dios.

Examen de Ingenios. The Examination of mens Wits. . . . By John Huarte. . . . Englished . . . by R.C. Esquire. . . . London, Printed by Adam Islip. 1604.

8°, text pp. 1–333.
(1) as in 1594.

[Rowlands, Samuel.]

Looke To It: For, Ile Stabbe Ye. Imprinted at London, by E. Alde, for W. Ferbrand, and George Loftes . . . 1604.*
4°.
(1) Tyrant kinges (p. 7), (2) Wicked magistrates (p. 8), (3) Curious diuines (p. 9), (4) Couetous lawyers (p. 10), (5) Vp-start courtier (p. 11), (6) Wealthye citizens (p. 12), (7) Greedy vsurer (p. 13), (8) Cursed swearers (p. 14), (9) Phisitions of the qvacksalvers crew (p. 15), (10) Gentlemen of base broode (p. 16), (11) Counterfayte captaine (p. 17), (12) Dissembling souldier (p. 18), (13) Vnkinde parents (p. 19), (14) Disobedient children (p. 20), (15) Drunkard (p. 21), (16) Perjurers (p. 22), (17) Godlesse athists (p. 23), (18) Miserable marchant (p. 24), (19) Deceitfull artificers (p. 25), (20) Wretched husbandmen (p. 26), (21) Swagg'ring ruffian (p. 27), (22) Proud gentlewomen (p. 28), (23) Odious quarreler (p. 29), (24) Disloyall traytor (p. 30), (25) Filthy pander (p. 31), (26) Lease-mongers (p. 32), (27) Adulterer (p. 33), (28) Idle huswife (p. 34), (29) Prodigall gallant (p. 35), (30) Gluttone (p. 36), (31) My fine dauncer (p. 38), (32) Ieffery Make-Shift (p. 39), (33) Spend-thriftes and ill husbandes (p. 40).

There were two editions in 1604. The one described here is STC 21398. Only one copy of 21399 is listed, that at Britwell Court, 1922.

Attributed to Rowlands by the STC and CBEL.

1605

Anonymous.

Willobie His Avisa Or The True Picture of a modest Maide, and of a chast and constant wife. . . . The fourth time corrected and Augmented. Imprinted at London by Iohn Windet. 1605.

4°, text ff. 1–72. In verse.
(1) as in 1594.

The only copy known is at Harvard. The second and third editions, of which no copies are known, are assigned by the STC to 1596 and 1599. See Pforzheimer No. 1068 n.

Crosse, Henry.

The Schoole of Pollicie: Or the Arraignment of State Abuses. London: Printed by V. Sims for N. Butter. 1605.*

(1–8) as in his Vertues Common-wealth, 1603.

A reissue of Vertues Common-wealth (1603) under another title.

1606

Anonymous.

The Picture of a Protestant Discoursinge the detestable heresies of ye popes and of Romishe religion.*

Arber, Stationers' Registers, III, 326.

This book was entered to Master [Richard] Ockold on July 18, 1606.

The Picture of No bodye. 1606.*

Arber, Stationers' Registers, III, 308.

This book was licensed to John Trundell on January 8, 1605/6. It may possibly be the book which, when published, was entitled No-body, and some-body, and was printed in 1606 for J. Trundle (STC 18597). On the other hand, a book by the title of No-body and somebody was entered in the Stationers' Registers on March 12, 1605/6 (Arber III, 316). There is no proof that they are identical.

The Retvrne From Pernassvs: Or The Scourge of Simony. Publiquely acted by the Students in Saint Iohns College in Cambridge. At London Printed by G. Eld, for Iohn Wright . . . 1606.

4°, text sigs. A4–Iv.

(1) John Marston (sig. B2v), (2) Beniamin Iohnson (sig. B2v), (3) A meere scholler (sig. D3v), (4) A vniuersity princox (sig. E2v), (5) Old Sir Raderick, a dissolute man (sig. E4v), (6) Amoretto, Sir Radericks sonne, a gull (sig. F).

There was another edition of the same year, STC 19310.

Barnes, Barnabe.

Fovre Bookes of Offices: Enabling Privat persons for the speciall seruice of all good Princes and Policies. Made and deuised by Barnabe Barnes. . . . London Printed at the charges of George Bishop, T. Adams, and C. Burbie. 1606.

4°, text pp. 1–210.

(1) Robert Devereux, Earl of Essex (p. 179).

[Breton, Nicholas.]

Choice, Chance, And Change: Or, Conceites in their Colours. . . . Imprinted at London for Nathaniell Fosbrooke . . . 1606.

4°, text sigs. B–K4.

(1) A finical asse (sig. I3v), (2) A foole, a swag-gering ruffe (sig. I3v), (3) A shamfast clovvn in gaie clothes (sig. I4), (4) A churle that was a great vsurer (sig. I4v), (5) A cheating companion (sig. I4v), (6) A gull that . . . was made a gentleman (sig. K), (7) A pander (sig. K), (8) A louing foole (sig. Kv), (9) A prodigall cockescomb (sig. Kv), (10) A fowle idle slut (sig. Kv), (11) A cunning tit (sig. K2), (12) A true souldier (sig. K2), (13) An honest man (sig. K2v), (14) A merry honest fellow (sig. K2v), (15) Of my selfe (sig. K3).

Attributed to Breton by the CBEL, and by Grosart, who reprinted it in 1881.

Breton, Nicholas.

The Wil Of Wit, Wils Wil, or Wils Wit . . . Containing fiue discourses . . . Newly corrected and amended, being the fift time Imprinted. Compiled by Nicholas Breton. . . . London, Printed by Thomas Creede, 1606.

4°, text sigs. B–I4v, Aa–Gg4, Aaa–Ddd4.

(1–8) as in 1597.

Bryskett, Lodowick.

A Discovrse Of Civill Life: Containing the Ethike part of Morall Philosophie. Fit for the instructing of a Gentleman in the course of a vertuous life. By Lod: Br. . . . London, Printed for VVilliam Apsley, 1606.

4°, text pp. 1–279.

(1) Youth (p. 100), (2) A magnanimous man (p. 232), (3) Justice (p. 248).

There was another issue of the same year, identical except printed for E. Blount (STC 3958).

[Dekker, Thomas.]

The Double PP, A Papist in Armes. Bearing Ten seuerall Sheilds. Encovntred By the Protestant. At Ten seuerall Weapons. A Iesuite Marching before them. . . . London, Imprinted by T.C. and are to be sold by John Hodgets . . . 1606.

4°, text sigs. A3–F2.

(1) The picture of a Jesuite (sig. A3), (2) A papist couchant, or the fawner (sig. C2), (3) A papist passant, or the plodder (sig. C2v), (4) A papist passand gardant, or the spie (sig. C3), (5) A papist variant, or the changeling (sig. C3v), (6) A papist volant, or the runaway (sig. C4), (7) A papist seminant, or the pope's husbandman (sig. C4v), (8) A papist saliant, or the ambusher (sig. D), (9) A papist rampant, or the cut throat (sig. Dv), (10) A papist umbreant, or the moldwarp (sig. D2), (11) A papist pendant, or the hanger on (sig. D2v), (12) Dynastes, or the nobleman (sig. E), (13) Apolectos, or councellor of estate (sig. Ev), (14) Antistes, or the bishop (sig. E2), (15) Dycastes, or the judge

(sig. E2v), (16) Academicos, or the schollar (Sig. E3), (17) Stratiotes, or the souldier (sig. E3v), (18) Emporos, or the merchant (sig. E4), (19) Nautes, or the sea-man (sig. E4v), (20) Arotes, or the ploughman (sig. F), (21) Technytes, or the artificer (sig. Fv).
BSC 2129. Pforzheimer No. 272.

Attributed to Dekker by the STC. There were two issues in 1606, of which the Pforzheimer copy is the second.

Dekker, Thomas.

Newes From Hell; Brought by the Diuell's Carrier. . . . Tho: Dekker. London Printed by R.B. for VV. Ferebrand . . . 1606.
4°, text sigs. B–H4v.
(1) Hell (sig. B3v), (2) Charon (sig. E2), (3) A souldier (sig. H2v).

Reprinted in 1607 (as A Knight's Conjuring).

Dekker, Thomas.

The Seuen deadly Sinnes of London: Drawne in seuen seuerall Coaches, Through the Seuen seuerall Gates of the Citie Bringing the Plague with them. . . . Tho: Dekker. At London, Printed by E.A. for Nathaniel Butter . . . 1606.
4°, text pp. 1–47, wrongly numbered 37.
(1) The politick bankrupt (p. 4), (2) Apishnesse (p. 32).

Several times reprinted.

Rich, Barnabe.

Faultes Faults, And Nothing else but Faultes. By Barnabie Rich . . . At London Printed for Ieffrey Chorleton . . . 1606.
4°, text ff. 1–63v.
(1) Jesters (f. 4), (2) Fashion-monger (f. 6v), (3) Malecontent (f. 7), (4) State ape (f. 7), (5) Traueller (f. 8), (6) Dauncer (f. 8v), (7) Covetous miser (f. 11), (8) Counterfeit souldiour (f. 12), (9) Frends (f. 15), (10) Ministers (f. 30), (11) Poets (f. 39), (12) Covetous magistrates (f. 41), (13) Courts of princes (f. 54), (14) Courtiers (f. 55v), (15) A vertuous and a vicious prince (f. 59).

1607

Anonymous.

The good hows-holder. 1607.*
s.sh.12°.

The only copy listed by the STC is in the British Museum.

Cleland, James.

Ἡρωπαιδεια, Or The Institvtion Of A Young Noble Man. By James Cleland. . . . At Oxford, Printed by Ioseph Barnes . . . 1607.
4°, text pp. 1–271.
(1) Ignorance and learning (p. 135), (2) An ig-

norant and a learned councellor (p. 135), (3) An ignorant and a learned warrior (p. 136), (4) An ignorant and a learned courtier (p. 137), (5) An ignorant and a learned lord (p. 138), (6) Vertue and vice (p. 164).

[Dekker, Thomas] and Wilkins, George.

Iests to make you Merie: With The Coniuring vp of Cock Watt, (the walking Spirit of Newgate) To tell Tales. Vnto which is Added, the miserie of a Prison, and a Prisoner. And a Paradox in praise of Serieants. Written by T.D. and George Wilkins. Imprinted at London by N.O. for Nathaniell Butter . . . 1607.
4°, text pp. 1–59 (wrongly numbered 63).
(1) What a iest is (p. 1), (2) A prisoner (p. 22), (3) Foysts (p. 26), (4) Morts (p. 28), (5) Lifts (p. 31), (6) Glimerers (p. 33), (7) Reachers (p. 35), (8) A foyst (p. 37), (9) Stals (p. 38), (10) Juglers (p. 43), (11) A mill, or break-house (p. 43), (12) A prison (p. 47), (13) Of a prison (p. 54, numbered 62), (14) Serieants (p. 57, numbered 58).

Attributed to Dekker by the STC.

[Dekker, Thomas.]

A Knights Conjuring, done in earnest. London, Printed by T.C. for W. Bailey. 1607.*
4°.

A reprint, with some revisions, of his Newes from Hell, 1606.

Johnson, Robert.

Essaies. 1607.*
See 1601.

Lloyd, Lodowick.

The Choyce of Iewels. By Lodowik Lloid Esquier. London, Printed by Thomas Purfoot. 1607.
4°, text pp. 1–39.
(1) Brave, bold women (p. 2), (2) Wise women (p. 6), (3) Women of faith (p. 7), (4) Warlike and victorious women (p. 9), (5) Women as rulers (p. 14), (6) Women of various countries and cities (p. 16), (7) Rare women (p. 22).

[Rowlands, Samuel.]

Diogenes Lanthorne. . . . London, Printed for Thomas Archer . . . 1628 [i.e., 1607?].
4°, text sigs. A3–F3.
(1) Mounsieur Vsurie (sig. A3v), (2) Bosting & presumption (sig. A4v), (3) Côtention (sig. B), (4) Hipocrisie (sig. Bv), (5) Swaggerer (sig. B2), (6) Detraction (sig. B2v), (7) Ielosie (sig. B3), (8) Discord (sig. B3v), (9) Sloath (sig. B4).

The Prologue is signed Samvell Rowlands. The Huntington copy seems to differ slightly from the Bodleian. The title page given above is from the Huntington. The date 1628 is printed on an extended margin and is considered an error.

[Rowlands, Samuel.]

Humors Ordinarie. London, Printed by E. Allde for W. Firebrand. 1607.*

Reprinted from The Letting of Humours Blood, 1600.

1608
Anonymous.

The cobler of Cannterburie. London: Printed by Nicholas Okes for Nathanael Butter . . . 1608.*

4°.

(1–5) as in 1590.

The only copy listed in the STC is in the British Museum.

[Dekker, Thomas.]

The Belman Of London. Bringing to light the most notorious villanies that are now practised in the Kingdome. . . . Printed at London for Nathaniel Bvtter. 1608.

4°, text sigs. B–I3v.

(1) An Vpright-man (sig. C3), (2) A ruffler (sig. C3v), (3) An angler (sig. C4), (4) A rogue (sig. C4), (5) A wilde rogue (sig. C4v), (6) A prigger of prancers (sig. D), (7) A palliard (sig. Dv), (8) A frater (sig. Dv), (9) A quire-bird (sig. D2), (10) An abraham-man (sig. D2), (11) A whipiacke (sig. D2v), (12) A counterfet cranke (sig. D2v), (13) A drummerar (sig. D2v), (14) A iack-man and a patrico (sig. D3), (15) An Irish toyle (sig. D3), (16) A swigman (sig. D3v), (17) A kinchin co (sig. D3v).

A cento compiled from materials in Awdeley, Harman, Greene, and others. There were three impressions in 1608. Attributed to Dekker by the STC. Lanthorne and Candle Light (1608 ff.) is called a second part of The Belman.

[Dekker, Thomas.]

The Belman of London. Bringing To Light The Most Notoriovs Villanies That Are Now Practised in the Kingdome. . . . The second Impression. Printed at London for Nathaniel Butter. 1608.

4°, text sigs. B–I2.

(1–17) as in first impression, 1608.

[Dekker, Thomas.]

The Belman of London. The Third Impression. London, Printed for N. Butter. 1608.*

4°.

(1–17) as in first impression of 1608.

The only copy recorded in the STC is in the British Museum.

[Dekker, Thomas.]

Lanthorne and Candle Light, or the second part of the Belman. London, Printed for J. Busbie, 1608.*

4°.

See 1609.
Pforzheimer No. 274 n.

Hall, Joseph.

Characters Of Vertves And Vices: In two Bookes: By Ios. Hall. London, Printed by Melch. Bradwood for Eleazar Edgar and Samuel Macham . . . 1608.

8°, text pp. 1–173.

(1) Wise man (p. 5), (2) Honest man (p. 13), (3) Faithfull man (p. 19), (4) Humble man (p. 27), (5) Valiant man (p. 33), (6) Patient man (p. 39), (7) True friend (p. 45), (8) Truly-noble (p. 51), (9) Good magistrate (p. 57), (10) Hypocrite (p. 71), (11) Busie-bodie (p. 79), (12) Superstitious (p. 87), (13) Profane (p. 93), (14) Male-content (p. 99), (15) Vnconstant (p. 107), (16) Flatterer (p. 113), (17) Slothfull (p. 119), (18) Couetous (p. 125), (19) Vaineglorious (p. 133), (2) Presumptuous (p. 141), (21) Distrustfull (p. 147), (22) Ambitious (p. 153), (23) Vnthrift (p. 161), (24) Enuious (p. 167).

Murphy 11–12. BSC 2131.

There was another edition of the same year (STC 12648a), differing only very slightly from the above.

Hall, Joseph.

Epistles. The Second Volume. Conteining two Decads. By Joseph Hall. London Printed by A.H. . . . 1608.

8°, text pp. 1–215.

(1) A good and faithful courtier (p. 99, Decade III, epistle x).

BSC 2132.

The first volume of Epistles contains no characters.

Middleton, Richard.

Epigrams And Satyres: Made by Richard Middleton, of Yorke, Gentleman. . . . London, Printed by Nicholas Okes for Joseph Harrison . . . 1608.*

In verse.

(1) Vaginius, (2) Belus, (3) Macer, (4) Histrionanus, (5) Nosyrus, (6) Dollabella, (7) Liberio, (8) Pulchrius, (9) Barbato, (10) Collegio, (11) Luscus, (12) Sapientio, (13) Jano, (14) Ridentius, (15) Graccius, (16) Calphurnius, (17) Pandulphoe.

The second part, beginning with number 7, has the title Times Metamorphosis.

[Rowlands, Samuel.]

Diogenes Lanthorne. . . . London Printed for T.P. [1608].

4°, text sigs. A3–F4.
(1–9) as in 1607.
Dated [1608] by the STC.

Vaughan, William.

The Golden-groue, moralized in three Bookes
. . . Made by W. Vaughan . . . The second
Edition . . . Imprinted at London by Simon
Stafford . . . 1608.

8°, text sigs. C–Dd6v.
(1–5) as in 1600.

1609

Anonymous.

Everie Woman in her Humor. . . . London,
Printed by E.A. for Thomas Archer . . .
1609.

4°, text sigs. A2–H4.
(1) A drunkard (sig. G4v).

[Dekker, Thomas.]

Lanthorne and Candle-Light. Or, The Bell-
Mans second Nights-walke. . . . The second
edition . . . London Printed for Iohn Busby
. . . 1609.

4°, text sigs. B2–L3v.
(1) The gull-groper (sig. Ev), (2) The wood
pecker (sig. E2), (3) The gull (sig. E2v), (4)
Ferrets (sig. E3), (5) A London tumbler (sig.
E4v), (6) Fawlconers (sig. F2), (7) Iacks of the
clock-house (sig. Gv), (8) Rancke riders (sig.
G2), (9) Moone men (sig. H), (10) A harlot,
or citty punck (sig. H4), (11) A horse-courser
(sig. Iv), (12) Iacke in a boxe (sig. K2), (13)
Quack-salving, or travelling empiricks (sig. K4v),
(14) Stragling scribling writers, or strowling
schoolemaister (sig. K4v).
Pforzheimer No. 274.

Reprinted 1612 (as O per se O), 1616 (as Villanies discovered), 1620 (ditto), 1630 (ditto), 1632 (as English
Villanies), 1638 (ditto), 1648 (ditto). Attributed to
Dekker by the STC. The reference in the subtitle is to
his The Belman of London, 1608.

Dekker, Thomas.

VVork For Armorours: Or, The Peace is
Broken. . . . Written by Thomas Dekker.
London, Printed for Nathaniel Butter . . .
1609.

4°, text sigs. B–G3.
(1) Discontent (sig. C2v), (2) Despaire and
Carelesnesse (sig. C2v), (3) Hunger (sig. C3),
(4) Sloth (sig. C3), (5) Repining (sig. C3), (6)
Industry (sig. C3v), (7) Beggery (sig. C3v),
(8) Couetousnesse (sig. D3v), (9) Prouidence
(sig. D3v), (10) Deceipt (sig. D4), (11) Violence (sig. D4), (12) Vsurie (sig. D4), (13)
Parsimonie (sig. D4v).

Nos. 1–7 are called Councellors to Pouerty, and 8–13
Councellors to Money.

Grahame, Simion.

The Anatomie Of Hvmours: VVritten By
Simion Grahame. . . . At Edinbvrgh. Printed
by Thomas Finlason. 1609.

4°, text ff. 1–74.
(1) A king (f. 1), (2) An vnjust servant (f. 3v),
(3) The wise servant (f. 3v), (4) A politick
matchavilian (f. 4v), (5) The yong aspyring gallant (f. 6v), (6) Poverty-stricken gallants (f. 8),
(7) A cowardly braggart captain (f. 9), (8) A
courtier (f. 10), (9) He who liues at home (f.
11), (10) A common souldier (f. 12), (11)
Misers (f. 13v), (12) A thieving steward (f.
14v), (13) A drunkard (f. 16v), (14) The charleton or quicksilver (f. 24), (15) Mountebank
(f. 25), (16) Ignorant medicenars (f. 24v), (17)
A Ianus-headed lawyer (f. 26), (18) Syranicall
wench (f. 29v), (19) A lady (f. 31), (20) Lustful man (f. 32v), (21) Coquette (f. 33, in verse),
(22) A peacable woman (f. 40), (23) Anger (f.
56v), (24) The malcontent (f. 59, in verse).

Hall, Joseph.

Salomon's Diuine Arts . . . By Joseph Hall.
At London, Printed by H.L. . . . 1609.

8°, in 2 parts, text pp. 1–174, 1–87.
(1) The liar (Part I, p. 49), (2) The slanderer (I,
50), (3) The dissembler (I, 52), (4) The flatterer (I, 52), (5) The contentious (I, 60), (6)
The covetous (I, 71), (7) The prodigal (I, 74),
(8) The slothful (I, 78), (9) The temperate man
(I, 83), (10) The modest man (I, 88), (11) The
humble man (I, 92), (12) The continent man
(I, 97), (13) The king (I, 108), (14) The counsellor of state (I, 119), (15) The courtier (I, 129),
(16) The good husband (I, 148), (17) The good
wife (I, 155).

Heywood, Thomas.

Troia Britanica: Or, Great Britaines Troy. A
Poem Deuided into XVII. seuerall Cantons,
intermixed with many pleasant Poeticall Tales.
Concluding with an Vniuersall Chronicle
from the Creation, vntill these present Times.
Written by Tho: Heywood. . . . London;
Printed by W. Jaggard, 1609.

6°, text pp. 1–466.
(1) A Puritan (p. 89, in verse).
Murphy 128. Pforzheimer No. 486.

[M., W.]

The Man In The Moone, Telling Strange
Fortunes, Or, The English Fortune Teller
. . . London Printed by I.W. for Nathaniel
Butter. 1609.

4°, text sigs. A2–H2.
(1) The drunkard, (2) The tobackonist, (3) The prodigal, (4) The serving-man, (5) The wicked woman, (6) The retainer, (7) The extortioner, (8) The glutton, (9) The parasite, (10) The wanton wife, (11) The jealous man, (12) The lover, (13) The virgin.
Murphy 121.

The address to the reader is signed W.M.

[Melton, Sir John.]

A Sixe-Fold Politician. By J.M. London: Printed by E.A. for J. Busby . . . 1609.
8°, text pp. 1–180.
(1) Ignorant politicians (p. 1), (2) Paules newes carriers, or foolish politicians (p. 23), (3) Usurping poets (p. 31), (4) Vain and ambitious travelers (p. 45), (5) Seminaries and Jesuits (p. 69), (6) Dangerous projectors (p. 93), (7) True statesmen (p. 107).

On the authorship, see J. Milton French, "Mute Inglorious Miltons," *Modern Language Quarterly*, I (1940), 367.

Rich, Barnabe.

Roome for a Gentleman, Or The Second Part Of Favltes Collected . . . for the true Meridian of Dublin. By Barnabe Rych Souldier. . . . London Printed by I.W. for Ieffrey Chorlton . . . 1609.
4°, text ff. 1–34 (misprinted 31).
(1) Vpstart women (f. 3v), (2) Apprentice souldiers (f. 19v), (3) Lawyers (f. 22v), (4) Opinion (f. 27).

[Rowlands, Samuel.]

The Knave Of Clubbes. . . . Printed at London for W. Ferebrand . . . 1609.
4°, text sigs. A3–F4v.
(1) A gull (sig. D2, in verse).

Attributed to Rowlands by the STC. The Epistle is signed S.R.

[Tuke, Thomas.]

The Picture of a True Protestant. London, Printed by N. Okes. 1609.*
BSC 2133.

[Tuvill, Daniel.]

Essayes, Morall and Theologicall. London, Printed by J.W. for E. Edgar. 1609.*
12°.
See his Vade Mecum, 1629.

Attributed to Tuvil by the STC. Initialed D.T.

1610
Rich, Barnabe.

A New Description of Ireland: Wherein is described the disposition of the Irish. . . . By Barnabe Rich, Gent. . . . Printed at London for Thomas Adams. 1610.
4°, text pp. 1–116.
(1) The Irish (p. 7), (2) The females (p. 11), (3) Citizens of Dublin (p. 59), (4) Irish Papists (p. 85).

Reprinted 1624 as A New Irish Prognostication.

[Sharpe, Roger.]

More Fooles yet. Written by R.S. At London, Printed for Thomas Castleton . . . An. 1610.
4°, text sigs. A4–E3v. In verse.
(1) Curio, a thriftie gallant (sig. A4v), (2) Zelopio, a confident cuckold (sig. B), (3) A variable humorist (sig. Bv), (4) A wondrous trauailer (sig. Bv), (5) A familiar tobacconist (sig. B2), (6) Criticus, a critical fool (sig. B3v), (7) A kind young man (sig. B4v), (8) Friuolus, an overconfident tennis player (sig. Cv), (9) Vinolentus, a drinker, a great obseruer (sig. C2), (10) An accomplisht gallant (sig. C2v), (11) Brutus, a conuertite (sig. C3v), (12) Mounsieur the Englishman (sig. D), (13) A penitent drunckard (sig. Dv), (14) Fatuus, a zany, a foole for companie (sig. Dv), (15) Fabulus, a man whose credit is not good (sig. E), (16) Furiosus, a bragging bully (sig. Ev), (17) Philosophaster, a second Diogenes (sig. E2).

Attributed to Sharpe by the STC.

1611
Coryat, Thomas.

Coryats Crudities. Hastily gobled vp in five Moneths trauells. . . . London, Printed by W.S. Anno Domini 1611.
8°, text pp. 1–655, plus appended poems, and preceded by some 200 pages of eulogy and the like unpaged.
(1) Thomas Coryat, the famous Odcombian, probably by Ben Jonson (sig. b of prefatory matter). Pforzheimer No. 218.

Coryat, Thomas.

The Odcombian Banqvet: Dished foorth By Thomas the Coriat. . . . Imprinted for T. Thorp. 1611.
4°, text sigs. A3–P4v.
(1) Thomas the Coryate, probably by Ben Jonson (sig. B).
Pforzheimer No. 219.

The verses following the character, which seem to be by the same writer, are an acrostic spelling out the name of Ben Jonson.

[Davies, John, of Hereford.]

The Scourge of Folly. Consisting of satyricall Epigramms . . . At London ·printed by E.A: for Richard Redmer.

8°, text pp. 1–264.

(1) Of iesting and iibing (sig. A5v), (2) Of poetry (sig. A7v), (3) Against Fuscus the vnciuill lawier (p. 4), (4) Of lascivious Laurentia (p. 35), (5) Against ouer-weening wit (p. 37), (6) Against amorous Andrugio (p. 39), (7) Against Congius his wit-stealing (p. 45), (8) Against Gorgonius his slovenry (p. 47), (9) Of Brunus his smoothnesse (p. 48), (10) Courtiers young and old (p. 50), (11) Of choosing a wife (p. 86), (12) Against Nefarius his base . . . lechery (p. 101), (13) Against Tuballus his time-keeping (p. 112), (14) Against Lubus his indirect purchasing (p. 117).

The two Huntington copies vary slightly. The characters listed above are chosen rather arbitrarily. Most of the poems in the volume might be called characters; those named are slightly longer than some of the rest. Attributed to Davies and dated 1611 by the STC.

[Rowlands, Samuel.]

The Knave of Clubbes. London, Printed for E. Allde, 1611.*

See 1609.

There were two editions of this year; Huntington has the only recorded copy of the first (STC 21388).

[Rowlands, Samuel.]

The Letting Of Humors Blood In The Head-Vaine. . . . Imprinted at London by W. White . . . 1611.*

8°, text sigs. A4–D6.

See 1600.

The only copy recorded in the STC is in the British Museum.

Stafford, Anthony.

Staffords Niobe: Or His Age Of Teares. The first Part. . . . The second Edition . . . Printed at London by Humfrey Lownes. 1611.

12°, in 2 parts, text pp. 1–202, 1–263.

(1) The seven ages of man (Part I, p. 100), (2) The monarch (II, 188), (3) The scholar (II, 195), (4) The soldier (II, 205), (5) The merchant (II, 212), (6) The shepherd (II, 214).

The first edition (STC 23129) also appeared in 1611.

1612

Adams, Thomas.

The Gallants Burden. A sermon. . . . By Tho. Adams . . . London Printed by W.W. for Clement Knight . . . 1612.

4°, text ff. 1–34.

(1) Atheistes (f. 16), (2) Epicures (f. 16v), (3) Libertines (f. 17), (4) Common prophane persons (f. 18).

Chapman, George.

Petrarchs· Seven Penitentiall Psalms, Paraphrastically Translated: With other Philo-sophicall Poems . . . Written by George Chapman. . . . London, Imprinted for Matthew Selman . . . 1612.*

8°, text pp. 1–94.

(1) Virgils epigram of a good man (sig. D8), (2) A great man (sig. Ev), (3) A sleight man (sig. E3v), (4) A good woman (sig. E5).

The only recorded copy of this edition is that in the Bodleian. The above information is taken from the reprint of Chapman's poems edited by Phyllis B. Bartlett in 1941. There have been other editions.

Cleland, James.

Ἡρωπαιδεια. 1612.*

See 1607.

The Bodleian copy is the only one recorded in the STC.

Davies, John, of Hereford.

[The Muses Sacrifice, Or Divine Meditations. By John Davies of Hereford. London, Printed by T.S. for G. Norton, 1612.]

8°, text ff. 1–172v.

(1) A happy man (f. 121), (2) True wealth (f. 123), (3) An angel-like man (f. 123v).

The title page is missing from the Harvard copy, as it was from all three copies which Grosart mentioned having seen. That given above is made up from a combination of the entry in the STC and that printed by Grosart.

[Dekker, Thomas.]

O per se O, or a new Cryer of Lanthorne and Candlelight. London, 1612.*

A reprint of Lanthorne and Candle Light, 1609. Pforzheimer No. 274 n.

[Maxwell, James.]

The Laudable Life, And Deplorable Death, of . . . Prince Henry. . . . By I.M. . . . London Printed by Edw: Allde, for Thomas Pauier . . . 1612.

4°, text sigs. B–F4v.

(1) Prince Henry (sig. B).

Peacham, Henry.

Minerva Britanna Or A Garden Of Heroical Deuises . . . Newly devised, moralized, and published, by Henry Peacham, Mr. of Artes. . . . London Printed . . . by Wa: Dight.

4°, text pp. 1–212. In verse.

(1) Princess Elizabeth (p. 14), (2) Phillip King of Spaine (p. 16), (3) D: Mauritio Hessiæ Lantgravio (p. 101), (4) Jacobum Magnae Britanniae Regem (p. 145).

Dated 1612 at the end of the text.

[Rowlands, Samuel.]

The Knaue of Harts. Haile Fellow. well met. . . . London: Printed by T.S. and are to be solde by George Loftus . . . 1612.

4°, text sigs. A2–F4v. In verse.
(1) A proud knaue (sig. B3v), (2) A shifting
knaue (sig. B4), (3) A lying knaue (sig. B4v),
(4) A whoring knaue (sig. C), (5) A dissembling
knaue (sig. Cv), (6) An hypocriticall knaue
(sig. C2), (7) A drunken knaue (sig. C2v), (8)
A swearing knaue (sig. C3), (9) A theeuing
knaue (sig. C3v), (10) A slothfull knaue (sig.
C4), (11) A busie knaue (sig. C4v), (12) A
prophane knaue (sig. D), (13) A prodigall
knaue (sig. Dv), (14) An ingratefull knaue
(sig. D2), (15) A couetous knaue (sig. D2v),
(16) An enuious knaue (sig. D3), (17) Beggery
embraceth whoredome (sig. D3v), (18) A guls
fray (sig. D4).

Attributed to Rowlands by the STC.

Stafford, Anthony.

Meditations, and Resolutions, Moral, Divine,
Politicall. Century I. Written for the instruc-
tion and bettering of Youth . . . By Antony
Stafford, Gent. There is also annexed an
Oration of Iustus Lipsius, against Calumnie;
translated out of Latine, into English. At
London, Printed by H.L. and are to be sold
by Thomas Saunders. 1612.

12°, text pp. 1–188.
(1) He who conforms his life to the lawes of a
true iudgement (p. 17), (2) Ambition (p. 43),
(3) A scholer, a true friend (p. 47), (4) The
worldling (p. 55), (5) Trauellers (p. 60), (6)
The miser (p. 118), (7) Calumny (p. 130), (8)
Curiosity (p. 147).

The whole oration of Lipsius against calumny, beginning
on p. 129, might be called an extended, digressive character.

1613

Adams, Thomas.

The White Devil, or the hypocrite uncased.
London: Printed by M. Bradwood for R.
Mab. 1613.*

4°, text pp. 1–62.
(1) Hypocrisie (p. 29), (2) A hypocrite (p. 31),
(3) A priuate theef (p. 37), (4) Public thieves
(p. 37), (5) Hypocritical magistrates (p. 41),
(6) The Pope (p. 41), (7) The hypocritical lawyer (p. 42), (8) The hypocritical official (p. 43),
(9) Hypocritical tradesman (p. 43), (10) Hypocritical ministers (p. 45), (11) Hypocritical landlords (p. 47), (12) Hypocritical inclosers (p. 48),
(13) Hypocritical taphouse-keepers (p. 48), (14)
Hypocritical flatterers (p. 49), (15) Hypocritical brokers (p. 50), (16) Hypocritical usurers
(p. 51).

The only copy recorded in the STC is in the New York
Public Library.

Adams, Thomas.

The VVhite Devil, Or The Hypocrite Vn-
cased: In A Sermon Preached at Pavls Crosse,
March 7. 1612. By Thomas Adams Minister
of the Gospell at Willington, in Bedford-shire.
. . . The second edition. London, Printed by
Thomas Snodham for Ralph Mab . . . 1613.

4°, text pp. 1–62.
(1–16) as in first edition of 1613.

Dekker, Thomas.

A Strange Horse-Race, At the end of which,
comes in The Catch-Poles Masqve. And
After That The Bankrouts Banquet: Which
done, the Diuell . . . makes his last will and
Testament, this present yeare. 1613. . . .
VVritten by Thomas Dekker. London, Printed for Ioseph Hunt . . . 1613.

4°, text sigs. B–G2.
(1) Blasphemous insolence, a proud Turke (sig.
C2), (2) Innocent humility, a Christian lady
(sig. C2), (3) A yong gallant, prodigallity (sig.
C2v), (4) A polliticke Belgicke, Hans-thrift (sig.
C2v), (5) A niggard, a vsurer (sig. C3), (6)
Hospitality (sig. C3), (7) An English knight
(sig. C4), (8) A Spanish don (sig. C4), (9)
Epicures (sig. D), (10) Lawyer (sig. D), (11)
A vicar (sig. Dv), (12) Capricious taylor (sig.
Dv), (13) Pride (sig. Dv), (14) Hypocrisie
(sig. E3), (15) Ingratitude (sig. E3v), (16) A
catch-poll (sig. F2), (17) A bankrout, that is
to say, a banker-out (sig. Gv).
Pforzheimer No. 280.

Johnson, Robert.

Essaies. 1613.*

See 1601.

Pemberton, William.

The Godly Merchant, Or The great gaine. A
Sermon preached at Paules-Crosse. Octob. 17.
1613. By William Pemberton . . . London
Printed by Edw. Griffin for Samuel Macham
. . . 1613.

8°, text pp. 1–126.
(1) Godlinesse and contentment (p. 21), (2)
The godly man and the vngodly man (p. 61),
(3) A godly man (p. 63).

[Rowlands, Samuel.]

The Knaue of Harts. Haile Fellow, well met.
. . . London, Printed for Iohn Bache . . .
1613.*

See 1612.

The only copy recorded in the STC is that of the British
Museum.

[Rowlands, Samuel.]

The Letting of Humours Blood in the Head-vaine. London, Printed by W.W. 1613.*
8°.
See 1600.

The Huntington copy is the only one recorded in the STC.

[Rowlands, Samuel.]

More Knaues Yet? The Knaues Of Spades And Diamonds. London: Printed for Iohn Tap . . .
4°, text sigs. A4–F4v.
(1) The picture of a pirat (sig. Bv, in verse), (2) To Machiauill the deuils statesman (sig. D2v, in verse), (3) To Mr. Mony-bag the vsurer (sig. D3, in verse), (4) The picture of a swagerer (sig. E2).

Attributed to Rowlands by the CBEL. The Epistle is signed S.R. The date is cut off the title page of the Huntington copy, from which these notes were made. It appears to be intact on the Bodleian copy.

[Tuvil, Daniel.]

The Dove and the Serpent. 1613.*
See 1614.

Wither, George.

Abvses Stript And whipt. Or Satirical Essayes. By George VVyther. Divided into two Bookes. . . . At London, Printed by G. Eld, for Francis Bvrton . . . 1613.

8°, text pp. 1–276, plus unnumbered leaves T5–V6v.
(1) Hate (p. 31), (2) Revenge (p. 43), (3) Choller (p. 52), (4) Ambition (p. 76), (5) Fear (p. 84), (6) Despaire (p. 92), (7) Hope (p. 96), (8) Compassion (p. 99), (9) Cruelty (p. 102), (10) Inconstancy (p. 180), (11) Presumption (p. 225).
Pforzheimer No. 1078.

There were at least five editions in 1613. Four are listed in the STC (25891–4); the fifth is described in the Pforzheimer Catalogue. The present notes are made from the Harvard copy of STC 25891. This volume was reprinted several times.

Wotton, Sir Henry.

Robert, late Earl of Salisbury.*
Manuscript.
Public Record Office (S.P. Dom. James I, Vol. LXIX, no. 59).

Catalogued in the Calendars of State Papers, Domestic Series, 1611–1618, p. 134. Printed in The Life and Letters of Sir Henry Wotton, ed. L. P. Smith, 1907, Vol. II, p. 487.

1614

Anonymous.

The Hvsband. A Poeme expressed In a Compleat Man. . . . London Printed for Lawrence L'isle . . . 1614.
8°, text sigs. B2–F7. In verse.
Begins: "Life was inspir'd, the first life was diuine."

Adams, Thomas.

The Deuills Banket. Described in foure Sermons. 1. The Banket propounded; begunne. 2. The second Seruice. 3. The breaking vp of the Feast. 4. The Shot or Reckoning. The Sinners Passing-Bell. Together with Phisicke from Heauen. Published by Thomas Adams. . . . London: Printed by Thomas Snodham for Ralph Mab . . . 1614.
4°, text pp. 1–341.
(1) Pride (p. 11), (2) Bribery (p. 12), (3) The calumniator (p. 66), (4) The flatterer (p. 69), (5) The idle man (p. 76), (6) The drunkard (p. 80), (7) The covetous man (p. 80), (8) The pope (p. 106).

The only copy listed in the STC is in the British Museum.

Adams, Thomas.

The White Devil, Or The Hypocrite Vncased: In A Sermon, Preached . . . By Thomas Adams . . . The third Edition reviewed and corrected by the Author. London, Printed by Thomas Purfoot for William Erondell . . . 1614.
4°, text pp. 1–62.
(1–16) as in 1613.

Brathwaite, Richard.

The Schollers Medley, Or, An Intermixt Discovrse Vpon Historicall And Poeticall Relations . . . By Richard Brathwayte Oxon. . . . London, Printed by N.O. for George Norton . . . 1614.
4°, text pp. 1–118.
(1) A flattering historian (p. 26), (2) The miser (p. 89), (3) The liberal man (p. 90), (4) The prodigal (p. 94).

In the Harvard copy, the date 1614 on the title page has been altered in pen to 1616. Reprinted 1638 (as A Survey of History), 1651 (as History Surveyed), 1652 (as History Re-surveyed).

Cooke, John.

Greenes Tu Quoque, Or, The Cittie Gallant. . . . Written by Io. Cooke Gent. . . . Printed at London for John Trundle. 1614.
4°, text sigs. B–M2.
(1) A usurer (sig. B3), (2) Longfield's mistress (sig. C), (3) A serving-man (sig. D2), (4) A gallant (sig. D3v), (5) Love (sig. H2), (6) Stains as an Italian (sig. I4).

[Corbet, Richard?]

The Times Whistle; or a new Daunce of seven Satires: wherevnto are annexed divers other Poems comprising Things Naturall, morall, & theologicall. Compiled by [R.C.] Gent. . . .*

Canterbury Cathedral Manuscript T.8.3.

(1) A boastful gallant, (2) Mistress Simula, the Puritan, (3) Sordido, a miser, (4) Moros, a demure fool, (5) A self-conceited coxcomb, (6) Madame Poppæa, a proud woman, (7) Epainnutus, a vain selfe-admiring gull, (8) Cervisius, a drunkard, (9) Bacchanal, an epicure in drink, (10) Misotochus, a hoarder of corn.

The date 1614 is assigned tentatively to this work in the reprint of 1871 and in the CBEL.

Overbury, Sir Thomas.

A Wife Novv The Widdow of Sir Thomas Overburye. Being A most exquisite and singular Poem of the choice of a Wife. Wherevnto Are Added many witty Characters, and conceited Newes, written by himselfe and other learned Gentlemen his friends. . . . London Printed for Lawrence Lisle . . . 1614.*

4°, text sigs. C4–F3v.

(1) A good woman, (2) A very very woman. Her next part, (3) A dissembler, (4) A courtier, (5) A golden asse, (6) A flatterer, (7) An ignorant glory-hunter, (8) A tymist, (9) An amorist, (10) An affected traveller, (11) A wiseman, (12) A noble spirit, (13) A old man, (14) A country gentleman, (15) A fine gentleman, (16) An elder brother, (17) A Welchman, (18) A pedant, (19) A servingman, (20) An host, (21) An ostler.

Murphy 15.

Overbury, Sir Thomas.

A Wife. The Second Impression. 1614*

See the first impression, 1614.
No copy is known.

Overbury, Sir Thomas.

A VVife. Novv The Wjddow Of Sir Tho: Overbvrye. Being A most exquisite and singular Poem of the choice of a Wife. Wherevnto Are Added many witty Characters, and conceited Newes, written by himselfe and other learned Gentlemen his friends. Dignum laude virum musa vetat mori. Cœlo musa beat. Hor: car: lib. 3. The third Impression; With addition of sundry other new Characters. London Printed by Edward Griffin for Lawrence Lisle . . . 1614.

4°, text sigs. A2–H4.

(1–21) as in first impression, 1614, (22) A good wife (sig. C4), (23) A melancholy man (sig. C4), (24) A sayler (sig. C4v), (25) A souldier (sig. C5).

Murphy 15. BSC 2136.

The paging of the added characters is confused, since there are other pages with the same signature marks, and these come between D4 and E. They may not have been inserted in all copies, since Murphy does not mention them.

Overbury, Sir Thomas.

A Wife. Now The Widdow Of Sir Tho: Overbvrye. Being A most exquisite and singular Poem of the choise of a Wife. Wherevnto Are Added many witty Characters, and conceited Newes, written by himselfe and other learned Gentlemen his friends: Dignum laude virum musa vetat mori, Caelo musa beat. Hor: Car: lib. 3. The fourth Impression, enlarged with more Characters, than any of the former Editions. London Printed by G. Eld, for Lawrence Lisle . . . 1614.*

4°, text sigs. C2–H3.

(1–25) as in the third impression, 1614, (26) A taylor, (27) A puritane, (28) A whore, (29) A very whore, (30) A happy life, by Sir Henry Wotton.

Murphy 16.

The only copy recorded in the STC is the Harmsworth, which is now presumably at Folger.

Overbury, Sir Thomas.

A Wife Now The Widow Of Sir Tho: Overbvrie Being A most exquisite and singular Poeme, of the choyse of a Wife. Wherevnto Are Added many witty Characters, and conceyted Newes, written by himselfe, and other learned Gentlemen his Friendes. Dignum laude virum Musa vetat mori, Cœlo Musa beat. Hor: Car: lib. 3. The fifth Impression, enlarged with more Characters, than any of the former Æditions. London, Printed by T.C. for Laurence Lisle . . . 1614.

4°, text sigs. A2–H4.

(1–30) as in fourth impression, 1614, (31) A mere common lawyer.

Murphy 17.

The new character is placed next to the last, just before Wotton's Character of a happy life.

[Tuvil, Daniel.]

The Dove and The Serpent. In which is conteined a large description of all such points and principles, as tend either to Conuersation, or Negotiation. Tuta velis. Tutus eris. London Printed by T.C. for Laurence L'isle . . . 1614.

4°, text pp. 1–92.
(1) The young (p. 53), (2) Old Men (p. 54), (3) Those of middle age (p. 56), (4) The noble (p. 58), (5) The rich (p. 58).
BSC 2137.

Attributed to Tuvil by the STC. The dedication is signed D.T.

Walker, William.

A Sermon Preached At The Fvnerals Of the Right Honourable, William, Lord Rvssell, Baron of Thornhaugh . . . Wherein is briefely set downe his godly Life . . . By William Walker . . . London: Printed for John Hodgets. 1614.
4°, text pp. 1–62.
(1) Lord Russell (p. 42 and p. 46).

1615
Anonymous.

The Pictvre Of A VVanton: her leawdnesse discouered. . . . London, Printed by W. White for T.P. . . . 1615.
4°, text sigs. A4–C4v.
(1) Popery (sig. C).

Not in STC. In Huntington Supplement.
The Huntington copy is the only one recorded.
A border-line character.

Adams, Thomas.

The Blacke Devill Or The apostate. Together With The Wolfe Worrying the Lambes. And The Spiritvall Navigator, Bovnd For the Holy Land. In three Sermons. By Thomas Adams. . . . London, Printed by William Iaggard, 1615.
4°, text pp. 1–78.
(1) The devill (p. 24), (2) The devill (p. 41), (3) The apostate (p. 68).
BSC 2138.

Adams, Thomas.

Englands Sicknes, Comparatively Conferred with Israels. Diuided into two Sermons, By Tho: Adams. . . . London Imprinted by E:G: for Iohn Budge, and Ralph Mab, 1615.
4°, text pp. 1–101.
(1) Impenitencie, and the impenitent man (p. 83).

Huntington has two copies which seem to be variant issues.

Adams, Thomas.

Mystical Bedlam, Or The VVorld Of Mad-Men. By Tho: Adams . . . London . . . Printed by George Purslowe, for Clement Knight . . . 1615.
4°, text pp. 1–82.

(1) The ambitious man (p. 10), (2) The epicure (p. 48), (3) The proud (p. 50), (4) The lustfull (p. 52), (5) The hypocrite (p. 54), (6) The auarous (p. 56), (7) The usurer (p. 58), (8) The drunkard (p. 61), (9) The idle man (p. 62), (10) The swearer (p. 63), (11) The liar (p. 63), (12) The busie body (p. 64), (13) The ungrateful (p. 65), (14) The flatterer (p. 65), (15) The angry man (p. 66), (16) The envious (p. 67), (17) The contentious man (p. 67), (18) The impatient (p. 68), (19) The vaine glorious (p. 69), (20) The papists (p. 69).
Murphy 122.

Adams, Thomas.

The Spirituall Nauigator Bovnd For the Holy Land. Preached at St. Giles without Cripplegate, on Trinity Sunday last, 1615. By Thomas Adams. . . . London, Printed by William Iaggard, 1615.
4°, text pp. 1–58.
(1) The worldling (p. 13), (2) The goodman (p. 21).

The British Museum Catalogue calls this Part III of The Blacke Devill.

Adams, Thomas.

The VVhite Devill Or The Hypocrite Vncased: To this fourth Impression are newly added . . . By Tho: Adams. London, Printed by Thomas Dawson, for William Arondell . . . 1615.
4°, text pp. 1–121.
(1–16) as in 1613.

Andrews, John.

The Anatomie of Basenesse. Or the Foure Quarters of a Knave; Flatterie, Ingratitude, Envie, Detraction . . . London, Printed for R. Redmer, 1615.*
4°.
(1) Of the flatterer, (2) Of the ingrateful, (3) Of the envious, (4) Of the detractor.

[Brathwaite, Richard.]

A strappado for the Diuell. Epigrams and Satyres. . . . By μισοσυκος . . . At London printed by I.B. for Richard Redmer . . . 1615.
8°, in two parts, text pp. 1–234, 1–104.
(1) The honest lawyer (p. 60), (2) A cashierd courtier (p. 64), (3) The courtier (p. 124).
Murphy 123.

Attributed to Brathwaite by the STC.

[Breton, Nicholas.]

Characters Vpon Essaies Morall, And Diuine, Written For those good Spirits, that will take them in good part, And Make vse of them to good purpose. . . . London Printed by Edw. Griffin, for Iohn Gwillim . . . 1615.

8°, text pp. 1–44.

(1) Wisdome (p. 1), (2) Learning (p. 6), (3) Knowledge (p. 9), (4) Practise (p. 12), (5) Patience (p. 15), (6) Loue (p. 17), (7) Peace (p. 20), (8) Warre (p. 23), (9) Valor (p. 25), (10) Resolution (p. 28), (11) Honor (p. 30), (12) Truth (p. 32), (13) Time (p. 34), (14) Death (p. 38), (15) Faith (p. 40), (16) Feare (p. 43).

Murphy 26. BSC 2139.

The dedication is signed Nich: Breton.

Hall, Joseph.

A Recollection of such Treatises as have bene heretofore seuerally published . . . By Jos: Hall . . . With addition of some others not hitherto extand. London Printed for Samvel Macham . . . 1615.

6°, text pp. 1–1111.

(1–24) as in Characters of Vertues and Vices, 1608, (25) The penitent man (p. 247), (26) A happy man (p. 250).

There was a variant edition of the same year (STC 12706a), printed for A. Johnson, S. Macham, and L. Lisle.

Overbury, Sir Thomas.

New And Choise Characters, of seuerall Authors: Together with that exquisite and unmatcht Poeme, The Wife, Written by Syr Thomas Ouerburie. With the former Characters and conceited Newes, All in one volume, With many other things added to this sixt Impression. Mar.—non norunt hæc monumenta mori. London Printed by Thomas Creede, for Laurence Lisle . . . 1615.

8°, text sigs. B–M8v.

(1–31) as in the fifth impression, 1614, (32) A meere scholler, (33) A tinker, (34) An apparatour, (35) An almanacke-maker, (36) An hypocrite, (37) A maquerela, in plain English, a bawd, (38) A chamber-mayde, (39) A precisian, (40) A fantastic Innes of Court man, (41) A meere fellow of an house, (42) A worthy commander in the warres, (43) A vaine-glorious coward in command, (44) A pirate, (45) An ordinary fencer, (46) A puny-clarke, (47) A footeman, (48) A noble and retir'd house-keeper, (49) An intruder into fauour, (50) A faire and happy milke-mayd, (51) An arrant horse-courser, (52) A roaring boy, (53) A drunken Dutchman, resident in England, (54) A phantastique. An improuident young gallant, (55) A button-maker of Amsterdam, (56) A distaster of the time, (57) A fellow of an house, (58) A meere petifogger, (59) An ingrosser of corne, (60) A diuellish vsurer, (61) A water-man, (62) A reuerend judge, (63) A vertuous widdow, (64) An ordinarie widdow, (65) A quack saluer, (66) A canting rogue, (67) A French cooke, (68) A sexton, (69) A Jesuite, (70) An excellent actor, (71) A franklin, (72) A purveior of tobacco, (73) A rimer.

Murphy 17. BSC 2140.

Stephens, John.

Essayes and Characters. Ironicall, and Instrvctive. The second impression. With a new Satyre in defence of Common Law and Lawyers: Mixt with reproofe against their common Enemy. With many new Characters, & diuers other things added; & euery thing amended. . . . By Iohn Stephens the yonger, of Lincolnes Inne, Gent. London, Printed by E: Allde for Phillip Knight . . . 1615.

8°, text pp. 1–421 (wrongly numbered 434).

(1–50) as in Satyrical Essayes, 1615, second title.

Murphy 29. BSC 2142. Pforzheimer No. 989.

Stephens, John.

Satyricall Essayes Characters And Others. Or Accurate and quick Descriptions, fitted to the life of their Subiects. . . . Iohn Stephens. London . . . Printed by Nicholas Okes, and are to be sold by Roger Barnes . . . 1615.

8°, text pp. 1–321.

(1) An impudent censurer (p. 129), (2) A compleate man (p. 133), (3) A good husband (p. 138), (4) A contented man (p. 142), (5) A good emperour (p. 147), (6) A worthy poet (p. 150), (7) An honest man (p. 155), (8) A detractor (p. 160), (9) An humorist (p. 165), (10) A coxcombe (p. 170), (11) A ranke observer (p. 175), (12) A parish polititian (p. 180), (13) A spendthrift (p. 185), (14) A ubiquitarie (p. 189), (15) A gamester (p. 193), (16) A novice (p. 197), (17) An epicure (p. 201), (18) A churle (p. 206), (19) An atheist (p. 211), (20) A lyar (p. 216), (21) A drunkard (p. 221), (22) A begging scholler (p. 226), (23) A iaylor (p. 231), (24) An informer (p. 235), (25) A base mercenary poet (p. 239), (26) A common player (p. 244), (27) A warrener (p. 249), (28) A huntsman (p. 253), (29) A falkoner (p. 257), (30) A farmer (p. 262), (31) An hostesse (p. 266), (32) A tapster (p. 270), (33) A lawyers clarke (p. 275), (34) A meere atturney (p. 280), (35) A crafty scrivener (p. 284), (36) A Welch client (p. 291), (37) A country bridegroome (p. 294), (38) A country bride (p. 298), (39) My mistresse (p. 301), (40) A gossip (p. 305), (41) An old woman (p. 309), (42) A witch (p. 312), (43) A pandar (p. 317).

Murphy 28. BSC 2141. Pforzheimer No. 988.

Reprinted 1615 (first, as Satyricall Essayes, with additional characters; second, as Essayes and Characters), 1631 (as New Essayes and Characters).

Stephens, John.

Satyrical Essayes Characters And Others. Or Accurate and quick Descriptions, fitted to the life of their Subiects. . . . Iohn Stephens. London, Printed by Nicholas Okes, and are to be sold by Roger Barnes . . . 1615.

8°, text pp. 1–434.

(1–43) substantially as in the previous edition or issue of 1615, (44) A friend (p. 401), (45) A sicke Machiauell pollititian (p. 405), (46) A page (p. 410), (47) An honest shepheard (p. 415), (48) A taylors man (p. 419), (49) A fidler (p. 423), (50) An executioner (p. 429).

Not in STC.

This entry has been made from the Harvard copy.

Aside from the change in pagination throughout, some of the titles are changed from the previous edition. Thus no. 10 here becomes A weake-train'd gull, no. 12 A simple polititian, no. 14 A ubiquitary, no. 19 An athiest, no. 33 A lawyers simple clarke, no. 34 A pettifogging atturny, no. 36 A wrangling Welch client, no. 37 A plaine country bridegroome, no. 38 A plaine countrey bride.

Tuke, Thomas.

The Christians Looking-Glasse . . . by Thomas Tvke . . . London, Printed by Nicholas Okes, and are to bee sold by Richard Bolton . . . 1615.

8°, text pp. 1–129.

(1) The proud person (p. 114).

The only copy recorded in the STC is at the Bodleian.

[Webbe, George.]

The Practice of Quietness. Six Sermons. London: Printed by E. Griffin for R. Mab. 1615.*

See 1638.

The only copy recorded in the STC is at Cambridge University.

Wither, George.

Abuses Stript and Whipt. 1615.*

(1–11) as in 1613, though with numerous changes.

1616

Anonymous.

The Character of a Player. 1616.*

Perhaps some relation to a character of the same type in Della Casa's The Rich Cabinet of the same year.

Adams, Thomas.

Diseases of the Sovle: A Discovrse Divine, Morall, And Physicall. By Tho. Adams. . . . London, Printed by George Purslowe for Iohn Budge . . . 1616.

4°, text pp. 1–74.

(1) Our braine-sicke nouelist (p. 5), (2) The in-

constant man (p. 8), (3) The angry man (p. 15), (4) The enuious man (p. 17), (5) The idle man (p. 20), (6) The couetous man (p. 23), (7) An vsurer (p. 29), (8) The proud man (p. 32), (9) The feareful man (p. 36), (10) The ambitious man (p. 40), (11) The lustfull man (p. 45), (12) The hypocrite (p. 49), (13) The prodigal man (p. 53), (14) The profane man (p. 56), (15) The secure man (p. 58), (16) The vaine-glorious man (p. 61), (17) The curious man (p. 64), (18) The flatterer (p. 67), (19) One weary of doing well (p. 70).

Murphy 122.

The titles used here are not always those put at the heads of the characters, but they best describe the types portrayed.

Adams, Thomas.

A Divine Herball Together with A Forrest of Thornes. . . . By Tho. Adams. . . . London, Printed by George Purslowe, for Iohn Budge . . . 1616.

4°, text pp. 1–157.

(1) Contemptible malecontents (p. 101, in the sermon entitled The Forrest of Thornes).

Some of the ideas in the third sermon, A Contemplation of the Herbes, are almost but not quite characters.

Adams, Thomas.

The Sacrifice Of Thankefulnesse. A Sermon . . . By Tho. Adams. Whereunto are annexed Fiue other of his Sermons . . . London, Printed by Thomas Purfoot for Clement Knight . . . 1616.

4°, 3 parts, pp. 1–105 (misprinted 103), 1–25, 1–45.

(1) Politicke hvnting: or, a discouerie of the cunning Esauities of our times (part I, p. 45), (2) Wilde boare . . . the depopulator (I, 77), (3) Hope (III, 6).

Beaumont, Francis, and Fletcher, John.

The Scornefvl Ladie. A Comedie . . . Written by Fra. Beavmont and Io. Fletcher, Gent. . . . London, Printed for Myles Partrich . . . 1616.

4°, text sigs. B–K2v.

(1) The hangers-on of young Loveless (sig. H2, act. iv, scene 1).

[Breton, Nicholas.]

The Good And The Badde, Or Descriptions of the Worthies, and Vnworthies of this Age. Where The Best may see their Graces, and the Worst discerne their Baseness. . . . London, Printed by George Purslowe for Iohn Budge . . . 1616.

4°, text pp. 1–40.

(1) A worthy king (p. 1), (2) An unworthy king

(p. 2), (3) A worthy queen (p. 3), (4) A worthy prince (p. 3), (5) An unworthy prince (p. 4), (6) A worthy privy councellor (p. 5), (7) An unworthy councellor (p. 5), (8) A nobleman (p. 6), (9) An un-noble man (p. 7), (10) A worthy bishop (p. 7), (11) An unworthy bishop (p. 8), (12) A worthy judge (p. 9), (13) An unworthy judge (p. 9), (14) A worthy knight (p. 10), (15) An unworthy knight (p. 11), (16) A worthy gentleman (p. 11), (17) An unworthy gentleman (p. 12), (18) A worthy lawyer (p. 13), (19) An unworthy lawyer (p. 13), (20) A worthy soldier (p. 14), (21) An untrained soldier (p. 15), (22) A worthy phisician (p. 16), (23) An unworthy phisician (p. 17), (24) A worthy merchant (p. 18), (25) An unworthy merchant (p. 19), (26) A good man (p. 19), (27) An atheist, or a most bad man (p. 20), (28) A wise man (p. 22), (29) A fool (p. 23), (30) An honest man (p. 23), (31) A knave (p. 24), (32) An usurer (p. 25), (33) A beggar (p. 26), (34) A virgin (p. 27), (35) A wanton woman (p. 27), (36) A quiet woman (p. 28), (37) An unquiet woman (p. 29, (38) A good wife (p. 30), (39) An effeminate fool (p. 30), (40) A parasite (p. 31), (41) A bawd (p. 32), (42) A drunkard (p. 33), (43) A coward (p. 33), (44) An honest poor man (p. 34), (45) A just man (p. 35), (46) A repentant sinner (p. 36), (47) A reprobate (p. 39), (48) An old man (p. 37), (49) A young man (p. 38), (50) A holy man (p. 39).
Murphy 27.

Attributed to Breton by the STC. Reprinted, with some modifications, in 1643 as Englands Selected Characters.

Casa, Giovanni della.

The Rich Cabinet Furnished with varietie Of Excellent discriptions, exquisite Charracters, witty discourses, and delightful Histories, Deuine and Morall. Together With Inuectiues against many abuses of the time: digested Alphabetically into common places, Wherevnto Is Annexed the Epitome of good manners, extracted from Mr. John de la Casa, Arch-bishop of Beneuenta. London Printed by I.B. for Roger Jackson . . . 1616.

8°, text ff. 1–166, plus sigs. Y6v–Aa4.
(1) Affinity (f. 1), (2) Anger (f. 2v), (3) Atheism (f. 5v), (4) Beauty (f. 7), (5) Birth (f. 9v), (6) Benefits (f. 10v), (7) Covetousness (f. 12v), (8) Cruelty (f. 15), (9) Courtesy (f. 17v), (10) The courtier (f. 18v), (11) Clergymen (f. 21), (12) A citizen (f. 27), (13) Country life (f. 28v), (14) A cuckold (f. 30), (15) Death (f. 32), (16) Diseases (f. 34v), (17) Drunkenness (f. 36v), (18) Effeminateness (f. 38v), (19) Eloquence (f. 39v), (20) Envy (f. 41), (21) Folly (f. 43v), (22) Fortune (f. 46v), (23) Friends (f. 48), (24) Gentry (f. 50v), (25) God (f. 58), (26) Grauity (f. 61), (27) Honor (f. 63), (28) Humility (f. 65), (29) Hypocrisy (f. 66), (30) Invections (f. 68), (31) Ignominy (f. 69v), (32) Idleness (f. 72), (33) Kings (f. 74), (34) Knowledge (f. 76), (35) Knavery (f. 79), (36) Laws (f. 81), (37) Lechery (f. 82v), (38) Love (f. 84v), (39) Liberty (f. 87v), (40) Merchant (f. 89), (41) Man (f. 90v), (42) Modesty (f. 92), (43) Money (f. 94), (44) Negligence (f. 96v), (45) Nobody (f. 97v), (46) Economie (f. 101), (47) Offices and Officers (f. 104v), (48) Order (f. 107), (49) Oaths (f. 108v), (50) Pleasure (f. 110v), (51) Poetry (f. 112), (52) Poverty (f. 113), (53) Player (f. 116), (54) Pride (f. 118), (55) Profit (f. 121), (56) Quietness (f. 122), (57) Reason (f. 124), (58) Religion (f. 126), (59) Remembrance (f. 129), (60) Resolution (f. 130), (61) A statesman (f. 132), (62) Scholars (f. 134), (63) A soldier (f. 135), (64) Shifting (f. 136v), (65) Singularity (f. 138v), (66) Sin (f. 139v), (67) Sorrow (f. 141), (68) Temperance (f. 143v), (69) Time (f. 145v), (70) A traveler (f. 147), (71) Troubles (f. 149), (72) Vanity (f. 151), (73) Valor (f. 153v), (74) Virtue (f. 155), (75) Wars (f. 157), (76) Wilfulness (f. 158v), (77) The world (f. 160), (78) Woman (f. 162v), (79) A whore (f. 164v).
BSC 2143.

Frequently listed under the name of Thomas Gainsford, the translator.

[Cornwallis, Sir William.]

Essayes of Certaine Paradoxes . . . London, Printed for T. Thorp . . . 1616.*
See 1617.
Pforzheimer No. 216.
There were two impressions in 1616.
The STC gives Cornwallis as the author.

[Davies, John, of Hereford.]

A Select Second Hvsband For Sir Thomas Overbvries Wife, Now A Matchlesse Widow. . . . London, Printed by T. Creede and Bernard Allsopp, for I. Marriott . . . 1616.
8°, text sigs. B–G4v.
(1) A choice husband (sig. B).
BSC 2144.
Attributed to Davies by the STC.

[Dekker, Thomas.]

The Belman of London. The Fourth Impression. London, Printed for N. Butter. 1616.*
4°.
(1–17) as in 1608.

[Dekker, Thomas.]

Villanies discovered by Lanthorne and Candlelight. London, 1616.*

Pforzheimer No. 274 n.

See his Lanthorne and Candle Light, 1609.

Healey, John.

Epictetvs Manuall. Cebes Table. Theophras-
tvs Characters. By Io. Healey. . . . London,
Printed by George Purslowe for Edward
Blount. 1616.

12°, text sigs. B–N11v.

(1) Characters, by Theophrastus (sig. I).

BSC 2145.

Huarte Navarro, Juan de Dios.

Examen de Ingenios. The Examination of
mens Wits. . . . By John Hvarte. . . . Englished . . . by R.C. Esquire. . . . London,
Printed by Adam Islip, for Thomas Adams.
1616.

8°, text pp. 1–333.

(1) as in 1594.

Jonson, Ben.

The Workes of Beniamin Jonson . . . London printed by W: Stansby, and are to be
sould by Rich: Meighen. Ano. D. 1616.

6°, text pp. 1–1015.

(1) Euery man ovt of his hvmovr (p. 73), (2)
Cynthia's Revels (p. 177), (3) Epicoene (p. 525).
Pforzheimer No. 559.

There are at least two other states or issues of this year:
one printed by Will Stansby, the other by William Stansby.
The contents are the same.

Overbury, Sir Thomas.

Sir Thomas Ouerburie His Wife, With New
Elegies vpon his (now knowne) vntimely
death. Whereunto are annexed, new Newes
and Characters, written by himselfe and other
learned Gentlemen. Editio Septima. London,
Printed by Edward Griffin for Laurence
L'isle . . . 1616.

8°, text sigs. ¶3–Q7.

(1–72) as (1–73) in sixth impression, 1615, but
with omission of no. 72, a purveior of tobacco.
Murphy 19. BSC 2146.

With the omission of no. 72, Wotton's Character of a
happy life becomes no. 72. The copy in the Boston Public
Library is defective, lacking title page and all pages before
A8. At the end someone has written in ink the name of
Lady Southwell, to whom the book has therefore been
ascribed.

Overbury, Sir Thomas.

Sir Thomas Ouerburie. His Wife. With New
Elegies vpon his (now knowne) vntimely
death. Whereunto are annexed, New Newes
and Characters, written by himselfe and other
Learned Gentlemen. The Eight Impression.

London, Printed by Edward Griffin for Laurence L'isle . . . 1616.*

8°, text sigs. C–Q8.

(1–72) as in seventh impression, 1616.

Murphy 20.

The Bodleian copy is the only one listed in the STC.

Overbury, Sir Thomas.

Sir Thomas Ouerbury His Wife. With Addition Of many new Elegies vpon his vntimely
and much lamented death. As Also New
Newes, and diuers more Characters, (neuer
before annexed) written by himselfe and other
learned Gentlemen. The ninth impression
augmented. London, Printed by Edward Griffin for Laurence L'isle, and are to be sold at
his shop at the Tigers head in Paules Church-
yard. 1616.

8°, text sigs. C–S3.

(1–72) as in eighth impression, 1616, (73) A
couetous man (sig. Q6v), (74) The proud man
(sig. Q8), (75) A prison (sig. R), (76) A prisoner (sig. R2v), (77) A creditour (sig. R4v),
(78) A sarieant (sig. R6v), (79) This yeoman
(sig. R8), (80) A iaylour (sig. S), (81) What a
character is (sig. S2v).

Murphy 20.

In the Huntington copy the deleted character of a purveior of tobacco (formerly no. 72) is written in MS on
sig. S3v.

Pemberton, William.

The Godly Merchant. 1616.*

See 1613.

The only copy listed in the STC is at Lincoln Cathedral.

Rich, Barnabe.

My Ladies Looking Glasse. Wherein May Be
Discerned A Wise Man From A Foole, A
Good Woman From A Bad . . . By Barnabe
Rich. . . . London, Printed for Thomas Ad-
ams. 1616.

4°, text pp. 1–74.

(1) Temporizer (p. 50), (2) The formalist (p.
50), (3) The fantasticke (p. 51), (4) The nini-
hammer (p. 51), (5) The newsmonger (p. 51),
(6) The malecontent (p. 53), (7) The amorist
(p. 54), (8) The courtier (p. 66), (9) The
counterfeit souldier (p. 66), (10) The lawyer
(p. 67).

[Tuke, Thomas.]

A Discourse Against Painting and Tincturing
of Women. . . . Whereunto is added the Picture of a Picture, or, The Character of a
Painted Woman . . . London for Edward
Marchant. 1616.

4°, text pp. 1–62.

(1) A painted wench, by Thomas Draiton (sig. Bv), (2) The picture of a picture, or, the character of a painted woman (p. 57).

Attributed to Tuke by the STC. There was another edition in the same year under the title, A Treatise against Painting.

Tuke, Thomas.

A Treatise Against Paintng [*sic*] and tinctvring of men and women . . . Whereunto is added The picture of a picture, or, the Character of a Painted Woman. By Thomas Tvke . . . London, Printed by Tho. Creed and Barn. Allsope for Edward Merchant . . . 1616.

4°, text pp. 1–62.
(1–2) as in A Discourse Against Painting, 1616.
Murphy 123. BSC 2147.

1617

Adams, Thomas.

The Sovldiers Honovr. . . . By Tho. Adams. . . . London, Printed by Adam Islip and Edward Blount . . . 1617.

4°, text pp. 1–33.
(1) The martialist (p. 23).

[Brathwaite, Richard.]

A Solemne Ioviall Disputation, Theoreticke and Practicke; briefely Shadowing The Lavv Of Drinking; Together, with the Solemnities and Controversies occurring . . . Faithfully rendred according to the originall Latine Copie. Θενοζψτηοπολις. At the Signe of Red-Eyes. CIƆ IƆC XVII.
[Inner title:] The Smoaking Age, Or, The Man in the mist: With The life and death of Tobacco. . . . CIƆ IƆC XVII.

8°, text pp. 1–194. The Smoaking Age begins on p. 99.
(1) Cornelius Vandunk (p. 62), (2) The scholar (p. 157), (3) The lawyer (p. 158), (4) The poet (p. 159).
BSC 2148.

Attributed to Brathwaite by the STC.

[Cornwallis, Sir William.]

Essayes Of Certaine Paradoxes. The second Impression, inlarged. London: Printed for Richard Havvkins . . . 1617.

4°, text sigs. A2–F4v.
(1) The praise of King Richard the Third (sig. A2), (2) The praise of nothing (sig. E3v).

Fennor, William.

The Compters Common-Wealth, Or A Voiage Made To an Infernall Iland long since dis-

couered by many Captaines, Seafaringmen, Gentlemen, Marchants, and other Tradesmen: Bvt The Conditions, Natures, and qualities of the people there inhabiting, and of those that trafficke with them, were neuer so truly expressed or liuely set foorth as By William Fennor His Maiesties Servant. London Printed by Edward Griffin for George Gibbes . . . 1617.

4°, text pp. 1–85.
(1) A prison (p. 9), (2) A iaylor (p. 58).
Murphy 124.

Reprinted 1619 (as The Miseries of a Iaile) and 1629 (as A True Description of . . . a Compter).

Hall, Joseph.

A Recollection of such Treatises. London, Printed for H. Fetherstone. 1617.*

Reprinted from 1615.

[Webbe, George.]

The Practice of Quietness. The second edition. 1617.*

See 1638.

Wither, George.

Abuses Stript and Whipt. 1617.
(1–11) as in 1613.

Young, Thomas.

Englands Bane, Or, The Description of Drunkennesse. Composed And Written By Thomas Yovng, sometimes Student of Staple-Inne. . . . London, Printed by William Iones, and are to be sold by Thomas Baylee . . . 1617.

4°, text sigs. B–F4.
(1) A drunkard (sig. F2v).

1618

Adams, Thomas.

The Happiness of the Church. Or, A Description Of those Spirituall Prerogatiues vvherewith Christ hath endowed her. Considered in some contemplations vpon part of the 12. Chapter to the Hebrewes. Together with certain other Meditations and Discourses . . . Being the Summe of diuerse Sermons . . . By Thomas Adams . . . London, Printed by G.P. for Iohn Grismand . . . 1618.

8°, two parts.
(1) The malicious slanderer (Part I, p. 171), (2) The griping vsurer (I, 171), (3) The destructiue depopulator (I, 171), (4) The oppressing landlord (I, 172), (5) The churlish cormorant (I, 172), (6) The proud gallant (I, 173), (7)

The fraudulent tradesman (I, 173), (8) The bribe-groping officer (I, 173), (9) The church-defrauder (I, 174), (10) The truth-hating Iesuite (I, 174), (11) Couetousnesse (I, 293), (12) The sad or melancholy foole (II, 77), (13) The glad or mad foole (II, 77), (14) The haughtie or ambitious foole (II, 78), (15) The naughtie or couetous foole (II, 78), (16) Pride (II, 159), (17) Prodigalitie (II, 160), (18) Enuie (II, 160), (20) Coueteousnes (II, 160), (21) Lust (II, 160), (22) Hypocrisie (II, 160), (23) Charitie (II, 161), (24) The ambitious (II, 200), (25) The flatterer (II, 201), (26) Ingrossers (II, 201), (27) The depopulator (II, 202), (28) Wealth (II, 233), (29) The inconstant man (II, 235), (30) The enuious eye (II, 312), (31) The dart, the angrie man (II, 321), (32) Dipsas, the drunkard (II, 321), (33) The crocodile, the hypocrite (II, 322), (34) The catterpillar, the couetous (II, 323), (35) The aspe, the traitours seminary (II, 324), (36) The sea-serpent (II, 325), (37) The stellion, the extortioner (II, 325).

[Mynshul, Geffray.]

Certaine Characters and Essayes of Prison and Prisoners Compiled By Novvus Homo A Prisoner in the Kings Bench . . . London Printed by William Iones . . . 1618.

8°, text sigs. A5 (first gathering) – D3.

(1) Of a prison, (2) Of a prisoner, (3) Of a creditor, (4) Of companions in prison, (5) Of visitants, (6) Of keepers, (7) Of jaylors.

Murphy 31.

The only recorded copy is in the British Museum.

The Epistle Dedicatorie (sig. A2) is dated Jan. 27, 1617 (i.e., 1617/8), and is signed Yarffeg Lluhsnym, an anagram of Mynshul's name. Some of the characters could be listed as two or more by separating them into different phases of the subjects.

[Mynshul, Geffray.]

Essayes And Characters Of A Prison And Prisoners. Written by G.M. of Grayes-Inne Gent. . . . Printed at London for Mathew Walbancke . . . 1618.

4°, text pp. 1–48.

(1–6) as in Certaine Characters, 1618 (omitting Of jaylors), (7) A locker vp at nights (p. 41), (8) A noble vnderstanding prisoner (p. 42).

Murphy 32. BSC 2149.

The dedication is signed Geffray Mynshvl.

Overbury, Sir Thomas.

Sir Thomas Ouerbury His Wife With Additions Of New Newes, and diuers more Characters, (neuer before annexed) written by himselfe and other learned Gentlemen. The tenth impression augmented. London, Printed by Edward Griffin for Laurence L'isle, and

are to be sold at his shop at the Tigers head in Pauls Church-yard. 1618.

8°, text sigs. ¶3–R3.

(1–81) as in ninth impression, 1616.

Murphy 21. BSC 2150

The title of No. 80 is here changed from A iaylour to A common cruell iaylour.

[Webbe, George.]

The Practice of Quietness. 1618.*

See 1638.

Not in STC. The only copy known to the editor is at Yale.

1619

Adams, Thomas.

The Happines of the Church. Or, A Description of those Spirituall Prerogatiues vvherewith Christ hath endowed her. Considered in some contemplations vpon part of the 12. Chapter to the Hebrewes. Together with certain other Meditations and Discourses. . . . By Thomas Adams . . . London, Printed by G.P. for Iohn Grismand . . . 1619.

4°, two parts, text pp. 1–429 (misprinted 443), 1–376 (misprinted 375).

(1–37) as in 1618.

The only copy recorded in the STC is at Huntington.

[B., A.D.]

The Covrt Of The Most Illvstrious and most Magnificent James, the first . . . London Printed by Edw: Griffin . . . 1619.

4°, text pp. 1–168.

(1) Wicked and ungodly courtiers (p. 91).

The Epistle Dedicatory and the Epistle to the Reader are signed A.D.B. The whole book is an extended character of a good courtier.

[Fennor, William.]

The Miseries Of A Iaile: Or, A True Description of a Prison . . . With many special Characters of Seriaunts, Key-turners, Keepers, Beadles, and other Officers . . . Pleasant, and not unprofitable. By F.W. London, for R.R. 1619.*

(1–2) as in The Compters Common–wealth, 1617.

Murphy 124.

The only copy recorded in the STC is at the Bodleian.

Hannay, Patrick.

A Happy Husband Or, Directions for a Maide to choose her Mate. As also, A Wives Behaviovr towards her Husband after Marriage. By Patricke Hannay, Gent. To which is adioyned the Good Wife; together with an Ex-

quisite discourse of Epitaphs . . . By R B.
Gent. . . . Printed at London for Richard
Redmer . . . 1619[–18].

8°, in 2 parts, text sigs. B–C8, B–L3v.
(1) A good wife, by Brathwaite (Part II, sig.
B2v), (2) A good husband, by Brathwaite (II,
B5v), (3) A description of death, by Brathwaite
(II, E7).

R.B. is identified with Brathwaite by the CBEL. Part II
bears a separate title page: Remains after Death . . . Imprinted at London by Iohn Beale 1618 (sig. C2).

[Heath, John.]

The Hovse of Correction: Or, Certayne
Satyricall Epigrams. Written by I.H. Gent.
Together with a few Characters, called Par
Pari: Or, Like to like, quoth the Deuill to
the Collier. . . . London, Printed by Bernard
Alsop, for Richard Redmer . . . 1619.

8°, text sigs. A4–D4v.
(1) A pirat (sig. D), (2) A drunkard (sig. Dv),
(3) A meere gallant (sig. Dv), (4) A curtizan
(sig. D2), (5) A gull traueller (sig. D2v), (6)
A swaggerer (sig. D3), (7) A broking scriuener
(sig. D3v), (8) A gamester at Irish (sig. D3v),
(9) An amorist (sig. D4).
Murphy 124. BSC 2162.

Hutton, Henry.

Follie's Anatomie: Or Satyres And Satyricall
Epigrams. . . . Compiled by Henry Hutton,
Dunelmensis. London Printed for Matthew
Walbanke . . . 1619.

8°, text sigs. A7–E3.
(1) A timist (sig. A7), (2) A letcher (sig. A8),
(3) Tom Tospot (sig. B), (4) Mounsier
Brauado, a foolish asse (sig. B2), (5) A tippling
poetaster (sig. B3), (6) Helluo, a glutton (sig.
B4v), (7) A demure wanton (sig. B6).

Taylor, John.

A Kicksey Winsey; or a Lerry Come-Twang,
Wherein John Taylor hath satyrically suited
800 of his bad debtors that will not pay him
for his return of his journey from Scotland.
London, Printed by N. Okes for M. Wal-
banck, 1619.*

8°. In verse.
(1) Those that have paid their subscriptions for
his journey to Scotland, (2) Those that would
pay if they could, (3) Those that are hard for
me to finde, (4) Those that will and doe daily
pay me in drinke and smoake, (5) Those that
are dead, (6) Those that are fled, (7) Those that
are as farre from honesty, as a Turke is from
true religion.

Reprinted 1624 as The Scourge of Basenesse. The contents
above are taken from the Spenser Society reprint.

Anonymous.

Haec-Vir: Or The Womanish Man. Being
an Answere to a late Booke intituled Hic-
Mulier. . . . London printed for I.T. . . .
1620.

4°, text sigs. A3–C4.
(1) A womanish man (sig. C).

[B., A.D.]

The Covrt Of The Most Illvstrious and most
Magnificent James, the First; King of Great-
Britaine . . . With Divers rvles, Most Pvre
Precepts, And Selected Definitions, liuely de-
lineated. . . . London Printed by Edw. Grif-
fin . . . 1620.

4°, text pp. 1–168.
(1) as in 1619.

Brathwaite, Richard.

Essaies Vpon The Five Senses, with a pithie
one upon Detraction. . . . By Rich: Brath-
wayt Esquire. . . . London, Printed by E:G:
for Richard Whittaker . . . 1620.

8°, text pp. 1–142.
(1) The author's opinion of marriage (p. 119),
(2) A shrew (p. 134).
Murphy 125. BSC 2134, 2153.

[Chandos, Grey Brydges, Fifth Baron.]

Horæ Subseciuæ. Observations And Discourses. . . . London, Printed for Edward
Blount . . . 1620.

8°, text pp. 1–542.
(1) An arrogant person (p. 4).
Attributed to Chandos by the STC.

[Dekker, Thomas.]

Villanies discovered. London, 1620.*
Pforzheimer No. 274 n.
A reprint of Lanthorne and Candle Light, 1609.

Dichante, George.

An Epitome Of The Worlds Woe, Wherein
is perspicuously discouered: the lamentable
miseries of the World, in these tempestuous
times, the infidelitie of fained friends, and
the ficklenesse of deceitefull fortune. Continued by way of Meditation and Resolution. By
Geo. Dichante, Gent. . . . London, Printed
by Thomas Cotes, and Richard Cotes, 1620.

8°, text pp. 3–34. In verse.
(1) Faithlesse friends (p. 15), (2) A friend (p.
16), (3) Petti-foggers (p. 22), (4) Mechanicke
men (p. 24), (5) The temporall man (p. 24), (6)
Tapsters (p. 26), (7) The cosenning broker (p.
27), (8) Our cleargy (p. 28).

Not in STC. Huntington Supplement, no. 6816+.
The Huntington copy seems to be unique.

[Ford, John.]

A Line of Life. Pointing at the Immortalitie
of a Vertuous Name. Printed by W.S. for
N. Butter . . . 1620.*
12°.
(1) A good man (p. 88 or 95).
Attributed to Ford by the STC.

[Jonson, Ben.]

Epicoene, or The silent Woman. A Comœdie.
Acted in the yeare 1609. . . . The Author
B.I. . . . London, Printed by William Stans-
by . . . 1620.
4°, text sigs. B–O4.
(1) A wife, by True-Wit (Act II, scene i), (2)
A wife, by Mrs. Otter (III, i).
There were two issues in 1620.
This play has been often reprinted.

[Rowlands, Samuel.]

The Night-Raven. By S.R. . . . London.
Printed by G: Eld for Iohn Deane. 1620.*
4°, text sigs. A3–E2v.
(1) A night swaggerer.
The Huntington copy is the only one mentioned in the
STC.
Attributed to Rowlands by the CBEL and the STC.

Rowlands, Samuel.

[A paire of spy-knaves. 1620?]*
(1) A fantastical knave (p. 8), (2) Usurer (p.
14), (3) A roaring boyes description (p. 15).
The only known copy, that in the British Museum, lacks
title page. This book was entered in the Stationers' Register in 1619 to P. Birch, and assigned in 1623 to R. Bird.

[Taylor, John.]

The praise of hemp-seed: with the voyage of
Mr. R Bird and the writer hereof in a boat of
brown-paper, to Quinborough in Kent. . . .
London, printed for Henry Gosson, 1620.*
4°.
(1) A cobbler, (2) A Brownist, or precise Amsterdam Puritane.
Attributed to Taylor by the STC.

1621

Adams, Thomas.

The White Devill Or The Hypocrite Vncased.
. . . fifth Impression . . . By Tho. Adams.
London, Printed for R. Higginbotham . . .
1621.*
4°.
(1–16) as in 1613.

[Breton, Nicholas.]

The Passion of a Discontented Minde. . . .
London, Printed by N. Okes for S. Albyn
. . . 1621.*
(1–2) as in 1601.

Hall, Joseph.

Meditations And Vowes, Diuine and Morall:
Seruing for direction in Christian and Ciuill
Practice. Newly enlarged with Caracters of
Vertues and Vices. By Ios. Hall. London,
Printed by William Stansby for Henrie Feth-
erstone. 1621.
12°, text pp. 1–796.
(1–26) as in A Recollection, 1615.
Murphy 12. BSC 2154.
Previous editions of Meditations and Vowes do not con-
tain the characters.

Hall, Joseph.

A Recollection of such Treatises as haue bene
heretofore seuerally published, and are nowe
reuised, corrected, augmented. By Jos: Hall
. . . With addition of some others not hitherto extant. London. Printed for Hen: Fetherstone . . . 1621.
6°, in 2 parts, text pp. 1–967, 1–166.
(1–26) as in 1615.

Mason, William.

A Handfvl Of Essaies. Or Imperfect offers.
By W: Mason Master of Arts. . . . London
Printed by Aug. Mathewes for Iohn Grismand
. . . 1621.
12°, text pp. 1–132.
(1) The covetous (p. 39), (2) Gluttons (p. 67),
(3) Envy (p. 122), (4) Flatterers (p. 127).

Rogers, Nehemiah.

Christian Curtesie: Or, St. Pavls Vltimum
Vale. Deliuered in two Sermons . . . By N.
Rogers . . . London, Printed by H.L. for
Edward Brewster . . . 1621.
4°, text pp. 1–77.
(1) Those who will give but not take comfort
(p. 49), (2) Enuy (p. 65), (3) The flatterer (p.
68), (4) The wrangling lawyer (p. 68).

Taylor, John.

The Praise, Antiquity, and Commodity, of
Beggery, Beggers, and Begging. By Iohn
Taylor. . . . At London Printed by E.A. for
Henry Gosson . . . 1621.
4°, text sigs. B–D3v.
(1) Beggars (sig. C2v, in verse), (2) Beggars
(sig. C4v, in prose).

Taylor, John.

Taylor's Goose, describing the wild goose. . . . E.A. for H. Gosson. 1621.*

(1) The tame goose, (2) The Winchester goose, (3) The taylers goose, (4) The praise of the gray goose wing, (5) The praise of the gooses quill, (6) The memorable honour of the goose sauing the capitoll at Rome, (7) Goostoft in Lincolnshire, (8) Goose Faire at Stratford Bow.

The original not being easily available, the above list of contents has been taken from the Spenser Society reprint of the Works of 1630.

1622

Adams, Thomas.

Eirenopolis: the citie of peace. London: Printed by A. Mathewes for J. Grismand. 1622.*

12°.

(1) Peace.

The only copy recorded in the STC is at the Bodleian. Reprinted 1630 as The Citie of Peace.

Bacon, Sir Francis.

The Historie Of The Raigne Of King Henry The Seuenth. Written By the Right Honourable, Francis, Lord Verulam, Viscount St. Alban. London, Printed by W. Stansby for Matthew Lownes, and William Barret. 1622.

4°, text pp. 1–248.

(1) The king (p. 233).

There have been frequent later editions.

Cooke, John.

Greenes Tu Quoque. London, Printed for T. Dewe. 1622.*

Reprinted from 1614.

Du Refuge, Eustache.

A Treatise Of The Court Or Instructions for Courtiers. Digested into two Books. Written in French by . . . Denys de Refuges . . . Done into English by Iohn Reynolds. Imprinted by A.M: for Will: Lee . . . 1622.

8°, in 2 parts, text pp. 1–189, 1–189.

(1) A choleric man (Part I, p. 112), (2) A fearful man (I, 115), (3) Old men (I, 128), (4) Rich men (I, 133).

Hannay, Patrick.

The Nightingale Sheretine and Mariana. A happy Husband. . . . by Patrick Hañay gent. . . . London printed for Nathaniel Butter. 1622.

8°, text pp. 1–250.

(1) A happy husband, second edition (p. 143).

Overbury, Sir Thomas.

Sir Thomas Ouerbury His Wife. With Additions Of New Characters, and many other

Wittie Conceits neuer before Printed. The eleuenth Impression. London, Printed for Laurence Lisle, and are to be sold by Henry Seile at the Tigers-head in Pauls Church-yard, 1622.

8°, text sigs. A2–V8v.

(1–81) as in ninth impression, 1616, (82) A dunce, by John Donne (sig. G3).

Murphy 21. BSC 2155.

[Scott, Thomas.]

The Interpreter Wherin three principall termes of State much mistaken by the vulgar are clearly unfolded. . . . Anno 1622.

8°, text pp. 2–16.

(1) A Puritan (p. 3), (2) A Protestant (p. 7), (3) A Papist (p. 15).

Murphy 126.

Attributed to Scott by Miss Murphy. There is also a manuscript version, n.d.

Taylor, John.

An Arrant Thiefe . . . With A Comparison betweene a Thiefe and a Booke. Written by Iohn Taylor. London: Printed by Edw: Allde, for Henry Gosson . . . 1622.

8°, text sigs. A5–C6v. In verse.

Begins: "I Lately to the world did send a *Whore*."

Not a very satisfactory example of character, because it is rather general and includes a number of types.

Taylor, John.

A Common Whore, VVith all these Graces Grac'd, Shee's very honest, beautifull and chaste. Written by Iohn Taylor. At London, Printed for Henry Gosson . . . 1622.

8°, text sigs. A3–B8v. In verse.

(1) A cheap whore (sig. A3), (2) A strange whore, common and yet honest (sig. A3v), (3) A comparison betwixt a whore and a book (sig. B6v).

Taylor, John.

The Water-Cormorant His Complaint: Against a Brood of Land-Cormorants. . . . By Iohn Taylor. . . . London, Printed by George Eld. 1622.

4°, text sigs. A4–F4. In verse.

(1) A Jesuite (sig. A4), (2) A separatist (sig. B), (3) A trust-breaker (sig. B2v), (4) A drunkard (sig. B4), (5) A prodigal country gallant (sig. C2), (6) An extortioner & a breaker (sig. C3v), (7) A basket justice (sig. C4v), (8) A cutpurse (sig. D2), (9) A good and a bad constable (sig. D3), (10) A London serieant and iaylor (sig. D4v), (11) A symonicall patron, and his penny clarke (sig. E2v), (12) A country yeoman (sig. E3v), (13) A figure flinger, or a couzning cunning man (sig. E4v), (14) A corrupted lawyer, and a knavish under-shriefe (sig. F2).

Wither, George.

Ivvenilia A Collection of those Poemes which were heretofore imprin-ted, and written by George wither. London printed for Iohn Budge . . . 1622.

8°, text sigs. A2–Qq8.

(1) Abuses Stript and Whipt (sig. A2).

There were two issues in this year. Abuses Stript and Whipt also appeared separately in 1622.

1623

Scott, Thomas.

The Proiector. Teaching A Direct, Svre, and ready way to restore the decayes of the Church and State both in Honour and Revenue. Delivered In A Sermon before the Iudges in Norwich, at Summer Assises there holden, Anno 1620. By Thomas Scot Batchelor in Diuinity. . . . Printed at London. 1623.

4°, text pp. 1–39.

(1) A just man (p. 5).

There were two other editions of the same year, one separate (STC 22082), and the other as part of Vox populi. Vox Dei (STC 22102).

[Taylor, John.]

[The praise of hemp-seed. 1623.]

4°, text pp. 1–34.

(1–2) as in 1620.

The Harvard copy lacks the title page.

1624

[Bolton, Edmund.]

Nero Caesar, Or Monarchie Depraved. An Hjstoricall Worke. . . . By the Translator of Lvcivs Florvs. London: Printed by T.S. for Thomas Walkley . . . 1624.

4°, text pp. 1–288.

(1) Boadicia, the warlick widdowe (p. 101).

Attributed to Bolton by the STC. An engraved title page is dated 1623.

[Brewer, Thomas.]

A knot of Fooles. Bvt, Fooles, or Knaues, or both, I care not, Here they are; Come laugh and spare not. Printed at London for Francis Groue . . . 1624.

4°, text sigs. A2–D2v.

(1) A miser (sig. A4), (2) A crafty tradesman (sig. A4v), (3) A woman's slave (sig. Bv), (4) A rotten post painted (i.e., a painted woman) (sig. Bv), (5) A drunkard (sig. B2), (6) A gamester (sig. B3), (7) A court zany (sig. B3v), (8) A gallant (sig. B4v), (9) A lawyer (sig. Cv), (10) A covetous physician (sig. Cv), (11) A lord (sig. C2).

The address to the reader is signed Tho. Brewer. Brewer uses no specific titles for his characters; these are the editor's.

[Rich, Barnabe.]

A New Irish Prognostication. 1624.*

(1–4) as in A New Description of Ireland, 1610.

[Rowlands, Samuel.]

The Night Raven. London, G. Eld for John Deane and Thomas Baily. 1624.*

(1) as in 1620.

The only copy recorded in the STC is at the Bodleian.

[Taylor, John.]

The Scourge of Basenesse. Or the old Lerry with a new Kicksey, and a new cum twang with the old Winsye. Wherein John Taylor hath curried or clapperclawed, neere a thousand of his bad Debters, etc. London, Printed by N.O. for M. Walbancke. [1619].*

(1–7) as in his Kicksey Winsey, 1619.

Dated [1619] by the British Museum Catalogue, but 1624 by the STC.

1625

Adams, Thomas.

The Holy Choice. London, Printed by A. Mathewes and J. Norton. 1625.*

4°.

(1) A good magistrate.

Gardyne, Alexander.

Characters And Essayes, By Alexander Garden. Aberdene, Printed by Edward Raban . . . 1625.

8°, text pp. 9–61.

(1) A worthie king (p. 9), (2) An vnworthie king (p. 10), (3) A worthie queene (p. 12), (4) A worthie prince (p. 13), (5) An vnworthie prince (p. 14), (6) A worthie counseller (p. 15), (7) An vnworthie councellor (p. 16), (8) A worthie noble-man (p. 16), (9) An ignoble-man (p. 18), (10) A worthie bishop (p. 19), (11) An vnworthie bishop (p. 20), (12) A worthie iudge (p. 21), (13) An unworthie iudge (p. 22), (14) A worthie knight (p. 23), (15) An vnworthie knight (p. 24), (16) A worthie gentleman (p. 25), (17) An vnworthie gentleman (p 26), (18) A worthie lawyer (p. 27), (19) An vnworthie lawyer (p. 28), (20) A worthie souldiour (p. 29), (21) An vntrained souldiour (p. 30), (22) A worthie physician (p. 31), (23) An vnworthie physician (p. 32), (24) A worthie merchand (p. 33), (25) An vnworthie merchand (p. 34), (26) A good man (p. 35), (27) A bad man, or atheist (p. 36), (28) A wise man (p. 37), (29) A

foole (p. 38), (30) A plaine honest man (p. 39), (31) A knaue (p. 40), (32) An vsurer (p. 41), (33) A beggar (p. 41), (34) A virgine (p. 43), (35) A wanton woman (p. 44), (36) A quyet woman (p. 45), (37) An vnquiet woman (p. 45), (38) A good wyfe (p. 46), (39) An effeminate man (p. 47), (40) A parasite (p. 48), (41) A baude (p. 49), (42) A drunkard (p. 50), (43) A coward (p. 51), (44) An honest poore man (p. 52), (45) A iust man (p. 54), (46) A repentant sinner (p. 55), (47) A reprobate (p. 56), (48) An holie man (p. 57), (49) An olde man (p. 58), (50) A young man (p. 60).

The only copy recorded in the STC is at the British Museum. Apparently plagiarized from Nicholas Breton's The Goode and the Badde, 1616.

Hall, Joseph.

The Works Of Joseph Hall. . . . London, Printed for Thomas Pauier, Miles Flesher, and Iohn Haviland. 1625.

fo, text pp. 1–1397.
(1) Meditations and vowes (p. 1), (2) Characters of vertves and vices (p. 173), (3) Salomons divine arts (p. 207), (4) Epistles (p. 275).
Murphy 13.

There were two other editions of the same year. One (STC 12635a) was printed for R. Moore; the other (STC 12635b) was printed for N. Butter.

Markham, Francis.

The Booke Of Honovr. Or, Five Decads Of Epistles Of Honovr. Written by Francis Markham. . . . London, Printed by Augustine Matthewes, and John Norton. 1625.

4°, text pp. 1–200.
(1) An absolute king (p. 198).

Robinson, John.

Observations Divine and Morale. . . . By John Robinson. . . . Printed in the Year M.DC.XXV.

4°, text pp. 1–324.
(1) Of councellors (p. 120), (2) People of lawful calling (p. 149), (3) Children (p. 308), (4) Young and old (p. 315).

Reprinted 1628 (as New Essayes), 1629 (ditto), 1638 (as Essayes).

Taylor, John.

An Arrant Thiefe. With a Comparison between a Thiefe and a Booke. London, Printed by E. All-de for H. Gosson. 1625.*
8°. In verse.
A reprint of 1622.

Taylor, John.

A Common Whore, with all these Graces grac'd. . . . London, Printed for H. Gosson. 1625.*

8°.
(1–3) as in 1622.

The only copy recorded in the STC is at the British Museum.

Wither, George.

The Schollers Pvrgatory, Discouered In the Stationers Common-wealth . . . By George VVither . . . Imprinted For the Honest Stationers.

8°, text pp. 1–131.
(1) An honest stationer (p. 116), (2) A meere stationer (p. 119).
Murphy 125.

Dated [1625?] by the STC.

1626

Bernard, Richard.

The Isle of Man. 1626.*
See 1627.

[Breton, Nicholas.]

Fantasticks: Seruing for A Perpetvall Prognostication. . . . London, Printed for Francis Williams. 1626.

4°, text sigs. A4–F3v.
(1) The world (sig. A4), (2) Loue (sig. A4v), (3) Money (sig. B), (4) The spring (sig. Bv), (5) Summer (sig. B2), (6) Haruest (sig. B2v), (7) VVinter (sig. B3), (8) January (sig. B3v), (9) February (sig. B4), (10) March (sig. B4v), (11) Aprill (sig. Cv), (12) May (sig. C2), (13) June (sig. C2v), (14) July (sig. C3), (15) August (sig. C3v), (16) September (sig. C4), (17) October (sig. C4v), (18) November (sig. D), (19) December (sig. Dv), (20) Christmas Day (sig. D2), (21) Lent (sig. D2v), (22) Good Friday (sig. D3), (23) Easter Day (sig. D3v), (24) Morning (sig. D4), (25) One of the clocke (sig. D4v), (26) Two of the clocke (sig. E), (27) Three of the clocke (sig. E2), (28) Foure of the clocke (sig. E2v), (29) Five of the clocke (sig. E3), (30) Sixe of the clocke (sig. E3v), (31) Seven of the clocke (sig. E4), (32) Eight of the clocke (sig. E4v), (33) Nine of the clocke (sig. F), (34) Ten of the clocke (sig. Fv), (35) Eleuen of the clocke (sig. F2), (36) Twelve of the clocke (sig. F2v), (37) Midnight (sig. F3), (38) The conclusion (sig. F3v).
Murphy 33.

Attributed to Breton by the STC.

[Breton, Nicholas.]

Pasqvils Mad-cappe, Throwne at the Corruptions of these Times. With His Message to Men of all Estates. . . . London Printed by A.M. for Francis Falkner . . . 1626.

4°, text sigs. A3–F4. In verse.
(1–7) as in 1600.

Cooke, Edward.

The Character of Warre doth instruct them
in the use of postures, in the use of fencing,
Wheeling, Count remarching, Doubling, Dis-
tances & the like. London: Printed by T. Purfoot. 1626.*

4°.
BSC 2156.

Overbury, Sir Thomas.

Sir Thomas Overbury His Observations In
His Travailes vpon the state of the XVII
provinces as they stood Anno Dom. 1609.
. . . Printed. MDC.XXVI.

4°, text pp. 1–28.
(1) People of the Low Countries (p. 8), (2)
People of France (p. 16).

Overbury, Sir Thomas.

Sir Thomas Ouerbury His VVife. VVith
Additions Of New Characters, and many
other witty conceits never before Printed. The
twelfth Impression. Dublin. Imprinted by
the Company of Stationers, Anno Domini.
1626.*

8°, text sigs. D3–Q8.
(1–82) as in eleventh impression, 1622.
Murphy 22. BSC 2157.

[Parrot, Henry.]

Cvres For The Itch. Characters. Epigrams.
Epitaphs. By H.P. . . London, Printed for
Thomas Iones . . . 1626.

8°, text sigs. A2–G8.
(1) A ballad-maker (sig. A2), (2) A tapster
(sig. A3v), (3) A drunkard (sig. A4v), (4) A
rectified young man (sig. A5v), (5) A young
nouices new yonger wife (sig. A7), (6) A common fidler (sig. A8v), (7) A broker (sig. Bv),
(8) A iouiall good fellow (sig. B2v), (9) A humorist (sig. B3v), (10) A malepart yong vpstart
(sig. B4v), (11) A scold (sig. B5), (12) A good
wife (sig. B6), (13) A selfe conceited parcell-
witty-old dotard (sig. B6v).
Murphy 34.

Attributed to Parrot by the STC. The address to the
reader is signed H.P. The collation is as follows: A4,
A–B8, B–E8, F12, G8.

Wither, George.

Ivvenilia. . . . London printed for Robert Al-
lott . . . 1626.*

8°, text sigs. A2–Qq8.
(1) as in 1622.

A reissue of 1622 with altered title page.

1627

Anonymous.

The Character Of A Christian As hee is distinguished from all Hypocrites And Hereticks
. . . London, Printed for Ralph Mab. 1627.

12°, text pp. 1–398.
(1) A disciple of Christ (p. 196), A Christian
(p. 206).
BSC 2158.

Bernard, Richard.

The Isle of Man: Or, The Legall Proceeding
in Man-shire against Sinne. . . . By R.B.
Rector of Batcomb. Somers. The fourth Edition much enlarged. London, Printed for
Edw. Blackmore . . . 1627.

12°, text pp. 1–303.
(1) Mr. Outside, a carnall securitan (p. 18), (2)
Sir Worldly Wise, a selfe-conceited earth-worme
(p. 19), (3) Sir Luke-warm (p. 20), (4) Sir
Plausible Civill (p. 20), (5) Mr. Machiavell (p.
21), (6) Libertine (p. 22), (7) Scrupulosity (p.
23), (8) The babbling Babylonian (p. 24).

First printed 1626; often reprinted.

[Bolton, Edmund.]

Nero Caesar Or Monarchie depraued An Historical work . . . Whereunto beside other
things is now newly added the authors priuat
account to k. James concerning ye same . . .
By The Translatour of L. Florvs London
CIɔ IɔCXXVII.

4°, text pp. 1–288, 1–16.
(1) as in 1624.

[Earle, John.]

[Characters.]*
Contains 46 characters.
Murphy 46.

The manuscript (Durham Cathedral, Hunter MS. 130)
is dated December 24, 1627. See 1628.

Overbury, Sir Thomas.

Sir Thomas Ouerbury His Wife. With Additions Of New Characters, and many other
Wittie Conceits neuer before Printed. The
twelfth Impression. London, Printed by I.I.
for Robert Swayne, and are to be sold at the
signe of the Bible in Britaines Bursse, 1627.

8°, text sigs. A–V8v.
(1–82) as in eleventh impression, 1622.
Murphy 22. BSC 2159.

[S., I.]

The Errors of Men Personated in Sundry Essaies. London: Printed for W. Barrengen.
1627.*

Attributed to I.S. as author by the STC.

Taylor, John.

An Armado, or Nauy, of 103. Ships & Other Vessels; who haue the Art to Sayle by Land, as well as by Sea. . . . By John Taylor. . . . London, Printed by E.A. for H. Gosson, 1627. 8°, text sigs. B–D3v.

(1) The lord-ship (sig. B), (2) Scholler-ship (sig. B2), (3) Lady-ship (sig. B2v), (4) Good fellow-ship (sig. B3v), (5) The apprentice-ship (sig. B5v), (6) The court-ship (sig. B6v), (7) The friend-ship (sig. B8), (8) The fellow-ship (sig. B8v), (9) The foot-man-ship (sig. C), (10) The horseman ship (sig. C2v), (11) The suretie-ship (sig. C6v), (12) The wor-ship (sig. C8v), (13) The huntsman-ship, or woodman-ship (sig. D2).

There was another edition in 1627 (STC 23726a).

1628

Cooke, John.

Greenes Tu Quoque. London, Printed by M. Flesher.*

A reprint of 1614. Dated [1628?] by the STC.

[Earle, John.]

Micro-cosmographie. Or, A Peece Of The World Discovered; Jn Essayes And Characters. Newly Composed for the Northerne parts of this Kingdome. . . . At London. Printed by W.S. for Ed: Blount. 1628.

12°, text sigs. B–K5v.

(1) A childe (sig. B), (2) A young rawe preacher (sig. B3), (3) A graue diuine (sig. B5), (4) A meere dull physitian (sig. B7v), (5) An alderman (sig. B10v), (6) A discontented man (sig. B12), (7) An antiquary (sig. Cv), (8) An aturney (sig. C3v), (9) A yonger brother (sig. C5v), (10) A meere formall man (sig. C7v), (11) A church-papist (sig. C9), (12) A selfe-conceited man (sig. C10v), (13) A tauerne (sig. C12v), (14) A too idly reserv'd man (sig. D2v), (15) A sharke (sig. D4v), (16) A carrier (sig. D6v), (17) An old coledge butler (sig. D7v), (18) An up-start countrey knight (sig. D9v), (19) An idle gallant (sig. D11), (20) A constable (sig. E), (21) A baker (sig. E2), (22) A cooke (sig. E3), (23) A young gentleman of the university (sig. E5), (24) A player (sig. E6v), (25) A downe-right scholler (sig. E8v), (26) A detractor (sig. E11), (27) A pot-poet (sig. Fv), (28) A plaine country fellow (sig. F3), (29) A forward bold man (sig. F6), (30) A young-man (sig. F8), (31) The common singing-men in cathedrall churches (sig. F10), (32) A pretender to learning (sig. F12), (33) A shop-keeper (sig. G2v), (34) A handsome hostesse (sig. G4, wrongly numbered 33), (35) A blunt man (sig. G5, wrongly numbered 34), (36) A criticke (sig.

G7, wrongly numbered 35), (37) A serjeant or catch-pole (sig. G8v, wrongly numbered 36), (38) A weake man (sig. G9v, wrongly numbered 37), (39) A tobacco-seller (sig. G12, wrongly numbered 38), (40) A plausible man (sig. G12v, wrongly numbered 38), (41) The worlds wise man (sig. H2v, wrongly numbered 40), (42) A bowle-alley (sig. H4v, wrongly numbered 41), (43) A surgeon (sig. H5v, wrongly numbered 42), (44) A shee-precise hypocrite (sig. H7v, wrongly numbered 43), (45) A contemplative man (sig. H11, wrongly numbered 44), (46) An vniuersitie dunne (sig. H12, wrongly numbered 45), (47) A scepticke in religion (sig. I2, wrongly numbered 46), (48) A partiall man (sig. I5, wrongly numbered 47), (49) A trumpeter (sig. I7, wrongly numbered 48), (50) A vulgar-spirited man (sig. I8, wrongly numbered 49), (51) A herald (sig. I10v, wrongly numbered 43), (52) A plodding student (sig. I11v, wrongly numbered 51), (53) Paules Walke (sig. K, wrongly numbered 52), (54) A stayed man (sig. K3, wrongly numbered 53).

Murphy 35.

[Earle, John.]

Micro-cosmographie. Or, A Peece Of The World Discovered; Jn Essayes And Characters. London, Printed by William Stansby for Edward Blount. 1628.

12°, text sigs. B–K5.

(1–54) as in 1628 edition printed for Edward Blount.

Murphy 36. BSC 2160, 2162.

The order is somewhat changed from the Blount edition.

[Earle, John.]

Micro-cosmographie. Or, A Peece Of The World Discovered; Jn Essayes And Characters. . . . London, Printed by William Stansby for Robert Allot. 1628.

12°, text sigs. B–K5.

(1–54) as in 1628 edition printed for Edward Blount.

Murphy 36.

[Earle, John.]

Microcosmographie. 4th edition. 1628.*

Murphy 38.

No copy of this issue has been located.

Hall, Joseph.

The Works Of Joseph Hall . . . London, Printed by I.H. for Ph. Stephens and Ch. Meredith . . . 1628.

fo, in 3 parts, text pp. 1–1321, 1–100, 1–75.

(1–4) as in 1625.

Murphy 13.

There was another edition of the same year (STC 12636), printed by John Haviland.

Jackson, John.

Ecclesiastes: the Worthy Church-Man. London, Printed for R. More. 1628.*

Overbury, Sir Thomas.

Sir Thomas Ouerburie His Wife. With Additions Of New Characters, and many other Wittie Conceits neuer before Printed. The thirteenth Impression. London, Printed for Robert Allot, and are to bee sold at the signe of the Beare in Pauls Church-yard. 1628.

8°, text sigs. A2–V8v.
(1–82) as in eleventh impression, 1622.
Murphy 23. BSC 2164.

Robinson, John.

New Essayes or Observations Divine and Morall. 1628.*

A reprint of his Observations Divine and Morale, 1625.

Rowlands, Samuel.

Diogenes Lanthorne. 1628.*

Reprinted from 1607.

1629
Adams, Thomas.

The Workes of Tho: Adams. Being the Svmme of His Sermons. . . . London . . . Tho. Harper for Iohn Grismand . . . 1629.

6°, text pp. 1–1240.
(1) The Gallants Burden (p. 1), (2) The White Devil (p. 32), (3) Englands Sickness (p. 302), (4) Diseases of the Soule (p. 440), (5) Mystical Bedlam (p. 478), (6) Peace (p. 995), (7) A Divine Herbal (p. 1016), (8) The Soldier's Honor (p. 1073).

[Andrews, Francis?]
Poems.*

(1) A monsieur (f. 87v).

This is a manuscript in the British Museum (Harleian MS. 4955).
This is a character of a Frenchman. The date 1629 is based on the fact that though the character is undated, the preceding piece is dated 1629. The character is reprinted in Gwendolen Murphy's A Cabinet of Characters, p. 42.

[Earle, John.]

Micro-cosmographie. Or, A Peece Of The World Discofered; In Essayes And Characters. The fift Edition much enlarged. London, Printed for Robert Allot . . . 1629.

12°, text sigs. B–M12.
(1–54) as in 1628, (55) A modest man (sig. B8), (56) A meere emptie wit (sig. C), (57) A

drunkard (sig. C8), (58) A prison (sig. D3), (59) A seruingman (sig. D7), (60) An insolent man (sig. E2v), (61) An acquaintance (sig. E4v), (62) A meere complementall man (sig. E8v), (63) A poore fiddler (sig. E10), (64) A medling man (sig. F3v), (64) A good old man (sig. F6v), (66) A flatterer (sig. F11v), (67) A high spirited man (sig. G4v), (68) A meere gull citizen (sig. G9), (69) A lascivious man (sig. G12), (70) A rash man (sig. H6v), (71) An affected man (sig. I), (72) A prophane man (sig. I11), (73) A coward (sig. K10v), (74) A sordid rich man (sig. L7), (75) A meere great man (sig. L10v), (76) A poore man (sig. M7v), (77) An ordinarie honest fellow (sig. N7).
Murphy 38. BSC 2166.

The order of the first 54 characters is entirely different from 1628. The new ones are mixed in with the old.

[Fennor, William.]

A True Description of the Lawes, Iustice, and Equity of a Compter . . . With a Character of a Iayle and Iaylor . . . The Nature of a Constable . . . And also A Description of a Sergeant his nature, slights, and properties, and in what fashions they oftentimes apparell themselves. London Printed 1629.*

(1–2) as in The Compters Common-wealth, 1617.
Murphy 124. BSC 2167.

Gaule, John.

Distractions, Or The Holy Madnesse. Feruently (not Furiously) inraged against Euill Men; or against their Euills. . . . By Iohn Gaule, Utriusque olim Academiæ. . . . London, Printed by Iohn Haviland, for Robert Allot. 1629.

12°, text pp. 1–490.
(1) The proud (p. 83), (2) The irefull (p. 196), (3) The covetous (p. 321).
Murphy 125. BSC 2168.

Lake, Arthur.

Sermons With some Religious and Divine Meditations. By . . . Arthvre Lake . . . London, Printed by W. Stansby for Nathaniel Butter. 1629.

6°, 3 parts paged 1–547, 1–322, 1–187, sigs. B–Qqqq4.
(1) Arthur Lake, by John Harris (?) (Part I, p. 1).

[Lenton, Francis.]

The Young Gallants Whirligigg: or Yovths Reakes. . . . Compiled and written by F.L. . . . London, Printed by M.F. for Robert Bostocke . . . 1629.

4°, text pp. 1–22. In verse.
Begins: "Leauing the learned Aciomes of old."
The character is that of a gallant.

M., R.

Mjcrologja. Characters, Or Essayes, Of Persons, Trades, and Places, offered to the City and Country. By R.M. . . . Printed at London by T.C. for Michael Sparke . . . 1629.

8°, text sigs. B–D8.
(1) A fantasticke taylor (sig. B), (2) A player (sig. B3), (3) A country shoo-maker (sig. B4v), (4) A rope maker (sig. B6), (5) A smith (sig. B7v), (6) A tobacconist (sig. C), (7) A cunning woman (sig. C2), (8) A cobler (sig. C3v), (9) A tooth-drawer (sig. C4v), (10) A tinker (sig. C6), (11) A fidler (sig. C7v), (12) A cunning horse-courser (sig. D), (13) Bethlem (sig. D2), (14) Ludgate (sig. D3), (15) Bridewell (sig. D4), (16) New-gate (sig. D7).
Murphy 46. BSC 2169.

The only known copy is in the Bodleian.

Robinson, John.

New Essayes or Observations Divine and Morall. 1629.*

A reprint of his Observations, 1625.
The only copy recorded in the STC is in the Bodleian.

[Tuvil, Daniel.]

Vade Mecum: A Manuall of Essayes Morall, Theologicall. Interwoven with moderne Observations, Historicall, Politicall. . . . London: Printed for I.S. and are to be sold by John Day . . . 1629.

12°, text pp. 1–246.
(1) Virtue (p. 1 and p. 18), (2) Child of vertue (p. 21), (3) True valour (p. 174), (4) A generous & heroic spirit (p. 179), (5) Vanity (p. 199).
Published earlier as Essayes, Morall and Theologicall, 1609.

1630

Anonymous.

The Tincker Of Turvey, his merry Pastime in his passing from Billingsgate to Gravesend . . . With these Persons . . . euery-One of them Telling his Tale . . . Euery Tale-Teller being Described in a Neate Character. . . . London. Printed for Nath: Butter . . . 1630.

4°, text pp. 1–72.
(1) Trotter, a tinker (p. 3), (2) Yerker, a cobbler (p. 11), (3) An ouer-growne cuckold (p. 22), (4) A cuckold & no cuckold (p. 22), (5) A horne-mad cuckold (p. 23), (6) A winking cuckold (p. 23), (7) An extempore cuckold (p. 23), (8) A Iohn hold-my-staffe-cuckold (p. 23), (9) A cuckold cryed vp (p. 23), (10) An antedated cuckold (p. 24), (11) Thumper, a smith (p. 24), (12) A gentleman (p. 34), (13) Sr. Rowland, a scholler (p. 56), (14) Bluster, a sea-man (p. 64).
Nos. 1, 2, 11, 12, 13, 14 are in verse.

Adams, Thomas.

The citie of peace. London, Printed by A. Mathewes for J. Griswold. 1630.*

fo.
(1) as in Eirenopolis, 1622.
The only recorded copy is in the British Museum.

Adams, Thomas.

Works.*

A reprint of 1629.

Brathwaite, Richard.

The English Gentleman: Containing Sundry excellent Rules or exquisite Observations, tending to Direction of every Gentleman, of selecter rank and qualitie; How to demeane or accommodate himselfe in the manage of publike or private affaires. By Richard Brathwait. . . . London, Printed by John Haviland, and are to be sold by Robert Bostock . . . 1630.

4°, text pp. 1–456, plus sigs. Nnn–Nnn2 unpaged.
(1) A gentleman (sig. Nnn).
BSC 2170, 2171.

The whole book might be considered as an extended character.

[Dekker, Thomas.]

Villanies discovered. London, 1630.*

A reprint of Lanthorne and Candle Light, 1609.
The only known copy is in the Bodleian.

[Earle, John.]

Micro-cosmographie. Or, A Peece Of The VVorld Discovered; In Essayes And Characters. The sixth Edition, augmented. . . . London, Printed by R.B. for Robert Allot . . . 1630.

12°, text sigs. B–N12.
(1–77) as in 1629.
Murphy 39.

[G., Sir R.]

Panacea: or Select Aphorisms Divine and Morall. London, Printed by Augustine Mathewes, 1630.*

(1) Prudence, (2) Fortitude, (3) Temperance, (4) Justice.
A second title page reads: A Characterisme of the Foure Cardinall Vertues. . . .

Overbury, Sir Thomas.

Sir Thomas Ouerbury His Wife, With Additions Of New Characters, and many other

Wittie Conceites neuer before Printed. The foureteenth Impression. London, Printed for Robert Allot, and are to be sold at the signe of the Beare in Pauls Church-yard. 1630.

8°, text sigs. A–V8v.

(1–82) as in eleventh impression, 1622.

Murphy 23. BSC 2171.

Taylor, John.

All The Workes Of Iohn Taylor The Water-Poet: Beeing Sixty and three in Number. . . . At London, Printed by J.B. for Iames Boler . . . 1630.

fo, 3 parts, text pp. 1–148, 1–343, 1–146.

(1) An Armado, or Navy (Part I, p. 76), (2) Taylors Goose (I, 104), (3) The Scourge of Basenesse . . . a Kicksey VVinsey (II, 33), (4) A Bawd (II, 91), (5) A Common Whore (II, 104), (6) An Arrant Thiefe (II, 113), (7) The Praise and Vertue of a Jayle and Jaylers (II, 125, wrongly numbered 115), (8) The VVater-cormorant (III, 1), (9) The Praise of Hemp-seed (III, 60).

Pforzheimer Catalogue No. 1006.

1631

Barclay, John.

The Mirrovr Of Mindes, Or, Barclay's Icon animorum, Englished by T.M. London, Printed by Iohn Norton, for Thomas Walkley . . . 1631.

12°, 2 parts, text pp. 1–332, 1–224.

(1) The four ages of man: childhood, youth, middle age, old age (Part I, p. 1), (2) France (I, 65), (3) Britain (I, 97), (4) Germany (I, 144), (5) Italy (I, 189), (6) Spain (I, 218), (7) Hungary, Polonia, Moscovia, and the other Northern nations (I, 242), (8) Turks and Jews (I, 280), (9) Men of various dispositions (II, 1), (10) Valiant minds (II, 40), (11) Amorous men (II, 78), (12) Kings and tyrants (II, 99), (13) Courtiers (II, 137), (14) Magistrates and lawyers (II, 171), (15) Divines (II, 199).

Brathwaite, Richard.

The English Gentlewoman drawne out to the full Body: Expressing what Habilliments do best attire her. . . . By Richard Brathvvait Esq. . . . London Printed by B. Alsop and T. Favvcet for Michaell Sparke . . . 1631.

4°, text pp. 1–231, plus sigs. Ff4–Gg3v unpaged, plus appendix.

(1) A perfect gentlewoman (sigs. ¶3v–¶¶2), (2) A perfect gentlewoman (sigs. ¶¶3v–*v), (3) Modesty (p. 168), (4) One who makes virtue her object (p. 199), (5) A lady of honour (p. 202), (6) A gentlewoman (sig. Ff4).

BSC 2172. Pforzheimer Catalogue No. 78.

The whole book might be considered an extended character.

Brathwaite, Richard.

Whimzies: Or, A New Cast of Characters. . . . London, Printed by F.K. and are to be sold by Ambrose Rithirdon . . . 1631.

[Inner title:] A Cater-Character, throwne out of a Boxe By an Experienc'd Gamester. . . . London, Imprinted by F.K. and are to be sold by A.R. 1631.

12°, in 2 parts, text pp. 1–211, 1–34.

(1) An almanack-maker (Part I, p. 1), (2) A ballad-monger (I, 8), (3) A corranto-coiner (I, 15), (4) A decoy (I, 25), (5) An exchange-man (I, 33), (6) A forrester (I, 40), (7) A gamester (I, 48), (8) An hospitall-man (I, 57), (9) A jayler (I, 65), (10) A keeper (I, 74), (11) A launderer (I, 82), (12), A metall-man (I, 90), (13) A newter (I, 98), (14) An ostler (I, 106), (15) A post-master (I, 115), (16) A quest-man (I, 122), (17) A ruffian (I, 130), (18) A sayler (I, 138), (19) A traveller (I, 147), (20) An vnder-sheriffe (I, 157), (21) A wine-soaker (I, 167), (22) A Xantippean (I, 173), (23) A yealous [sic] neighbour (I, 186), (24) A zealous brother (I, 196), (25) An apparator (II, 1), (26) A painter (II, 8), (27) A pedler (II, 18), (28) A piper (II, 26).

Murphy 47. BSC 2173, 2174, 2174*.

Attributed to Brathwaite by the STC. A variant of the present title page of the Cater-Character reads: to be sold by R.B.

Jonson, Ben.

The Nevv Inne. Or, The light Heart. . . . By the Author, B. Ionson. . . . London, Printed by Thomas Harper, for Thomas Alchorne . . . MDCXXXI.

8°, text sigs. B–H2v.

(1) The persons of the play (sig. (*)8v).

Pforzheimer Catalogue No. 552.

Reprinted several times.

Lenton, Francis.

Characterismi: Or, Lentons Leasvres. Expressed In Essayes And Characters, Neuer before written on. By F.L. Gent. . . . London, Printed by I.B. for Roger Michell. 1631.

12°, text sigs. B–H3.

(1) A state politician (sig. B), (2) A gallant courtier (sig. B2v), (3) A young barrester (sig. B4v), (4) A comissary (sig. B6), (5) A parasite or flatterer (sig. B7v), (6) An vxorious man (sig. B9), (7) A country widdow (sig. B10), (8) A chambermaid (sig. B11v), (9) A broken citizen (sig. C), (10) An old bawd (sig. C3), (11) A pandor (sig. C4v), (12) A countrey girle or darling (sig. C6), (13) A lawyers clarke (sig.

C7v), (14) A carle, or farmer tenant (sig. C9v), (15) A double benefic't parson (sig. C11v), (16) A young schoolmaster (sig. Dv), (17) A countrey alewife (sig. D3v), (18) An aldermans daughter (sig. D5), (19) A prodigall (sig. D7v), (20) An vsurer (sig. D9v), (21) A broker (sig. D12), (22) A thraso or braggadotia (sig. Ev), (23) A sempster shopkeeper (sig. E3v), (24) A prostitute or common whore (sig. E5v), (25) An ordinary gamester (sig. E7), (26) An host (sig. E9v), (27) A common drunkard (sig. E12), (28) An elder brother (sig. F2), (29) A yong Innes a Court gentleman (sig. F4), (30) A lowcountrey common souldier (sig. F6), (31) A gentleman-vsher (sig. F9), (32) A cuckold (sig. F10v), (33) An informer (sig. F12v), (34) A bachelour (sig. G2), (35) An vndershriefe (sig. G3v), (36) A drawer (sig. G5), (37) A good husband (sig. G6v), (38) A constant man (sig. G8), (39) A iealous man (sig. G10), (40) A desperate man (sig. G11v), (41) A true friend (sig. H).
Murphy 48.

The Epistle Dedicatory is signed Fra. Lenton.

[Rowlands, Samuel.]

Diogenes Lanthorne. . . . London, Printed for Robert Bird . . . 1631.

4°, text sigs. A2–E4v.
(1–9) as in 1607.

Saltonstall, Wye.

Picturae Loquentes. Or Pictvres Drawne forth in Characters. With a Poeme of a Maid. By Wye Saltonstall. . . . London, Printed by Tho. Cotes, and are to be sold by Tho. Slater . . . 1631.*

12°, text sigs. A8–F6.
(1) The world, (2) An old man, (3) A woman, (4) A widdow, (5) A true lover, (6) A country bride, (7) A ploughman, (8) A melancholy man, (9) A young heire, (10) A scholler in the university, (11) A lawyers clearke, (12) A townesman in Oxford, (13) An usurer, (14) A wandring rogue, (15) A waterman, (16) A sheapheard, (17), A ielous man, (18) A chamberlaine, (19) A maide, (20) A baylye, (21) A petty countrey faire, (22) A countrey alehouse, (23) A horse race, (24) A farmers daughter, (25) A keeper, (26) A gentlemans house in the countrey.
Murphy 50. BSC 2175.

Stephens, John.

New Essayes And Characters. With a new Satyre in defence of the Common Law, and Lawyers: Mixt with reproofe against their Enemy Ignoramus. Written by Iohn Stephens the younger, of Lincolnes Inne, Gent. . . . London, Printed for Luke Faune . . . 1631.

8°, text pp. 1–421 (wrongly numbered 434).
(1–50) as in his Satyricall Essayes, 1615 (later edition).
Murphy 31. Pforzheimer Catalogue No. 989 n.

[Tuvil, Daniel.]

Vade mecum . . . By D.T. London: Printed for I.S. and are to be sold by Iohn Day and Daniel Pakeman . . . 1631.

12°, text pp. 1–250.
(1–5) as in 1629.

1632

[Dekker, Thomas.]

English Villanies six severall Times prest to death. 1632.*

Pforzheimer Catalogue No. 274 n.
A reprint of Lanthorne and Candle Light, 1609.

Lenton, Francis.

Spare time. Expressed in essayes and characters, never before written on. By F.L. Gent. London, Printed for James Boler, 1632.*

A reprint of Characterismi, 1631.
Described in Catalogue 321 of Gregory's Book Store, Bath, item 19.

Lupton, Donald.

London and the Covntrey Carbonadoed and Quartred into seuerall Characters. By D. Lupton. . . . London. Printed by Nicholas Okes. 1632.

8°, text pp. 1–143.
(1) London (p. 1), (2) The Tower (p. 5), (3) St. Paules Church (p. 9), (4) The Bridge (p. 14), (5) The Thames (p. 18), (6) Exchanges old and new (p. 22), (7) Cheapeside (p. 27), (8) Innes of Court, and Chancery (p. 31), (9) Smithfield (p. 35), (10) Bridewell (p. 38), (11) Ludgate and Counters (p. 42), (12) Newgate (p. 46), (13) Turnebyll-streete (p. 50), (14) Hounsditch and Long-lane (p. 55), (15) Charterhouse (p. 58), (16) Christs-hospitall (p. 63), (17) Paris-Garden (p. 66), (18) Artillery (p. 70), (19) Bedlam (p. 74), (20) Play-houses (p. 79), (21) Fencing-schooles (p. 83), (22) Dancing-schooles (p. 87), (23) Fisher-women (p. 91), (24) Scavengers and goldfinders (p. 94, misprinted 49), (25) [Here begins The Country Carbonadoed] The countrey (p. 97), (26) Hospitality (p. 100), (27) Enclosures (p. 104), (28) Tenants by lease (p. 108), (29) Tenants at will (p. 112), (30) Countrey schoole-maisters (p. 115), (31) Country ushers (p. 119), (32) Country chaplaines (p. 123), (33) Ale-houses (p. 127), (34) Apparators (p. 131), (35) Constables (p. 136), (36) Currantoes or weekly newes (p. 140).
Murphy 51. BSC 2176.

Overbury, Sir Thomas.

Sir Thomas Overbury His Wife. With Additions Of New Characters, and many other Wittie Conceits never before Printed. The fifteenth Impression. . . . London, Printed by R.B. for Robert Allot, and are to be sold at the signe of the Beare in Pauls Church-yard. 1632.

8°, text sigs. A2–V8v.
(1–82) as in eleventh impression, 1622.
Murphy 23. BSC 2177.

Rogers, Nehemiah.

[General title page] The True Convert. . . . By Nehemiah Rogers . . . London, Printed by George Miller for Edward Brewster . . . 1632.
[First sub-title] The Indvlgent Father . . . or an Exposition On The Parable Of The Prodigall Or Lost Sonne . . . London . . . 1632.
[Second sub-title] The Watchfull Shepheard . . . in an Exposition On The Parable of the Lost Sheep . . . 1632.
[Third sub-title] The Good Hovsewife With Her Broome And Candle: or an Exposition On The Parable of the Lost Groat . . . 1632.

8°, in 3 parts, pp. 1–406, 1–264, 1–196.
(1) Properties of fooles naturall to every wicked man (Part I, p. 26), (2) Signs of an humbled soule (I, 184), (3) Magistrates, ministers, lawyers, tradesmen (II, 64).

1633

Barclay, John.

The Mirror Of Minds: Or, Barclay's Jcon animorum. Englished, By Tho. May, Esq. . . . London, Printed by I.B. for Thomas Walkley . . . 1633.

12°, text pp. 1–380.
(1–15) as in 1631.

Brathwaite, Richard.

The English Gentleman. . . . The second Edition. . . . By Richard Brathwait. . . . London, Printed by Felix Kyngston . . . 1633.

4°, text pp. 1–456, plus sigs. Hh–Hh2v unpaged.
(1) as in 1630.
BSC 2178.

Donne, John.

Ivvenilia: Or Certaine Paradoxes, And Problems, Written By I. Donne. . . . London, Printed by E.P. for Henry Seyle . . . 1633.

4°, text sigs. A3–H4v.
(1) Old and young men (sig. C4v).

A border-line example of character. There were two editions in 1633.

[Earle, John.]

Micro-cosmographie. Or, A Piece Of The World Discovered; In Essayes And Characters. The sixth Edition, augmented. . . . London, Printed by E.A. for Robert Allot. . . . 1633.

12°, text sigs. B–N12v.
(1–77) as in 1629, (78) A suspitious or jealous man (sig. N11).
Murphy 40. BSC 2179.

Hall, Joseph.

The Works of Joseph Hall. London: Printed by M. Flesher for N. Butter. 1633.*

2 tomes.
(1–4) as in 1625.

Lemnius, Levinus.

The Touchstone of Complexions. London, Printed by E.A. for M. Sparke, 1633.*

A reprint of 1581.

[May, Thomas.]

The Reigne Of King Henry The Second, Written in Seaven Bookes . . . London, Printed by A.M. for Benjamin Fisher . . . 1633.

8°, text sigs. B–Ov.
(1) Henry II (sig. N).
Pforzheimer Catalogue No. 686.

The Harvard copy collates as above. Some copies, however, apparently extend to sig. O8v and include further characters, which the Pforzheimer Catalogue describes as "single and comparative characters, in prose, recto O3–recto [O7]."

[Price, Lawrence.]

A Compleate Gentle-woman Described by her feature, Her person slender, her beauty admirable, her wit excellent, her carriage modest, her behaviour chast, with her constancie in love. To the tune of Sabina. London, Printed for J. Wright. [1633]*

s.sh.fo, in 2 parts. In verse. Black letter.
Attributed to Price by the STC, which dates it [1633]. It is signed L.P.

Shirley, James.

The Wittie Faire One. A Comedie. . . . By Iames Shirley. . . . London, Printed by B.A. and T.F. for Wil. Cooke . . . 1633.

4°, text sigs. B–K2.
(1) Fuddle, a foolish knight, by Aimwell (Act II, scene ii).

Webbe, George.

The Practice of Quietness: Directing a Christian how to live quietly in this troublesome

World. The Sixth Edition. London, for M.F. 1633.*

See 1638.
The only recorded copy is in the British Museum.

1634

Anonymous.

Cacoethes Leaden Legacy: Or His Schoole of ill manners: Wherein it is fainedly supposed that Cacoethes being ready to die, did bequeath this Leaden Legacy of Counsell to his two sons, Slovanio and Nerebeegood, instructing them in many points of slovanry and ill husbandry . . . Printed at London for Thomas Lambert . . .

12°, text sigs. A2–A11v. Black letter.
(1) A slovenly man (sig. A3), (2) An impious or worthless man (sig. A8v).

Dated 1634 by the STC.
The only recorded copy is in the Bodleian.

The Phantastick Age: or, The Anatomy of Englands vanity, In wearing the fashions Of severall Nations, With good exhortations, Against transmutations. To the tune of, O Women monstrous, &c. [Two Parts] London Printed for Thomas Lambert.*

In verse. Black letter.
Begins: "Audience audience gallants all."
Dated [1634?] by the STC.
The only recorded copy is in the British Museum.

Blaxton, John.

The English Vsvrer . . . Collected By Iohn Blaxton . . . London. Printed by Iohn Norton, and are to bee sold by Francis Bovvman, in Oxford. 1634.

4°, text pp. 1–84.
(1) A usurer (p. 48).

Another issue is identical with this except that the title page reads: sold by Iohn Long, in Dorchester, 1634.
A copy of this variant, not noticed in the STC, is at Harvard.

Blaxton, John.

The English Usurer. Or, Usury Condemned, By The most Learned, and Famous Divines of the Church of England. Collected By Iohn Blaxton . . . The second Impression. Corrected by the Authour. . . . London, Printed by Iohn Norton, and are to be sold by Francis Bowman, in Oxford. 1634.

4°, text pp. 1–80.
(1) as in the first impression, 1634.

[Brathwaite, Richard.]

A Strange Metamorphosis of Man, transformed into a VVildernesse. Deciphered in Characters. . . . London, Printed by Thomas Harper, and are to be sold by Lawrence Chapman . . . 1634.

12°, text sigs. B–I10.
(1) The lyon (sig. B), (2) The squirill (sig. B3v), (3) The bramble (sig. B5v), (4) The stagge (sig. B7v), (5) The golden myne (sig. B10), (6) The hedgehog (sig. B12), (7) The Pike (sig. C2v), (8) The rock (sig. C4v), (9) The goat (sig. C6v), (10) The eccho (sig. C9), (11) The lake (sig. C12), (12) The coalepit (sig. D3), (13) The beare (sig. D5v), (14) The mustard-seed (sig. D8), (15) The goose (sig. D10v), (16) The horse (sig. Ev), (17) The hawk (sig. E4v), (18) The elephant (sig. E8), (19) The gnat (sig. E10v), (20) The mole (sig. F2), (21) The peacocke (sig. F4), (22) The batte (sig. F6v), (23) The mosse (sig. F9), (24) The ant (sig. F11), (25) The ivie (sig. Gv), (26) The daw (sig. G3v), (27) The snake (sig. G5v), (28) The crab (sig. G7v), (29) The ape (sig. G10), (30) The owle (sig. G11v), (31) The snayle (sig. Hv), (32) The swallow (sig. H3), (33) The oak (sig. H5), (34) The dog (sig. H6v), (35) The parat (sig. H8v), (36) Tobacco (sig. H10v), (37) The bay-tree (sig. H12), (38) The vine (sig. I2), (39) The fox (sig. I4), (40) The primrose (sig. I6v).

Attributed to Brathwaite by the STC.

Hall, Joseph.

The Works of Joseph Hall. Tom. I. London, Printed by Io. Haviland . . . 1634.

6°, text pp. 1–764.
(1–4) as in 1625.
Murphy 13.

Hall, Joseph.

The Works Of Joseph Hall . . . London, Printed for Ph. Stephens and Ch. Meredith . . . 1634.

6°, text pp. 1–1353.
(1–4) as in 1625.
Murphy 13.

Rowlands, Samuel.

Diogenes Lanthorne. 1634.*
Reprinted from 1607.

[Rowlands, Samuel.]

The Night Raven. London, W. Jones for T. Baily. 1634.*
Reprinted from 1620.
The only recorded copy is in the British Museum.

Warwick, Arthur.

Spare minutes; or, resolved meditations. Second edition. R. B[adger] for W. Hammond, 1634.*
4°.

See entry under 1821.
The only copy recorded in the STC is in the Bodleian. Another edition of the same year, also called the second, 12° and printed by G. M[iller] for W. Hammond, is also given in the STC. The only copy listed is the Harmsworth. There is no record of either the first or the third edition.

Young, Thomas.

England's Bane. 1634.*

Reprinted from 1617.

1635

Baldwin, William.

A Treatise Of Morall Philosophie . . . by William Bauldwin, and now the ninth time since inlarged by Thomas Palfreyman. . . . London, Printed by William Stansby.

8°, text ff. 1–189v. In black letter.
(1) Aristotle (f. 3v), (2) Anarchasis (f. 4v), (3) Antisthenes (f. 5v), (4) Anaxagoras (f. 6), (5) Archilaus (f. 7), (6) Aristippus (f. 7v), (7) Agesilaus (f. 8v), (8) Alexander Seuerus (f. 8v), (9) Alexander Magnus (f. 9), (10) Ambrose (f. 9v), (11) Augustus Caesar (f. 9v), (12) Bias (f. 9v), (13) Chilon (f. 10v), (14) Cicero (f. 11v), (15) Crates Thebanus (f. 11v), (16) Diogenes (f. 13v), (17) Democritus (f. 15), (18) Demosthenes (f. 15), (19) Ennius (f. 15v), (20) Epimenedes (f. 17), (21) Galenus (f. 15v), (22) Hermes (f. 16), (23) Horace (f. 18), (24) Homer (f. 18), (25) Isocrates (f. 18v), (26) Iustinus (f. 19), (27) Iustitianus (f. 19v), (28) Lycurgus (f. 19v), (29) Marcus Aurelius (f. 20), (30) Myson (f. 20), (31) Pithagoras (f. 21), (32) Periander (f. 23), (33) Pherisides (f. 24), (34) Plato (f. 24v), (35) Plutarch (f. 26), (36) Photion (f. 26v), (37) Philip (f. 27), (38) Plinie (f. 27v), (39) Plautus (f. 27v), (40) Pittachus Mitelinus (f. 28), (41) Pirrhus (f. 28), (42) Pacuuius (f. 28v), (43) Pompeius (f. 28v), (44) Quintilianus (f. 29), (45) Solon (f. 29v), (46) Socrates (f. 29v), (47) Seneca (f. 34v), (48) Sigismond Emp (f. 35), (49) Thales (f. 35), (50) Theopompus (f. 36v), (51) Theophrastus (f. 36v), (52) Xenophon (f. 37v), (53) Xenocrates (f. 38), (54) Zeno Elvates (f. 39).

Of this work, first published about 1547, at least eighteen editions are recorded before 1640 in the STC. Only this one has been included here.

Brathwaite, Richard.

A Character of Honour.*

The Bodleian has a copy of this character, supposed to be a fragment of a unique copy of The English Gentleman (Douce frag. b.1.89). But see the entry under 1641.

Brathwaite, Richard.

Essaies Vpon The Five Senses, Revived by a new Supplement. . . . By Ric: Brathvvayt Esquire. The Second Edition, revised and en-

larged by the Author. . . . London. Printed by Anne Griffin, and are to bee sold by Henry Shephard . . . 1635.

12°, text pp. 1–316.
(1–2) as in 1620.

[Habington, William.]

Castara. . . . The second Edition. . . . London. Printed by B.A. & T.F. for Will: Cooke . . . 1635.

12°, text pp. 1–167.
(1) A mistris (sig. A6v), (2) A wife (p. 71), (3) A friend (p. 147).
Murphy 127. BSC 2181.

The characters, which are in prose, were not included in the first edition of Castara, 1634.

Hall, Joseph.

The Character of Man; Laid forth in a Sermon preach't at the Court March 1. 1634 by the L. Bishop of Exceter. London, Printed by M. Flesher, for Nat. Butter. 1635.*
8°.
BSC 2182.

[Price, Lawrence.]

A Complete Gentlewoman. 1635.*

A reprint of 1633.
This edition is not mentioned in the STC, and no copy has been found.

Rous, John.

Diary.*

4°, text pp. 1–176. Manuscript.
(1) The new churchman (under date of 1635, in verse).

In 1856 the manuscript was in the library of Dawson Turner. Its present location is not known. The character is quoted by Rous as one of several poems which came out in 1635, apparently not composed by Rous himself.

Saltonstall, Wye.

Picturae Loquentes, Or Pictvres Drawne forth in Characters. With a Poeme of a Maid. By Wye Saltonstall. The second Edition enlarged. . . . London, Printed by Tho. Cotes, and are to be sold by William Hope . . . 1635.

12°, text sigs. A9–H6.
(1–26) as in 1631, (27) A fine dame (sig. F6v), (28) A country dame (sig. F8v), (29) A gardiner (sig. F11), (30) A captaine (sig. G), (31) A poore village (sig. G3), (32) A merry man (sig. G4v), (33) A scrivener (sig. G6v), (34) The tearme (sig. G9), (35) A mower (sig. G10v), (36) A happy man (sig. G12), (37) An arrant knave (sig. H2v), (38) An old waiting gentlewoman (sig. H4v).
Murphy 50. BSC 2183, 2184.

Scott, William.

An Essay Of Drapery; or, the compleate citizen. Trading Iustly. Pleasingly. Profitably. By William Scott. . . . London, Printed by Eli All-de, for Stephen Pemell . . . 1635.

12°, text pp. 1–169.

(1) A good draper (p. 3).

Taylor, John.

An Armado. 1635.*

A reprint of 1627.

Taylor, John.

An Arrant Thiefe . . . With a Comparison betweene a Thiefe and a Booke. Written by Iohn Taylor. Printed at London for Henry Gosson. 1635.

8°, text sigs. A5–C7v. In verse.
Begins: "I Lately to the world did send a *Whore*."
A reprint of 1622.

Taylor, John.

A Bawd. A vertuous Bawd, a modest Bawd: As Shee Deserves, reproove, or else applaud. Written by John Taylor. Printed at London for Henry Gosson. 1635.

8°, text sigs. A3–C8.
(1) A flattering hireling preacher (sig. A5v, in verse), (2) A bawd (sig. Bv).

Taylor, John.

A Common Whore With all these graces grac'd, Shee's very honest, beautifull and chaste. Written By Iohn Taylor. Printed at London for Henry Gosson. 1635.

8°, text sigs. A4–C6. In verse.
(1–3) as in 1622.

[Taylor, John.]

A most Horrible, Terrible, Tollerable, Termagant Satyre: Most fresh and newly made, and prest in Print, And if it bee not lik'd, the Divells in't.

8°, text pp. 1–33.
(1) The avaricious or covetous man, and projector (p. 5), (2) The bragging rogue (p. 14), (3) The mountebanke, or quacksalver (p. 19), (4) The alchimist (p. 23), (5) The hypocrite (p. 25), (6) The whoore (p. 31).

Not in STC. There is a copy at Huntington.
Some verses on sig. A3, signed W. Gainsford, are addressed to his friend John Taylor, "the Author of this most wholesome following Blackmouth'd biting Satire." Attributed to Taylor by the CBEL, which assigns it to the date 1635. It was however licensed in the Stationers' Registers on February 23, 1638/9.

Warwick, Arthur.

Spare minutes. Fourth edition. G. M[iller] for W. Hammond, sold by M. Sparke, 1635.*

12°.
A reprint of 1634.

1636

[Habington, William.]

Castara. The second edition. B. A[lsop] and T. F[awcet] for W. Cooke, 1636.*

A reprint of 1635, called by the STC another issue of 1635. The Harmsworth copy is the only one recorded by the STC.

Healey, John.

Epictetvs Manuall. 1636.*

A reprint of 1616.
The only copy recorded by the STC is in the Bodleian.

[Heywood, Thomas.]

A True Discourse of the Two infamous upstart Prophets, Richard Farnham Weaver of White-Chappell, and John Bull Weaver of Saint Butolphe Algate . . . Written by T.H. Printed at London for Thomas Lambert . . . 1636.

4°, text pp. 1–19.
(1) An innovator in religion, or a hypocrite (p. 2).
Murphy 127.

Lenton, Francis.

Lentons Leisvres Described, in divers Moderne Characters. By Francis Lenton, Her Maiesties Poet. . . . Imprinted at London, 1636.

12°, text sigs. B–H3.
(1–41) as in his Characterismi, 1631.
The only copy recorded in the STC is at Huntington.

Nemesius.

The Natvre Of Man, a learned and usefull Tract written in Greek by Nemesius, surnamed the Philosopher. . . . Englished, And divided into Sections . . . by Geo: Wither. London: Printed by M.F. for Henry Taunton . . . 1636.

12°, text sigs. A–Ff6.
Pforzheimer Catalogue No. 1085.

An extended essay which might possibly be called a character. Reprinted 1657 as The Character of Man.

Warwick, Arthur.

Spare minutes; or, resolved meditations. Fifth edition. G. M[iller] for W. Hammond, sold by M. Sparke, 1636.*

12°.
A reprint of 1634.

1637

Jordan, Thomas.

Poeticall Varieties: Or, Varietie Of Fancies.
. . . By Tho. Jordan . . . London, Printed by
T.C. for Humphry Blunden . . . 1637.

4°, text pp. 1–52.
(1) A whore (p. 25, in verse).
Pforzheimer Catalogue No. 565.
Reprinted 1646 as Love's Dialect.

[Parker, Martin.]

Harry White his humour, so neare as may be
set forth by M.P. . . . Printed at London, for
Thomas Lambert.*

8°.
Begins: "Very good sir but why Harry White's
humour?"
Dated [1637?] by the STC.
The only recorded copy is in the Bodleian.

Warwick, Arthur.

Spare minutes. Sixt Edition. G. M[iller] for
W. Hammond, 1637.*

12°.
A reprint of 1634.

1638

Brathwaite, Richard.

A Survey Of History: Or, A Nursery for Gentry . . . By Richard Brathwait Esquire, Oxon.
. . . Imprinted at London by I. Okes, for Ias-
per Emery . . . 1638.

4°, text pp. 1–415.
(1–4) as in The Schollers Medley, 1614.
Pforzheimer Catalogue No. 82.

[Dekker, Thomas.]

English villanies seven severall times prest to
death, now the eighth time discovered. M.
Parsons, sold by J. Becket, 1638.*

4°.
Reprinted from Lanthorne and Candle Light,
1609.
Pforzheimer Catalogue No. 274 n.

[Earle, John.]

Micro-cosmographie. Or, A Piece Of The
VVorld Discovered; In Essayes And Characters. The seventh Edition augmented. . . .
London, Printed by I.L. for Andrew Crooke
. . . 1638.

12°, text sigs. A7–M12v.
(1–78) as in 1633.
Murphy 40. BSC 2185.

Johnson, Robert.

Johnson's Essayes, expressed in sundry ex-

quisite fancies. M. P[arsons] for R. Wilson,
1638.*

12°.
Reprinted from 1601.

[Mynshul, Geffray.]

Essayes and Characters of a Prison and Prisoners. Written by G.M. of Grayes-Inne, Gent.
With some new Additions. . . . Printed at
London by I.O. for Mathew Walbancke . . .
1638.

4°, text pp. 1–49.
(1–8) as in second entry under 1618.
Murphy 33.

Overbury, Sir Thomas.

Sir Thomas Overbury His Wife. With Additions of New Characters, and many other
Witty Conceits never before Printed. The Sixteenth Impression. . . . London, Printed by
Iohn Haviland, for A. Crooke, and are to be
sold at the signe of the Beare in Pauls Church-
yard. 1638.

8°, text sigs. A2–V8v.
(1–82) as in eleventh impression, 1622.
Murphy 24. BSC 2186.

Peacham, Henry.

The Truth of our Times: Revealed out of one
Mans Experience, by way of Essay. Written
by Henry Peacham. London: Printed by
N.O. for Iames Becket . . . 1638.

12°, text pp. 1–203.
(1) A clown (p. 123), (2) A religious honest
man (p. 145).
BSC 2187.

Peacham, Henry.

The Valley of Varietie: or, Discourse fitting
for the Times . . . By Henry Peacham. . . .
London, Printed by M.P. for Iames Becket
. . . 1638.

12°, text pp. 1–174.
(1) Of the strange mixture of vertue and vice,
in the natures and dispositions of manie men
(p. 54), (2) The extreme madnesse, and vaine
pride of some great persons in former ages (p.
86).

Robinson, John.

Essayes; or, Observations Divine And Morall.
. . . By Iohn Robinson. The second Edi-
tion . . . London, Printed by I.D. for I.
Bellamie . . . 1638.

12°, text pp. 1–566.
(1–4) as in Observations, 1625.

[Tuvil, Daniel.]

Vade Mecum . . . By D.T. . . . The third Edition. London: Printed by E.P. for J.S. . . . 1638.

12°, text pp. 1–250.
(1–5) as in 1629.

[Webbe, George.]

The Practise of Quietnes: Directing a Christian how to liue quietly in this troblesome World. The 7th Edition. Profitably amplified by the Author. . . . London Printed by M.F. and are sold by Geo. Edwards . . . 1638.

12°, text pp. 1–278.
(1) Quietness, and a quiet man (chap. 2, p. 7).

[Younge, Richard.]

The Drunkard's Character, Or, A True Drunkard with such sinnes as reigne in him, viz. Price . . . Lively set forth in their colours . . . By R. Iunius. London, Printed by R. Badger, for George Latham . . . 1638.*

8°, text pp. 1–863.
(1) A drunkard (p. 37).
BSC 2188.

Reprinted 1639(?) as Sinne Stigmatizd, 1646(?) (in brief summarized form), and 1649 as The Odious . . . condition of a Drunkard.

1639

Daniel, George.

Ecclesiasticus.*
(1) A wise man (chap. 39).
A manuscript, now in the British Museum.

Du Bosc, Jacques.

The Compleat VVoman. VVritten in French by Monsieur Du-Boscq, and by him after severall Editions reviewed, corrected, and amended: And now faithfully Translated into English, by N.N. London, Printed by Thomas Harper and Richard Hodgkinson, 1639.

4°, in two parts, text pp. 1–66, 1–87.
(1) The learned women (Part II, p. 23), (2) The dissolute woman (II, 57).
BSC 2189.

Neither of these characters is very good, but the second is better than the first.

Fuller, Thomas.

The Historie of the Holy Warre; By Thomas Fuller. . . . Printed by Thomas Buck, one of the Printers to the Universitie of Cambridge, 1639.

4°, text pp. 1–286.

(1) Frederick II (p. 160).
Pforzheimer Catalogue No. 390.
There were several later editions.

Hall, Joseph.

The Works of Joseph Hall.*
Murphy 13. Pforzheimer Catalogue II, 439.

Reprinted from 1634.
Not in STC.
Dated 1639–1662 by the Pforzheimer Catalogue, which points out that though there is no dated principal title page, the individual titles are dated all the way from 1639 to 1647 (Volume I), and 1662 (Volume III).

Hodson, W.

The Holy Sinner, a Tractate meditated on some Passages of the Storie of the Penitent Woman in the Pharisee's house. Cambridge: Printed for A. Crooke, 1639.*
BSC 2190.

Lenton, Francis.

Characterismi. 1639.*
A reprint of 1631.
Not in STC.
Hazlitt, Handbook to Early English Literature, 1869, p. 333.

[Pick, Samuel.]

Festum Voluptatis, Or the Banquet of Pleasure . . . containing . . . Love-Posies, Songs, Sonnets . . . Satyrs . . . By S.P. Gent. London: Printed by E.P. for Bernard Langford . . . 1639.

4°, text pp. 1–54.
(1) Tom Tospot (p. 22), (2) Insatiate woman (p. 23), (3) Of gracelesse grace, a whore (p. 25).
The epistle dedicatory is signed Samuel Pick.

[Taylor, John.]

A Juniper Lecture. The Second Impression. London: Printed by J.O. for W. Ley. 1639.

12°, text pp. 1–236.
(1) A wicked woman (p. 196).
Attributed to Taylor by the STC.
No copy of the first impression is known.
The only recorded copy of the second impression is at Huntington.

[Younge, Richard.]

Sinne Stigmatizd; Or, The Art to Know savingly, Believe rightly, Live Religiously. . . . By R. Junius. London, Printed for G. Latham . . .

8°, text pp. 1–863 (but inexact, since the paging is erroneous in several places).
(1) As in The Drunkard's Character, 1638.
BSC 2191.

Two inner titles are dated 1638, but the McAlpin copy is dated in pencil 1639. A reprint of The Drunkard's Character, 1638.

1640

Anonymous.

The caracter of a true subject on the loyall fidelity of the Lord Marquesse Huntleys &c.*

Nothing further is known of this title.

A Timely Advice. Or, A Treatise Of Play, and Gaming. Wherein is shewed how far forth it is lawfull to use such Play: And how dangerous and hurtful by excesse to abuse it. . . . London, Printed by Th. Harper for Richard Stevenson, and are to be sold at his shop in Princes street neere Lincolns Inne fields. 1640.*

(1) A gamester (p. 119).

BSC 2193.

The only recorded copy is in the British Museum.

The Wandering-Jew, Telling Fortunes to English-men . . . London; Printed by John Raworth, for Nathaniel Butter. 1640.*

4°, text pp. 17–67.

(1) The courtier, (2) The drunkard, (3) An alderman's prodigall sonne, (4) The tobacco-taker, (5) The good lawyer, (6) The wanton wife, (7) The prentice, (8) The serving-man, (9) The extortioner, (10) The glutton, (11) The jealous man, (12) The fond fantastic lover, (13) The witch, (14) The roaring boy, (15) The voluntary bankrupt, (16) The sergeant of London, (17) The thief, (18) The hangman.

BSC 2195. Murphy 121.

The preface to the reader is signed with the pseudonym Gad Ben-arod, Ben Balaam, Ben-Ahimoth, Ben-Baal, Ben-Gog, Ben-Magog. Adapted from W.M.'s The Man in the Moon, 1609.

[Brathwaite, Richard.]

Ar't asleepe Husband? A Boulster Lecture; Stored With all variety of witty jeasts, merry Tales, and other pleasant passages; Extracted, From the choicest flowers of Philosophy, Poesy, antient and moderne History. Illustrated with Examples of incomparable constancy, in the excellent History of Philocles and Doriclea. By Philogenes Panedonius. O nox longa! — Hor. London, Printed by R. Bishop, for R.B. or his Assignes. 1640.

8°, text pp. 1–318, plus sigs. Y–Y4 unnumbered.

(1) A gentleman usher (p. 161).

BSC 2192. Pforzheimer Catalogue No. 76 and Addenda, III, 1277.

Attributed to Brathwaite by the STC. Variant imprints of the same year are known.

Brome, Richard.

The Sparagvs Garden: A Comedie. Acted in the year 1635. . . . The Author Richard Brome. . . . London, Printed by J. Okes, for Francis Constable . . . 1640.

4°, text sigs. B–L4v.

(1) Doctor Thou-Lord (sig. D).

[Dekker, Thomas.]

The Belman of London. The fift impression. London, Printed for M. Flesher. 1640.*

4°.

(1–17) as in 1608.

The only recorded copy is in the British Museum.

[Habington, William.]

Castara . . . The third Edition. . . . London Printed by T. Cotes, for Will. Cooke . . . 1640.

12°, text pp. 1–228.

(1–3) as in 1635, (4) A holy man (p. 169).

Murphy 127.

[Howell, James.]

Δενδρολογια. Dodona's Grove, Or, The Vocall Forrest. By I.H. Esqr. . . . By T:B. for H. Mosley . . . 1640.

4°, text pp. 1–219.

(1) Sacra Jovi Quercus. A character of Druina (p. 5), (2) Ampelona (p. 7), (3) Elaiana (p. 13), (4) Leoncia (p. 21), (5) Itelia (p. 25), (6) Cardenia (p. 44), (7) Monticolia (p. 46), (8) Lurana (p. 48), (9) Adriana (p. 91).

BSC 2194. Pforzheimer Catalogue No. 512.

According to keys in later editions, Druina stands for England, Ampelona for France, Elaiana for Spain, Leoncia for Flanders, Itelia for the Low Countries, Cardenia for Scotland, Monticolia for Wales, Lurana for Ireland, and Adriana for Venice. Attributed to Howell by the STC.

Jonson, Ben.

The Magnetic Lady: Or, Hvmors Reconcil'd. A Comedy Composed By Ben: Iohnson . . . London, Printed M.CD.XL.

4°, text pp. 5–64.

(1) Parson Palate, by Compasse (Act I, scene ii), (2) Mrs. Placentia Steele, by Mrs. Polish (I, iv).

Not in STC. Perhaps a detached section of his VVorkes, vol. II, 1640.

There is a copy at Harvard.

This play has been reprinted.

Jonson, Ben.

Q. Horatius Flaccus: His Art of Poetry . . . Englished By Ben: Jonson. . . . With other Workes of the Author, never Printed before. . . . London: Printed by J. Okes, for John Benson . . . 1640.*

12°, text pp. 1–138.

(1) King James, by the fortune teller in The Gypsies Metamorphosed (p. 58).

Pforzheimer Catalogue No. 548.

According to the Pforzheimer Catalogue no unmutilated copy of this edition is known. The Gypsies Metamorphosed was acted in 1621. There is a contemporary manuscript in Jonson's hand in the Huntington.

Jonson, Ben.

The Workes of Beniamin Jonson. London, R. Bishop, sold by A. Crooke, 1640.*

fo.

Reprinted from 1616.

Jonson, Ben.

The VVorkes Of Benjamin Jonson. The second Volume. . . . London. Printed for Richard Meighen, 1640.

6°, various pagings.

(1) The Magnetick Lady, (2) Timber, or, discoveries, (3) The Gypsies Metamorphos'd.

Pforzheimer Catalogue No. 560.

Martin Mar-Prelate.

A Dialogve, Wherin Is Plainly Layd Open the Tyrannicall Dealing Of Lord Bishops Againt Gods Children. . . . Published, by the worthy Gentleman Dr. Martin Mar-Prelat . . . Reprinted in the time of Parliament, Anno Dom. 1640.

4°, text sigs. A3–D2v.

(1) A Puritan (sig. D2, in verse).

Murphy 128.

This character does not appear in the 1589 edition. Reprinted 1643 (as The Character of a Puritan).

Mill, Humphrey.

A Nights Search. Discovering the Nature and Condition of all sorts of Night-Walkers. . . . By Humphry Mill. . . . London, Printed by Richard Bishop . . . 1640.

8°, text pp. 1–283. In verse.

(1) A modest, wise poet (p. 7).

[Stafford, Anthony.]

Honour and Vertue, Triumphing over the Grave. Exemplified in a faire devout life, and Death . . . of Edward Lord Stafford, London: Printed by J. Okes, for Henry Seile . . . 1640.

4°, text pp. 1–90, wrongly numbered 92, and 42 pages of elegies.

(1) Edward [or rather Henry], Lord Stafford (p. 25), (2) Prudencie (p. 72).

Attributed to Stafford by the STC.

There was another edition of the same year, sold by J. Lownds (STC 23126).

Warwick, Arthur.

Spare minutes. G. M[iller] for W. Hammond, sod [sic] by F. Eglesfield, 1640.*

12°.

Reprinted from 1634.

1641

Anonymous.

A Charitable Church Warden, or an Hypocrite anatomized. Set forth in a Discourse betweene two Church Wardens, one of them being an honest man, and that's a wonder. London: Printed for John Thomas, 1641.*

4°, text pp. 1–8.

Thos. I, 43.

The Earl of Strafford characterized in a Letter sent to a Friend in the Country. 1641.*

fo.

BSC 2205.

A manuscript which has not been traced.

The Frogges of Egypt, or the Caterpillers of the Common-Wealth truely Dissected and laid open; with the Subjects Thankefulnesse unto God for their deliverance from that Nest of Vermine. Printed in the yeare 1641.*

4°, text pp. 1–6. Partly in verse.

(1) Monopolists.

Thos. I, 26.

Three Choice Characters of Marriage.*

BSC 2199.

Known only from the Bliss Sale Catalogue, this title may be a selection from Richard Brathwaite's books, such as his English Gentleman, English Gentlewoman, or Essaies upon the Five Senses, all of which bear upon the subject of marriage and are reasonably close to the date suggested.

The True Character Of An Untrue Bishop. With A Recipe at the end, how to recover a Bishop if hee were lost. . . . London, Printed in the Yeare 1641.

4°, text pp. 1–10.

Begins: "If you aske me of what calling hee is."

Murphy 97. Thos. I, 39. BSC 2197.

Brathwaite, Richard.

The English Gentleman; And The English Gentlevvoman: Both In one Volvme couched, and in one Modell portrayed . . . The Third Edition revised, corrected, and enlarged. By Richard Brathvvait Esq. . . . London, Printed by Iohn Dawson. 1641.

4°, text pp. 1–406.

(1) as in 1630, (2) A gentlewoman (p. 397).

Pforzheimer Catalogue No. 79.

Some copies, as for instance the Huntington, contain also: (3) A character of honour (sig. aaaa). This is also known separately; see the entry under 1635.

Brathwaite, Richard.

The English Gentlewoman. Drawne out to the full body . . . By Richard Brathwait . . . London, Printed by I. Dawson, 1641.

4°, text pp. 271–395.

(1) as (2) in The English Gentleman, 1641.

The Harvard copy, from which this note is taken, is bound as part of Time's Treasury, 1652, but has a title page as above. It is probably a section from The English Gentleman, 1641. It is not identical with the work of the same title of 1631.

Brugis, T.

The Discovery Of A Proiector. Shewing the beginning, progresse, and end of the Projector and his Projects. Also the Projectors last Will and Testament, with an Epitaph to his memory. By T. Brugis, Gent. . . . London, Printed by R.H. and are to be sold by Lawrence Chapman, and William Cooke . . . 1641.

4°, text ff. 1–36, wrongly numbered 34.

(1) A projector (sig. B2, unnumbered, and inserted between original sigs. B and B2).

Cheeke, Sir John.

The Trve Svbject To The Rebell. Or The Hvrt of Sedition, How Greivovs It Is to a Common-wealth. written By Sᵣ Iohn Cheeke Knight (Tutor and Privy-Councellour to King Edward the Sixt.) 1549. Whereunto is newly added by way of Preface a briefe discourse of those times, as they may relate to the present, with the Authors life. Oxford, Printed by Leonard Lichfield . . . Anno Dom. 1641.

4°, text pp. 1–64.

(1) Sir John Cheeke, by Gerald Langbaine (sig. b4).

Poor example of character.

Daye, John.

The Parliament Of Bees, With their proper Character. Or A Bee-hive furnisht with twelve Hony-Combes, as Pleasant as Profitable. Being an Allegoricall description of the actions of good and bad men in these our daies. By Iohn Daye, Sometimes Student of Caius Colledge in Cambridge. . . . London: Printed for William Lee . . . 1641.

4°, text sigs. B4–H2v.

(1) Prorex, or the master bee (sig. B4), (2) Elimozynus, or the hospitable bee (sig. C2v), (3) Thraso, or the plush bee (sig. C4), (4) Armiger, or the field bee (sig. Dv), (5) Poetaster (sig. D3v), (6) The rivals (sig. E2), (7) Parsimonious, or thrifty bee (sig. E4), (8) Inamorato, the passionate bee (sig. F), (9) Pharmacopolis, the quack-salver (sig. F3), (10) Foenerator, the usuring bee (sig. F4v), (11) Oberon (sig. G2v), (12) Rexacillum (sig. G4).

BSC 2200.

[Fannant, Thomas.]

A True Relation of that Memorable Parliament began at Westminster in the tenth yeare of the Reigne of K. Richard the second, with a character of the said King.*

(1) Richard II.

Thos. I, 15.

Attributed to Fannant by Halkett and Laing.

Gentili, Robert.

The Antipathy betweene the French and Spaniard Englished by Robert Gentilys. Sold by H. Martine . . . 1641.*

(1) Of the nobleness & valor of the French (chap. 6), (2) Of the nobleness & valor of the French nation (chap. 7), (3) The contrariety & antipathy of the soul and body of the Spaniards & the French (chap. 11).

BSC 2201.

Reprinted 1642 (as The French-man and the Spaniard), 1704 (ditto).

[Heywood, Thomas.]

Machiavel. As He lately appeared to his deare Sons, the Moderne Proiectors. Divulged for the pretended good of the Kingdomes of England, Scotland, and Ireland. Printed by authority: In the yeare of Grace 1641. London: Printed by J.O. for Francis Constable . . . 1641.

4°, text sigs. A3–D4v.

(1) A projector in general (sig. B2), (2) Wine projectors (sig. C4v), (3) Wine-license farmers (sig. D), (4) Tobacco projectors (sig. Dv), (5) Salt projectors (sig. D2), (6) Rag-projectors (sig. D2), (7) Card projectors (sig. D2v), (8) Butter projectors (sig. D2v), (9) Soap projectors (sig. D3), (10) Coal-projectors (sig. D3), (11) Corporation-projectors (sig. D4).

BSC 2202.

There are one or more variant issues of this work, differing in slight points of title and the like. A somewhat wider variation is that which bears the title Machiavels Ghost, etc. (thereafter almost identical with the above).

Jonson, Ben.

Timber: Or, Discoveries; Made Vpon Men And Matter. . . . By Ben: Iohnson. . . . London, Printed M.DC.XLI.*

(1) The true artificer (p. 41), (2) The man vehement in study (p. 44), (3) Bacon (p. 101).
This has been reprinted.

[Jordan, Thomas.]

A Medicine For The Times. Or, An Antidote Against Faction. Written, By T.J. Containing these Cures, viz. . . . London. Printed for Robert Wood. 1641.

4°, text sigs. A2–A4v.
(1) A roundhead (sig. A3v).

Jordan, Thomas.

Pictures Of Passions, Fancies, & Affections. Poetically Deciphered, in Variety of Characters. By Tho: Jordan, Gent. . . . London, Printed by R. Wood.

8°, text sigs. B–E4v. In verse.
(1) The parliament of England (sig. Bv), (2) A compleat man (sig. B2v), (3) A drunkard (sig. B4), (4), A melancholly man (sig. B5v), (5) A plundering coward (sig. B7), (6) A valiant man at arms (sig. B8v), (7) A complemental man (sig. C2), (8) A rustick (sig. C3v), (9) A seaman (sig. C5), (10) A common souldier (sig. C6v), (11) A roaring boy (sig. C8), (12) A usurer (sig. Dv), (13) A prison (sig. D3), (14) A rash man (sig. D4v), (15) A corrupt lawyer (sig. D6), (16) A noble spirit (sig. D7v), (17) A mountebanck (sig. D8), (18) A whore (sig. E2), (19) A virtuous wife (sig. E3v).
Murphy 53.

The title page as given above is taken from the Huntington copy. That in the British Museum is a variant, naming the author only by his initials, T.J., but adding the full name of the printer, Robert Wood, and the date, 1641. The Bodleian copy is like the Huntington.

Naunton, Sir Robert.

Fragmenta Regalia. Written by Sr Robert Naunton, Master of the Court of Wards. Printed Anno Dom 1641.

4°, text pp. 1–49, wrongly numbered 43.
(1) Queen Elizabeth (p. 1), (2) The Earl of Leicester (p. 13), (3) Radclife Earle of Sussex (p. 16), (4) Secretary William Cecill (p. 17), (5) Sir Philip Sidney (p. 21), (6) Sir Francis Walsingham (p. 22), (7) Willoughbie (p. 23), (8) Sir Nicholas Bacon (p. 24), (9) Knowles (p. 26), (10) Perrot (p. 27), (11) Hatton (p. 32), (12) Effingham (p. 32), (13) Packington (p. 32), (14) Hunsdowne (p. 32), (15) Rauleigh (p. 33), (16) Grevile (p. 36), (17) Essex (p. 36), (18) Buckhurst (p. 34), (19) Mountiou (p. 42), (20) Robert Cecill (p. 38), (21) Vere (p. 41), (22) Worcester (p. 42).
Thos. I, 18.

The page numbers are badly confused through most of the book. They are given here as they are printed.

[Peacham, Henry.]

The Worth of a Peny: Or, A Caution to keep Money. . . . By H.P. Master of Arts. London, Printed by R. Hearne. 1641.

4°, text pp. 1–35.
(1) The covetous person (p. 3), (2) The symptomes of a minde dejected, and discontent for want of money (p. 14).
The dedication is signed Hen. Peacham. This edition is not mentioned by Miss Murphy, who gives 1647 as the earliest.

Richards, Nathaniel.

Poems Sacred and Satyricall. . . . By Nathaniel Richards: Printed at London by T. Paine, for H. Blunden . . . 1641.

8°, text pp. 1–178.
(1) The Iesvite (p. 45, in verse).

[Scott, Thomas.]

The Interpreter. . . . Incerto Authore. . . . Printed in the yeare 1641.

4°, text sigs. A–C2.
(1–3) as in 1622.
Murphy 126. BSC 2203.

[Taylor, John.]

The complaint of M. Tenter-hooke the Projector, and Sir Thomas Dodger the Patentee. . . . London, by E.P. for Francis Coles. 1641.*

s.sh.fo. In verse.
(1) A projector, (2) A patentee.
An unsigned, undated copperplate of the patentee is ascribed to Hollar. The figure at the head of Taylor's broadside looks like a poor imitation of Hollar's. The copperplate bears a couplet at the top:
Who am I, who am I like, what nobody.
Sure I'me the Picture of a Pattenty.
At the bottom are twelve lines of verse beginning, "Loe! here is he, whose Hogs-head now doth vent."

[Taylor, John?]

Lvcifers Lacky, Or, The Devils new Creature. Being The true Character of a dissembling Brownist, whose life is hypocriticall, instructions Schismaticall, thoughts dangerous, Actions malicious, and opinions impious. With the Relation of their repulse from the Parliament house upon Thursday the 4. of December And the reason why Constables had warrants in the City and Liberties of London to take up men to guard the Parliament-house upon Friday the 12. of December, 1641. [ornament] London, Printed for John Greensmith. 1641.

4°, text sigs. A2–A3v.
(1) Hypocritical fanatics [tub-preachers] (sig. A2).
Murphy 97. Thos. I, 46.
Attributed to Taylor by the McAlpin Catalogue.

Watts, Richard.

The Young Mans Looking-Glass. Or, A summary Discourse between the Ant and the Grasshopper. ∴ . . Together with Certaine Characters, Epigrams, and other Poems. By Richard Watts. Printed at London for Edward Blackmore . . . An. 1641.*

8°, in 3 parts, text pp. 1–46 (misprinted 44), 1–22, 1–22.

(1) A common drunkard (Part I, p. 35), (2) An host (I, 37).

Murphy 129.

1642

Anonymous.

The Character of an Atturney.*

A manuscript in the Bodleian.

The character of an honest, and worthy Parliament-man.*

s.sh.fo.

See 1689. This may be a mistaken dating for the same publication.

The Discription, Causes, and Discovery, or Symptomes of a Church Papist, or Popish Protestant, which may stand in stead this Year. 1642. London, for J.T. 1642.*

4°, text pp. 1–8.

(1) A church papist (sig. A3).

Thos. I, 105.

An Exact Description Of A Roundhead, And A Long-Head Shag-Poll: Taken our of the purest Antiquities and Records. Wherein are confuted the odious aspersions of Malignant Spirits: Especially in answer to those most rediculous, absurd and beyond comparison, most foolish Baffle-headed Pamphlets sent into the World by a Stinking Locust, viz. The Devill turn'd Round-Head. The Resolution of the Round-Head. The Vindication of the Round-Head. and Jourdan the Players ex-exercising . . . London, Printed for George Tomlinson . . . 1642.

4°, text pp. 3–8.

(1–2) as in A Short, Compendious . . . Description, 1642.

The Iesuits Character. Or, A Description of the wonderfull Birth, wicked Life, and wretched Death, of a Jesuite. . . . London, Printed by Edw. Griffin. 1642.

4°, 4 leaves unpaged.

Begins: "A Iesuit is the *Nimblest pated Fellow* that the Pope hath to *send.*"

Thos. I, 207.

The Lively Character Of The Malignant Partie . . . By one who cordially affects his Soveraigne, and really respects the Parliament. . . . Published and Printed in the yeare of Feares and Jealousies, plots, projects, and policies, designes, dangers, and discoveries. 1642.

4°, text pp. 2–8.

(1) Papists (p. 2), (2) The prelaticall partie (p. 3), (3) Part of the nobilitie and gentry (p. 4), (4) Delinquents and fugitives (p. 5), (5) Evill counsellors, corrupted judges, and ambitious lawyers (p. 5), (6) The Hotspurres of the time, or cavaliers (p. 7).

Murphy 79. Thos. I, 178. BSC 2207.

The Right Character of A True Subject. Profitably declaring, How every man in this time of danger ought to square all his actions, that he may neither be taxed of disobedience to the Maiesty of the King, nor want of duty to the wisome of the Parliament. 1642.

4°, text pp. 1–4.

Begins: "How difficult a thing it is to observe a mean."

Thos. I, 150.

The Round-head Uncovered, being a moderate triall of his spirit with a distinction betwixt the Round heads and such as Papists call Puritans. London, Printed for George Lindsey. 1642.*

Thos. I, 141.

A Short, Compendious, And True Description Of the Round-Heads, and the Long-Heads, Shag-polls, briefly declared, with the true discovery both of the time and place of both their Originall begin-nings, deduced and drawn out of the purest and re-finedst Antiquities or Records of Time. Or, An Answer To a most ridiculous, absurd, and beyond comparison, most foolish Baffle, sent into the world by a stinking Locust, And Intituled, The Devil Turn'd Round-Head. . . . Printed in the yeer, 1642.

4°, text pp. 1–9.

(1) A roundhead (p. 2), (2) A shag-poll locust (p. 5).

Thos. I, 129.

Reprinted as An Exact Description, 1642.

The Soundheads Description of the Roundhead. Or The Roundhead Exactly Anatomized. . . . In the yeare of the Roundhead his hopes confounded. 1642. London, for I.B. 1642.*

4°, text pp. 1–12.

Thos. I, 116.

Browne, Humphrey.

A Map Of The Microcosme, Or, A Morall Description Of Man. Newly compiled into Essayes: By H. Browne. . . . London, Printed by T. Harper, for John Williams . . . 1642.

12°, texts sigs. A8–I5v.

(1) Man, (2) A learned man, (3) A lustful man, (4) A factious hypocrite, (5) A covetous wretch, (6) An angry man, (7) An envious man, (8) A fortune-teller, (9) Fortune, (10) The common people, (11) A flatterer, (12) A brainsick man, (13) A scandalous scholar, (14) A lawyer, (15) A physitian, (16) A good woman, (17) A proud woman, (18) A prodigall man, (19) Truth.
Murphy 53. BSC 2206.

Some copies (e.g., that in the British Museum) have a variant title page: Printed by T. Harper, for John Harrison.

[Earle, John.]

A Trve Description Of The Pot-Companion Poet: Who Is the Founder of all the Base and Libellous Pamphlets lately spread abroad. Also A Character of the Swil-bole Cook. . . . London, Printed for R.W. 1642.*

4°, text sigs. A2–A4v.

(1) A pot-poet (sig. A2), (2) A swil-bole cook (sig. A3v).
Murphy 44. BSC 2208.

Fuller, Thomas.

The Holy State. By Thomas Fuller, B.D. and Prebendarie of Sarum. . . . Cambridge: Printed by Roger Daniel for John Williams . . . 1642.

4°, text pp. 1–442.

(1) The good wife (p. 1), (2) The good husband (p. 8), (3) The good parent (p. 12), (4) The good child (p. 14), (5) The good master (p. 17), (6) The good servant (p. 19), (7) The good widow (p. 24), (8) The constant virgin (p. 34), (9) The elder brother (p. 44), (10) The younger brother (p. 47), (11) The good advocate (p. 51), (12) The good physician (p. 53), (13) The controversial divine (p. 60), (14) The true church antiquary (p. 69), (15) The general artist (p. 72), (16) The faithful minister (p. 80), (17) The good parishioner (p. 93), (18) The good patron (p. 95), (19) The good landlord (p. 99), (20) The good master of a college (p. 102), (21) The good schoolmaster (p. 109), (22) The good merchant (p. 113), (23) The good yeoman (p. 116), (24) The good handicraftsman (p. 119), (25) The good soldier (p. 119 [the paging is erroneous here]), (26) The good sea-captain (p. 128), (27) The good herald (p. 141), (28) The true gentleman (p. 149), (29) Natural fools (p. 180), (30) A moderate man (p. 206), (31) The favorite (p.

237), (32) The wise statesman (p. 257), (33) The good judge (p. 270), (34) The good bishop (p. 277), (35) The true nobleman (p. 296), (36) The court lady (p. 300), (37) The ambassador (p. 319), (38) The good general (p. 326), (39) The prince or heir apparent (p. 336), (40) The king (p. 349), (41) The harlot (p. 357), (42) The witch (p. 365), (43) The atheist (p. 378), (44) The hypocrite (p. 388), (45) The heretic (p. 393), (46) The rigid Donatists (p. 396), (47) The liar (p. 404), (48) The common barretour (p. 408), (49) The degenerous gentleman (p. 411), (50) The traitor (p. 418), (51) The tyrant (p. 425).
Murphy 55. Pforzheimer No. 392.

There is also an engraved title page.
Miss Murphy omits three characters from her list: (29) Natural fools, (30) A moderate man, and (46) The rigid Donatists.

[Gentili, Robert.]

The French-man And The Spaniard. Or, The two Great Lights of the world, displayed in lively Characters, representing the Antipathy of their Humours and different Dispositions. With an Impartiall Survey of the Customes of both those Nations. By R.G. Gent. London, Printed for Humphrey Mosley . . . 1642.

12°, text sigs. B–M10.

(1–3) as in The Antipathy betweene the French and Spaniard, 1641.
BSC 2209.

[Hausted, Peter.]

A Satyre Against Seperatists, Or, The Conviction Of Chamber-Preachers, and other Chismaticks contrary to the Discipline of This our Protestant Profession. By A.C. Generosus. . . . London, Printed for A.C. 1642.

4°, text pp. 2–8. In verse.
Begins: "I have beene where so many Brownists dwell."

This is a character of a separatist preacher.

[Heywood, Thomas.]

Hogs Caracter Of A Projector. Wherein Is Disciphered The manner and shape of that Vermine. . . . London, Printed for G. Tomlinson. July 15, 1642.

4°, text pp. 1–6.
Begins: "He is a Mongrill by birth."
Murphy 54. Thos. I, 136. BSC 2210.

A reprint, with some changes, of A Projector in General, in Heywood's Machiavel, 1641. The Huntington copy has a variant title page.

[Howell, James.]

Instructions for Forreine Travell. . . . London, Printed by T.B. for Humphrey Mosley . . . 1642.

12°, text pp. 1–236.

(1) A Frenchman and a Spaniard (p. 63), (2) An ingenious and discerning traveller (p. 189).

Attributed to Howell by the CBEL.

[Jordan, Thomas.]

The Christian Souldier. Or, Proparation For Battaile. A Legend containing true Rules for a Souldier . . . Published by a well-willer to the Gown and Sword, T.J. . . . London, Printed for Edward Christopher. 1642.

4°, text pp. 2–6.

(1) A perfect souldier (p. 4), (2) Your coward (p. 4).

Attributed to Jordan by the Huntington Library Catalogue.

L., W.

The courts of justice corrected and amended. Or the corrupt lawyer, untrust, losht and quasht. Wherein the partial judge, counsellour, great mover, whispering informer, favourite at the bar are fully displayed, convicted and directed. London, Printed for G. Lindsey, 1642.*

(1) The menial, (2) The counsellor.

Thos. I, 145.

Naunton, Sir Robert.

Fragmenta Regalia. 1642.*

A reprint of 1641.

[Peacham, Henry.]

A Paradox, In The Praise Of A Dunce, To Smectymnuus. By H.P. . . . London, Printed for Thomas Paybody . . . 1642.

4°, text pp. 1–5.

Begins: "When I undertook this subject, and seriously bethought me of the title."

Murphy 129. Thos. I, 85.

Reresby, Sir John.

Characterismes of Errors [?] and Abuses of these our times daylie acted by too many. Written (as a Parenthesis to my more troublesome Occasions) to refresh myself delight my friends & incite the Conscious Perusers to Reformation. Done by Sʳ. J: R:

A manuscript in the Harvard College Library, signed and dated 1 January 1642.

(1) A gentleman usher (p. 31), (2) A younge sinister justice (p. 43), (3) A roaringe boy (p. 53), (4) A bonny country hostesse (p. 63), (5) A common parasite (p. 73), (6) A lords younger sonne (p. 83), (7) A counterfeit criple (p. 91), (8) A religions counterfeit (p. 103), (9) A wan-

dring fidler (p. 119), (10) An innkeeper (p. 135), (11) A cooke (p. 149, incomplete).

According to the accompanying bill of sale the manuscript originally contained 31 characters corresponding to the 31 epigrams at the beginning of the book. Part of the title page and the latter part of the manuscript are torn away.

T., G.

Roger The Canterburian, That cannot say Grace for his Meat, with a low-crown'd Hat before his Face. Or The Character of a Prelaticall Man affecting great Heighths. Newly Written, by G.T. London, Printed for William Larmar, 1642.

4°, text pp. 1–6.

Begins: "Roger the *Canterburian* is a Man made up of a Soule and a Body like *Ananias*."

Murphy 99.

Sometimes attributed to John Taylor.

[Taylor, John.]

The Anatomy Of The Separatists, alias, Brownists, the factious Brethren in these Times. Wherein This seditious Sect is fairely dissected . . . London, Printed in the yeare, 1642.

4°, text pp. 1–6.

Begins: "Such is the all-daring and Lewd Licentiousnesse."

Murphy 99. Thos. I, 108.

Attributed to Taylor by the Thomason Catalogue.

Taylor, John.

A Cluster of Coxcombes, Or, A Cinquepace of five sorts of Knaves and Fooles: Namely, The Donatists, Publicans, Disciplinarians, Anabaptists, and Brownists; The Originals, Opinions, Confutations, and (in a word) their Heads Roundly jolted together. Also shewing how in the Raignes of sundry Kings, and in the late Q. Elizabeths Raign the Anabaptists have bin burnt as Hereticks, and otherwayes punished. And that the Sect of the Brownists is so new, that many are alive who knew the beginning of it. With other sects displayed. By John Taylor. [woodcut] July 13. Printed for Richard Webb, 1642.*

4°, text fols. 1–4.

Thos. I, 135.

[Taylor, John.]

A description Of The Round-Head and Rattle-Head. . . . London, Printed for J. Sweeting. 1642.

4°, text pp. 1–6. In verse.

(1) The round-head (p. 1), (2) The rattle-head

(p. 3), (3) The roaring cavalier (p. 6).
Murphy 99. Thos. I, 148.

Attributed to Taylor by Halkett and Laing.

[Taylor, John.]

The Devil Turned Round-Head: Or, Pluto
become a Brownist.

4°, text sigs. A2–A4v.
(1) Roundheads (sig. A3).

Reprinted as Taylor's by the Spenser Society, with tentative date 1642.

[Taylor, John.]

Heads of all Fashions . . . Allegorically shewing the Diversities of Religion in these distempered times. . . . London Printed for Iohn
Morgan . . . 1642.

4°, text pp. 2–8. In verse.
(1) A round-head, both at randome and couched
(p. 3), (2) A square head (p. 4), (3) A solid head
(p. 4), (4) An empty head (p. 4), (5) An hollow
head (p. 4), (6) A full head (p. 4), (7) A deepe
head (p. 5), (8) A great head (p. 5), (9) A little
head (p. 5), (10) A long head (p. 5), (11) A
short head (p. 5), (12) A tall head (p. 5), (13) A
flat head (p. 6), (14) A strong head (p. 6), (15)
A weake head (p. 6), (16) A thick head (p. 6),
(17) A thin head (p. 6), (18) A plaine head (p.
6), (19) A forked head (p. 7), (20) A smooth
head (p. 7), (21) A rugged head (p. 7), (22) A
loger head (p. 7), (23) A narrow head (p. 7),
(24) A broad head (p. 7), (25) A blocke head
(p. 7), (26) A light head (p. 8), (27) A heavy
with some other whole and halfe heads (p. 8).
Thos. I, 115.

Attributed to Taylor by the CBEL.

[Taylor, John?]

A Puritane Set forth In his Lively Colours: or
K. James his description of a Puritan. Whereunto is added, The Round-heads Character,
With The Character of an Holy Sister. All
fitted for the times. . . . London, Printed for
N.B. 1642.

4°, text pp. 1-6. In verse except no. 1.
(1) A puritan, (2) A roundhead, (3) A holy sister.
Murphy 98. Thos. I, 159.

Attributed to Taylor doubtfully by Halkett and Laing.

[Ward, Robert?]

The Anatomy of Warre. By R. W. London:
Printed for John Dalham and Richard
Lownds. 1642.*
Thos. I, 199.

Ward is probably the author since both the STC and the
CBEL attribute Animadversions of Warre, 1639, to him.
The present title may possibly be a revision or reprint of
that. The Character of Warre, 1643, it seems likely, must
be somehow related.

1643

Anonymous.

An Abstract of some late Characters. Or, How
the principall means appointed for our Reformation is become the maine fuell of our Wickednes. Laid downe in Sundry Characters of
L. Bishops. Dumb Dogs. Non-Residenciaries.
Men-Pleasers. Unpreaching Ministers, that
Edify to damnation, By their Scandalous Living. False wresting Mis-applying The Scripture. . . . London . . . James Crumpe . . .
1643.

4°, text pp. 1–45.
(1) Dumb dogs (p. 3), (2) Non-residenciaries
(p. 3), (3) Men-pleasers (p. 4), (4) Unpreaching
ministers (p. 8).
BSC 2212. Thos. I, 286.

The Character of a Prince. 1643.*

The Cities Warning-Peece, in the Malignants
description and Conversion: or, the Roundhead turn'd Poet, Where a Feast of Prose and
Verse invite Curiosity to be nibling. Written
long since, but Printed in the Yeere That every
Knave and foole turn'd Cavaleere. [1643.]*

4°, text pp. 1–8 (?)
(1) a Malignant (p. 2).
Thos. I, 238.

The Thomason copy is dated in manuscript Feb. 27,
1642 (i.e., 1643).

The King no Tyrant: or the Character of them
both. Being the true Mirrour of a Commonwealth. Containing the severall sorts of government, and how a King may be known, and
distinguished from a Tyrant. As also, what
are the Lawes, Magistrates, and Counsellors
which conduce to the establishment of a perfect Commonwealth. Printed according to
order. London, Printed for Laurence Chapman. 1643.*

4°, text pp. 1–6.
(1) A king (p. 2), (2) A tyrant (p. 5).

The pious Life and Death of Mr. Josiah Shute,
Who left us on the 22. day of June. 1643.*
(1) Josiah Shute.

The Reformado, Precisely Charactered by a
Transformed Churchwarden, at a Vestry,
London. The Motion of the World this day
Is mov'd the quite contrary way. . . . Printed
in the yeare 1643.

4°, text sigs. A2–C1v.
(1) An able pastor (sig. B3).
Murphy 129. Thos. I, 249. BSC 2215.

The Right Character of a True Subject. 1643.*
Reprinted from 1642.

A strange Sight to be seen at Westminster.
. . . [colophon] Oxford, Printed for Wil.
Web. 1643.
s.sh.fo. In verse.
(1) The state mountebanke (p. 1).
Murphy 129.
The title given is that of the first poem on the sheet. The
State Mountebanke begins lower down on the first column.

Three severall and different Characters Of the
Cardinall Duke of Plessis Richelieu; The late
potent Manager of the French Monarchie, and
well-nigh Grand Arbitrator of the rest of Europe. London, for Francis Constable. 1643.*
4°, text pp. 1–13.
Thos. I, 276.

The True Character of such as are Malignants
in the Kingdome of Scotland, Also the indic-
tion of a publike fast by the Commissioners of
the generall Assembly. London, Printed for
Henry Overton, 1643.*
Thos. I, 231. BSC 2211.

Twenty Lookes Over all the Rovnd-Heads
that ever lived in the world. . . . 1643.
4°, text sigs. A2–A4v.
(1) Heathenish round-heads (sig. A2), (2)
Round-head vowers (sig. A2v), (3) Aged round-
heads (sig. A2v), (4) David's round-heads (sig.
A2v), (5) Round-head mourners (sig. A2v), (6)
Israelitish round-heads (sig. A2v), (7) Round-
head Corinths (sig. A3), (8) Golgothan round-
heads (sig. A3), (9) Feminish round-heads (sig.
A3), (10) Oxford round-heads (sig. A3), (11)
English round-heads (sig. A3v), (12) Essex
round-heads (sig. A3v), (13) Women round-
heads (sig. A3v), (14) Court round-heads (sig.
A3v), (15) Round-head cat (sig. A3v), (16)
Round-head friers (sig. A4), (17) Round-head
citizens (sig. A4), (18) Strange round-heads (sig.
A4v), (19) Round-head separatists (sig. A4v),
(20) Round-heads of the time (sig. A4v).
Thos. I, 223.

[Breton, Nicholas.]
Englands Selected Characters, Describing the
good and bad Worthies of this Age. . . . London, Printed for T.S. 1643.
4°, text pp. 1–14.
(1) A worthy king (p. 1), (2) An unworthy king
(p. 1), (3) A worthy queen (p. 2), (4) An unworthy queen, or woman (p. 2), (5) A worthy
prince (p. 3), (6) An unworthy prince (p. 3),

(7) A worthy privy counsellor (p. 4), (8) An unworthy privy councellor (p. 4), (9) A worthy
nobleman (p. 4), (10) An unworthy nobleman
(p. 5), (11) A worthy bishop or minister (p. 5),
(12) An unworthy bishop or minister (p. 6), (13)
A worthy judge (p. 6), (14) An unworthy judge
(p. 7), (15) A worthy knight and soldier (p. 7),
(16) An unworthy knight and soldier (p. 7),
(17) A worthy gentleman (p. 8), (18) An unworthy gentleman (p. 8), (19) A worthy lawyer
(p. 9), (20) An unworthy lawyer (p. 9), (21) A
worthy soldier (p. 10), (22) An untrained soldier
(p. 10), (23) A worthy physician (p. 11), (24)
An unworthy physician (p. 11), (25) A Jesuit
reprobated (p. 12), (26) A cowardly cavalier (p.
12), (27) A bawd of the black guard (p. 13),
(28) A malignant knave a hatcher of plots (p. 13).
Murphy 28. Thos. I, 269. BSC 2213.
Some copies have a title page reading: Printed for Thomas
Slater. This work is a reprint, with some changes, of The
Good and the Badde, 1616.

[Cowley, Abraham.]
A Satyre, The Puritan and the Papist. By a
Scholler in Oxford. 1643.*
Published anonymously, but attributed to Cowley in Wit
and Loyalty Reviv'd, 1682.

Davenport, Robert.
A Valiant Martyr A Spiritvall Coward A
Weeping Convert An Acceptable Sacrifice
And A Hovse On Fire. By R.D.*
Manuscript, 4°, 9 leaves.
(1) A martyr, (2) A spiritual coward (in verse),
(3) A weeping convert, (4) An acceptable sacri-
fice.
Autograph MS in possession of G. Thorn-Drury in 1921.
He reprinted it in A Little Ark, 1921. He dated it as be-
ing before 1643.

Martin Mar-Prelate.
The Character Of A Puritan; And His Gal-
limaufrey of the Antichristian Clergie; prepared with D. Bridges Sawce for the present
time to feed on. By the worthy Gentleman,
D. Martin Mar-Prelat, Doctor in all the Faculties, Primate and Metropolitan. . . . Printed
in the time of Parliament. 1643.
4°, text sigs. A3–D2v.
(1) A Puritan (sig. D2), in verse.
Murphy 128. Thos. I, 228. BSC 2214.
A reprint of A Dialogue Wherin is Plainly Layd Open the
Tyrannicall Dealing of Lord Bishops, 1640.

[Palmer, Herbert.]
The Upright Protestant, As He Was Reformed
From The Superstitious errours of Popery in
the happy Reignes of Edward the 6th, Qu.
Elizabeth, and K. Iames of blessed memory.

. . . London, Printed for George Lindsey . . . 1643.

4°, text pp. 1–6.

Begins: "A True Reformed PROTESTANT is one that beleeves things, his reason cannot comprehend."

Murphy 59. Thos. I, 255.

Subtitled: The Characters of a Beleeving Protestant, in Paradoxes, and seeming Contradictions. Reprinted with some changes as The Character of a Believing Christian, 1645.

Staples, George.

A Character of a Traitor. [1643?]*

Manuscript, 16 pages, in the Public Record Office, London (S.P. Dom., Vol. CCCCXCIX, no. 58).

Described in the Calendar of State Papers, Domestic Series, 1641–43 (p. 540) as "Two short Latin poems . . . followed by stanzas in English entitled 'A Character of a Traitor' having evident reference to Archbishop Laud, to whom a dedication in Latin is prefixed 'Ab amplitudinis et virtutum tuarum devotissimo cultore, G. Staplaeo.' "

[Ward, Robert?]

The Character of Warre; or, the miseries thereof discected and laid open from Scripture and experience. By R.W. London: Printed for James Williams. 1643.*

Thos. I, 279.

The Anatomy of War, 1642, probably by the same author, is possibly an earlier version of the present title.

1644

Anonymous.

The Character of a Cavalier.*

BSC 2303 (a nineteenth-century transcript).

No copy of a manuscript or book dated 1644 has been found. This title may be a mistaken reference to one of the books of this year by Symmons or Taylor (q.v.), or the date may be wrong. See 1647.

A Nest of Perfidious Vipers: Or, The Second Part Of The Parliaments Kalendar Of Black Saints. Pictured forth in a second Arraignment or Jayl-delivery of Malignants, Jesuites, Arminians, and Cabinet Counsellors, being the Fatall Engineers, Plotters, and Contrivers of Treasons against the Parliament, our Religion, Laws, and Lives. . . . London, Printed according to Order, for G. Bishop. Septemb. 21. 1644.

4°, text pp. 2–8.

(1) Black saints (p. 2), (2) Basilisks or bishops (p. 2), (3) Wren (p. 3), (4) Mountague (p. 4), (5) White (p. 5), (6) Prince Rupert (p. 5), (7) Prince Maurice (p. 6), (8) The Marquis of Hartford (p. 6), (9) The Duke of Richmond (p. 7), (10) Lord Keeper Littleton (p. 7), (11) Lindsey (p. 7), (12) Huntington (p. 7), (13) Cockatrices, i.e., the queen and others (p. 8), (14) Curled winding snakes (p. 8), (15) Dangerous adders (p. 8).

Thos. I, 341.

Some of these sections are almost too brief to be characters.

[Cleveland, John.]

The Character Of A London Diurnall. . . . Printed in the Yeare 1644.

4°, text pp. 1–8.

Begins: "A Diurnall is a puny Chronicle."

Murphy 60. BSC 2216. Thos. I, 360.

Dated by the Thomason Catalogue January, 1644/5. Contains 36 lines. There were at least three distinct editions in this year.

[Cleveland, John.]

The Character Of A London Diurnall. . . . Printed in the Yeare, 1644.

4°, text pp. 1–6.

Begins: "A Diurnall is a puny Chronicle."

Murphy 60.

Designated by Miss Murphy and Huntington as second edition. Contains 38 lines.

[Cleveland, John.]

The Character Of A London Diurnall. . . . Printed in the Yeare, 1644.

4°, text pp. 1–6.

Begins: "A Diurnall is a puny Chronicle."

Murphy 61.

Third edition, 38 lines.

[Cooke, William.]

The true Character of a Noble Generall: Seen and Allowed of by his Excellencie, The Earl of Essex. Written in Prose and Verse. London, Printed by Iohn Hammond, 1644.*

4°, text pp. 1–6.

(1) The true description of a noble generall (sig. A2).

Thos. I, 329.

The dedication is signed William Cooke.

[Featley, Daniel.]

Sacra Nemesis, The Levites Scourge, Or Mercurius Britan. Civicvs Disciplin'd. Also Diverse remarkable Disputes and Resolvs in the Assembly of Divines related, Episcopacy asserted, Truth righted, Innocency vindicated against detraction. . . . Oxford, Printed by Leonard Lichfield . . . 1644.

4°, text pp. 1–92.

(1) Britanicus (p. 1).

Thos. I, 336. BSC 2217.

Attributed to Featley by the CBEL.

[Heywood, Thomas.]

Machiavels Ghost as he lately appeared. 1644.*

A reprint of 1641. No copy of an edition of 1644 has been found.

[Howell, James.]

Δενδρολογια. Dodona's Grove, Or The Vocall Forrest. The Second edition . . . with an Addition of two other Tracts: viz. Parables, reflecting upon the Times, And England's Teares for the present VVarres. By J.H. Esquire. . . . Printed in the Yeare, 1644.

4°, text pp. 1–172.
(1–9) as in 1640.
Thos. I, 353. BSC 2194.

Palmer, Herbert.

Memorials of Godlinesse and Christianitie . . . Printed by G.M. for Tho. Underhill. 1644.*
See 1657.
Thos. I, 304.

Symmons, Edward.

A Military Sermon, Wherein By the word of God, the nature and disposition of a Rebell is discovered, and the Kings true Souldier described and Characterized: Preached at Shrewsbury, March 3. 1643. to His Majesties Army there under the Command of the High and most Illustrious Prince Rupert. By Edw. Symmons Chaplaine to the Life-guard of the Prince of Wales. . . . Oxford, Printed by Henry Hall, in the Yeare 1644.

4°, text pp. 1–44.
(1) A rebel (p. 7), (2) A complete cavalier (p. 22).
Murphy 130. BSC 2219.

Symmons, Edward.

A Militarie Sermon . . . By Edw. Symmons . . . Oxford, Printed by Henry Hall, in the Yeere 1644.*

4°, text pp. 1–32.
(1–2) as in A Military Sermon, 1644.
Murphy 130. Thos. I, 325.

Miss Murphy considers this title a London counterfeit reprint of the other issue.

Taylor, John.

The Noble Cavalier Caracterised, And A Rebellious Caviller Cauterised. By John Taylor.

4°, text pp. 1–8.
Begins: "To begin roundly, soundly, and profoundly, The *Cavalier* is a Gentleman."

The CBEL dates this work 1647 (?), but a reference to Wither's Campo-Musae (1643) at the end makes an earlier date more likely.

1645

Anonymous.

The Character of a Roundhead.*
BSC 2303 (a nineteenth-century transcript).

A Character Of An Antimalignant, Or Right Parliamentier; Expressing plainly his opinion concerning King and Parliament. Published by Authoritie. . . . London, Printed by F.N. for Robert Bostock . . . 1645.

4°, text pp. 1–6.
Begins: "An *Antimalignant*, or right *Parliamentier*, is one who layes aside."
Murphy 100. Thos. I, 388. BSC 2221.

The Character Of An Oxford-Incendiary. . . . [colophon] London printed for Robert White.

4°, text pp. 1–8.
Begins: "An *Oxford Incendiary* is a Court Salamander."
Murphy 101. Thos. I, 374. BSC 2198, 2213.
The Thomason Catalogue dates this work 1645.

A Character Of The New Oxford Libeller, In answer to his Character of a London Diurnall. Published according to order. London, Printed by M.S. for H.B. . . . 1645.*

4°, text pp. 1–5.
Begins: "He is a Gentleman grown lousie."
Murphy 60. Thos. I, 361.

A Full Answer To A Scandalous Pamphlet, Intituled, A Character of a London Diurnall. Published by Authoritie. London, Printed by F.P. for Francis Coles and Lawrence Blaikeloke . . . 1645.*

4°.
Murphy 60. Thos. I, 372. BSC 2222.

The Moderate Presbyterian. . . . London, Printed by R.B. . . . 1645.

4°, text pp. 1–14.
Begins: "First, That in the most proper sence."
Thos. I, 451.

A New Anatomie, Or Character of a Christian, or Round-head. Expressing His Description, Excellencie, Happiness, and Innocencie. . . . London, Printed for Robert Leybourne . . . 1645.*

8°, text pp. 1–13.
Murphy 100. BSC 2220. Thos. I, 402.

The Oxford Character of the London Diurnall examined and answered. [colophon] Printed by M.B. 1645.*
Murphy 60. BSC 2222. Thos. I, 369.

The true Character of Mercurius Aulicus. . . . London, Printed by T. Forcet . . . 1645.*

4°, text pp. 1–8.
Begins: "His very Name speaketh him a Courtier."
Murphy 101.

Cheynell, Francis.

The Man of Honour, Described In a Sermon, Preached before the Lords of Parliament, In the Abbey Church at Westminster, March 26. 1645. . . . By Francis Cheynell. . . . London, Printed by J.R. for Samuel Gellibrand . . . 1645.

4°, text pp. 1–67.
Begins: "A Sad Text, fit to be considered."
Thos. I, 368.

[Gayton, Edmund.]

Chartæ Scriptæ: Or A New Game At Cards, Call'd Play By The Booke. . . . Printed in the Year, 1645.

4°, text pp. 1–24. In verse.
(1) The knave of clubs (p. 6).
Thos. I, 407.

[Harding, W. N. H.]

The Academy of Complements. . . . The sixt Edition. . . . London . . . A. Badger, for H. Mosley . . . 1645.

12°, text pp. 1–290.
(1) The love-sick picture drawer, or the perfections of ever to be admired Clarinda (p. 102).

The character does not occur in the earlier editions of the book. Attributed to Harding by the CBEL. The Author's Preface is signed Philomusus.

[Howell, James.]

Dendrologia. 1645.*

Reprinted from 1640.

[May, Thomas.]

The Character Of A Right Malignant. [1645.]*

4°, text pp. 1–7.
Begins: "He is one that professes love to the Protestant-Religion."
Murphy 100. BSC 2218, 2221. Thos. I, 360.

The Thomason copy is attributed in MS. to Thomas May and dated Feb. 1/2, 1644 (i.e., 1644/5).

Milton, John.

Poems Of Mr. John Milton, Both English and Latin, Compos'd at several times. Printed by his true Copies. . . . Printed and publish'd according to Order. London, Printed by Ruth Raworth for Humphrey Moseley . . . 1645.

8°, in 2 parts, text pp. 1–120 (English) and 1–87 (Latin).

(1) L'Allegro, the cheerful man (p. 30), (2) Il Penseroso, the melancholy man (p. 37).
Reprinted hundreds of times.

[North, Dudley, third Baron.]

A Forest of Varieties. First Part. London Printed by Richard Cotes, 1645.

4°, text pp. 1–243. Part II has a separate title page.
(1) A king (p. 85), (2) A good counsellor (p. 87), (3) A good Parliament man (88, misprinted 87), (4) A good courtier (p. 89, misprinted 88), (5) A gentleman (p. 90), (6) A supplement to the gentleman (p. 92), (7) A favorite (p. 94), (8) A divine (p. 96), (9) A physitian (p. 98), (10) A lawyer (p. 99), (11) A souldier (p. 100).
Murphy 130.

The British Museum has North's autographed copy.

[Palmer, Herbert.]

The Character Of A believing Christian. Set forth in Paradoxes, and seeming Contradictions. Imprimatur, Joseph Caryl. London, Printed, for Richard Wodenothe, at the Star, under Peters Church in Cornhill, 1645.

8°, text pp. 1–11.
Begins: "A Christian is one that believeth things his reason cannot comprehend."
Murphy 59. Thos. I, 387.

A reprint, under different title, of The Upright Protestant, 1643.

[Taylor, John.]

The Rebells Anathematized and Anatomized. Or, a Satyricall Salutation to the Rabble of Seditious, Pestiferous Pulpit-praters. . . . Oxford, 1645.*

4°. In verse.
Thos. I, 377.
Attributed to Taylor by the CBEL.

Vicars, John.

The Picture of independency lively yet lovingly delineated. By John Vicars. Printed by John Macock and are to be sold by Michael Spark junior.*
Thos. I, 367.

1646

Anonymous.

The Picture of an English Antic, with a List of his ridiculous Habits, and Apish Gestures. Maids, where are your hearts become? Look you what here is! 1646.*
Thos. I, 475.

The Zealous Soldier. 1646.*
s.sh.fo. In verse.
Thos. I, 433.

Geree, John.

The Character of an old English Pvritan, Or Non-Conformist. By John Geree M.A. and Preacher of the Word sometime at Tewksbury, but now at Saint Albans. Published according to Order. . . . London, Printed by W. Wilson for Christopher Meredith . . . 1646.

4°, text pp. 1–6.
Begins: "The Old English Puritane was such an one, that honoured God (*a*) above all."
Murphy 101. Thos. I, 430. BSC 2224, 2225.

Another edition of the same year is virtually identical except for some variations in the title page. It is printed by A. Miller instead of by W. Wilson. Reprinted 1649, 1659, 1660 (as A Vindication of Calvin), [1670?] (as The Character of an Old English Protestant), 1672, 1673 (as The Character of the Sober Non-Conformist).

Jordan, Thomas.

Loves Dialect. 1646.*
A reprint of Poeticall Varieties, 1637.

Mill, Humphrey.

The Second Part of The Nights Search . . . By Humphrey Mill . . . London, Printed for Henry Shepheard . . . 1646.

8°, text pp. 1–163. In verse.
(1) Types of bawd and whore (p. 1), (2) Types of drunkard (p. 7), (3) Types of thief and lecher (p. 13), (4) A degenerate lord (p. 38), (5) A foul hag (p. 38), (6) A lecherous carpenter (p. 44), (7) A poetaster (p. 55), (8) A group of sharks (p. 64), (9) A constable (p. 71), (10) A physician (p. 76), (11) A wanton couple (p. 80), (12) A vicious lawyer (p. 97), (13) Various criminals (p. 126).

[Sheppard, Samuel.]

The times Displayed In Six Sestyads . . . London, Printed and are to be sold by J. P. at his shop neer the Sessions house in the Old Bayly. 1646.

4°, text pp. 5–24. In verse.
(1) A presbyter (p. 6), (2) An independent (p. 7), (3) An Anabaptist (p. 9), (4) A Brownist (p. 9), (5) A familist (p. 10), (6) An antinomian (p. 11), (7) A libertine (p. 13), (8) An Arminian (p. 15), (9) A Protestant (p. 17), (10) Of the Pope (p. 19).
Thos. I, 479.

The Dedication is signed S. Sheppard. The British Museum calls the author Simon Sheppard, the Huntington Samuel Sheppard. The characters are very poor.

Vicars, John.

The Schismatick Sifted. Or, The Picture of Independents, Freshly and Fairly Washt-over again. . . . By John Vicars. . . . London . . .

Nathanael Webb, and William Grantham . . . 1646.

4°, text pp. 1–43.
(1) A truly godly-man (p. 8).
Thos. I, 446.

Vines, Richard.

The Hearse Of The Renowned, The Right Honourable Robert Earle of Essex . . . As it was represented in a Sermon, preached in the Abbey Church at Westminster, at the Magnificent Solemnity of his Funerall, Octob. 22. 1646. By Richard Vines. . . . London, Printed by T.R. and E.M. for Abel Roper . . . 1646.

4°, text pp. 1–38.
(1) Robert, Earl of Essex (p. 29).
Thos. I, 470.

Wortley, Sir Francis.

Characters And Elegies. By Francis VVortley, Knight and Baronet. . . . Printed in the Yeere, CIƆ IƆC XLVI.

4°, text pp. 1–68.
(1) His royall Majestie (p. 1), (2) The Queenes Majestie (p. 3), (3) The hopefull prince (p. 5), (4) The illustrious James, Duke of York (p. 7), (5) A noble generall (p. 8), (6) A true English Protestant, or true cavallier (p. 11), (7) An antinomian, or anabaptisticall independent (p. 14), (8) A Jesuite (p. 16), (9) A northern lady, as she is wife, mother, and sister (p. 18), (10) The politique neuter (p. 21), (11) The citie paragon (p. 23), (12) A sharking committee-man (p. 25), (13) Britannicus his pedigree. A fatall prediction of his end (p. 26), (14) The phoenix of the court (p. 28).
Murphy 131. Thos. I, 452. BSC 2226.

Rosenbach's English Poetry to 1700, 1941, item 828, advertised a copy with presentation inscription from the author to Lady Abigail Sherard, with a long autobiographical note and corrections throughout.

[Younge, Richard.]

The Drunkards Character. [1646?].*
s.sh.fo.
Begins: "A Drunkard is the annoyance of Modesty."
Thos. I, 436.

Probably a summary or abstract of the long edition of 1638.

1647

Anonymous.

A Catalogue of the severall Sects and Opinions in England and other Nations. With a briefe rehearsall of their false and dangerous tenents. London, Printed for W.H. 1647.
s.sh. Partly in verse.
Thos. I, 488.

The Character of a Cavaliere, with his Brother Seperatist. Both striving which shall bee most active in dividing the two Nations, now so happily, by the blessing of God, united. . . . London, Printed for W.H. 1647.

4°, text pp. 1–6.
(1) A seperatist (p. 2), (2) A cavalier (p. 5).
Murphy 132. BSC 2228. Thos. I, 502.

The Character Of An Agitator. . . . Printed in the Yeare 1647.

4°, text pp. 3–7.
Begins: "An *Agitator* is a late spurious *Monster* of *John Lilburnes* generation."
Murphy 103. Thos. I, 569. BSC 2227.

A fresh Whip For all scandalous Lyers. Or, A true description of the tvvo eminent Pamphliteers, or Squib-tellers of this Kingdome. With a plaine and true Relation of their Tricks and Devices wherewith they use to couzen and cheate the Common-wealth. London printed. 1647.*

4°, text pp. 1–6.
(1) The Diurnall-writer, (2) The Perfect Occurrence-writer.
Murphy 63.

Looke about you, or the Faultfinder and Critical Observer.*

Thos. I, 533.

The Portratt of the Politicke Christian Favorite. 1647.*

Eyre, Stationers' Registers, I, 265. Entered to Mercy Meighen and Gabr. Beadle, March 8, 1646/7.

Study to be quiet: Or, a short View of the Miseries of Warre, With the Necessity of Peace. Also, The Character of a Peaceable Man: whose Motto is, I am for Peace, Psal. 120. vers. 7. By a Dyer. London: Printed for B. Alsop, 1647.*

4°, text sigs. A–A4.
(1) A peaceable and quiet man (sig. A3, in verse).
Murphy 132. BSC 2234. Thos. I, 545.

This piece has no connection with Study to be Quiet: A Serious and Seasonable Advice, 1680.

Terrible Newes from Scotland . . . By a Gentleman imployed in the Service for the Publique, and dedicated to the Commissioners of Scotland. . . . London, Printed for T.W. 1647.*

4°, text pp. 1–6.
(1) The Scots (p. 5).
Murphy 132. Thos. I, 545.

A Vindication Of the late Archbishop of York, from a Scurrulous Libel . . . Printed in the Yeer. 1647.

4°, text pp. 3–8.
(1) John Williams, Archbishop of York (p. 3).
BSC 2235.

[Birkenhead, Sir John.]

The Assembly-Man.*

The date is uncertain. There may not have been any edition before 1663 (*q.v.*).

[Cleveland, John.]

The Character of a Country Committee-Man with the Ear-mark of a Sequestrator.*

The existence of this edition is dubious. See 1649.

[Cleveland, John.]

The Character of a Diurnal-Maker. By J.C. 1647.*

An uncertain edition. See 1654.

[Cleveland, John.]

The Character Of A London-Diurnall: With severall select Poems: By the same Author. . . . Printed in the Yeere CIƆ IƆC XLVII.

4°, text pp. 1–50. 17 poems.
Begins: "A *Diurnall* is a puny Chronicle."
Murphy 61. Thos. I, 494. BSC 2229, 2230 (this or other editions of 1647).

There were at least six distinct editions or issues of this year; see below.

[Cleveland, John.]

The Character Of A London Diurnall: With severall select Poems. By the same Author. . . . Printed in the Yeere CIƆ IƆC XLVII.

4°, text pp. 1–50. 17 poems.
Begins: "A *Diurnall* is a puny Chronicle."
Murphy 61.

Some copies of this title page have a colon after Poems.

[Cleveland, John.]

The Character of A London-Diurnall: VVith severall select Poems: By the same Author. Optima & novissima Editio. Printed in the Yeere CIƆ IƆC XLVII.

4°, text pp. 1–50. 18 poems.
Begins: "A *Diurnall* is a puny Chronicle."

[Cleveland, John.]

The Character Of A London-Diurnall: With severall select Poems. By the same Author. Novissima & castigatissima Editio. . . . Printed in the Yeere CIƆ IƆC XLVII.

4°, text pp. 1–56. Contains 20 poems.
Begins: "A *Diurnall* is a puny Chronicle."
Murphy 61.

[Cleveland, John.]

The Character Of A London-Diurnall: With severall select Poems: By the same Author. Optima & novissima Editio. Printed in the Yeere CIↃ IↃC XLVII.

4°, text pp. 1–56. 22 poems.
Begins: "A *Diurnall* is a puny Chronicle."

[Cleveland, John.]

The Character of a London-Diurnall: With severall select Poems: By the same Author. Optima & novissima Editio. Printed in the Yeare 1647.

4°, text pp. 3–52. 23 poems.
Begins: "A *Diurnall* is a puny Chronicle."

[Cleveland, John.]

The Character Of A Moderate Intelligencer With some select Poems. Written by the same Author. J.C.

4°, text pp. 1–12.
(1) A moderate intelligencer (p. 1), (2) The zealous sectary (p. 6).
Murphy 62. Thos. I, 506.
Dated April 29, 1647, in the Thomason Catalogue.

Cook, John.

What The Independents Would have, Or, A Character, Declaring some of their Tenents, and their desires to disabuse those who speak ill of that they know not. Written By John Cook of Grays Inne Barrister. London, Printed for Giles Calvert, 1647.

4°, text pp. 1–16.
(1) An Independent (p. 3).
Thos. I, 552. BSC 2231.

Duncon, John.

The Holy Life and Death of the Viscountess Falkland. 1647.*
(1) Elegy on Lady Falkland by Jasper Mayne.

[Felltham, Owen.]

A Perfect Description of . . . Scotland. 1647.*
The date 1647 is given by the CBEL. See 1649.

[Ford, Thomas.]

The Times Anatomiz'd, In severall Characters. By T.F. . . . London, Printed for W.L. Anno, MDCXLVII.

12°, text sigs. B–E12.
(1) A good king (sig. B2), (2) Rebellion (sig. B3), (3) An honest subject (sig. B4v), (4) An

hypocriticall convert of the times (sig. B6v), (5) A souldier of fortune (sig. B8), (6) A discontented person (sig. B9v), (7) An ambitious man (sig. B10v), (8) The vulgar (sig. B12), (9) Errour (sig. C), (10) Truth (sig. C2v), (11) A selfe-seeker (sig. C4), (12) Pamphlets (sig. C5), (13) An envious man (sig. C6), (14) True valour (sig. C7), (15) Time (sig. C8), (16) A newter (sig. C9v), (17) A turn-coat (sig. C11v), (18) A moderate man (sig. C12v), (19) A corrupt committee-man (sig. D2), (20) A sectary (sig. D4v), (21) War (sig. D6v), (22) Peace (sig. D8), (23) A drunkard (sig. D9v), (24) A novice-preacher (sig. D12v), (25) A scandalous preacher (sig. E2v), (26) A grave divine (sig. E4), (27) A selfe-conceited man (sig. E5v), (28) An inconstant man (sig. E6v), (29) Religion (sig. E8), (30) Death (sig. E9v).
Murphy 63. BSC 2232. Thos. I, 709.
The Thomason copy has a MS note on the title: "T. Ford, servt to Mr. Sam. Man."

M., N.

A True Account and Character of the Times, Historically and Politically Drawne by a Gentleman to give Satisfaction to his Friend in the Countrey. By N.M.*

4°, text pp. 1–3.
The date 1647 is taken from Bliss's manuscript notes, I, 313.

N., B.

The true Character tending to Love. Or a short Treatise Wherein is showed how Christians ought to love their Christian Brethren. By a Lover of Charity, B.N. London, Printed for R. Wodenoth . . . 1647.*

4°, text pp. 1–13.
Thos. I, 498. BSC 2233.

Palmer, Herbert.

Memorials of Godliness. 1647.*
See 1657.

[Peacham, Henry.]

The Worth Of A Peny: Or A Caution to keep Money. . . . By H.P. . . . London, Printed, Ann. Dom. 1647.

4°, text pp. 1–35.
(1–2) as in 1641.
Murphy 133. Thos. I, 534.

[Taylor, John.]

A Recommendation to Mercurius Morbicus. Together With A fair Character upon his worth. . . . Printed in the Yeer 1647.

4°, text pp. 3–8.
(1) Mercurius Morbicus (p. 5).
Murphy 103. Thos. I, 562.

A satire on Henry Walker. Attributed to Taylor by the CBEL.

Tel-troth, Thomas.

The True Character Of An Ordinance Of Parliament in generall. Written by Tho. Tel-troth . . . Printed at Amsterdam 1647.

4°, text pp. 1–8.
Begins: "An Ordinance of Parliament (without the Royall assent)."

Venning, Ralph.

Orthodoxe Paradoxes, or a beleiver clearing truth by seeming contradictions. With an appendix, called the Triumph of assurance. By Ralph Venning. Printed by E.G. for I. Rothwell, and Hanna Allen. 1647.*

Text pp. 1–119.
See 1650.
Thos. I, 499.

1648

Anonymous.

An Agitator Anotomiz'd: Or, The Character of an Agitator. . . . Printed in the Yeare, MDCXLVIII.

4°, text sigs. A–A3v.
Begins: "He is a small peece of earth."
Murphy 104. Thos. I, 605.

The Hunting of the Fox or the Sectaries Dissected In a Parallel betweene them, and Foxes . . . London Printed in the Yeare 1648.

4°, text pp. 3–48.
(1) The fox and sectaries (p. 15).
Thos. I, 661.

Independency Stript & VVhipt. Or, Iretons Petition, And The Royall Proiect, Examined and Confuted. Together with The Character of an Independent. Written by a lover of his Country, for the information of all such who hate Slavery, and love to live Freemen. . . . Printed in the Year. 1648.

4°, text pp. 1–14.
(1) An Independent (p. 14).
Murphy 133. Thos. I, 701.

Bacon, Sir Francis.

The Remaines Of The Right Honorable Francis Lord Verulam Viscount of St. Albanes. . . . Being Essayes and severall Letters to severall great Personages. London, Printed by B. Alsop, for Lawrence Chapman . . . 1648.

4°, text pp. 1–103.
(1) A believing Christian, in paradoxes, and seeming contradictions (p. 88).
Murphy 59. BSC 2196.

A reprint of The Character of a Believing Christian, by Herbert Palmer, 1645.

C., T.

A Glass for the Times, By Which According to the Scriptures, you may clearly behold the true Ministers of Christ, how farre differing from false Teachers. . . . Collected by T.C. a Friend to Truth. London, Printed by Robert Ibbitson. 1648.

4°, text pp. 1–8.
(1) The gospell minister (p. 1), (2) False prophets (p. 2).
Thos. I, 656.

[Cleveland, John?]

Midsummer-Moone. Or Lvnacy-Rampant. Being A Character of Master Cheynell, the Arch Visitor of Oxford, and Mungrell-President of Saint John Baptist's Colledge. With a Survey of the three Renegado-fellowes Web, Inkersell and Lownds. . . . Printed, An. Dom. 1648.

4°, text pp. 1–6.
(1) Cheynell (p. 1), (2) Inkersell (p. 5), (3) Web. (p. 6), (4) Lownds (p. 6).
Thos. I, 656.

On Thomas Winyard as the possible author, see note to J. Cleaveland Revived, 1660.

Cook, John.

What the Independents would have. 1648.*
(1) as in 1647.

[Dekker, Thomas.]

English Villanies prest to death. 1648.*
Pforzheimer Catalogue No. 274 n.
Reprinted from Lanthorne and Candle Light, 1609.

[Felltham, Owen.]

Three Months Observation of the Low Countries, Especially Holland. 1648.*
Said by the CBEL to be a pirated form of A Brief Character of the Low Countries. See 1652, 1659.

Fuller, Thomas.

The Holy State. By Thomas Fuller, B.D. and Prebendarie of Sarum. . . . The second Edition enlarged. . . . Cambridge: Printed by R.D. for John Williams . . . 1648.

6°, text pp. 1–460.
(1–51) as in 1642.
Murphy 57.
There is also an engraved title page.

Mede, Joseph.

The Works. 1648.*
See 1672.

Sedgwick, William.

The Leaves of the Tree Of Life: For the healing of The Nations. . . . William Sedgwick. . . . London, Printed by H. for Giles Calvert . . . 1648.

4°, text pp. 1–121.
(1) The clergy (p. 32), (2) The king in his raised estate (p. 71).

Border line examples of character.

Terrey, Mr.

Caracters of the heart. [1648?]*

Eyre, Stationers' Registers, I, 286.

Entered to Master Stephens, January 14, 1647/8; formerly held in copartnership between him and Mr. Meredith.

[Younge, Richard.]

A Touch-Stone To try by our knowledge, belief, and life Whether we be Christians in name onely, or Christians in deed. Or, The Character of a true Beleever, that walks in some measure answerable to the Gospell, his Christian profession, and the millions of mercies he hath received. By R.Y. of Roxwell in Essex. . . . Printed at London, and are to be sold by Andrew Crooke . . . 1648.

8°, text pp. 1–30.
(1) A true beleever (p. 1).
Murphy 133. Thos. I, 693.

Reprinted 1653 (as The Whole Duty of a Christian).

1649
Anonymous.

A Hue And Crie After Cromwell: Or, The Cities Lamentation for the losse of their Coyne and Conscience . . . Nol-Nod. Printed in the Year of no Liberty, 1649.

4°, text pp. 1–5.
Begins: "Oyes, Oyes, Oyes: If any manner of Man, or Woman."
Thos. I, 759.

New News from the Old Exchange. Or, The Common-Wealth of Vertuous Ladies lively decyphered: being a modest answer to an immodest scurrulous Phamphlet . . . Intituled, Newes from the New-Exchange. Not Printed in the Yeare of Women without Grace, but in that yeare when the Author of it with thousands more, manifestly have showed themselves to be almost gracelesse. [1650.]*

4°, text pp. 1–9.
(1) T.B., author of The New Exchange.
Thos. I, 789.

Thomason dates this March 16, 1649/50. It is on the border line of character-writing, and contains several portraits of ladies which are almost characters.

Cherbury, Edward Herbert, First Baron Herbert of.

The Life And Raigne Of King Henry The Eighth. Written By the Right Honourable Edward Lord Herbert of Cherbury. . . . London, Printed by E.G. for Thomas Whitaker . . . 1649.

4°, text pp. 1–575.
(1) An analytical character or dissection of Henry the Eighth, by J[ames]. H[owell]. (between sigs. A4 and B), (2) Cautious councellours (p. 3), (3) Cardinal Wolsey (p. 314), (4) Thomas Cromwell (p. 462), (5) Henry VIII (p. 570).
Pforzheimer Catalogue No. 463.

[Cleveland, John.]

The Character Of A Country Committee-man, With the Eare-marke of a Sequestrator. . . . London, Printed in the Yeare, 1649.

4°, text pp. 1–5.
Begins: "A Committee man by his name should be one that is possessed."
Murphy 62. Thos. I, 764.

The dedication is signed I:C. There may have been an earlier edition in 1647.

[Cleveland, John.]

The Hue and Cry After Sir John Presbyter. With Hair in Characters, and Lugs in Text. His Fingers thicker then the Prelat's Loyn's. [1649.]*

s.sh.fo.
Thos. I, 741.

The Thomason copy is dated May 4, 1649.

[Felltham, Owen.]

A Perfect Description Of The People and Country Of Scotland. By James Howel, Gent. London, Printed for J.S. 1649.

4°, text pp. 3–8.
Begins: "First; for the Country, I must confess, it is good for those that possess it."
Thos. I, 750.

On the authorship, see the note to Felltham's Batavia, 1672. Also variously attributed to James Howell and Sir Anthony Weldon.

Geree, John.

The Character of an old English Pvritane, Or Non-Conformist. By John Geree M.A. and late Preacher of the Word at Saint Faiths. Published according to Order. [ornament] London, Printed by A. Miller for Christopher Meredith at the Crane in Pauls Church-yard. 1649.*

4°, text pp. 1–6.
Begins: "The Old English Puritane was such an one, that honoured God above all."
Murphy 102.

Miss Murphy considers this part of the same edition as the 1646 issue by Miller.

[Howell, James.]
Dendrologia. 1649.*
Reprinted from 1640.

Philo Regis.
The right picture of King Olivre, from top to toe. That all the World may a false Rebell know. Whereunto is added, His Genealogy, and the Memorialls of all his Worthy Acts from the beginning of his reign, to his present routing in Ireland. By Philo Regis. . . . Printed at the Signe of the Traytors Head . . . 1649.*
4°, text pp. 1–8.
(1) Oliver Cromwell (p. 1).
Thos. I, 781.

More specifically, the verse picture and the prose genealogy might be called characters.

[Vicars, John.]
Speculum scripturale schismaticorum or a Scripture Looking-Glasse, most exactly characterizing all sorts of Schismaticks. Printed for T.M. 1649.*
s.sh.fo.
Thos. I, 762.
Attributed to Vicars by the Thomason Catalogue.

Younge, Richard.
The Odious, Despicable, and Dreadfull condition of a Drunkard; drawn to the Life by Junius Florilegus. . . . Or, A hopeful way to cure Drunkennesse. . . . London, Printed by R. Cotes, 1649.*
(1) A drunkard (p. 22).
BSC 2236.
An abridgment of The Drunkard's Character, 1638.

1650

Anonymous.
The Mirrour Of Complements. Or, A Manuall Of Choice, requisite, and compendious Curiosities wherein Gentlemen, Ladies, Gentlewomen, and all others, may practise Complementall and amorous expressions . . . Exactly Performed, with Addition of witty Songs, Sonnets, Poems, Epigrams, Essays, Characters, &c. The fourth Edition, with very many Additions . . . London, Printed by T.H. and are to bee sold by F. Coles, R. Harper, and W. Gilbertson . . . 1650.

12°, text pp. 1–240.
(1) Against Fuscus an uncivill lawyer (p. 146, in verse), (2) On Gryphus the vsurer (p. 146, in verse), (3) On the choice of a wife (p. 149, in verse), (4) A good man (p. 167), (5) A true friend (p. 171), (6) A good wife (p. 174), (7) Of a mistresse, or rather what a mistresse ought to be (p. 177), (8) A detracter (p. 184), (9) A rash man (p. 187), (10) A weake man (p. 188), (11) An affected man (p. 191), (12) A plausible man (p. 192), (13) A worldly wise man (p. 194), (14) A prophane man (p. 196), (15) A timerous man (p. 197), (16) A partiall man (p. 199), (17) A vulgar spirited man (p. 200), (18) A busie or a medling man (p. 202), (19) A plain countrey fellow (p. 204), (20) The difference between an acquaintance and a friend (p. 206), (21) An insolent man (p. 209), (22) An idly reserved man (p. 211), (23) A selfe conceited man (p. 212), (24) A formall man (p. 214), (25) A discontented man (p. 216), (26) A witty man unlettered (p. 217), (27) A modest man (p. 219), (28) A bold man (p. 222), (29) A poore man (p. 224).

Most of these characters are taken from Davies or Earle. This is a different work from The Mirror of Complements of 1635 (STC 17979).

[Bulwer, John.]
Anthropometamorphosis: Man Transform'd; Or, The Artificiall Changeling. Historically Presented, In the mad and cruel Gallantry, Foolish Bravery, ridiculous Beauty, Filthy Finenesse, and loathsome Lovelinesse of most Nations . . . And An Appendix of the Pedigree of the English Gallant. By J.B. Surnamed, The Chirosopher. . . . London, Printed for J. Hardesty . . . 1650.
12°, text pp. 1–263.
(1) The national gallant (sig. A2, in verse), (2) The pedigree of the English gallant (p. 256).

The dedication is signed John Bulwer, and there is a portrait of him at sig. A4v. Many chapters in this strange work approach closely to the character form.

[Cleveland, John?]
The Character of Mercurius Politicus.
4°, text pp. 1–8.
Begins: "The *Mercurius Politicus* is the *Paper Militia.*"
Thos. I, 809.

The Thomason copy is dated August 14, 1650. Attributed dubiously to Cleveland by the CBEL.

[Cleveland, John?]
[The Second Character of Mercurius Politicus. 1650.]
4°, text pp. 1–8.
Begins: "*Mercurius Politicus* is our Sir *Roger.*"
Thos. I, 814.

The Harvard copy, from which this note was made, lacks the title page. The Harvard Catalogue attributes it to Marchamont Nedham. The CBEL gives it to Cleveland. Thomason dated it October 23, 1650.

Cowley, Abraham.

The guardian; A Comedie. Acted before Prince Charls His Highness At Trinity-Colledg in Cambridge, upon the twelfth of March, 1641. Written by Abraham Cowley. London, Printed for John Holden . . . 1650.

4°, text sigs. A3–F3v.
(1) Dogrel, a bad poet (Act I, scene iv), (2) Cutter (I, v).

[Earle, John.]

Micro-Cosmographie. Or, A piece of the World Characteriz'd; In Essayes and Characters. . . . London, Printed by W. Bentley, for William Shears . . . 1650.*

12°, text pp. 1–105.
(1–54) as in 1628.
Murphy 41.

[Earle, John.]

Micro-cosmographie. Or, A piece of the World Characteriz'd; In Essayes and Characters. . . . London, Printed by W. Bentley, for William Shears . . . 1650.*

12°, text pp. 1–131.
(1–74) as in 1629, but omitting nos. 68, 71, and 76.
Murphy 41.

Fry, John.

The Clergy in their Colovrs; Or A brief Character of them. . . . By John Fry, a Member of the Parliament of England. . . . London, Printed for Giles Calvert . . . 1650.

8°, text pp. 1–60.
Begins: "As I fancy not the sheltring my self under any mans wings."
Thos. I, 818.

The whole book is a diffuse character of unworthy ministers. It is a poor example of character.

Gobert, John.

A True and Lively Character of a Right Communicating Church Member; Laid down in 18 Arguments. London: Printed by C. Sumptner. 1650.*
BSC 2238.

[Howell, James.]

Dendrologia. 1650.*
Reprinted from 1640.

Howell, James.

Instructions And Directions for Forren Travell. . . . By James Howell. . . . London,

Printed by W.W. for Humphrey Moseley . . . 1650.

12°, text pp. 1–140.
(1–2) as in 1642.
Thos. I, 796.

La Chambre, Marin Cureau de.

The Characters of the Passions. Written in French by the Sieur de la Chambre, physitian to the Lord Chancellor of France. Translated into English. Printed by Tho. Newcomb, for John Holden. 1650.*
Thos. I, 790.

Naunton, Sir Robert.

Fragmenta Regalia. 1650.*
Reprinted from 1641.

[Neville, Henry.]

Newes from the New Exchange, Or The Commonvvealth Of Ladies, Dravvn to the Life, in their severall Characters and Concernments. . . . London, Printed in the year, of Women without Grace, 1650.

4°, text pp. 1–21 (misprinted 2).
(1) Lady Carlisle (p. 3), (2) Lady Peterburgh (p. 3), (3) Lady Salisbury (p. 4), (4) Lady Sands (p. 4), (5) Lady Devonshire (p. 4), (6) Lady Cranborn (p. 5), (7) Lady Forster (p. 5), (8) Lady Prat (p. 6), (9) Mrs. Hamlyn (p. 6), (10) Lady Hungerford (p. 7), (11) Lady Kingsmell (p. 7), (12) Lady Rutland (p. 7), (13) Mrs. Luson (p. 8), (14) Lady Fairfax (p. 8), (15) Mistris Duns (p. 10), (16) Lady Middlesex (p. 10), (17) Lady Marchioness of Winchester (p. 11), (18) Lady of Bath (p. 11), (19) Lady Monmouth (p. 11), (20) Lady Stanhope (p. 12), (21) Lady Mountague (p. 12), (22) Lady Newport (p. 13), (23) Lady Elizabeth Darcy (p. 13), (24) Lady Cullen (p. 14), (25) Lady Crompton (p. 15), (26) Madam Peterborough (p. 16), (27) Madam Peter (p. 16), (28) Mrs. Phil. Mohun (p. 16), (29) Mistris Harris (p. 17), (30) Mistris Campbell (p. 18), (31) Lady Wildgoose (alias Velledicus, alias Mistris Salkeld) (p. 18), (32) Lady Stapleton (p. 19), (33) Lady Campion (p. 19), (34) Lady Cromwell (p. 19).
Thos. I, 784. BSC 2240.
Attributed to Neville by the Thomason Catalogue.

[Sanderson, Sir William.]

Aulicus Coquinariæ: or a Vindication In Answer To A Pamphlet, Entitvled The Court and Character of King James. Pretended to be penned by Sir A. W. and published since his death, 1650. . . . London, Printed for Henry Seile . . . 1650.

4°, text pp. 1–205.
(1) Queen Elizabeth (p. 1), (2) The Earl of Essex

(p. 40), (3) Robert Cecil (p. 52), (4) Henry Howard Earl of Northampton (p. 65), (5) Sir Walter Ralegh (p. 74), (6) Prince Henry (p. 144), (7) James I (p. 200).
Thos. I, 830. BSC 2242.

Attributed to Sanderson by the CBEL. Poor examples of character.

Venning, Ralph.

Orthodoxe Paradoxes, Theoreticall and Experimentall . . . By Ralph Venning . . . The third Edition . . . London Printed by E.G. for I. Rothwell . . . and Hanna Allen . . . 1650.

8°, text pp. 1–44.
(1) A beleever (p. 1).

The book consists of many short paragraphs, most of which begin: "He beleeves." The whole book is one extended character.

W., S.

The Constant Man's Character. Intended to be sent first as a Letter From A Gentleman in the Country, to a Gentleman his esteemed Friend and Country man, a Member of the House of Commons. Since inlarged into a Discourse by way of humble Advice to keep him from Revolting. . . . Printed at London for Giles Calvert . . . 1650.

4°, text pp. 1–77.
Begins: "Sir, I know not how this discourse may relish."
Thos. I, 789.

The tract is signed "S.W." and dated February, 1649. The Thomason Catalogue dates it March 18, 1650. Not a true Theophrastan character.

Ward, Walter.

A True Character of Injustice and Oppression. or a Relation of the Suit in Chancery between Harris and Ward. 1650.*
BSC 2241.

[Weldon, Sir Anthony.]

The Court And Character Of King James. Written and taken by Sir A:W. being an eye, and eare witness. . . . London: Printed by R.I. and are to be sold by John Wright . . . MDCL.

8°, text pp. 1–197.
(1) James I (p. 177).
Thos. I, 813. BSC 2242, 2246.
Attributed to Weldon by the CBEL.

Younge, Richard.

England's Unthankfulness striving with God's Goodness. The Fourth Edition.*

Dated [1650?] by the British Museum Catalogue. See 1653.

1651

[Boate, Arnold.]

The character of a trulie vertuous and pious woman, as it hath been acted by Mistris Margaret Dongan (wife to Doctor Arnold Boate) in the constant course of her whole life, which she finished at Paris 17. Aprilis 1651. Paris, by Ste. Maucroy for the author, 1651.*
BSC 2243.

The preface, though unsigned, speaks of Mrs. Boate as "my . . . most beloved consort."

Brathwaite, Richard.

History Surveyed in a brief Epitomy. 1651.*
Pforzheimer Catalogue, I, 100.

A reissue of A Survey, 1638.

Cartwright, William.

The Siedge: Or, Love's Convert, A Tragi-Comedy. Written by Mr. William Cartwright. . . . London, Printed for Humphrey Moseley . . . 1651.

8°, text pp. 91–180.
(1) A waiting-woman, Euthalpe, by Pyle (Act II, Scene ii), (2) An ideal state (II, ii), (3) A tyrant's concubine (II, iv).

[Cleveland, John.]

The Character of a London-Diurnall. 1651.*
Reprinted from 1647.

[Cleveland, John.]

The Hue and Cry after Sir John Presbyter. 1651.*
Reprinted from 1649.

[Cleveland, John.]

Poems. By J.C. With Additions. [ornament] Printed in the Year 1651.

8°, text pp. 1–78. 28 poems.
(1) The Hue and Cry after Sir John Presbyter (p. 13), (2) A London-diurnall (p. 59), (3) A country-committee-man (p. 71).

The Huntington Library calls this first of the editions of 1651.

[Cleveland, John.]

Poems. By J.C. With Additions. [ornament] Printed in the Year, 1651.

8°, text pp. 1–91. 32 poems and letters.
(1) as in first edition of 1651.

The Huntington Library catalogues this temporarily as the second edition.

[Cleveland, John.]

Poems. By J.C. VVith Additions. [ornament] Printed in the Yeare, 1651.

8°, in two parts, text pp. 1–91, 1–14. 32 poems and letters.
(1–3) as in first edition of 1651, (4) The mixt assembly (Part I, p. 37), (5) On J.W. A.B. of York (I, 63).
Murphy 135.

The Huntington Library catalogues this as the third edition.

[Cleveland, John.]

Poems. By J.C. VVith Aditions. [ornament] Printed in the Yeare, 1651.

8°, text pp. 1–77. 32 poems and letters.
(1–5) as in third edition of 1651.
Murphy 135.

The Huntington Library catalogues this as the fourth edition.

Davenant, Sir William.

Gondibert: An Heroick Poem, Written by Sr William D'Avenant. . . . London, Printed by Tho. Newcomb for John Holden . . . 1651.

4°, text pp. 1–344.
(1) Love (p. 21, preface), (2) Wit (p. 26, preface).
Thos. I, 825. Pforzheimer Catalogue No. 252.

There were two editions in 1651. Several presentation copies are known.

[Junius.]

The Character of a Cockney. 1651.*

In verse.

Undoubtedly simply another title for Alazono-Mastix, 1652, which is dated by Thomason January 1, 1652.

Overbury, Sir Thomas.

Observations Upon the Provinces United And On the State of France. Written By Sr Thomas Overbury. . . . London. Printed by T. Maxey . . . 1651.

8°, text pp. 1–80.
(1–2) as in Sir Thomas Overbury His Observations, 1626.

[Peters, Hugh?]

The none-such Charles his character: extracted, Out of divers Originall Transactions, Dispatches and the Notes of severall Publick Ministers, and Councellours of State as wel at home as abroad. Published by Authority. London, Printed by R.I. and are to be sold by John Collins . . . MDCLI.

8°, text pp. 1–196.
(1) Charles I and James I (*passim*).
Thos. I, 823.

Attributed to Peters in the DNB, though listed anonymously by the CBEL.

Sheppard, Samuel.

Epigrams Theological, Philosophical, And Romantick. Six Books, Also The Socratick Session, Or The Arraignment and Conviction, of Julius Scaliger, with other Select Poems. By S. Sheppard. London, Printed by G.D. for Thomas Bucknell . . . 1651.

8°, text pp. 1–263 (misprinted 257, pp. 117–120 and 147–148 being repeated).
(1) A Callidonian (p. 113), (2) The prodigall (p. 123, misprinted 119), (3) An alderman (p. 124, misprinted 120), (4) An accomplist man (p. 174, misprinted 168).
Murphy 134. BSC 2244.

[Sheppard, Samuel.]

The Joviall Crew; or, the Devill turned Ranter, being a character of the Roaring Ranters of these times, represented in a Comedy with their Prodigious Pranks and Rude Revellings. Written by S.S. Gent. Printed for W. Say. 1651.*

Thos. I, 824.

[Weldon, Sir Anthony.]

The Court and Character Of King James. Whereunto is now added The Court of King Charles . . . With some Observations upon Him in stead of a Character. Collected and perfected by Sir A. W. . . . Printed at London by R.I. and are to be sold by J. Collins . . . 1651.

8°, text pp. 1–226.
(1) as in 1650, (2) Charles I (p. 215).
BSC 2245.

Wotton, Sir Henry.

Reliquiae Wottonianae, Or, A Collection Of Lives, Letters, Poems, With Characters Of Sundry Personages: And other Incomparable Pieces of Language and Art. By the curious Pensil of the Ever Memorable Sr Henry Wotton Kt, Late, Provost of Eton Colledg. London: Printed by Thomas Maxey, for R. Marriot, G. Bedel, and T. Garthwait. 1651.

12°, text pp. 1–540.
(1) Of Robert Devereux, Earl of Essex; and George Villiers, Duke of Buckingham: Some observations by way of parallell (p. 1), (2) The differences and disparity between the estates and conditions [of Buckingham and Essex] (p. 37), (3) Ferdinando Medici (p. 359), (4) Sir Richard Weston (p. 388), (5) A happy life (p. 522).
Thos. I, 825. BSC 2247, 2248.

Many other biographical sketches are called characters in the table of contents and elsewhere, but most of them are not strictly such.

1652

Anonymous.

A Looking-Glass for a Drunkard, Or a Drunkard Defined. London, Imprinted for J.D. and are to be sold by George Wilford in little Britain neer the Hospitall gate. 1652.*
s.sh.fo.
Begins: "A Drunkard is the annoyance of Modesty."
Thos. I, 877.

A true and exact Character of the Low Countreys; especially Holland, Or, The Dutchman anatomized, and truly dissected. Being the Series of three Moneths Observations of the Country, Customes, Religions, Manners, and Dispositions of the People. A Tract very admirable and sententious, no lesse pleasant then profitable to peruse. London, Printed for William Ley, 1652.*
Thos. I, 864.

Brathwaite, Richard.

History Re-surveyed. 1652.*
Reprinted from The Schollers Medley, 1614.

Brathwaite, Richard.

Time's Treasury: Or, Academy for Gentry. . . . And a Supplement, Entituled, The Tvrtle's Trivmph: Summing up all in an Exquisite Character of Honour. By Ri: Brathwait Esq. . . . London, Printed for Nath: Brooke . . . 1652.
4°, in 3 parts, text pp. 1–454, 1–47 (Supplement), plus sigs. aaaa–bbbb2 unpaged.
(1) The English gentleman (Part I, p. 1), (2) A roarer (I, 23), (3) A timist, or trimmer (I, 138), (4) A timonist, or misanthrope (I, 141), (5) A wanton (I, 143), (6) A man deserving our friendship (I, 154), (7) Court-comets (I, 186), (8) An ambitious waster of time (I, 189), (9) A voluptuous man (I, 190), (10) A covetous person (I, 191), (11) A gentleman (I, 255), (12) The English gentlewoman (I, 271), (13) A gentlewoman (I, 397), (14) Honour (sig. aaaa, unpaged).
Pforzheimer Catalogue No. 79 note.
A reissue of The English Gentleman, 1641, with some changes.

Castaniza, Jean.

The Christian Pilgrime in his spiritual Conflict and Conquest. Paris, 1652.*
(1) The animal, carnal and sensual man (sig. b7v), (2) The hypocondriacal, hypocritical and counterfeit man (sig. b8v), (3) The spiritual, supersensual & perfect man (sig. b9v).

Attributed to Castaniza by Halkett and Laing. Translated by Crowther and Vincent. There were several other editions, sometimes under slightly different titles.

Cook, John.

Monarchy No creature of Gods making, &c. Wherein is proved by Scripture and Reason, that Monarchicall Goverment is against the minde of God. . . . By Iohn Cooke . . . Printed at Waterford in Ireland, by Peter de Pienne, in the yeare of our Lord God, 1651[/2].
8°, text pp. 1–134.
(1) Henry Ireton (sig. g).
BSC 2251.
There seems to have been a different edition, printed by Peter de Pienne to be sold in London by Thomas Brewster, 1652, but I have not seen it. Dated 1651/2 by the Huntington Library.

Donne, John.

Paradoxes, Problems, Essayes, Characters, Written By Dr Donne Dean of Pauls. To which is added a Book of Epigrams, Written in Latin by the same Author; translated into English by J. Maine, D.D. . . . London, Printed by T.N. for Humphrey Moseley . . . 1652.
12°, text pp. 1–224.
(1) A Scot at the first sight (p. 65, misprinted 56), (2) A dunce (p. 67).
Murphy 134. Thos. I, 889.
Number 2 first appeared in Overbury's Wife, 1622, q.v.

[Du Refuge, Eustache.]

Arcana Aulica: Or Walsingham's Manual; Of Prudential Maxims, For The States-Man And the Courtier. London, Printed for James Tong, and are to be sold by John Williams . . . 1652.
(1) The choleric prince (p. 32), (2) The sanguine man (p. 34), (3) The melancholy prince (p. 35), (4) The phlegmatic prince (p. 37).
A translation, according to the CBEL, from Du Refuge's Traité de la Cour, 1616(?). There were several other translations.

[Felltham, Owen.]

A Brief Character of the Low Countries. 1652.*
See 1659.
This may have appeared under the pirated form of Three Months Observation of the Low Countries, Especially Holland. See the 1648 edition of that title.

[Felltham, Owen.]

Three Months Observation of the Low Countries. 1652.*
Reprinted from 1648.

Fuller, Thomas.

The Holy State. By Thomas Fuller, B.D. and Prebendarie of Sarum. . . . The third Edition. . . . London: Printed by R.D. for John Williams . . . 1652.

6°, text pp. 1–510.
(1–51) as in 1642.
Murphy 57.

Herbert, George.

Herbert's Remains. Or, Sundry Pieces Of that sweet Singer of the Temple, Mr George Herbert, Sometime Orator of the University of Cambridg. Now exposed to publick Light. London, Printed for Timothy Garthwait . . . 1652.

12°, text pp. 1–168.
(1) A priest to the temple (p. 1).
Murphy 135. Thos. I, 890. BSC 2389. Pforzheimer Catalogue No. 464.

The whole book is a character of a priest to the temple, and there is a separate title page by that title. Each of the 37 chapters might be called an individual character, but it seems wiser to consider them simply as subdivisions.

Junius Anonymous.

Alazono-Mastix: or the Character of a Cockney: in a Satyricall Poem. Dedicated (as a New-years-gift) to the Apprentices of London. By Junius Anonymous. A London Apprentice. London, Printed by R.I. 1652.*

4°, text pp. 1–16. In verse.
Thos. I, 858.

The Thomason Catalogue dates this January 1, 1652.

[Lockier, Lionel.]

The Character of a Time-Serving Saint: Or, The Hypocrite anatomized, and thorowly dissected. To the Tune of the Three Cheaters.*
s.sh.fo. In verse.
Begins: "The Heavens do frown, the earth doth groan."
Thos. I, 873.

Dated June 5, 1652, in the Thomason Catalogue. The last stanza gives the author's name: "Men do me *Lionel Lockier* name."

[Sheppard, Samuel.]

The Weepers: or, The bed of Snakes broken. Wit Vitiated, and made a Pander to Wickednesse; Instanced in a Pack of Knaves (calling themselves Servants to the late King) worthy the Anger of the present Age; and the wonder and indignation of all Posterity. Six Cupping-Glasses, clapt to the cloven Feet of the six Dæmons, who Govern the times by turns from Munday to Saturday Annually. . . . By S.S.

London, Printed for Thomas Bucknell . . . 1652.

4°, text pp. 1–12.
(1) A meagre Levite (p. 6), (2) An apothecary (p. 6), (3) Another broken citizen (p. 6), (4) Two lawyers (p. 6), (5) Two drapers (p. 7), (6) A major (p. 7), (7) Britanicvs-Divrnall (p. 8), (8) Diurnal (p. 8), (9) The Commonwealths Weekly Intelligence (p. 9), (10) Democritus (p. 10), (11) Politicus (p. 11), (12) The Scout (p. 11), (13) Perfect Passages (p. 12).
Thos. I, 885.

Attributed to Sheppard by the CBEL.

Taylor, John.

A Juniper Lecture. With the description of all sorts of women, good and bad. The Third Impression, with additions. London: Printed for William Ley. 1652.*

Thos. I, 890.

A reprint of 1639.

Venning, Ralph.

Orthodoxe Paradoxes, Theoretical and Experimental. The fifth edition. 1652.*

Reprinted from 1650.

Younge, Richard.

The Character of a Formal Hypocrite. Printed by J. Bel for J. Crumpe.*

BSC 2253.

Younge, Richard.

England's Unthankfulness striving with God's Goodness for the Victory. London: Printed by R. and W.L. for J. Crump, 1652.*

See 1653.
BSC 2254.

1653

[Brome, Richard.]

The City Wit, Or, The VVoman wears the Breeches. A Comedy. London, Printed by T.R. for Richard Marriot, and Thomas Dring . . . 1653.

8°, text sigs. A4–G4.
(1) Mrs. Sneakup (sig. A6), (2) Mr. Sneakup (sig. A6v), (3) Dr. Pulse-feel, actually Crasy in disguise (sig. B6v), (4) A courtier (sig. Cv), (5) Crasy (sig. E3v).

Attributed to Brome by the CBEL. It has been reprinted.

[Bulwer, John.]

Anthropometamorphosis: Man Transform'd; Or, The Artificiall Changling. . . . Scripsit J.B. Cognomento Chirosophus. M.D. . . . London, Printed by William Hunt, Anno Dom. 1653.

4°, text pp. 1–559.
(1–2) as in 1650.
Pforzheimer Catalogue No. 115.
Some copies are said to have the date printed as 2653.

[Cleveland, John.]

The Character of a Diurnal-Maker. By J.C.
1653.*
See 1654.

[Cleveland, John.]

Poems. By J.C. With Additions, never before
Printed. [Ornament: clasped book and double
line about page] Printed in the Yeare 1653.
8°, text pp. 1–107.
(1–3) as in first edition of 1651.
Murphy 136.

[Cleveland, John.]

Poems. By J.C. With Additions, never before
Printed. [Ornament: book, with initials W
and S] Printed in the Yeare, 1653.
8°, text pp. 1–106.
(1–3) as in first edition of 1651.
Murphy 136.

Flecknoe, Richard.

Miscellania. Or, Poems of all sorts, with divers
other Pieces, Written by Richard Fleckno.
Dedicated to the most excellent of her Sexe.
London, Printed by T.R. for the Author,
M.D.C.LIII.
8°, text pp. 1–146.
(1) A joviall companion (p. 11), (2) An English
merchant, resident in forrain parts (p. 132), (3)
A petty French lutenist abroad (p. 134), (4) A
new ignoramus in religion (p. 136).
Murphy 64. Thos. II, 8.

Gauden, John.

Hieraspites A Defence by way of Apology For
The Ministry and Ministers Of The Church
of England: Humbly Presented To the Con-
sciences of all those that excell in Virtve. By
John Gauden, D.D. and Minister of that
Church at Bocking in Essex. . . . Printed for
Andrew Crooke . . . 1653.
4°, text pp. 1–594.
(1) True saints characters (p. 2), (2) Good ministers (p. 58), (3) Antiministerial pretenders to
gifts (p. 208), (4) An excellent bishop (p. 273).
Thos. II, 21. BSC 2256.

Lenton, Francis.

Lentons Characters: Or witty and ingenious
Descriptions Of Severall Professions, presented
to all judicious Readers. Written for his owne,
and now published for others Recreation. . . .

London, Printed for Richard Harper, in Smithfield, near the Hospitall Gate. 1653.*
12°, text pp. 1–164.
(1–41) as in his Characterismi, 1631.
Murphy 49.

[Marvell, Andrew.]

The Character of Holland.*
See 1665.
No copies of an edition of this year have been found. This
note may refer to a manuscript version.

[Master, William.]

Λογοι Εὐκαιροι. Essayes and Observations
(Characters) with Meditations and Prayers
etc. By a student of Theologie. London:
Printed by R.W. for R. Davis in Oxon. 1653.*
(1) The vain man's self-miracle (p. 24), (2) The
commonwealth meere wits (p. 33), (3) The all-
most Christian (p. 88).
BSC 2255.
Attributed to Master by the CBEL. The propriety of including this item in the bibliography is in some doubt.

[Webbe, George.]

The Practice of Quietness. The Eighth Edition. 1653.*
Reprinted from 1638.

Wilson, Arthur.

The History Of Great Britain, Being The Life
And Reign Of King James The First, Relating To what passed from his first Access to the
Crown, till his Death. By Arthur Wilson, Esq.
. . . London, Printed for Richard Lownds . . .
1653.
4°, text pp. 1–292.
(1) James I (p. 289). Also many portrait-characters too brief to record.
There were two editions in this year.

[Y., D.]

Legenda lignea: With An Answer To Mr.
Birchleys Moderator. (Pleading for a Tolera-
tion of Popery.) And a Character of some
hopefull Saints Revolted to the Church of
Rome. . . . London, Printed in the Year 1653.
8°, text pp. 1–238.
(1) Revolters to Rome (p. 131).
Thos. I, 890. BSC 2257.
The Epistle to the Reader is signed D.Y.

Younge, Richard.

The Character of a True Believer. 1653.*
Probably an inexact reference to The Whole Duty Of A
Christian, 1653.

Younge, Richard.

Englands Vnthankfulness striving with Gods
Goodness, for the Victory . . . By R. Younge,

Florilegus. . . . The fourth Impression. . . . [colophon] London, Printed by R. and W.L. for James Crump. . . .

8°, text pp. 1–30.
(1) The loose libertine (p. 25), (2) A formall hypocrite, or civil justiciary (Chap. X, sect. 1).

The various editions of this work listed in this bibliography are somewhat uncertain. The British Museum calls its earliest edition the fourth and dates it [1650?]. That issue may be identical with the above. The McAlpin copy contains only one of the two characters listed above, the first; but Mr. Greenough's notes state that both are in the British Museum copy. The McAlpin copy is bound with several other books under the general title page of The Christian Library, 1655. The author promises further characters but ends abruptly without furnishing them.

[Younge, Richard.]

Philarguromastix. Or, The Arraignment of Covetousness, and Ambition, in our great and greedy Cormorants . . . Together with the lively, and lovely Characters, of Justice, Thankfulnesse, Contentation, Frugality, Liberality . . . By Junius Florilegus. . . . [colophon] London, Printed by J.L. 1653.

8°, 2 parts, pp. 1–23, 1–22.
(1) The covetous cormorant or judge (p. 1), (2) A corrupt lawyer (p. 14).
BSC 2260.

Despite the title, there are no characters of justice, thankfulness, etc.

Younge, Richard.

The Whole Duty Of A Christian: Or, The Character of a true Beleever, that walks in some measure answerable to the Gospel, his Christian profession, and the millions of Mercies he hath received. . . . The second Impression, much inlarged. By R.Y. of Roxwell in Essex. [colophon] London, Printed by R. & W. Leybourn. 1653.*

8°, text pp. 1–61.
(1) as in A Touch-Stone to try, 1648.
BSC 2259.

1654

Anonymous.

The Character of a Protector.*

s.sh.fo. In verse.
Begins: "What's a Protector? Its a stately thing."
Thos. II, 73.

A manuscript in Thomason's hand.

Aylett, Robert.

Divine, And Moral Speculations in Metrical Numbers, Upon Various Subjects. By Doctor R. Aylet, one of the Masters of the High Court of Chancery. . . . London, Printed for Abel Roper . . . 1654.

8°, 4 parts, text pp. 1–480, 1–44, 1–118, 1–28.
(1) Heavenly love (p. 21), (2) Humility (p. 33), (3) Repentance (p. 44), (4) Faith (p. 58), (5) Hope (p. 72), (6) Justice and righteousness (p. 83), (7) Truth (p. 95), (8) Mercy (p. 107), (9) Patience (p. 120), (10) Fortitude (p. 131), (11) Heavenly knowledge (p. 141), (12) Zeal and godly jealousye (p. 152), (13) Temperance (p. 162), (14) Bounty (p. 173), (15) Spiritual and heavenly joy (p. 184), (16) Wisdom and prudence (p. 195), (17) Obedience (p. 206), (18) Meekness (p. 216), (19) Gods word (p. 227), (20) Prayer (p. 238), (21) Peace and concord (p. 361), (22) Chastity (p. 373), (23) Constancie (p. 376), (24) Courtesie or humanity (p. 395), (25) Gravity (p. 406), (26) Frugality or thrift (p. 418), (27) Providence (p. 430), (28) Diligence (p. 442), (29) Care and labour (p. 454), (30) Death (p. 465).
Thos. II, 53.

All the characters occur in Part I of the book. Nos. 1–20 are part of The Song of Songs, 21–25 of Five Moral Meditations, and 26–30 of Five Divine and Moral Meditations.

Blount, Thomas.

The Academy of Eloquence.*

See 1656.
Thos. II, 55.

[Bulwer, John.]

Anthropometamorphosis.*

Pforzheimer Catalogue No. 115 n.

Reprinted from 1650.

[Cleveland, John.]

A Character Of A Diurnal-Maker. By J.C. . . . London, Printed in the Yeare, 1654.

8°, text pp. 1–12.
Begins: "A Diurnall-Maker is the Sub-Almoner of History."
Murphy 62. BSC 2261. Thos. II, 46.

There were two distinct editions of 1654. References to earlier editions in 1647 and 1653 have been found, but the books themselves have not been traced, and may never have existed.

[Cleveland, John.]

Poems By J.C. With Additions, never before Printed. [conventional ornament, *not* book and initials W S] Printed in the Year, 1654.

8°, in 2 parts, text pp. 1–107, 1–12.
(1–3) as in first edition of 1651. (4) A diurnal-maker (Part II, p. 1).
Murphy 136. BSC 2261.

[Cleveland, John.]

Poems. By J.C. With Additions, never before Printed. [ornament: book, with initials W s] Printed in the Yeare, 1654.

8°, in 2 parts, text pp. 1–107, 1–12.
(1–4) as in other edition of 1654.
Pforzheimer Catalogue No. 185.

[Du Refuge, Eustache.]

Arcana Aulica; or, Walsingham's Manual of
Prudential Maxims for the States-Man and the
Courtier. London: Printed by T. C. for John
Wright. 1654.*

Text pp. 1–153.
Thos. II, 89.

Reprinted from 1652.

Erbery, William.

The Great Earthquake, Revel. 16.18, Or, Fall
Of all the Churches. Discovering the Apostasie
of purest Churches. . . . By William Erbery.
London, Printed for Giles Calvert . . . 1654.

4°, text pp. 3–52.
(1) The author, by J.W. (preface, sig. A2).
Thos. II, 75.

A rather poor example of character.

Farnworth, Richard.

A Character Whereby the false Christs, or
Antichrists, Seducers, false Prophets, and
house-creepers may be Known. . . . By one
known to the world by Richard Farnworth.
. . . [London, Printed by Giles Calvert . . .
1654].

4°, text pp. 1–14.
Thos. II, 90.

Contains no true characters.
In the Harvard copy the author's name is printed as Horn-
worth, but is changed in contemporary writing to Farnworth. Part of the title page is trimmed off. Though this
book is not accurately described as a character, it is included
here because of its title.

Flecknoe, Richard.

A Relation of ten Years Travells In Europe,
Asia, Affrique, and America . . . By Richard
Fleckno . . . London, Printed for the Author,
and are to be sold by

8°, text pp. 1–176.
(1) The Earl of Strafford (p. 4), (2) An English
merchant, resident in forrain parts (p. 89, in a
letter dated 1650), (3) Persons in a play, The
Temple of Friendship, on which Flecknoe was
then occupied (p. 147).
Murphy 64.

The Bodleian dates this work [1654?]. Neither the Bodleian copy nor the Harvard gives any indication of printer
or date.

Nicolls, Ferdinando.

The Life and Death Of Mr. Ignatius Jurdain,
One Of The Aldermen of the City of Exeter;
Who departed this Life July 15th. 1640. . . .

Drawn up and published by Ferd. Nicolls,
Minister of the Gospel at Mary Arches, Exon.
. . . London, Printed for Tho. Newberry . . .
1654.

4°, text pp. 1–22.
(1) Ignatius Jurdain (p. 3).
Thos. I, 2.

North, John.

A True Looking Glass for all the Oppressed
. . . Peoples of England with a Catalogue and
Character of the Enemies of Liberty. 1654.*

[Phillips, John?]

Tyrants and Protectors Set forth In their Colours. Or, The Difference between Good and
Bad Magistrates; In several Characters, Instances and Examples of both. . . . By J.P.
London, Printed for H. Cripps and L. Lloyd
. . . 1654.

4°, text pp. 1–52.
(1) A tyrant, or homo homini demon (p. 1), (2)
A protector, or homo homini deus (p. 27).
Thos. II, 69.

Whitlock, Richard.

Ζωοτομια, Or, Observations On The Present
Manners Of The English: Briefly Anatomiz-
ing the Living by the Dead. With An Usefull
Detection Of The Mountebanks of both Sexes.
By Richard Whitlock, M.D. Late Fellow of
All-Souls Colledge in Oxford. London, Print-
ed by Tho. Roycroft, and are to be sold by
Humphrey Moseley . . . 1654.

8°, text pp. 1–568.
(1) The honest Adamite (p. 17), (2) The quacking hermaphrodite (p. 45), (3) The peoples physitian (p. 62), (4) The Valentinian doctor (p.
101), (5) Medicinal observations & characters,
containing I. a live dissection of selfe-killers, and
their accessories, or of patients and their tenders
(p. 109), (6) A scholar (p. 185), (7) The wise
chapman (p. 264), (8) The chair-man (p. 319),
(9) The loadstones touch-stone, trying, who's the
magnetick lady (p. 321), (10) The grand schismatick (p. 357), (11) The faithfull chirurgeon
(p. 384), (12) The levellers (p. 419).
Thos. II, 55. BSC 2263.

Wotton, Sir Henry.

Reliquiae Wottonianae. 1654.*
Reprinted from 1651.

1655

[Culpeper, Thomas, the younger.]

Morall Discourses And Essayes, Upon Severall
Select Subjects. Written, By T.C. Esquire. . . .

London, Printed by S.G. for Charles Adams . . . 1655.

12°, text pp. 1-184.

(1) Princely valour (p. 32), (2) Tutor, or governour (p. 72), (3) Sycophants (p. 104), (4) Youth (p. 119), (5) Old sinner (p. 123), (6) Magnanimity (p. 168), (7) Taciturn man (p. 174), (8) Temperance (p. 177).

Thos. II, 122.

Ascribed to Culpeper by the CBEL.

[Du Refuge, Eustache.]

Arcana Aulica. 1655.*

Reprinted from 1652.

Fuller, Thomas.

The Church-History of Britain; From the Birth of Jesus Christ. Untill the Year M.DC.-XLVIII. Endeavoured by Thomas Fuller. . . . London, Printed for John Williams . . . 1655.

4°, 11 books, separate paging for about every 2 books.

(1) Thomas Cromwell (Book V, p. 231), (2) Richard Hooker (IX, 216), (3) Sir Francis Bacon (X, 89), (4) James I (XI, 113), (5) Archbishop Laud (XI, 216), (6) Archbishop Williams (XI, 225).

There were several later editions.

Gayton, Edmund.

Wil: Bagnal's Ghost. Or the Merry Devill Of Gadmvnton. In his peramulation of the Prisons of London. By E. Gayton, Esq;. London, Printed by W. Wilson, for Thomas Johnson . . . 1655.

4°, text pp. 1-48.

(1) A prison (p. 36), (2) A serjeant (p. 39), (3) A true friend (p. 41), (4) A friend in a corner, or helplesse friend (p. 42).

Murphy 140. Thos. II, 135.

[Hobbes, Thomas.]

A Briefe Of The Art Of Rhetoriqve . . . London Printed by Tho. Cotes. . . .

12°, text pp. 1-202.

(1) Young men (chap. 14), (2) Old men (chap. 15), (3) Middle-aged men (chap. 16), (4) The nobility (chap. 17), (5) The rich (chap. 18), (6) Men in power (chap. 19).

The CBEL lists two editions as [1637?] and [1655?]. It is not clear which the present edition is. The title does not occur in the STC. Reprinted 1681 (as The Whole Art of Rhetoric).

[Lupton, Donald.]

The Quacking Mountebanck, Or The Jesuite turn'd Quaker. In a witty and full Discovery of their Production and Rise, their Language, Doctrine, Discipline, Policy, Presumption, Ignorance, Prophanes, Dissimulation, Envy, Uncharitablenes, with their Behaviours, Gestures, Aimes and Ends. All punctually handled and proved, to give our Country men timely Notice to avoid their Snares and subtile Delusions, Simulata Sanctitas Duplicata Iniquitas. By One Who Was An Eye And Ear Witnesse of their Words and Gestures in their new hired great Tavern Chappell, Or the great Mouth within Aldersgate. London, Printed for E.B. at the Angell in Pauls-ChurchYard, 1655.

4°, text pp. 3-20.

Begins: "These severall Texts of Holy Scripture." Murphy 104. Thos. II, 115.

The Thomason copy has a manuscript note on the title page, "written by mr. Lupton." The whole pamphlet is a character of a Quaker.

Newcastle, Margaret Cavendish, Duchess of.

The Worlds Olio. Written by the Right Honorable, the Lady Margaret Newcastle. . . . London: Printed for J. Martin and J. Allestrye . . . 1655.

4°, text pp. 1-216.

(1) The self-conceited fool (p. 68), (2) The learned fool (p. 68), (3) The superstitious fool (p. 69), (4) The venturous fool (p. 69), (5) The busie fool (p. 70), (6) The vain-glorious fool (p. 70), (7) The affected fool (p. 71), (8) The good ruler or judge (sig. Ff4, unpaged).

[Nicolls, Ferdinando.]

The Life and Death Of Mr. Ignatius Jurdain. The Second Edition. 1655.*

Reprinted from 1654.

Overbury, Sir Thomas.

Sir Thomas Overbury His Wife. With Additions Of New Characters, and many other Witty Conceits never before Printed. London, Printed for William Shears . . . 1655.*

4°, text sigs. C4v–Q8.

(1–82) as in twelfth impression of 1626.

Murphy 24. BSC 2264.

Palmer, Herbert.

Memorials of Godliness & Christianity. Part II. Containing . . . the Character of a Christian in Paradoxes . . . The fifth Edition corrected. By Herbert Palmer. . . . London, Printed by A.M. for T. Underhill . . . 1655.*

See 1657.

[Phillips, John.]

A Satyr Against Hypocrites . . . Printed in the Year, 1655.

4°, text pp. 1-22. In verse.

(1) A non-conformist preacher (p. 4).

This character is too short to be a proper example of the type but is included for completeness. There were numerous later editions of the work. Attributed to Phillips by the CBEL.

Wall, Thomas.

A Comment on the Times: or a Character of the Enemies of the Church. 1655.*

See 1659.

Younge, Richard.

A Christian Library, Or, A Pleasant and Plentiful Paradise Of Practical Divinity, in ten Treatises Of sundry and select Subjects . . . By R. Younge, of Roxwel in Essex, Florilegus. London, Printed by R. and W. Leybourn, and are to be sold and only sold by James Crumpe . . . 1655.

8°, several titles separately paged.
(1) The Seduced Soul Reduced, (2) A Hopefull Way to cure . . . Swearing, (3) The Blemish of Government, (4) Philarguromastix, (5) Englands Unthankfulness.

1656

Bacon, Sir Francis.

The Mirrour of State and Eloquence. Represented in the Letters of Sr Francis Bacon, Lord Verulam, To Queen Elizabeth, King James and other Personages. Together with the Character of a true Christian. Printed for Lawrence Chapman. 1656.*

(1) A true Christian, by Herbert Palmer.
Thos. II, 165.

Blount, Thomas.

The Academy of Eloquence: Containing a Compleat English Rhetoriqve, Exemplified. . . . By Tho. Blount Gent' The Second Edition with Additions. . . . London: Printed by T.N. for Humphrey Moseley . . . 1656.

12°, text pp. 1–231.
(1) Beauty (p. 53), (2) Constancy (p. 57), (3) Death (p. 62), (4) Friendship (p. 69), (5) Inconstancy (p. 70), (6) Hope (p. 72), (7) Jealousy (p. 73), (8) Joy (p. 74), (9) Love (p. 76), (10) Man commended (p. 84), (11) King Charles, by Sir Henry Wotton (p. 88), (12) Nature (p. 91), (13) Silence and secrecy (p. 91), (14) Sorrow (p. 92), (15) Vanity (p. 100), (16) Virtue (p. 100), (17) Women commended (p. 101), (18) Women discommended (p. 113), (19) The world (p. 116), (20) Youth (p. 117).

[Cleveland, John.]

Poems. By J.C. With Additions, never before Printed. [ornament: book, initials W S] Printed in the Yeare, 1656.

8°, in 2 parts, text pp. 1–107, 1–8.
(1–4) as in 1654.

A second copy at Huntington, otherwise practically identical, contains 15 additional pages of poems and letters, etc.

Collop, John.

Poesis Rediviva: Or, Poesie Reviv'd. By John Collop M.D. . . . London, Printed for Humphrey Moseley . . . 1656.

8°, text pp. 1–110.
(1) The poet (p. 1), (2) A Jesuite (p. 9), (3) A presbyter (p. 11), (4) Prophanum vulgus: the people (p. 13), (5) Sectaries (p. 15), (6) The enthusiasticks (p. 16), (7) The Beraean (p. 16), (8) Fiduciaries (p. 17), (9) Loyal friendship (p. 25), (10) A compleat gentleman (p. 30).
BSC 2265. Thos. II, 135.

The Thomason copy is dated Nov. 30, 1655.

[Crooke, Samuel?]

The Hypocrite Unmasked. Published by John Dolling [or Downing?].*

Referred to in Crooke's Τα Διαφεροντα as a spurious, botched piece, in which Crooke's characters were "almost reduced to as much dishonour, as Jezebel's carcasse" (Address to the reader, dated Dec. 12, 1657).

Hardy, Nathaniel.

Wisdomes Character And Counterfeit. Deliniated in two Sermons. The one on the Epistle of St. James, chap. 3.17 The other on the Gospel of St. Matth. chap. 2.8. By Nath. Hardy, Minister of Gods Word, and Preacher to the Parish of St. Dionis Back-Church. . . . London, Printed by J.P. for John Clark, and are to be sold at his Shop under St. Peters Church in Corn-hil, 1656.*

4°, in 2 parts, text pp. 1–35, 1–31.
(1) Wisdomes character: or, the queen of graces (Part I), (2) Wisdomes counterfeit: or, Herodian policy (Part II).

This title hardly deserves admission as a character.

Jacombe, Thomas.

The Active and Publick Spirit. Handled in a Sermon, preached at Pauls, October 26, 1656. London, Printed by T.R. for Philemon Stephens. 1656.*

(1) A public spirited man (p. 25).
Thos. II, 164.

[King, Philip.]

The Surfeit. To A B C. London, Printed for Edw. Dod at the Gun in Ivy-lane. 1656.

12°, text pp. 1–82.
(1) The Romanist (p. 73).

Attributed to Philip King by the Huntington Library. The introduction is signed P.K. (p. 13).

Pierce, Thomas.

The Sinner Impleaded in his own Court, wherin are represented the Great Discouragements from Sinning, which the Sinner receiveth from Sin itselfe. By Tho: Pierce. London, Printed by R. Norton for Richard Royston. 1656.*

See 1670.

Thos. II, 158.

S., J.

The Picture of a New Courtier, drawn in a Conference between Mr. Timeserver, and Mr. Plainheart. In Which is discovered the abominable Practises and horrid Hypocrisies of the Usurper, and his time-serving Parasites. By J.S. London, Printed in the year of Englands great trouble and slavery . . . 1656.*

4°, text pp. 1–16.

Thos. II, 145.

T., R.

A Character Of A Female-Cockney, Brought upon the publike Theater To be Judged, Censured, and Condemned by his Friends and Assistants in the late-revived work of Labour-In-Vain. . . . By R.T. . . . London, Printed for John Harrison . . . 1656.

4°, 4 leaves, unpaged and unsigned.

Begins: "A *Cockney* is one who being *conceived*."

Tate, Faithful.

The Character of Cruelty in the Workers of Iniquity, and Cure of Contention among the People of God: held forth in two sermons, preached in the day of publick Humiliation upon occasion of the late sad persecution in Piedmont. London, Printed for G. Sawbridge. 1656.*

12°, in 2 parts.

BSC 2266.

Younge, Richard.

The Blemish of Government. 1656.*

See 1658.

1657

Anonymous.

The Difference Between An Usurper And a Lawfull Prince, Explained In their several Characters, for the satisfaction of all men. . . . Printed in the year, 1657.

4°, text pp. 1-11.

(1) An usurper (p. 1), (2) A lawfull prince (p. 5).

Thos. II, 173.

B., I.

Heroick Education, or choice maximes and instructions for the training up of youth. By I.B. Gent. Printed for William Hope, and Henry Herringman. 1657.*

(1–3) Three kinds of pedants (sigs. D3–D6), (4) Good governours (Chap. 6).

Thos. II, 162.

Possibly the date should be 1656, as both the CBEL and the Thomason Catalogue date the work. There is also some doubt whether the characters named above are genuine examples of the type.

Bacon, Sir Francis.

Resuscitatio, Or, Bringing into Publick Light Severall Pieces of the Works . . . of . . . Francis Bacon. . . . By William Rawley . . . London, Printed by Sarah Griffin, for William Lee . . . 1657.

4°, text pp. 1–282.

(1) Sir Francis Bacon, by Rawley (sig. b2), (2) In Happy Memory of Elizabeth, Queen of England, by Bacon (p. 181).

Bacon, Sir Francis.

Several Letters, Written By This Honourable Authour, To Queen Elizabeth, King Iames . . . London, Printed by F.L. for William Lee . . . 1657.

4°, text pp. 1–192.

(1) In Happy Memory of Elizabeth (p. 181).

This should probably be part of Resuscitatio (*q.v.*), but like Several Discourses, 1661 (*q.v.*), it does not so appear in the Harvard copy. It is therefore here recorded separately.

[Cleveland, John.]

Poems By J.C. With Additions, never before Printed. [conventional ornament, *not* book and initials] Printed in the Year, 1657.

8°, in 2 parts, text pp. 1–107, 1–12.

(1–4) as in 1654.

Murphy 136. BSC 2267.

A second Huntington copy, otherwise practically identical, contains an additional 15 pages at the end.

[Davenant, Sir William.]

The First Days Entertainment at Rutland-House, By Declamations and Musick: After the manner of the Ancients. By Sr. VV.D. London, Printed by J.M. for H. Herringman . . . 1657.

8°, text pp. 1–91.

(1) London, described by a Parisian (p. 45), (2) Paris, described by a Londoner (p. 66).

Thos. II, 167.

Attributed to Davenant by the CBEL.

[H., J., and others.]

Two Essays of Love And Marriage. Being A Letter written by a Gentleman to his Friend, to disswade him from Love. And an Answer thereunto by another Gentleman. Together with some Characters and other Passages of Wit. Written by Private Gentlemen for recreation. . . . London, Printed for Henry Brome . . . 1657.

12°, text pp. 1–123.

(1) A whore (p. 54), (2) A patentee (p. 58), (3) A politick (p. 63), (4) A clubber (p. 68), (5) A politick citizen (p. 71), (6) A schismatick (p. 77), (7) A gallant (p. 84), (8) A ballad-maker (p. 90), (9) A self-conceited fellow (p. 94), (10) A city wit (p. 101), (11) A humourist (p. 109), (12) A fudler (p. 115), (13) A solicitor (p. 120). Murphy 71. BSC 2272.

The various letters are signed by J.H., A.B., J.S., and J.B.

Jacombe, Samuel.

Moses his Death: Opened and applyed, in a Sermon At Christ-Church in London, Decemb. 23, MDCLXI. at the Funeral of Mr. Edward Bright. . . . By Samuel Jacombe. . . . London, Printed for Adoniram Byfield . . . 1657.

4°, text pp. 1–50 plus sigs. H2–Kv.

(1) Edward Bright (p. 41).

Thos. II, 170.

Jacombe, Thomas.

The Active and Publick Spirit, Handled in a Sermon, Preached at Pauls, October 26th. 1656. By Thomas Jacomb, Minister at Martins-Ludgate, London. . . . London, Printed by T.R. for Philemon Stephens . . . and Abel Roper . . . 1657.

4°, text pp. 1–46.

(1) as in 1656.

[May, Thomas.]

The Life Of A Satyricall Puppy, Called Nim. Who Worrieth All Those Satyrists He Knowes, And Barkes At The Rest. By T.M. London, Printed by for Humphrey Moseley . . . 1657.

8°, text pp. 1–118.

(1) The Hollanders (p. 69), (2) A whore (p. 84).

Nemesius.

The Character Of Man. Or, His Nature exactly displayed, in a Philosophicall Discourse, by the Learned Nemesivs. Now made English. London, Printed for Rob. Crofts . . . 1657.*

BSC 2268.

British Museum.

A reissue of The Nature of Man, 1636.

Palmer, Herbert.

Memorials Of Godlines & Christianity. In three Parts. Part I. Containing Meditations. . . . The seventh Edition corrected and enlarged by the Author Herbert Palmer, B.D. late Master of Queens-Col. Camb. London, Printed by A.M. for Tho. Underhill . . . 1657.

12°, text pp. 1–116.

(1) A Christian in paradoxes and seeming contradictions (p. 53), (2) Visible godliness (p. 69). BSC 2270.

In part a reworking of his The Upright Protestant, 1643, and The Character of a Believing Christian, 1645.

Smith, Henry.

Sermons. Edited by Thomas Fuller. 1657.*

(1) Henry Smith, by Thomas Fuller.

There were at least two later editions.

[Sprigg, William.]

Philosophicall Essayes with Brief Adviso's. Accommodated to the Capacity of the Ladyes and Gentlemen, sometime Students of the English Academy, lately Erected at London. . . . London, Printed by J.S. for R. Blaggrave . . . 1657.

12°, text pp. 1–105.

(1) A covetous man (p. 32), (2) A melancholy man (p. 36), (3) A physitian (p. 40), (4) A foole or naturall (p. 43), (5) An hypocrite (p. 44), (6) Souldiers (p. 78). Murphy 140. BSC 2353.

Attributed to Sprigg doubtfully by the CBEL.

Venning, Ralph.

Orthodox Paradoxes, Theoretical and Experimental . . . By Ralph Venning . . . The seventh Edition . . . London, Printed by S.G. for J. Rothwell . . . 1657.

8°, in 2 parts, text pp. 1–36, 1–39.

(1) as in 1650.

Wall, Thomas.

A Comment on the Times: or a Character of the Enemies of the Church. By Thomas Wall. Printed for the Author, 1657.*

BSC 2273.

See 1659.

Watson, Thomas.

The Upright Mans Character And Crown. Preached in a Sermon. . . . March 29. 1657. By Thomas Watson . . . London, Printed for Ralph Smith . . . 1657.

8°, text pp. 1–54.

Begins: "Sincerity is of Universal importance to a Christian."

BSC 2274.

An extended but genuine character.

[Webbe, George.]

The Practice of Quietness. The Ninth Edition. 1657.*

See 1638.

1658

Anonymous.

The Low Dutch character'd, their Butter Box opened, and their Juggles Apprehended and Reprooved. 1658.*

[Austin, Samuel.]

Naps Upon Parnassus. A sleepy Muse nipt and pincht, though not awakened . . . together with two Satyrical Characters of his Own, of a Temporizer, and an Antiquary . . . London, Printed by express Order from the Wits, for N. Brook . . . 1658.

[Inner title] Two Exact Characters, One of a Temporizer. The other of an Antiquarian. . . . Printed by the same Order.

8°, text sigs. A–H4.

(1) A temporizer (sig. E8), (2) An antiquarian (sig. F2v).

Murphy 140. BSC 2275. Thos. I, 210. Pforzheimer Catalogue I, 26.

Attributed to Austin by Murphy.

Bergerac, Hercule Savinien de Cyrano de.

Satyrical Characters, And handsome Descriptions In Letters, Written to severall Persons of Quality. . . . By Monsieur De Cyrano Bergerac. Translated out of the French, By A Person of Honour. London, Printed for Henry Herringman. . . . 1658.

8°, text pp. 1–174.

(1) A red-hair'd lady (p. 33), (2) A country house (p. 36), (3) Against a detractor (p. 70), (4) Against a plagiary (p. 85), (5) Against physitians (p. 114).

Thos. II, 208. BSC 2277.

Brathwaite, Richard.

The Honest Ghost, Or A Voice From The Vault. . . . London, Printed by Ric. Hodgkinsonne. 1658.

8°, text pp. 1–326.

(1) A trapanner (p. 94), (2) A tar-paulin (p. 98), (3) The ape of honour (p. 127), (4) The ape of pleasure (p. 135), (5) The ape of vaine-glory (p. 142), (6) The ape of fancy (p. 148), (7) The ape of fashion (p. 156), (8) The ape of observa-

tion, or traveller (p. 161), (9) The court ape (p. 172), (10) The city ape (p. 182), (11) The country ape (p. 191), (12) The church ape (p. 200), (13) The judiciall ape (p. 210), (14) The politicall ape (p. 221), (15) The chymicall ape, or alchemist (p. 229), (16) An ape of pleasure (p. 240), (17) The selfe-conceited ape (p. 241), (18) The formall fashion monger (p. 242), (19) The observing ape (p. 243), (20) Silk-worme, a courtly-carpet-ape (p. 251), (21) City-mammon (p. 252), (22) The country boar (p. 253), (23) A church-chuffer (p. 224), (24) A profiteer (p. 255), (24) A politick state underminer, of Machiavels opinions late refiner (p. 256), (26) A mountebank physician (p. 257).

No. 23 is called, in the character, a "formal apish timist" and "a zeale-pretending halting Laodicean." Attributed to Brathwaite by the CBEL. On p. 288 it bears an "Anagram *composed on his friends Name*," reading "Virtue hath but bare credit," which, it is true, contains Brathwaite's name, but leaves some letters over.

[Brewer, Thomas.]

A Knot of Fooles. 1658.*

Reprinted from 1624.

Crook, Samuel.

Τα Διαφεροντα, Or, Divine Characters In Two Parts, Acutely Distinguishing the more Secret and Undiscerned Differences Between 1. The Hypocrite . . . And The True Christian . . . By that late burning and shining Lamp, Master Samuel Crook, B.D. late Pastor of Wrington in Somerset. . . . By C.B. and W.G. London, Printed for A.B. and are to be sold by Joseph Cranford . . . 1658.

4°, text pp. 1–634.

(1) Of hypocrisie, and of hypocrites in general (Part I, chap. 2), (2) Satan, the arch-hypocrite, and father of hypocrites (I, 3), (3) The natural hypocrite (I, 4), (4) The moral hypocrite (I, 5), (5) The civil hypocrite (I, 6), (6) The political hypocrite (I, 7), (7) The theatrical hypocrite (I, 8), (8) The heretical hypocrite (I, 9), (9) The schismatical hypocrite (I, 10), (10) The superstitious hypocrite (I, 11), (11) The ignorant hypocrite (I, 12), (12) The prophane hypocrite (I, 13), (13) The worldly hypocrite (I, 14), (14) The religious hypocrite (I, 15), (15) The stinted hypocrite (I, 16), (16) The waxing hypocrite (I, 17), (17) The temporary hypocrite (I, 18), (18) The preaching hypocrite (I, 19), (19) The hearing hypocrite (I, 20), (20) The praying hypocrite (I, 21), (21) The inspired hypocrite (I, 22), (22) The beleeving hypocrite (I, 23), (23) The hoping hypocrite (I, 24), (24) The fawning hypocrite (I, 25), (25) The repenting hypocrite (I, 26), (26) The counterfeit convert (I, 27), (27) The fearing hypocrite (I, 28), (28) The patient hypocrite (I, 29), (29) The obedient

hypocrite (I, 30), (30) The talking hypocrite (I, 31), (31) The idle hypocrite (I, 32), (32) The zealous hypocrite (I, 33), (33) The judging hypocrite (I, 34), (34) The libertine hypocrite (I, 35), (35) The scandalous hypocrite (I, 36), (36) A Christian clogged with original corruption (Part II, chap. 2), (37) A Christian disadvantaged by parentage or defects of body (II, 3), (38) A Christian labouring under natural defects of the mind (II, 4), (39) A Christian transported with passions (II, 5).
BSC 2276 (as The Hypocrite and the True Christian).

[Elys, Edmund.]

Divine Poems. With A Short Description of Christian Magnanimity. By E.E. . . . Oxon. Printed by H. Hall, for R. Blagrave. 1658.

8°, text pp. 1–45.

(1) A magnanimous man (sig. D).

Flecknoe, Richard.

Enigmaticall Characters, All Taken to the Life, from several Persons, Humours, & Dispositions. By Rich. Fleckno. Anno Dom M.D.C.-LVIII.

8°, text pp. 1–135 (misprinted 125).

(1) Of a lady of excellent conversation (p. 1), (2) Of one that is the foyle of good conversation (p. 4), (3) Of an excellent companion (p. 6), (4) Of one that zanys the good companion (p. 8), (5) Of one that imitates the good companion another way (p. 10), (6) Of an irresolute person (p. 12), (7) Of a fantastique lady (p. 14), (8) Of a green-sicknesse girle (p. 16), (9) Of a talkative lady (p. 18), (10) Of a taciturne person (p. 20), (11) Of a Dutch waggoner (p. 22), (12) Of a huge overvaluer of himself (p. 24), (13) Of an ordinary French laquey (p. 26), (14) Of a suspitious person (p. 28), (15) Of raillerie (p. 30), (16) Of one who troubles her selfe with every thing (p. 32), (17) Of one who troubles himself with nothing (p. 34), (18) Of a chambermaid (p. 38), (19) Of a noblemans chaplain (p. 40), (20) Of an impertinent governant (p. 42), (21) Of a school of young gentlewomen (p. 44), (22) Of a novice (p. 47, misprinted 46), (23) Of a fille devote, or a ghostly daughter (p. 49), (24) Of an immitable widdow (p. 51), (25) Of a more immitable widdow (p. 53), (26) Of a fifth-monarchy man (p. 55), (27) Of an importunate visitant (p. 57), (28) Of a French dancing-master in England (p. 59), (29) Of your town-talkers (p. 61), (30) Of a horrible wicked deboished person (p. 63), (31) Of a valiant man (p. 65), (32) Of a proud one (p. 65), (33) Of an all-admirable person (p. 65), (34) Of a gallant warriour (p. 68), (35) Of a miserable old gentlewoman (p. 70), (36) Of a ladies little dog (p. 72), (37) Of your ladies coronel [colonel] (p. 74), (38) Of

a school-boy (p. 76), (39) Of one that shall be namelesse [a ruffian] (p. 78), (40) Of pretty sweet innocence (p. 80), (41) Of a scrupulous honour (p. 82), (42) Of a fleerer (p. 84), (43) Of a make-bate (p. 86), (44) Du tour a la mode (p. 88), (45) Of a changeable disposition (p. 90), (46) Of a physition (p. 92), (47) Of the authors idea, or of a character (p. 92), (48) Of a dull-fellow (p. 94), (49) Of a bold abusive wit (p. 96), (50) Of troublesome kindnesse [i.e., a person who is troublesome] (p. 104), (51) Of a Jansenist (p. 100), (52) Of a certain nobleman (p. 103), (53) Of an other [nobleman] (p. 104), (54) Of a natural beauty (p. 106, in verse), (55) Of an artificial beauty (p. 107), (56) Of a petty-politick (p. 109), (57) Of a hom-bred country-gentleman (p. 111), (58) Of a common acquaintance (p. 113), (59) Of a young envoy (p. 115), (60) Of a degenerate lord (p. 117), (61) Of a high-spirited man (p. 119), (62) Of a proud one [woman] (p. 121), (63) Of low spirited man (p. 123), (64) Of a petty French lutenist in England (p. 125), (65) Of a flatterer (p. 127), (66) Of a faire and virtuous lady (p. 129), (67) Of a quarrelsome coxcomb (p. 130), (68) Of a complementer (p. 132), (69) Of a young enamourist (p. 134).
Murphy 64. BSC 2278.

Since No. 62 repeats No. 32, the actual total is only 68. Reprinted 1665 (as Fifty-five Enigmatical Characters, as Sixtynine Enigmatical Characters, and in part in Rich. Flecknoe's Aenigmaticall Characters), 1673 (in part, in A Collection of the Choicest Epigrams), 1677 (as Seventy Eight Characters).

[Heydon, John?]

Advice to a Daughter. In opposition to the Advice to a Sonne. By Eugenius Theodidactus. London, Printed by J. Moxon, for Francis Cossinet. 1658.*

(1) A meere scholar, (2) A proud man, (3) A plotter, (4) A good wife, (5) A good woman, (6) The same continued, (7) An affected traveller, (8) A time-server.

Attributed to Heydon by the Thomason Catalogue, but the references to Heydon in the book itself (pp. 8, 150–151) make such an assumption awkward.

[Phillips, Edward.]

The Mysteries Of Love & Eloquence, Or, the Arts of Wooing and Complementing . . . A Work, in which are drawn to the Life, the Deportments of the most accomplisht Persons, the mode of their Courtly Entertainments . . . London, Printed for N. Brooks . . . 1658.

8°, in 2 parts, text pp. 1–288, 1–70.

(1) A hector, a bold spirited lover (p. 5), (2) The picture of the poet's mistress (p. 51), (3) The choice of a gentleman vsher (p. 53).
Thos. II, 213.

Attributed to Phillips by the CBEL. The Preface and the Dedicatory Epistle are signed E.P. Reprinted 1685 and 1699 (as The Beau's Academy).

Starkey, George.

Pyrotechny Asserted And Illustrated, To be the surest and safest means For Arts Triumph over Natures Infirmities. . . . By George Starkey, who is a Philosopher by Fire. London, Printed by R. Daniel, for Samuel Thompson . . . 1658. 8°, text pp. 1–172.
(1) A preposterous searcher after natures secrets (p. 57), (2) Him, who so searcheth natures secrets, as to reap profit thereby (p. 63).

Wall, Thomas.

A Comment on the Times. 1658.*
See 1659.

[Wharton, Sir George.]

A Second Narrative Of The Late Parliament (so called.) Wherein . . . is given an Account of their Second Meeting . . . Together with an Account of three and forty of their Names, who were taken out of the House, and others that sate in the Other House . . . with a Brief Character and Description of them. All humbly presented to Publique View By a Friend to the good Old Cause of Justice . . . Printed in the Fifth Year of Englands Slavery under its New Monarchy, 1658.

In 2 parts, text pp. 5–12, 1–36.
(1) Richard Cromwel (Part II, p. 1), (2) Commissioner Fiennes (II, 1), (3) Henry Lawrence (II, 2), (4) Lieutenant-General Fleetwood (II, 2), (5) Colonel Disbrow (II, 3), (6) Lord Viscount Lisle (II, 3), (7) Sir Gilbert Pickering (II, 4), (8) Walter Strickland (II, 4), (9) Sir Charles Ousely (II, 4), (10) Mr. Rouse (II, 5), (11) Major General Skippon (II, 5), (12) Colonel Sydenham (II, 6), (13) Col. Mountague (II, 6), (14) Colonel Philip Jones (II, 7), (15) Commissioner Lisle (II, 7), (16) Chief Justice Glyn (II, 8), (17) Bulstrode Whitlock (II, 8), (18) William Lenthal (II, 9), (19) Mr. Cleypole (II, 9), (20) Lord Faulconbridge (II, 9), (21) Colonel Howard (II, 10), (22) Lord Broghil (II, 10), (23) Colonel Pride (II, 11), (24) Colonel Hewson (II, 11), (25) Colonel Barkstead (II, 12), (26) Colonel Ingoldsby (II, 12), (27) Colonel Whaly (II, 13), (28) Colonel Goff (II, 13), (29) Colonel Berry (II, 14), (30) Colonel Cooper (II, 14), (31) Alderman Pack (II, 15), (32) Alderman Tichborn (II, 15), (33) Sir William Roberts (II, 16), (34) Colonel John Jones (II, 17), (35) Mr. Edmond Thomas (II, 17), (36) Sir Francis Russel (II, 17), (37) Sir William Strickland (II, 18), (38) Sir Richard Onsloe (II, 18), (39) Mr. John Fiennes (II, 19), (40) Sir John Hubbard (II, 19), (41) Sir Thomas Honywood (II, 19), (42) Lord Ewre (II, 20), (43) Mr. Hampden, (now Lord Hampden) (II, 20), (44) Sir Arthur Haslerigg (II, 21).
Thos. II, 227. BSC 2279.
Attributed to Wharton by the Huntington Library.

Wright, Thomas le.

An Exact Character or Narrative of the late right Noble, and Magnificent Lord, Oliver Cromwell . . . Written . . . for the present perusal of all honest Patriots . . . Vivet post funera Virtus. London, Printed for G.E. & C. 1658.*
4°, text pp. 1–8.
Begins: "He was born at Huntington, of Honourable Parents."

Wright, Thomas le.

A more Exact Character and Perfect Narrative of the late right Noble, and magnificent Lord, Oliver Cromwell, Together with a brief Recapitulation . . . With His Decease on Friday, the 3d of Septemb 1658 . . . London, for J. Jones, 1658.*
Begins: "He was born at Huntington, of Honourable Parents."

Younge, Richard.

The Blemish of Government, the Shame of Religion, the Disgrace of Mankind; or, a Charge drawn up against Drunkards, and presented to his Highness the Lord Protector . . . By R. Younge of Roxwell in Essex. . . . [colophon] Printed by A.M. and are to be sold by Henry Crips . . . and James Crump . . . 1658.
8°, text pp. 1–16.
(1) A drunkard (p. 5).
The whole book is virtually a character of a drunkard.

1659
Anonymous.

Anti-Quakerism, or, A Character of the Quakers Spirit . . . 1. Being a precise Puritan. 2. An Anabaptist. 3. A Seeker. 4. A Ranter. 5. A Quaker, and indeed what not, all things, and nothing. By which Character may . . . see the deceitfulness of his own imagination . . . and watch himself accordingly. London, Printed for the Author, Anno Dom 1659.*
s.sh.fo.
(1) Quakers.
Murphy 141. Thos. II, 275.
Dated January 5, 1660, in the Thomason Catalogue.

A Character Of France. To which is added, Gallus Castratus. Or, An Answer To A Late

Slanderous Pamphlet, called The Character of England. . . . London, Printed for Nath. Brooke . . . 1659.
12°, text pp. 1–38.
Begins: "Being to describe this Large Continent."
BSC 2284.

A Character of King Charles II. Written by a Minister of the word. Printed by D. Maxwell. 1659.*
Thos. II, 237.
Probably reprinted 1660 as A Character of His most Sacred Majesty, and 1661 as The Character of Charles II.

The character of the late upstart House of Lords. Together with some reflections on the carriage and government of his late Highness. By a friend to the good old cause. London, Printed in the year 1659.*
4°, text pp. 1–55.

The Character Or Ear-Mark Of Mr. William Prinne Bencher of Lincolnes-Inne. In which are contain'd many seasonable, and Wholsome Exhortations to the same. . . . London, Printed in the year MDCLIX.
4°, text pp. 1–5.
Begins: "It was once a saying of the famous Aristotle."
Thos. II, 233. BSC 2285.

The Leveller: Or, The Principles & Maxims Concerning Government And Religion, Which are Asserted by those that are commonly called, Levellers. London, Printed for Thomas Brewster . . . 1659.
4°, text pp. 3–16.
Begins: "When the Sect of the Christians first arose."
Thos. II, 223. BSC 2294.

The Pourtraiture Of His Royal Highness, Oliver Late Lord Protector &c. In His Life and Death; With a short View Of His Government. . . . London, Printed by T.N. for Edward Thomas . . . 1659.
12°, text pp. 7–69.
(1) Oliver Cromwell (p. 7 and passim through book).

Cleveland, John.
J. Cleaveland Revived: Poems, Orations, Epistles, And other of his Genuine Incomparable Pieces, never before publisht. With some other Exquisite Remains of the most eminent Wits of both the Universities that were his Con-

temporaries. . . . London, Printed for Nathaniel Brooke . . . 1659.
8°, text pp. 1–127.
(1) The Puritan (p. 58).
Murphy 63, 138.
Some copies appear to contain also: (2) The protector.

Cleveland, John.
Poems. By John Cleavland. With Additions, never before Printed. [ornament: book and initials] Printed for W. Shears . . . 1659.
8°, text pp. 1–219.
(1–4) as in 1654.
Murphy 63, 136.

[Elys, Edmund.]
Divine Poems. 1659.*
Reprinted from 1658.

[Evelyn, John.]
A Character Of England, As it was lately presented in a Letter, to a Noble Man of France. Londons Printed for Jo. Crooke . . . 1659.
12°, text pp. 1–71.
Begins: "My Lord, You command me to give you minute account."
BSC 2281, 2287.
Attributed to Evelyn by the CBEL. There were three editions in 1659 and another in 1700 under the title of A Journey to England.

[Evelyn, John.]
A Character of England. Second edition. 1659.*

[Evelyn, John.]
A Character Of England, As it was lately presented in a Letter, to a Noble Man of France. With Reflections upon Gallus Castratus. The third Edition. London, Printed for John Crooke . . . 1659.
12°, text pp. 1–66.
Begins: "You command me to give you minute account."
Thos. II, 237. BSC 2282, 2283.

[Felltham, Owen.]
A Brief Character Of the Low-Countries Under the States Being three weeks observation of the Vices and Vertues of the Inhabitants. . . . London, Printed for H.S. and are to be sold by Rich. Lowndes . . . 1659.
12°, text pp. 1–100.
(1) A Dutchman (p. 27).
BSC 2282, 2288. Thos. II, 345.
Attributed to Felltham by the CBEL. There is said to have been an earlier edition in 1652. The CBEL states that it also appeared in pirated form in 1648 and 1652 as Three Months Observations of the Low Countries, Especially Holland.

[Felltham, Owen.]

A Perfect Description of the People and Countrey of Scotland . . . London, Printed for Rich. Lownds. 1659.

12°, text pp. 1–21.
Begins: "First for the Country, I must confess."
BSC 2283, 2295.

Flecknoe, Richard.

The Idea of His Highness Oliver, late Lord Protector, &c. With certain brief Reflexions on his Life. London, Printed Anno 1659.*

(1) Oliver Cromwell (p. 66).

Gadbury, John.

The Nativity of the late King Charls, Astrologically and Faithfully performed; with Reasons in Art, Of the Various Success, and Misfortune Of His whole Life. . . . By John Gadbury. . . . London, Printed by James Cottrel. 1659.

8°, text pp. 1–128.
(1) Charles I (p. 15).
Thos. II, 255. BSC 2289.

Geree, John.

The Character Of an Old English-Pvritan Or Non-Conformist. By John Geree M.A. and late Preacher of the Word at Saint Albans. Published according to Order. . . . London, Printed in the Year, 1659.

4°, text pp. 1–6.
Begins: "The Old English Puritane was such an one, that honoured God above all."

[Heydon, John?]

Advice to a Daughter. In Opposition to the Advice to a Sonne. The second edition. London, Printed by J. Moxon, for Francis Cossinet. 1659.*

(1–8) as in 1658.
Thos. II, 223.

Larkin, Edward.

Speculum Patrum: A Looking-Glasse Of The Fathers . . . To which are added, The Characters of some of the Chief Philosophers, Historians, Grammarians, Orators, and Poets. By Edward Larkin. . . . London: Printed for Henry Eversden . . . 1659.

8°, in 2 parts, text pp. 1–99, 9–223.
(1) Hermes (Part II, p. 9), (2) Pythagoras (II, 10), (3) Democritus (II, 12), (4) Heraclytus (II, 13), (5) Socrates (II, 14), (6) Plato (II, 16), (7) Epicurus (II, 17), (8) Zeno (II, 18), (9) Chrysippus (II, 20), (10) Cleanthes (II, 21), (11) Anaxagoras (II, 22), (12) Carneades (II, 23), (13) Aristoteles (II, 24), (14) Diogenes (II, 26), (15) Theophrastus (II, 28), (16) Seneca (II, 29), (17) Plinius (II, 31), (18) Plutarchus (II, 32), (19) Apollonius Tyan (II, 34), (20) Epictetus (II, 36), (21) Arianus (II, 37), (22) Plotinus (II, 39), (23) Porphyrius (II, 40), (24) Maximus Tyrius (II, 41), (25) Boethius (II, 42), (26) Hippocrates (II, 44), (27) Galenus (II, 46), (28) Thucidides (II, 53), (29) Zenophon (II, 55), (30) Polybius (II, 56), (31) Herodotus (II, 57), (32) Dyonysius Halicarnassius (II, 58), (33) Caius Julius Caesar (II, 59), (34) Velleius Parterculus (II, 60), (35) Diodorus Siculus (II, 62), (36) Crispus Salustius (II, 63), (37) Titus Livius (II, 65), (38) Valerius Maximus (II, 67), (39) Quintus Curtius (II, 70), (40) Cornelius Tacitus (II, 72), (41) Lucius Annæus Florus (II, 74), (42) Josephus (II, 76), (43) Suetonius Tranquillus (II, 78), (44) Junianus Justinus (II, 80), (45) Pausanias (II, 81), (46) Herodianus (II, 83), (47) Procopius (II, 84), (48) Ammianus Marcellinus (II, 86), (49) Varro (II, 93), (50) Athenaeus (II, 95), (51) Julius Pollux (II, 96), (52) Aulus Gellius (II, 97), (53) Martianus Capella (II, 98), (54) Suidas (II, 99), (55) Cœlius Rhodoginus (II, 101), (56) Erasmus (II, 102), (57) Budæus (II, 104), (58) Julius Scaliger (II, 105), (59) Camerarius (II, 106), (60) Casaubonus (II, 107), (61) Josephus Scaliger (II, 108), (62) Justus Lipsius (II, 110), (63) Janus Gruterus (II, 111), (64) Caspar Barthius (II, 112), (65) Antiphon (II, 113), (66) Gorgias (II, 115), (67) Isocrates (II, 116), (68) Demosthenes (II, 117), (69) Æschines (II, 119), (70) Lysias (II, 120), (71) Demades (II, 121), (72) Cicero (II, 122), (73) Marcus Seneca (II, 125), (74) Petronius Arbiter (II, 126), (75) Hermogenes (II, 128), (76) Quintilianus (II, 129), (77) Lucianus (II, 130), (78) Elianus (II, 132), (79) Aristides (II, 133), (80) Symmachus (II, 134), (81) Orpheus (II, 143), (82) Alcæus (II, 144), (83) Sappho (II, 146), (84) Musæus (II, 147), (85) Homerus (II, 148), (86) Hesiodus (II, 151), (87) Pindarus (II, 153), (88) Anacreon (II, 154), (89) Theognis (II, 155), (90) Theocritus (II, 156), (91) Aratus (II, 157), (92) Lycophron (II, 158), (93) Æschylus (II, 159), (94) Sophocles (II, 161), (95) Euripides (II, 162), (96) Menander (II, 164), (97) Aristophanes (II, 165), (98) Plautus (II, 166), (99) Terentius (II, 168), (100) Callimachus (II, 170), (101) Afranius (II, 171), (102) Lucilius (II, 172), (103) Accius (II, 175), (104) Ennius (II, 177), (105) Lucretius (II, 178), (106) Catullus (II, 180), (107) Virgilius (II, 183), (108) Corn. Gallus (II, 185), (109) Horatius (II, 187), (110) Ovidius (II, 189), (111) Manilius (II, 192), (112) Tibullus (II, 193), (113) Propertius (II, 194), (114) Gratius (II, 197), (115) Seneca (II, 198), (116) Persius (II, 199),

(117) Pedo Albin (II, 201), (118) Pomponius Secundus (II, 202), (119) Arunt. Stella (II, 203), (120) Juvenalis (II, 205), (121) Valerius Flaccus (II, 207), (122) Silius Italic. (II, 208), (123) Lucanus (II, 210), (124) Martialis (II, 211), (125) Statius (II, 212), (126) Ausonius (II, 214), (127) Oppianus (II, 216), (128) Claudianus (II, 217), (129) Prudentius (II, 218), (130) Sidonius (II, 220), (131) Pontianus Paul. (II, 221), (132) Dracontius (II, 223).
Thos. II, 229. BSC 2291.

Maidston, John.

[A letter to John Winthrop, dated March 24, 1659.*]
(1) Oliver Cromwell.
Printed in A Collection of the State Papers of John Thurloe, 1742.

[North, Dudley, third Baron.]

A Forest Promiscuous Of Several Seasons Productions. The Entrance, Or, First Part. . . . London, Printed by Daniel Pakeman. 1659.
4°, text pp. 1–331.
(1–11) as in 1645, (12) A supplement to the churchman (p. 94, following A divine).
Murphy 131.

Osborne, Francis.

A Miscellany of Sundry Essayes, Paradoxes, and Problematicall Discourses, Letters and Characters; Together with Politicall Deductions from the History of the Earl of Essex, Executed under Queen Elizabeth. By Francis Osborn Esquire. London, Printed by John Grismond, 1659.
12°, text pp. 1–260.
(1) Of honour (p. 119), (2) On a deboshed souldier (p. 187), (3) On a cook (p. 195), (4) Of an host (p. 197).
Murphy 141. Thos. II, 224.

Stubbe, Henry.

Malice Rebuked; or, A Character of Richard Baxters Abilities, and a vindication of Sir Henry Vane from his aspersions in his Key for Catholicks. By Henry Stubbe.*
Text pp. 1–60.
Thos. II, 258.

Swinnock, George.

Ουρανος και ταρταρος. Heaven & Hell Epitomized. 1659.*
Reprinted in 1663.

Wall, Thomas.

A Comment On the Times, or, A Character of The Enemies of the Church. Written by Thomas Wall . . . London, Printed for the use and benefit of Thomas Gibbs, Gent, 1659.
8°, text pp. 1–51.
Hardly a real character despite the title.

1660

Anonymous.

A Briefe Description Or Character Of the Religion and Manners of the Phanatiques In Generall. Scil. Anabaptists, Independents, Brovvnists, Enthusiasts, Levellers, Quakers, Seekers, Fift-Monarchy-Men, & Dippers. Shewing and Refuting their Absurdities by due Application, Reflecting much also on Sir John Præcisian and other Novelists. . . . London Printed, and are to be sold by most Stationers; 1660.*
8°, text pp. 1–52.
(1) Phanaticks in generall.
Murphy 105. Thos. II, 335.

The Character of a Phanatique. . . . [colophon] London, Printed for Henry Marsh . . . 1660.
s.sh.fo.
Begins: "A *Phanatique* is the Mushroom of distemper."
Murphy 105. Thos. II, 297. BSC 2303.
The phrase quoted is the beginning of the character proper. There is about half a page of introductory material, which begins: "To the performing of this task it will be necessary."

The Character Of A Presbyter, or Sr. Iohn anatomized. . . . London, Printed for John Calvin . . . 1660.
4°, text pp. 1–9.
Begins: "I will first present him in Grosse."
Murphy 106. Thos. II, 322.

The Character of an Anabaptist. As it was presented to some Lords of His Majestys Right Honourable Privy Council, for His Majesty, upon Thursday the 24th of January, 1660. . . . [Colophon:] London, Printed by J. Clowes, for P.C. 1660.*
s.sh.fo. In verse.
Begins: "An Anabaptist is so called, for being baptized according to Scriptures."
Thos. II, 356.
The date 1660 in the title means 1660/1.

A Character Of His most Sacred Majesty King Charles the IId. . . . By a Minister of the Word, Who hath for a long time desired, and daily Prayed for the happy Settlement of Church and State within the three Nations of

England, Scotland and Ireland In Truth, &
Peace, & Order . . . London, Printed by D.
Maxwell. 1660.

8°, text pp. 1–37.
Begins: "I. That His Majesty was a Prince unto
whom the Lord had given."
BSC 2295.

Dated Apr. 26, 1660, in contemporary manuscript on the
Harvard copy. The opening words quoted above are from
the beginning of the character proper on p. 9. Preceding
this is a long Apologie.

The Character Of Italy: Or, The Italian Anatomiz'd By An English Chyrurgion. . . . London: Printed for Nath. Brooke . . . 1660.

12°, text pp. 1–93.
Begins: "That this *Epitome* should suit."
Thos. II, 327. BSC 2282.

The Character Of Spain: Or, An Epitome Of
Their Virtues and Vices. . . . London: Printed for Nath. Brooke . . . 1660.

12°, text pp. 1–93.
(1) Spain (p. 1), (2) A Spaniard (p. 5).
Thos. II, 327. BSC 2282.

The Character of the Rump. . . . London,
Printed in the Year 1660.

4°, text pp. 1–6.
Begins: "A Rump is the hinder part of the many-
headed Beast."
Thos. II, 294. BSC 2296.

The Faithful, yet Imperfect Character Of a
Glorious King, King Charles I. His Country's
and Religions Martyr. Written by a Person of
Quality. . . . London, Printed for Richard
Royston . . . 1660.

8°, text pp. 1–71.
Begins: "If it be true, that the Eye-Catechism."
Thos. II, 353. BSC 2293.

A Murmurer described.*

Manuscript, location unknown.

A manuscript copy, of the eighteenth or nineteenth century,
is known.

O. Cromwell's Thankes To The Lord Generall, Faithfully presented by Hugh Peters In
another Conference. Together with an Hue
and Cry After Mercurius Politicus. London,
Printed by M.T.

4°, text pp. 1–14.
(1) An hue and cry after Mercurius Politicus (p.
10, in verse).

Dated 1660 by the Harvard Catalogue and May 10, 1660,
by the Thomason Catalogue.

A Short View Of The Life and Actions Of
The Most Illustrious James Duke Of York,

Together with his Character. . . . London:
Printed for Henry Marsh. 1660.*

4°, text pp. 1–26.
(1) James, Duke of York (p. 24).

The True Characters of the Educations, Inclinations, and several Dispositions for all those
bloody and barbarous persons who sate as
Judges upon the life of our late King Charls I.
Printed for Edward Thomas. 1660.*

Thos. II, 350.

Youths Lookinglass, wherein they may behold
the frailties . . . of all things under the sun
. . . Printed for J. Williamson . . . [1660?].*

8°, text pp. 1–16. In verse.
(1) Youth, (2) Old age.

Adis, Henry.

A Fannaticks Mite Cast into the Kings Treasury: Being A Sermon Printed to the King, Because not Preach'd before the King. By Henry
Adis, a Baptized Believer . . . London, Printed for the Author an Upholdster . . . 1660.

4°, text pp. 1–64.
(1) A gospel-church, & minister (p. 12).
Thos. II, 348.

Baxter, Richard.

The True Catholick, and Catholick Church
Described. And The vanity of the Papists,
and all other Schismaticks . . . discovered and
shamed. By Richard Baxter. . . . London,
Printed by A.M. and F. Tyton . . . 1660.

12°, text pp. 1–335.
(1) A true Christian (p. 87).
Thos. II, 306.

A poor example of character.

Baxter, Richard.

The Vain Religion of the Formal Hypocrite.
1660.*

(1) The religious formalist.

Beaumont, Robert.

Loves Missives To Virtue. With Essaies. By
Robert Beaumont. London, Printed by William Godbid . . . 1660.

8°, text pp. 1–116.
(1) A gentleman improved by foreign travel (p.
82), (2) A gentleman not improved by foreign
travel (p. 83).

Caton, William.

Truth's Caracter of Professors And their
Teachers . . . By . . . William Caton. London, Printed for Thomas Simmons . . . 1660.

4°, text pp. 5–56.
(1) Professors (p. 5), (2) Their teachers (p. 16).
BSC 2292.

Cleveland, John.

J. Cleaveland Revived: Poems, Orations, Epistles, And other of his Genuine Incomparable Pieces . . . This second Edition . . . is enriched with the Authors Midsummer-Moon, or Lunacy-rampant; Being an University Character, a short Survey of some of the late Fellows of the Colledges. Now at last publisht from his Original Copies, by some of his intrusted Friends. . . . London, Printed for Nathaniel Brooke . . . 1660.

8°, text pp. 1–190.
(1) as in 1659, (2) A protector (p. 78), (3) Midsummer-moon (p. 179).
Murphy 138. BSC 2286, 2298. Thos. II, 445.

Miss Murphy thinks that Midsummer-moon is by Thomas Winyard, since Wood wrote his name against it in his own copy and in MS Rawl. D. 945.

[Ellis, Clement.]

The Gentile Sinner, Or, England's Brave Gentleman: Characterized Jn a Letter to a Friend, Both As he is, and as he should be. . . . Oxford, Printed by Henry Hall, for Edward and John Forrest, 1660.

8°, text pp. 1–261.
(1) The gallant (p. 9), (2) His nature in generall (p. 15), (3) His calling or imploiment (p. 20), (4) His education and breeding (p. 23), (5) His habit and garbe (p. 28), (6) His language and discourse (p. 31), (7) His religion and conversation (p. 39), (8) The degenerate gentleman (p. 48), (9) The provident gentleman (p. 53), (10) The prudent gentleman (p. 60), (11) The peaceable gentleman (p. 69), (12) The stately gentleman (p. 75), (13) The true gentleman (p. 98), (14) His generall character (p. 100), (15) His chief honour and dignity (p. 105), (16) His outside and apparell (p. 108), (17) His discourse and language (p. 113), (18) His behaviour and civility (p. 122), (19) His inside (p. 126), (20) His command over himselfe (p. 129), (21) His magnanimity and humility (p. 133), (22) His charity and temperance (p. 139), (23) His valour and prudence (p. 144), (24) His behaviour in both fortunes (p. 149), (25) His respect and affection for his country (p. 156), (26) His studies and recreations (p. 162), (27) His good-husbandry (p. 170), (28) His religion (p. 172), (29) A satyrical character of a gentleman (p. 200).
Murphy 141. BSC 2291.

These characters blend into each other to form larger groups; indeed the whole book is really an extended character of a gentleman. The Dedicatory Epistle is signed C.E. Later editions have Ellis's name on the title page.

[Felltham, Owen.]

A Brief Character Of the Low-Countries Under the States. Being three weeks observation of the Vices and Vertues of the Inhabitants . . . London, Printed for H.S. and are to be sold by Rich. Lowndes . . . 1660.

12°, text pp. 1–100.
(1) as in 1659.
Thos. II, 345. BSC 2283.

The Harvard copy is bound with A Perfect Description of . . . Scotland, 1659.

Flecknoe, Richard.

Heroick Portraits With other Miscellary Pieces, Made, and Dedicate to His Majesty. By Rich. Flecknoe. . . . London, Printed by Ralph Wood, for the Author. 1660.

8°, text sigs. B–I4v.
(1) A fine, nice dame (sig. F3), (2) A modern casuist (sig. F4v), (3) A curious glutton (sig. F5v), (4) The shee-gamester (sig. F6v), (5) A formal schollar (sig. F7v), (6) A gallant French monsieur (sig. F8v), (7) A lady of the time (sig. Gv), (8) A Dutch frow (sig. G3), (9) A bilk courtier (sig. G4v), (10) A busie body (sig. G5v), (11) An English inn (sig. G7), (12) A lazie disposition (sig. H5), (13) A sighing lover (sig. H6), (14) A strange disposition (sig. H7), (15) A timorous disposition (sig. H8).
Murphy 66. BSC 2300.

In addition to the characters named, there are portraits of many living people, especially members of the court. Reprinted in part in 1665 (in Rich. Flecknoe's Aenigmatical Characters), 1673 (in A Collection of the Choicest Epigrams).

[Fletcher, Henry?]

The Perfect Politician: Or A Full View Of the Life and Actions . . . of O. Cromvvell. Whereunto is added His Character . . . London: Printed by I. Cottrell, for William Roybould . . . and Henry Fletcher . . . 1660.

8°, text pp. 1–359.
(1) Oliver Cromwell (p. 346).

Authorship uncertain but generally attributed to Fletcher. The address to the reader is signed I.S.

[G., J.]

A Letter from an Honourable Person in London, To a small Friend of his in Lancashire, Conteining the Character of a certain constant Practiser of Rebellion, now pretending to Loyalty.

s.sh.fo.
(1) A certain constant practiser of rebellion, now pretending to loyalty (p. 1).

The text is signed J.G.

[Geree, John.]

A Vindication of Calvin: Or, The Old English Puritan No Enemy to Kingly Power. Published according to Order. [ornament] London, Printed in the Year 1660.*

4°, text pp. 1–8.

Begins: "The Old English Puritane was such an one, that honoured God above all."

A reprint of The Character of an old English Puritan, 1646.

H., R.

New Atlantis . . . Continued by R.H. . . . London, Printed for John Crooke . . . 1660.

8°, text pp. 1–101.

(1) Persons that strike at the root of monarchy (sig. b4).

The epistle dedicatory and the preface are signed R.H. The author may possibly be Richard Head.

Heydon, John.

Idea of the Law charactered from Moses to King Charles. Whereunto is added the Idea of Government and Tyranny. Printed for the Author, 1660.*

BSC 2301. Thos. II, 321.

[Ingelo, Nathaniel.]

Bentivolio And Urania, In Four Bookes. By N.I. D.D. London: Printed by J.G. for Richard Marriott . . . MDCLX.

fo, text pp. 1–283.

(1) Inganna, craft (p. 75), (2) Inhabitants of Piacenza, lovers of pleasure (p. 76), (3) Pigerrimo, a sluggish person (p. 79), (4) Discontented women (p. 98), (5) Apiston, one that doth not rashly assent, but doubts till he sees reason for his belief (p. 102), (6) Pammelaenians, the ignorant (p. 121), (7) The obedient ignorant (p. 125), (8) An ignorant person (p. 126), (9) Catasarkus, fleshly, corpulent (p. 131), (10) Divers orders of ghostly people (p. 136), (11) Tuphlecon the late governor of Kenapistis (p. 150), (12) The Kenapistians, lovers of ease (p. 151), (13) Inhabitants of Tapinophrosyne, humble people (p. 193), (14) Theoprepians, virtuous people (p. 229), (15) Theosebes, a religious person (p. 237), (16) Sophrosynians, temperate people (p. 253), (17) Charity (p. 262).

The dedication is signed N. Ingelo.

[Jones, Andrew?]

The Dreadful Character of a Drunkard. Fourth Edition. 1660.*

See 1678.

Jordan, Thomas.

Pictures of Passions, Fancies, and Affections, poetically deciphered in Variety of Characters. London: Printed by R. Wood.*

8°.

Reprinted from 1641.

Matthew, Sir Tobie.

A Collection of Letters, Made by Sr Tobie Mathews, Kt. Wth A Character of . . . Lucy Countesse of Carleile . . . London, Printed for Hen. Herringman . . . 1660.

8°, text pp. 1–356.

(1) Lucy, Countess of Carleile (sig. A4).

Thos. II, 349.

P., W.

The Character Of That Glorious Martyred King, Charles I: Being A Brief Description Of His Religious Reign, from his Coronation to his unhappy Death. By W.P., Esq. London, Printed for T.B. 1660.*

4°, text pp. 1–6.

Pierce, Thomas.

The Sinner impleaded in his own Court . . . Whereunto is added the grand Character of a Christian.*

See 1670.

Spelman, Clement.

Character of the Oliverians; written by Clement Spelman, son of Sir Henry Spelman, and published 1660.*

[Tuke, Sir Samuel.]

A Character Of Charles the Second Written By an Impartial Hand, and exposed to Publick View For Information of the People. . . . London, Printed for Gabriel Bedell . . . 1660.

4°, text pp. 3–14.

Begins: "If the Naturalists pretend to give a reason."

BSC 2294, 2297. Thos. II, 305.

Attributed to Tuke or George Morley by Halkett and Laing. There is a variant edition of the same year, printed by D. Maxwell.

[Winyard, Thomas.]

Midsummer-Moon. 1660.

See John Cleveland's J. Cleaveland Revived, 1660.

1661

Anonymous.

Character of Cardinal Mazarine.*

Perhaps identical with An Impartial Character of . . . Mazarine, 1661.

The Character of Charles II by a minister of the Word. 1661.*

Perhaps a reissue of A Character of His Most Sacred Majesty King Charles the IId, 1660.

An Impartial Character of that famous Politician and late admired Minister of State, Cardinal Mazarine, De mortuis nil nisi Bonum. London, Printed in the year 1661.*

4°, text pp. 1–10.
Thos. II, 363. BSC 2306.

Manes Presbyteriani: Or The Monuments Of The Kirk. . . . All compiled and laid together. . . . London, Printed for the Reverend Classes, in the year 1661.

4°, in 2 parts, text pp. 1–16, 1–31.
(1) The late Marques of Arguile (part ii, p. 10).

B., F.

The Character of Sr. Arthur Haslerig The Church-Thief. By F.B. Gent.*

s.sh.fo.
Begins: "The Royal beams of his late Majesties favour had no sooner began."
Thos. II, 358.

Dated January, 1661, by the Thomason Catalogue.

Bacon, Sir Francis.

Resuscitatio, Or, bringing into Pvblick Light Several Pieces Of The Works . . . Of the Right Honourable Francis Bacon . . . The Second Edition . . . By William Ravvley . . . London, Printed by S. Griffin, for William Lee . . . 1661.

4°, 2 parts, text pp. 1–323, 1–122.
(1–2) as in 1657, (3) Julius Caesar (Part I, p. 283), (4) Augustus Caesar (I, 288).

Bacon, Sir Francis.

Several Discourses Written, in the Dayes of King James . . . By the Right Honourable Francis Bacon . . . London, Printed by S. Griffin, for William Lee . . . 1661.

4°, text pp. 197–288.
(1) Julius Caesar (p. 283), (2) Augustus Caesar (p. 288).

According to the Harvard Library Catalogue, this book is part of Bacon's Resuscitatio, 1661, q.v. It is part of a volume of which the first piece is Several Letters, 1657. Though paging is consecutive, there is no inclusive title page for the whole volume.

Barksdale, Clement.

Memorials of Worthy Persons.*

(1) Joseph Hall, (2) John Donne, (3) Sir William Cokain, (4) Sir Thomas Bodley, (5) Bishop Jewell, (6) George Herbert, (7) Bishop Usher, (8) John Hales, (9) R. Evelyn, (10) Bishop Lake, (11) Edward Peyton, (12) Archbishop Laud, (13) Archbishop Usher, (14) Thomas Brandeston, (15) John Dod, (16) Joseph Mede, (17)

Josias Shute, (18) Sir Francis Bacon, (19) Thomas Jackson, (20) Lady Falkland.

Charleton, Walter.

A Character Of His most Sacred Majesty Charles the Second, King of Great Britain France and Ireland . . . Written by Dr Charleton, Physician in Ordinary to His Maiestie. . . . London, Printed for Henry Herringman . . . 1661.

4°, text pp. 1–23.
Begins: "*Seneca* the *Rhetorician* reports."
BSC 2307.

An inside title reads: An Imperfect Pourtrait of His Sacred Majesty, etc.
A different work from the anonymous publication of similar title in the same year.

Cleveland, John.

Poems. By John Cleavland. With Additions never before Printed. [ornament] London, Printed for John Williams . . . 1661.

8°, text pp. 1–233 (last page erroneously numbered 15).
(1–4) as in 1654.
Murphy 63, 137.

[Denham, Sir John.]

The True Presbyterian Without Disguise: Or, A Character Of A Presbyterians Wayes and Actions, in Verse. Difficile est Satyram non scribere, namquis iniquae Tam patiens urbis tam ferreus, ut teneat se? Juv. [ornament] London, Printed in the Year, 1661.

4°, text pp. 1–6. In verse.
Begins: "A Presbyter is such a Monstrous thing."
Murphy 106. Thos. II, 365. BSC 2312.

The edition of 1680 bears Denham's name on the title page. Included in several editions of Edward Ward's The Secret History of the Calves-Head Club.

[Du Gard, Thomas.]

Confused Characters of Conceited Coxcombs: Or, A dish of Trayterous Tyrants, dressed with Verjuice and pickeled too posterity. Together with their Camp-retinue and Fems Covert. By Verax Philobasileus. . . . London, Printed by T.M. for Typographus . . . 1661.*

4°.
(1) A courtier, (2) A conceited statesman, (3) A meere polititian, (4) An upstart pragmaticall, (5) A justice of peace, (6) A high constable, (7) A juryman rustick, (8) A church-warden, (9) A baily or serjeant, (10) A lawyer in common, (11) An informer, (12) A flatterer, (13) Of a temporizer, (14) A finnicall London citizen, (15) A Hide Park lady, (16) The good old cause, (17)

A detracting empirick, (18) A colledge butler, (19) A university beadle, (20) A covetueus usurer, (21) A Cambridge minion, (22) A pune pragmatick pulpit-filler, (23) An old hording hagg.

Murphy 73. BSC 2313, 2314.

No copy has been located. The description is taken from the reprint of 1860, *q.v.* Attributed to Du Gard by Hazlitt.

Ellis, Clement.

The Gentile Sinner, Or, England's Brave Gentleman: Characterized In a Letter to a Friend, Both As he is, and as he should be. By Clem. Ellis, M.A. Fellow of Qu. Coll. Oxon. The Second Edition. . . . Oxford, Printed by A. and L. Lichfield, for Edward and John Forrest. 1661.

8°, text pp. 1–261.
(1–29) as in 1660.
Murphy 142. BSC 2308.

[Felltham, Owen.]

Lusoria: Or Occasional Pieces. With A Taste Of Some Letters. . . . London: Printed for Anne Seile . . . 1661.

4°, text pp. 3–102.
(1) A Brief Character of the Low Countries (p. 45).

Attributed to Felltham by the CBEL. A Brief Character has its own separate title page, 1661, but is paged as part of Lusoria. The New York Public Library copy is bound with, but not paged as part of, Resolves, 1661.

Felltham, Owen.

Resolves . . . The Eighth Impression. With New and several other Additions . . . By Owen Felltham. . . . London: Printed for Peter Dring . . . MDCLXI.

4°, text pp. 1–394.
(1) A brief character of the Low Countries (p. 45).

The earlier editions do not contain the character. Reprinted numerous times.

[Gatford, Lionel?]

Essayes and Characters. . . . Written by L.G. . . . London, Printed in the year, 1661.*

12°, text pp. 1–83.
(1) Of man in general, (2) A religious prince, (3) A reverend divine, (4) A vertuous woman, (5) A rigid Presbyterian, (6) A debaucht courtier, (7) An university bedle, (8) A phanatick, (9) A whore, (10) A happy rustick, (11) A beastly drunkard, (12) An ignorant old man, (13) A player, (14) A mechanick magistrate, (15) A scandalous minister, (16) A loyal subject, (17)

A male content, (18) A noble spirit, (19) A bad wife, (20) The R. . . . Parliament.

Murphy 72.

Glanvill, Joseph.

The Vanity of Dogmatizing: Or Confidence in Opinions Manifested in a Discourse Of The Shortness and Vncertainty Of Our Knowledge. . . . By Jos. Glanvill. . . . London, Printed by E.C. for Henry Eversden . . . 1661.*

8°, text pp. 1–250.
(1) A noble or generous man (p. 233).
Thos. II, 365.

Reprinted 1931 by The Facsimile Text Society. This note is taken from that edition.

Goddard, Thomas.

Miscellanea; Or, Serious, Useful Considerations, Moral, Historical, Theological. Together with the Characters Of A True Believer In Paradoxes and Seeming Contradictions. An Essay. . . . By Tho. Goddard, Gent. . . . London: Printed by E.C. for Tho. Williams . . . and Will. Thompson . . . 1661.

4°, in 2 parts, text pp. 1–152, 1–23, and four leaves unpaged.
(1) God (Part I, p. 1), (2) Jesus Christ (I, 7), (3) The Holy Ghost (I, 19), (4) Sin and sinners (I, 23), (5) The world, and the brightest jewell in its crowne, soveraignty (I, 34), (6) Loyalty, and rebellion (I, 42), (7) Riches (I, 46), (8) Covetousness; and covetous persons (I, 51), (9) Pleasure (I, 61), (10) Health (I, 65), (11) Saving faith, and sincere love (I, 67), (12) Repentance (I, 74), (13) Prayer (I, 80), (14) An upright or sincere man (I, 84), (15) An hypocrite (I, 89), (16) Affliction (I, 92), (17) Patience (I, 102), (18) Baptism (I, 105), (19) The sacrament of the Lord's Supper (I, 109), (20) Of preaching (I, 113), (21) Pious ministers (I, 116), (22) Self-making preachers or seducers (I, 124), (23) A bad conscience (I, 133), (24) A good conscience (I, 134), (25) Life (I, 137), (26) Of death (I, 144), (27) The Characters of a true beleever, in paradoxes, and seeming contradictions. An essay. By Tho. Goddard, Gent. (II, 1).
BSC 2309, 2310.

There was another edition of the same year, printed by E.C. for R. Gammon.

Nedham, Marchamont.

The True Character Of A Rigid Presbyter: With A Narrative of the Dangerous Designes of the English and Scotish Covenanters . . . Also, The Articles of their Dogmatical Faith, And the inconsistency thereof with Monarchy. To which is added, A short History of the English Rebellion: Compiled in Verse, By

Marchamont Nedham; And Formerly extant, in his Mercurius Pragmaticus. London: Printed by the Assignes of J. Calvin . . . 1661.

4°, text pp. 1–83 (misprinted 93).

Begins: "To give you an exact Character of him, is impossible."

Murphy 142. BSC 2305.

The parts of the book beginning on pp. 1, 12, and 29 are more appropriately called characters than the rest. There was a second edition the same year.

P., M.

A Character of Coffee and Coffee-Houses. By M.P. . . . London, Printed for John Starkey . . . 1661.*

4°, text pp. 1–10.

[Perrinchief, Richard.]

The Syracusan Tyrant: Or, The Life Of Agathocles. With some Reflexions on the practices of our Modern Usurpers. . . . London, Printed by J.F. for R. Royston . . . MDCLXI.

8°, text pp. 1–263.

(1) An usurper (p. 10), (2) The tyrant Agathocles (p. 259).

The Dedication is signed R.P. Reprinted as The Sicilian Tyrant, 1676.

Powell, Vavasour.

[Hebrew characters] Or The Bird in the Cage, Chirping Four distinct Notes to his Consorts abroad. . . . By Vava. Powell. . . . London, Printed, for L.C. . . . 1661.*

(1) A true Christian (p. 94).

Stevenson, Matthew.

The Twelve Moneths . . . By M. Stevenson . . . London, Printed by M.S. for Thomas Jenner . . . 1661.

4°, text pp. 1–59.

(1) January (p. 1), (2) February (p. 6), (3) March (p. 11), (4) April (p. 16), (5) May (p. 21), (6) June (p. 26), (7) July (p. 31), (8) August (p. 36), (9) September (p. 41), (10) October (p. 45), (11) November (p. 50), (12) December (p. 55).

Murphy 34.

Based on Breton's Fantasticks and amplified. Each character is preceded by a woodcut.

Verax, Philadelphus.

The Knavish Merchant, now turn'd Warehouseman, characterized: Or a severe scourge for an unjust cruel, and unconscionable adversary. By Philadelphus Verax, a cordial friend to T. Crocker, Merchant.*

Thos. II, 367.

This is an attack on Richard Neave. Dated April 20, 1661, by the Thomason Catalogue.

1662

Barksdale, Clement.

Characters and Historical Memorials, on the Lives and Actions of England's late Worthies, in Church and State. London, Printed for J.W. 1662.*

12°.

(1–20) as in Memorials, 1661.

BSC 2315.

Barksdale, Clement.

Memorials of Worthy Persons. The Third Decad. By Cl. Barksdale. . . . Oxford, Printed by A. & L. Liechfield . . . 1662.

8°, text pp. 1–104.

(1) Edward VI, by Heylyn (p. 1), (2) Lady Jane Grey, by Heylyn (p. 13, misprinted 31), (3) Sir John Cheke, by Langbane (p. 24), (4) Archbishop Whitgift, by Sir George Paul (p. 31), (5) Richard Hooker, by Gauden (p. 53), (6) Lancelot Andrewes, by John, Bishop of Ely (p. 62), (7) Ralph Brounrig, Bishop of Exeter, by Gauden (p. 69), (8) Thomas Gataker, anon. (p. 77), (9) Henry Hammond, by John Fell (p. 83), (10) Miles Smith, Bishop of Gloucester, by John Stephens (p. 94).

[Brome, Alexander?]

Rump: Or An Exact Collection Of the Choycest Poems and Songs Relating To The Late Times. By the most Eminent Wits, from Anno 1639 to Anno 1661. London, Printed for Henry Brome . . . and Henry Marsh . . . 1662.

8°, in 2 parts, text pp. 1–376, 1–200.

(1) The character of a roundhead, 1641 (Part I, p. 42).

Pforzheimer Catalogue No. 842.

Attributed to Brome doubtfully by the Pforzheimer Catalogue.

Cleveland, John.

J. Cleaveland Revived: Poems, Orations, Epistles, And other of his Genuine Incomparable Pieces. With some other Exquisite Remains of the most eminent Wits of both the Universities that were his Contemporaries. This third Edition, besides many other never before publisht Additions, is enriched with the Authors Midsummer-Moon, or Lunacy-Rampant: Being an University Character, a short Survey of some of the late Fellows of the Colledges. Now at last publisht from his Original Copies, by some of his intrusted Friends. . . . London, Printed for Nathaniel Brook . . . 1662.

8°, text pp. 1–182.

(1–3) as in 1660.

Murphy 63, 139. BSC 2318.

Cleveland, John.

Poems. By John Cleavland. With Additions, never before Printed. [ornament and motto] London, Printed for W. Shears . . . 1662.

8°, text pp. 1–235.
(1–4) as in 1654.
Murphy 63, 137. BSC 2318.

[Felltham, Owen.]

A Brief Character of the Low Countries. Printed for R. Lowndes. 1662.*
BSC 2319.

Fuller, Thomas.

The History of the Worthies of England. 1662.*
(1) Thomas Allen, (2) Sir Nicholas Bacon, (3) Bishop Brownrigg, (4) William Butler.
Reprinted several times.

Gadbury, John.

The Nativity of the late King Charles. 1662.*

Leyburn, George.

Holy Characters Containing A Miscellany of Theologicall Discourses That Is Theology, Positive, Scholasticall, Polemicall, and Morall . . . Written by George Leyburn, Doctor of Divinity . . . Devided into Two Books. Printed at Doway, By Baltazar Bellier. An. 1662. With Privilege.

In 2 parts, text pp. 1–343, 1–403.
(1) Of a Christian (I, 55), (2) Of a Christian persecuted for Christ's sake (I, 61), (3) Of a wit-believer (I, 74), (4) Of a singular doctor (I, 78), (5) The covetous man (I, 284), (6) A detractor (I, 316), (7) A slothful man (I, 332), (8) Of a missionary priest (I, 335).
BSC 2320.

Powell, Vavasour.

[Hebrew characters] Or The Bird in the Cage, Chirping Four distinct Notes to his Consorts abroad . . . By Vava. Powell. The second Edition Corrected and Enlarged. . . . London Printed, for L.C. . . . 1662.

8°, text pp. 1–142.
(1) as in 1661.
BSC 2321.

[Sikes, George.]

The Life and Death of Sir Henry Vane, Kt. . . . Printed in the year, 1662.

4°, text pp. 3–162.
(1) Sir Henry Vane (pp. 7 and 93).
Attributed to Sikes in the CBEL. Sometimes attributed to Sir Roger L'Estrange.

Swinnock, George.

The Christian-mans Calling: Or, A Treatise Of Making Religion ones business. . . . By George Swinnock . . . London, Printed by J.B. for Thomas Parkhurst . . . 1662[–65].

4°, 2 vols.
(1) He that makes religion his business (Vol. I, p. 22), (2) A tradesman that minds his employment (I, 31), (3) A good neighbour (II, 48), (4) A vicious man (II, 142), (5) A drunken man (II, 143), (6) Unsactified persons (II, 703).

[Taylor, John?]

The Traytors Perspective-glass. . . . Whereunto is added Three Perfect Characters of those late-executed Regicides, Viz. Okey, Corbet, and Barkstead . . . faithfully delineated by I.T. Gent. . . . London, Printed by H.B. for Phil. Stephens the younger . . . 1662.

4°, text pp. 1–43.
(1) John Okey (p. 28), (2) Miles Corbet (p. 32), (3) John Barkstead (p. 36).
BSC 2322.
Attributed to Taylor by the Huntington Library. There were two different impressions in 1662.

[Woolnoth, Mr.]

The Coffee Scuffle, occasioned by a Contest Between a Learned Knight, And A Pitifull Pedagogue. With The Character of a Coffee-House. London, Printed and are to be sold at the Latine Coffee House 1662.*

(1) Dull pedagogue, (2) Learned knight, (3) Grotius, (4) A coffee-house.
The British Museum copy has a manuscript note, "This is thought to be made by one Woolnoth."

1663

Anonymous.

The Character of a Detractor. 1663.*

The Character of a Lecturer.*

4°, text pp. 1–9.

Coffee, its vertues set forth by Lord Bacon, Parkington, Sir G. Sandys, and J. Howel. W.G. for J. Playford. 1663.*
4°.
BSC 2325.

The Maiden's Complaint against Coffee, or the Coffee-House discovered, besieged, stormed, taken, untyled, and laid open to publick View in a Merry Conference. . . . London, Printed for J. Jones. 1663.*
BSC 2324.

Raillerie a la Mode Consider'd: Or The Supercilious Detractor. A Joco-serious Discourse; shewing the open Impertinence and Degenerosity of Publishing Private Pecques and Controversies to the World. Occasionally Written. To a Young Gentleman, to shew the Odium of this Ingentile Humour, and to direct him in the best choice of Men and Books. . . . London, Printed by T.R. and N.T. for Henry Million . . . MDCLXIII.

8°, text pp. 1–70.
(1) A detractor (p. 51), (2) A worthy man described (p. 58).
Murphy 146. BSC 2328.
In the Huntington copy the date has been altered in ink to 1673 by the addition of another X. Miss Murphy considers the earlier date a printer's error, which he remedied by this means or by substituting, as in the British Museum copy, a new title page.

Reason and Judgement: or, Special Remarques Of the Life Of the Renowned Dr. Sanderson, Late Lord Bishop of Lincoln. . . . Oxford: Printed by J.W. for Will. Thorne. 1663.

4°, text pp. 3–92.
(1) Dr. Sanderson (p. 3).

Aretino, Peter.
The Sixth Part of the Wandering-whore Revived. In a dialogue Between Magdalena, a crafty Bawd, etc. London, Printed for John Johnson 1663.*
(1) Lucretia, a famous courtesan.

Barksdale, Clement.
Memorials Of Worthy Persons. (Lights and Ornaments Of The Church of England.) The Fourth Decad. By Cl. Barksdale. . . . Oxford, Printed by A. and L. Lichfield, 1663.

8°, text pp. 1–135.
(1) John Colet, by Erasmus (p. 1), (2) John Langly, by Edward Reynolds (p. 17), (3) Thomas Morton, by Barwick (p. 23), (4) George Herbert, anon. (p. 45), (5) Joseph Hall, by himself (p. 68), (6) Sir Thomas More, by J.H. (p. 88), (7) Sir Henry Wotton, by Izaac Walton (p. 99), (8) William Bedel, by Izaac Walton and Joseph Hall (p. 121), (9) Anthony de Dominis, by Barwick (p. 127), (10) Abraham Wheelock, anon. (p. 133).

[Birkenhead, Sir John.]
The Assembly-man: Written in the Year 1647. . . . London: Printed for Richard Marriot . . . 1662/3.

4°, text pp. 5–22.
Begins: "An *Assembler* is part of the *States*' Chattels."
Murphy 106. BSC 2316 and 2317.

Birkenhead, Sir John.
Cabala or An Impartial Account of the Non-Conformists Private Designs, Actings and Wayes. London, Printed in the year 1663.*
(1) A lecturer.
BSC 2323.

[Casa, Giovanni della.]
The Refin'd Courtier.*
See 1679.

Cowley, Abraham.
Cutter of Coleman-Street. A Comedy. The Scene London, in the year 1658. Written by Abraham Cowley. London, Printed for Henry Herringman . . . 1663.

4°, text pp. 1–70.
(1) Worm, a pretended Royalist (Act I, Scene vi).
Pforzheimer Catalogue No. 226.
A revision of his earlier The Guardian, 1650.

Fuller, Thomas.
The Holy State. By Thomas Fuller, B.D. and Prebendarie of Sarum. . . . The fourth Edition . . . London: Printed by John Redmayne for John Williams . . . 1663.*
fo, text pp. 1–460.
(1–51) as in 1642.
Murphy 58.
There is also an engraved title page.

[Harding, W. N. H.]
The Academy of Complements. . . . The last Edition. . . . London . . . Tho. Leach, and Tho. Child, 1663.
(1) as in 1645, (2) A character of complements (p. 320).

[Jones, Andrew?]
The Dreadful Character of a Drunkard. Tenth Edition. London: Printed for Elizabeth Andrews. 1663.*
See 1678.
BSC 2326.

Lenton, Francis.
Characters: Or, Wit and the World In Their proper Colours. Presented to the Queens most Excellent Majestie. By a person of Quality. . . . London: Printed for Samuel Speed . . . MDCLXIII.
12°, text sigs. B–H3.
(1–41) as in his Characterismi, 1631.
Murphy 50. BSC 2327.

Swinnock, George.
Ουρανος και Ταρταρος. Heaven & Hell Epitomized. The true Christian Characterized.

as also an Exhortation with Motives, Means and Directions to be speedy and serious about the work of Conversion. By George Swinnock, sometime Fellow of Balliol Colledge in Oxford, and Preacher of the Gospel, late at Great-Kimbel in the County of Bucks. . . . London, Printed for Tho. Parkhurst . . . 1663.*

4°, text pp. 1–220.
BSC 2329.

1664

Anonymous.

The Dutch Drawn to the Life, In I. An Exact Description and Character of the several Provinces of the Netherlands. . . . London, Printed for Tho. Johnson . . . and H. Marsh . . . 1664.

12°, text pp. 1–156.
(1) The Dutch people (p. 64), (2) Henry Nassau, 1500 (p. 126).
BSC 2332.

The first part, despite the promise of the title, is not a character. Neither of those listed is actually very good.

B., P.

Juvenilia Sacra, Or Divine Youthfull Meditations; Consisting Of a Dialogue between Christ and the Soul. A Preparation to the Lords Supper. Characters of the Pious and Impious Man. Of the Good, and Wicked Woman. The Foure Quarters of the Year. Ten Historicall, Ten Scripture, and Ten Occasional Applications. By, P.B. Gent. London, Printed by Tho. Mabb, for John Playfere . . . 1664.

8°, text pp. 1–131.
(1) A pious man (p. 37), (2) The impious man (p. 44), (3) The good woman (p. 50), (4) The wicked woman (p. 55).
Murphy 143. BSC 2330.

Blount, Thomas.

The Academy of Eloquence. Third Edition. 1664.*

[C., O.]

The Conduct And Character Of Count Nicholas Serini, Protestant Generalissimo of the Auxiliaries in Hungary, The most Prudent and resolved Champion of Christendom. . . . London, Printed for Sam. Speed . . . 1664.

12°, text pp. 1–168.
(1) Serini (*passim*, but especially on pp. 74 and 108).
BSC 2339.

The address to the reader is signed O.C.

Crossman, Samuel.

The Young Man's Monitor. Or A modest Offer toward the Pious, and Vertuous Composure of Life from Youth to Riper Years. By Samuel Crossman, B.S. London, by J.H., 1664. See his The Young Man's Calling, 1685.
BSC 2331.

de la Chambre, Marin Cureau.

The Art to know Men. 1664.*
See 1665.

[Earle, John.]

Micro-Cosmographie: Or, a Piece of the World Discover'd; In Essayes, And Characters. The eighth Edition. . . . London, Printed by R.D. for P.C. 1664.

12°, text pp. 1–276.
(1–78) as in 1633.
Murphy 42. BSC 2334.

Ellis, Clement.

The Gentile Sinner; Or, England's Brave Gentleman: Character'd In a Letter to a Friend. Both As he is, and as he should be. By Clem. Ellis, M.A. Fellow of Qu. Coll. Oxon. The Third Edition. . . . Oxford, Printed by A. and L. Lichfield, for Edward and John Forrest. 1664.

8°, text pp. 1–261.
(1–29) as in 1660.
Murphy 142. BSC 2335.

Flecknoe, Richard.

Love's Kingdom. A Pastoral Trage-Comedy. . . . By Richard Flecknoe. . . . London, Printed by R. Wood . . . 1664.

8°, text pp. 1–81.
(1) A good actor (Burbage) (sig. G6v, in his A Short Discourse of the English Stage).

Ingelo, Nathaniel.

Bentivolio And Urania, The Second Part. In Two Books: By Nath. Ingelo, D.D. London, Printed by J. Grismond for Richard Marriott . . . 1664.

fo, text pp. 1–385.
(1) Theone, a divine mind (p. 3), (2) Plutocopians, people who take pains for nothing but wealth (p. 9), (3) Orthocrinon, one that makes a true estimate of things (p. 24), (4) Anaxagathus, a good king (p. 47), (5) Alethon, an excellent prince (p. 52), (6) Antitheus, an anti-God (p. 128), (7) Pasenantius, a perverse man (p. 152), (8) Dogmapornes, one who believes chiefly in sensual pleasure (p. 153), (9) Philedones, a lover of pleasure (p. 154), (10) Medenarete, who

esteems vertue to be nothing (p. 156), (11) Scepticus, one of the Pyrrhonian sect (p. 161), (12) Hypsagoras, a lofty speaker, one who believes nothing (p. 162), (13) Antigraphus, one that is an opposer of the Holy Scriptures (p. 165), (14) Anaxanacton, Jesus Christ (p. 245), (15) Calliphon, a wise statesman (p. 289).

Mackaile, M.
Moffet-Well and Oyley-Well, with Character of Mr. Culpeper and his Writings. Edinburgh. 1664.*
BSC 2336.

Mede, Joseph.
The Works. 1664-63.*
See 1672.

Newcastle, Margaret Cavendish, Duchess of.
CCXI. Sociable Letters, Written By The Thrice Noble, Illustrious, and Excellent Princess, The Lady Marchioness Of Newcastle. . . . London, Printed by William Wilson, Anno. Dom. M.DC.LXIV.
4°, text pp. 1-453.
(1) Mrs. P. I., an altered woman, on being a sanctified soul (p. 103), (2) Mrs. H.O., a wit (p. 147), (3) A wise man (independent of the mode) (p. 134).

Overbury, Sir Thomas.
Sir Thomas Overbury His Wife. With Additions of New Characters: And many other Witty Conceits never before Printed. The Seventeenth Impression. London, Printed for John Playfere . . . 1664.
8°, text sigs. A8–V8.
(1-82) as in twelfth impression of 1626.
Murphy 25. BSC 2337.

Peacham, Henry.
The VVorth of a Peny, Or, A Caution to keep Money. . . . By Henry Peacham . . . Now newly reprinted . . . London, Printed by S. Griffin, for William Lee . . . 1664.
4°, text pp. 1-34, wrongly numbered 38.
(1-2) as in 1641.
Murphy 133.

Person, Samuel.
An Anatomical Lecture Of Man. Or A Map of the Little World, Delineated in Essayes and Characters. By Samuell Person, Late of Kings Colledge, Cambridge. London, Printed by T. Mabb, for Samuell Ferris . . . 1664.
8°, text pp. 1-95.
(1) A character (p. 1), (2) The world (p. 6),

(3) A man (p. 9), (4) A wise man (p. 13), (5) A fool (p. 22), (6) A knowing man (p. 28), (7) An ignorant man (p. 35), (8) A covetous man (p. 39), (9) A free spirited, or a liberal man (p. 44), (10) A proud self-conceited man (p. 47), (11) A meere physitian (p. 51), (12) A divine (p. 53), (13) A grammarian (p. 57), (14) A logician (p. 59), (15) A rhetorician, or an orator (p. 61), (16) An arithmetician (p. 63), (17) A musitian (p. 66), (18) A geometrician (p. 69), (19) An astronomer (p. 72), (20) Nemo (p. 75), (21) A gyant (p. 76), (22) A melancholy man (p. 78), (23) A souldier (p. 81), (24) A child (p. 83), (25) A critick (p. 85), (26) Riches (p. 88), (27) Fortune (p. 90), (28) A virgin (p. 92), (29) Death (p. 94).
Murphy 74. BSC 2338.
No. 1 is taken from Overbury, nos. 11 and 24 from Earle.

[Philips, Katherine.]
Poems. By the Incomparable, Mrs. K.P. London, Printed by J.G. for Rich. Marriot . . . 1664.
8°, text pp. 1-242. In verse.
(1) La grandeur d'esprit, a virtuous man (p. 171).
Attributed to Katherine Philips by the CBEL. There were several later editions.

Scattergood, Anthony.
Jethro's Character of Worthy Judges. An Assize-Sermon Preached At Northampton March 22. 1663. By Antonie Scattergood D.D. London: Printed by J.G. for Richard Marriott, and are to be sold at his Shop under St. Dunstans Church in Fleet-street. 1664.*
4°, text pp. 1-39.

1665
Anonymous.
The Character Of A Coffee-House. Wherein Is contained a Description of the Persons usually frequenting it, with their Discourse and Humors, As Also The Admirable Vertues of Coffee. By an Eye and Ear Witness. . . . Printed in the Year, 1665.
4°, text pp. 1-10. In verse.
Begins: "A Coffee-house, the learned hold."
Murphy 76.

Character of the five Sectaries: namely Presbyterian, Independent, Anabaptist, Quaker, and Fifth-Monarchy Man. Concluding with Remarks to King Charles the Second. 1665.*

The Dutch Boare Dissected, or a Description of Hogg-Land. . . . [colophon] London, Printed, 1665.*

s.sh.fo.
Begins: "What makes the wiser Mackerell to stay."
A character of a Dutchman.

Brathwaite, Richard.

The Captive-Captain: Or, The Restrain'd Cavalier; Drawn to his full Bodie in these Characters; I. Of a Prison. II. The Anatomy of a Jayler. III. A Jaylers Wife. IV. The Porter. V. The Century. VI. The Fat Prisoner. VII. The Lean Prisoner. VIII. The restrain'd Cavalier, with his Melancholy fancy. Presented, and Acted to Life in a Suit of Durance; an Habit suiting best with the Place of his Residence. Nullus extra te Carcer. London Printed by J. Grismond, 1665.*

8°, text pp. 1–189.
(1) A prison, (2) A jailor, (3) A jailor's wife, (4) A porter, (5) A century [i.e., sentry], (6) A fat prisoner, (7) A lean prisoner, (8) A restrained cavalier, (9) A countrey commissioner, (10) A state-competitor, (11) A phanatic.
Murphy 75.
Attributed to Brathwaite by the CBEL.

Casa, Giovanni della.

The Arts of Grandeur and Submission.*
See 1670.

Cleveland, John.

Poems. By John Cleaveland. With Additions, never before Printed. [ornament: crown and globe] London, Printed by S.G. for John Williams . . . 1665.

8°, text pp. 1–232.
(1–4) as in 1654.
Murphy 63, 137. BSC 2340.

Crouch, John.

Belgica Caracteristica, or The Dutch Character. Being Nevvs from Holland. A Poem. By John Crouch, Gent. The second Impression, Improv'd. . . . London, Printed by Edward Crouch . . . 1665.

8°, text pp. 1–8. In verse.
Begins: "Where are our Mighty Dutch? still weather-bound?"
BSC 2341.
A reprint of his The Dutch Embargo, 1665.

Crouch, John.

The Dutch Imbergo, Upon their State Fleet; Or, Nevvs from Holland. A Poem. By John Crouch. Gent. London, Printed by Edward Crowch . . . 1665.

4°, text pp. 3–8. In verse.
Begins: "Where are our Mighty Dutch? still Weather-bound."
A dubious example of character. Reprinted 1665 as The Dutch Embargo and again in 1665 as Belgica Caracteristica.

Crouch, John.

The Dutch Embargo, Upon their State Fleet; or, Nevvs from Holland. A Poem. By John Crouch. Gent. The second impression, Improv'd. London, Printed by Edward Crowch . . . 1665.

4°, text pp. 1–8. In verse.
Begins: "Where are our Mighty Dutch? Still Weather-bound?"
A reprint of The Dutch Imbergo, 1665.

de la Chambre, Marin Cureau.

The Art How to know Men, Originally written. By the Sieur De La Chambre . . . Rendred into English By John Davies of Kidwelly . . . London, Printed by T.R. . . . M.DC.-LXV.

8°, text pp. 1–330.
(1) Of the figure of man's parts (p. 21), (2) Wherein the beauty of the woman consists (p. 31), (3) Prudence (p. 167), (4) Justice (p. 171), (5) Temperance (p. 175), (6) Fortitude (p. 180).
A border-line example of character.

Flecknoe, Richard.

Fifty-five Enigmatical Characters, All Very exactly drawn to the Life, from several Persons, Humours, Dispositions. Pleasant and full of Delight. By R.F. Esq; London, Printed for William Crook . . . 1665.

8°, text pp. 1–135.
(1–69) as in Enigmaticall Characters, 1658.
Murphy 66.

Flecknoe, Richard.

Rich. Flecknoe's Ænigmatical Characters. Being Rather a new Work, then new Impression of the old. . . . London, Printed by R. Wood, for the Author, in the Year 1665.

8°, text pp. 1–118.
(1–56) characters reprinted from previous books of 1653, 1658, and 1660, (57) Of an excellent actor (p. 2), (58) Of an eager disputant (p. 5), (59) Of a dairy (p. 16, in verse), (60) Of absence. To the Lady —— (p. 18), (61) Of the same lady [one who silences calumny] (p. 19), (62) Of a stage critick (p. 32), (63) Of a shrewd old Catholick gentlewoman (p. 42), (64) Of the patrons lives (p. 46, in verse), (65) Of a grave formal sir (p. 53), (66) Of a table disputant (p. 61), (67) Of a Flaunders devote (p. 62), (68) Of liberty (p. 66, in verse), (69) Of a mendicant

Irish priest (p. 69), (70) Of a changeable disposition (p. 72), (71) Of a good honest Catholick (p. 75), (72) Of your fanatick reformers (p. 83), (73) Of an English papist ass (p. 96), (74) Of a chymerical poet (p. 106), (75) Of a too ordinary courtier (p. 107), (76) Of an old lady, who lookt ill upon him (p. 114, in verse), (77) Another on the same (p. 115), (78) Of Mrs. Stuart (p. 117, in verse).
Murphy 67.

[Flecknoe, Richard.]

Sixtynine Enigmatical Characters, All Very exactly drawn to the Life. From several Persons, Humours, Dispositions. Pleasant And full of Delight. The second Edition by the Author R. F. Esquire. London, Printed for William Crook . . . 1665.

12°, text pp. 1–150.
(1–69) as in his Enigmatical Characters, 1658.
Murphy 66. BSC 2342.

[Gother, John.]

A Papist Mis-represented, and Represented: Or. A Twofold Character Of Popery. . . . By J.L. Printed Anno Domini 1665.*

(1) A papist mis-represented, (2) A papist represented.
BSC 2343.
Continued in The Catholic Representer, 1687, and in The Papist Misrepresented, Third Part, 1687.

[Head, Richard.]

The English Rogue Described, In The Life Of Meriton Latroon, A Witty Extravagant. Being a compleat History of the Most Eminent Cheats Of Both Sexes. . . . London, Printed for Henry Marsh . . . 1665.

8°, 4 vols.
(1) A bottle of canary (Vol. I, p. 63), (2) The definition of a prison (I, 75), (3) An hector or trapan (I, 80).
Murphy 143.
Attributed to Head by the CBEL. A second part appeared in 1668.

Jordan, Thomas.

Pictures of Passions, Fancies and Affections; poetically deciphered in a Variety of Characters. 1665.*
Reprinted from 1641.

[Marvell, Andrew.]

The Character Of Holland. . . . [colophon] London, Printed by T. Mabb for Robert Horn . . . 1665.

fo, text pp. 1–7. In verse.
Begins: "Holland, that scarce deserves the name of Land."
Attributed to Marvell by the CBEL.

Patrick, Simon.

The Parable of the Pilgrim: Written to a Friend. By Symon Patrick. B.D. London, Printed by Robert White for Francis Tyton . . . 1665.

4°, text pp. 1–527.
(1) A safe guide (p. 12), (2) One of our conceited believers (p. 197), (3) A true friend (p. 393).

Waterhouse, Edward.

The Gentleman's Monitor; Or, a Sober Inspection Into The Vertues, Vices, and Ordinary Means, Of the Rise and Decay Of Men and Families. . . . By Edw. Waterhous, Esq; London, Printed by T.R. for R. Royston . . . MDCLXV.

8°, text pp. 1–493.
(1) An old English noble or gentle-man (p. 365).

Wilson, John.

The Projectors, A Comedy By, John Wilson . . . London, Printed for John Playfere . . . and William Crook . . . 1665.

4°, text pp. 1–63.
(1) Sir Gudgeon Credulous, a projector (p. 5), (2) A usurer, Suckdrie (p. 14), (3) A good wife (p. 25).

1666

Alsop, George.

A Character Of the Province of Mary-Land . . . By George Alsop. London . . . T.J. for Peter Dring . . . 1666.

8°, text pp. 1–118.
Begins: "Mary-Land is a Province situated."
BSC 2344.

Flecknoe, Richard.

A Farrago Of several Pieces. Newly written by Richard Flecknoe. Being a Supplement To His Poems, Characters, Heroick Pourtraits, Letters, and other Discourses formerly Published by him. . . . London, Printed for the Author, 1666.

8°, text pp. 1–84.
(1) Margaret, Dutches of Newcastle (p. 28), (2) One who changes day into night (p. 44), (3) A French taylor (p. 46), (4) An old batchellor (p. 48), (5) An excellent wife (p. 53), (6) Your new irreligious order (p. 55), (7) Wit (p. 58).
Murphy 68.

[Head, Richard.]

The English Rogue Described, In The Life Of Meriton Latroon . . . London: Printed for Fra: Kirkman . . . 1666.

8°, in 3 parts, text pp. 1–112, 1–160, 1–131.
(1–3) as in 1665.
Murphy 144.

Molloy, Charles.

Hollands Ingratitude: Or, A Serious Expostulation With the Dutch. Shewing their Ingratitude to this Nation, and their inevitable Ruine, without a speedy Compliance and Submission To His Sacred Majesty Of Britain. By Charles Molloy of Lincolns-Inn, Gent. London: Printed by T.J. for Fr. K. . . . 1666.
4°, text pp. 11–48.
(1) A Dutchman (p. 44), (2) A Frenchman (p. 46).
Murphy 144. BSC 2345.

Smith, John.

Pourtract of Old Age. Printed by J. Macock. 1666.*
BSC 2398.
According to the BSC, the title page is dated 1666 and the imprimatur 1676.

Spurstow, William.

The Spiritual Chymist: or Six Decads Of Divine Meditations On several Subjects. By William Spurstow D.D. . . . London, Printed for Philip Chetwind, 1666.
8°, text pp. 1–182.
(1) William Spurstow, by an anonymous writer (sig. A6v).

Tanner, Thomas, G.J.E.

Euphuia, or the Acts and Characters of a Good Nature. London, for John Crook, 1666.*
8°.
(1) A free and ingenuous spirit or magnanimous man (p. 14), (2) A courteous person (p. 100).
BSC 2347.

Watson, Thomas.

The Godly Mans Picture, Drawn with a Scripture-Pensil. Or Some Characteristical Notes of a Man that shall go to Heaven. By Thomas Watson . . . London, Printed for Thomas Parkhurst . . . 1666.
8°, text pp. 1–363.
(1) A godly man (p. 15).
BSC 2348.
Very long, but yet essentially a character. The running title of a considerable section of the book (pp. 15–270) is The Character of a Godly Man.

[Wild, Robert.]

The Loyal Nonconformist; or, an Account what he dare swear, and what not. . . . Printed in the Year, 1666.

s.sh.fo. In verse.
Begins: "I fear an Oath, before I swear to take it."
Murphy 107.
This is a character in the first person singular. It was reprinted twice. It is attributed to Wild by the CBEL.

[Winstanley, William.]

Poor Robin's Character of France: Or, France Painted to the Life. In A Briefe Dialogue Of The Description of that Nation, their Manners, Customs, Complements, Language, Discourse, &c. As Also, An exact Character of the City of Paris . . . of their Gentry, Peasants, Women, &c. By Poor Robin, Knight of the Burnt-Island, a Well willer to the French Taylors. Printed in the Year 1666.*
4°, text pp. 1–31.
(1) Gentry (p. 7), (2) Frenchwomen (p. 16), (3) French cities and great towns (p. 17), (4) The old women of Parry (p. 29).
BSC 2346.
Attributed to Winstanley because he frequently wrote under the pseudonym of Poor Robin.

1667

Anonymous.

A Hue and Crie after the Earl of Clarendon. . . . Printed in the Year of Clarendon's Confusion 1667.*
In verse.
Begins: "From Dunkirk-House there lately ran away/A Traytor, whom you are desir'd to stay."

News from the Coffe-House; In which is shewn their seueral sorts of Passions, Containing Newes from all our Neighbour Nations. A Poem. . . . London, Printed by E. Crowch for Thomas Vere . . . 1667.*
s.sh.fo. In verse.
Murphy 76.
Reprinted 1672 as The Coffee-House Or News-Mongers Hall.

A true Character of Sundry Trades and Callings: Or a New Ditty of Innocent Mirth. 1667.*
The word Trades in the title may be an error for Traits.

Baxter, Richard.

Of Redemption of Time.*
(1) A Christian woman, (2) Sensual ladies and gentlewomen, (3) A fleshly brute.

[Butler, Samuel.]

The Character Of A London Scrivener. Printed in the Year MDCLXVII.

4°, text pp. 1-10.

Begins: "A *London* Scrivener Is a Creature begot by a *Pen*."

BSC 2349 and 2351.

Ascribed to Butler by the Huntington Library.

[Kirke, Thomas.]

A Modern Account of Scotland: being an exact Description of the People and their Manners. Written by an English Gentleman from thence. 1667.*

(1) Scotland, (2) A Scottish student of divinity.

Mackenzie, Sir George.

[First title] Moral Gallantry. A Discourse, Wherein the Author endeavours to prove, that Point of Honour (abstracting from all other tyes) obliges men to be Vertuous. And that there is nothing so mean (or unworthy of a Gentleman) as Vice. By Sir George Mackenzie. . . . Edinburgh, Printed for Robert Broun . . . 1667.

[Second title] A Moral Paradox: Maintaining, That it is much easier to be Vertuous then Vitious. By Sir George Mackeinzie. . . . Edinburgh, Printed for Robert Broun . . . 1667.

8°, two parts, text pp. 21-136, 5-87.

(1) A philosopher (Part II, p. 76).

Newcastle, Margaret Cavendish, Duchess of.

The Life Of The Thrice Noble, High and Puissant Prince William Cavendishe, Duke, Marquess, and Earl of Newcastle . . . Written By . . . Margaret . . . His Wife. London, Printed by A. Maxwell . . . 1667.

fo, text pp. 1-199.

(1) William, Duke of Newcastle (p. 147).

Several times reprinted.

Patrick, Simon.

The Parable of the Pilgrim. 1667.*

Reprinted from 1665.

Peacham, Henry.

The Worth of a Peny, or A Caution to keep Money. Now newly reprinted according to Order, and made more publick than heretofore: with some Additions of Notes in the Margin. . . . London, Printed by S. Griffin for William Lee, 1667.

4°, text pp. 1-34, wrongly numbered 33.

(1-2) as in 1641.

Murphy 133.

The Huntington copy, from which this note was made, lacks the title page. The title as given is taken from an unverified work-card.

[Price, Lawrence?]

The Vertuous Wife Is the Glory of her Husband; Or, A good Woman in her Proper Colours. Shewing at large the Rare Endowments, Excellent qualities, that are as Ornaments and Jewels, which bedeck the breast of the truly Vertuous Woman. Also ten Characters, or rare Jewels, hanging in the Crown of the vertuous Wife, who is the Glory of her Husband, the honour of her age, the mirrour of her Sex, the best Earthly Portion in the world. Likewise many examples, as well Modern as Divine, Queens, Princes, and Ladies, eminent for Vertue and Goodness. Lastly, A few counsels to all young men to be wary in their choice, if ever they would obtain, that portion of portions, and Incomparable Jewel, the Good Wife. Prov. 31.30 [quoted] By L.P. A well-wisher to all Good Women. Printed for T. Passenger, at the three Bibles on the middle of London-Bridge. 1667.*

8°, text pp. 1-21. Black letter.

(1) The vertuous wive's character, (2) Her person, (3) Her parts, (4) Her religion, (5) Her temper, (6) Her conduct, (7) Her conversation.

Murphy 77. BSC 2350.

Attributed to Price by the DNB. The whole book might be considered a character of an exemplary wife.

Wells, Jeremiah.

Poems Upon Divers Occasions. With A Character Of A London Scrivener. . . . London, Printed for John Crosley . . . 1667.

8°, text pp. 1-138, plus 8 leaves unnumbered.

(1) A London scrivener (p. 129).

Murphy 145. BSC 2351.

1668

Anonymous.

The Characters Or Pourtraicts Of The Present Court Of France: Wherein is described The King, the Princes, the Generals and the principal Ministers of State, &c. Written Originally in French. Made English by J.B. Gent. London: Printed by J.C. for Thomas Palmer . . . 1668.

8°, text pp. 1-135.

(1) King Louis XIV (p. 3), (2) The king's family (p. 13), (3) The queen-mother (p. 30), (4) Monsieur, the king's brother (p. 37), (5) Prince Lewis (p. 42), (6) The Duke (p. 51), (7) The Prince of Conty (p. 55), (8) Mlle. de Montpensier (p. 58), (9) The House of Vendosme (p. 64), (10) The Duke of Guise (p. 69), (11) The House of Longueville (p. 77), (12) The House of Soissons (p. 80), (13) The House of Courtenay (p.

82), (14) Cardinal de Retz (p. 88), (15) Cardinal Antonio (p. 96), (16) The chancellor (p. 99), (17) M. Colbert (p. 104), (18) M. Tellier (p. 110), (19) M. de Lionne (p. 113), (20) M. Foucquet (p. 117), (21) M. de la Mignon (p. 121), (22) The Duke de S. Agnan (p. 124), (23) The Duke de Crequi (p. 127), (24) The Duke de Novailles (p. 130), (25) The Duke de Mazarine (p. 133).

These are characters in hardly more than name.

The Whores Dialogue, briefly discovering the cheats, abuses and trappaning trades which they drive, their ways to entice young cullies, their alluring looks, &c; as also a brief character of a lady of pleasure . . . by P.L. for T. Passenger, on London Bridge, 1668.*

Cleveland, John.

J. Cleaveland Revived: Poems, Orations, Epistles, And other of his Genuine Incomparable Pieces . . . This Fourth Edition . . . is enriched with the Authors Midsummer-Moon, or Lunacy-Rampant. Being an University Caracter, a short survey of some of the late fellows of the Colledges. Now at last publisht from his Original Copies by some of his intrusted Friends. . . . London, Printed for Nathaniel Brooks . . . 1668.

8°, text pp. 1–182.
(1–3) as in 1660.
Murphy 63, 139. BSC 2354.

Cowley, Abraham.

The Works of Mr. Abraham Cowley. Consisting of Those which were formerly Printed: And Those which he Design'd for the Press, Now Published out of the Authors Original Copies. London, Printed by J.M. for Henry Herringman . . . 1668.

4° (prefatory pages folio), text sigs. D–Ddd2.
(1) Abraham Cowley, by Thomas Sprat (sig. A), (2) Cutter of Coleman Street, (3) The Puritan and the Papist.
Often reprinted.

Ellis, Clement.

The Gentile Sinner. The Fourth Edition. Oxford: Printed by Henry Hall, for Edward and John Forrest. 1668.*

Murphy 142. BSC 2352.
Reprinted from 1660.

Gailhard, Jean.

The Present State of the Princes and Republicks of Italy . . . with a character of Spain. London, 1668.*

Hardy, Nathaniel.

The Royal Common-wealths man: Or, King David's Picture, Represented in a Sermon Preached at the Solemnity of the Funeral of Sir Tho. Adams Knight and Baronet, and Alderman of London. . . . On the 10th of March, 1667. By Nath. Hardy, D.D.D.R. . . . In the Savoy. Printed by Tho. Newcomb, for William Grantham, at the Sign of the Black Bear in Westminster-Hall. 1668.*

4°, text pp. 1–40.

[Head, Richard, and Kirkman, Francis.]

The English Rogue Continued, In the Life Of Meriton Latroon . . . The Second Part. Licensed Feb. 22. 1668. London: Printed for Francis Kirkman . . . 1668.

8°, text pp. 1–374 (misprinted 366).
(1) A taylor (p. 109), (2) A list of 26 kinds of rogues (p. 132), (3) A canting rogue (p. 139), (4) A libertine zealot (p. 286).
Murphy 144.

The dedication is signed Fra. Kirkman. Nos. 1 and 3 are taken from Overbury, no. 2 from Harman.

Willan, Leonard.

The Perfect States-Man, or, Ministers of State . . . Savoy, Printed by T. Newcomb, 1668.*

Text pp. 1–198.

1669

Anonymous.

Character of Moderation. 1669.*

The Freshman's Speech. Characters and Verses. Manuscript, dated 1669.*
BSC 2357.

[Charleton, Walter.]

Two Discourses. I. Concerning the Different Wits of Men: II. Of The Mysteries of Vintners. . . . London, Printed by R.W. for William Whitwood . . . 1669.

8°, text pp. 1–230.
(1) The ready or nimble wit (p. 54), (2) The ranging wit (p. 62), (3) The slow but sure wit (p. 74), (4) The indoles or ample wit (p. 79), (5) The malignant wit (p. 112).

Cleveland, John.

Poems. By John Cleaveland. With Additions, never before Printed. [ornament: crown] London, Printed by J.R. for John Williams, 1669.

8°, text pp. 1–230.
(1–4) as in 1654.

Murphy 63, 137. BSC 2354. Pforzheimer Catalogue No. 186.

[Earle, John.]

Micro-cosmographie: Or, a Piece of the World Discovered; In Essayes, And Characters. The Ninth Edition. . . . London, Printed by Thomas Ratcliffe and Thomas Daniel for Philip Chetwind. 1669.

12°, text pp. 1–276.
(1–78) as in 1633.
Murphy 42. BSC 2356.

[Felltham, Owen.]

A Brief Character of the Low Countries under the States. 1669.*

The existence of this edition has not been verified. If it is correct, it must be a reprint of 1659.

Gailhard, Jean.

The Present State of the Princes and Republicks of Italy . . . with a Character of Spain. London, 1669. 2nd edition.*

Reprinted from 1668.

Ingelo, Nathaniel.

Bentivolo and Urania, In Six Books. By Nathaniel Ingelo D.D. The Second Edition. . . . London, Printed for T. Dring . . . 1669.

4°, in 2 parts, text pp. 1–171, 1–219.
(1–17) as in Part I, 1660, (18–32) as (1–15) in Part II, 1664.

[Jones, Andrew?]

The Dreadful Character of a Drunkard. Glasgow: Sanders. 1669.*
See 1678.

Mackenzie, Sir George.

[First title] Moral Gallantry. A Discourse . . . By Sir George Mackenzie. . . . Printed at Edenburgh, and Re-printed at London, by J. Streater, 1669.
[Second title] A Moral Paradox . . . By Sir George Mackenzie. . . . Printed at Edenburgh, and Re-printed at London, by J. Streater, 1669.

12°, in 3 parts, text pp. 1–124, 1–89, 1–38.
(1) as in 1667.

Naylor, Joseph.

Life of Thomas Morton.*
(1) Thomas Morton.

Peacham, Henry.

The worth of a Penny. London, Printed by S. Griffin. 1669.*
Murphy 133.

[Price, Lawrence.]

The Vertuous Wife. 1669.*

1670

Anonymous.

The Character Of a true and false Shepherd: With A general admonition to Ministers, being very seasonable for the present times. . . . Printed in the Year 1670.

4°, text pp. 2–24.
Begins: "It is worthy of examination."

The Old Pudding-pye Woman set forth in her Colours.*

The True Character of Sundry Traites and Callings, Or a new Ditty of Innocent Mirth. London.*

Reprinted from 1667.

Bacon, Sir Francis.

Resuscitatio; or, bringing into Public Light several pieces of the Works . . . of Sir Francis Bacon . . . the third edition. By William Rawley. 1670.*

4°, text sigs. B–Ov.
(1) as (1) in 1657.

In the Harvard copy used for this note the title page is lacking.

Blount, Thomas.

The Academy of Eloquence. Fourth Edition. 1670.*

Casa, Giovanni della.

The Arts Of Grandeur and Submission . . . Written in Latin by Joannes Casa . . . and rendered into English. By Henry Stubbe Oxon. Now Physician at Warwick. The Second Edition. . . . London, Printed by T.J. for William Lee . . . 1670.

8°, text pp. 1–68.
(1) Rich men (p. 16), (2) Men newly made rich (p. 18), (3) Men that are in power (p. 20), (4) The poorer sort (p. 20).

de la Chambre, Marin Cureau.

The Art to know Men. 1670.*

[Eachard, John.]

Some Observations upon the Answer to an Enquiry into the Grounds and Occasions of the Contempt of the Clergy. 1670.*

Attributed to Eachard by the CBEL. See 1671.

[Felltham, Owen.]

A Perfect Description of . . . Scotland. 1670.*
See his Batavia, 1672.

[Geree, John.]

The Character Of an Old English Protestant; Formerly Called A Puritan; Now a Non-Conformist.

s.sh.fo.

Murphy 108.

<small>This sheet bears no date or printer's name. The Bodleian copy is dated in manuscript (by Anthony Wood?): "St. Peters day 1670." A reprint of Geree's The Character of an Old English Puritan, 1646.</small>

[Hickeringill, Edmund.]

Priestcraft, its Character and Consequences. Second Edition. Printed by B. Bragge.*

BSC 2361.

<small>There were other editions.</small>

[Kirke, Thomas.]

A Modern Account of Scotland: being an exact description of the Country, and a true Character of the People and their Manners. Written by an English Gentleman from thence.*

Palmer, Herbert.

Memorials Of Godliness & Christianity. In Three Parts. Part. I. Containing Meditations. . . . The Tenth Edition Corrected and Enlarged. By Herbert Palmer, B.D. late Master of Queens Col. Camb. London, Printed for Henry Million . . . 1670.

12°, text pp. 1–119.

(1–2) as in 1657.

Patrick, Simon.

The Parable of the Pilgrim. 1670.*

Pierce, Thomas.

The Signal Diagnostick Whereby We are to judge of our own Affections . . . By Tho. Pierce. D.D. London, Printed by R.N. for R. Royston . . . 1670.

4°, text pp. 1–167.

(1) One that truly loves Christ (p. 41).

Pierce, Thomas.

The Sinner Impleaded In His Own Court . . . The Third Edition . . . By Tho. Pierce Rector of Brington . . . London, Printed by R.N. for R. Royston . . . 1670.

4°, text pp. 1–256.

(1) The man of pride (p. 27), (2) The covetous and worldly man (p. 28), (3) The envious malicious man (p. 30), (4) The rageful impatient man (p. 32), (5) The man of lust and uncleanness (p. 33), (6) The very followers of Eudoxus (p. 34), (7) The reveller (p. 35), (8) The highway-thief (p. 35).

[Preston, Richard Graham, Viscount.]

Angliæ Speculum Morale; The Morale State Of England, With The several Aspects it beareth To Virtue and Vice. . . . London, Printed for Henry Herringman . . . 1670.

8°, text pp. 1–187.

(1) The noble man (p. 8), (2) The courtier (p. 17), (3) The gentleman (p. 24), (4) The gallant or hector (p. 31), (5) The virtuoso (p. 38), (6) The divine (p. 47), (7) The physitian (p. 52), (8) The lawyer (p. 57), (9) The poet (p. 65), (10) The woman (p. 73), (11) The maid (p. 80), (12) The wife (p. 84), (13) The widow (p. 94). BSC 2360.

<small>Attributed to Preston by the CBEL.</small>

Willan, Leonard.

The Exact Politician, Or, Compleat Statesman: Briefly and Methodically Resolved into such Principles, whereby Gentlemen may be Qualified for the Managment of any Publick Trust. . . . Written by Leonard Willan Esq. . . . London: Printed for Dorman Newman . . . MDCLXX.

fo, text pp. 1–198.

(1) Prudence (p. 27).

BSC 2362.

1671

Bacon, Sir Francis.

Resvscitatio Or, bringing into Pvblick Light Several Pieces Of The Works . . . Of . . . Francis Bacon. . . . The Third Edition. . . . Together With his Lordships Life. By William Rawley. . . . London Printed by S.G. and B.G. for William Lee . . . 1671.

4°, 8 parts, separately paged.

(1–4) as in 1661.

[Eachard, John.]

Some Observations Upon The Answer To an Enquiry into the Grounds & Occasions Of The Contempt Of The Clergy: With some Additions. In a Second Letter to R.L. By the same Author. London, Printed for N. Brooke . . . 1671.

8°, text pp. 1–200.

(1) A young pert soph. from the universities (p. 142), (2) The small ingeniosa or experimenteer (p. 146), (3) The young gentleman of fashion (p. 149), (4) The modish, grave, and well considering gentleman (p. 150), (5) The tearer and confounder of all that belongs to divinity (p. 161), (6) The disciples of Mr. Hobbes (p. 196).

<small>There were three editions in 1671.</small>

[Head, Richard.]

The Character Of A Quaker In his true and

proper Colours; Or, The Clownish Hypocrite Anatomized. . . . Licensed and Entred according to Order. London, Printed for T. Egglesfield. 1671.

4°, text pp. 1–17.
Begins: "A Quaker is a *Vessel of Phanaticisme* drawn off to the Lees."
Murphy 108.

The address to the reader is signed R.H. D'Foe's Answer to the Quakers Catechism, 1706, is almost a reprint.

[Head, Richard.]

The English rogue . . . London, Printed for Francis Kirkman . . . 1671.

8°, text sigs. B–Hhh8v. (Part I only.)
(1–3) as in 1665.
Murphy 144.

Herbert, George.

A Priest To The Temple . . . By Mr. George Herbert . . . The Second Edition . . . London, Printed by T. Roycroft . . . 1671.

8°, text pp. 1–139.
(1) as in Herbert's Remains, 1652.
Murphy 135.

Lake, John.

Στεφανος Πιστου: or the True Christians Character & Crown. Described in a Sermon . . . at the Funeral of Mrs. William Cade. London, by William Godbid. 1671.*

(1) Mrs. William Cade.
BSC 2364.

Probably reprinted 1690 as The Character of a True Christian.

Newcastle, Margaret Cavendish, Duchess of.

The World's Olio . . . The Second Edition. . . . London, Printed by A. Maxwell, in the Year 1671.

4°, text pp. 1–424.
(1–8) as in 1655.

Panton, Edward.

Speculum Juventutis: or, a true Mirror; where Errors in Breeding Noble and Generous Youth, with the Miseries and Mischiefs that usually attend it, are clearly made manifest; as likewise Remedies for every growing Evil. . . . By Capt. Edw. Panton, Patrophilus. . . . London, Printed for Charles Smith, and Thomas Burrell . . . 1671.

8°, text pp. 1–403.
(1) Proud persons (p. 143), (2) A civil well-bred person (p. 150), (3) The young (p. 171), (4) Old men (p. 172), (5) Men of middle age (p. 174), (6) Nobles (p. 174), (7) The rich (p. 174).

[Rudyard, Thomas?]

The Libeller Characteriz'd By his own Hand. In Answer To A Scurrilous Pamphlet, Intituled, The Character of a Quaker, &c. . . . Printed in the Year, 1671.

4°, text pp. 1–8.
Begins: "He is an entire lover of his *Party*."
Murphy 109.

This book is signed T.R.

1672

Anonymous.

The Coffee House Or News-Mongers Hall. In which is shewn their seueral sorts of Passions, Containing Newes from all our Neighbour Nations. A Poem. . . . London, Printed by E. Crouch, for T. Vere . . . 1672.

s.sh.fo. In verse.
Murphy 76.

A reprint of News from the Coffee-House, 1667.

The Fox Unkennel'd; Or, The Whiggs Idol. By a Young Nobleman of the University of Oxford. . . . London, Printed by J. Benson in the Strand. [1672?]

s.sh.fo. In verse.
Begins: "If Men are deem'd for Loyalty."
Murphy 145.

A character of James Butler, first Duke of Ormond, or of a good soldier and statesman in general.

The Phanatick Anatomized. . . . [colophon] London, Printed, Anno Domini: 1672.

s.sh.fo. In verse.
Begins: "A True Phanatick to Anatomize."
Murphy 146.

Plus Ultra Or The Second Part Of the Character of a Quaker With Reflections on a Pittiful Sheet, Pretended to be an Answer to the Former. . . . London, Printed, and are to be sold by the Booksellers of London, or else where. 1672.

4°, text pp. 1–12.
Begins: "A Quaker is an *Everlasting Argument*."
Murphy 109.

An answer to Rudyard's The Libeller Characterized, 1671.

Bona, Giovanni.

Manuductio ad Cœlum: Or, A Guide To Eternity; Extracted out of the Writings of the Holy Fathers, And Antient Philosophers. Written originally in Latine, By John Bona . . . And now done into English. London, Printed by A.C. for Henry Brome . . . 1672.

8°, text pp. 1–239.
(1) The angry man (p. 47), (2) A proud man (p. 68), (3) A man of fortitude (p. 199), (4) A magnanimous man (p. 205), (5) An humble man (p. 231), (6) A perfect man (p. 236).
Murphy 145.

The translation is by Sir Roger L'Estrange. In later editions the title is sometimes as above, sometimes A Guide to Eternity. The short poem published under this title in 1681 is so different that it is not included here.

Cherbury, Edward Herbert, First Baron Herbert of.

The Life and Raigne of King Henry the Eighth. 1672.*
Reprinted from 1649.

[Eachard, John.]

Some Observations upon the Answer To an Enquiry into the Grounds & Occasions Of The Contemt Of The Clergy . . . By the same Authour. The Fourth Edition. London, Printed by E. Tyler . . . 1672.
8°, text pp. 1–220.
(1–6) as in 1671.

Ellis, Clement.

The Gentile Sinner. The Fifth Edition. 1672.*
Murphy 142.

[Felltham, Owen.]

Batavia: Or The Hollander displayed: In Brief Characters & Observations . . . Also, A Perfect Description Of the People & Country Of Scotland. London, Printed for G. Widdowes . . . 1672.
12°, text pp. 1–89.
(1) Hollanders (p. 17), (2) The Scotch (p. 81).

At p. 71 there is a separate title page: A Perfect Description Of The People And Country of Scotland. London, Printed for Rich. Lownds, 1670. But the paging is continuous. The authorship of this and some other pieces attributed to Felltham in the present volume is uncertain. A Perfect Description is sometimes attributed to James Howell and sometimes to Sir Anthony Weldon.

Geree, John.

The Character Of an Old English Puritan, Or Non-Conformist. By John Geree M.A. and late Preacher of the Word at St. Albans. Published according to Order. London; Printed in the Year, 1672.*
4°, text pp. 1–6.
Begins: "The Old English Puritane was such an one, that honoured God above all."
Murphy 102. BSC 2128, 2366.

[Head, Richard.]

The Character of a Quaker, in his true and proper Colours, Or The Clowning Hypocrite

anatomized. The First Part. Sic oculos, sic Ille manus, sic ora movebat. Licensed and Entered according to order. London, Printed and are to be sold by the Booksellers of London or else-where. 1672.*
4°, text pp. 1–17.
Begins: "A Quaker is a Vessel of Phanaticisme."
BSC 2365.

[Head, Richard, and Kirkman, Francis.]

The English Rogue . . . London, Printed for Francis Kirkman . . . 1672.*
8°, 4 parts in 2 vols.
(1–3) as in 1665, (4–7) as (1–4) in 1668.
Murphy 143.

[Le Pays, René.]

The Drudge: Or The Jealous Extravagant. 1672.*
See 1673.

[Marvell, Andrew.]

The Character Of Holland. London, Printed for Rob. Horn . . . 1672.
4°, text pp. 1–5. In verse.
Begins: "*Holland*, that scarce deserves the name of Land."
BSC 2367.

Mede, Joseph.

The Works Of The Pious and Profoundly-Learned Joseph Mede, B.D. . . . London, Printed by Roger Norton, for Richard Royston . . . MDCLXXII.
6°, text pp. 1–923.
(1) Joseph Mede, anonymous (p. xiv).

[Ramesey, William.]

The Gentlemans Companion: or, a Character of True Nobility, and Gentility: In the way of an Essay. By a Person of Quality. . . . London, Printed by E. Okes, for Rowland Reynolds . . . 1672.
8°, text pp. 1–242.
(1) Superstitious persons (p. 41), (2) The truly generous person (p. 144).
BSC 2369.

Attributed to Ramesey by the CBEL.

[Walker, Obadiah.]

Of Education. 1672.*
See 1673.

[Winstanley, William.]

Poor Robins Character of a Dutch-Man, As also his Predictions On the affairs of the United Provinces Of Holland. Together With a brief

Epitomy of the Ingratitude of the Dutch, and their barbarous cruelties committed on the English . . . London, Printed for Benjamin Harris . . . 1672.

4°, text pp. 1–6.
Begins: "*Europe* now being the Stage of Action."
Murphy 146. BSC 2368.

Attributed to Winstanley because he frequently used Poor Robin as a pseudonym.

Wotton, Sir Henry.

Reliquiæ Wottonianæ: Or, A Collection Of Lives, Letters, Poems: With Characters Of Sundry Personages: And other Incomparable Pieces of Language and Art. . . . By . . . Sir Henry Wotton Kt. The Third Edition, with large Additions. London, Printed by T. Roycroft, for R. Marriott, F. Tyton, T. Collins, and J. Ford, 1672.

8°, text pp. 1–582.
(1–5) as in 1651.

Maggs Brothers (Mercurius Britannicus, no. 72, 1942, item 965) offered a presentation copy from Izaak Walton to his daughter Anne Hawkins.

1673

Anonymous.

The Character Of A Coffee-House, With The Symptomes Of A Town-Wit. With Allowance, April 11th. 1673. . . . London, Printed for Jonathan Edwin . . . 1673.

fo, text pp. 1–6.
Begins: "A Coffee-House is a *Lay-Conventicle*."
Murphy 76. BSC 2371, 2372, 2373.

A different work from the same title in 1665.

The Character Of A Papist. . . . London, Printed in the Year 1673.

4°, text pp. 1–8.
(1) A papist (p. 3), (2) A papist (p. 7, in verse).
Murphy 109.

Holborn-Drollery, Or, The Beautiful Chloret Surprized In The Sheets: All the Love-Songs and Poems with which she hath been Treated this Long-Vacation being Publish'd. To which is Annexed, Flora's Cabinet Unlocked. . . . London: Printed for Robert Robinson . . . 1673.

8°, text pp. 1–96. In verse.
(1) On jealousie (or a jealous husband) (p. 81), (2) On melancholy (p. 83).

The London Prodigal, Or the Unfortunate Spendthrift. . . . London, Printed by J.W. for R.C. . . . 1673.

s.sh.fo. In verse.
Begins: "Oft have I wonder'd at the various state."
Murphy 146.

The play entitled The London Prodigall, 1605, sometimes attributed to Shakespeare, is an entirely different work.

Raillerie a la Mode Consider'd . . . MDC-LXXIII.

See note to 1663.

Bona, Giovanni.

A Gvide to Heaven: Or Morall Instrvctions Compiled Partly out of the Maximes of holy Fathers, and partly out of the Sentences of Antient Philosophers. Written in Latin by the Reverend Father D. John de Bona. . . . Translated into English by Iames Price. Printed at Roan: 1673.

8°, text pp. 1–216.
(1–6) as in his Manuductio ad Cœlum, 1672.
Murphy 146. BSC 2370.

Though by a different translator, this version of Bona's work has substantially the same contents as L'Estrange's.

[C., S.]

The Art Of Complaisance Or The Means to oblige in Conversation. . . . London, Printed for John Starkey . . . 1673.

12°, text pp. 1–180.
(1) A sanguine prince (p. 106), (2) A choleric man (p. 148), (3) A fearful man (p. 151), (4) A youth (p. 165), (5) An old man (p. 169), (6) A man of middle age (p. 172), (7) Those of noble birth (p. 174), (8) The rich (p. 174), (9) The powerful (p. 175).

Largely an adaptation of Eustache du Refuge's Traité de la Cour [1616?], according to the CBEL.

Dare, Josiah.

Counsellor Manners His Last Legacy To His Son . . . By Josiah Dare . . . London, Printed for Edward Gough . . . 1673.

8°, text pp. 1–156.
(1) An ideal wife (p. 87).

Based on Della Casa's Galateo. Attributed to Dare by the CBEL. A border-line example of character.

Flecknoe, Richard.

A Collection Of the choicest Epigrams And Characters Of Richard Flecknoe. Being rather a New Work, then a New Impression of the Old. . . . Printed for the Author. 1673.

4°, in 2 parts, text pp. 1–99, 1–64.
(1–44) characters reprinted from previous editions of 1658, 1660, 1665, and 1666 (Part I), (45) Of these characters (Part II, p. 1), (46) Of a running head (II, 2), (47) Of our modern censurers

(II, 5), (48) Of a common newsmonger (II, 6), (39) Of poetry and its abuse (II, 14), (50) Of an unconstant disposition (II, 17), (51) Of a profess'd coward (II, 20), (52) Of a meer libertine (II, 25), (53) Of one ridiculously proud of his estate (II, 36), (54) Of a modern fanatick sectary (II, 37), (55) Of a gentleman turned clown (II, 44), (56) Old age (II, 47), (57) Of a tepid timorous Christian (II, 51), (58) Of a mischievous disposition (II, 54), (59) Of an honest man (II, 59), (60) Of a rich miser (II, 61), (61) Of one who is never content (II, 61), (62) Kindness (II, 62), (63) Of the Parliament, in answer to the ignorant objections of some strangers (II, 63).

Murphy 68. BSC 2376.

Reprinted 1677 (as Seventy Eight Characters).

Geree, John.

The Character Of the Sober Non-Conformist. By John Geree M.A. and late Preacher of the Word at St. Albans. Published According to Order. London; Printed in the Year, 1673.

4°, text pp. 1–6.
Begins: "The Old English Puritane was such an one, that honoured God above all."
Murphy 103. BSC 2377.
A reprint of Geree's The Character of an Old English Puritan, 1646.

[H., J., and others.]

Essays Of Love and Marriage: Being Letters written by two Gentlemen; One dissuading from Love, the other an Answer thereunto. With some Characters and other Passages of Wit. . . . London, Printed for H. Brome . . . 1673.

12°, text pp. 1–103.
(1–13) as in Two Essays of Love and Marriage, 1657.
Murphy 72.

[Head, Richard.]

The Canting Academy, Or, The Devils Cabinet Opened. . . . London, Printed by F. Leach for Mat. Derw, and are to be sold by the Booksellers. 1673.

12°, text pp. 1–192.
(1) The upright man (p. 59), (2) A ruffler (p. 65), (3) Anglers (p. 68), (4) Rogues (p. 69), (5) Wild rogues (p. 70), (6) Priggers of prancers (p. 71), (7) Palliards or clapperdogeons (p. 73), (8) Fraters (p. 77), (9) Quire birds (p. 77), (10) Abram-men (p. 78), (11) Whip-jacks (p. 78), (12) Mumpers (p. 79), (13) Dommerars (p. 81), (14) Jack-men (p. 81), (15) Patrico's (p. 82), (16) Irish toils or swig-men (p. 82), (17) Kyncheon coes (p. 83), (18) Glymmerers (p. 84), (19) Bawdy-baskets (p. 85), (20) Autem-morts (p.

85), (21) Strowling-morts (p. 86), (22) Doxies (p. 86), (23) Dells (p. 87), (24) Kynchin-morts (p. 87), (25) The high-pad (p. 88), (26) The low-pad (p. 93), (27) The gilt (p. 94), (28) The budge (p. 95), (29) The ken-miller (p. 96), (30) The huff (p. 97), (31) The file and bulker (p. 99), (32) The moon-curser (p. 101), (33) The bawd, pimp, and whore (p. 102), (34) The shop-lift (p. 106), (35) The night-walker and diver (p. 107).

The characters are taken from Head's English Rogue and from Awdeley and Dekker; see Studies in Philology, XXXVIII (1941), 470.
Attributed to Head by the CBEL.

Ingelo, Nathaniel.

Bentivolo And Urania. In Six Books. By Nathanael Ingelo D.D. The Third Edition . . . London, Printed by T.R. . . . MDCLXXIII.

4°, in 2 parts, text pp. 1–171, 1–219.
(1–32) as in 1669.

Jackson, Thomas.

The Works Of The Reverend And Learned Divine, Thomas Jackson, D.D. . . . In Three Volumes. . . . London: Printed by Andrew Clark, for John Martyn, Richard Chiswell, and Joseph Clark . . . MDCLXXIII.

4°, 3 vols.
(1) Thomas Jackson, by E. Vaghan (Vol. I, sig. *).

[Kirkman, Francis.]

The Unlucky Citizen: Experimentally Described In The Various Misfortunes Of an Unlucky Londoner . . . Intermixed with severall Choice Novels . . . London, Printed by Anne Johnson, for Fra. Kirkman . . . 1673.

8°, text pp. 1–296.
(1) A vicious stepmother (p. 157), (2) A kind master (p. 171).
The preface is signed F.K., and Kirkman's portrait is the frontispiece.

Le Pays, René.

The Drudge: or the Jealous Extravagant. A Piece of Gallantry. . . . London, Printed for Henry Herringman . . . 1673.

8°, text pp. 1–98.
(1) The Duke of Savoy (p. 3), (2) Lycidas, a cavalier skilled in any other virtues than military ones (p. 12), (3) Zelotide, a covetous charmer (p. 15).
Le Pays's signature occurs in several places: for example, on p. 98. The epistle dedicatory is signed J.B. [i.e., John Bulteel?]. Attributed to Le Pays by the CBEL.

Mayo, Richard.

The Life of Edmund Staunton. 1673.*
(1) Edmund Staunton.

Overbury, Sir Thomas.

The Illustrious Wife, viz. that excellent Poem, Sir Thomas Overburie's Wife, illustrated by Giles Oldisworth, nephew to the same Sir T. O. 1673.*

Mentioned in Rimbault's Overbury. No copy has been found.

Patrick, Simon.

The Parable of the Pilgrim. Fourth edition. 1673.*

[Ramesey, William.]

The Character Of A Quack-Astrologer: Or, The Spurious Prognosticator Anatomiz'd. . . . London, Printed, and are to be Sold at the Book-sellers Shops, 1673.

4°, text sigs. A3–C4v.
Begins: "A Quack Astrologer is a *Gypsy* of the upper Form."
Murphy 83. BSC 2374, 2375.

[Walker, Obadiah.]

Of Education Especially of Young Gentlemen. In Two Parts. Oxon. At the Theater. Ann. 1673.

8°, text pp. 1–291.
(1) A good educator (p. 25), (2) His title of gentleman (p. 54), (3) The proud man (p. 87).
Attributed to Walker by the CBEL.

[Walker, Obadiah.]

Of Education. Especially of Young Gentlemen. In Two Parts. The Second impression with additions. Oxon. At the Theater Ann. 1673.

12°, text pp. 1–280.
(1–3) as in first impression, 1673.

1674

Anonymous.

An Answer To The Geneva Ballad . . . [colophon] Printed in the year, 1674.

s.sh.fo. In verse.
Begins: "Of all the *Drolsters* in the Town."

This is a character of "Spruce," a "sacred *Proteus* that can, Blend *Gospel* with the *Alchoran*," and that "takes *Texts* from *Leviathan*."

The Character of a bawd: or, a description of their ways and means how they get money, by impoverishing others to enrich themselves. . . . London, Printed for J. Hose, 1674.*
Bibliotheca Heberiana, I, 73. Bernard Quaritch, General Catalogue, No. 22589.

Flos Ingenii vel Evacuatio Descriptionis. Being an Exact Description of Epsam, and

Epsam Wells . . . London Printed in the year 1674.*
s.sh.fo.
(1) Epsom Wells.

Gallantry A-la-mode, A Satyrical Poem, In III Parts. Representing the Vanities of several Humours of this present Age. . . . London, Printed by T.R. & N.T. for the Author . . . 1674.

8°, text pp. 1–138. In verse.
(1) Time (p. 69), (2) Formality (p. 79).

The Women's Petition against Coffee. 1674.*
BSC 2388.

[Butler, Samuel.]

The Geneva Ballad. To the Tune of 48. London: Printed for Henry Brome . . . MDC-LXXIV.

s.sh.fo. In verse.
Begins: "Of all the *Factions* in the Town."

There were two editions of this year. The character is of a Presbyterian parson.

[Cotton, Charles.]

The Compleat Gamester: Or, Instructions How to play at Billiards, Trucks, Bowls, and Chess. . . . London: Printed by A.M. for R. Cutler, and are to be sold by Henry Brome . . . 1674.

8°, text pp. 1–232.
(1) A gamester (p. 21), (2) A bowling-ally (p. 49).

The character of a bowling-ally borrows heavily from Earle. Attributed to Cotton by the CBEL.

Davies, John, of Kidwelly, translator.

Prudential Reflections, Moral Considerations, and Stoical Maximes. Written originally in the Spanish Tongue. English'd by J.D. of Kidwelly. London: Printed by Jas. Cotterel. 1674.*
(1) A wise man (p. 171), (2) A good man (p. 172).

Flatman, Thomas.

Poems and Songs. By Thomas Flatman. London, Printed by S. and B.G. . . . 1674.

8°, text pp. 1–140.
(1) The happy man (p. 50), (2) A belly god (p. 118).

Golborne, J.

A Friendly Apology, In the behalf of the Womans Excellency: Together with some Examples of Women-Worthies. As also the Character of a Virtuous and Accomplished Woman

. . . Written in verse by J. Golborne, some-time Fellow of Trinity Colledge near Dvblin. . . . London, Printed, for Henry Mortlock . . . 1674.

12°, text pp. 1–68. In verse.
(1) A virtuous and accomplished woman (p. 48).

[H., J., and others.]

Essays of Love and Marriage. Being Letters written by two Gentlemen . . . 1674.*

A reprint of Two Essays of Love and Marriage, 1657.

[Head, Richard.]

The Canting Academy, or Villanies Discovered. The Second Edition. London, Printed by F. Leach for Mat. Drew. 1674.*

(1–35) as in 1673.

Vincent, Samuel.

The Young Gallant's Academy. . . . To which is added, The Character of a Town-Huff. Together with The Character of a right Generous and well-bred Gentleman. By Sam. Vincent. London, Printed by J.C. for R. Mills . . . 1674.

8°, text pp. 1–100.
(1) A proud, huffing, self-conceited, foppish and lascivious young gallant (p. 73), (2) A true, noble, liberal, and stayed gentleman (p. 87).
Murphy 147. BSC 2378, 2379.

A variant issue giving the author's name as Sam. Overcome is in the Bodleian. The book as a whole is a modernization of Dekker's Gull's Hornbook. The two characters named are based chiefly on Overbury and Earle. See also an article by William Sloane in Modern Language Notes, LIII (1938), 114.

Wilkinson, H.

Characters of a Sincere Heart. Oxford, L. Lichfield. 1674.*
BSC 2380.

1675

Anonymous.

An answer To the Character of an Exchange-wench: Or A Vindication Of An Exchange-woman. London . . . Thomas Croskill. 1675.

4°, text pp. 1–6.
Begins: "An Exchange-Woman does as far exceed a meer Gentle-Woman. . . ."
BSC 2388. Murphy 83.

The Ape-Gentle-vvoman, Or The Character Of An Exchange-Wench. . . . London, Printed for Francis Pye. 1675.

4°, text pp. 1–6.
Begins: "She's a Huffing piece of Puff-past."
BSC 2388. Murphy 83.

The Batchellors Answer To The Maids Complaint Or The Young Men's Vindication. . . . London Printed for J. Coniers . . . 1675.

4°, text pp. 3–8.
(1) Designing women (p. 3).
BSC 2388.

The Character of a Dutchman.*

Perhaps a reference to Poor Robin's Character of a Dutchman, by (?)Winstanley, 1672.

The Character Of A Fanatick: By a Person of Quality. . . . London, Printed in the Year 1675.

4°, text pp. 3–8.
Begins: "He is a person of a more Exercised faith."
Murphy 110. BSC 2381.

The Character of a Pawnbroker. 1675.*

Possibly related in some fashion to Winstanley's (?) Four for a Penny; Or, Poor Robin's Character of an Unconscionable Pawn-broker, 1678.

The Character Of A Pilfering Taylor, Or a True Anatomy Of Monsieur Stich, In all his Tricks and Qualities. London, Printed in the Year 1675.

4°, text pp. 1–6.
Begins: "A Tailor is a Sorry piece of Mortality."
Murphy 84. BSC 2382.

The Character of a Scold. 1675.*

Perhaps an earlier form of Poor Robin's Character of a Scold, by Winstanley (?), 1678.

The Character Of A Soliciter. Or the Tricks and Quillets of a Pettyfogger. With his manifold Knaveties, Cheats, Extortions, and other Villanies. . . . London, Printed for K.C.I.F. 1675.

4°, text pp. 1–5.
Begins: "A Soliciter is a Pettyfogging Sophister."
Murphy 84. BSC 2388.

The Character of a Tallyman.*

This piece may perhaps have some relation to Winstanley's (?) Four for a Penny, 1678, which contains The Character of a Tallyman.

The Character Of A Town-Gallant; Exposing The Extravagant Fopperies of some vain Self-conceited Pretenders to Gentility and good Breeding. . . . London, Printed for W.L. 1675.

4°, text pp. 2–8.
Begins: "A *Town-Gallant* is a Bundle of *Vanity*."
Murphy 84. BSC 2384 and 2388.

The Character Of A Town-Misse . . . London, Printed for W.L. 1675.

4°, text pp. 3–8.
Begins: "A Miss is a new Name."
Murphy 85. BSC 2385, 2388.

There were two issues this year, chiefly differentiated by
the ornament on the title page. One bears a fleuron, the
other a globe.

The Character of an Ill-Husband. 1675.*

The Character Of An Informer. Wherein His
Mischeivous Nature, and Leud Practises are
Detected. . . . London, Printed for T.P. 1675.*
4°, text pp. 1–5.
Begins: "An Informer (I mean of the baser
sort)."
Murphy 110. BSC 2386.

Reprinted 1682, with some additions, as The Second Character of an Informer.

The Holborne Hector, or the Character of a
profane debauched Gentleman. London,
Printed for C.N. and are to be sold in the High
Way to Tybourn. 1675.*
4°, text pp. 1–6.
BSC 2390.

The Maids Complaint against the Batchelors
. . . London, Printed for J. Coniers . . . 1675.
4°, text pp. 3–8.
Begins: "Though Grave People tell us that Mod-
esty."
BSC 2388.

A character of a bachelor.

[Manuscript.]*
(1) A Popish priest (p. 172, no. 59b).
Royal Society (Misc. MS. 83).

The character is not dated, but most of the rest of the
manuscript is earlier than 1680.

News from Covent-Garden: or, The Town-
Gallants Vindication. Being the Debates and
Result of a famous Club of Wits, and Men of
Humours and Intrigues, assembled for the
Damning of the late Character. London,
Printed for J.T. 1675.
4°, text pp. 3–7.
Begins: "Several pretended Gallantissimo's of the
Town."
BSC 2384, 2388.

This is an answer to the Character of a Town-Gallant.

The Town Misses Declaration and Apology;
or, an Answer to the Character of a Town-
Misse: London, Printed for J.T., 1675.
4°, text pp. 3–7.
(1) A town-misse (p. 5).
BSC 2385. Murphy 85.

Barksdale, Clement.
Memorials. Examples Of Memorable Men To
awaken this Age to greater care of Good
Learning And True Religion . . . London,
For John Barksdale . . . 1675.
8°, text pp. 1–135.
(1–10) as in Memorials . . . The Fourth Decade, 1663.

[Charleton, Walter.]
Two Discourses. 1675.*
Reprinted from 1669.

[Earle, John.]
The Character Of A Tavern. With A brief
draught of a Drawer. . . . London, Printed
for D.A. 1675.
4°, text pp. 1–6.
Begins: "A Tavern is an Academy of Debauch-
ery."
Murphy 45. BSC 2383.

An adaptation of Earle's character of a tavern in his Micro-
cosmographie.

Freeman, Goodlove [pseud.?].
The Downfall Of The Bailiffs: Or a Lash for
your Bumms. Wherein The oppressions, extortions, and villanies of Catch-Poles, Serjeants,
Bailiffs, and Marshals-men, with their Yeomen,
Followers, and under Litter of Setting-Dogs,
are fully exposed and detected in their proper
colours. By Goodlove Freeman, Esquire. London, Printed for Thomas Grumbleton. 1675.
4°, text pp. 1–5.
(1) A sergeant (p. 2), (2) A common bayliff (p.
3), (3) A marshals-man (p. 3), (4) Yeomen,
followers, setters, etc. (p. 4), (5) A gaoler (p. 5).

[Hausted, Peter.]
[First title page] Ad popvlvm: Or, A Lecture
To The People. With A Satyre Against Separatists. London, Printed in the Late Times,
and now Reprinted 1675.
[Second title page] A Satyre Against Separatists. Or, The Conviction Of Chamber-
Preachers, And Other Schismaticks contrary
to the Discipline of this our Protestant Profession. London, Printed 1675.
4°, text sigs. A3–D4.
(1) A separatist preacher (sig. Dv).
The Satyre is reprinted from 1642.

[Hausted, Peter.]
A Satyre against Separatists. Or, The Con-
viction of Chamber-Preachers . . . London,
Printed 1675.

4°, text sigs. C4–D4.

Begins: "I have been where so many Brownists dwell."

Probably a detached section of his Ad Popvlvm, 1675.

[Head, Richard.]

The Miss Display'd, With all Her Wheedling Arts and Circumventions. . . . By the Author of the First Part of the English Rogue . . . London, Printed and are to be sold by the several Booksellers. 1675.

8°, text pp. 1–133.

(1) Ignatius, a lustful gallant who pretends piety (p. 17), (2) Cornelia, a successful courtisan (*passim*, but especially p. 127).

[Head, Richard.]

Proteus Redivivus: or the Art of Wheedling, or Insinuation, Obtain'd by General Conversation, and Extracted from the several Humours, Inclinations, and Passions of both Sexes, respecting their several Ages, and suiting each Profession or Occupation. Collected and Methodized By the Author of the First Part of the English Rogue. . . . London, Printed by W.D. . . . 1675.

8°, text pp. 1–352.

(1) Pretender to learning (p. 9), (2) Reserved wheedler (p. 18), (3) Dissimulating wheedle (p. 22), (4) Flattering wheedle (p. 27), (5) Humble wheedle (p. 37), (6) Civil wheedle (p. 43), (7) Affable wheedle (p. 46), (8) Plausible man (p. 48), (9) The wheedle in general (p. 49), (10) The sanguine man (p. 56), (11) Cholerick man (p. 62), (12) Phlegmatick man (p. 64), (13) Melancholy man (p. 68), (14) Dissembling wheedler (p. 88), (15) She-wheedle (p. 118), (16) Voluptuous wheedle (p. 120), (17) Hating, or selfish, wheedle (p. 129), (18) Wheedle's use of acquaintance (p. 143), (19) Gentile town-shift (p. 160), (20) Ordinary town-shift (p. 173), (21) Tavern wheedle (p. 182), (22) Barmaid (p. 188), (23) Town-shift in a coffee-house (p. 197), (24) Quacking astrological doctor (p. 206), (25) Self-edifying phanatick cheat (p. 231), (26) Covetous phanatick cheat (p. 249), (27) The shop-keeper (p. 252), (28) Practicing apothecary (p. 257), (29) Country lawyer (p. 271), (30) Pettifogger (p. 279), (31) Catch pole (p. 296), (32) Prison (p. 308), (33) Cellarman or tapster (p. 317), (34) Country hostess (p. 325), (35) Wheedling hostess (p. 334), (36) Master of a ship (p. 336), (37) The scrivener (p. 349).

Murphy 147.

Much of this work is borrowed or copied from Earle.

Herbert, George.

A Priest to the Temple. Or, The Country Parson His Character and Rule of Holy Life

By Mr. Geo. Herbert . . . The Third Impression. London, Printed by T.R. . . . 1675.

12°, text pp. 1–166.

(1) as in Herbert's Remains, 1652.

Murphy 135. BSC 2389.

Ingelo, Nathaniel.

Bentivolio and Urania. 1675.*

Reprinted from 1669.

S., J.

The Starr-Prophet Anatomiz'd & Dissected: Or, Judicial Astrologie, And The Astro-Mancers . . . By J.S. a Lover of all Laudable Arts and Sciences. [woodcut] London, Printed for M.D. Anno Domini. 1675.*

4°, text pp. 1–39.

(1) A quack ass-trologer (p. 1).

Murphy 83.

The character seems to be taken, with some changes, from William Ramesey's The Character of a Quack Astrologer, 1673.

Smith, Samuel.

The Character Of A Weaned Christian. Or The Evangelical Art of promoting Self-Denial. Being an Essay, alluding to the Severities and Advantages of Infant-Weaning, both Pleasant and Profitable. Grounded On Psal. 131.V.2,3. By S.S. M.S. Formerly Fellow of St. John Bapt. Coll. Oxon, now Minister of the Gospel in London. . . . London, Printed for Dorman Newman . . . 1675.*

8°, text pp. 1–143.

(1) A saint or weaned mortified Christian (p. 14), (2) The same (p. 62).

BSC 2391.

Traherne, Thomas.

Christian Ethicks: or, Divine Morality. Opening the Way to Blessedness, By the Rules of Vertue And Reason. By Tho. Traherne . . . London, Printed for Jonathan Edwin . . . 1675.

8°, text pp. 1–577.

(1) A perfect soul (p. 17), Divine goodness (p. 147), (3) Living power in the goodness of God (p. 157), (4) Repentance (p. 252), (5) Valour (p. 335), (6) Cowardice (p. 337), (7) Patience (p. 362), (8) Meekness (p. 378), (9) Humility (p. 400), (10) Contentment (p. 423), (11) Magnanimous soul (p. 449), (12) Modesty (p. 464), (13) Liberal man (p. 473), (14) Grateful soul (p. 543), (15) Man truly vertuous (p. 465), (16) A God-like man (p. 574).

[Winstanley, William.]

Poor Robins Character, Of an Honest Drunken Curr: With a Relation of the Frollicks of his Life, and Conversation. And his Epitaph. . . . London, Printed by E.C. for C. Hussey . . . 1675.

4°, text pp. 3–8.

Begins: "He's a Pickel'd Youth to be sure."

Attributed to Winstanley by Miss Murphy (edition of 1686).

[Winstanley, William.]

Poor Robin's True Character of a Scold, or, the Shrews Looking-Glass. Dedicated to all Domineering Dames, Wives Rampant, Cuckolds Couchant, and Henpeckt Sneaks in City or Country. 1675.*

See 1678.

1676

Anonymous.

The Art Of Making Love: Or, Rules For The Conduct Of Ladies and Gallants In their Amours . . . London, Printed by J. Cotterel for Richard Tonson . . . 1676.

12°, text pp. 1–180.

(1) A valiant man (p. 85).

According to the Address to the Reader, "part of this Book is taken from the Gallant Morale of Monsieur Boulanger."

The Character Of A Quack-Doctor, Or The Abusive Practices Of Impudent Illiterate Pretenders to Physick Exposed. . . . Licensed and Entered According to Order. . . . London, Printed for Thomas Jones, in the Year 1676.

fo, text pp. 1–6.

Begins: "A Quack-Doctor is one of the Epidemical Diseases of this Age."

Murphy 85. BSC 2392.

The New Art to Live Without Money: Or, The Town-Shift Uncas'd. Composed For the Edification of the Freshmen Of Ale-Satia. By A Select Committee Of Tatter'd Poets, Younger Brothers, and Whimsie-board Players. . . . London: Printed for D.M. in the Year 1676.

4°, text pp. 3–8.

Begins: "A True Spunger is a walking Ghost."

A Warning for House-keepers, or, A Discovery of all sorts of Thieves . . . Written by one who was a Prisoner in Newgate. London, Printed for T. Newton, 1676.*

(1) A tongue-padder, (2) A private thief.

Agrippa, Henry Cornelius.

[Of the Vanity . . . of Arts. 1676.]

8°, text pp. 1–368.

(1–9) as in 1569.

The title page is missing in the Rutgers copy, used for these notes. Though this is a different translation from that of 1569 and 1575, the content is substantially the same.

C., H.

The Character Of An Honest Lawyer. By H.C. Φιλόνομιον . . . Licensed. Aug. 29th. 1676. Roger L'Estrange. . . . London, Printed for Jonathan Edwin . . . 1676.*

fo, text sigs. A2–B2.

Murphy 86. BSC 2393.

Chevreau, Urbain.

The Mirror of Fortune: or, the true Character of Fate and Destiny, &c. &c. Written in French by Monsieur Chevreau, and newly translated into English by D. Decoisnon. In the Savoy. Printed by T.N. and are to be sold by Sam. Lowndes. 1676.*

8°.

[Cotton, Charles.]

The Compleat Gamester. 1676.*

Dryden, John.

Aureng-Zebe: A Tragedy. . . . Written by John Dryden. . . . London: Printed by T.N. for Henry Herringman. . . . 1676.

4°, text pp. 1–86.

(1) A courtier without wit (dedication, sig. A2).

Pforzheimer Catalogue No. 319.

Often reprinted.

[Earle, John.]

Micro-cosmographie. Printed for S. Crouch. 1676.*

(1–78) as in 1633.

BSC 2395.

This is the edition of 1669 with a new title page.

Etheredge, Sir George.

The Man of Mode, Or, Sr Fopling Flutter. A Comedy. . . . By George Etheredge Esq;. Licensed, June 3. 1676. Roger L'Estrange. London, Printed by J. Macock, for Henry Herringman . . . 1676.

4°, text pp. 1–96.

(1) Sir Fopling Flutter, a fop (Act I, scene i, p. 12).

Pforzheimer Catalogue No. 360.

Frequently reprinted.

Flatman, Thomas.

Poems And Songs. By Thomas Flatman. The Second Edition With Additions and Amendments. . . . London, Printed by S. and B.G.

for Benjamin Took . . . and Jonathan Edwin . . . 1676.

8°, text pp. 1–141.

(1–2) as in 1674.

Guidott, Thomas.

A Discourse of Bathe . . . with An Account of the Lives, and Character of the Physicians of Bathe. By Tho. Gvidott . . . London, Printed for Henry Brome . . . 1676.

8°, text pp. 1–200.

(1) The physicians of Bathe (p. 163; fifteen sketches).

BSC 2396.

Mazarine, Ortesia de la Porte, Duchess of.

The Memoires Of The Dutchess Mazarine, Out of French. London Printed, and are to be Sold by William Cademan . . . 1676.

8°, text pp. 1–130.

(1) The Duchess of Mazarine (p. 115).

There were several other editions, both in 1676 and in other years.

[Perrinchief, Richard.]

The Sicilian Tyrant: or, The Life of Agathocles. London, Printed by J. Grover for R. Royston . . . 1676.

8°, text pp. 1–278.

(1–2) as in The Syracusan Tyrant, 1661.

The preface to the reader is signed Rich. Perrinchiefe. From the tone of the address it is evident that Oliver Cromwell is the real usurper in view.

[Ramesey, William.]

The Gentleman's Companion. 1676.*

Reprinted from 1672.

Shadwell, Thomas.

The Virtuoso. A Comedy. . . . Written by Thomas Shadwell. . . . London, Printed by T.N. for Henry Herringman . . . 1676.

4°, text pp. 1–100.

(1) Sir Nicholas, the virtuoso (p. 9).

There were several later editions.

[Williams, Nathaniel?]

Imago Sæculi: The Image Of The Age, Represented in Four Characters. Viz, The Ambitious Statesman. Insatiable Miser. Atheisticall Gallant. Factious Schismatick. . . . By the same Authour. N.W. . . . Oxford, Printed by H.H. and L.L. for John Nixon. 1676.

8°, text pp. 1–108. In verse.

(1) The ambitious statesman (p. 1), (2) The insatiable miser (p. 25), (3) The atheisticall gallant (p. 49), (4) The factious schismatick (p. 77).

BSC 2399.

Sometimes attributed to N. West.

1677

Anonymous.

Character of the English by a French Author. 1677.*

The Devil and Broker Or A Character Of A Pawn Broker In A Merry Dialogue. . . . London, Printed for J.C. 1677.

4°, text pp. 1–7.

Begins: "A Certain North-Country Man by name John *Plugg*."

Poor Robin's Visions: wherein is described the present Humours of the Times; the Vices and fashionable Fopperies thereof . . . Discovered in a dream. London: Arthur Boldero, 1677.*

(1) Charon (p. 43).

The Present State Of Christendome And The Interest of England, With a Regard to France. In a Letter to a Friend. London, Printed by J.B. for H. Brome . . . 1677.

4°, text pp. 1–28.

(1) The English (p. 5).

BSC 2401.

The character, given in both French and English, is taken from the Politique de France.

The Smithfield Jockey: Or, the Character and Original Of A Horse-Courser. With the Tricks and Rogueries Of An Ostler. Published for the benefit of Gentlemen and others. London, Printed for W.D. 1677.*

[cancel-title:] A Whip For A Jockey: Or, A Character Of An Horse-Courser. London, Printed for R.H. 1677.

8°, text pp. 1–29.

Murphy 86.

The cancel-title is found in a copy in the Bodleian, described by Miss Murphy.

A Whip For A Jockey: Or, A Character Of An Horse-Courser. London, Printed for R.H. 1677.

8°, text pp. 1–29.

See The Smithfield Jockey, 1677, for which this is a cancel-title.

The Young Maids Character of an Ungrateful Batchellor: Being a full discovery of all those Tricks, Cheats, and Delusions, whereby young men do often deceive, and many times ruine their too credulous Sweethearts. Written by one who has undergone the Martyrdom of their cruelty, and would have all her loving Sisters beware the same fate, 1677.*

Bragge, Robert.

The Life and Death of the Godly Man Exemplified in a funeral sermon on the Rev. Thos. Wadsworth, London, for Dorman Newman, 1677.

4°, text pp. 1–32.

(1) Thomas Wadsworth.

[C., S.]

The Art of Complaisance Or The Means to oblige in Conversation. . . . The Second Edition. London . . . John Starkey . . . 1677.

12°, text pp. 1–180.

(1–9) as in 1673.

Cleveland, John.

Clievelandi Vindiciæ; Or, Clieveland's Genuine Poems, Orations, Epistles, &c. Purged from the many False & Spurious Ones Which had usurped his Name, and from innumerable Errours and Corruptions in the true Copies. To which are added many Additions never Printed before: With an Account of the Author's Life. Published according to the Author's own Copies. London, Printed for Obadiah Blagrave . . . 1677.

8°, text pp. 1–239.

(1–4) as in his Poems, 1654.

Murphy 63, 138.

Cleveland, John.

Clievelandi Vindiciæ: Or, Clieveland's Genuine Poems, Orations, Epistles, &c. Purged from The many False and Spurious Ones which had usurped his Name, And from innumerable Errours and Corruptions in the True Copies. To which are added many never Printed before, with an Account of the Author's Life. Published according to the Author's own Copies. London, Printed for Robert Harford . . . 1677.

8°, text pp. 1–239.

(1–4) as in Blagrave edition of 1677.

Cleveland, John.

Clievelandi Vindiciæ; Or, Clieveland's Genuine Poems, Orations, Epistles, &c. Purged from the many False & Spurious Ones Which had usurped his Name, and from innumerable Errours and Corruptions in the True. To which are added many never Printed before.

Published according to the Author's own Copies. London, Printed for Nath. Brooke . . . 1677.

8°, text pp. 1–239.

(1–4) as in Blagrave edition of 1677.

Murphy 138. BSC 2400.

[Felltham, Owen.]

A Brief Character of the Low Countries. 1677.*

Reprinted from 1659.

[Flecknoe, Richard.]

Seventy Eight Characters Of So many Vertuous and Vitious Persons. Written, By one well acquainted with most of them. London, Printed for Publick Use. 1677.

8°, text pp. 1–64.

(1–61) as in A Collection of the Choicest Epigrams, 1673, omitting two from that list, (62) Of a bold abusive person (p. 47), (63) Of an exceptious person (p. 48).

Murphy 69.

Long, Thomas.

The Character Of A Separatist: Or, Sensuality the Ground Of Separation. To which is Added, The Pharisees Lesson, on Matth. IX. xiii. And An Examination Of Mr. Hales Treatise of Schisme. By Thomas Long, B.D. and Prebendary of St. Peter's Exon. . . . London, Printed for Walter Kettilby . . . 1677.

8°, text pp. 1–102.

(1) A separatist (p. 3).

Not precisely a character in the sense of the present work, but included because of its title.

Peacham, Henry.

The Worth of a Penny. London, Printed by S. and B.G. for Thomas Lee, 1677.*

Reprinted from 1641.

Walker, Obadiah.

Of Education. . . . The Third Impression. Oxford, 1677.*

BSC 3161.

Reprinted from 1673.

Wycherly, William.

The Plain-Dealer. A Comedy. . . . Written by Mr Wycherley. . . . Licensed Jan. 9. 1676. Roger L'Estrange. London, Printed by T.N. for James Magnes and Rich. Bentley . . . M.DC.LXXVII.

4°, text pp. 1–96.

(1) A woman of the age (Act II, scene i, p. 19).

Pforzheimer Catalogue No. 1102.

Frequently reprinted.

1678

Anonymous.

The Character Of a true English Souldier. . . .
Written by a Gentleman of the New-rais'd
Troops. With Allowance. Ro. L'Estrange.
London: Printed for D.M. 1678.*
4°, text pp. 1–8.
Murphy 88.

The Character Of A Turbulent, Pragmatical
Jesuit And Factious Romish Priest. Licensed,
October 15, 1678. London: Printed for Langley
Curtis . . . 1678.
4°, text pp. 2–8.
Begins: "A Turbulent Pragmatical Jesuite, is the
Bell-weather of the *Roman* Shepherds Flock."
Murphy 111. BSC 2402.

The Mystery Of Mony-catching, Or The
Character Of An Importunate-Dunn: With
The most approved means, for a persecuted
Debtor, to avoid or pacify him. With Allow-
ance. London Printed for D.M. 1678.
4°, text pp. 3–8.
Begins: "An *Importunate-Dunn*, is the Quintes-
sence of Vexation."

The Present State Of Christendome And The
Interest of England, With a Regard to France.
In a Letter to a Friend. London, Printed by
J.B. for H. Brome . . . 1678.
4°, text pp. 1–28.
(1) as in 1677.

A Scourge For Poor Robin; Or, The Exact
Picture Of A Bad Husband. Drawn to the
Life, by an Experienc'd Female-Hand, to Revenge her Injured Sex, for the Abusive Truths
Of the late Character Of A Scold. With Allowance. London: Printed for L.C. 1678.
4°, text pp. 3–8.
(1) A bad husband (p. 4).
Murphy 87. BSC 2404.

Barrow, Isaac.

Sermons preached upon several occasions.
London, 1678.*
(1) An upright walker.

Barrow, Isaac.

Several Sermons Against Evil-Speaking. By
Isaac Barrow D.D. late Master of Trinity Col-
ledge in Cambridge, and one of His Majestie's
Chaplains in Ordinary. London, Printed for
Brabazon Aylmer . . . 1678.

8°, two parts, text pp. 1–243, 1–140.
(1) Slander (Part I, p. 181), (2) The slanderer
(I, 217), (3) A detractor (II, 4).
There have been several editions of Barrow's collected
works.

Baxter, Richard.

A Sermon Preached At The Funeral Of That
Holy, Painful, and Fruitful Minister of Christ,
Mr. Henry Stubbs . . . By Richard Baxter.
Printed in the Year, 1678.
8°, text pp. 3–48.
(1) Henry Stubbs (p. 23).

Bona, Giovanni.

Precepts and Practical Rules For A truly Christian Life, Being A Summary of Excellent Directions to follow the narrow way to Bliss. In
two Parts. Written Originally in Latin By
John Bona. Englished by L.B. London:
Printed by M. Clark, for H. Brome . . .
MDCLXXVIII.
12°, two parts, text pp. 1–108, 1–126.
(1) A true Christian (Part I, p. 50), (2) A proud
man (II, 72), (3) A humble man (II, 79).
An entirely separate work from Bona's Manuductio ad
Coelum.

Buckinghamshire, John Sheffield, Duke of.

The Character of an Ugly Woman, or an Hue
and Cry after Beauty, 1678.*

[Butler, Samuel.]

The Geneva Ballad. To the Tune of 48. . . .
[colophon] London: Printed for H. Brome
. . . M.DC.LXXVIII.
s.sh.fo. In verse.
Begins: "Of all the *Factions* in the Town."

Gailhard, Jean.

The compleat gentleman: Or Directions For
the Education of Youth As to their Breeding
at Home And Travelling Abroad. . . . By J.
Gailhard . . . In the Savoy: Printed by Tho.
Newcomb, for John Starkey . . . 1678.
4°, in 2 parts, text pp. 1–102, 1–196.
(1) Some nations (Part II, p. 178).

[Head, Richard.]

Madam Wheedle, or the Fashionable Miss Discovered. 1678.*
Probably a reprint of The Miss Display'd, 1675.

[Jones, Andrew?]

The Dreadful Character of a Drunkard. Or,
The Odious and Beastly sin of Drunkenness,
Described and Condemned . . . Printed by
A.D. & T.H. for W. Thackeray . . . 1678.

8°, text sigs. A2–B4v. Black letter.
Begins: "The Prophet Habakkuk in the foregoing verses."

Patrick, Simon.

The Parable of the Pilgrim . . . By Symon Patrick D.D. Chaplain in Ordinary to His Majesty. The Fifth Edition. London, Printed by Robert White for Francis Tyton . . . 1678.
4°, text pp. 1–527.
(1–3) as in 1665.

Walker, Anthony.

Εὕρηκα, Εὕρηκα. The Virtuous Woman found Her Loss Bewailed, and Character Exemplified in a Sermon . . . Preached at the Funeral of . . . Mary, Countess Dowager of Warwick . . . Felsted in Essex, April 30, 1678. London, Printed for Nathaniel Ranew, 1678.*
8°.
(1) Mary, Countess Dowager of Warwick.

Walton, Izaak.

The Life Of Dr. Sanderson, Late Bishop of Lincoln. Written by Izaak Walton. . . . London, Printed for Richard Marriott. 1678.
8°, text sigs. a–o7.
(1) Robert Sanderson (sig. k).
Pforzheimer Catalogue No. 1053.
Reprinted many times.

[Winstanley, William.]

Four for a Penny: Or, Poor Robin's Character Of an Unconscionable Pawn-Broker, And Ear-Mark of an Oppressing Tally-Man: With A friendly Description of A Bum-Bailey, And his Merciless Setting-Cur, or Follower. With Allowance. London: Printed for L.C. 1678.
4°, text pp. 2–8.
(1) An unconscionable pawn-broker (p. 2), (2) An oppressing tally-man (p. 6), (3) A bumbailey (p. 7), (4) His merciless setting-cur, or follower (p. 7).
Murphy 87. BSC 2403.
Attributed to Winstanley by Miss Murphy.

[Winstanley, William.]

Poor Robin's Intelligence Reviv'd; Or, A Narrative Of the late Dreadful Battels Between The Potent Prince de l'Or, And the Grand Duke of Penuria, alias Ragland. . . . London: Printed for L.C. 1678.
4°, text pp. 2–8.
(1) Discontent (p. 4), (2) Despair (p. 4), (3) Sloth and Carelessness (p. 4), (4) Repining (p. 5), (5) Don Projectoro (p. 5), (6) Signior Gulletto, Marquis of Bowzington (p. 5), (7) Duke

Humphrey, Earl of Hungary (p. 5), (8) Covetousness (p. 5), (9) Parsimony (p. 5), (10) Violence (p. 5), (11) Deceit (p. 6), (12) Usury (p. 6).
Winstanley frequently wrote under the pseudonym of Poor Robin.

[Winstanley, William.]

Poor Robin's True Character Of A Scold: Or, The Shrews Looking-glass. Dedicated To all Domineering Dames, Wives Rampant, Cuckolds Couchant, and Henpeckt Sneaks, In City or Country. With Allowance. London: Printed for L.C. 1678.
4°, text pp. 3–8.
Begins: "A Rank Scold is a Devil of the Feminine Gender."
Murphy 87. BSC 2404.
Attributed to Winstanley by Miss Murphy.

1679

Anonymous.

An Answer To The Mantuan, Or, False Character, lately wrote against Womankind. . . . [colophon] London, Printed in the Year 1679.
s.sh.fo. In verse.
Begins: "A Vertuous Woman, O ye Gods! who dare/ Presume to speak or write her Character?"

The Court of Honour, Or, The Vertuous Protestant's Looking-Glass: Being The True and Lively Characters (or Descriptions of the Chief and most Noble Worthies that maintain any Pious Prince's Crown . . . VVritten by a Royalist, a Person of Quality: One that fears God, and Honoureth the King. . . . Printed by A. Purslow, and Tho. Haly. 1679.
4°, text pp. 2–8.
(1) A worthy king (p. 2), (2) A worthy prince (p. 2), (3) A worthy covnsellor (p. 3), (4) A worthy nobleman (p. 3), (5) A worthy bishop or minister (p. 4), (6) A worthy judge (p. 4), (7) A worthy knight and commander in the warrs (p. 4), (8) A worthy gentleman (p. 5), (9) A worthy lawyer (p. 5), (10) A worthy sovldier (p. 6), (11) A worthy physitian (p. 6).
BSC 2406.
V. B. Heltzel shows (Modern Language Notes, LIII [1938], 587) that these characters come from Breton's The Good and the Badde, 1616.

The Jesuits Character. Written by a Member of the Popish Club. To the Black-Smiths Tune, Which no body can deny. . . . [colophon] London, Printed in the Year 1679.
s.sh.fo. In verse.
Begins: "The Jesuits they are a sort of Men."
Murphy 111.

An entirely different work from The Iesuits Character, 1642.

A Letter on the Subject of the Succession. . . . Printed at London, 1679.
fo, text pp. 1–9.
(1) The Duke of York (p. 4).

A Nest of Plots Discovered; or, A Rod for the Romish Iesuits . . . Printed in the Year 1679, for the General Assembly of Hawkers.
s.sh.fo.
Begins: "Is Hell broke loose?"
This is a character of a Jesuit.

A Rod for Rome Or, A Description of the Popish Clergye Their Popes, Cardinals, Jesuites, Monks, Fryers, In Their Proper Colours. . . . [colophon] London, Printed for F. Coles.
s.sh.fo. In verse.
Begins: "Describe the *Romish Jesuites*, who can do't."
Murphy 111.
The British Museum copy is dated in a contemporary hand, 1679.

[The third Advice to A Painter, How to draw the Effigies of the Whore of Rome. Whose Character is Lively represented by a Bad Woman. 1679?]
fo, text pp. 1–4.
Begins: "If you'l observe the Whore, as stript and strip'd."
BSC 2405.
The Harvard copy, from which this note was made, lacks the title page.

Turbulent Conspiracies: Or, The Roman-Catholiques Enormities against the Metropolitans of England. . . . Setting forth the Character of a Jesuit in his proper colours. . . . With Allowance. Printed by Ann Pursloe, and Thomas Haly, in the Year, 1679.
4°, text pp. 1–6.
(1) A Jesuit (p. 2).
BSC 2421.

The Weekly Character: Being the Character Of A Pope. . . . London, Printed in the Year 1679.
4°, text pp. 3–7.
Begins: "The Pope is one that braggs much of his Ancestors."
BSC 2412.
On the verso of p. 7 is the announcement: "The Reader may be pleased to take notice that every Wednesday a Character will come out, as occasion shall offer." This issue bears the notation Numb. I. at the head of the title.

Bacon, Sir Francis.
Baconiana. Or Certain Genuine Remains of Sr. Francis Bacon. . . . London, Printed by J.D. for Richard Chiswell . . . 1679.
8°, text pp. 3–104.
(1) Bacon, by Peter Heylin (p. 263), (2) Bacon, by Sprat (p. 264), (3) Bacon, by Cowley (p. 267).
Pforzheimer Catalogue No. 25.

[Care, Henry?]
The Weekly Pacquet Of Advice from Rome . . . London: Printed for, and are to be sold by Langley Curtis . . . 1679[–83].
4°, 5 vols.
(1) A Romish priest (Vol. II, p. 337, for April 30, 1680).
Attributed to Care by the CBEL.

[Casa, Giovanni della.]
The Refin'd Courtier, Or A Correction of several Indecencies crept into Civil Conversation. . . . London, Printed for R. Royston . . . 1679.
12°, text pp. 1–233.
(1) A person of brittle humor (p. 66).
The dedication is signed N.W. The preface to the reader states that the book is a paraphrase of Casa's Galateus.

Du Bosc, Jacques.
The Compleat Woman. 1679.*
BSC 2189.
Reprinted from 1639.

Ellis, Clement.
The Gentile Sinner. Or England's brave gentleman character'd. Oxford, Printed for H. Hall, 1679.*
Murphy 142. BSC 2407.

[Head, Richard.]
Proteus Redevivus: or the Art of Wheedling: or Insinuation . . . Collected and Methodized By the Author of the First Part of the English Rogue. . . . London, Printed by W.D. and are to be sold by most Booksellers, 1679.
8°, text pp. 1–352.
(1–37) as in 1675.
Murphy 148.

[Jones, Andrew?]
The Dreadful Character of a Drunkard. By Andrew Jones. Printed by the Heir of A. Anderson, Scotland. 1679.*

[Kirke, Thomas.]
A Modern Account Of Scotland; Being An exact Description of the Country, And a True

Character Of The People and their Manners. Written from thence by an English Gentleman. Printed in the Year, 1679.

4°, text pp. 1–17.
(1–2) as in 1667.
BSC 2417.

[Marvell, Andrew.]

The Character of Popery and Arbitrary Government. 1679.*
BSC 2405.
See 1689.

Shadwell, Thomas.

A True Widow. A Comedy . . . Written by Tho. Shadwell. . . . London, Printed for Benjamin Tooke . . . 1679.

4°, text pp. 1–79.
(1) Mr. Prig (p. 7).
Pforzheimer Catalogue No. 876.

South, Robert.

Sermons Preached upon Several Occasions. 1679.*
See 1737.

Whitlock, Richard.

Zootomia, or Morall Anatomy of the Living by the Dead in Observations, Essays, Characters, &c. P. Parker, 1679.*
BSC 2413.

1680

Anonymous.

The Car-Man's Poem: Or Advice to a Nest of Scriblers.

s.sh.fo. In verse.
Begins: "Car-Men turn Poets now, why may not I?"
Murphy 112.
The copy in the British Museum is dated in MS, Feb. 2, 1679/80. The poem is a character of a satirist.

The Character Of A Town-Gallant; Exposing the Extravagant Fopperies of some vain Self-conceited Pretenders to Gentility, and good Breeding . . . FINIS. London, Printed for Rowland Reynolds in the Strand, 1680.

fo, text pp. 1–4.
Begins: "A town gallant is a bundle of vanity."
Murphy 84.

The Character Of A Town-Miss. . . . [Colophon] London, Printed for Rowland Reynolds in the Strand, 1680.

fo, pp. 1–4.
Begins: "A Miss is a new name."
Murphy 85.

The Character of a True Englishman. 1680.*

The Character Of An English-Man.

s.sh.fo, text pp. 1–2. In verse.
Begins: "By the first Principles of Mother Earth."
Murphy 112.
Dated conjecturally 1681 by the British Museum Catalogue and 1680 by the Huntington Library Catalogue.
A mock imprimatur at the end is signed by Nath. Lee.

The Genius of True English-men. . . [colophon] London, Printed for Francis Smith . . . 1680.

s.sh.fo. In verse.
Begins: "The Free-born *English* Generous and Wise."

The Honest Briton's Character of Himself. [1680?]*

In verse.
Begins: "To all whom it may concern to know me, greeting."

An Hue and Cry after R. Ls. . . . [colophon] Printed for Tom. Tell-Troth. [c. 1680.]

fo, text pp. 1–4.
Begins: "O Yes! O Yes! O Yes! If there be any Man in Town."
Murphy 112.
A character of Sir Roger L'Estrange. There were two slightly different editions.

The Knavery Of Astrology Discover'd, In Observations Upon Every Month, of the Year 1680. Together With the Nature of the Seven Planets, &c. By Tim. Tell-Troth, Star-Gazer to the Great Mogvl. . . . London, Printed for T.B. and R.E. 1680.

4°, text pp. 5–20.
(1) Saturn (p. 5), (2) Jupiter (p. 5), (3) Mars (p. 6), (4) The svn (p. 6), (5) Venus (p. 7), (6) Mercury (p. 7), (7) The moon (p. 8).

Lex Talionis. . . . Poor Robin turn'd Robin the Devil: Being his exact Character. Written by one that had his Friend, formerly most egregiously abused by him, to his great Disparagement, and greater Prejudice . . . [1680?]*
s.sh.fo.
Begins: "He is a Meddler of those things that doth not concern him."

Looke about you, or the Fault-finder and criticall Observer characterizing himself and others.*
BSC 2418.
Probably a reprint of 1647.

The Old Pudding-pye woman set forth in her colours.———. London. Printed for F. Coles, T. Vere, J. Wright, and J. Clark.

s.sh.fo. In verse.
Begins: "There was an Old wife and she sold pudding-pye."

A Pattern Or President For Princes To Rule By, And For Subiects To Obey By. . . . London, Printed for William Miller . . . 1680.

4°, text pp. 3–39.
(1) The most renowned Queen Elizabeth (p. 3).
BSC 2419.
The whole book bears the running title, A Lively Character of the most Renowned Queen Elizabeth.

Philo-Carolus: Consisting of Three Poems, (Viz.) A Canto upon the Plot. A Satyr against Atheism. And A Panegyrick Upon our most Gracious Sovereign K: Charles II. London, Printed for Norman Nelson . . . 1680.

4°, text pp. 1–21. In verse.
(1) An atheist (p. 7).

Presbytery Truly Display'd, Or An Impartial Character Of The Presbyterian. Being A Vindication of that Sanctified Party, from the Virulent Calumnies of some Foul-mouth'd Detractors in this Modern Age. London, Printed in the Year M.DC.LXXX.

fo, text pp. 1–6.
(1) A presbyter (p. 2).

Baxter, Richard.

A Sermon Preached at the Funeral of that Faithful Minister of Christ Mr. John Corbet. With his True and Exemplary Character. By Richard Baxter. London, Printed for Thomas Parkhurst. . . .

4°, text pp. 1–36.
(1) John Corbet (p. 28).
BSC 2414.
Dated 1680 by BSC.

Baxter, Richard.

A True Believer's Choice and Pleasure, instanced in the Exemplary Life of Mrs. Mary Coxe.*

(1) Mrs. Coxe.

Bona, Giovanni.

A Guide To Eternity: Extracted out of the Writings Of The Holy Fathers, And Ancient Philosophers. Written Originally in Latine, By John Bona: And now done into English, By Roger L'Estrange, Esq; The Second Edi-

tion. London, Printed for Hen. Brome . . . 1680.

12°, text pp. 1–188.
(1–6) as in first edition of 1672.
Murphy 146.

[Buckinghamshire, John Sheffield, Duke of, and Dryden, John.]

An Essay Upon Satyr, Or, A Poem On the Times . . . To which is Added, A Satyr against Separatists. London, Printed for Tho: Dring. . . . 1680.

4°, text pp. 1–88. In verse.
(1) A silenced minister (p. 82).
The postscript is signed A.C. (i.e., Abraham Cowley?). Attributed to Buckinghamshire and Dryden by Halkett and Laing. The Satyr against Separatists had first been published in 1642; it was probably written by Peter Hausted.

[Butler, Samuel.]

The Geneva Ballad. 1680.*

A re-issue of 1674.

[Care, Henry?]

The Popes Harbinger. . . . Printed by A. Godbid, for L.C. 1680.

4°.
(1) A true Englishman (p. 168).

Copp, Abiezar.

A Character of a true Christian. Written by Abiezar Copp. The Tune is, The Fair Nimphs. . . . London, Printed by T.D: sold by La: Curtiss. 1680.

s.sh.fo. In verse.
Begins: "A Christian true doth love/ his Father that's above."
Murphy 88.

[Cotton, Charles.]

The Compleat Gamester. 1680.*

Reprinted from 1674.

Denham, Sir John.

The True Presbyterian Without Disguise: Or, A Character Of A Presbyterians Ways and Actions. By Sir John Denham, Knight. . . . London: Printed for J.B. 1680.

s.sh.fo, text pp. 1–2.
Begins: "A Presbyter is such a Monstrous thing."
Murphy 106. Pforzheimer Catalogue No. 287.

[Fletcher, Henry?]

The perfect politician: Or, A Full View Of the Life and Actions . . . Of O. Cromwel. . . . The Second Edition. Whereunto is added His Character. . . . London, Printed in the Year 1680.

8°, text pp. 1-294.
(1) as in 1660.

[Head, Richard.]

The English Rogue . . . London, Printed for
Francis Kirkman . . . 1680.

8°, text pp. 1-402.
(1-3) as in 1665.
Murphy 144.

Mantuanus, Baptista Spagnuoli.

Mantuan English'd, and Paraphras'd: Or, The
Character Of A Bad Woman. Mant. Ecl.
3. . . .

fo, text pp. 1-4. In verse.
Begins: "A Bad Woman! Heav'n bless us, Sirs!
Who dare."
Murphy 88. BSC 2408.

Dated [1680?] by the British Museum. The source is
actually Mantuan's fourth eclogue, not the third.

[Mee, Dr.]

The Character of a Compleat Physician or
Naturalist. London, Printed for E.H.*

4°, text pp. 1-8.
BSC 2415.

The author's name is written in manuscript on the title
page of the British Museum copy. Dated [1680?] by the
British Museum Catalogue.

Power, Laurence.

The Righteous Mans Portion. Delivered in a
Sermon At The Obsequies Of The Noble and
Renowned Gentleman, Henry St John Es-
quire: Who was unfortunately Killed by the
Tories on Tuesday the 9th of September, 1679.
. . . Together with a short Character of his
Life, and the way and manner of his Death.
By Laur. Power, M.A. . . . London, Printed
by J.M. for Henry Bonwicke . . . 1680.

4°, text pp. 1-29.
(1) Henry St. John (p. 23).

[Rapin, Rene.]

Instructions for History: With A Character of
the most Considerable Historians, Ancient and
Modern. Out of the French, By J. Davies Of
Kidwelly. London, Printed by A.G. and J.P.
. . . M.DC.LXXX.

8°, text pp. 1-134.
(1) The characters of persons (chap. 20), (2) A
judgment of historians (chap. 28).
BSC 2420.

Chapter 20 is virtually an essay on character-drawing.

Reyner, Samuel.

A Sermon Preached At The Funeral Of The
Right Honourable Denzell Lord Holles . . .

By Samvel Reyner . . . London, Printed for
William Churchill Bookseller in Dorchester,
MDCLXXX.

4°, text pp. 1-28.
(1) Denzell Lord Holles (p. 18).

[Tate, Nahum?]

Characters of an accomplished Virgin and
Wife.

4°. Manuscript.
BSC 2416.

A manuscript formerly owned by Bliss, location now unknown. Presumably the author was Nahum Tate; see his
A Present for the Ladies, 1692.

Walker, Anthony.

Eureka, Eureka. The Virtuous woman Found.
Second edition. 1680.*

[Warren, Albert.]

An Apology for the Discourse of Humane
Reason, Written by Ma. Clifford, Esq; being a
Reply to Plain Dealing. With the Author's
Epitaph and Character. . . . London, Printed
for Walter Davis . . . 1680.*

(1) Martin Clifford (p. 144).
BSC 2422.

1681

Anonymous.

The Caracter Of A Leading Petitioner. . . .
[colophon] London, Printed for W. Davis,
1681.

s.sh.fo, text pp. 1-2.
Begins: "He is an Insect produc'd by the Car-
rion."
Murphy 113. BSC 2427.

The Character.

s.sh.fo. In verse. No imprint.
Begins: "The Lords and Commons having had
their doom."
This is an invective against the Roman Catholics.

The character Of A Church-Papist . . . [colo-
phon] London, Printed for John Kidgell . . .
1681.

s.sh.fo.
Begins: "A Church-Papist divides his Religion
between his Conscience and his Pocket."
Murphy 113. BSC 2427.

The Character Of A Disbanded Courtier. . . .
[colophon] London, Printed for N. Thompson, Anno Dom. 1681.

s.sh.fo.
Begins: "He was born with an aspiring Mind."

The Character Of A Fanatick in General, By what other Name however he may be more specially distinguished. [colophon] London: Printed for N.T. 1681.

fo, text pp. 1–4.
Begins: "He is a person of a more exercis'd Faith."
Murphy 110.
A reprint of The Character of a Fanatick, 1675.

The Character of a good Clergy-man. A Worthy Observation, but Scarce Example, in This Degenerate Age.*
Broadside.
Mr. Greenough's notes refer to this broadside as being in the possession of Sir Charles Firth. It is reprinted in Firth's edition of Macaulay's History of England, I, 320.

The Character Of A Good Man, Neither Whig nor Tory. . . . [colophon] London, Printed for Jonathan Robinson . . . 1681.

s.sh.fo, text pp. 1–2.
Begins: "He is one whose Name is Christian."
Murphy 113. BSC 2426.

The Character Of A Jesuit. . . . [colophon] London, Printed for J. Newton. 1681.

s.sh.fo, text pp. 1–2.
Begins: "He is a Peccant Humour of the Body Politick."
Murphy 113. BSC 2427.

The Character Of A Modern Sham-Plotter. . . . [colophon] London: Printed for R. Janeway in Queens-Head-Ally in Pater-Noster-Row.
s.sh.fo.
Begins: "He is the Common Enemy of Honest Mankind."
Murphy 114. BSC 2427.
Not to be confused with The Character of a Sham-Plotter, by Edmund Hickeringill (?), 1681.

The Character Of A Modern Whig, Or An Alamode True Loyal Protestant. . . . [colophon] London, Printed for John Smith . . . 1681.

s.sh.fo, text pp. 1–2.
Begins: "He is a Certain Insect bred in the Corruption of the late Rebellion."
Murphy 114. BSC 2427.

The Character Of A Rebellion, And what England May expect from one. Or, The Designs of Dissenters Examined by Reason, Experience, And the Laws and Statutes of the Realm. London, Printed for Benj. Tooke, 1681.

fo, text pp. 1–18.
Begins: "He does not deserve the name of an Englishman."
BSC 2425.
An answer to Settle's Character of a Popish Successour.

The Character Of An Ignoramus Doctor . . . [colophon] London; Printed by M.T. 1681.
s.sh.fo, text pp. 1–2.
Begins: "An Ignoramus Doctor is a certain Duncical Dolt."
BSC 2427.

The Character Of An Ill-Court-Favourite: Representing the Mischiefs That flow from Ministers of State, When they are More Great than Good . . . Translated out of French. Printed for T. Davis, in the year 1681.

fo, text pp. 3–19.
Begins: "He that stands by and observes the supple Addresses."
Mr. Greenough considered this barely a character, if at all.

The Character Of An Vnjust Judge. Or An Unjust Judge Painted To The Life. . . . [colophon] London printed for T.VV. 1681.
s.sh.fo, text pp. 1–2.
Begins: "He is a Certain kind of Animall."
Murphy 113.

The Character Of Those Two Protestants in Masquerade, Heraclitus, And The Observator. . . . [colophon] London, Printed for E. Ryddal. 1681.
s.sh.fo.
Begins: "They are Teeming Animals."
BSC 2427.

The Character Of Wit's Squint-Ey'd Maid, Pasquil-Makers. . . . [colophon] London, Printed for W. Davis, 1681.
s.sh.fo. In verse.
Begins: "What Puppy Plays are entering now the Stage?"
BSC 2428.
A poor example of a character.

The Dissenter Truely Described. . . . [colophon] London, Printed by N. Thompson, Anno. Dom. 1681.
s.sh.fo. In verse.
Begins: "What shall a glorious Nation be o'rthrown."

The Genius of True English-men. . . . [colophon] London, Printed for Francis Smith. . . .
s.sh.fo. In verse.
Begins: "The Freeborn English Generous and Wise."

Murphy 149.

A reprint of 1680. Or, since the only evidence of date is the manuscript date 18 April 1681 on one of the copies in the British Museum, this edition may be identical with that of 1680, and the date may be simply that of its acquisition by its owner.

Grimalkin, Or, The Rebel-Cat: A Novell. Representing the Unwearied Attempts of the Beasts of his Faction Against Sovereignty and Succession Since the Death of the Lyons in the Tower. . . . London, Printed for the Author, 1681.

fo, text pp. 1–13.
(1) The spirit of the Whig rebellion, considered as a cat (p. 12).

The Phanatick in his Colours: Being a Full and Final Character of a Whig; in a Dialogue between Tory and Tantivy. . . . London: Printed for N. Thompson. 1681.

fo, text pp. 1–4.
Begins: "Well, Tory, did not I tell thee we should vex those Plotting Countermining Whigs to the heart?"
Murphy 115. BSC 2427.

The Presbyterians described In the Character of their Predecessours The Pharisees. . . . [Colophon:] London: Printed for W. Hinchman . . . 1681.

s.sh.fo, text pp. 1–2.
Begins: "*Josephus*, though himself a Pharisee, gives this Character of them."

Presbytery Truly Display'd: Or An Impartial Character Of The Presbyterian; Being A Vindication of that Sanctified Party from the Virulent Calumnies of some Foul-mouth'd Detractors in this Modern Age. To which is annexed The Ballad of the Cloak. London, Printed for the Author, and sold by W.L. . . . 1681.

fo, text pp. 1–6.
(1) as in 1680.
BSC 2434.

The Reformed Papist, Or High-Church-Man. Characterized in Reflections on his Principles and Designs. . . . [Colophon] London, Printed for J. Blackborne 1681.

fo, text pp. 1–4.
Begins: "It is an old Charge managed against many of the Church of *England*."
BSC 2427.

Twelve Ingenious Characters: or Pleasant Descriptions of the Properties of Sundry Persons and Things. 1681.*

See 1686.

No trace of this edition has been found.

A., T.

Religio Clerici. . . . By T.A. London: Printed for Henry Brome . . . 1681.

12°, text pp. 1–96.
(1) A minister of the Church of England (p. 82).

Baxter, Richard.

Faithful Souls Shall Be With Christ, The Certainty Proved and their Christianity Described, and Exemplified in the truly Christian Life and Death of . . . Henry Ashhvrst Esq; Citizen of London. . . . By Richard Baxter. . . . London, Printed for Nevil Simmons . . . 1681.

4°, text pp. 1–60.
(1) Henry Ashhurst (p. 36).

Baxter, Richard.

A Search For The English Schismatick: By the Case and Characters, I. Of the Diocesan Canoneers. II. Of the present Meer Nonconformists . . . By Richard Baxter, One of the Accused. London: Printed for Nevil Simmons . . . 1681.

4°, text pp. 1–44.
(1) The papists (p. 1), (2) The passive conformists (p. 3), (3) The sectaries (p. 4), (4) Mere present nonconformists (p. 5), (5) Diocesan canoneers, or zealots for imposition of conformity (p. 7), (6) Mere nonconformists (p. 29).
Murphy 148.

Rather poor examples of character.

[Birkenhead, Sir John.]

The Assembly-Man. Written in the Year 1647. . . . London, Printed for Walter Davis . . . 1681.

4°, text pp. 5–16.
Begins: "An *Assembler* is part of the *States* Chattels."
Murphy 107.

Probably the date 1681 means 1681/82, since some copies are so catalogued.

[Buckinghamshire, John Sheffield, Duke of.]

The Character of a Tory . . . . [colophon] London, Printed for William Inghall the Elder Bookbinder. 1681.

s.sh.fo, text pp. 1–2.
Begins: "A *Tory* is a *Monster* with an *English Face*."
Murphy 114. BSC 2426.

Attributed to Buckinghamshire by Halkett and Laing, and included in his Works later. There are references to earlier editions of 1659 and 1679, but both must be mistakes. The latter may be the date of composition.

[D'Urfey, Thomas.]

The Progress Of Honesty: Or, a View Of A Court And City. A Pindarique Poem. By T.D. . . . London: Printed for Joseph Hindmarsh . . . 1681.

fo, text pp. 1–23. In verse.
(1) Honesty (paragraph 3), (2) Error (par. 4), (3) Beauty (par. 6), (4) King Titus (par. 8), (5) Resolution (par. 9), (6) Discord (par. 10), (7) Marcian (par. 11), (8) Loyal Clytus (par. 13), (9) Brave Cleon (par. 13), (10) Hophni or Achitophel (par. 14), (11) A wastrel (par. 15).

There were two editions in 1681, the other being 4°, text pp. 1–32.

[Fletcher, Henry?]

The Perfect Politician: Or a full View of the Life and Actions military and Civil of O. Cromwell. Containing also a History of the late Civil War so far as he was concerned therein. The third edition corrected and enlarged. Whereunto is added His Character; and a Compleat Catalogue of all the Honours conferr'd by him on several Persons. Qui nescit dissimulare, nescit regnare. London, Printed for J. Crumpe. 1681.*

8°, text pp. 1–283.
(1) as in 1660.
BSC 2429.

[Hickeringill, Edmund.]

The Character Of A Sham-Plotter or Man-Catcher. . . . [colophon] London, Printed For Ab. Green, 1681.

s.sh.fo, text pp. 1–2.
Begins: "A *Sham-Plotter* (to begin with his Pedigree) is the *Spawn* of a *Papist*."
Murphy 114.

Reprinted in Hickeringill's Works, 1716. Not to be confused with the anonymous The Character of a Modern Sham-Plotter [1681?].

[Hobbes, Thomas.]

The Whole Art of Rhetoric. 1681.*

See A Briefe of the Art of Rhetorique [1655?].

[Jones, Andrew?]

The Dreadful Character of a Drunkard. Printed by T.H. for W. Thackeray. 1681.*

L'Estrange, Sir Roger.

The Character Of A Papist in Masquerade; Supported By Authority and Experience. In Answer to the Character Of A Popish Successor. By Roger L'Estrange. London, Printed for H. Brome . . . 1681.

4°, text pp. 1–85.
Begins: "*The Character of a Popish Successor* were an excellent *Piece* in the kinde."
BSC 2431.

Hardly a real character; rather a step-by-step refutation of The Character of a Popish Successor.

[L'Estrange, Sir Roger.]

Machiavil's Advice To His Son. Newly Translated out of Italian into English Verse. By R.L. Esq; . . . [colophon] London, Printed for T. Burrel, 1681.

fo, text pp. 1–8. In verse.
Begins: "Come hither Son, and learn thy Fathers Lore."

This is a character of a projector.

Milton, John.

Mr John Milton's Character of the Long Parliament and Assembly of Divines. In MDCXLI. Omitted in his other Works, and never before Printed, And very seasonable for these times. . . . London: Printed for Henry Brome . . . 1681.

4°, text pp. 1–11.
Begins: "Of these who sway'd most."
BSC 2432.

Several times reprinted. An early manuscript version is in the Harvard College Library. The Pforzheimer Catalogue states (under item 710) that "several early manuscripts" are known.

Palmer, Herbert.

Memorials of Godliness and Christianity. Printed for S. Crouch. 1681.*
BSC 2433.

[Phillips, John.]

The Character Of A Popish Successor, And What England May Expect From such a One. Part the Second. . . . London: Printed, and are to be sold by Richard Janeway, MDCLXXXI.

fo, text pp. 1–34.
Begins: "It might seem strangely preposterous."
BSC 2424.

Attributed to Phillips by the CBEL. Hardly a true character.

[Phillips, John.]

The Character Of a Popish Successour Compleat: In Defence of the First Part. . . . London: Printed for J. Graves . . . 1681.

fo, text pp. 1–35.
Begins: "The first Allegation Mr L'Estrange makes."

Attributed to Phillips by Halkett and Laing. Not a true character.

[Préfontaine, César François Oudin, Sieur de.]

The Extravagant Poet. A comical Novel. Translated out of French by G.R. Gent. London, Printed for B.M., 1681.*

(1) Brindestoc, a thief.

Attributed to Préfontaine by Halkett and Laing.

[Settle, Elkanah.]

The Character Of A Popish Successour, And What England May Expect From Such a One. Humbly offered to the Consideration of Both Houses Of Parliament, Appointed to meet at Oxford, On the One and twentieth of March, 1680/1. London, Printed for T. Davies. MDCLXXXI.

fo, text pp. 1–36.
(1) A Popish successour (p. 4).

Attributed to Settle by Halkett and Laing. Sometimes ascribed to John Phillips. There were at least three editions in 1681, of which Huntington has the third.

[Thompson, N.?]

An Answer to a late Pamphlet, entituled, A Character of a Popish Successor. 1681.*

1682

Anonymous.

The Character Of A disbanded Courtier. Dedicated to the Author of that Famous Speech, Call'd, The Speech of a Noble Peer. By a Person of Quality. . . . [colophon] London, Printed for R.J. 1682.

fo, text pp. 1–4.
Begins: "He was Born of a considerable Family, Heir to a Fortune above contemptible."
BSC 2435.

A different work from the same title of 1681.

The Character of a Disbanded Peer.*

Possibly an alternative title for The Character of a Disbanded Courtier, 1682, q.v.

The Character Of A Protestant Jesuite. . . . [colophon] London, Printed for W. Davis, 1682.

s.sh.fo, text pp. 1–2.
Begins: "He is a Person of a more exercised Faith."
Murphy 112. BSC 2435.

A reprint of A Character of a Fanatick in General, 1681. Miss Murphy dates [1680?] since the final figure in the Bodleian copy is cropped.

The Character Of A Through-Pac'd Tory, Ecclesiastical Or Civil. London, Printed for Joseph Collier. 1682.

4°, text pp. 1–10.

Begins: "That he is a man of haste, you may know."
Murphy 116. BSC 2436.

The Character Of A Trimmer, Neither Whigg nor Tory . . . [colophon] London, Printed for T.S. in the Year 1682.*

s.sh.fo.
Murphy 116.

There are references to various works with this title in 1683, 1684, and 1685. They may not all be identical. They seem to be entirely distinct, in any case, from the work of this title by George Savile, Marquis of Halifax, which first appeared in 1688.

The Character Of A True Protestant. . . . [colophon] London, Printed for T.S. in the Year 1682.

s.sh.fo, text pp. 1–2.
Begins: "He is one that professeth the Doctrine."
Murphy 115.

A Character Of The True Blue Protestant Poet: Or, The Pretended Author Of The Character Of A Popish Successor. . . . [colophon] London: Printed for A. Banks, 1682.

fo, text pp. 1–4.
Begins: "One would believe it almost Incredible."
BSC 2424.

A Desription Of His Majesties True and Loyal Subjects, Scandalously called Toreys . . . [colophon] London: Printed by J. Wallis for Randall Taylor. 1682.*

s.sh.fo, text pp. 1–2.
Murphy 115.

The Dying Mans Destiny, And The Living Mans Duty, Opened. And Applyed in a Sermon Preached On Board the Loyal-Eagle, etc. At the Solemn Obsequies of Mr. Richard Bernard, Chyrurgeon. . . . London, Printed for Dorman Newman, 1682.*

(1) Richard Bernard (p. 34).

Fore-warn'd, Fore-arm'd. 1682.*
See 1684.

The Hypocritical Christian: Or The Conventicling Citizen Displayed. Shewing the Refractory temper of the Whiggish Party of the Town, in Opposition to the Establish't Religion, and their Disaffection to Monarchy. . . . [colophon] London Printed by George Croom . . . 1682.

fo, text pp. 1–4. In verse.
Begins: "Well! for a careful foresight, sober wit."

The Hypocritical Whigg Displayed. . . . [colophon] London, Printed for C.H. Anno Domini 1682.

s.sh.fo. In verse.
Begins: "What shall a *Glorious Nation* be o'rthrown."
Murphy 149.

The Informers Lecture To his Sons, instructing them in the mysteries of that Religion. . . . [colophon] London, Printed for Joseph Collier . . . 1682.

s.sh.fo, text pp. 1–2.
Begins: "Come, children, come, and learn your Fathers trade."
A character of an informer in the first person plural.

The Informers Looking-Glass, In which he may see himself while he is maliciously prosecuting Dissenting Protestants. . . . [colophon] London: Printed and are to be sold by Joseph Collier. 1682.

s.sh.fo.
Begins: "An Informer is the Spawn of Envy conglutinated to a spiteful Revenge."
Murphy 115.

A New Ballad, Or, The True-Blew-Protestant Dissenter: With their sad Lamentation for their late Loss in Aldersgate-Street. To the Tune of the Down-fall of Anthony. . . . Printed for W. Davis . . . 1682.

s.sh.fo. In verse.
Begins: "When *Jeroboams* Calves were rear'd."

A Pillar Erected to the Memorial of Popish-Nat, shewing how unlike the Best, and how like the worst of Men he is. . . . [colophon] London Printed for J. Jones. 1682.

s.sh.fo. In verse.
Begins: "In Holy-Record we do read."
This is a character of Nat Thompson.

The Second Character Of An Informer: Wherein His Mischievous Nature And Leud Practises Are Detected. London, Printed for S.M. 1682.*

4°, text pp. 1–6.
Murphy 111.
A re-issue of The Character of an Informer, 1675, with some additions.

The Second Part of the Character of a Good-Man. Neither Whig nor Tory. . . . [colophon] London, Printed for Jonathan Robinson . . . 1682.

s.sh.fo.
Begins: "He is one who endeavors to imitate."
Murphy 111.

This Ages Rarity: The Emblem of a Good Servant Explain'd. [colophon] London, Printed in the Year 1682.*

Burnet, Gilbert.

The life and Death of Sir Matthew Hale, Kt. . . . Written by Gilbert Burnett, D.D. London, Printed for William Shrowsbery . . . 1682.

8°, text pp. 1–128.
(1) Sir Matthew Hale (p. 71).

Coppinger, Matthew.

Poems, Songs And Love-Verses, Upon several Subjects. By Matthew Coppinger Gent. London, Printed for R. Bentley, and M. Magnes . . . 1682.

8°, text pp. 1–128.
(1) On a wife (p. 121).

Cowley, Abraham, and others.

Wit and Loyalty Reviv'd, In a Collection of some smart Satyrs In Verse and Prose on the late Times. By Mr. Abraham Cowley, Sir J. Berkenhead, and the Ingenious Author of Hudibras, &c. . . . London Printed, for W. Davis. 1682.

4°, text pp. 1–35.
(1) The Puritan and the papist, by Cowley (p. 1), (2) An holy sister (p. 8, in verse), (3) The assembly-man, 1647, by Sir John Birkenhead (p. 9).
Murphy 149.

Flatman, Thomas.

Poems And Songs. By Thomas Flatman. The Third Edition With Additions and Amendments. . . . London, Printed for Benjamin Tooke . . . 1682.

8°, text pp. 1–170.
(1–2) as in 1674.
There were two issues in this year.

Freeman, Samuel.

The Israelite Indeed. A Sermon Preached at the Funeral of Mark Cottle Esq; Late Register of the Prerogative-Office, on Thursday, Jan. 5, 1681. By Sam. Freeman, M.A. and Rector of St. Ann's Aldersgate, London. London, Printed for Edward Gellibrand . . . 1682.

4°, text pp. 1–31.
(1) An Israelite (p. 1), (2) Mark Cottle (p. 24).

Gailhard, J.

Two Discourses. The first concerning a Private Settlement at Home after Travel. The second concerning the Statesman, or Him who is in Publick Employments. London, Printed for Walter Davis. 1682.*

(1) The Prince of Condé (p. 173).

[Hicks, W.]

Grammatical Drollery, Consisting of Poems & Songs. . . . By W.H. London: Printed for Tho. Fox . . . 1682.

8°, text pp. 1–117.

(1) On a beautiful miss (p. 105, in verse).

Attributed to Hicks by the CBEL.

Ingelo, Nathaniel.

Bentivolio And Urania, In Six Books. By Nathanael Ingelo, D.D. . . . The Fourth Edition, with large Amendments . . . London: Printed by A.M. and R.R. for Dorman Newman. 1682.

fo, in 2 parts, text pp. 1–171, 1–219.

(1–32) as in 1669.

[L'Estrange, Sir Roger.]

The Observator. 1682.*

See 1684.

Long, Thomas.

The Character of a Separatist. London, Printed for W. Kettilby. 1682.*

Arber, Term Catalogues, I, 288.

Reprinted from 1677.

[Northleigh, John.]

The Parallel . . . Closing with a Disparity between A True Patriot and A Factious Associator. London, Printed for B. Tooke . . . and T. Sawbridge, MDCLXXXII.

fo, text pp. 1–34.

(1) A true patriot (p. 30), (2) A factious associator (p. 31).

An Associator is one who desires to exclude the Duke of York from the throne.

[Pordage, Samuel.]

Azaria and Hushai, A Poem. . . . London, Printed for Charles Lee, An. Dom. 1682.

4°, text pp. 1–38.

(1) Chemerarims, priests of the hellish brood (p. 2), (2) Hushai (p. 9), (3) Eliakim (p. 10).

Attributed to Pordage by the CBEL. Sometimes attributed to Elkanah Settle.

[Pordage, Samuel.]

Azaria and Hushai. A Poem. . . . The Second Editon, Revised and Amended. London, Printed for Charles Lee, An. Dom. 1682.

4°, text pp. 1–38.

(1–3) as in first edition of 1682.

[Richard, William?]

Wallography; or the Britton Described: Being A Pleasant Relation of a Journey into Wales. London, Printed for Obadiah Blagrave, 1682.*

(1) A Welshman.

The character occurs between pp. 80 and 91.

[W., T.]

The Poets Complaint, A Poem. To which is added The Character of Poetry; Written in Prose. . . . London, Printed for D. Brown . . . 1682.

4°, text pp. 1–20.

(1) Poetry (p. 17).

BSC 2437.

1683

Anonymous.

The Character of a Trimmer. . . . [colophon] London: Printed for Jo: Hindmarsh . . . 1683.

s.sh.fo. In verse.

Begins: "Hang out your *Cloth*, and let the *Trumpet* sound."

See note to 1682.

The Character Of A True-Protestant Ghostly Father. . . . [colophon] London, Printed for Richard Waite. 1683.

s.sh.fo, text pp. 1–2.

Begins: "He is a Jesuite disguis'd."

Murphy 116.

Excelling Contemplations. 1683.*

(1) Lord Arthur Capel (p. 6).

The Loyal Livery-Mens Hue and Cry after Sir John Presbyter. London, Printed for Robert Miller at the Blew Bible in Bedford Street Covent-Garden. 1683.*

s.sh.fo. In verse.

Begins: "With Hair in Characters, and Lugs in Text."

This seems to be a reprint of (John Cleveland's?) Hue and Cry after Sir John Presbyter (1649?).

Sphinx Lvgdvno-Genevensis Sive Reformator Proteus. Containing the True Character Of Sanctified Legion. Together with His Relations, Associates, and Retinue . . . London, Printed for R. Sollers, MDCLXXXIII.

4°, text pp. 1–22.
(1) Sanctified legion (p. 1), (2) A presbyter (p. 12).
Murphy 151. BSC 2294, 2439.

A., D.

The Whole Art Of Converse: Containing Necessary instructions for all Persons, of what Quality, and Condition so ever. With the Characters of the four Humours, of the English and French, as to their way of Conversing. By D.A. Gent. London, Printed for Joseph Hindmarsh, Bookseller to his Royal Highness, &c. 1683.*
BSC 2438.

A., P.

The Character Of An Honest Man; Whether Styled Whig Or Tory, And his opposite, the Knave. Together With some short Reflections on some Passages in a late Pamphlet, called the Character of a Popish Successor, and Considerations thereupon. By a Lover of Truth and Peace. . . . London: Printed for Randal Taylor. 1683.
fo, text pp. 3–20, wrongly numbered 16.
(1) The honest man (p. 4), (2) The knave or hypocrite (p. 4, in parallel columns).
Murphy 150. BSC 2426.
The Huntington Library entry ascribes this to P.A. with the note that he acknowledged it in the dedication to his Sober and Serious Considerations, 1685.

Blount, Thomas.

The Academy of Eloquence. Fifth Edition. 1683.*
Reprinted from 1656.

Gaskarth, John.

A Sermon Preached upon the first occasion After The Death Of His Grace John Duke of Lavderdale, In The Chapel at Ham. By John Gaskarth, his late Graces Chaplain, and Fellow of Pembroke-Hall in Cambridge. . . . London, Printed for Walter Kettilby . . . 1683.
4°, text pp. 1–42.
(1) Good governors (p. 1), (2) The Duke of Lauderdale (p. 25).

Heraclitus's Ghost [pseudonym.]

The Character Of A Church-Trimmer. By Heraclitus his Ghost. . . . [colophon] London, Printed for W.A. in the Year 1683.
s.sh.fo.
Begins: "A Church-Trimmer is the *Beelzebub*."
Murphy 116. BSC 2435.

[Hoy, Thomas.]

Agathocles The Sicilian Usurper. A Poem. Mutato Nomine, de Te Fabula narratur. . . . London, Printed for J.C. and are to be sold by Walter Davis . . . 1683.
fo, text pp. 1–32.
(1) Agathocles (i.e., Oliver Cromwell) (p. 11).

[Norris, John?]

A Murnival of Knaves: Or, Whiggism Plainly Display'd. . . . London: Printed for James Norris . . . 1683.
4°, text pp. 1–36.
(1) Jack Presbyter (p. 3).
This is a character of a Presbyterian.

[Sacheverell, Henry.]

The Character Of A Low-Church-Man: Drawn in an Answer To the True Character of a Church-man; Shewing the False Pretences to That Name. Humbly Offer'd to all Electors of Parliament and Convocation. The Third Edition. . . . Printed, and Sold by the Booksellers of Great-Britain.
8°, text pp. 1–24.
Begins: "It cannot but be visible to every Man."
The frontispiece is a portrait of Sacheverell. Since this is an answer to West's True Character of a Churchman, 1683, it must date from that year or later. The first and second editions have not been found.

Tillotson, John.

A Sermon Preached at the Funeral of the Reverend Benjamin Whichcot, D.D. and Minister of S. Lawrence Jewry, London, May 24th, 1683. London, Printed by M. Flesher, 1683.*
4°.
(1) Benjamin Whichcot (p. 31).
His works have been published in several editions.

[Walker, Obadiah.]

Of Education. Especially of Young Gentlemen In Two Parts. The Fourth Impression. . . . Oxford. Printed at the Theater for Amos Curteyne Ann. 1683.
6°, text pp. 1–339.
(1–3) as in 1673.

[West, Richard.]

The True Character of a Churchman showing the False Pretences to that Name. 1683.*
See 1700.

[Williams, Nathaniel?]

Imago Sæculi. 1683.*
Reprinted from 1676.

1684

Anonymous.

The Character of a Trimmer. 1684.*

Manuscript.
BSC 2440.
See note to 1682.

A Character Of London-Village; By a Countrey-Poet. . . . [colophon] London, Printed for J. Allen. 1684.

s.sh.fo. In verse.
Begins: "A *Village*! Monstrous! 'Tis a mighty Beast,/*Behemoth*, or *Leviathan* at least."
Murphy 151. BSC 2435.

Fore-warn'd, Fore-arm'd: Or, A Caveat to Batchelors, In The Character of a Bad Woman. . . . [colophon] London, Printed by T. Snowden, 1684.

s.sh.fo. In verse.
Begins: "A *Bad Woman*! Heav'n bless us, Sirs, who dare/Approach so near, to write her *Character*?"

The Nature, Nobility, Character, and Complement of Money. . . . London, Printed for William Thackeray . . . MDCLXXXIV.

s.sh.fo. In verse.
Begins: "In this word more is comprehended."

Allestree, Richard.

Forty Sermons. 1684.*
(1) Allestree, by John Fell.

Bacon, Sir Francis.

Baconiana.*
Reprinted from 1679.

Dunton, John.

The Pilgrim's Guide From the Cradle to his Death-bed . . . Represented to the Life in a Delightful new Allegory, wherein the Christian Traveller is more fully and plainly Directed than yet he hath been by any in the Right and Nearest way to the Celestial Paradise. . . . By John Dunton late Rector of Aston Clinton. London, Printed for John Dunton . . . MDCLXXXIV.

12°, text pp. 1–306.
(1) A safe guide for the pilgrim (p. 7).

[D'Urfey, Thomas.]

The Malecontent; A Satyr: Being the Sequel of the Progress of Honesty, Or A View Of Court and City. London, Printed for Joseph Hindmarsh . . . 1684.

fo, text pp. 1–30.
(1) Rich Gallus (par. xiv), (2) Loyal Cleon (par. xvii), (3) Just Solon (par. xvii).
Attributed to D'Urfey by the CBEL.

[Head, Richard.]

Proteus Redivivus . . . Compil'd and Publish'd formerly by R.H. but now Reprinted with Additions in every Chapter . . . By the same Author. London. Printed for W.D. and are to be sold by most Booksellers of London and Westminster, 1684.*

12°, text pp. 1–322.
(1–37) as in 1675.
Murphy 148.

[Ker, Patrick.]

Flosculum Poeticum. Poems Divine and Humane, Panegyrical, Satyrical, Ironical. By P.K. London, Printed for Benjamin Billingsley . . . 1684.

4°, text pp. 1–88. In verse.
(1) A lie and a liar (p. 78), (2) A fortune-teller (p. 80), (3) Drunkenness (p. 83), (4) Tipsy Tom, the metropolitan of drinkers (p. 84), (5) A cuckold, by D.N.B. (p. 86).
BSC 2441.
Attributed to Ker by the CBEL.

Kettlewell, John.

A Funeral Sermon For The Right Honourable, The Lady Frances Digby, Who Deceased At Coles-Hall in Warwickshire, on the 29th of September, 1684. By John Kettlewell, Vicar of Coles-Hill in Warwickshire. London, Printed for Robert Kettlewell . . . MDCLXXXIV.

4°, text pp. 1–33.
(1) Lady Frances Digby (p. 15).

L'Estrange, Sir Roger.

The Observator, in Dialogue. The First Volume. By Roger L'Estrange, Esq. . . . London, Printed by G. Bennet, for William Abington . . . MDCLXXXIV.

s.sh.fo (each number).
(1) A discourse of trimmers, an account of their humour, and practice (no. 241, Nov. 15, 1682; continued Nov. 16, Nov. 20, Dec. 11, Dec. 27, Feb. 21, 1682/3, April 30, 1683, Sept. 12, Nov. 26, Dec. 3, 1684, Dec. 4), (2) A false accuser (Oct. 3, 1683), (3) An honest man (Nov. 28, 1683).

Oldham, John.

Remains of Mr. John Oldham in Verse and Prose. London: Printed for Jo. Hindmarsh . . . 1684.

8°, text pp. 1–130.
(1) A certain ugly old p—— (p. 111).
Murphy 116. BSC 2442.

The Character, which is of a preacher, has a separate title page, also dated 1684.

Oldham, John.

The Works of Mr. John Oldham, Together with his Remains. London: Printed for Jo. Hindmarsh . . . 1684.

8°, each part separately paged.
(1) Remains, which in turn contains The Character of a Certain Ugly Old P—— (p. 109).

Reprinted numerous times. The Remains were also published separately.

Salgado, James.

The Manners And Customs Of the Principal Nations of Europe. Gathered together by . . . James Salgado, a Spaniard . . . and Translated into English by the Author's care, Anno 1684. . . . [Colophon] London, Printed by T. Snowden for the Author. 1684.

fo, text pp. 1–4.
(1) brief characters of the German, English, French, Italian, and Spanish nations, topically arranged.

Thorne, Edmond.

A Funeral Sermon upon the . . . death of Col. Edward Cook; Who died in London, January 29, 1683/4. London, by T.B. for Walter Davies. 1684.*
(1) Col. Edward Cook (p. 27).

1685
Anonymous.

. . . Being an Excellent New Poem, Containing The Character of Titus Oates, Who sometimes went under the Notion of the Salamanca Doctor. . . . London, Printed by J.M. in the Year MDCLXXXV.

s.sh.fo. In verse.
Begins: "Approach good people, here's (for pence a peece)."

The top line of the title has been entirely trimmed off in the Harvard copy, from which this note was made.

The Character of a Trimmer. 1685.*
See note to 1682.

A Character of the True-Blue Protestant Poet. 1685 (?).*
A reprint of 1682?

. . . Containing ane Encomiastic Character of the Famous [City] of Dumbrittain. Printed Anno 1685.*
s.sh.fo.

The Signet Library copy is mutilated, so that the whole title is not available. This notice comes from Bliss's letter to Laing (June 8, 1840), inserted in his copy of Earle in the Bodleian.

Epipapresbyter, Grand-Child to Smectymnus. Or, The Worlds Hue and Cry after Titus Oates. Ordain'd Doctor of Deviltry, at Salamanca. London, Printed by George Croom . . . 1685.*

4°, text pp. 1–2. In verse.
Begins: "Come hark and hear and draw me nigh."

Abercromby, David.

A Discourse Of Wit. By David Abercromby, M.D. . . . London, Printed for John Weld . . . 1685.

12°, text pp. 1–236.
(1) A pretender to wit (p. 41), (2) A great wit (p. 102).

[Buckinghamshire, John Sheffield, Duke of.]

The Character of a Tory.*

[Burnet, Gilbert.]

The Life of William Bedell, D.D. Bishop of Kilmore in Ireland. London, Printed for John Southby . . . MDCLXXXV.

8°, text pp. 1–487.
(1) William Bedell (p. 218).

Attributed to Burnet by the CBEL.

[Crossman, Samuel.]

The Young Man's Calling: Or The Whole Duty of Youth. London, Printed for Nath. Crouch. 1685.*

(1) The truly virtuous young man (chap. 6), (2) What the vertuous young man is and ought to be (chap. 7), (3) Civil and loving society.

A reprint of his The Young Man's Monitor, 1664.

Crowne, John.

Sir Courtly Nice: Or, It cannot Be. A Comedy. . . . Written by Mr. Crown. London, Printed by H.H. Jun. . . . M.DC.LXXXV.

4°, text pp. 1–60.
(1) Sir Courtly Nice, a fop (p. 11).

[Eachard, John.]

Some Observations Upon The Answer To an Enquiry into the Grounds & Occasions Of The Contempt Of The Clergy. With some Additions. In a Second Letter to R.L. By the same Authour. The Fifth Edition. London, Printed by R. Holt, for Obadiah Blagrave . . . 1685.

8°, text pp. 1–222.
(1–6) as in 1671.

[Gother, John.]

A Papist Mis-represented and Represented: or, A Two-fold Character of Popery. . . . By J.L. Printed Anno Dom. 1685.

4°, text pp. 1–127.
(1–2) as in 1665.
BSC 2444, 2448.

Heyrick, Thomas.

The Character of a Rebel. A Sermon Preached at Market Narborow, On the 26th of July, 1685. Being the day of Thanksgiving Appointed for His Majesties Victory over the rebels. London, Printed for Samuel Heyricke, 1685.*

Though the whole sermon is ostensibly a character, parts of it are definitely in character-form, e.g., p. 13.

[Hildesley, Mark.]

Religio Jurisprudentis: Or, The Lawyer's Advice to His Son . . . Per Philanthropum. . . . London, Printed for J. Harrison . . . and R. Taylor . . . Anno Regni Regis Jacobi II. Primo, 1685.*

12°, text pp. 1–168.
(1) A down-right jurisprudent (p. 166, in verse).
Murphy 151. BSC 2445.

Attributed to Hildesley on the authority of a note in the Bodleian copy. The original manuscript, undated, is in the British Museum.

Mackenzie, Sir George.

[First title] Moral Gallantry . . . By Sir George Mackenzie. . . . London, printed by T.B. . . . MDCLXXXV.
[Second title] A Moral Paradox . . . By Sir George Mackenzie. . . . London, printed by T.B. . . . MDCLXXXV.

12°, in 3 parts, text pp. 1–124, 1–89, 1–38.
(1) as in 1667.

[Phillips, Edward.]

The Mysteries of Love & Eloquence, Or, the Arts of Wooing and Complementing. . . . London, Printed by James Rawlins, for Obadiah Blagrave . . . 1685.

8°, text pp. 1–318, 1–70.
(1–3) as in 1658.

[Taubman, Matthew.]

Loyal Poems And Satyrs Upon the Times, Since the beginning of the Salamanca Plot, Written by several Hands. Collected by M.T. . . . London, Printed for John Smith . . . 1685.

8°, text pp. 1–128. In verse.

(1) The hypocritical Christian. or the conventicling citizen (p. 34), (2) Sejanus, or the popular favourite (p. 70), (3) The true Presbyterian without disguise, by Sir John Denham (p. 80), (4) The dissenter (p. 87), (5) The sollicitous citizen (p. 90).
BSC 2446.
The Epistle is signed Mat. Taubman.

Wotton, Sir Henry.

Reliquiae Wottonianae. 1685.*
Reprinted from 1651.

1686

Anonymous.

The Character And Qualifications Of An Honest Loyal Merchant. Licensed, and Entered according to Order. . . . London: Printed by Robert Roberts. MDCLXXXVI.

4°, text pp. 1–14.
Begins: "The Loyal Honest Merchant is an Universal Tradesman."
Murphy 88. BSC 2447.

The Character of Love, guided by Inclination, instanced in two true Histories. Translated out of the French. 1686.*

Twelve Ingenious Characters: Or, Pleasant Descriptions, Of the Properties Of Sundry Persons & Things. Viz. [in two columns] An Importunate-Dunn. A Serjeant or Bailiff. A Paun-broker. A Prison. A Tavern. A Scold. A Bad Husband. A Town-Fop. A Bawd. A Fair and Happy Milk-Maid. The Quacks Directory. A Young Enamourist. Licensed, June the 2d. 1686. R.P. London: Printed for S. Norris, and are to be Sold by most Booksellers. 1686.*

8°, text pp. 1–48.
(1) An importunate-dunn, (2) A serjeant or bailiff, (3) A pawn-broker, (4) A prison, (5) A tavern, (6) A scold, (7) A bad husband, (8) A town-fop, (9) A bawd, (10) A fair and happy milk-maid, (11) The quacks directory, (12) A young enamourist.
Murphy 89.

Nos. 4 and 5 come from Earle, No. 8 from The Character of a Coffee-House (1673), No. 10 from Overbury, No. 12 from Flecknoe (according to Miss Murphy). Much of the contents is included in H.C.'s England's Jests Refin'd, 1686.

Abercromby, David.

A Discourse of Wit. By David Abercromby, M.D. . . . London, Printed for John Weld . . . 1686.*
Reprinted from 1685.

Behn, Aphra.

La Montre: Or The Lover's Watch. By Mrs.
A. Behn. London, Printed by R.H. for W.
Canning . . . 1686.

8°, text pp. 1–243.
(1) The coquet (p. 43, in verse), (2) Sincerity
(p. 92, in verse).

According to the CBEL, this was translated from Baltha-
zarde Bonnecorse. There was an earlier edition in 1685.
It was reprinted numerous times.

Brown, Thomas.

Works.*

See 1707.

[C., H.]

England's Jests Refin'd and Improved. . . .
To which are added Twelve ingenious Characters drawn to the life. 1686.*

(1) Of a character, (2) Of an importunate dun,
(3) Of a serjeant, or baylif, and his setting-cur,
(4) Of a paunbroker, (5) Of a prison, (6) Of a
tavern, (7) Of a scold, (8) Of a bad husband, (9)
Of a town-fop, (10) [numbered 11] A fantastick
lady, (11) [numbered 10] Of a young enamourist, (12) Of an honest drunken cur, (13) Of a
natural beauty (in verse).
Arber, Term Catalogues, II, 170, 180.

All but four of the characters seem to have been taken
from Twelve Ingenious Characters, 1686. No. 12 is probably from Winstanley's Poor Robin's Character of an
Honest Drunken Cur, 1686 (earlier edition, 1675).

Casa, Giovanni della.

The Refin'd Courtier, Or, A Correction of several Indecencies crept into Civil Conversation.
Written originally in Italian by John Casa . . .
made English, by N.W. London, Printed for
Matth. Gilliflower . . . MDCLXXXVI.

12°, text pp. 1–233.
(1) as in 1679.

Flatman, Thomas.

Poems And Songs, By Thomas Flatman. The
Fourth Edition, With many Additions and
Amendments. . . . London, Printed for Ben-
jamin Tooke . . . 1686.

8°, text pp. 1–280.
(1–2) as in 1674.
Some copies are on thick paper.

[Gother, John.]

A Papist Mis-represented and Represented.
1686.*

Reprinted from 1665.

Nourse, Timothy.

A Discourse upon the Nature and Faculties of
Man in Several Essayes: With some Consid-

erations upon the Occurrances of Human Life.
London: Printed for Jacob Tonson. 1686.*

(1) Talkers (chap. 28), (2) The solitary man
(chap. 29), (3) The business man (chap. 30),
(4) Study (chap. 31), (5) A rich man (conclusion).

Sherlock, William.

A Sermon Preached at the Funeral Of the Reverend Benj. Calamy, D.D. and late Minister
of St. Lawrence Jewry, London, Jan. 7th,
1685/6, by William Sherlock, D.D., Master of
the Temple, and Chaplain in ordinary to his
Majesty. London, Printed for John Amery,
1686.*

See 1702.

Walker, Anthony.

Eureka, Eureka, The Virtuous Woman
Found. 1686.*

Reprinted from 1678.

[Winstanley, William.]

Poor Robins Character Of an Honest Drunken
Cur: With A Relation Of The Frolicks Of His
Life & Conversation. And his Epitaph. Licens'd, Septemb. 28, 1686. London: Printed
for John Harris . . . 1686.*

4° text pp. 1–8.
Begins: "He's a pickl'd Youth to be sure."
Murphy 89.

1687

Ayres, Philip.

Lyric poems, Made in Imitation of the Italians.
Of which, many are Translations From other
Languages. . . . By Philip Ayres Esq; Li-
censed, R.L.S. London, Printed by J.M. for
Jos. Knight and F. Saunders . . . 1687.

8°, text pp. 1–167. In verse.
(1) His friend, W.B. Esq. (p. 11).

[C., H.]

England's Jests Refin'd and Improv'd. 1687.*
(1–13) as in 1686.
Eyre, Term Catalogues, II, 201.

Cleveland, John.

The Works of Mr. John Cleveland, Containing his Poems, Orations, Epistles, Collected
into One Volume, With the Life Of the Author. London, Printed by R. Holt, for Obadiah Blagrave . . . 1687.

8°, text pp. 1–514.
(1–4) as in his Poems, 1654, (5) A protector (p.
343), (6) A Puritan (p. 355).
Murphy 63, 139.

[Cotton, Charles.]

How to Play at Billiards. 1687.*

A reprint of his Compleat Gamester, 1674.

Gamaches, Father Cyprian de.

Some Characters, distinguishing a real Christian. . . . Done originally in French by Father Cyprian de Gamaches. 1687.*

[Gother, John.]

The Catholic Representer, Or The Papist Misrepresented And Represented. Second part. Published with Allowance. London, Printed by Henry Hills . . . 1687.

fo, text pp. 1–88.
(1) The papist misrepresented, (2) The papist represented.

A continuation of A Papist Mis-represented and Represented, 1665. The two characters are in parallel columns.

[Gother, John.]

The Papist Misrepresented and Represented . . . Third part. Published with allowance. London, Printed by H. Hills . . . 1687.

4°, text pp. 1–61.
(1) A continuation of the two parallel characters begun in the edition of 1665.

[Heyrick, Thomas.]

The New Atlantis. 1687.*

Attributed to Heyrick by the CBEL. Reprinted 1689 (as A True Character of Popery and Jesuitism), 1690 (ditto).

Oldham, John.

Remains. 1687.*

Patrick, Simon.

The Parable of the Pilgrim . . . By Symon Patrick, D.D. Dean of Peterburgh. The Sixth Edition Corrected. . . . London, Printed for Richard Chiswell . . . MDCLXXXVII.

4°, text pp. 1–527.
(1–3) as in 1665.

Peacham, Henry.

The Worth of a Penny. 1687.*

Reprinted from 1641.

Walker, Anthony.

The Virtuous Woman Found, her Loss bewayl'd, and Character Exemplified in a Sermon preached at the funeral of the Rt. Hon. Mary, Countess Dowager of Warwick. London, Printed by Nat. Ranew, 1687.*

(1) as in 1678.

[Walker, Obadiah.]

Of Education. The Fifth Impression. 1687.*

1688

Anonymous.

Character. . . . [colophon] Tot de Hague, gedruckt door Hans Verdraght, 1688.

s.sh.fo.
Begins: "In Answer to your last, wherein you desire me to give a Character of our Prince."
BSC 2435.

This is a character of the Prince of Orange, later William III.

An Exclamation Against Julian, Secretary to the Muses; With the Character of a Libeller. By a Person of Quality.

fo, text pp. 1–4. In verse.
Begins: "Thou Common Shore of this Poetick Town."
Murphy 152. BSC 2405.

This is a character of a libeller. The date is uncertain.

To That Most Lamentable . . . Scribler Bavius. . . . [colophon] Printed for the Coffeehouses, 1688.

fo, text pp. 1–4.
(1) Bavius (p. 1).
BSC 2451.

Behn, Aphra.

Three Histories . . . By Mrs. A. Behn. London, Printed for W. Canning . . . 1688.
[Inner title:] The Fair Jilt: Or, The History of Prince Tarquin and Miranda. Written by Mrs. A. Behn. London, Printed by R. Holt, for Will. Canning . . . 1688.

8°, 3 parts.
(1) A fop (Part II, p. 2).

Bona, Giovanni.

Manuductio ad Coelum. Third Edition. 1688.*
Murphy 146.

[Buckinghamshire, John Sheffield, Duke of.]

The Character of a Tory. 1688.*
Reprinted from 1681.

[Gother, John.]

Pulpit-Sayings, or, the Characters of the Pulpit-Papist Examined. In Answer to the Apology for the Pulpits, and in Vindication of the Representer against the Stater of the Controversie. With Allowance. London, Printed by Henry Hills . . . 1688.

4°, text pp. 1–58.
(1) The "pulpit-Papist," or preacher hostile to the Catholic church (a running account through most of the essay).

[Halifax, Charles Montagu, Earl of.]

The Man of Honour, Occasion'd by the Post-script of Pen's Letter.*

4°, text pp. 1–4. In verse.
Begins: "Not all the Threats or Favours of a Crown."
BSC 2465, 2466.

Attributed to Halifax by the CBEL, which dates it [1688?].

[Halifax, George Savile, Marquis of.]

The character Of A trimmer. His Opinion of I. The Laws and Government. II. Protestant Religion. III. The Papists. IV. Foreign Affairs. By the Honourable Sir W.C. London, Printed in the Year, MDCLXXXVIII.

4°, text pp. 1–43.
Begins: "Our Trimmer hath a great Veneration."
BSC 2294.

Although attributed on the title page here and often else-where to Sir W[illiam] C[oventry], this is given by the CBEL and other authorities to Halifax. See also note to the anonymous The Character of a Trimmer, 1682.

[Halifax, George Savile, Marquis of.]

The Lady's New Years Gift, or Advice to a Daughter . . . London, Printed . . . by Ran-dall Taylor . . . 1688.*

A unique copy of this first edition is said to have been in the possession of Simpkin and Marshall in 1926.

[Halifax, George Savile, Marquis of.]

The Lady's New-years Gift: Or, Advice To A Daughter. The Second Edition Corrected by the Original. London, Printed for Matt. Gilly-flower . . . and James Partridge . . . 1688.

12°, text pp. 1–164.
(1) A good kind of woman (p. 104), (2) A good humoured woman (p. 105), (3) A vain woman (p. 135), (4) A woman who is both vain and affected (p. 140).

[Halifax, George Savile, Marquis of.]

The Ladies New Year's Gift. Third Edition. 1688.*

[Penton, Stephen.]

The Guardian's Instruction, Or, The Gentle-man's Romance: Written for The Diversion and Service of The Gentry. . . . London, Printed for the Authour, and sold by Simon Miller . . . 1688.

12°, text pp. 1–90.
(1) A young lady fit for a person of quality (p. 29), (2) A raw and unqualified schoolmaster (p. 31), (3) A patron (p. 41), (4) A plain-dealing tutor (p. 48).
BSC 2452.

The Harvard copy bears an old manuscript note on the title page: By Stephen Penton.

[Shannon, Francis Boyle, first Viscount.]

Several Discourses and Characters, addressed to the Ladies of the Age; Wherein the Vanities of the Modish Women are discovered. Writ-ten, at the Request of a Lady, by a Person of Honour. . . . Printed for C. Wilkinson; and sold by T. Salusbury. 1688.*

8°.
See 1689.
Arber, Term Catalogues, II, 238.

[Shirley, John.]

The Triumph of Wit, and Ingenuity display'd in its Perfection. Being the newest and most usefull Academy, In Three Parts. Printed for Nicholas Bodington . . . 1688.*

(1) A wheedler (p. 202), (2) An abraham-man (p. 205).

There were several later editions. Miss Gertrude Noyes, in Studies in Philology, XXXVIII (1941), 464, discusses it at some length, pointing out the sources of its material in Awdeley, Harman, Head, and others. There are prob-ably more characters than those mentioned above.

Tate, Nahum.

A Pastoral In Memory Of his Grace The Illus-trious Duke of Ormond; Deceased July the 21st. 1688. . . . Written by N. Tate. London, Printed, and to be sold by Randal Taylor . . . MDCLXXXVIII.

fo, text pp. 1–15. In verse.
(1) The Duke of Ormond (p. 10).

1689

Anonymous.

The Character of a Grumbletonian, or The New Malcontent. London, Printed by Rich-ard Janeway, 1689.*

s.sh.fo, text pp. 1–2.
Begins: "A Grumbletonian! What's that — in the Pope's Name? Why, 'tis the First and Second Part of Hickeringill."

The Character Of A Prince. London: Printed, and are to be sold by Randall Taylor . . . 1689.

4°, text pp. 3–8.
Begins: "There are four Virtues properly called Regal."
Murphy 152. BSC 2453.

There is also a title page in Dutch dated 1688. Not prop-erly a character, in the sense of this bibliography. Perhaps reprint of 1643.

The Character Of a True English Protestant Souldier; With That of a Doublet-Pinking Bully-Hec, Or, A Cowardly-Spirited Animal,

Who dares not Venture his Life in the Service of his Country. . . . [colophon] London, Printed by E.W. for J. Gibbs. 1689.*

4°, text pp. 1–4.

(1) A souldier, (2) A coward.

Murphy 90.

The Character Of an Honest, and Worthy Parliament-Man.

s.sh.fo, text pp. 1–2.

Begins: "I hope the Reader will not be so unwise."

The Huntington copy is bound with other tracts dated 1689. Baldwin (*PMLA*, XIX [1904], 106) dates it 1642.

The Character Of An Irish-Man: Or, A Dear-Joy Painted to the Life. . . . [colophon] Printed in the Year 1689.

4°, text pp. 1–4.

Begins: "Since the Arrival of the Teague-Land Troops."

Mr. Greenough felt disinclined to include this title.

The Character Of His Royal Highness William Henry Prince Of Orange. . VVith Allowance. London: Printed for Randall Taylor . . . MDCLXXXIX.

fo, text pp. 3–7.

Begins: "When the Almighty designs a Great Hero."

Characters and Discourses, wherein the Vanities of Modish Women are Discovered. C. Wilkinson, 1689.*

BSC 2455.

A Collection Of The Newest and Most Ingenious Poems, Songs, Catches, &c. Against Popery, Relating to the Times. Several of which never before Printed. . . . London, Printed in the Year MDCLXXXIX.

4°, text pp. 1–23.

(1) The converts (p. 2, in verse).

The Converts contains satirical portraits of (a) the Earl of Peterborough, (b) the Earl of Salisbury, and (c) the Earl of Sunderland.

His Grace the Duke of Schomberge's Character, according to the Ignorant Notions that The Irish Papists in Jreland Have form'd of Him. . . . [colophon] London, Printed for William Beale.

s.sh.fo, text pp. 1–2.

Begins: "The Antients never Design'd their Heroes for any great Work."

The character proper begins at the top of page 2.

The Muses Farewel to Popery and Slavery . . . London, Printed for N.R. . . . 1689.

8°, text pp. 1–144, 1–95 (supplement).

(1) Old England, in allusion to a piece of Tacitus De Vita Agricolae (p. 52).

The Portrait of the Trimmer. 1689.*

Begins: "A true blew Priest, or Lincey Woolsey Brother."

Modified from Butler's Hudibras, I, iii, 1225 ff.

Seven Papers. Viz. . . . II. The Character of Popery. . . . London, Printed, and are to be sold by R. Baldwin . . . MDCLXXXIX.

4°, text pp. 1–42.

(1) Popery (p. 6).

Taken from Mr. Andrew Marvell's Character of Popery, 1689.

A Sixth Collection of Papers Relating to the present Juncture of Affairs. Containing I. The Character of the Prince of Orange. London, Printed, and sold by R. Baldwin.*

(1) The Prince of Orange.

Apparently reprinted from the anonymous Character, 1688.

The Trimers Character.*

Begins: "Who Can in the Twinkling of an Eye."

The Vision of Pasquin, or, a Character of the Roman Court, Religion, and Practices. Together with an Account of the Arts of the Popes Nephews to get Money, the Tricks of the Priests to fill the Churches Coffers by Masses for the Dead, The Policy of the Jesuites to cully Princes, and cheat Christendom. As also an Exact Description of Purgatory and Hell. In a Dialogue between Pasquin and Marforio. Translated out of Italian. . . . London: Printed and are to be Sold by Richard Baldwin . . . 1689.*

4°, text pp. 1–64.

BSC 2461.

[Buckinghamshire, John Sheffield, Duke of.]

The Fourth (and Last) Collection of Poems, Satyrs, Songs, &c. Containing . . . X. An Essay upon Satyr. By. Mr. Dr——den . . . Most of which never before Printed. London, Printed Anno Dom. 1689.*

4°, text pp. 1–33.

(1) Buckingham, (2) Shaftesbury, (3) Halifax, (4) Chancellor Finch, (5) Sedley, (6) Rochester.

Gould, Robert.

Poems Chiefly consisting of Satyrs and Satyrical Epistles. By Robert Gould . . . London . . . MDCLXXXIX.

8°, text pp. 1–310. In verse.
(1) A satyr upon man (p. 195, a collection of many minute characters).

[Halifax, George Savile, Marquis of.]

The Character Of A Trimmer. . . . By the Honourable, Sir W. Coventry. The Second Edition, carefully Corrected . . . Licensed December 27. 1688. London, Printed for Richard Baldwin . . . MDCLXXXIX.
4°, text pp. 1–43.
Begins: "Our Trimmer hath a great Veneration."
BSC 2457.

[Halifax, George Savile, Marquis of.]

The Character Of A Trimmer. . . . By the Honourable, Sir W. Coventry. The Third Edition, carefully Corrected, and cleared from the Errors of the first Impression. Licensed and Entred according to Order. London, Printed for Richard Baldwin . . . MDCLXXXIX.
4°, text pp. 1–36.
Begins: "Our Trimmer hath a great Veneration."

[Halifax, George Savile, Marquis of.]

The Character of the Protestants of Ireland, Impartially set forth in a Letter, In Answer to Seven Queries . . . London, Printed for Dorman Newman . . . MDCLXXXIX.
4°, text pp. 1–30.
Begins: "That I have not sooner performed my Promise."
BSC 2454.

[Head, Richard.]

The English Rogue. 1689.*
Reprinted from 1665.

Heyrick, Thomas.

A True Character of Popery and Jesuitism. The New Atlantis, a poem in Three Books; with some Reflections upon The Hind and the Panther. By Thos. Heyrick, M.A. 1689.*
A reprint of The New Atlantis, 1687.

Hickeringill, Edmund.

The Ceremony-Monger, His Character. In Five Chapters. . . . By E. Hickeringill . . . Edinburgh, Re-printed in the year, 1689.
8°, text pp. 6–80.
Begins: "As Black as my Ceremony-monger is."
BSC 2458.

Marvell, Andrew.

Mr. Andrew Marvell's Character Of Popery. January 17. 168$\frac{8}{9}$. This may be Printed. Rob.

Midgley. London, Printed for Richard Baldwin . . . MDCLXXXIX.
4°, text pp. 3–8.
(1) The Pope (p. 5).
BSC 2459.

Plunket, Captain Thomas.

The Character of A Good Commander, Together with a Short Commendation Of the Famous Artillery (More properly Military) Company of London; also A Brief Encomium on the Great Duke, and Worthy Prince, Elector of Brandenbourg. Lastly Plain Dealing with Treacherous Dealers. Wherenuto [sic] is Annexed The General Exercise of the Prince of Orange's Army. By Captain Tho. Plunket. Licensed, March the 4th. 1689. London, Printed for William Marshal . . . 1689.
4°, in 2 parts, text pp. 1–55, 3–12. In verse.
(1) A good commander (part I, p. 1).

Selden, John.

Table-Talk: Being The Discourses Of John Selden Esq; Or His Sence Of Various Matters . . . Relating especially to Religion and State. . . . London, Printed for E. Smith, in the Year MDCLXXXIX.
4°, text pp. 1–60.
(1) Gentlemen (p. 21), (2) King (p. 27).
Pforzheimer Catalogue No. 859.
Several times reprinted.

[Settle, Elkanah.]

The Character of a Popish Successour. 1689.*
Reprinted from 1681.

[Shannon, Francis Boyle, first Viscount.]

Several Discourses and Characters Address'd To The Ladies of the Age. Wherein The Vanities Of The Modish Women Are Discovered. Written at the Request of a Lady, by a Person of Honour. London, Printed for Christopher Wilkinson . . . 1689.
8°, text pp. 1–199.
(1) The Welch people (p. 25), (2) A happy marriage (p. 53), (3) A governing wife (p. 56), (4) An amorous gallant (p. 81), (5) Content (p. 94), (6) A young widow (p. 98), (7) Proud, brisk, ranting widows (p. 110), (8) Vicious sparks (p. 114), (9) Misses (i.e., whores) (p. 115), (10) A pretender to wit (p. 128), (11) Censorious ladies (p. 132), (12) Extravagant London ladies (p. 141), (13) Extravagant English gallants (p. 150), (14) Praise (p. 155), (15) Pride (p. 185).
BSC 2455.
Attributed to Shannon by the British Museum Catalogue.

1690

Anonymous.

The Character Of A Jacobite, By what Name or Title soever Dignifyed or Distinguish'd, — Written by a Person of Quality. . . . London, Printed for the Author. 1690.

4°, text pp. 1–28.

Begins: "*Jacobites* in general are a sort of Animals."

Murphy 90. BSC 2294, 2462.

The Character Of A Williamite: Being the Reverse of a late unlicens'd Treatise, Entituled, The Character of a Jacobite, By what name or Title soever Dignify'd or Distinguish'd; Written by a Person of Quality. . . . London, Printed for Richard Baldwin . . . 1690.

4°, text pp. 1–28 (pp. 23–28 misprinted 25–30).

(1) A Williamite in general (p. 2), (2) A Williamite in the House of Commons (p. 5), (3) A Williamite in the country (p. 6), (4) A Williamite among the clergy (p. 9), (5) The dignify'd Williamite (p. 18), (6) The Williamite citizen (p. 20), (7) The Williamite souldier (p. 23, misprinted 25), (8) A Williamite sailor (p. 27, misprinted 29).

Murphy 91. BSC 2463.

The Character of the Man with no Honour. In verse. Manuscript.*

BSC 2466.

Probably an answer to Halifax's The Man of Honour [1688?].

Characters of the Chief Ministers and Favourites during the reigns of Edw. & Richard II in Sir Robert Howard's History. London: Pr. by F. Collins for Thomas Fox at the Angel in Westminster Hall. 1690.*

4°.

See Howard's History, 1690, below.

[Manuscript.]*

(1) A king (p. 105).

MS. Tanner 89 in the Bodleian.

The Murmurers. A Poem. To which is added the Character of a Grumbletonian.*

Mentioned in a list of books, printed for Dorman Newton at the King's Arms in the Poultrey, at the end of A Vindication Of The Proceedings Of The Late Parliament &c., London, 1690.

The Muses Farewel to Popery & Slavery, The Second Edition. . . . London: Printed for S. Burgess . . . 1690.

8°, text pp. 1–224, 1–20 (supplement).

(1) as in 1689.

The School of Politicks: Or, The Humours Of A Coffee-House. A Poem. . . . Licensed, Apr. 15, 1690. London, Printed for Richard Baldwin . . . 1690.

4°, text pp. 1–24.

(1) Discontented men (p. 14).

BSC 2387.

Sherlockianus Delineatus: Or, The Character of a Sherlockian. Occasion'd By Dr. Sherlock's late Book, or Reasons for taking the Oath of Allegiance to their Majesties K. William and Q. Mary. . . . [colophon] London, Printed, for the Author, and are to be sold by most Booksellers. 1690.

s.sh.fo., text pp. 1–2.

Begins: "Dr. *Sherlock* having, more especially of late."

Ellis, Clement.

The Gentile Sinner. The seventh edition. 1690.*

Murphy 142.

[Giffard, Martha Temple, Lady.]

The Life and Character of Sir William Temple, Bart. Written by a particular Friend.

Manuscript.

Begins: "Sir William Temple was descended."

This manuscript, said to have been written about 1690, was in 1930 in the possession of Rev. J. C. Longe, Spixworth Park, near Norwich, England. See Temple's Early Essays and Romances, ed. G. C. Moore-Smith, Oxford, 1930, in which it is reprinted.

Heyrick, Thomas.

A True Character of Popery and Jesuitism. The new Atlantis, a Poem in Three Books: with some Reflections on 'The Hind and the Panther.' The Second Edition. By Tho. Heyrick M.A. Sold by T. Basset at the George in Fleet Street. 1690.*

A reprint of The New Atlantis, 1687.

Howard, Sir Robert.

The History of the Reigns of Edward and Richard II. With Reflections and Characters Of Their Chief Ministers and Favourites . . . Written in the Year 1685. By the Honourable Sr Robert Howard. . . . London: Printed by F. Collins . . . 1690.

4°, text pp. 1–183.

(1) Edward I, Edward II, Edward III, and Richard II compared (p. 174).

BSC 2464.

Lake, John.

The Character of a true Christian described in a Sermon . . . By John Locke [Lake?] D.D., late Rector of that Parish and late Lord Bishop of Chichester . . . Printed for O. Blagrave, 1690.*

(1) Mrs. William Cade.
Arber, Term Catalogues, II, 298.
Probably a reprint of Lake's Στεφανος Πιστου, 1671.

Mather, Cotton.

The Serviceable Man. . . . By Cotton Mather . . . Boston, Printed by Samuel Green . . . 1690.

8°, text pp. 1–64.
(1) A serviceable man (p. 1).
Very poor example of character.

Plunket, Thomas.

The Character of a Good Army, &c. Being A few Hints touching the Gallantry and Fidelity of the Army in the Late Wars . . . Written by Capt. Tho. Plunket; who was himself in that Army from first to last. . . . London, Printed in the Year 1690.

12°, text pp. 3–24.
(1) Cromwell as general (p. 6), (2) Cromwell's army (p. 8), (3) Commission officers (p. 8), (4) The army, by a chaplain of General Fairfax (p. 15), (5) The army (p. 19).

[Shannon, Francis Boyle, first Viscount.]

Several Discourses and Characters.*
Reprinted from 1689.

Walker, Anthony.

The Holy Life of Mrs. Elizabeth Walker, Late Wife of A.W.D.D. Rector of Fyfield in Essex. London, Printed by J. Leake, 1690.*

(1) Mrs. Walker.
The Preface to the Honoured Friends of my late Dear Wife is signed Anthony Walker.

[West, Richard.]

The True Character of a Churchman. 1690.*
See 1700.
BSC 2467.

1691

Anonymous.

The Character Of A Biggoted Prince; And What England May Expect from the Return of such a One. . . . London: Printed, for Richard Baldwin . . . 1691.

fo, text pp. 1–22.
(1) A biggoted prince [the deposed James II]

(p. 1), (2) The present king [William III] (p. 17), (3) The present queen (p. 18).
BSC 2469.

A Satyr Against the French. . . . Licens'd, December 6. 1690. London Printed . . . by Randal Taylor . . . 1691.

4°, text pp. 1–30.
(1) A French lover (p. 20).
BSC 2471.

The School of Politicks. 1691.*
Reprinted from 1690.

Burgess, Daniel.

Characters of a Godly Man . . . By Daniel Burgess . . . London, Printed for Tho. Parkhurst . . . 1691.*

8°, text pp. 1–128.
(1) The gracious man (p. 57), (2) The best Christians, by Bishop Wilkins (p. 124).
Murphy 152. BSC 2468.

Mackenzie, Sir George.

The Moral History of Frugality VVith its opposite Vices, Covetousness, Niggardliness, Prodigality, and Luxury Written by the Honourable Sir George Mackenzie. . . . London: Printed for J. Hindmarsh . . . 1691.

8°, text pp. 1–95.
(1) The frugal Dutch (p. 19), (2) The covetous man (p. 31), (3) The niggardly man (p. 63), (4) The luxurious man (p. 77).

Mather, Cotton.

Ornaments for the Daughters of Zion. 1691.*
See 1694.

S., S.

The Character of a Christian, or The Evangelical Art of promoting self-denial. Being an Essay alluding to the severities and advantages of Infant-weaning; grounded on *Psal.* 131. v.2,3. By S.S., M.A. In Octavo. Price, bound, 1s.*

Arber, Term Catalogues, I, 186.

Tate, Nahum.

Characters Of Vertue and Vice. Described in the Persons of The Wise-Man . . . Attempted in Verse From A Treatise Of The Reverend Joseph Hall, Late Lord Bishop of Exeter. By N. Tate. London, Printed for Francis Saunders . . . 1691.

4°, text pp. 1–32. In verse.
(1) The man of wisdom (p. 1), (2) The valiant man (p. 4), (3) The truly noble (p. 7), (4) The

patient man (p. 10), (5) The true friend (p. 13), (6) The hypocrite (p. 17), (7) The superstitious (p. 20), (8) The profane (p. 23), (9) The busy-body (p. 27), (10) The envious (p. 30). Murphy 14. BSC 2470.

Adapted from Hall's Characters of Vertues and Vices, 1608.

[Ward, Edward.]

The Poet's Ramble after Riches, or a Night's Transactions upon the Road Burlesqued. 1691.*

See 1710.

[Wood, Anthony à.]

Athenæ Oxonienses. . . . To which are added, The Fasti or Annals . . . London: Printed for Tho. Bennet . . . MDCXCI[–II].

fo, 2 vols.
(1) John Milton (Vol. I, col. 883).

Quoted in Toland's Life of Milton as a "character." Probably many other similar passages could be selected. Wood's book has been reprinted.

1692
Anonymous.

A Brief Character of Ireland, with some Observations of the Customs, &c., of the meaner sort of the Natural Inhabitants of that Kingdom. — Non seria semper. Licensed, Nov. 16, 1691. Printed for W.C. and are to be sold by R. Taylor, 1692.*

BSC 2473. Arber, Term Catalogues, II, 384.

A brief Character of the Protector, Oliver Cromwell . . . In a seasonable speech . . . in the House of Commons . . . in March 1659. Sold by R. Taylor. 1692.*

Arber, Term Catalogues, II, 429.

Chuse which you will be. London, Printed for R. Halyard, 1692.*

BSC 2472.

Said by Bliss to be a reprint of The Character of a Bigotted Prince, 1691.

[Boyer, Abel.]

The English Theophrastus, or the Manner of the Age, being the modern Characters of the Court, the Town, and the City. London: 1692.*

See 1702.

Burnet, Gilbert.

A Discourse Of The Pastoral Care. Written By the Right Reverend Father in God, Gilbert, Lord Bishop of Sarum. London: Printed by R.R. for Ric. Chiswell . . . MDCXCII.

8°, in 2 parts, text pp. 1–52, 1–40.
(1) A true clergyman (p. 2).

Burnet, Gilbert.

A Sermon Preached at the Funeral Of The Honourable Robert Boyle; At St. Martins in the Fields, January 7. 1691/2. By the Right Reverend Father in God, Gilbert Lord Bishop of Sarum. London; Printed for Ric. Chiswell . . . MDCXCII.

4°, text pp. 5–40.
(1) A good man (p. 18), (2) Robert Boyle (p. 35).

[Charleton, Walter.]

Two Discourses. 1692.*

Reprinted from 1669.

[Dorrington, Theophilus.]

The Excellent Woman Described By Her True Characters And Their Opposites. Licensed and entered. . . . London, Printed for Joseph Watts . . . MDCXCII.

8°, text pp. 1–304.
(1) Well-read and ill-read women (p. 1), (2) Good and bad conversationalists (p. 31), (3) Cheerful and melancholy women (p. 51), (4) Virtuous and superstitious women (p. 82), (5) Chaste and loose women (p. 91), (6) Courageous and timid women (p. 102), (7) Constant and inconstant women (p. 112), (8) Prudent and imprudent women (p. 123), (9) Learned and ignorant women (p. 131), (10) Kind and unkind women (p. 163), (11) Debauched women (p. 176), (12) Jealous women (p. 183), (13) Complaisant or flattering women (p. 216).
BSC 2474.

The dedication is signed T.D.

[Gildon, Charles.]

Miscellany Poems Upon Several Occasions . . . London, Printed for Peter Buck . . . 1692.

8°, text pp. 1–112.
(1) The beaux, an epigram, by Mr. Tho. Brown (p. 45, in verse).
Attributed to Gildon by the CBEL.

Hickeringill, Edmund.

The Good Old Cause: Or, The Divine Captain Characteriz'd. In A Sermon . . . Vpon II Sam. X.12. . . . By Edm. Hickeringill, Rector of the Rectory of All-saints in Colchester. Licens'd according to Order, Feb. 1. 169½. London, Printed for John Dunton . . . 1692.

4°, text pp. 1–32.
(1) Souldiers of fortune (p. 7), (2) A hector (p. 9), (3) A religious rogue (p. 12).

Hollingworth, Richard.
The Character of King Charles I. From the Declaration of Mr. Alexander Henderson . . . Upon his Death-Bed. . . . By Rich. Hollingworth, D.D. London Printed, and are to be Sold by R. Tayler . . . 1692.
4°, text pp. 1–28.
(1) Charles I (sig. B2).

Jonson, Ben.
Works. 1692.*
Pforzheimer Catalogue No. 561.
Reprinted from 1616.

Mather, Cotton.
Ornaments for the Daughter of Zion. 1692.*
See 1694.

Matthew, Sir Tobie.
A Collection of Letters, Made By Sr Tobie Mathews, Kt. With A Character of the Most Excellent Lady, Lucy Countess of Carlisle . . . Published by the Revd Dr J Donne. London, Printed for Tho. Horne . . . 1692.
8°, text pp. 1–356.
(1) as in 1660.

St. Evremond, Charles de Marguetel de Saint-Denis, Seigneur de.
Miscellaneous Essays: By Monsieur St. Euremont. Translated out of French. With A Character, By A Person of Honour here in England. Continued By Mr. Dryden. London, Printed for John Everingham . . . 1692 [–94].
8°, 2 vols.
(1) St. Evremond, by Dryden and others (preface), (2) Of Augustus (I, 85), (3) Of Tiberius (I, 105), (4) Monsieur de Lionne (I, 124), (5) Courtiers (I, 125), (6) The comparison of Caesar and Alexander (I, 128), (7) Persons who despise the new and value the old (I, 195), (8) A judgment upon Petronius (I, 241), (9) The man who does good as a duty (I, 259), (10) Other friends, whose only prospect is their own satisfaction (I, 261), (11) Hypocrites at court (I, 268), (12) Those, who can't leave the court, and yet are vexed at every thing which passes there (I, 269), (13) Persons who mind their employments (I, 271), (14) Persons who consult their pleasures (I, 272), (15) Reformers (I, 272), (16) Reasonable persons (I, 276), (17) So-called friends (I, 352),

(18) The heart (I, 355), (19) A woman that is not, and never will be found (I, 370).
BSC 2746.

[Tate, Nahum.]
A Present For The Ladies: Being An Historical Vindication Of The Female Sex. To which is added, The Character Of an Accomplished Virgin, Wife, and Widow, In Verse. London, Printed for Francis Saunders . . . 1692.
8°, text pp. 1–101, 1–22. In verse.
(1) The virgin (Part II, p. 1), (2) The wife (II, 7), (3) The widow (II, 14).
Murphy 152. BSC 2416, 2475.
Attributed to Tate by the CBEL, and acknowledged by him in 1693.

1693
Anonymous.
The Humours, And Conversations Of The Town, Expos'd in Two Dialogues, The First, of the Men. The Second, of the Women. London, Printed for R. Bentley . . . and J. Tonson . . . 1693.
12°, text pp. 1–139.
(1) A meer beau (p. 58), (2) A rake-hell (p. 60), (3) A comical poet (p. 74), (4) The merchant (p. 95), (5) The country gentleman of middle estate (p. 99), (6) The broken gentleman, or country spunger (p. 99), (7) The country farmer (p. 100).
The characters are presented by means of dialogues between Mr. Jovial, Mr. Pensive, and Mr. Sociable.
Others might be added, but these seem truest to type.

The Modern Fanatical Reformer: Or, The Religious State-Tinker. . . . To the Tune of, Liggan Water. . . . [colophon] London, Printed for (Rich.) Kell . . . 1693.*
s.sh.fo. In verse.
Murphy 153.

The Petition of the Ladies of London and Westminster to the Honourable House for Husbands. Printed for Mary Want-Man, &c. 1693.*
BSC 2388.

[Blount, Charles.]
Reasons Humbly offered for the Liberty of Unlicens'd Printing. To which is Subjoin'd, The Just and True Character of Edmund Bohun, The Licenser of the Press, 1693.
Text pp. 3–32.
(1) Edmund Bohun, by J.M. (p. 10).
Much of the book is a reprint of Milton's Areopagitica, but the character is not by him. Attributed to Blount by the CBEL.

Bohun, Edmund.

The Character Of Queen Elizabeth. Or, A Full and Clear Account of Her Policies. . . . Her Virtues and Defects. Together with The Characters of Her Principal Ministers of State. . . . Collected and Faithfully Represented, By Edmund Bohun, Esquire. . . . London: Printed for Ric. Chiswell . . . MDCXCIII.

8°, text pp. 1–376.

(1) Queen Elizabeth (p. 1), (2) Robert Dudley, Earl of Leicester (p. 75), (3) Robert Devereux, Earl of Essex (p. 85), (4) Thomas Ratcliff, Earl of Sussex (p. 89), (5) William Cecil, Lord Burleigh (p. 90), (6) Peregrine, Lord Willoughby (p. 94), (7) Sir Francis Walsingham (p. 95), (8) Mary, Queen of Scots (p. 97), (9) Sir Nicholas Throgmorton (p. 98), (10) Thomas Howard, Duke of Norfolk (p. 141), (11) The Duke of Alva (p. 184), (12) Sir William Fitzwilliams (p. 228), (13) Nicholas Sanders (p. 363).

BSC 2477.

Bona, Giovanni.

Manuductio ad Coelum. Fourth Edition. 1693.*

Murphy 146.

Reprinted from 1672.

[C., H.]

England's Jests Refin'd and Improv'd. . . . To which are added XIII. Ingenious Characters Drawn to the Life. The Third Edition. London, Printed for John Harris. 1693.*

Reprinted from 1686.

de Gombaud, M. Jean Ogier.

A Discourse of Christianity. . . . And shewing the way to a Holy Life, in the Character of a true Christian. Written Originally in French by the famous Monsieur de Gombaud; and now done into English by P. Lorrain. . . . London, Printed for S. Lowndes. 1693.*

12°.

Arber, Term Catalogues, II, 438.

D'Urfey, Thomas.

The Richmond Heiress: Or, A Woman Once in the Right. A Comedy . . . Written by Mr. D'Vrfey. London, Printed for Samuel Briscoe . . . 1693.

4°, text pp. 1–64.

(1) A man of the town (p. 14).

The Dramatis Personae also contains brief characters of the people in the play.

Hickeringill, Edmund.

The Ceremony-Monger his Character. Reprinted in the year 1693.*

BSC 2478.

Reprinted from 1689.

[Penn, William.]

Some Fruits of Solitude: In Reflections And Maxims Relating to the Conduct Of Human Life. Licens'd, May 24. 1693. London: Printed for Thomas Northcott . . . 1693.

12°, text pp. 1–134.

(1) A general character of man (p. 8), (2) A covetous man (p. 30), (3) A friend (p. 39), (4) Partiality (p. 100).

Attributed to Penn by the CBEL.

[Settle, Elkanah.]

The Character of a Popish Successour. 1693.*

Reprinted from 1681.

Tate, Nahum.

A Present For The Ladies: Being An Historical Account Of Several Illustrious Persons Of The Female Sex. To which is added, The Character of an Accomplish'd Virgin, Wife, and Widow, in Verse. Written by N. Tate, Servant to Their Majesties. The Second Edition Corrected, with Additions. London, Printed for Francis Saunders . . . 1693.

8°, in 2 parts, text pp. 1–101, 1–22. In verse.

(1–3) as in 1692.

Murphy 153.

1694

Anonymous.

The Gentleman's Journal: Or The Monthly Miscellany . . . London, Printed . . . by Richard Baldwin . . . 1694.

4°, text pp. 5–276.

(1) a fop (p. 228, Aug.–Sept.; in verse.)

The True Conduct Of Persons Of Quality. Translated out of French. London, Printed for Walter Kettilby . . . MDCXCIV.

8°, text pp. 1–191.

(1) A sincere man (p. 110), (2) A cowardly and faint-hearted man (p. 117).

Agrippa, Henry Cornelius Agrippa.

Of the Vanity . . . of Artes. 1694.*

Reprinted from 1569.

[Astell, Mary?]

A Serious Proposal to the Ladies. 1694.*

See 1697.

Blount, Sir Thomas Pope.

De Re Poetica: Or, Remarks Upon Poetry. With Characters And Censures Of The Most Considerable Poets. Whether Ancient or Modern. Extracted out of the Best and Choicest Criticks. By Sir Thomas Pope Blount. London, Printed by Ric. Everingham, for R. Bently . . . MDCXCIV.

4°, 2 parts, text pp. 1–129, 1–248.
(1) Aeschylus (p. 1), (2) Anacreon (p. 5), (3) Apollonius Rhodius (p. 7), (4) Aratus (p. 9), (5) Aristophanes (p. 11), (6) Aristotle (p. 15), (7) Ausonius (p. 19), (8) Beaumont and Fletcher (p. 21), (9) Ariosto (p. 27), (10) Boccaccio (p. 29), (11) Buchanan (p. 32), (12) Callimachus (p. 36), (13) Catullus (p. 38), (14) Chaucer (p. 41), (15) Claudian (p. 45), (16) Cowley (p. 48), (17) Dante (p. 56), (18) Davenant (p. 58), (19) Denham (p. 65), (20) Donne (p. 67), (21) Ennius (p. 69), (22) Euripides (p. 72), (23) Flaccus, Valerius (p. 75), (24) Fracastorius (p. 77), (25) Grotius (p. 80), (26) Gyraldus (p. 83), (27) Heinsius (p. 85), (28) Hesiod (p. 88), (29) Homer (p. 99), (30) Horace (p. 99), (31) Ben Jonson (p. 104), (32) Juvenal (p. 113), (33) Lucan (p. 118), (34) Lucilius (p. 124), (35) Lucretius (p. 127), (36) Martial (p. 131), (37) Milton (p. 135), (38) Oldham (p. 138), (39) Appian (p. 142), (40) Ovid (p. 145), (41) Persius (p. 154), (42) Petrarch (p. 160), (43) Petronius (p. 164), (44) Mrs. Phillips (p. 168), (45) Pindar (p. 171), (46) Plautus (p. 174), (47) Propertius (p. 179), (48) Prudentius (p. 183), (49) Rapin (p. 186), (50) The Earl of Rochester (p. 188), (51) Sannazarius (p. 192), (52) Sappho (p. 195), (53) Seneca (p. 197), (54) Shakespear (p. 202), (55) Sidney (p. 206), (56) Sophocles (p. 209), (57) Spenser (p. 213), (58) Statius (p. 217), (59) Suckling (p. 220), (60) Tasso (p. 222), (61) Terence (p. 227), (62) Theocritus (p. 230), (63) Tibullus (p. 233), (64) Vida (p. 235), (65) Virgil (p. 238), (66) Waller (p. 243). BSC 2479.

All the characters are in Part II.

Burnet, Gilbert.

A Sermon Preached at the Funeral Of The Most Reverend Father in God John By the Divine Providence, Lord Archbishop of Canterbury . . . By the Right Reverend Father in God, Gilbert Lord Bishop of Sarum. London, Printed for Ri. Chiswell . . . MDCXCIV.

4°, text pp. 1–36.
(1) John, Archbishop of Canterbury (p. 10).
There were two editions in 1694.

Collier, Jeremy.

Miscellanies: In Five Essays. I. Vpon the Office of a Chaplain. . . . By Jeremy Collier, M.A. London, Printed for Sam. Keeble . . . 1694.

8°, text pp. 1–188.
(1) An atheist (sig. A3v, prefixed to The Office of a Chaplain).

[Du Refuge, Eustache.]

Arcana Aulica. 1694.*
Reprinted from 1652.

[H., N.]

The Ladies Dictionary; Being a General Entertainment For the Fair-Sex: A Work Never attempted before in English. . . . London: Printed for John Dunton . . . 1694.

8°, text pp. 1–528.
(1) A bawd (p. 45), (2) A good child (p. 133), (3) A huff (p. 186), (4) A good husband (p. 198), (5) Fame (p. 233), (6) Good parents (p. 370), (7) A town beau (p. 404), (8) A virgin (p. 436), (9) A vain woman (p. 451), (10) A good wife (p. 472), (11) A good widow (p. 481).
Gertrude E. Noyes (Studies in Philology, XXXVIII [1941], 471 ff.) shows that many of the cant terms in this work are taken verbatim from Head's The Canting Academy. In the Philological Quarterly, XXI (1942), 129, she also points out that the contents in general are a *mélange* of borrowings from Heywood, Fuller, Brathwaite, Halifax, and numerous others. The dedication is signed N.H.

Mather, Cotton.

Ornaments for the Daughters of Zion. Or the Character and Happiness of a Virtuous Woman . . . Written by Cotton Mather. Tertullian's Advice for the Ornament of Women . . . In English. . . . London, Printed for Tho. Parkhurst . . . 1694.

12°, text pp. 1–144.
(1) A virtuous woman (pp. 1, 12), (2) The virtuous maid (p. 95), (3) The virtuous wife (p. 101), (4) The virtuous mother (p. 118), (5) The virtuous widow (p. 131).

[Penton, Stephen.]

New instructions To The Guardian: Shewing That the last Remedy to Prevent the Ruin, Advance the Interest, and Recover the Honour of this Nation . . . London, Printed for Walter Kettilby . . . 1694.

12°, text pp. 1–143.
(1) A purs-proud clown who oppresseth his minister (p. 130).
The Epistle Dedicatory is signed: Stephen Penton.

Rogers, Thomas.

A Posie for Lovers: Or The Terrestrial Venus Unmaskt. In Four Poems Viz. I. The Tempest, or Enchanting Lady. II. The Luscious

Pennance, or the Fasting Lady. III. The Feign'd Innocence, or the Jealous and Whining lady. IV. To an Old Gamesome Madame. . . . London, Printed for Thomas Speed . . . 1694. 4°, text pp. 1–23.
(1) Dorinda (p. 3), (2) Lausania, once a flirt, now a scold (p. 9).

[Shower, John.]
Some Account of the Holy Life and Death of Mr. H. Gearing, citizen of London . . . With the trial and character of a real Christian. London, Printed by J.D. for J. Lawrence. 1694.*
(1) Henry Gearing.
BSC 2481.
The "character" of a real Christian mentioned in the title is not a true character.

Tate, Nahum.
A Present for the Ladies . . . to which is added, The Character of an Accomplished Virgin and Widow in Verse. By N. Tate, Servant to their Majesties. London: Printed for F. Saunders, 1694.*
Reprinted from 1692.

Willard, Samuel.
The Character Of a Good Ruler. As it was Recommended in a Sermon Preached before his Excellency the Governour . . . of Massachusetts-Bay . . . on May 30. 1694. . . . By Samuel Willard . . . Boston Printed by Benjamin Harris, for Michael Perry . . . 1694. 4°, text pp. 1–31.
Begins: "Whether the Ordination of *Civil Government.*"
A poor character, consisting chiefly of exhortation.

1695
Anonymous.
Characters Of Gentlemen That have been put in to The Ladies Invention.*
s.sh.fo.
(1) A little beau of the city-strain, (2–16) Fifteen other brief characters.

Characters of Several Ingenious designing Gentlemen, Who have lately Put in to the Ladies Invention. Which is intended to be drawn as soon as full.*
s.sh.fo.
(1) A person of quality, (2–14) Thirteen other brief characters.
This is a different work from Characters of Gentlemen. The former is preceded by a woodcut of a stag's head,

this by a crested ram and a herald on horseback. At the bottom of this is an advertisement referring to the former as having come "on Friday last" and as not being "Genuine."

[Astell, Mary?]
A Serious Proposal to the Ladies.*
See 1697.

[Crossman, Samuel.]
The Young Man's Calling: Or, The Whole Duty of Youth. London, Printed for Nath. Crouch. 1695.*
(1–3) as in 1685.

[Dorrington, Theophilus.]
The Excellent Woman Described by her True Characters And their Opposites: Being A Just and Instructive Representation of the Vertues and Vices of the Sex. . . . In Two Parts. Done out of French, by T.D. London, Printed for John Wyat . . . 1695.
8°, in 2 parts, text pp. 1–304, 3–336.
(1–13) as in 1692, (14) The coquette (Part II, p. 48), (15) The superstitious (II, 192), (16) Of the modest and scandalous (II, 236), (17) The passionate and indifferent (II, 254).
BSC 2483.

[H., N.]
The Ladies Dictionary. 1695.*
Reprinted from 1694.

[Houghton, John.]
A Collection For Improvement of Husbandry and Trade. Friday, March 22, 1694/5. [no. 138.]
fo, 4 pages, unnumbered.
(1) A physician.
The first number bears Houghton's name, as does the later collected edition of 1727.

P., A.
Divine Characters, with a short Catechise (entitled Children's Bread) by A.P. Printed in the year 1695.*
8°.
BSC 2482.

Peacham, Henry.
The Worth of a Penny. London, Printed for Samuel Keble. 1695.*
Reprinted from 1641.

[Ward, Edward.]
Female Policy Detected. 1695.*
See the description of the undated edition.

1696

Anonymous.

A Character Of Mr. Blaw's Book, Entituled Suadela Victrix. [1696?]

4°, text pp. 1–8. No date or printer.
Begins: "You desired me to be at the Pains."
Though bearing no indication of printer or date, this book is dated tentatively 1696 by the Harvard catalogue.

The Character Of The Beaux, In Five Parts. I. Of a nice Affected Beaux. II. A Hector, or Bully Beaux. III. A Country Beaux. IV. A City Beaux. V. A Spruce Beaux, alias, a Lawyer's Clerk. To which is Added: The Character Of A Jacobite. Written by a Young Gentleman. London: Printed in the Year, 1696.*

4°, text pp. 1–46.
(1) A nice affected beaux, (2) A hector, or bully beaux, (3) A country beaux, (4) A city beaux, (5) A spruce beaux, alias, a lawyer's clerk, (6) A Jacobite.
Murphy 92.

[Astell, Mary?]

The Character of the Wisest Men.*

[Astell, Mary?]

A Serious Proposal to the Ladies.*
See 1697.

Baxter, Richard.

Reliquiæ Baxterianæ: Or, Mr. Richard Baxter's Narrative Of The most Memorable Passages Of His Life And Times. Faithfully Publish'd from his own Original Manuscript, By Matthew Sylvester. . . . London: Printed for T. Parkhurst, J. Robinson, J. Lawrence, and J. Dunton. MDCXCVI.

4°, 4 parts, text pp. 1–448, 1–200, 1–132, 1–18.
(1) Fairfax (Vol. I, p. 48), (2) Cromwell (I, 98).
Many other items are designated characters in the table of contents, but they are not characters in the sense used in this bibliography. The Fairfax is not a very good example.

[Buckinghamshire, John Sheffield, Duke of.]

The Character Of Charles II. King of England. With a Short Account Of his being Poyson'd. Written by a Person of Honour. With an Introduction exhibiting the Different Characters given him by the several different Parties of Roman Catholicks, Churchmen, and Dissenters, &c. By Another Hand. London Printed, and are to be Sold by Richard Baldwin . . . 1696.

8°, text pp. 1–14.
Begins: "I have pitch'd on this Character of King Charles."
BSC 2484.
Attributed to Buckinghamshire by the CBEL.

Cibber, Colley.

Love's Last Shift; Or, The Fool in Fashion. A Comedy. . . . Written by C. Cibber. . . . London, Printed for H. Rhodes . . . 1696.

4°, text pp. 1–103.
(1) Sir Novelty Fashion, by Elder Worthy (Act I, Scene i), (2) Beau Noisy, by Young Worthy (III, ii).

[Cotton, Charles.]

The Compleat Gamester. 1696.*
Reprinted from 1674.

[Drake, Judith?]

An Essay In Defence of the Female Sex. In which are inserted the Characters Of A Pedant, A Squire, A Beau, A Vertuoso, A Poetaster, A City-Critick, &c. In a Letter to a Lady. Written by a Lady. . . . London, Printed for A. Roper and E. Wilkinson . . . and R. Clavel . . . 1696.

8°, text pp. 1–148.
(1) A pedant (p. 27), (2) A country squire (p. 30), (3) Vanity (p. 60), (4) A bully (p. 62), (5) A scowrer (p. 64), (6) A beau (p. 68), (7) A poetaster (p. 79), (8) A coffee-house politician (p. 87), (9) A vertuoso (p. 96), (10) A sham lover (p. 115), (11) An envious man (p. 116), (12) A city-critick (p. 119).
Murphy 153. BSC 2485.
Attributed to Judith Drake by the CBEL, but occasionally to Mary Astell by other bibliographies. See A. H. Orphan, JEGP, XII (1913), 262. There were two editions in 1696.

[Eachard, John.]

Some Observations Upon The Answer To an Enquiry into the Grounds and Occasions Of The Contempt Of The Clergy. With some Additions. In a Second Letter to R.L. By the same Author. The Sixth Edition. London, Printed for E. Blagrave, and Sold by the Booksellers of London and Westminster, 1696.

8°, text pp. 1–188.
(1–6) as in 1671.

Foxcroft, John.

The Character and blessing of a Virtuous Wife; With other particulars relating to the Marriage state, practically considered in a discourse on Proverbs 19th. 14th. By John Foxcroft, Rector of Wyfardby in Leicestershire. 1696.*

Arber, Term Catalogues, II, 600.

[H., N.]

The Ladies Dictionary. 1696.*
Reprinted from 1694.

[Halifax, George Savile, Marquis of.]

The Ladies New Years Gift. Fifth Edition. 1696.*

Reprinted from 1688.

[Meriton, L.?]

Pecuniæ Obediunt Omnia Money Does Master all Things, A Poem Shewing the Power and Influence of Money over all Arts, Sciences, Trades, Professions, and ways of Living, in this Sublunary World. . . . York, Printed by John White, for the Author, and Sold by Tho: Baxter . . . 1696.

8°, text pp. 1–115.

(1) Divines (no. 6), (2) Domestic chaplains (no. 7), (3) Non-conformists (no. 8), (4) The Quakers (no. 9), (5) Persons in high employment (no. 10), (6) Judges (no. 11), (7) Justices of the peace (no. 12), (8) Lawyers (no. 13), (9) Attorneys (no. 14), (10) The spiritual-court men (no. 15), (11) Clerks of the crown (no. 17), (12) The under sheriff (no. 18), (13) The sheriff's seal-keeper (no. 19), (14) Bailiffs (no. 20), (15) Goalers (no. 21), (16) (entry cancelled), (17) Sea officers (no. 23), (18) Privateers (no. 24), (19) Land officers (no. 25), (20) Skippers (no. 26), (21) Merchants (no. 27), (22) Seamen and land soldiers (no. 28), (23) The custome officers (no. 29), (24) Sergeants at armes (no. 30), (25) Surveyors of land (no. 31), (26) Stewards (no. 32), (27) Astrologers (no. 33), (28) Officers of the excise (no. 34), (29) Messingers (no. 35), (30) Common informers (no. 36), (31) Church wardens (no. 37), (32) Chief constables (no. 38), (33) Conservators of rivers (no. 39), (34) Post boys (no. 40), (35) Doctors (no. 41), (36) Apothecaries (no. 42), (37) Romish priests (no. 43), (38) Clerks to J.P.'s (no. 44), (39) Gripeing landlords (no. 46), (40) Gamesters (no. 47), (41) Schoolmasters (no. 48), (42) Petty constables (no. 49), (43) Mountibancks (no. 50), (44) Dancing masters (no. 51), (45) Public waites (no. 52), (46) Fencing masters (no. 53), (47) The bell man (no. 54), (48) Highwaymen (no. 55), (49) Usurers (no. 56), (50) Clippers and coiners (no. 58), (51) Musicians (no. 59), (52) Sextons (no. 60), (53) The common crier (no. 61), (54) Miners (no. 62), (55) Common fowlers (no. 63), (56) Arms painters (no. 64), (57) Farmers husband-men and graysiers (no. 66), (58) Millers (no. 67), (59) Gardeners (no. 69), (60) The provident country housewife (no. 70), (61) Butter buyers and factors (no. 75), (62) Corn merchants and maltsters (no. 76), (63) Jobbers of cattle (no. 77), (64) Butter searchers (no. 78), (65) Farryers (no. 79), (66) The horse jockey (no. 80), (67) Badgers (no. 82), (68) A gentleman shepherd (no. 83), (69) Inn keepers (no. 84), (70) Vintners (no. 85), (71) Wine merchants (no. 86), (72) Porters (no. 87), (73) Hackney coachmen (no. 88), (74) Footmen (no. 89), (75) Hostlers (no. 90), (76) Common carriers (no. 91), (77) Tapsters (no. 92), (78) Drapers and merchants (no. 93), (79) Taylors (no. 94), (80) Milliners (no. 95), (81) Barbers (no. 96), (82) Chyrurgions (no. 97), (83) Drugists (no. 98), (84) Shoomakers (no. 99), (85) Watchmakers (no. 100), (86) Upholsterers (no. 101), (87) Jack of all trades (no. 102), (88) Sword cutlers (no. 103), (89) Sadlers (no. 104), (90) Coach makers (no. 105), (91) Braziers and pewterers (no. 106), (92) Cabinet makers (no. 107), (93) Goldsmiths (no. 108), (94) Grocers (no. 109), (95) The tobacconist (no. 110), (96) Joyners and carpenters (no. 111), (97) Butchers (no. 112), (98) Sempstresses and haberdashers (no. 113), (99) Scotch pedlers (no. 114), (100) Booksellers (no. 115), (101) Printers (no. 116), (102) Higglers (no. 117), (103) Petty chapmen (no. 118), (104) Traveling petty booksellers (no. 119), (105) Linen-weavers (no. 120), (106) Hardware men (no. 121), (107) Tanners (no. 122), (108) Woolen weavers (no. 123), (109) Hawking pedlers (no. 124), (110) Glovers (no. 125), (111) Common Brewers (no. 126), (112) The ale house keeper (no. 127), (113) Apprentizes (no. 129), (114) City carmen (no. 120), (115) Country colliers (no. 131), (116) Pavers (no. 132), (117) Fishermen (no. 133), (118) Brickmakers (no. 134), (119) Carters (no. 135), (120) Glassmen (no. 136), (121) Bowl-sellers (no. 137), (122) Coopers (no. 138), (123) Traveling potters (no. 139), (124) Oatmeal sellers (no. 140), (125) Sellers of roots (no. 141), (126) Sellers of bread (no. 142), (127) Country rope-makers (no. 143), (128) Fish-drivers (no. 144), (129) Sievers and basket-makers (no. 145), (130) Country salters (no. 146), (131) Tinkers and bow-sewers (no. 147), (132) Thatchers (no. 148), (133) Chimney sweepers (no. 149), (134) Kennell rakers, and ragg gatherers (no. 150), (135) The jakes-farmer, or gold-finder (no. 151), (136) Cowherds (no. 152), (137) Common swineherds (no. 153), (138) The common daily cryes, in and about London (no. 154), (139) Gripeing and oppressing mortgagees (no. 155), (140) Berge men or loyter men (no. 156), (141) Intelligencers or news-mongers (no. 157), (142) Ferry men (no. 158), (143) Water men (no. 159), (144) Common strumpets (no. 160).

Murphy 155. BSC 2486.

This book is an answer to An Essay in Defence of the Female Sex, by Judith Drake.

Shannon, Francis Boyle, first Viscount.

Discourses and Essays, Useful for the Vain Modish Ladies and their Gallants. . . . In Two Parts. Written by . . . Francis Lord Viscount Shannon. . . . The Second Edition, with new Additions. London: Printed for John Taylor . . . 1696.

8°, in 2 parts.

(1) A would-be vertuous woman (part I, p. 3), (2) Envious woman (I, 6), (3) Conceited women (I, 7), (4) Another sort of vertuous wives (I, 24), (5) Sir John Sucklin, a Venus Philosopher (I, 44), (6) Paulina, a virtuous woman (I, 51), (7) A drolling, abusive wit (I, 129), (8) Solomon's character of a covetous person (I, 139), (9) Praise (I, 155), (10) A pious contemplative man (II, 1), (11) Vain pretending wits (II, 34), (12) Elder brothers (II, 65), (13) Lawyers (II, 126), (14) Swearers (II, 186).

BSC 2487.

Starkey, George.

Pyrotechny Asserted. 1696.*

Reprinted from 1658.

[Sympson, Ez.]

A farther Essay Relating to the Female-Sex. Containing Six Characters, and Six Perfections. With the description of Self-Love. To which is added, A Character Of a Compleat Beau. London, Printed for A. Roper and E. Wilkinson . . . 1696.

8°, text pp. 1–115.

(1) A coquette (p. 1), (2) Hypocrites (p. 14), (3) The opinionate: or, conceited female (p. 29), (4) An avaricious housekeeper (p. 41), (5) A gamester (p. 51), (6) The litigious (p. 62), (7) A beau (p. 105).

Murphy 155.

Attributed to Sympson by the British Museum Catalogue. A reply to An Essay in Defence of the Female Sex, 1696, by Judith Drake.

1697

Anonymous.

Poems on Affairs of State: from The time of Oliver Cromwell, to the Abdication of K. James the Second. Written by the greatest Wits of the Age . . . With some Miscellany Poems by the same: Most whereof never before Printed. . . . Printed in the Year 1697.

8°, text pp. 1–240 (misprinted 260). In verse.

(1) The true Englishman, 1686 (p. 171), (2) Portsmouth's looking-glass (p. 174), (3) The English, in allusion to Tacit. de Vit. Agric. (p. 140).

No. 2 is a character of the Duke of Portsmouth. There were a number of editions during the following twenty years.

Poems on Affairs of State. The Second Part. Written during the Reign of K. James the II. against Popery and Slavery, and his Arbitrary Proceedings. By the most Eminent Wits. . . . Now Carefully Collected, and Published from the Originals. London, Printed in the Year 1697.

8°, text pp. 1–224. In verse.

(1) The man of honour (p. 1), (2) Old England (p. 37), (3) Dispensing judges (p. 41), (4) Fumbumbis: or the north-country-mayor (p. 140).

No. 2 is a reprint of No. 3 in the first part, 1697.

[Astell, Mary?]

A Serious Proposal To The Ladies; For The Advancement of their True and Greatest Interest. In Two Parts. By a Lover of her Sex. London: Printed for Richard Wilkin . . . 1697.

(1) A vain young lady (p. 30), (2) A prudent lady (p. 58), (3) A virtuous lady (p. 66), (4) An old maid (p. 101).

Burgess, Daniel.

The Golden Snuffers: Or, Christian Reprovers, and Reformers, Characterized, Cautioned, and Encouraged. A Sermon Preach'd unto the Societies for Reformation of Manners, in London, Feb. 15, 1696/7. By Daniel Bvrgess. . . . London, Printed by J. Darby, for T. Parkhurst . . . 1697.

8°, text pp. 7–80.

(1) The internal reprover (p. 17), (2) The ecclesiastical reprovers (p. 17), (3) The natural reprovers (p. 18), (4) The despotical reprovers (p. 18), (5) The fraternal brotherly reprovers (p. 19), (6) The pure gold (p. 21).

Collier, Jeremy.

Essays upon Moral Subjects. 1697.*

See 1703–09.

[Defoe, Daniel.]

An Essay upon Projects. London: Printed by R.R. for T. Cockerill . . . MDCXCVII.

4°, text pp. 1–336.

(1) A meer projector (p. 23), (2) The honest projector (p. 35).

Attributed to Defoe by the CBEL.

[Drake, Judith.]

An Essay In Defence of the Female Sex. . . . The Third Edition with Additions. . . . London, Printed for A. Roper . . . and R. Clavel . . . 1697.*

8°, text pp. 1–148.

(1–12) as in 1696.

Murphy 154.

[Halifax, George Savile, Marquis of.]

The Character Of A Trimmer. . . . By the

Honourable Sir W. Coventry. Corrected and Amended by a Person of Honour. The Third Edition. London, Printed for Rich Baldwin . . . 1697.

12°, text pp. 1–105.
Begins: "Our Trimmer, as he has a great Veneration."
BSC 2488.
A reprint of 1688.

Heyrick, Thomas.

The Character of a Rebel; a Thanksgiving Sermon, on 2 Sam. xv. ii. 1697.*
Reprinted from 1685.

Nourse, Timothy.

A Discourse upon the Nature and Faculties of Man. 1697.*
Reprinted from 1686.

Rogers, Timothy.

The Character of a Good Woman . . . in a Funeral Discourse . . . Occasion'd by the Decease of Mrs Elizabeth Dunton . . . With an Account of Her Life and Death; and Part of her Diary . . . By Timothy Rogers, M.A. London: Printed for John Harris . . . 1697.

8°, text pp. 1–174.
(1) A good woman (p. 9 and p. 132).

[Vanbrugh, Sir John.]

Aesop. A Comedy. . . . London, Printed for Thomas Bennet . . . 1697.

4°, text pp. 1–76.
(1) Aesop (p. 3).
There were later editions.

Vanbrugh, Sir John.

The Provok'd Wife: A Comedy . . . By the Author of . . . The Relapse . . . London, Printed by J.O. for R. Wellington . . . and Sam. Briscoe . . . 1697.

4°, text pp. 1–78.
(1) Lady Fanciful, a foolish woman about town (Act I, scene i).
Pforzheimer Catalogue No. 1020.
Often reprinted.

1698

Anonymous.

Herodian's History of the Roman Emperors. . . . With a Character of the Ancient Britains, done from the Greek, by a Gentleman at Oxford. Printed for J. Hartley. 1698.*
Arber, Term Catalogues, II, 238.

Collier, Jeremy.

Essays upon several moral subjects. The third edition. 1698.*
See 1703–09.

[Dare, Josiah.]

Counsellor Manners His Last Legacy To His Son: Enriched and Embellished With Grave Adviso's, Excellent Histories, and Ingenious Proverbs, Apologues, and Apothegms. [motto] The Third Edition, Corrected. London, for E.G. 1698.*
(1) as in 1673.

Huarte Navarro, Juan de Dios.

Examen de Ingenios: Or, The Tryal of Wits. . . . Published Originally in Spanish by Doctor Juan Huartes. And made English from the most Correct Edition by Mr. Bellamy. . . . London, Printed for Richard Sare . . . MDC-XCVIII.

8°, text pp. 1–502.
(1) as in 1594.

Mather, Cotton.

A Good Man making a Good End. The Life and Death of the Reverend Mr. John Baily. . . . By Cotton Mather. . . . Boston in N.E. Printed by B. Green . . . 1698.

8°, text pp. 3–88.
(1) A Christian (p. 58).

[Meriton, L.?]

Pecuniæ obediunt Omnia. Money Masters all Things: Or, Satyrical Poems, Shewing the Power and Influence of Money over all Men, of what Profession or Trade soever they be. To which are added, A Lenten Litany, by Mr. C--d, a Satyr on Mr. Dryden, and several other Modern Translators; also a Satyr on Women in general: Together with Mr. Oldham's Character of a certain Ugly old P--. . . . Printed, and Sold by the Booksellers of London and Westminster, 1698.

8°, text pp. 1–132.
(1–143) as (1–144) in 1696, but omitting no. 132, (144) Agents to regiments (no. 46), (145) Players (no. 49), (146) Dyers (no. 70), (147) Carpenters (no. 78), (148) Salesmen (no. 103), (149) Truckers (no. 104), (150) Mintmen (no. 110), (151) Bakers (no. 121), (152) Mealmen (no. 122), (153) Vestry keepers (no. 145), (154) Apple-sellers (no. 146), (155) Porters (no. 149), (156) Park keepers (no. 162), (157) Warreners (no. 166), (158) A certain ugly old P——, by Oldham (p. 125).
Murphy 156.

Miege, Guy.

Miege's last and best French Grammar . . . To
which is added . . . Characters, both in French
and English. . . . By Guy Miege, Gent;, Author of the French Dictionary. London:
Printed for W. Freeman. 1698.*

Arber, Term Catalogues, III, 67.

Milton, John.

A Complete Collection of the Historical, Political, and Miscellaneous Works of John Milton
. . . In Three Volumes. To which is Prefix'd
The Life of the Author . . . Amsterdam, Fin-
ish'd in the Year M.DC.XC.VIII.

4°, 3 vols.
(1) John Milton, by John Toland (Vol. I, p. 46).
The Life of which this portrait-character is a part is signed
I.T. and dated Sept. 3, 1698 (p. 47). Milton's works
have been reprinted numerous times, as has also this character.

Orrery, Charles Boyle, Fourth Earl of.

Dr. Bentley's Dissertations On The Epistles of
Phalaris, And The Fables of AEsop, Examin'd
By the Honourable Charles Boyle . . . Lon-
don, Printed for Tho. Bennet . . . 1698.

8°, text pp. 1–290.
(1) A good critic (p. 224).
There were two editions in 1698.

Sidney, Algernon.

Discourses concerning government . . . London, Printed, and are to be sold by the booksellers of London and Westminster, 1698.*

(1) Good and bad magistrates (p. 342).
Reprinted several times.

Theophrastus.

Characters. 1698.*
See 1714.

W., J.

Youth's Safety; or, advice to the younger sort,
of either sex . . . laying open to the wickid
practices . . . of Sharpers . . . to cheat . . .
1698.*

(1) A gentile town-shift (chap. 3), (2) A town-
shark (chap. 4), (3) A sharper (chap. 5), (4) A
beau (chap. 6), (5) Of a rake (chap. 7), (6) A
lewd woman.

[Ward, Edward.]

The London Spy. . . . By the Author of the
Trip to Jamaica. London, Printed for J. Nutt
. . . 1698[–1700].*

fo, in 18 parts.
(1) The former apprentice who now dresses like

a beau (part i, p. 5), (2) The spark who plays
the decayed gentleman (part i, p. 6), (3) The
highwayman who plays the ex-officer (part i, p.
6), (4) A rascal of varied talents (part i, p. 7), (5)
A projector (part i, p. 9), (6) A man who grew
rich by too frequent marriages (part i, p. 10), (7)
A peripatetic (part iii), (8) A member of the
Royal Society (part iii), (9) A vintner (part iv),
(10) A quack (part vi, in verse), (11) Gamesters
(part vii), (12) A pettifogger (part viii), (13)
A footsoldier (part viii), (14) A modern critic
(part x), (15) A victualler (part xv), (16) A
common victualler (part xv, in verse), (17) A
confidence man (part xv, in verse), (18) A modern reformer of vice, or, a reforming constable
(part xv), (19) The same (part xvi, in verse),
(20) A master of a vessell (part xvi, in verse),
(21) An Irishman (part xvi), (22) A beau (part
xvi), (23) A stockjobber (part xvi), (24) A
banker (part xvii, in verse), (25) A gossip (part
xvii, in verse), (26) A prize-fighter (part xviii,
in verse).

Attributed to Ward by the CBEL. The titles given are
not always Ward's, since he often omits titles.

[Ward, Edward.]

The Poet's Ramble after Riches. 1698.*
See 1710.

[Ward, Edward.]

Sot's Paradise. 1698.
See 1699.

[Ward, Edward.]

A Trip to Jamaica: With a True Character Of
The People and Island. By the Author of Sot's
Paradise. The Third Edition. London, Printed
in the Year, 1698.

fo, text pp. 5–16.
(1) Jamaica (p. 14), (2) Of Port-Royal (p. 15),
(3) Of the people (p. 16).
Attributed to Ward by the CBEL, which gives 1698 as the
first edition.

[Webb, James.]

An Encomium or Short Character Of The
Gracious and Virtuous Mrs. Lucy Webb; Who
Departed this Life, Nov. 13, 1698. Dublin;
Printed at the back of Dick's Coffee House in
Skinner Row 1698.*

The Dedication is signed James Webb.

1699

Anonymous.

A brief Character of Ireland, with some Observations of the Customs, &c.*

Probably a reprint of 1692.

The Country Gentleman's Vade Mecum: or his Companion for the Town. In Eighteen Letters, from a Gentleman in London, to his Friend in the Country, Wherein he passionately disswades him against coming to London, and Represents to him the Advantages of a Country Life, in Opposition to the Follies and Vices of the Town. . . . London, Printed for John Harris . . . 1699.

8°, text pp. 1–148.

(1) A sot (p. 27), (2) A beau (p. 30), (3) A gamester (p. 32), (4) A procurer (p. 103), (5) A bawd (p. 107), (6) A hilt (p. 110), (7) A bully (p. 118), (8) A setter (p. 120), (9) A sponger (p. 128).

Reprinted as The Tricks of the Town Laid Open, 1746, 1747, 1927.

The English Martial, Wherein He hath given a Diverting Idea of the Men and Things of both Ages, In Select Epigrams, Together with his Life, and Manner of turning Poet. To be continued monthly. This for January 1698/9. . . . London, Printed and Sold by A. Baldwin . . . 1698/9.

fo, text pp. 1–18.

(1) The king (p. 3), (2) The favorite (p. 4), (3) The statesman (p. 5), (4) The traitor (p. 6), (5) The loyalist (p. 7), (6) The rabble (p. 8), (7) The nobleman (p. 9), (8) The dukes (p. 9), (9) The duchesses (p. 10), (10) The lords (p. 10), (11) The knights (p. 11), (12) The squires (p. 12), (13) The ladies (p. 12), (14) The gentlemen (p. 13), (15) The commons (p. 14), (16) The man (p. 14), (17) The woman (p. 15), (18) The boy (p. 16), (19) The girl (p. 16), (20) The world (p. 17).

BSC 2489.

A Hue and Cry After A Man-Midwife, Who has Lately Deliver'd the Land-Bank of their Money. . . . [colophon] London, Printed in the Year, 1699.

s.sh.fo., text pp. 1–2. In verse.

Begins: (1) "If any Good Person, in Country or Town."

A character of a projector.

The Stage Acquitted. Being A Full Answer to Mr Collier . . . With A Vindication of King Charles the Martyr . . . To which is added, The Character of an Animadverter . . . London, Printed for John Barnes . . . and sold by M. Gilliflower . . . D. Brown . . . and R. Parker . . . MDCXCIX.

8°, text pp. 1–185.

(1) An animadverter (p. 181).

A Trip to Holland, Being A Description Of The Country, People and Manners: As also some Select Observations On Amsterdam. [eight lines of verse quoted from the Dutch Hudibras] Printed in the Year, 1699.

fo, text pp. 1–12.

(1) The country and the people (p. 3), (2) Of Amsterdam (p. 10).

BSC 2492.

Sometimes attributed erroneously to Edward Ward. In the Preface the author refers to Ward's Trip to Jamaica and says that "if I am not so Witty as the Plantation Author I am somewhat Wiser."

A Trip to Ireland, Being A Description Of The Country, People and Manners: As also some Select Observations On Dublin. . . . Printed in the Year, 1699.

fo, text pp. 1–12.

(1) Ireland and the Irish (p. 3), (2) Of Dublin (p. 10).

BSC 2492, entitled A Journey to Ireland, is probably the same work under a variant or erroneous title.

Erroneously attributed to Edward Ward. The author refers in the preface to "two other Authors (viz. those of the Trips to Jamaica and Holland)"; since Ward was almost surely the author of the first of these titles, he can hardly have been the author of the present work.

The True Character of the Spirit and Principles of Socinianism. London, 1699.*

Brown, Thomas.

A Collection of Miscellany Poems, Letters, &c. By Mr. Brown, &c. To which is added, A Character Of A Latitvdinarian. London, Printed for John Sparks . . . 1699.

8°, in 2 parts, text pp. 1–251 (misprinted 351), 1–15.

(1) A latitudinarian (Part II, p. 2).

Murphy 156. BSC 2490.

Brown, Thomas.

A Journey to Scotland.*

BSC 2492.

Brown, Thomas.

Works.*

See 1707.

Cleveland, John.

The Works of Mr. John Cleveland . . . With the Life of the Author. London, Printed for O.B. . . . 1699.

8°, text pp. 1–514.

(1–6) as in 1687.

Dunton, John.

The Dublin Scuffle: Being A Challenge Sent By John Dunton, Citizen of London, To

Patrick Campbell, Bookseller in Dublin. . . . London, (Printed for the Author) and are to be Sold by A. Baldwin . . . and by the Booksellers in Dublin. 1699.

8°, in 2 parts, text pp. 1–16, 1–544.
(1) A woman of sence (p. 319), (2) The Dissenters in Ireland (p. 331), (3) Quakers (p. 331), (4) Catholics (p. 332).

D'Urfey, Thomas.

The Famous History and Fall of Massaniello . . . The Second Part. Written by Mr. Durfey London: Printed for J. Nutt . . . 1699.

4°, in 2 parts, text pp. 1–52, 1–50.
(1) The Dutch (Act I, Scene ii, Pimpwell's speech to Ursala).

Other speeches of Pimpwell form a sort of satyrical character of the English.

[D'Urfey, Thomas.]

Wit and Mirth; or Pills to purge Melancholy, etc. Part II, with several new songs. 1699.*
(1) The beau's character.

Gailhard, Jean.

The true character of the Spirit and Principles of Socinianism. By J. Gailhard, Gent. London, for J. Hartley. 1699.*
BSC 2493.

[H., J., and others.]

Essays of Love and Marriage . . . 1699.*
Arber, Term Catalogues, III, 125, 159.

A reprint of Two Essays of Love and Marriage, 1657.

[Halifax, George Savile, Marquis of.]

The Character of a Trimmer. 1699.*
Reprinted from 1688.

[Halifax, George Savile, Marquis of.]

The Ladies New Years Gift. Sixth Edition. 1699.*
Reprinted from 1688.

La Bruyère, Jean de.

The Characters, Or The Manners of the Age. By Monsieur De La Bruyere of the French Academy. Made English by several hands. With the Characters of Theophrastus, Translated from the Greek. And A Prefatory Discourse to them, by Monsieur de La Bruyère. To which is added, A Key to his Characters. London, Printed for John Bullord, and sold by Matt. Gilliflower . . . Ben Tooke . . . Christopher Bateman . . . and Richard Parker . . . MDCLXXXXIX.

4°, in 2 parts, text pp. 1–451, 1–45.
(1) Of polite learning (Part I, p. 6), (2) Of personal merit (I, 34), (3) Of women (I, 52), (4) Of the heart (I, 81), (5) Of society and conversation (I, 96), (6) Of the goods of fortune (I, 123), (7) Of the city (I, 148), (8) Of the court (I, 164), (9) Of the great (I, 197), (10) Of the soverain or commonwealth (I, 219), (11) Of man (I, 243), (12) Of judgment (I, 301), (13) Of the fashion (I, 341), (14) Of certain customs (I, 366), (15) Of the pulpit (I, 396), (16) Of the wits of the age (I, 413), (17) Of dissimulation (II, 1), (8) Of flattery (II, 3), (19) Of impertinence (II, 5), (20) Of rusticity (II, 6), (21) Of wheedling (II, 8), (22) Of villany (II, 11), (23) Of loquacity (II, 12), (24) The news-monger (II, 14), (25) Of impudence occasioned by covetousness (II, 16), (26) Of sordid frugality (II, 17), (27) A brazen-fac'd fellow (II, 19), (28) Of unseasonable conversation (II, 21), (29) A busie body (II, 23), (30) Of stupidity (II, 24), (31) Brutality (II, 26), (32) Of superstition (II, 27), (33) A splenetic man (II, 28), (34) Of distrust (II, 30), (35) A sloven (II, 31), (36) A troublesome fellow (II, 33), (37) Vain glory (II, 34), (38) A niggard (II, 35), (39) Of ostentation (II, 37), (40) Of pride (II, 39), (41) Of cowardice (II, 40), (42) Of an oligarchical government &c. (II, 42), (43) Of those that begin to learn in old age (II, 43), (44) Of slander (II, 44).

Numbers 1–16 are by La Bruyère; the reminder are by Theophrastus. The latter are dated 1698.

Orrery, Charles Boyle, Fourth Earl of.

Dr. Bentley's Dissertations. 1699.*
Reprinted from 1698.

[Penn, William.]

Fruits of Solitude. 1699.*
Reprinted from 1693.

[Pettis, Mr., or Pittis?]

Characters of Several Ingenious Designing Gentlewomen, Who have lately put in to the Ladies Invention. Which is Intended to be drawn as soon as full.*
s.sh.fo.
(1) A certain worthy merchant, (2–17) [Sixteen other brief characters].

According to a note in The Postboy of February 23, 1699, the author was one Pettis or Pittis. The work is mentioned in An Elegy on the Death of the Author of the Characters, &c. of the Ladies Invention, who dyed on the 13th of this Instant at the Rose Spunging-House. Probably inspired by the anonymous Character of Several Ingenious designing Gentlemen, 1695. The date is not certain.

[Phillips, Edward.]

The Beau's Academy. 1699.*
Reprinted from Mysteries of Love and Eloquence, 1658.

[Shower, John.]

Some Account of the Holy Life and Death of Mr. H. Gearing . . . With the trial and character of a real Christian. London, 1699.*

Reprinted from 1694.

Tate, Nahum.

An Essay Of A Character Of the Right Honourable Sir George Treby Kt. Lord Chief Justice of His Majesty's Court of Common-Pleas. Address'd to the Learned Dr. Fowke: By N. Tate, Servant to His Majesty. . . . [colophon] London: Printed by R. Roberts, for the Author. MDCXCIX.

fo, text pp. 1–4.
(1) Dr. Fowke (p. 1), (2) Sir George Treby (p. 2).

[Toland, John.]

The Life of John Milton, Containing, besides the History of his Works, Several Extraordinary Characters of Men and Books, Sects, Parties, and Opinions. . . . London, Printed by John Darby . . . M.DC.XC.IX.

8°, text pp. 5–155.
(1) John Milton (pp. 9, 149, 152).
BSC 2494.

The Life has been several times reprinted; one of the latest editions is in The Early Lives of Milton, edited by Helen Darbishire, London, 1932.

[Walker, Obadiah.]

Of Education. Especially of Young Gentlemen. The Sixth Edition, Enlarged. London, Printed by H. Gellibrand, for Richard Wellington . . . And are to be Sold by Bernard Lintott . . . 1699.

12°, text pp. 1–299.
(1–3) as in 1673.

[Ward, Edward.]

The Poet's Ramble after Riches. 1699.*

See 1710.

[Ward, Edward.]

Sot's Paradise: Or, The Humours of a Derby-Ale-House, With A Satyr Upon The Ale. The Second Edition. . . . London, Printed in the Year, 1699.

fo, text pp. 5–16. In verse.
(1) A sage old bard (p. 7), (2) A wit (p. 7), (3) A scholar (p. 9), (4) A captain (p. 10), (5) A dapper blade (p. 10), (6) A drone (p. 11), (7) A spark (p. 11), (8) Teague, an Irish barber (p. 12).
BSC 2491.
Attributed to Ward by the CBEL.

[Ward, Edward.]

A Trip to Jamaica, with a true Character of the People and Island. 1699.*

BSC 2492.
Reprinted from 1698.

[Ward, Edward?]

A Trip To New-England. With A Character Of The Country and People, both English and Indians. [ornament] London, Printed in the Year, 1699.

fo, text pp. 3–16.
(1) Of Boston, and the inhabitants (p. 5), (2) Of the country in general (p. 8), (3) Of the native English in general (p. 10), (4) Of the beasts (p. 13), (5) First of the Moos-Deer (p. 13), (6) Of the Bear (p. 13), (7) Of the raccoon (p. 14), (8) Of the wild-cat (p. 14), (9) Of the porcupine (p. 14), (10) Of the beaver (p. 14), (11) Of the jackall (p. 15), (12) Of the Indians, and first of the men (p. 15), (13) Of their women (p. 16), (14) Of their food (p. 16), (15) Their distempers (p. 16).

1700

Anonymous.

An Answer to a late Abusive Pamphlet entituled The True Born Englishman Together with a True Character of a True Englishman.*

The British Excise-Man Dismounted, with his Character.*

4°, 2 leaves unpaged. In verse.
BSC 2500.

The Character Of A Whig, Under Several Denominations. To which is added, The Reverse, or the Character of a true Englishman, in Opposition to the former. London, Printed, and are to be Sold by the Booksellers of London and Westminster. 1700.

8°, text pp. 1–134.
(1) A sowre, malcontented Whig, &c. (p. 1), (2) A busie, impertinent, intermedler in government (p. 2), (3) The hypocritical preaching Whigs under every denomination (p. 5), (4) The factious, seditious, illiterate Whig lawyer (p. 15), (5) A bold, treacherous, Whig attorney (p. 28), (6) The juggling Whig physician (p. 34), (7) The university toping Whig physician (p. 36), (8) The decayed gentleman Whig physician (p. 40), (9) The mechanick, or scoundrel Whig physician (p. 42), (10) The traveller, or strawling Whig physician (p. 45), (11) The blustering pendantick poetical physician (p. 47), (12) The astrological Whig physician (p. 49), (13) The chimical Whig physician (p. 52), (14) The stately

methodical Whig physician (p. 55), (15) An amphibious latitudinarian, aldermanlike Whig (p. 58), (16) The sence-less, upstart Whig country gentleman (p. 62), (17) The church Whig, or the ecclesiastical bifarius (p. 72), (18) A slasher, or a tirannical ignorant pedagogue (p. 79), (19) A politick, tricking, over-reaching, trading Whig (p. 83), (20) The shifter, or Jacobite Whig (p. 86), (21) The republican Whig Jacobite (p. 89), (22) The scurrilous and seditious Whig writer (p. 94), (23) A Whig trimmer, or a jack of all sides (p. 98), (24) A Whiggish false pretending friend (p. 106), (25) A precise hypocritical coquet (p. 108), (26) A covetous griping usurer and extortioner (p. 113), (27) A wheedling cheating scrivener (p. 115), (28) The reverse, or the character of a true Englishman, in quality of a statesman (p. 122), (29) A private subject (p. 124), (30) A clergy-man (p. 125), (31) An upright lawyer (p. 128), (32) A learned physician (p. 129), (33) A true English country gentleman (p. 132).
Murphy 92. BSC 2497.

A Character of France. 1700.*
8°.
BSC 2498.

An Essay Upon Rewards And Punishments, According to the Practice of the Present Times. . . . London: Printed for W. Shaw.
4°, text pp. 1–44.
Begins: "Rewards and *Punishments* are allow'd."
BSC 2605.
A border-line example of character. The essay might be called an extended character of John Walter.
The date is uncertain.

An Explanation of the Vices of the Age . . . Printed and Sold by J. Evans.
Text pp. 2–8.
(1) A sot (p. 2).
Some copies are said to have the imprint: Printed and sold at No. 41, Long Lane. The date is uncertain.

The Lively Character of a Contented And Discontented Cuckold, Ala-mode de Anglitere, By what Names or Titles soever distinguished. With an Apology for, and a Defence of the Fair and Tender Sex. Suited for the Meridian of London. [colophon] Sold by the Booksellers of London and Westminster, 1700.
4°, text pp. 1–4.
Begins: "I shall make no Preface to the following Epistle."
BSC 2496.

The Natives: An Answer to the Foreigners . . . London: Sold by John Nutt . . .

fo, text pp. 2–19. In verse.
(1) The natives (p. 2), (2) The foreigners (by John Tutchin) (p. 3).
John Tutchin's The Foreigners was published in 1700. The two characters face each other on opposite pages.

The Picture Of the first Occasional Conformist (Job I. 6) Drawn in Little. . . .
fo, text pp. 1–4. In verse.
Begins: "A Picture I must Paint, but yet."
BSC 2521.
Since Defoe is among those satirized, the probable date is 1700 or later.

The Reformado precisely characterized. 1700.*
Reprinted from 1643.

A Step to Oxford: or a mad Essay on the Reverend Mr. Tho. Creech's Hanging himself (as 'tis said) for Love. London Printed in the Year 1700.*
4°, text pp. 1–23.
(1) Mr. Creech's mistress (p. 20).
BSC 2499.

A Succinct Description Of France, Wherein is a Character Of The People, Customs, &c. Of That Kingdom. Sent by a Gentleman now Travelling there, to his Friend in England. Dedicated to . . . Dr. Martin Lister. . . . Printed in the Year 1700.
4°, text pp. 1–70.
(1) A Frenchman (p. 11), (2) A French woman (p. 14).

Wit's Cabinet: A Companion For Gentlemen and Ladies. London, Printed by T. Morris at the Looking Glass on London Bridge.*
(1) The lover's description of his mistress (p. 104), (2) An exact description of a complete beauty (p. 104), (3) A drunkard (p. 141).
The date is uncertain.

Brown, Thomas.

Amusements Serious And Comical . . . By Mr. Brown. Printed for John Nutt. 1700.
8°, text pp. 1–160.
(1) The court (p. 15), (2) A professed courtier (p. 15), (3) Londoners (p. 23), (4) Bedlam (p. 34), (5) Westminster Hall (p. 39), (6) The playhouse (p. 48), (7) A quack physician (p. 93), (8) Coffee houses (p. 115), (9) The city circle (p. 132), (10) A pretentious talker (p. 148), (11) A touchy man (p. 152), (12) The publick (p. 156).
According to the CBEL, this work is based on Dufresny's Amusements Sérieux et Comiques, 1699.

Brown, Thomas.

A Collection of Miscellany Poems. 1700.*

Reprinted from 1699.

Congreve, William.

The Way of the World, A Comedy. . . . Written by Mr. Congreve . . . London; Printed for Jacob Tonson . . . 1700.

4°, text pp. 1–89.
(1) Millamant, by Mirabell (Act I, Scene i, p. 6).
Often reprinted.

[Defoe, Daniel.]

The Six Distinguishing Characters of a Parliament-Man; Address'd to the Good People of England. . . . London: Printed in the Year MDCC.

fo, text pp. 1–23.
Begins: "The Disuse, or Distrust."
BSC 2501.
Attributed to Defoe by the CBEL.

[Defoe, Daniel.]

The True-Born Englishman. A Satyr. . . . Printed in the Year MDCC.

4°, text pp. 1–71. In two parts.
Begins: "Speak, Satyr, for there's none can tell like thee."
Attributed to Defoe by the CBEL.

[Evelyn, John.]

A Journey to England. 1700.*

Reprinted from A Character of England, 1659.

Gloucester, William, Duke of.

English-Latin Theme Book.*
(1) A tyrant.
A manuscript at Christ Church, Oxford.

[H., J., and others.]

Essays of Love and Marriage . . . 1700.*
(1–13) as in Two Essays of Love and Marriage, 1657.
Arber, Term Catalogues, III, 190, 202.

[Halifax, George Savile, Marquis of.]

Advice to a Daughter. 1700.*

Reprinted from The Lady's New Years Gift, 1688.

[Halifax, George Savile, Marquis of.]

The Character of a Trimmer.*

Probably a copy of 1688.
A manuscript described in Maggs Brothers' Catalogue 717, 1942. A similar manuscript is offered in Quaritch's Catalogue 629, 1945.

Halifax, George Savile, Marquis of.

Miscellanies By . . . The Late Lord Marquess Of Halifax. Viz. I. Advice to a Daughter. II.

The Character of a Trimmer. . . . London: Printed for Matt. Gillyflower . . . 1700.

8°, 7 parts, each item having separate pagination.
(1) The Lady's New-Year's-Gift: Or, Advice To A Daughter, (2) The Character of a Trimmer.

[Kirke, Thomas.]

A Modern Account of Scotland: Being an exact Description of the Country, and a true Character of the People and their Manners. Written from thence by an English Gentleman. Printed in the Year. 1700.*

Reprinted from 1667.

La Bruyère, Jean de.

The Characters or Manners of the Age. By Mons. de la Bruyere . . . with the Characters of Theophrastus. . . . The Second Edition corrected and enlarged . . . Printed for J. Bullard. 1700.*

(1–44) as in 1699.

[Price, Lawrence.]

The Virtuous Wife. A Poem. In Answer to the Choice, That would have No Wife. . . . London . . . by J. Nutt . . . MDCC.

fo, text pp. 3–7.
(1–7) as in 1667.

St. Evremond, Charles de Marguetel de Saint-Denis, Seigneur de.

The Works Of Mr de St.-Evremont. In II Volumes. Translated from the French. . . . London: Printed for Awnsham and John Churchill . . . 1700.

8°, 2 vols.
(1–10) as (1–10) in Miscellaneous Essays, 1692, (11) as (19) *ibid.*

Scarron, Paul.

The whole Comical Works of Monsr. Scarron, containing I. His Comical Romance of a Company of State-Players. II. All his Novels and Histories. III. His Select Letters, Characters, &c. Translated by Mr. T. Brown, Mr. Savage, and others. London, Printed by S. & J. Sprint, 1700.*

8°, in 3 parts.
There were numerous later editions.

[T., C.]

A Short Account and Character of Spain, etc. London, 1700.*

See 1701.

[Tate, Nahum.]

An Essay Of A Character Of the Late Right Honourable Sir George Treby Kt Lord Chief

Justice of His Majesty's Court of Common-Pleas. . . . [colophon] London: Printed by R. Roberts, and Sold by A. Baldwin . . . 1700.

s.sh.fo. In verse.

(1–2) as in 1699.

[Tutchin, John.]

The Foreigners. A Poem. Part I. . . . London, Printed for A. Baldwin . . . MDCC.

fo, text pp. 3–11. In verse.

(1) The Dutch (p. 6), (2) Bentir (p. 7), (3) Keppeck (p. 10).

According to the CBEL, Part I was all that was published.

[Ward, Edward.]

The London Spy. 1700.*

Reprinted from 1698.

[Ward, Edward.]

The Poet's Ramble after Riches.*

See 1710.

[Ward, Edward.]

The Reformer, Exposing the Vices of the Age: In Several Characters . . . London, Printed by J. How. 1700.*

(1) The vitious courtier, (2) The debauch'd person, (3) The factious hypocrite, (4) The wet Quaker, (5) The covetous miser, (6) The prodigal son, (7) The city letcher, (8) The insatiate wife, (9) The amorous maid, (10) The beau apprentice, (11) The city mob, (12) The country squire.

BSC 2502.

[Ward, Edward.]

Sot's Paradise. 1700.*

Reprinted from 1699.

[Ward, Edward.]

A Step to the Bath: with a Character of the Place. London, Printed and Sold by J. How . . . 1700.

fo, text pp. 3–16.

(1) The bath (p. 16).

BSC 2495.

Attributed to Ward by the CBEL.

[Ward, Edward.]

A Trip To Jamaica: With a True Character Of The People and Island. By the Author of Sot's Paradise. The Seventh Edition. [ornament] Londod [sic], Printed and Sold by J. How . . . 1700.

fo, text pp. 5–16.

(1–3) as in 1698.

Reproduced in facsimile in his Five Travel Scripts, 1933.

[Ward, Edward.]

The Wealthy Shop-keeper: Or, The Charitable Citizen. A Poem. London: Printed, and are to be Sold by the Booksellers. MCC. [sic].

fo, text pp. 3–16. In verse.

Begins: "With Stars Propitious from his Birth he's blest."

[West, Richard.]

The True Character Of A Church-Man, Shewing The False Pretences to that Name.

s.sh.fo, text pp. 1–2.

Begins: "It is commonly observ'd, and we have too often felt."

BSC 2503.

Attributed to West by Halkett and Laing.

The date is not certain.

Willard, Samuel.

The Truly Blessed Man . . . By Samuel Willard . . . Boston in N.E. Printed by B. Green, and J. Allen, for Michael Perry. 1700.

8°, text pp. 7–652.

(1) The pardoned man (p. 9).

1701

Anonymous.

The Character Of King William III. . . . [colophon] London, Printed and Sold by Henry Hills. . . .

s.sh.fo.

Begins: "The Head, Hand and Heart of the Confederacy."

The date is uncertain.

[Astell, Mary?]

A Serious Proposal to the Ladies.*

Reprinted from 1694.

[B., E.]

Scotland Characterized . . . By the Author of, The Trip to North-Wales. 1701.*

[B., E.]

A Trip To North-Wales: Being A Description of that Country and People. Vincit qui Patitur. London: Printed in the Year, 1701.

fo, text pp. 1–12.

(1) Wales and its people (p. 1).

The Epistle Dedicatory to W.—— T.—— Esq. and the Preface are signed E.B. Frequently attributed to Edward Ward.

[Boyer, Abel.]

Letters of Wit, Political and Moral. 1701.*

(1) A Short Account and Character of Spain, by C.T. (p. 293).

[Davenant, Charles?]

The True Picture Of A Modern Whig, Set forth in a Dialogue Between Mr. Whiglove & Mr. Double, Two Under-Spur-Leathers to the late Ministry. London: Printed in the Year, 1701.

8°, text pp. 3–96.

(1) A modern Whig (p. 42).

Attributed to Davenant by the Harvard Catalogue. There were several other editions in the same year. A border line example of character.

[Defoe, Daniel.]

The True-Born Englishman. 1701.*

Reprinted from 1700.

Dering, Sir Edward.

The Most Excellent Maria, in a Brief Character. By . . . Sir Edward Dering. . . . London: Printed by R. Roberts . . . 1701.

8°, text pp. 1–261.

Begins: "Great and unsearchable are the Works."

BSC 2504.

An extended character of Lady Dering.

[H., J., and others.]

Essays of Love and Marriage. 1701.*

Arber, Term Catalogues, III, 236.

Reprinted from Two Essays of Love and Marriage, 1657.

[Halifax, George Savile, Marquis of.]

The Ladies New Years Gift. Seventh edition. 1701.*

Reprinted from 1688.

Herbert, George.

A Priest to the Temple: or the Country Parson's Character, and Rule of Holy Life. By Mr. G. Herbert . . . The Fourth Edition. London: Printed for Benj. Tooke . . . 1701.

12°, text pp. 1–141.

(1) as in Herbert's Remains, 1652.

Murphy 135. BSC 2505.

[Sacheverell, Henry.]

The Character of a Low-Church-man . . . in answer to the True Character of a Church man . . . . 1701.*

Reprinted from 1683.

[T., C.]

A Short Account And Character Of Spain: In A Letter from an English Gentleman now residing at Madrid, to his Friend in London. London: Printed and are to be sold by the Booksellers of London and Westminster. 1701.

fo, text pp. 1–20.

Begins: "Having, Dear Sir, acquainted you before with my Passage from Plymouth to Corunna."

BSC 2506.

Signed at the end, C.T.

[Ward, Edward.]

The Poet's Ramble after Riches. 1701.*

See 1710.

Warwick, Sir Philip.

Memoires Of the reigne of King Charles I. With A Continuation to the Happy Restauration of King Charles II. By Sir Philip Warwick, Knight. . . . London, Printed for Ri. Chiswell . . . 1701.

8°, text pp. 1–437.

(1) Charles I (pp. 1, 64, 346), (2) Archbishop Laud (p. 78), (3) Bishop Williams (p. 92), (4) Bishop Juxon (p. 93), (5) The Marquis of Hamilton (p. 102), (6) The Earl of Strafford (p. 109), (7) Oliver Cromwell (p. 247), (8) General Monke (p. 408).

[West, Richard.]

The True Character of a Church-Man, Shewing the False Pretences to that Name. 1701.*

4°, text pp. 1–4.

Reprinted from 1700.

1702

Anonymous.

Religion tossed in a Blanket: a brief Character of some false Professors of Religion. 1702.*

BSC 2509.

The True Character Of A Virtuous Wife; Being a Wedding Sermon [on Prov. xxi, 14] Preached on Board the English Admiral; Wherein a Virtuous Wife is compar'd both unto a Merchants Ship, and a Man of War. London, Printed for M. Fabian . . . 1702.*

Text pp. 1–34.

[Boyer, Abel?]

The English Theophrastus: Or, The Manners of the Age. Being the Modern Characters of the Court, the Town, and the City. . . . London, Printed for W. Turner . . . R. Basset . . . and J. Chantry . . . 1702.

8°, text pp. 1–383.

(1) Authors, wits, etc. of various kinds (p. 1), (2) Women of various types (p. 28), (3) A beau (p. 51), (4) A country squire (p. 58), (5) Courtiers (p. 110), (6) Tale-bearers (p. 128), (7) False pretenders (p. 187), (8) True and false friends (p. 197), (9) Kings and courtiers (p. 230).

BSC 2511.

[Brown, Andrew.]

The Character Of The True Publick Spirit . . . Printed in the Year, M.DCC.II.

4°, text pp. 1–152.

Begins: "Many Men have their proper *Genius*."

Too long and preachy to be a good character.

Brown, Thomas.

Amusements Serious And Comical, Calculated for the Meridian of London. By Mr. Tho. Brown. The 2d Edition, with large Improvements. London: Printed, and Sold by the Booksellers of London and Westminster, 1702.

8°, text pp. 1–184.

(1–12) as in 1700, (13) An antiquated beau (p. 17), (14) A gay courtier (p. 18), (15) A superannuated general (p. 19), (16) A quarrelsome actress (p. 53), (17) An irascible man (p. 164).

The order of the characters has been changed from 1700.

[C., H.]

England's Jests Refin'd and Improv'd. 1702.*

Reprinted from 1686.

[Davenant, Charles?]

The Old and Modern Whig Truly Represented. Being A Second Part of His Picture. And A Real Vindication Of His Excellency the Earl of Rochester, His Majesty's Lord Lieutenant of Ireland. . . . London: Printed in the Year 1702.

4°, text pp. 1–69.

Begins: "The Detraction of Great and Good Men is indeed the common Fate."

[Davenant, Charles?]

Tom Double Return'd out of the Country: Or, The True Picture Of A Modern Whig, Set forth in a Second Dialogue Between Mr. Whiglove and Mr. Double, At the Rummer Tavern in Queen-street. . . . The Second Edition. London: Printed in the Year, 1702.

8°, text pp. 3–96.

(1) A modern Whig (p. 3), (2) Caleb Casehard-en'd, a Presbyterian parson (p. 15).

There were two editions in 1702.

A border line example of character.

[Defoe, Daniel.]

Characters of the Court of Hanover. 1702.*

See 1714.

There are said to have been two impressions in 1702. This may possibly be an alternative title for Characters of the Royal Family; if so, it has no relation to 1714.

[Defoe, Daniel.]

Characters Of The Royal Family, Ministers of State, And of All the Principal Persons In The French Court. With a Short Account Of The French King's Revenue, And of His Land and Naval Forces. Written by a French Nobleman to his Friend in England. London: Printed for Frances Coggan . . . And Sold by John Nutt . . . 1702.

fo, text pp. 1–28.

(1) The king (p. 1), (2) Madam Maintenon (p. 2), (3) The Dauphin (p. 3), (4) Monsieur, the late Duke of Orleans (p. 3), (5) The Duke of Burgundy (p. 4), (6) The Duke of Anjou (p. 4), (7) The Duke of Berry (p. 4), (8) The present Duke of Orleans (p. 4), (9) Monsieur the Prince (of Condé) (p. 5), (10) The Duke of Bourbon (p. 5), (11) The Prince of Conti (p. 5), (12) The Duke of Maine (p. 6), (13) The Count of Toulouse (p. 6), (14) The Duke of Vendosme (p. 7), (15) The Grand-Prior of France (p. 7), (16) Cardinal of Bouillon (p. 7), (17) The Duke of Rheims (p. 7), (18) The Duke of Bouillon (p. 8), (19) Paul de Beauvillers, Duke of St. Aignan (p. 8), (20) The Duke d'Aumont (p. 8), (21) The Duke of Gevres (p. 8), (22) The Duke of la Tremouille (p. 9), (23) The Duke of Rochefoucaut (p. 9), (24) Monsieur John Racine (p. 9), (25) Monsieur Bontemps (p. 10), (26) Mareschal Duke of Noailles (p. 10), (27) Mareschal Duke of Duras (p. 11), (28) Mareschal Duke of Lorge (p. 11), (29) Mareschal Duke of Villeroy (p. 11), (30) Michael Francis le Tellier Marquis of Courtenaux (p. 13), (31) The Prince of Soubise (p. 13), (32) The Duke of Chevreuse (p. 13), (33) Marechal Duke of Boufflers (p. 13), (34) The Duke of Lauzun (p. 15), (35) The Duke of Armagnac (p. 15), (36) The Marquis of Beringhen (p. 15), (37) The Bishop of Meaux (p. 16), (38) The Archbishop of Cambray (p. 16), (39) The Duke of Uzes (p. 16), (40) The Duke of Vantadour (p. 17), (41) Monsieur de Sully (p. 17), (42) Monsieur de Lesdiguieres (p. 17), (43) Monsieur de Brissac (p. 17), (44) Monsieur de Channes (p. 18), (45) Monsieur de Richelieu (p. 18), (46) Monsieur de Luxembourg (p. 18), (47) Monsieur d'Estrees (p. 18), (48) Monsieur de Mazarin (p. 18), (49) Monsieur de Vivonne (p. 19), (50) Monsieur de Foix-Rendant (p. 19), (51) Monsieur de Coalin (p. 19), (52) Monsieur de Choiseul (p. 19), (53) Monsieur de la Ferte Senneterre (p. 20), (54) Monsieur de Charrots (p. 20), (55) Monsieur Rosen (p. 20), (56) Monsieur de Vauban (p. 20), (57) The Duke d'Harcourt (p. 20), (58) The Marquis of Villars (p. 21), (59) Monsieur de Megryny (p. 21), (60) Louis Boucherat (p. 21), (61) The Marquis of Chateauneuf (p. 21), (62) The Marquis of Barbesieux (p. 21), (63) Jean Baptist Colbert, Marquis of Torcy (p. 22), (64) Monsieur de Pont-Chartrain (p. 22), (65) Monsieur le Comte d'Aubigny (p.

22), (66) Mareschal Catinat (p. 23), (67) Mareschal Boufflers (p. 23).
BSC 2510.

Each section is headed: Character XXV, etc. The length varies from a few lines to a page, but all are of the character type.

[Defoe, Daniel.]
Essays upon Several Projects. 1702.*

Reprinted from An Essay upon Projects, 1697.

[Dunton, John.]
The History of Living Men: Or, Characters of the Royal Family, the Ministers of State, and the Principal Natives of the Three Kingdoms . . . Dedicated to His Royal Highness, Prince George of Denmark. London, Printed and are to be Sold by E. Mallet . . . 1702.
4°, text pp. 1–118.
(1) Queen Anne (p. 1), (2) Prince George of Denmark (p. 31), (3) Dowager Queen Catherine of England (p. 50), (4) Princess Sophia (p. 52), (5) Thomas, Archbishop of Canterbury (p. 56), (6) James, Duke of Ormond (p. 66), (7) James, Duke of Queensberry (p. 84), (8) Laurence, Earl of Rochester (p. 92), (9) Sir Thomas Littleton (p. 104), (10) Gilbert Heathcot (p. 113).
BSC 2512.

The dedication is signed John Dunton.

Dunton, John.
Letters from New England.*

See John Dunton's Letters from New-England, 1867.

[Gildon, Charles.]
Miscellany Poems upon Several Occasions . . . By T.B. Gent. Sold by J. Nutt. 1702.*
fo.
(1) as in 1692, (2) A wise man, (3) A lady's lapdog, (4) Revenge, (5) Vanity display'd, or the beaux anatomized.
Arber, Term Catalogues, III, 299.

The description is taken from the entry in Arber.

[Grascome, Samuel?]
The Character of a True Church-of-England-Man . . . [colophon] London, Printed by D. Edwards for N.C. in the Year 1702.*
4°, text pp. 1–8.
Begins: "Next to the name *Christian*, I think there is scarce a more honourable Name than that of *Protestant*."
BSC 2509.

The authorship of this piece is very uncertain. It is attributed to Grascome by Halkett and Laing, but often to Henry Sacheverell.

La Bruyère, Jean de.
The Characters, Or The Manners of the Age. By Monsieur de la Bruyere. Made English by several hands. With The Characters of Theophrastus. . . . The Third Edition. London, Printed for F. Leach, and Sold by Tho. Newborough . . . J. Nicholson . . . R. Parker . . . and B. Tooke, 1702.
8°, in 2 parts, text pp. 1–382, 1–38.
(1–44) as in 1699.

[Leslie, Charles.]
The New Association of . . . Moderate-Church-Men, with the Modern-Whigs and Fanaticks . . . By a True-Church-Man. . . . The Third Edition Corrected. Printed and Sold by the Booksellers of London and Westminster. 1702.
4°, text pp. 1–21.
(1) Moderate-church-men (p. 1).
BSC 2294.

Attributed to Leslie by the Harvard catalogue.

Mather, Cotton.
Magnalia Christi Americana: Or, The Ecclesiastical History of New-England. . . . In Seven Books. . . . By . . . Cotton Mather . . . London, Printed for Thomas Parkhurst . . . MDCCII.
4°, in 7 parts, text pp. 1–38, 1–75, 1–238, 125–222, 3–100, 1–88, 3–118.
(Some fifty or more characters of early American ministers.)

Mather, Cotton.
The Pourtraiture of a Good Man: Drawn with the Pencils of the Sanctuary. Printed for Benjamin Eliot. 1702.*

Mather, Increase.
The Excellency Of A Publick Spirit Discoursed: In a Sermon, Preached in the Audience of the General Assembly of the Province of the Massachusetts Bay in New England, May 27, 1702. . . . By Increase Mather . . . Boston in New-England: Printed by B. Green, & J. Allen, for Nicholas Boone . . . 1702.
6°, text pp. 1–84.
(1) The publick spirited man (p. 1), (2) The righteous man (p. 39), (3) Jesus Christ, the morning star (p. 64).

The three characters are rather diffuse, being sermons. Their titles, respectively, are as follows: (1) The Publick Spirited Man, (2) The Righteous Man A Blessing, (3) The Morning Star.

Penn, William.
Some Fruits of Solitude, in Reflections and Maxims relating to the Conduct of Human

Life, in two parts. London, Printed for T. Northcott, 1702.*

Reprinted from 1693.
Part II is entitled More Fruits of Solitude.

[Sacheverell, Henry.]

The Character Of A Low-Church-man: Drawn In Answer To The True Character of a Church-Man: Shewing the false Pretences to That Name. . . . Printed in the Year, 1702.

fo, text pp. 3–28.
Begins: "It cannot but be Visible to Every Man."
BSC 2294, 2509.

There were at least two editions of this year, differing in size, paging, etc.

Sedley, Sir Charles.

The Miscellaneous Works Of the Honourable Sir Charles Sedley, Bart. Containing Satyrs, Epigrams, Court-Characters, Translations, Essays, and Speeches. . . . The Death of Marc Antony: A Tragedy never before Printed . . . from the Original Manuscripts, by Capt. Ayloffe. London: Printed . . . by J. Nutt . . . 1702.

8°, in 3 parts, text pp. 1–213, 1–24, 3–64.
(1) A rich husband (Part I, p. 169).

Sherlock, William.

Sermons Preach'd upon Several Occasions. By W. Sherlock, D.D. . . . The Second Edition. London, Printed for William Rogers . . . 1702.

8°, 2 vols.
(1) Sermon II. Preach'd at the Funeral of the Reverend Benjamin Calamy . . . Jan. 7. 1685/6 (Vol. I, p. 33).

There were several other editions.

[Tutchin, John.]

The Observator. 1702.*

(1) A coxcomb (no. 13), (2–9) Other characters (nos. 94, 95, 96, 103, 107, 108, 109, 110).

The editor has not been able to check this item to discover the contents of the other numbers listed above.

[Ward, Edward.]

The Character of a Covetous Citizen, Or, A Ready Way to get Riches. A Poem. London, Printed, and are to be Sold by the Booksellers of London and Westminster. 1702.

fo, text pp. 3–16. In verse.
Begins: "The Man who dotes on Gold, how curs'd his Fate!"
BSC 2508.

Attributed to Ward by the Harvard Library. A reissue, with some changes, of his The Wealthy Shop-keeper, 1700.

[Ward, Edward.]

The City Madam, and the Country Maid: or, Opposite Characters Of a Virtuous Housewifely Damsel, and a Mechanick's Town-Bred Daughter. By the Author of The Pleasures of a Single Life, &c. London: Printed for John Nutt . . . 1702.

fo, text pp. 1–12.
(1) A half-bred-gentlewoman: or, a mechanick's daughter's education in town (p. 1), (2) A rural virgin: or, a rich farmer's housewifely daughter (p. 7).

Attributed to Ward by the CBEL.

[Ward, Edward.]

Female Policy Detected. 1702.*

See the notes on the undated edition.

Warwick, Sir Philip.

Memoirs of the Reign of King Charles I. 1702.*

Reprinted from 1701.

[West, Richard.]

The True Character Of A Church-Man, Shewing The False Pretences to that Name. Together with the Character Of A Low Church-Man Drawn in Answer to it. With Remarks. London, Printed for A. Baldwin . . . MDCCII.

4°, text pp. 1–63.
(1) A church-man (p. 1), (2) A low church-man, by Henry Sacheverell (p. 7).
BSC 2513.

1703

Anonymous.

The Apostates: Or The Noble Cause of Liberty Deserted. A Satyr. With the Character of a late L--d Li------nt. And a Comparison between the Fate of Troy and that of Israel. London; Printed for Eliz. Mallet . . .*

fo, text pp. 1–12.
(1) A lord lieutenant.

The date is uncertain because the lower part of the title page is torn off the British Museum copy, from which the note was made. This work seems to be a different poem from John Tutchin's The Apostates, 1701.

A Character of an Ecclesiastick; And Observations on the late Controversies of the Dissenters; With a brief Encomium on the Late Bp. of Worcester. 1703.*

4°.
Arber, Term Catalogues, III, 331.

The English Monster: or, the Character of an Occasional Conformist. London: Printed, and

are to be Sold by most Booksellers in London and Westminster, 1703. Price 2d.*
4°.
BSC 2515.

The true Picture of an ill Practiser of the Law. In a Dialogue between a Sollicitor and his intended Client.*
Arber, Term Catalogues, III, 349.

Wit's Cabinet: A Companion For Gentlemen and Ladies. Eleventh Edition. 1703.*
Reprinted from 1700.

Barnes, Joshua.
The Good Old Way, with the Character of an Honest Man. London: Printed for W. Turner, 1703.*
8°.
(1) An honest man.
BSC 2514.

[Brathwait, Richard.]
The Smoaking Age: or, the Life and Death of Tobacco. Containing plenty of pregnant Passages, pleasant Allusions, liberal and unforc'd Relations: Accomodated with the Strength of Ingenuity and Invention, and adapted to the Humour of the present Age. London, by John Nutt, 1703.*
Reprinted from A Solemne Ioviall Disputation, 1617.

[Brown, Thomas.]
Marriage Ceremonies, as now used in all Parts of the World. To which is added The Fantastick Adventures of Sir E-- H-- with his Seven Wives. 1703.*
(1-7) Seven unpleasant wives.

Chudleigh, Lady Mary.
Poems on Several Occasions . . . By the Lady Chudleigh. London, Printed by W.B. . . . 1703.
8°, in 2 parts, text pp. 1-125, 1-73.
(1) The happy man (p. 35, in verse).

Collier, Jeremy.
Essays Upon Several Moral Subjects. In Two Parts. . . . By Jeremy Collier, M.A. The Fifth Edition. London: Printed for Daniel Brown . . . J. Nicholson . . . B. Took . . . and G. Strahan . . . 1703[-09].
8°, in 4 parts.
(1) A person of honour (Part I, p. 90), (2) An atheist (I, 183), (3) A man of confidence (II, 102), (4) A covetous man or miser (II, 142), (5)

The man of interest (IV, 36), (6) The covetous man (IV, 90), (7) The spendthrift (IV, 91), (8) The coward (IV, 224), (9) The flatterer (IV, 241).

[Gordon, James.]
The Character Of A Generous Prince Drawn from the great Lines of Heroick Fortitude. . . . By a Hearty Well-Wisher of Her Majesties Government. . . . London, Printed for Edw. Evets . . . 1703.
8°, text pp. 1-439.
(1) Happy princes, by St. Augustine (p. 353), (2) Queen Elizabeth (p. 409), (3) Charles I (p. 418).
BSC 2516.
Attributed to Gordon by Halkett and Laing.
The word Lines in the title is a misprint for Lives.

Halifax, George Savile, Marquis of.
Miscellanies. 1703.*
Reprinted from 1700.

Spooner, Lawrence.
A Looking-Glass for Smoakers: Or, The Danger of the Needless or Intemperate Use of Tobacco. . . . A Poem. By Law. Spooner. London, Printed for A. Baldwin . . . 1703.
8°, text pp. 17-104. In verse.
(1) Tobacco, personified (p. 98 and *passim*).

[Spooner, Lawrence.]
Mirth and Wisdom, in a Miscellany of Different Characters, Relating to Different Persons, and Perswasions. . . . London, Printed for B. Bragg . . . 1703.*
8°, text pp. 1-56.
(1) A Presbyterian, or a female hypocrite, (2) A beau, (3) A Whig, (4) A lawyer's clerk, or, a pot-poet, (5) An attorney, (6) A detractor, (7) A bowling-green, (8) A surgeon, (9) A player, (10) A tavern, (11) A coquet, (12) A pinnershall text-driver, (13) An unsanctify'd dun, or a cruel creditor, (14) A bayliff's follower, (15) The exchange, (16) Will's coffee-house, (17) A wit, (18) A flatterer, (19) A high-flyer, (20) A drunkard, (21) A prison, (22) A courtier, (23) A handsom bar-keeper, (24) A young rake (25) A whore-master, (26) A pretender to learning, (27) A tobacconist, (28) An upstart sheriff, or a country justice, (29) A sceptick in religion, (30) A stock-jobber.
BSC 2517.
A medley, with minor changes, of selections from Earle and other writers. Reprinted in 1708 as Hickelty Pickelty.

[Ward, Edward.]
The London-Spy. Compleat, In Eighteen-Parts. By the Author of the Trip to Jamaica.

London, Printed and Sold by J. How . . .
1703.
8°, text pp. 1–437.
(1–26) as in 1698.

Warwick, Sir Philip.
Memoirs of the Reign of King Charles I.
1703.*
Reprinted from 1701.

[West, Richard.]
The True Character of a Churchman. Lon-
don, Printed for A. and J. Churchill. 1703.*
Arber, Term Catalogues, III, 357.
Reprinted from 1700.

1704

Anonymous.
The Character of a Modern Whig. 1704.*
Reprinted from 1681.

The Dissenter. . . . London, Printed in the
Year 1704.
4°, text pp. 3–60. In verse.
(1) A Puritan (p. 27).

A Just and Impartial Character of the Clergy
of the Church of England . . . London, Sold
by A. Baldwin. 1704.*
Arber, Term Catalogues, III, 402, 413.

The Pictures Of A High Flyer. . . . [colo-
phon] London: Printed in the Year 1704.*
4°, text pp. 1–4.
Begins: "A High-Flyer is a Monster, with an
English-Face."
BSC 2519, 2521.
There were at least two editions in 1704.

The Picture Of A Low-Flyer. London . . .
1704.*
4°, text pp. 1–4.
Begins: "A Low Flyer is an inconsiderable Animal."
BSC 2521.

Poems on Affairs of State, From 1640. to this
present Year 1704. Vol. III. Printed in the
Year 1704.
8°, text pp. 1–468. In verse.
(1) The wolf justice (p. 187), (2) The pension-
ers (p. 330), (3) The weasel uncas'd, or, the in
and outside of a priest drawn to the life (p. 361),
(4) Lackworth's lively character (p. 431), (5)
The character (p. 453).
No. 1 is a character of Lord Chief Justice Scroggs.

A Step to Oxford: in which is comprehended
An Impartial Account of The University:

With a Pleasant Relation of such Passages as
befel the Author in his Journey. London,
Printed in the Year, MDCCIV.*
fo, text pp. 1–10.
Characters of Oxford colleges.
An entirely different work from the similarly entitled work
of 1700.

[Birkenhead, Sir John.]
The Assembly-man. Written in the Year 1647.
But proves the True Character of (Cerberus)
The Observator, MDCCIV . . . London,
Printed in the Year 1704.*
4°, text pp. 1–22.
Begins: "An Assembler is part of the State's Chat-
tles."

Brown, Thomas.
Amusements Serious and Comical. 1704.*
Reprinted from 1702.

Brown, Thomas.
A Collection Of all the Dialogues, written by
Mr. Thomas Brown: One of them Entituled,
Democratici Vapulantes, Being a Dialogue between Julian, and others, was never before
Printed. To which are added, His Translations and Imitations of several Odes of Horace,
of Martial's Epigrams, &c. London: Printed
and sold by John Nutt . . . 1704.
8°, text pp. 1–388.
(1) A pretended saint (p. 150), (2) Dissenters
(p. 289).

[Brown, Thomas.]
Marriage Ceremonies: As now Used in all
Parts of the World . . . By Seignior Goya.
The Third Edition, 1704.*
Reprinted from 1703.

[Darrell, William.]
A Gentleman Instructed.*
See 1707.

Dunton, John.
The New Practice of Piety. 1704.*
(1) A moderate or right Christian.

[Gentili, Robert.]
The Frenchman and the Spaniard display'd in
lively Characters. 1704.*
(1–3) as in 1642.
Arber, Term Catalogues, III, 401.

Halifax, George Savile, Marquis of.
Miscellanies By the Late Lord Marquis of
Halifax . . . London: Printed for W. Rogers
. . . 1704.

8°, text pp. 1–364.
(1–2) as in 1700.

[Head, Richard.]

The Character of a Quaker in his true and proper colours. 1704.*

Reprinted from 1671.

[Leslie, Charles.]

The Rehearsal. . . . London, Printed and Sold by the Booksellers of London and Westminster. 1704[–09].

s.shs.fo. (each number).

(1) The tackers (Vol. I, no. 21, Dec. 16–23, 1704), (2) A tacker (I, no. 35, March 24–31, 1705), (3) Mr. Hickeringil (I, no. 195, March 29, 1707), (4) A Whigg as to the church (III, no. 15, May 22, 1708).

Attributed to Leslie by CBEL. The earliest issues were entitled The Observator.

Peacham, Henry.

The Worth of a Penny. 1704.*

Reprinted from 1641.

Perrault, Charles.

Characters . . . Of The Greatest Men . . . in France, During the Last Century. By Monsieur Perrault. Now Render'd into English, by J. Ozell. Printed for Bernard Lintott, 1704[–05].

8°, 2 vols.

(1) Armand John du Plessis (Vol. I, p. 1), (2) Peter de Berulle (I, 6), (3) Henry de Sponde (I, 11), (4) Peter de Marca (I, 15), (5) John Peter Camus (I, 20), (6) Anth. Godeau (I, 24), (7) John Francis Senault (I, 28), (8) Anth. Arnauld (I, 33), (9) James Sirmond (I, 38), (10) Denys Petau (I, 42), (11) John Morin (I, 47), (12) Louis de Bourbon (I, 52), (13) Viscount de Turenne (I, 56), (14) Blaise Francis (I, 61), (15) Peter Seguier (I, 66), (16) Louis Thomassin (I, 71), (17) William du Vair (I, 76), (18) The President Jeannin (I, 80), (19) Paul Phelybeaux (I, 85), (20) John-Baptiste Colbert (I, 89), (21) William de Lamoignon (I, 94), (22) President de Thou (I, 98), (23) Hierome Bignon (I, 102), (24) Nicolas Claude Fabri de Peiresc (I, 105), (25) Papire Masson (I, 109), (26) Scevola de Sainte Marthe (I, 113), (27) Paul Pellisson Fontanier (I, 118), (28) Peter du Puy (I, 123), (29) Robert Arnauld (I, 127), (30) Anth. Rossignol (I, 131), (31) Rene Descartes (I, 135), (32) Anth. le Maistre (I, 140), (33) Peter Gassendi (I, 144), (34) Char. de Fresne (I, 148), (35) Claude Perrault (I, 152), (36) Francis de Malherbe (I, 158), (37) John Louis Guez, Sieur de Balzac (I, 162), (38) Vincent Voiture (I, 166),

(39) John Francis Sarrafin (I, 171), (40) Peter Corneille (I, 175), (41) John Baptiste Poquelin de Moliere (I, 179), (42) Philip Quinault (I, 184), (43) John de la Fontaine (I, 188), (44) John Baptiste Lully (I, 192), (45) Francis Mansart (I, 196), (46) Nicolas Poussin (I, 201), (47) Charles le Brun (I, 205), (48) Eustache le Sueur (I, 210), (49) Blaise Pascal (I, 214), (50) Achilles de Harlay (I, 219), (51) James Davi du Perron (II, 1), (52) Cardinal d'Ossat (II, 6), (53) Nicolas Coeffteau (II, 11), (54) Vincent de Paul (II, 14), (55) John de Launot (II, 18), (56) Peter Lallemant (II, 23), (57) Sebastian le Nain de Tillemont (II, 28), (58) John-Baptiste Santevil (II, 33), (59) Hierom Vignier (II, 38), (60) Father Fr. de Combesis (II, 43), (61) Marin Mersenne (II, 47), (62) Henry de Loraine (II, 51), (63) Maximilian de Bethune (II, 55), (64) Mareschal de Meilleraye (II, 59), (65) Mareschal de Gramont (II, 62), (66) Mareschal Luxembourg (II, 65), (67) John de Gassion (II, 70), (68) Abraham de Fabert (II, 74), (69) Abraham du Quesne (II, 80), (70) Honorius D'Urfé (II, 85), (71) Claude Berbier du Metz (II, 89), (72) Sebastian de Pontault, de Beaulieu (II, 94), (73) James de Soleisel (II, 98), (74) Michael de Tellier (II, 102), (75) John-Baptiste Colbert (II, 107), (76) Pomponius de Bellievre (II, 112), (77) Francis Pithou (II, 116), (78) Nicolas le Fevre (II, 120), (79) Francis la Mothe le Vayer (II, 125), (80) Joseph Justus Scaliger (II, 129), (81) Nicholas Rigault (II, 134), (82) Oliver Patru (II, 138), (83) Ismael Bouilleau (II, 142), (84) Barthelmy d'Herbelot (II, 147), (85) John Racine (II, 152), (86) David Blondel (II, 156), (87) Adrian Valois (II, 160), (88) Samuel Bochart (II, 165), (89) Giles Menage (II, 168), (90) Isaac de Benserade (II, 173), (91) John de la Quintinie (II, 178), (92) John Varin (II, 183), (93) Philip Collot (II, 187), (94) Simon Vouet (II, 192), (95) James Blanchart (II, 196), (96) Claude Melan (II, 200), (97) Francis Chauveau (II, 203), (98) Robert Nanteuil (II, 207), (99) Peter Mignard (II, 212), (100) James Calot (II, 217), (101) Claude Ballin (II, 221).
BSC 2520.

[Shippen, William.]

Faction Display'd. A Poem. . . . From a Correct Copy. London: Printed in the Year 1704.

4°, text pp. 1–20.

(1) Moro (p. 3), (2) Ario (p. 4), (3) Patriarcho (p. 5), (4) Mysterio (p. 5), (5) Clodio (p. 7), (6) Sigillo (p. 9), (7) Narcisso (p. 12), (8) Orlando (p. 12), (9) Bathillo (p. 13).

In the Harvard copy these characters are identified in the margin in an old manuscript hand as follows: (1) Some [the rest cut off], (2) Burnett, (3) Canterbury, (4) Loy'd, (5) Wharton, (6) Sommers, (7) Devonshire, (8) Peterborough, (9) Halifax.

[Shippen, William.]

Moderation Display'd: a poem . . . By the Author of Faction Display'd. London: Printed in the Year 1704.

4°, text pp. 1–20. In verse.
(1) A moderate statesman (p. 7).

[Shower, John.]

Some Account of the Holy Life and Death of Mr. Henry Gearing, Late Citizen of London . . . With the Trial and Character of a Real Christian, collected out of his Papers . . . Boston in New-England . . . for Samuel Phillips . . . 1704.

12°, text pp. 1–134.
(1) as in 1694.

[Swift, Jonathan.]

The Character of Richard St--le, Esq. 1704.*
See 1713.

[Ward, Edward.]

Female Policy Detected, or the Arts of a designing Woman laid open: with a Character of a vertuous Woman or Wife indeed. B. Harris, 1704.*

See the undated edition.
BSC 2522.

[Ward, Edward.]

In Imitation of Hudibras. The Dissenting Hypocrite, Or Occasional Conformist . . . London, Printed in the Year 1704.

4°, text pp. 1–78. In verse.
(1) An occasional conformist (p. 14), (2) A covenanter (p. 19), (3) An observator (p. 46).

Yalden, Thomas.

An Essay on the Character of Sir Willoughby Aston Late of Aston in Cheshire, a Poem. London, 1704. By Tho. Yalden, dated at Magd. Coll. Oxon.*
BSC 2518.

1705

Anonymous.

The Character Of A Modern Whig, Or the Republican in Fashion. 1705.*
Begins: "A modern Whig is a new book."

The Character Of A Sneaker. . . . London Printed in the year MDCCV.

4°, text pp. 1–5.
Begins: "A *Sneaker* is Something so very like *Nothing*."
BSC 2524.

The Invisible-Observator: or The Town Discover'd; With The Character of a Religious Informer. London, Printed, and Sold by S. Malthus, in London-House-Yard, 1705.*

(1) A religious informer.

A Kit-Kat C--b Describ'd. . . . London, Printed in the Year 1705.

4°, text pp. 3–8.
Begins: "Is an Ens Rationis."

[Bellegarde, Jean Baptiste Morvan de.]

Reflections upon ridicule. 1705.*
See 1707.

Blackwell, Samuel.

The Character and Duty of a Loyal Subject, and a Good Patriot. In An Assize Sermon Preach'd at Northampton, Jvly the 18th. 1705. By Samuel Blackwell . . . London: Printed by S.H. for Awnsham and John Churchill . . . MDCCV.

4°, text pp. 1–20.
Begins: "The Publick Welfare is the desire . . . of all truly Honest and Good Men."

Brown, Thomas [and Ward, Edward, and others].

A Legacy for the Ladies. Or, Characters of Women of the Age. By the late ingenious Mr. Thomas Brown. With A Comical View of London and Westminster; Or, The Merry Quack; wherein Physick is Rectified for both the Beaus and the Ladies . . . To which is Prefixt, The Character of Mr. Tho. Brown, and his Writings, Written by Dr. Drake. London, Printed by H. Meere, for S. Briscoe, and Sold by J. Milt . . . 1705.

8°, text pp. 1–192.
(1) Mr. Thomas Brown, and his writings (p. i), (2) A wanton woman (p. 1), (3) The modest woman (p. 9), (4) A pretended godly woman (p. 16), (5) The religious woman (p. 25), (6) The witty woman (p. 31), (7) The prudent woman (p. 37), (8) The house-wife, or penurious woman (p. 43), (9) The good house-wife (p. 50), (10) The gaming woman (p. 34), (11) The diligent woman (p. 61), (12) The litigious woman (p. 66), (13) A quiet woman (p. 72), (14) Self-love, or the predominant passion of women, by Mr. Brown (p. 77), (15) A true-born Dutch skipper, by Mr. Edward Ward (p. 176, in verse), (16) A Welshman, by Mr. Edward Ward (p. 181, in verse), (17) A barren adulteress, by Mr. Edward Ward (p. 192, in verse).
BSC 2523.

Many of these characters are translated from Mme. de Pringy's Les Differens Caractères des Femmes du Siecle, 1694.

[Butler, Samuel.]

The Geneva Ballad. To the Tune of 48. . . . [colophon] London, Printed in the Year 1705.
s.sh.fo. In verse.
Begins: "Of all the *Factions* in the town."
There were two editions in 1705.

Defoe, Daniel.

Good Advice to the Ladies, &c. The Second Edition. With the Character of a Beau. London: Printed by R. Smith and J. Nutte. 1705.*
4°. In verse.
BSC 2525.
The CBEL mentions editions of 1702 and 1728 (under the title A Timely Caution, or Good Advice to the Ladies), but whether the character of a beau occurs in these other editions is not certain.

[Dunton, John.]

The Character of a Tacker. To which is added, The Character of an Anti-Tacker By the same Hand. . . . [colophon] London, Printed in the Year, 1705.
s.sh.fo, text pp. 1–2.
(1) A tacker (p. 1), (2) An anti-tacker (p. 2).
In Charles Leslie's The Rehearsal, No. 21 (Dec. 12–23, 1704), is the statement: "John Dunton, in his *Athenian Catachism*, N. 17, of *Wednesday* this *December* 13 has Publish'd The Character of a Tacker." The present work is probably a reprint.

Dunton, John.

The Life and Errors of John Dunton Late Citizen of London; Written by Himself in Solitvde. . . . Together with the Lives and Characters of a Thousand Persons now Living in London . . . London, Printed for S. Malthus, 1705.
8°, 2 vols.
(1 . . .) An enormous number of portrait-characters, too numerous to be listed.

Dunton, John.

The New Practice of Piety: Writ in Imitation of Dr. Browne's Religio Medici. . . . Together with, I. The Character of a Moderate (or Right) Christian. . . . London, 1705.*
Reprinted from 1704.

Dunton, John.

Plain French: or, a Satyr upon the Tackers. To which is added The Character of a True Patriot. Written to caution and direct English Free-holders in the Choice of a new Parliament; and particularly the Electors in Bucks.

By John Dunton, a Free-holder of the same Country. The Fourth Edition, Corrected and Enlarged. . . . London: Printed in the Year 1705.*
(1) A tacker (p. 9), (2) An anti-tacker (p. 35), (3) A true patriot.

Mather, Cotton.

A Faithful Man, Described and Rewarded. Some Observable & Serviceable Passages in the Life and Death of Mr. Michael Wigglesworth. . . . By Cotton Mather. . . . Boston: Printed by B. Green . . . 1705.
8°, text pp. 1–48.
Begins: "'Tis the Voice of our Glorious Commander."

[Shippen, William.]

Faction Display'd. A Poem. . . . Now first Correctly Published, with large Amendments, and the Addition of several Characters. . . . London: Printed in the Year 1705.
4°, text pp. 1–38. In verse.
(1–9) as in 1704.

[Shippen, William.]

Moderation Display'd. 1705.*
Reprinted from 1704.

[Shippen, William.]

The Sequel: Or Moderation Further Display'd, a Poem. By the Author of Faction Display'd. . . . Printed in the Year 1705.
4°, text pp. 1–20.
(1) Nabal, a trusty Whig and friend (p. 5), (2) Burso, the incorruptible (p. 9), (3) Loyal Zebo (p. 10), (4) Seth (p. 10), (5) Euphronius (p. 11).

Walker, Sir Edward.

Historical Discourses, upon Several Occasions. . . . By Sir Edward Walker . . . London: Printed by W.B. for Sam. Keble . . . 1705.
4°, text pp. 1–369.
(1) Thomas, Earl of Arundel, 1651 (p. 221).
The character is dated "Iselsteyne the 7th of June 1651."

[Ward, Edward.]

The Secret History of the Calves-Head Club . . . The Fifth Edition . . . With A Character of a Presbyterian; Written by Sir John Denham, Knight. London, Printed, and Sold by the Booksellers of London and Westminster, 1705.
4°, text pp. 11–138.
(1) A Calves-Head Clubman (p. 21), (2) The royal martyr King Charles I, by Mr. Butler (p.

122), (3) The true Presbyterian without disguise: or, a character of a Presbyterian's ways and actions, by Sir John Denham (p. 129, in verse).

Attributed to Ward by the CBEL. In the first edition, 1703, there were no characters. Maggs Brothers (Catalogue 717, 1942) advertised an edition published in Dublin in 1705.

Webbe, George.

The Practice of Quietness, Directing a Christian How to live Quietly In this troublesome World. By Dr. George Webb, Lord Bishop of Limerick in Ireland. London, Printed by J. Downing, 1705.*

Reprinted from 1638.

1706
Anonymous.

The Beau's Character in the Comedy call'd Hampstead Heath. Sett and Sung by Mr. Ramondon.

s.sh.fo. In verse with music.
Begins: "A Wigg that's full, an empty Skull."

Thomas Baker's Hampstead Heath was acted in 1705 and printed in 1706. It seems likely that this broadside should be dated 1706.

The Management Of The Tongue. Under these following Heads. . . . Done out of French. London. Printed by D. Leach, for H. Rhodes . . . 1706.

8°, text pp. 1–272.
(1) Of conversation (p. 1), (2) The babbler (p. 22), (3) The silent man (p. 33), (4) The witty man (p. 40), (5) The droll (p. 44), (6) The jester (p. 46), (7) The disputer (p. 52), (8) The opiniator (p. 64), (9) The heedless and inconsiderate man (p. 66), (10) The complimenter (p. 69), (11) The man who praises others (p. 71), (12) The flatterer (p. 85), (13) The lyar (p. 94), (14) The boaster (p. 96), (15) The ill tongue (p. 103), (16) The swearer (p. 108), (17) The promiser (p. 110), (18) The novelist (p. 115), (19) The tale-bearer (p. 120), (20) The adviser (p. 124), (21) The reprover (p. 130), (22) The instructor (p. 137), (23) The man, who trusts others, or is trusted with a secret (p. 152), (24) The tongue of women (p. 158), (25) The language of love (p. 167), (26) The complaining man (p. 175), (27) The comforter (p. 179).

[Bellegarde, Jean Baptiste Morvan de].
Reflections upon Ridicule. 1706.*
See 1707.

[Defoe, Daniel.]
The Character of a True Englishman, Not to be found in the Number Five, Viz. I. A Honorary Levite; 2. A Tacker; 3. A Non-juror; 4. A Popelin; 5. A Zam-zum-mim of High

Church. . . . [colophon] Printed in the Year, 1706.*
4°, text pp. 1–4.
Begins: "I. I find it less difficult to describe, than to find out a true *Englishman*."
Reprinted in some copies of his The Review, 1706, or perhaps merely bound in.

[Defoe, Daniel.]
D'Foe's Answer to the Quakers Catechism: Or, A Dark Lanthorn for a Friend of the Light. London, Printed in the year 1706.*
Murphy 108.
Almost a reprint of Richard Head's The Character of a Quaker, 1671. The verses to the reader are signed "D'Foe, &c."

[Defoe, Daniel.]
The Review. 1706.*
Contains: (1) A true English-man &c. (Vol. IV, following no. 175), (2) A true English-man, not to be found in the Number Five, viz. 1. A honorary Levite; 2. A Tacker; 3. A Non-juror; 4. A Popelin; 5. A Zam-zummin of High-Church (Vol. IV, following p. 700, paged 1–4 separately).
These are not found in the facsimile edition of The Review. They may be separate publications which were bound into one or more copies of The Review. The Huth-Shaw set contained them.

Dunton, John.
Dunton's Whipping-Post: or, A Satyre upon Everybody. To which is added a Panegyrick on the most deserving gentlemen and ladies in the three Kingdoms. With the Whoring Packet. . . . London, B. Bragg. 1706.*

[Halifax, Charles Montague, Earl of.]
The Man of Honour, Or the Character Of A True Country Man. Printed in the Year M.D.CC.VI.*
4°, text pp. 1–7. In verse.
Begins: "Not all the Threats or Favours of a Crown."
Reprinted from 1688.

[Kennett, White.]
A Complete History of England . . . In Three Volumes . . . London: Printed for Brab. Aylmer . . . 1706.
fo, 3 vols.
(1) Archbishop Laud, by Clarendon (Vol. III, p. 61), (2) Charles I, by Clarendon (III, 173), (3) Cromwell, by Clarendon (III, 209), (4) Tillotson, by Burnet (III, 679).

[Le Clerc, Jean.]
The Life and Character of Mr. John Locke. 1706.*

See his An Account of . . . John Locke, 1713.
Pforzheimer Catalogue no. 614.

[Sacheverell, Henry.]

The Character of a Low-Church-Man; Drawn in an Answer to the True Character of a Church-man; Shewing the False Pretences to That Name. Humbly Offer'd to all Electors of Parliament and Convocation. The Second Edition. [mottoes] Printed in the Year 1706.*

4°, text pp. 1–22.

Reprinted from 1683.

[Swift, Jonathan?]

The Swan-Tripe Club. A Satyr. Printed at Dublin . . . 1706.*

(1–10) as in The Tripe Club, 1706.

[Swift, Jonathan?]

The Tripe Club. A Satyr. . . . By the Author of the Tale of a Tub. London; Printed for Jacob Tonson . . . MDCCVI.

fo, text pp. 3–20. In verse.

(1) Borachio, son of Pudding and eternal Beef (p. 6), (2) Egregious Magpye (p. 7), (3) Firedrake, a senator (p. 7), (4) Grimberd, who scorns his age (p. 8), (5) Nut-brain, a dagglegown of large renown (p. 9), (6) Sooterkin, of melancholy spleen (p. 10), (7) Crab (p. 11), (8) Musty Pot (p. 11), (9) Great Moon-Calf (p. 11), (10) Trady Meaning (p. 11).

Attributed doubtfully to Swift by the CBEL. There was another edition in 1706 under the title of The Swan Tripe-Club.

[Ward, Edward.]

The London Spy. 1706.*

Reprinted from 1698.

[Ward, Edward.]

The Secret History of the Calves-Head Club . . . The Sixth Edition . . . With A Character of a Presbyterian, Written by Sir John Denham, Knight. And the Character of a Modern Whig; or, The Republican in Fashion . . . by B. Bragge . . . London Printed . . . by B. Bragge . . . 1706.

4°, in 2 parts, text pp. 11–104, 1–55.

(1–3) as in 1705, (4) A modern Whig: or, the Republican in fashion (Part II, p. 49).

1707

Anonymous.

A Character of a Turn-Coat: Or, The True Picture of an English Monster . . . Printed in the Year, MDCCVII.*

s.sh.fo. In verse with woodcuts.

Begins: "If Kings are Gods, as Scripture says they be."

BSC 2303 (19th century manuscript copy).

Character of Sir G. Treby. 1707.*

BSC 2303 (19th century manuscript copy).

The Ladies Characterized. 1707.*

Arber, Term Catalogues, III, 558.

From the entry in Arber, the book appears to include sketches of about 34 ladies.

The Life and Character of St. Whig. 1707.*

Arber, Term Catalogues, III, 571.

The Management of the Tongue. The Second Edition. London, Printed by D.L. for H. Rhodes. 1707.*

BSC 2527.

Reprinted from 1706.

The Several Qualities Of The British Court, Characteris'd. D. of Marlborough, L. Orford, E. of Godolphin, D. of Ormond, The Lord Chancellor, L. Hallifax, E. of Pembroke, E. of Sunderland, D. of Somerset, L. Granby, D. of Newcastle, L. Hartington, D. of Devonshire, L. Kingston, D. of Richmond, L. Mordaunt, E. of Lindsey, L. Stemford, L. Wharton, L. Portland, L. Summers. London, Printed in the Year 1707.

Text pp. 1–8. In verse.

Begins: "Brave Marlbro' who preserves our Capital."

Baxter, Richard.

The Practical Works Of the Late Reverend and Pious Mr. Richard Baxter, In Four Volumes. . . . London: Printed for Thomas Parkhurst . . . Jonathan Robinson . . . and John Lawrence . . . 1707.

4°, 4 vols.

(1) Directions for weak distemper'd Christians (Vol. II, p. 930), (2) A sound confirm'd Christian (II, 963, the second part of no. 1), (3) The vain religion of the formal hypocrite (IV, 445, misprinted 437), (4) A sermon preached at the funeral of Henry Stubbs (IV, 881), (5) A true believer's choice . . . Mrs. Mary Coxe (IV, 889), (6) Faithful souls shall be with Christ . . . Henry Ashurst (IV, 899), (7) A sermon preached at the funeral of John Corbet (IV, 911), (8) Of redemption of time (IV, 951).

[Bellegarde, Jean Baptiste Morvan de.]

Reflexions Upon Ridicule; Or, What it is that makes a Man ridiculous; and the Means to avoid it. Wherein are Represented The different Manners and Characters of Persons of the Present Age. . . . London: Printed for Tho. Newborough . . . D. Midwinter . . . and Benj. Tooke . . . MDCCVII.

[Part II:] Reflexions upon the Politeness of Manners; with Maxims for Civil Society. Being the Second Part of the Reflections upon Ridicule By the same hand . . . London, Printed for Tho. Newborough . . . MDCCVII.

8°, two parts, text pp. 5–390, 1–287.

(1) An indiscreet man (Part I, p. 43), (2) Affected men (I, 77), (3) A vain man (I, 97), (4) A morose man (I, 166), (5) An impertinent man (I, 189), (6) Those who live only for themselves (I, 247), (7) A capricious man (I, 317), (8) The discreet man (II, 76), (9) The complaisant man (II, 133), (10) Doritius (II, 208).

The two parts are sometimes found separately. These are not very good characters, and other choices would easily be possible.

[Brown, Thomas?]

A Walk around London and Westminster.*

(1) A tavern (sig. Aaa2), (2) A barmaid (sig. Aaa3, in verse), (3) a Tavern-keeper (sig. Aaa4), (4) The vintner's help-mate (sig. Aaa5).

Brown, Thomas.

The Works of Mr. Thomas Brown, In Prose and Verse; Serious, Moral, and Comical. . . . To which is prefix'd, A Character of Mr. Tho. Brown and his Writings, by James Drake . . . London, Printed for Sam. Briscoe and Sold by B. Bragg . . . 1707[–1711].

8°, 4 vols.

(1) Mr. Tho. Brown & his writings. Written by James Drake (Vol. I, Sig. A5), (2) The Highlander (I, 150, in verse), (3) A Comical View of . . . London & Westminster (I, 43, second numbering), (4) Letters from the Dead to the Living (II, 1, containing an attorney, p. 589), (5) Amusements, Serious & Comical (III, 1), (6) A Walk Round London (III, 1 of 3rd numbering), (7) Algernon Sidney's Letter of Advice (III, 118), (8) The Character of a Puritan (IV, 183, in verse), (9) The Jacobite clergy (IV, 262), (10) A Letter from a Gentleman in Holland, to his Friend in England [or] Character of the Dutch Women (IV, 415, wrongly numbered 135).

[Darrell, William.]

A Gentleman Instructed In the Conduct of a Virtuous and Happy Life. Written for the Instruction of a Young Nobleman. The Third Edition. London, Printed for E. Smith, and are to be sold by Rich. Wilkin . . . 1707.

12°, in 2 parts, text pp. 1–164, 1–464.

(1) A libertine (Part I, p. 159), (2) An atheist (I, 160).

Attributed to Darrell by the CBEL.

[Davenant, Charles?]

The True Picture Of A Modern Whig Reviv'd. Set forth in a Third Dialogue Between Whiglove and Double, At Tom's Coffee-Hovse in Covent Garden. London: Printed in the Year, 1707.

4°, text pp. 5–72.

(1) An old Whig and a modern Whig contrasted (p. 44), (2) A low ch----man, or liberty of conscience sinner (p. 45).

[Dunton, John.]

The Pulpit-Fool. A Satyr. . . . London: Printed in the Year MDCCVII.

4°, text pp. 1–66. In verse.

(1) S--- (p. 26), (2) An independent-pulpit-fool (p. 57).

The S--- of the first character is Dr. Sacheverell.

[Dunton, John.]

The Second Part Of The Pulpit-Fool. A Satyr. Containing, A Distinct Character of the most Noted Clergy-Men in the Queens Dominions, both Church-men and Dissenters. London: Printed for B. Bragge . . . 1707.

fo, text pp. 4–40.

(1) Archbishop Tenison (p. 25), (2) Bishop Burnet (p. 26), (3) Stanhope (p. 27), (4) Hoadly (p. 28), (5) Norris (p. 28), (6) Moss (p. 29), (7) Flamstead (p. 30), (8) Gravener (p. 31), (9) Stennet (p. 31), (10) Roswel (p. 33), (11) Showers (p. 33), (12) Lewis (p. 34), (13) Franks (p. 34), (14) Clark (p. 35), (15) Palmer (p. 35), (16) Mauduits (p. 35), (17) Freke (p. 35), (18) Calamy (p. 36), (19) Viret (p. 37), (20) Thomas D--- (p. 38), (21) Adekiah (p. 38), (22) Nobs (p. 38), (23) Chinner's sons (p. 38), (24) Y--- (p. 39), (25) Sangator (p. 39), (26) Moderate-men, or trimmers (p. 39).

[H., J., and others.]

Essays of Love and Marriage. 1707.*

Arber, Term Catalogues, III, 536.

Reprinted from Two Essays of Love and Marriage, 1657.

[Halifax, Charles Montagu, Earl of.]

The Man of Honour. 1707.*

Reprinted from 1688.

Hamilton, William.

The Exemplary Life and Character Of James Bonnell, Esq; Late Accomptant General of Ireland. By William Hamilton. . . . The

Third Edition, with Additions . . . London, Printed and Sold by Joseph Downing . . . 1707.

8°, text pp. 1–278.

(1) His father's character (p. 2), (2) His own character (p. 79), (3) His character in short (p. 237), (4) A Church of England man (p. 243).

[Harding, W. N. H.]

Essays Serious and Comical with Characters, satyrical and panegyrical, Letters amorous and gallant, Miscellaneous Poems, the English Epigrammatist, and the Instructive Library. By a person of quality. London: Printed by R.J. for B. Bragg. 1707.*

8°.

BSC 2526. Arber, Term Catalogues, III, 536.

Attributed to Harding by the CBEL.

Quevedo Y Villegas, Francisco Gomez de.

The Comical Works. Translated by John Stevens. 1707.*

(1) The night adventurer.

There were numerous later editions.

Theophrastus.

Characters. 1707.*

See 1714.

[Ward, Edward.]

Mars Stript of his Armour. 1707.*

See 1709.

[Ward, Edward.]

The Secret History of the Calves-Head Club . . . The Sixth Edition . . . London. Printed . . . by B. Bragge . . . 1707.

4°, text pp. 1–138.

(1–4) as in 1706.

[Ward, Edward.]

[The Wooden World Dissected, In The Characters Of I. A Ship of War . . . by Edward Ward. London, 1707.]

12°, text pp. 1–107.

(1) A ship of war (p. 1), (2) A sea-captain (p. 6), (3) A sea-lieutenant (p. 24), (4) A sea-chaplain (p. 37), (5) A master of a ship of war (p. 47), (6) The purser (p. 55), (7) The surgeon (p. 60), (8) The gunner (p. 67), (9) The carpenter (p. 71), (10) The boatswain (p. 76), (11) The sea-cook (p. 82), (12) The midshipman (p. 87), (13) The captain's steward (p. 92), (14) A sailor (p. 95).

Attributed to Ward by the CBEL. The title above is taken from the Harvard copy, in which the original title page, now missing, has been replaced by a typewritten sheet.

1708

Anonymous.

The Battel of Audenard. A Poem . . . With the Characters of the General Officers, who were present in the Engagement. . . . London, Printed and Sold by H. Hills . . . For the Benefit of the Poor. 1708.

8°, text pp. 4–15.

(1) Lumley (p. 10), (2) Orkney (p. 11), (3) Cadogan (p. 12), (4) Webb (p. 13), (5) Campbell (p. 13), (6) Stairs (p. 13), (7) Temple (p. 13).

BSC 2528.

The Character of a good Man, neither Whig nor Tory. 1708.*

Probably a reprint of 1681.

The Character of a High Church-Man, in Answer to the Pretended Character of a Low-Church-Man. To which is Added, Jack in an Office: Or, Fools will be meddling. An Upstart Gentleman: Or, A Beggar on Horseback. The Fawning News-monger : Or, The Knave in Fashion. The griping Usurer: Or, The Devil for Money. The Tricking Shop-Keeper: Or, The Best Side Outward. The High-Church-Man: Or, The Best at last. Written by Dr. B---s. London: Printed by J. Smith, near Fleet-Street. 1708.*

Probably contains six characters as indicated in the title.

The Character Of An Ill-Court-Favourite: Representing the Mischiefs That flow from Ministers of State When they are More Great than Good. . . . Translated out of French. London: Printed in the Reign of King Charles II. and Reprinted 1708.

fo, text pp. 3–24.

Begins: "He that stands by and observes the *supple* Addresses."

BSC 2529.

Reprinted from 1681.

The Dutch Riddle: or, A Character of A H--ry Monster, Often found in Holland. 1708.*

A Friendly Letter in three parts . . . III. Shewing some marks of a Christian, or the Character of a good man. The second edition.*

Hickelty Pickelty: Or A Medly Of Characters Adapted to the Age. Relating to different Persons and Perswasions. . . . London, Printed in the Year, 1708.

8°, text pp. 2–16.
(1) A Presbyterian, or a female hypocrite (p. 2), (2) A beau (p. 3), (3) A Whig (p. 3), (4) A lawyer's clerk, or a pot-poet (p. 4), (5) An attorney (p. 5), (6) A detractor (p. 5), (7) A bowling green (p. 6), (8) A surgeon (p. 6), (9) A player (p. 7), (10) A tavern (p. 7), (11) A coquet (p. 8), (12) A Pinner's Hall text driver (p. 9), (13) An unsanctified dun, or a cruel creditor (p. 9), (14) A bailiff's follower (p. 10), (15) The Exchange (p. 10), (16) Will's Coffee House (p. 11, title only, no text), (17) A wit (p. 11), (18) A flatterer (p. 11), (19) A high flyer (p. 11), (20) A drunkard (p. 12), (21) A prison (p. 12), (22) A courtier (p. 12), (23) A handsome barkeeper (p. 13), (24) A young rake (p. 13), (25) A whoremaster (p. 13), (26) A pretender to learning (p. 14), (27) A tobacconist (p. 14), (28) An upstart sheriff, or a country justice (p. 14), (29) A sceptic in religion (p. 15), (30) A stockjobber (p. 16).
BSC 2530, 2531.
A reprint of Spooner's Mirth and Wisdom, 1703.

The Manners of the Age. Being the Modern Characters of the Court, the Town, and the City. The third edition. 1708.*

Mirth in Ridicule: or, a Satyr against Immoderate Laughing. Containing the Follies too often found in . . . London, Printed: And Sold by J. Morphew. 1708.*
In verse.
(1) A sea-officer, (2) A land-officer, (3) A courtier, (4) A lawyer, (5) A priest, (6) A merchant, (7) A scholar, (8) A poet, (9) A miser, (10) The ladies, (11) A maid, (12) A strumpet, (13) A beau, (14) A gamester, (15) A quack, (16) A plotter, (17) A libertine.

The True Characters of, Viz. A Deceitfull Petty-Fogger, Vulgarly call'd Attorney. A Know-all Astrological Quack, or, Feigned Physician. A Female Hypocrite, or, Devil in Disguise. A Low-Churchman, or, Ecclesiastical Bifarius. A Trimmer, or, Jack of All Sides, &c. . . . London: Printed by J. Jones . . . 1708.
8°, text pp. 3–16.
(1) A deceitful petty-fogger (p. 3), (2) A know-all astrological quack (p. 6), (3) A female hypocrite (p. 7), (4) A low-churchman (p. 10), (5) A trimmer (p. 13).

Brown, Thomas.
Works. 1708.*
Reprinted from 1707.

Claudian.
Strena Kal. Januariis. 1708. . . . Edinburgh Printed by the Author January 1. 1708.*
s.sh.fo.
(1) The happy man (p. 1).
This is a translation of Claudian's "Felix qui propriis," which appears in a parallel column with it. The translation is given as by A.S.V.D.M.D.

[Defoe, Daniel.]
A Review Of The State Of The British Nation. Vol. V. London: Printed in the Year MDCCIX.*
Text pp. 1–632. 158 numbers. Each number is 4 pages.
(1) A covenanter, i.e., an abjuration-taking Jacobite (no. 35, June 16, 1708).

Dunton, John.
The New Practice of Piety. 1708.*
Reprinted from 1704.

[Dunton, John.]
Stinking Fish: Or, A Foolish Poem, Attempted by John the Hermit. Part I. To be continu'd till the Hermit has cry'd all his Stinking Fish. i.e. Publish'd A Secret, as well as Publick History, of all the Fools and Knaves in the World. . . . London: Printed by R. Tookey, and . . . Sold by John Morphew . . . MDCCVIII.
4°, text pp. 1–89.
(1) The boy, or fool in petticoats (p. 29), (2) A maid (p. 33), (3) A green-sickness fool (p. 34), (4) A talkative woman (p. 34), (5) A fantastick woman (p. 35), (6) A precise or hypocritical woman (p. 36), (7) A humble man (p. 52), (8) A mere complimental man (p. 57), (9) A noble (or wise) man (p. 64), (10) A noble fool (p. 65), (11) A lord's chaplain (p. 65), (12) A tacker (p. 74), (13) A detractor (p. 77).
These are footnotes, in prose, to the verse, and are taken from Earle, Overbury, Flecknoe, Hall, and others. The Harvard copy contains as frontispiece a portrait of Dunton's father, Mr. John Dunton, late minister of Aston Clinton.

La Bruyère, Jean de.
The Characters. 1708.*
Reprinted from 1699.

[Swift, Jonathan.]
The Sentiments of a Church of England Man, with Respect to Religion and Government. Written in the Year 1708.*
See his Miscellanies, 1711.

[Swift, Jonathan?]
A Trip to Dunkirk. 1708.*

Listed by the CBEL as one of the works frequently attributed to Swift.

[Ward, Edward.]

The Modern World Disrob'd: Or, Both Sexes Stript of their pretended Vertue. In Two Parts. First, Of the Ladies. Secondly, Of the Gentlemen. With Familiar Descant upon every Character. . . . London, Printed for G.S. and sold by J. Woodward . . . 1708.

8°, text pp. 1–224, paged continuously. Part II begins with no. 16. In verse and prose.

(1) The formal precisian; or, the devout lady (p. 1), (2) The female student; or, the learned lady (p. 10), (3) She muses as she uses: or, the censorious lady (p. 21), (4) The cunning wanton: or, the intriguing lady (p. 28), (5) The Countess of Brandipolis: or, the toping lady (p. 37), (6) The dissatisfy'd wife: or, the jealous lady (p. 44), (7) Bad luck to him that has her, or, the gaming lady (p. 51), (8) Female secresy: or, the prying lady (p. 58), (9) From the spinning-wheel, to the coach: or, Golden Joan made his worship's lady (p. 65), (10) High birth, but no fortune: or, the depending lady (p. 72), (11) The fashionable bawd: or, the lady's confident (p. 80), (12) The great man's prostitute: or, the original of an actress taken into keeping (p. 88), (13) Miss Buxom: or, the golden-lock'd lady unmarry'd (p. 97), (14) The modern quality: or, the upstart lady (p. 105), (15) The hospitable house-keeper: or, the bountiful lady (p. 113), (16) The modish gentleman: or, the climbing courtier (p. 119), (17) The corrupt statesman: or, the compleat courtier (p. 127), (18) The trimming guide: or, the avaricious priest (p. 134), (19) The beau-officer: or, the coward in commission (p. 142), (20) The ambitious mercenary: or, the climbing lawyer (p. 148), (21) The prodigal upstart; or, the citizen turn'd gentleman (p. 153), (22) The severe magistrate: or, the proud man in authority (p. 162), (23) Riches acquir'd before discretion: or, the young extravagant heir just come to an estate (p. 169), (24) The states-man's minion: or, the politick understrapper (p. 178), (25) The promissory gentleman: or, the fashionable friend (p. 186), (26) The temporizing zealot: or, the religious mammonist (p. 193), (27) The dignify'd adulterer: or, the libertine of title (p. 201), (28) Sir Narcissus Foplin: or, the self-admirer (p. 210), (29) The worthy patriot: or, the true English nobleman (p. 217).

Attributed to Ward by the CBEL. Reprinted as Adam and Eve Stript of their Furbelows, 1710, 1714.

[Ward, Edward.]

The Wooden World Dissected, In The Characters Of I. A Ship of War. . . . By a Lover of the Mathematicks. The Second Edition, Corrected and Amended by the Author. London, Printed . . . for H. Meere . . . 1708.

12°, text pp. 1–107.
(1–14) as in 1707.
BSC 2532.

1709

Anonymous.

A British Janus. Anglice a Timeserver.*
s.sh.fo. In verse.
Begins: "A British Janus with a double face."

The Character of a Modern Whig. 1709.*
Reprinted from 1681.

The Character of a Whig, Under Several Denominations. To which is added, The Reverse, or the Character of a true English-Man, in Opposition to the former. London, Printed, and are to be sold by the Booksellers of London and Westminster. 1709.*

8°, text pp. 1–134.
(1–33) as in 1700.
Murphy 93.

The Life and History of Lewis XIV. Present King of France and Navarre. In Eight Parts. . . . London: Printed for John Morphew . . . MDCCIX[–XVII].

fo, 2 vols.

(1) The most Christian King [Louis XIV] (Vol. I, appendix, p. 5), (2) The Viscount de Turenne (p. 49), (3) The late Duke of Orleans (p. 51), (4) M. de Vautan (p. 51), (5) The Marquis de Barbesiens (p. 51), (6) The Duke of Burgundy (p. 52), (7) The Duke of Anjou (p. 53), (8) The Duke of Berry (p. 53), (9) The Duke of Orleans (p. 53), (10) The Prince of Conti (p. 53), (11) The Duke of Maine (p. 54), (12) The Duke of la Rochefoucaut (p. 55), (12) The Marshal Duke of Villeroy (p. 56), (13) The Prince of Soubize (p. 57), (14) The Marshal Duke of Boufflers (p. 57), (15) The Archbishop of Cambray (p. 59), (16) Marshal Catinat (p. 60), (17) Paul de Beauvilliers (p. 61), (18) The Marshal Duke of Noailles (p. 61), (19) The King (Vol. II, p. 1189).

Mirth diverts all Care: Being excellent new Songs, composed by the most Celebrated Wits of the Age. . . . London: Printed by J. Morphew. 1709.*

(1) A good parson, (2) The leveller.
Arber, Term Catalogues, III, 621.

The Rump. or a Satyr on the Ladies High Tails; Being a Lampoon privately dispensed at Tunbridge Wells, in the year 1707. By a

Water-Drinker with characters of the most noted water-drinkers. 1709.*

Scrinia Reclusa: or brief Remarks upon the Reigns of several of our English Princes; with the Characters of their Favourites. 1709.*

The True Church-Man Set in a Just and Clear Light: Or, An Essay Towards the Right Character Of A Faithful Son of the Established Church. London, Printed for Richard Sare, at Gray's-Inn-Gate in Holbourn, 1709.*
Arber, Term Catalogues, III, 626.

Browne, Simon.
The True Character of the Real Christian or Sincere Good Man. From Psal. CXIX, 113. By Simon Browne, Minister in Portsmouth. Wherein the Nature of a Religious Hatred to Vain Thoughts, etc. are proved to be the Property of the True Christian. London, Printed by R. Brugis for Ralph Sympson. 1709.*
8°, text pp. 1–344.
BSC 2534.

Brown, Thomas.
Works. 1709.*
Reprinted from 1707.

Burnet, Gilbert.
A Sermon Preached at the Funeral of the . . . Archbishop of Canterbury. 1709.*
Reprinted from 1694.

[Cotton, Charles.]
The Compleat Gamester. 1709.*
Reprinted from 1674.

[Darrell, William.]
The Gentleman Instructed. 1709.*
(1–2) as in 1707.

[Davenant, Charles?]
The True Picture of a Modern Whig Reviv'd. 1709.*
Reprinted from 1707.

[Fenton, Elijah.]
Oxford And Cambridge Miscellany Poems . . . London: Printed for Bernard Lintott. . . .
8°, text pp. 1–400.
(1) Claudian's Old Man of Verona (p. 18), (2) Cato's character (p. 40), (3) A friend (p. 244).
Ascribed to Fenton by the Harvard Catalogue and by the CBEL.

[Gandouet, F.]
The French Politick Detected, with the Characters of the French Politicians display'd in IV. Parts. By Way of Allegory. Bristol, Printed by W. Bonny. 1709.*
BSC 2535.

[Heywood, James.]
Erubescite Momi: the ladies advocate, or a compendious character of the most illustrious and celebrated beauties in Manchester, by a Well-wisher to the Town. 1709.*

[Manley, Mary de la Rivière.]
The Female Tatler. By Mrs. Crackenthorpe . . . [colophon] Sold by B. Bragge . . . 1709.
fo, each issue s.sh., text pp. 1–2.
(1) An old fool (no. 13).
Attributed by the CBEL to either Mrs. Manley or Thomas Baker.

[Pits, or Pittis, John.]
The Character of a Primitive Bishop, in a Letter to a Non-Juror. . . . By a Presbyter of the Church of England. London, Printed for B. Bragge . . . 1709.*
BSC 2533.
There are two copies in the Bodleian. One bears a manuscript note, "By John Pits," and the other, "By Pittis."

[Shippen, William.]
Faction Display'd. A Poem. . . . From a Corrected Copy. London: Printed and sold by H. Hills . . . 1709.
8°, text pp. 4–16. In verse.
(1–9) as in 1704.

[Shippen, William.]
Moderation Display'd: A Poem. . . . By the Author of Faction Display'd. London: Printed and Sold by H. Hills . . . 1709.
8°, text pp. 5–16.
(1) as in edition of 1704, (2) Anno (p. 7), (3) Hortensio (p. 7), (4) Suado (p. 7), (5) Urbano (p. 8), (6) Sempronia (p. 8), (7) Jano (p. 9), (8) Moloch (p. 10).

[Steele, Sir Richard, Addison, Joseph, and others.]
The Tatler. By Isaac Bickerstaff Esq. . . . Tuesday, April 12. 1709. . . . [colophon] London: Printed for the Author, 1709[–10].
Each number s.sh.fo, text pp. 1–2. 289 numbers.
(1) An absent lover (no. 1), (2) Chloe and Clarissa (no. 4), (3) The Duke of Marlborough (no. 5), (4) Alexander and Caesar (no. 6), (5) A coquette and a coxcomb (no. 7), (6) Timon,

from La Bruyère (no. 9) (7) Verus (no. 14), (8) Characters at Bath (no. 16), (9) Sophronius, a gentleman, and Jack Dimple, a pretty fellow (no. 21), (10) Col. Brunett, a very pretty fellow (no. 24), (11) A rake (no. 27), (12) The author's three nephews (no. 30), (13) Characters at Epsom (no. 36), (14) Lord Nowhere, Will Shoestring, and Umbra (no. 38), (15) Will Whynot, a questioner (no. 41), (16) Aspasia (no. 42), (17) Florio and Senecio (no. 45), (18) Aurengzebe (no. 46), (19) Sir Taffety Trippet (no. 47), (20) Nestor and Varillus (no. 52), (21) Emilia (no. 57), (22) Actaeon (no. 59), (23) Men of fire (no. 61), (24) Cleontes (no. 64), (25) A battle-critic (no. 65), (26) A club of gamesters (no. 73), (27) Hippocrates (no. 78), (28) The dappers (no. 85), (29) Inventory of a beau (no. 113), (30) Sir Hannibal (no. 115), (31) Castabella, a prude, and Lydia, a coquette (no. 126), (32) The club at the Trumpet (no. 132), (33) Lovemore and his wife, an affectionate couple (no. 150), (34) Characters in conversation described as instruments of music (no. 153), (35) The upholsterer (no. 155), (36) Tom Folio (no. 158), (37) Sir Timothy Tittle (no. 165), (38) Tom Modely (no. 166), (39) Mr. Betterton (no. 167), (40) Impudence and absurdity (no. 168), (41) A country gentleman (no. 169), (42) Horace (no. 173), (43) Martius and Aristaeus (no. 176), (44) Wilks and Cibber (no. 182), (45) Regulus (no. 183), (46) Desdemona (no. 188), (47) Sam Bickerstaff and his family (no. 189), (48) Polypragmon (no. 191), (49) Characters in a stage-coach (no. 192), (50) Tom Courtly (no. 204), (51) Jack Gainly and his sister Gatty (no. 206), (52) A gentleman (no. 207), (53) The most agreeable companion (no. 208), (54) Tom Trueman (no. 213), (55) Tom Mercet (no. 219), (56) Plumbeus and Levis (no. 246).

Often reprinted.

[Ward, Edward.]

The History Of The London Clubs. Or, The Citizens' Pastime. . . . By the Author of the London Spy. . . . London, Printed by J. Dutton . . . 1709.*

(1) The lying club (p. 7), (2) The Yorkshire club (p. 11), (3) The thieves' club (p. 14), (4) The beggars' club (p. 16), (5) The broken shopkeepers' club (p. 18), (6) The basket-woman's club (p. 20).

Attributed to Ward by the CBEL. Reprinted 1709 (two parts), 1746 (as a Compleat and Humorous Account of all the Remarkable Clubs and Societies in the Cities of London and Westminster), 1756, 1896. The Second Part of the London Clubs was reprinted [1720?].

[Ward, Edward.]

The London-Spy Compleat, In Eighteen Parts. The First Volume of the Author's Writings.

The Fourth Edition. London, Printed and Sold by J. How . . . MDCCIX.

8°, text pp. 1–439.

(1–26) as in 1698.

[Ward, Edward.]

Mars stript of his Armour: or, the Army Display'd in all its true Colours. Containing the characters . . . [24 types] . . . By a Lover of the Mathematicks. London . . . Printed by J. Woodward . . . and B. Bragge . . . 1709.

6°, text pp. 1–107.

(1) An army in general (p. 1), (2) A regiment, or battalion (p. 8), (3) A captain-general (p. 17), (4) A lieutenant-general (p. 20), (5) A major-general (p. 26), (6) A brigadier-general (p. 31), (7) A colonel (p. 39), (8) A lieutenant-colonel (p. 46), (9) A major (p. 50), (10) A captain of the guards (p. 53), (11) An aide-de-camp (p. 61), (12) A partizan (p. 63), (13) A spy (p. 67), (14) A captain (p. 71), (15) A lieutenant (p. 78), (16) An ensign (p. 81), (17) An adjutant (p. 84), (18) A quartermaster (p. 88), (19) The chaplain of a regiment (p. 90), (20) The surgeon (p. 96), (21) A sergeant (p. 100), (22) A grenadier (p. 102), (23) A private centinel (p. 104), (24) A provost (p. 106).

BSC 2531.

Attributed to Ward by the CBEL.

1710

Anonymous.

An Auction Of State Pictures; Containing a Most Curious Collection Of Original Low-Church Faces: Drawn Exactly to the Life By A High-Church Limner. Enter'd in the Hall, according to Order. MDCCX.

4°, text pp. 5–20.

(1) Dr. Tenison, Archbishop of Canterbury (p. 5), (2) Gilbert Burnet, Bishop of Salisbury (p. 6), (3) Dr. Moore, Bishop of Ely (p. 7), (4) Dr. Cumberland, Bishop of Peterborough (p. 7), (5) Dr. Fowler, Bishop of Gloucester (p. 8), (6) Dr. Trimnell, Bishop of Norwich (p. 8), (7) Dr. Wake, Bishop of Lincoln (p. 9), (8) Lord Halifax (p. 10), (9) Charles fifth Baron Mohun (p. 11), (10) The Earl of Manchester (p. 11), (11) The Earl of Orford (p. 12), (12) The Duke of Bedford (p. 16), (13) The Duke of Newcastle (p. 17), (14) William first Earl Cowper (p. 19), (15) The Duke of Marlborough.

The book consists of a series of sketches of various Whiggish bishops and lords that were opposed to Dr. Sacheverell. All together there are 26 satirical "pictures" set in the framework of an auctioneer's patter as he offers them for sale. Though none are identified in the text, those listed above are labeled in contemporary hand in the Newberry copy.

A brief and true Character and Account of Edmund Grindal, D.D. Sometime Archbishop of Canterbury. Published to rectify some Misapprehensions taken up of that most reverend and godly Prelate. &c. London: Printed for A. Baldwin, near the Oxford Arms in Warwick Lane. 1710.*

8°, text pp. 1–30.
(1) Archbishop Grindal (p. 7).
BSC 2537.

There was another edition of the same year, printed and sold by H. Hills (BSC 2536).

The Character Of The London Mobb. London, Printed for D. Browne, 1710.*

s.sh.fo.
Begins: "The London Rabble, vulgarly call'd *The Mobb*."

It is not certain that the title as quoted is complete. Some other words may precede it.

Chuse which you Please: Or, Dr. Sacheverell, And Mr. Hoadley, Drawn to the Life. Being a Brief Representation Of The Respective Opinions of each Party . . . London: Printed and Sold by the Booksellers of London and Westminster, 1710.

4°, text pp. 3–8.
Begins: "I have great Reason to believe."

A Collection Of Poems, For and Against Dr. Sacheverell. The Third Part. London, Printed in the year 1710.*

(1) A modern addresser (p. 37), (2) A receipt to make a stiff-rumpt Presbyterian (p. 40).

A Collection Of Poems, &c. For and Against Dr. Sacheverell, And On other Affairs of State; most of them never before Printed. The Fourth Part. . . . London, Printed in the year MDCCX.

4°, text pp. 3–40.
(1) The priest without religion (p. 13, in verse).

The Constable's Hue and Cry after Whores and Bawds, etc. London, printed for John Smith, near Charing Cross.*

8°, text pp. 1–8.
(1) A bawd (p. 6).

The Description Of A Presbyterian; Humbly Address'd to those Gentlemen, that by the Imputation Of The High Church Are lately Added to that Famous Party. [motto] Printed, in the Yeare 1710.*

8°, text pp. 1–16.
Begins: "Gentlemen: you see whither you are brought at last."

Dr. Sacheverell's Picture Drawn to the Life: Or, A True Character Of A High-Flyer. Of Use to all those who admire Originals. . . . [colophon] London Printed, and Sold by J. Baker . . . 1710.

4°, text pp. 1–8.
Begins: "A *High-Flyer* is a Monster with an *English* Face, a *French* Heart, and an *Irish* Conscience."

A Dream: or, The force of Fancy. A Poem, containing Characters of the company now at the Bath. 1710.*

The Husband, A Poem. Expressed in A Compleat Man. . . . London: Printed and Sold by H. Hills . . . 1710.

8°, text pp. 3–16. In verse.
Begins: "Life was inspir'd, the first Life was Divine."

A reprint from 1614.

A Receipt How to make a Right Presbyterian In Two Days. [colophon] Printed in the Year 1710 And Entred in the Hall-Book.*

s.sh.fo.
Begins: "Take the Herbs of Hypocrisie and Ambitions of each two Handfulls."

Shining Character of a Public-Spirited Man. 1710.*

The State-Bell Man's Collection of Verses for . . . 1711. 1710.*

(1) A noble-man (no. 1).

The Tacking-Club: Or, A Satyr On Doctor S---ll, And His Bulleys. Printed in the Year MDCCX.

4°, text pp. 3–8. In verse.
Begins: "Attend you Fools, your Character is such."

A satire on Henry Sacheverell, but rather a denunciation of him than strictly a character.

View here the Pourtrait of a Factious Priest . . . Engrav'd, and Printed at Amsterdam: 1710.*

s.sh.fo.
BSC 2538.

[Bellegarde, Jean Baptiste Morvan de.]
Reflections upon Ridicule. 1710.*
Reprinted from 1707.

[Cotton, Charles.]

The Compleat Gamester. 1710.*

Reprinted from 1674.

[Dare, Josiah.]

Counsellor Manners His Last Legacy etc. By Sir. R.L.S. . . . London, Printed for J. &. B. Sprint . . . and G. Conyers . . . 1710.

8°, text pp. 5–120.

(1) as in 1673.

[Defoe, Daniel.]

The Character Of A Modern Addresser. . . . London Printed. Sold by John Baker . . . 1710.

4°, text pp. 3–8.

Begins: "A *Modern Addresser* is one that has *Life* and *Fortune* in one Hand."

Attributed to Defoe in the Boston Public Library.

[Distaff, John.]

A Character of Don Sacheverellio, Knight of the Firebrand; In A Letter To Isaac Bicker-staff Esq; Censor of Great Britain. Dublin: Printed and Sold by Francis Higgins, Book-maker; and to be had of A. Baldwin, in London. [1710?]

8°, text pp. 3–16.

Begins: "As You have been frequently Comple-mented."

BSC 2540.

The "letter" is dated March 16, 1710, and signed John Distaff.

Dunton, John.

Athenianism: Or, The New Projects of Mr. John Dunton. . . . with . . . Characters . . . London: Printed by Tho. Darrack . . . 1710.

8°, in 2 parts, text pp. 1–224, 11–360.

(1) The Dublin courtship, or Dunton's character of Madame Singer (Part I, p. 1), (2) Dignify'd and Distinguish'd: or, a character of the most eminent conformists in the Queen's dominions (I, 61), (3) The court and character of Queen Mary (I, 76), (4) Dunton's shadow: or the character of a summer friend (I, 101), (5) Dun-ton: or, the projector of the rhiming frolick: being a merry character of himself, the meanest of all the poetick-tribe (I, 206), (6) Dissenting clergy (II, 141), (7) The beggar mounted — be-ing a satyr on some mushrome gentlemen and ladies (II, 304), (8) The man of honour, or true gentleman, riding post to Heaven (II, 317).

[Grascome, Samuel?]

The Character Of A True Church of England-Man. Exclusive of Dr. West, Mr. Hoadly And Their Adherents . . . Enter'd Pursuant to the late Act of Parliament. London: Printed, and are to be Sold by John Morphew . . . MDCCX.

4°, text pp. 3 (misprinted 1)–8.

Begins: "In the last Century there was no Name more Honourable than that of a *Protestant*."

A reprint, with some modifications, of 1702.

[Leslie, Charles?]

The true Church-man, and Loyal Subject. Fear God. Honour the King. 1 Pet. II. 17. London, Printed for J. Morphew near Station-er's-Hall. 1710.*

8°, text pp. 1–168.

BSC 2539.

Place, Conyers.

The True English Revolutionist, Or; The Happy Turn, Rightly Taken. By Conyers Place, A.M. Printed for W. Taylor, 1710.

8°, text pp. 1–68.

Begins: "The True English Revolutionist, believes in God."

[Povey, Charles.]

The Visions of Sir Heister Ryley . . . Letters representing . . . The Characters of Vertue, Beauty . . . Vol. I. London: Printed for the author . . .

4°.

(1) A sordid ambitious wretch (no. 5, p. 20), (2) A gentlewoman (no. 21, p. 81), (3) A certain banished courtier (no. 26, p. 103).

The separate numbers are all dated, these three being Aug. 30, Oct. 6, and Oct. 18, 1710. Attributed to Povey by the CBEL.

[Sacheverell, Henry.]

The Character of a Low-Church-Man. 1710.*

Reprinted from 1683.

[Shaftesbury, Anthony Ashley Cooper, Earl of.]

Soliloquy: Or, Advice To An Author. . . . London, Printed for John Morphew . . . M.DCC.X.

8°, text pp. 1–196.

(1) A man of breeding and politeness (p. 176).

Attributed to Shaftesbury by the Harvard College Library.

Stillingfleet, Edward.

The Works of that Eminent and most Learned Prelate Dr. Edw. Stillingfleet, Late Lord Bishop of Worcester. Together With His Life and Character. In Six Volumes. . . . Lon-don: Printed by J. Heptinstall, for Henry and George Mortlack . . . MDCCX.

fo, 6 vols.

(1) Stillingfleet (Vol. I, p. 42).

The life and character, which is attributed by the CBEL to Samuel Butler, was reprinted separately in 1735.

[Swift, Jonathan?]

The Swan Tripe-Club: A Satyr, On The High-Flyers; In the Year 1705. . . . London: Printed and Sold by the Book-sellers of London and Westminster, 1710.

8°, text pp. 3–16.
(1–10) as in his Tripe Club, 1706.

[Ward, Edward.]

Adam and Eve stripped of their furbelows. Second edition. 1710.*

Reprinted from The Modern World Disrob'd, 1708.

[Ward, Edward.]

The Poet's Ramble after Riches . . . London: Printed and Sold by J. How . . . 1710.

4°, text pp. 3–19.
(1) An encomium on his noble steed (p. 6).
Attributed to Ward by the CBEL.

1711

Anonymous.

The Character Of A True Churchman. In A Letter From A Gentleman in the City, To His Friend in the Country. London, Printed for John Baker . . . 1711.

4°, text pp. 3–16.
Begins: "He is one, who is not only called a Christian, but is in Truth and Reality such."

Honesty the Best Policy: or the Mischiefs of Faction Shewed in the Character of an High, and a Low-Church Clergyman. London, Printed for J. Morphew . . . MDCCXI.*

8°, text pp. 1–16.
Begins: "I cannot help being. . . ."

The London Bawd, with her Characters and Life, discovering the various and subtile Intrigues of Lewd Women. London: Printed for John Gwillim, 1711.*

The Picture Of A Church Militant. An Original, after the Modern manner. For the Use of St. Stephen's Chapel, and humbly Subscrib'd to A Member of the Lower House of Convocation. By the Author of the Blackbird's Tale. London, Printed for S.B. and Sold by J. Morphew. 1711.*

Text pp. 1–13. In verse.

Brown, Thomas.

Works.*

Reprinted from 1707.

[Defoe, Daniel.]

The Conference; Or, Gregg's Ghost: With The Character of a Puritan and a Holy Sister, by K. James the First. London: Printed for J. Baker . . . 1711.

4°, text pp. 5–40.
(1) A Tory (p. 16), (2) A Whig (p. 22), (3) Faction (p. 24), (4) A tantivy-man (p. 27), (5) The Examiner and his brother Abel (p. 29), (6) A holy sister (p. 38, in verse).

[Defoe, Daniel.]

The History of the October Club: From its Original to this Time. By a Member. London: Printed in the Year, 1711.

4°, text pp. 1–86.
(1) The October Club (p. 1).
BSC 2531 (as The Character of the October Club).

Attributed by the CBEL to Defoe as The Secret History etc.

[Defoe, Daniel.]

R...'s on both Sides. In which are the Characters of Some R...'s not yet describ'd; With a True Description of An Old Whig, and a Modern Whig; an Old Tory, and a Modern Tory; High-flyer, or Motly; As also of a Minister of State. By the same Author. London, Printed for John Baker . . . 1711.

4°, text pp. 1–36.
(1) An old Whig (p. 9), (2) A modern Whig (p. 10), (3) An old Tory (p. 20), (4) New High-flyer (p. 24), (5) Modern Tory (p. 27), (6) Good and bad ministers of state (p. 29).
BSC 2542.

Attributed to Defoe by the CBEL. There were two editions in 1711.
The "R..." in the title stands for "Rogue."

Drummond, William.

The Works of William Drummond, of Hawthornden. Consisting of Those which were formerly Printed, and Those which were design'd for the Press. Now published from the Author's Original Copies. . . . Edinburgh: Printed by James Watson, in Craig's-Closs, 1711.

fo, in 2 parts, text pp. 1–243, pp. 1–56.
(1) A perfect anagram (Part I, p. 230), (2) An anti-covenanter (II, 56).

H., S., Misodolus.

Do no Right, Take no Wrong; or The Way of the World Displayd. . . . The whole intermixt with . . . Satyrical Characters. . . . By S. H. Misodolus. . . . London: Printed for Robert Gifford . . . 1711.

12°, text pp. 1–152.

(1) A knave (p. 11), (2) An ale-draper or victualler (p. 103), (3) A scrivener (p. 113), (4) A tailor (p. 115), (5) A baker (p. 116), (6) A bricklayer (p. 117), (7) A pawnbroker (p. 119), (8) A sergeant or bailiff (p. 121), (9) His follower (p. 122), (10) A prison (p. 124), (11) An importunate dun or cruel creditor (p. 127), (12) A stock-jobber (p. 131), (13) A surgeon (p. 133), (14) An attorney, solicitor, or pettifogging lawyer (p. 135), (15) A vintner (p. 136), (16) A handsome barkeeper (p. 138), (17) A tobacconist (p. 139), (18) A player (p. 140), (19) A courtier (p. 141), (20) An upstart sheriff or country justice (p. 143), (21) The master of a ship (p. 144, in verse), (22) The master of an inn (p. 146), (23) A drawer or tapster (p. 148), (24) A chamberlain (p. 150), (25) A hostler (p. 151).

[Leslie, Charles?]

The True Church-Man and Loyal Subject. London, Printed for H. Clements at the Half Moon. 1711.

Arber, Term Catalogues, III, 660.

[Puckle, James.]

The Club: Or, A Dialogue Between Father and Son. . . . London: Printed for the Author; and Sold by S. Crouch . . . 1711.*

See 1713.

Shaftesbury, Anthony Ashley Cooper, Earl of.

Characteristics. 1711.*

(1) as in his Soliloquy, 1710.

Frequently reprinted.

[Steele, Sir Richard, Addison, Joseph, and others.]

The Spectator. 1711.*

See 1712.

[Swift, Jonathan.]

Miscellanies in Prose and Verse. London: Printed for John Morphew . . . MDCCXI.

8°, 2 vols.

(1) The Sentiments of a Church of England-Man With Respect to Religion and Government. Written in the Year, 1708 (Vol. I, p. 95).

The Miscellanies appeared in numerous states and at various dates after 1711. Attributed to Swift by the CBEL.

[Swift, Jonathan.]

A Short Character of His Ex. T.E. of W.L.L. of I——. With An Account of some smaller Facts, during His Government, which will not be put into the Articles of Impeachment. London: Printed for William Coryton . . . 1711.

8°, text pp. 3–29.

(1) Thomas Earl of Wharton (p. 5).

BSC 2543.

There were several editions in 1711, and at least two others of uncertain date later. Attributed to Swift by the CBEL.

[Trapp, Joseph.]

The Character And Principles Of the Present Set of Whigs. . . . London: Printed for John Morphew . . . 1711.

4°, text pp. 3–48.

Begins: "By Whigs I do not mean these who are heartily well affected."

A border line example of character.

1712

Anonymous.

The Character of a Jesuit.*

BSC 2303 (a nineteenth-century manuscript copy of it).

Presumably a reprint of 1681.

Observations and Remarks upon the Lives & Reigns of King Henry VIII, King Edward VI, Queen Mary I, Queen Elizabeth, & King James. With particular Characters after the Earl of Clarendon's method of all their Favourites; and the most Eminent and Illustrious Persons both in church and State that flourished in England during those Reigns. Collected from Publick Histories & Private Memoirs. By the author of the History of England in 2 vols. London, Printed for Charles King and are to be sold by John Morphew, 1712.*

8°, text pp. 1–361.

BSC 2548.

Scrinia Reclusa: or brief Remarks upon the Reigns of several of our English Princes; with the Characters of their Favourites. 1712.*

Reprinted from 1709.

Whig and Tory. 1712.*

See 1713.

Bona, Giovanni.

Manuductio ad Coelum. Sixth Edition. 1712.*

Murphy 146.

Reprinted from 1672.

[Burnet, Sir Thomas?]

A Certain Information Of a Certain Discourse. That happen'd at a Certain Gentlemans House, In a certain County. Written by a certain Person then present . . . The Third Edition. London: Printed, and Sold by John Baker . . . 1712.

4°, text pp. 1–79.

(1) Philologus, the compleat pattern of the country gentleman (p. 2), (2) Scudiero, a county squire, the perfect reverse of Philologus (p. 3), (3) Daribeus, an honest man, though a dissenting parson (p. 4).

Attributed to Burnet by the Huntington Catalogue and others. There was a second edition in the same year. The first edition has not been traced.

[Burnet, Sir Thomas?]

Our Ancestors as wise as we. . . . London: Printed for A. Baldwin . . . 1712.

4°, text pp. 3–34.

(1) Agricola (p. 13), (2) Raymond (p. 15), (3) Sir Walter Raleigh (p. 16), (4) The D[uke]. of M[arlborough?]. (p. 18), (5) Edward II (p. 24), (6) Richard II (p. 26), (7) Henry VI (p. 27), (8) James I (p. 29).

BSC 2544.

[Burnet, Sir Thomas?]

The True Character of An Honest Man: Particularly With relation to the Publick Affaire. . . . London Printed: And Sold by J. Baker . . . 1712.

4°, text pp. 1–32.

(1) An honest man (p. 3), (2) An honest prince (p. 4), (3) An honest minister (p. 5), (4) An honest peer (p. 11), (5) An honest commoner (p. 14), (6) An honest judge (p. 16), (7) An honest lawyer (p. 17), (8) An honest writer (p. 18), (9) An honest clergyman (p. 23).

BSC 2544.

The dedication is signed Timon.

[Burnet, Sir Thomas?]

Truth, if you can find it: Or, A Character Of the Present M---y and P---t. In a Letter to a Member of the March Club. . . . London: Printed, and Sold by the Booksellers, 1712.

4°, text pp. 3–37.

(1) The E--l of Ox---d (p. 14), (2) Mr. St. J---ns (p. 17), (3) The D--e of O----d (p. 18), (4) The D--e of M-----h (p. 21), (5) The E--l of G-----n (p. 23).

BSC 2549, 2550, 2544.

The whole piece is a sort of character of the ministry.

Hoffman, Francis.

An Impartial Character Of the Noble Family of the Most Honourable the Earl of Oxford and Mortimer, Lord High Treasurer of Great Britain Sir Robert Harley Grand-Father formerly Governor of Dunkirk. Written by Francis Hoffman, Gent.*

[Second title:] The Character, Or the Most Honourable Sir Edward Harley, Father.

[Third title:] The Character Of the Most Honourable Robert Harley Earl of Oxford and Mortimer, Lord High-Treasurer of Great-Britain. London, Printed by A. Hinde in Peterborough Court in Fleetstreet, 1712. Price one Penny.

fo, text pp. 1–6.

(1) The family of the Earl of Oxford, (2) Sir Edward Harley, (3) Robert Harley, Earl of Oxford.

BSC 2547.

Holles, Denzil Holles, first Baron.

The British Constitution Consider'd, With A Character Of The Court And Parliament In The Year 1676. In a Letter from Denzil Lord Hollis. . . . London, Printed for A. Baldwin, 1712.

8°, text pp. 1–15.

(1) The French (p. 5), (2) English government (p. 8), (3) The Parliament (p. 10).

[Pope, Alexander.]

Miscellaneous Poems and Translations. By Several Hands. . . . London: Printed for Bernard Lintott . . . 1712.

8°, text pp. 3–376.

(1) Chaucer's characters, or the introduction to the Canterbury Tales, by Thomas Betterton (p. 245).

Attributed to Pope by the CBEL. Not true characters.

Raleigh, Sir Walter.

Instructions for Youth, Gentlemen and Noblemen. By Sir Walter Raleigh, Lord Treasurer Burleigh, Cardinal Sermonetta, And Mr. Walsingham. London: Printed for Randal Minshull . . . MDCCXII.*

(1) Arcana Aulica, by Eustache de Refuge (p. 103).

[Settle, Elkanah.]

The Character of a Popish Successor, and what England may Expect from such a One. First Printed about the year 1680 And now Reprinted with a Preface containing the Reasons of it. London, Printed in the year 1712.*

(1) as in 1681.

Sewell, George.

The Patriot. A Poem, Inscrib'd To the Right Honourable Robert Earl of Oxford, &c. Lord High Treasurer Of Great-Britain. By Mr. George Sewell. . . . London: Printed for E. Curll . . . 1712.

fo, text pp. 1–10.

Begins: "A Patriot Soul by Nature is design'd."

Shower, John.

Enoch's Translation. A Funeral Sermon Upon the Sudden Death of Dr. Nehemiah Grew, Fellow of the College of Physicians. . . . By John Shower. London: Printed by J.R. for John Clark . . . 1712.

4°, text pp. 1–22.
(1) Nehemiah Grew (p. 16).

[Steele, Sir Richard, Addison, Joseph, and others.]

The Spectator. . . . London: Printed for S. Buckley . . . 1712[–15].

8° and 12°, 8 vols.
(1) The Spectator (no. 1), (2) The Club (no. 2), (3) Arietta (no. 11), (4) Aurelia and Fulvia (no. 15), (5) The Ugly Club (no. 17), (6) The starers (no. 20), (7) Laetitia and Daphne (no. 33), (8) Leonora (no. 37), (9) Women called Picts (no. 41), (10) The Hebdomadal Club (no. 43), (11) An old beau and Hegatissa, a modern Pict (no. 48), (12) Eubulus (no. 49), (13) A new set of loungers (no. 54), (14) Sir Fopling Flutter, Dorimant, and Harriet (no. 65), (15) The Everlasting Club (no. 72), (16) The idols (no. 73), (17) A fine gentleman, Vocifer, and Ignotus (no. 75), (18) An absent man, by la Bruyere (no. 77), (19) Harry Tersett and Varilas (no. 100), (20) Will Honeycomb and various pedants (no. 105), (21) Will Wimble (no. 108), (22) Laertes and Irus (no. 114), (23) Peter the Great (no. 139), (24) Various beauties (no. 144), (25) A man of wit and pleasure (no. 151), (26) Women's men (no. 156), (27) A Jezebel (no. 175), (28) Zealots (no. 185), (29) Jilts (no. 187), (30) The salamanders (no. 198), (31) A female pander (no. 205), (32) The Club of She-Romps (no. 217), (33) Classes of female orators (no. 247), (34) Irus (no. 264), (35) A beau's head (no. 275), (36) Polycarpus (no. 280), (37) A coquette's heart (no. 281), (38) Male jilts (no. 288), (39) Emilia (no. 302), (40) The Mohock Club (no. 324), (41) Prince Eugene (no. 340), (42) A devotee (no. 354), (43) The Club of Parish Clerks, and The Lawyers' Club (no. 372), (44) Acasto (no. 386), (45) English oratory (no. 407), (46) Callisthenes, Acetus, and Minutius (no. 422), (47) Sempronia, a matchmaker (no. 437), (48) Charles II (no. 462), (49) Manilius (no. 467), (50) Dick Eastcourt (no. 468), (51) Tom Puzzle and Will Dry (no. 476), (52) A Templar in love (no. 485), (53) Erastus, Letitia, Tawdry, and Flavilla (no. 506), (54) A tavern-tyrant (no. 508), (55) William III (no. 516), (56) A shoeing-horn (no. 536), (57) Sir Roger de Coverley (no. 544), (58) The Widows' Club (no. 561).

First published 1711. Often reprinted.

[Ward, Edward.]

Female Policy Detected: Or, The Arts of a Designing Woman Laid Open. By E.W. Author of the London-Spy, and Trip to Jamaica. Treating . . . III. A True Character of a Vertuous Woman; or, Wife indeed. To which is added, A Poetical Discription of a Widow, Wife, and Maid. London, Printed and Sold by B. Harris, 1712.*

BSC 2552.
See the undated edition.

[Ward, Edward.]

The Poetical Entertainer: Or, Tales, Satyrs, Intrigues, &c. . . . To be publish'd as often as occasion shall offer. Numb. II. London . . . J. Morphew . . . M DCC XII.

4°, text pp. 3–40.
(1) A certain rattling Whig, lately taken notice of at Will's (p. 3, in verse).

Attributed to Ward by the CBEL.

[Wharton, Thomas, Marquis of?]

The Character Of A Certain Whigg. . . . [colophon] Printed in the Year 1712.

s.sh.fo. In verse.
Begins: "Industrious, unfatigue'd in FACTION's Cause."
BSC 2545.

1713

Anonymous.

The Character Of A Modern Tory; in A Letter to a Friend. . . . London: Printed for T. Harrison . . . and A. Baldwin . . . 1713.

4°, text pp. 3–24.
Begins: "A *Modern* Tory is a *Monster* with an *English* Face." (This is p. 12, where the character proper begins.)

The Monitor. 1713.*
fo.
See M. Smith, An Entire Set of the Monitors [1715?].

Whig and Tory: Or, Wit on both Sides. Being A Collection Of State Poems . . . The Second Edition. London, Printed for E. Curll . . . 1713.

4°, in 4 parts.
(1) The Character of a Modern Addresser (Part III, p. 37).

[Blackmore, Sir Richard, and others.]

The Lay monk.*

See his Lay Monastery, 1714.

Brown, Thomas.

The Lover's Secretary: or, the Adventures of Lindamira, The second edition. 1713.*

(1) Lindamira's portraiture of her old suitor (p. 18), (2) Cleomidon (p. 55), (3) A chaplain and an old lady (p. 65), (4) Lindamira's character of her friend (p. 82), (5) Lindamira's character of Octavius, a jealous husband (p. 163).

[Burnet, Sir Thomas?]

A Certain Information Of a Certain Discourse. That happen'd at a Certain Gentlemans House, In a certain County. Written by a certain Person then present . . . The Fourth Edition. London: Printed, and Sold by John Baker . . . 1713.

4°, text pp. 1–79.
(1–3) as in 1712.
BSC 2544.

[Burnet, Sir Thomas.]

Some New Proofs, By which it Appears that the Pretender Is Truly James the Third. London: Printed for J. Baker . . . 1713.

4°, text pp. 1–28.
(1) The L--d V---- B---- (sig. A3).

There were several editions in this same year. Reprinted 1714. In the 1745 reprint the dedication is changed, so that this character is omitted.

[Davenant, Charles?]

Dr. D--nant's Prophecys. A. Baldwin, 1713.*
BSC 2544.

The preface is subscribed T. Double.

[Deslandes, A.F.B.]

A Philological Essay: or Reflections on the Death of Free-Thinkers. With the Characters of the most eminent Persons of both sexes antient and modern, that died pleasantly and unconcern'd. By Monsieur D--- of the Royal Academy of Sciences. Translated from the French by Mr. B---. London, Printed by J. Baker. 1713.*

8°, text pp. 1–128.
BSC 2552.

The translator was A. Boyer.

[H., S., Misodolus.]

The Young-Mans Counsellor Or The Way of the World Displayd: In several Profitable Essays, Serious and Comical . . . intermixt with . . . Satyrical Characters . . . The Second Edition. London, Printed for Robert Gifford, 1713.*

Reprinted from Do No Right, 1711.
Described by William Sloane in Modern Language Notes, LIII (1938), 114.

Henry, Matthew.

A Sermon Preach'd upon Occasion of the Funeral Of the Reverend Mr. Daniel Burgess, Minister of the Gospel . . . By Matthew Henry . . . With a short Account concerning him. London: Printed for John Lawrence . . . Em. Mattews . . . MDCCXIII.

4°, text pp. 3–38.
(1) Daniel Burgess (p. 32).

La Bruyère, Jean de.

The Characters. 1713.*
Reprinted from 1699.

La Bruyère, Jean de.

The Works Of Monsieur De La Bruyere. In Two Volumes. . . . The Sixth Edition, Revis'd by the Paris Edition: With an Original Chapter, Of the Manner of Living With Great Men: Written after the Method of M. Bruyere, By N. Rowe, Esq;. London: Printed for E. Curll . . . and J. Pemberton . . . MDCCXIII.

8°, 2 vols.
(1–44) as in his The Characters, 1699.

[LeClerc, Jean.]

An Account of the Life and Writings of Mr. John Locke, Author of the Essay Concerning Humane Understanding. The Second Edition, Enlarged. London: Printed for John Clarke . . . and E. Curll . . . 1713.

4°, text pp. 1–63.
(1) Lord Ashley (p. 8), (2) John Locke (p. 50).

The preface notes that this was "first written . . . by Mr. LeClerc." First published as The Life and Character of Mr. John Locke, 1706, and reprinted with that title, 1714, 1740.

Le Clerc, John.

A Funeral Oration Upon The Death of Mr. Philip Limborch, Professor of Divinity among the Remonstrants at Amsterdam . . . by Mr. John Le Clerc. Translated from the Latin. London; Printed for A. Baldwin . . . M.-DCC.XIII.

4°, text pp. 1–31.
Begins: "If we consider the Nature. . . ."

Appended to Limborch's Compleat System or Body of Divinity, 2nd edition, London, 1713, Vol. I.

Palmer, Herbert.

Memorials of Godliness and Christianity. In Three Parts . . . By H. Palmer, B.D. . . . The Eighth Edition. Boston, Printed & Sold by Timothy Green . . . 1713.

6°, in 3 parts, text pp. 1–36, 1–28, 1–18.
(1–2) as in 1657.

Puckle, James.

The Club: or, a Dialogue Between Father and Son. . . London: Printed for the Author, James Puckle. 1713.

6°, text pp. 5–84.

(1) Buffoon (p. 9), (2) Critic (p. 10), (3) Detractor (p. 12), (4) Envioso (p. 14), (5) Flatterer (p. 16), (6) Hypocrite (p. 20), (7) Impertinent (p. 22), (8) Knave (p. 23), (9) Moroso (p. 26), (10) Newsmonger (p. 29), (11) Opiniator (p. 30), (12) Wiseman (p. 44), (13) Newsmonger, by his wife, Xantippe (p. 46), (14) Youth (p. 50).

[Puckle, James.]

The Club. In A Dialogue Between Father and Son. . . . The third Edition. London: Printed for the Author, 1713.

6°, text pp. 7–70.

(1–14) as in preceding edition of 1713.

BSC 2554.

St. Evremond, Charles de Marguetel de Saint-Denis, Seigneur de.

Memoirs of the Duchess of Mazarin. Written in Her Name by the Abbot of St. Real. . . . To which are added, Some Pieces attributed to Monsieur De St. Evremond, and by him approved. Printed in the Year, 1713.

8°, 2 vols.

(1–11) as (1–10, 19) in 1692.

Vol. I is virtually two volumes with separate signatures and pagination. Pp. 3–208 contain the memoirs; pp. i–clx (new pagination and signatures) contain the life of St. Evremond; pp. 1–368 (signatures continuous from the life of St. Evremond) contain miscellaneous essays and writings. Volume II bears the title page: The Works of Monsieur De St. Evremond, Vol. II. . . . London, Printed for J. Churchill [and others] . . . MDCCXIV. Another edition or state occurs in three volumes dated 1714 but with additional title page for Vol. I.

Smith, Jeremiah.

The Right Reformer's Character and Duty. In A Sermon Preach'd at Salters-Hall, To The Societies For Reformation of Manners, In the Cities of London and Westminster, 29th June, 1713. By Jeremiah Smith. Published at their Request. London, Printed for John Lawrence . . . and N. Cliff and D. Jackson . . . 1713.

4°, text pp. 1–40.

Begins: "Man's Recovery from Corruption and Misery."

Too long and hortatory to be a true character.

[Steele, Sir Richard, and others.]

The Guardian. . . . [colophon] London: Printed for J. Tonson . . . 1713.

(1) The author and his family (no. 1), (2) Sir Harry Lizard (no. 6), (3) Mr. Charwell (no. 9),

(4) A fine gentleman (no. 34), (5) A pretty gentleman (no. 38), (6) A lion (no. 71), (7) Peer the comedian (no. 82), (8) A good master (no. 87), (9) The Short Club (no. 91, 92), (10) The Tall Club (no. 108), (11) Female gamesters (no. 120), (12) The Silent Club (no. 121), (13) The Terrible Club (no. 143), (14) A mistress of a family, from Proverbs (no. 168).

Reprinted many times.

[Swift, Jonathan.]

The Character Of Richard St--le, Esq; With some Remarks. By Toby, Abel's Kinsman. . . . London, Printed for J. Morphew . . . 1713.

4°, text pp. 1–32.

Begins: "Sir, I have sent you the late Performances of Mr. St--le."

Listed by the CBEL under Swift, but with the added note: "[By William Wagstaffe?]." There are some indications of an earlier edition in 1704. There were two other editions in 1713, differing from the present only very slightly, the principal change being the insertion of "The Second Edition corrected" and "The Third Edition" on the title page.

Theophrastus.

The Moral Characters of Theophrastus. . . . From the French of Monsr. De La Bruyere. The Sixth Edition. London, Printed in the year 1713.*

See 1714.

[Ward, Edward.]

The History Of The Grand Rebellion . . . With the Impartial Characters of the most Famous and Infamous Persons . . . Digested into Verse. . . . In Three Volumes . . . London: Printed for J. Morphew . . . MDCCXIII.

8°, 3 vols. In verse.

(1) Queen Elizabeth (Vol. I, p. 1), (2) King James I (I, 4), (3) The Duke of Buckingham (I, 19), (4) Lord-Keeper Coventry (I, 21), (5) The House of Commons in 1625 (I, 23), (6) The Earl of Bristol (I, 38), (7) The Lord Bacon (I, 41), (8) The Lord Archbishop Abbot (I, 62), (9) The Earl of Portland (I, 65), (10) The Earl of Manchester (I, 68), (11) The Earl of Arundell (I, 82), (12) The Earl of Pembroke (I, 84), (13) The Lower House (I, 86), (14) The Earl of Montgomery (I, 91), (15) The Earl of Dorset (I, 93), (16) The Earl of Carlisle (I, 96), (17) The Earl of Holland (I, 106), (18) The Earl of Essex (I, 110), (19) Sir John Cope, and Sir Dudley Carleton (I, 112), (20) Duke Hamilton (I, 122), (21) Mr. Attorney-General Noy (I, 126), (22) Sir Harry Vane, the father (I, 128), (23) Sir Harry Vane, the son (I, 130), (24) The Earl of Northumberland (I, 140), (25) The Earl of

Lindsey (I, 142), (26) The Lord Cottington (I, 144), (27) The Earl of Bedford (I, 152), (28) The Lord Viscount Say (I, 154), (29) The Lord Mandevile (I, 156), (30) Mr. John Pym (I, 167), (31) Mr. John Hambden (I, 170), (32) Mr. St. John (I, 173), (33) Mr. Nathaniel Fiennes (I, 177), (34) Archbishop Laud (I, 183), (35) Bishop Juxon (I, 188), (36) Dr. Williams, Bp. of Lincoln (I, 191), (37) Sir John Finch, Lord-Keeper (I, 199), (38) Lord-Keeper Littleton (I, 201), (39) Sir Francis Windebank (I, 216), (40) Mr. William Pryn (II, 223), (41) Dr. John Bastwick (II, 224), (42) Mr. Henry Burton (II, 226), (43) General Lesly, Earl of Leven (II, 233), (44) Sir Denzil Hollis (II, 236), (45) The Earl of Bedford, the son (II, 237), (46) The Earl of Salisbury (II, 249), (47) The Earl of Berkshire (II, 251), (48) The Lord Dunsmore (II, 252), (49) The Earl of Leicester (II, 253), (50) The Earl of Strafford (II, 268), (51) The Marquis of Hertford (II, 270), (52) The Lord Savil (II, 273), (53) The Lord Brook (II, 276), (54) The Short Parliament (II, 278), (55) The Earl of Southampton (II, 294), (56) The Duke of Richmond (II, 296), (57) The Earl of Newcastle (II, 299), (58) The Lord Seymour (II, 302), (59) The Earl of Warwick (II, 320), (60) The Lord Viscount Falkland (II, 323), (61) Sir John Colepeper (II, 328), (62) Sir Edward Nicholas (II, 330), (63) The Lord Hopton (II, 361), (64) The Earl of Sutherland (II, 363), (65) The Earl of Carnarvan (II, 364), (66) Sir John Banks (II, 367), (67) Sir Peter Wych (II, 369), (68) Prince Rupert (II, 379), (69) Prince Maurice (II, 382), (70) Sir Bevil Greenvil (II, 384), (71) The Lord Goring (II, 386), (72) The Earl of Northampton (II, 397), (73) The Earl of Lindsey (II, 399), (74) The Lord Digby (II, 401), (75) The Earl of Litchfield (II, 404), (76) The Lord Fairfax (II, 414), (77) Sir Thomas, son of the Lord Fairfax (II, 415), (78) Sir Arthur Haslerig (II, 419), (79) The Earl of Kingston (II, 421), (80) Sir George Lisle (II, 432), (81) Sir Charles Lucas (II, 435), (82) The Lord Capel (II, 437), (83) The Royal Martyr [Charles I] (II, 446), (84) Sergeant Bradshaw (III, 461), (85) The high court of justice (III, 462), (86) Colonel Hewson (III, 464), (87) The Marquis of Montrose (III, 474), (88) David Lesley (III, 478), (89) Duke Hamilton (III, 487), (90) The Earl of Derby (III, 489), (91) Mr. Love (III, 492), (92) The Earl of Norwich (III, 505), (93) The Earl of Lautherdale (III, 508), (94) Major-General Harrison (III, 519), (95) Mr. John Lilburne (III, 521), (96) Oliver Cromwell (III, 534), (97) Ireton (III, 537), (98) Colonel Penruddock (III, 545), (99) Dr. John Hewet (III, 547), (100) Fleetwood, Lord-Deputy of Ireland (III, 553), (101) Major-General Desborough (III, 555), (102) The Duke of Ormond (III, 565), (103)

The Marquis of Argyle (III, 567), (104) Major-General Lambert (III, 577), (105) Colonel Ludlow (III, 579), (106) General Monk (III, 595). BSC 2556.

These are entitled characters, and accompanied usually by engravings. Many of the characters are taken from Clarendon and other previous writers.

[Ward, Edward.]

The Poetical Entertainer: Consisting of Epigrams, Satyrs, Dialogues, &c. . . . Numb. V. London . . . J. Woodward . . . and J. Morphew . . . MDCCXIII.

4°, text pp. 3–40.
(1) A bottle-definition of that fall'n angel, call'd, a Whig (p. 22, in verse).

[Ward, Edward.]

The Whigs Unmask'd: Being The Secret History Of The Calf's-Head Club. . . . To which are added, Several Characters by Sir John Denham, and other valuable Authors. . . . The Eighth Edition, with large Additions. London Printed: And Sold by J. Morphew . . . MDCCXIII.

8°, text pp. 1–224.
(1–4) as in his The Secret History of the Calves-Head Club, 1706, (5) The royal martyr, King Charles I, by Butler (p. 220).

1714

Anonymous.

The Character Of An Ill-Court Favourite. . . . Printed in the Year 1714. and Sold by F. Burleigh. . . .

4°, text pp. 5–38.
Begins: "He that stands by and observes the *supple* Addresses."
A reprint of 1681.

Churchill's Annals. 1714.*
See 1722.

The Enigmatical Court: Or, A Key To The High-German Doctor. Being The Characters of those Men whose Actions are a Mystery. To which is prefix'd, A List of several Eminent Persons. Part I. . . . London, Printed, and Sold by J. Baker . . . 1714.

4°, text pp. 3–21.
(1) Dr. Hermodactyl (p. 3), (2) Harry Gambol (p. 11), (3) Rub (p. 14), (4) Codicil (p. 16), (5) Smut (p. 18), (6) Atty Brogue (p. 20).

The Monitor. 1714.*
8°.
See M. Smith, An Entire Set of the Monitors, 1715.

Perkin's-Cabal, Or The Mock Ministry Characteriz'd. . . . London. Printed for A. Boulter . . . and S. Popping . . . and Sold by the Book-sellers of London and Westminster. 1714.*

4°, text pp. 1–12. In verse.
Begins: "First O---d's execrable Name."
BSC 2559.

The True Character of an Ill-Court Favourite. 1714.*

Probably a variant title for The Character of an Ill-Court-Favourite, 1714.

Two very odd characters, tho' the Number may be Even of the Whigg Flesh-Fly and the industrious Tory-bee, with a Hymn written by the Bee, and set to Musick of his Wings (with Character of F--c H-ffm--n, author of the Englishman). Printed for the Author, 1714.*

BSC 2561.

[Blackmore, Sir Richard and others.]

The Lay-Monastery. Consisting of Essays, Discourses, &c. Publish'd singly under the Title of the Lay-Monk. London: Printed by Sam. Keimer . . . M.DCC.XIV.

6°, text pp. 1–239. 40 numbers.
(1) The members of the society (no. 2), (2) The secretary of the society (no. 2), (3) An uncritical book-collector (no. 8), (4) The atheist (no. 14), (5) Hypocrites and dissemblers (no. 23), (6) Will Oscitant, a sedentary person, Tom Langer, a sportsman, and Prudentius, who avoids both excesses (no. 28), (7) Fools (no. 34), (8) An old-fashioned justice of the peace (no. 36), (9) A womanish man (no. 36).

A reprint of the Lay Monk, 1713. Attributed to Blackmore by the CBEL. There was a second edition in the same year.

[Burnet, Sir Thomas.]

Some New Proofs.*
BSC 2544.
Reprinted from 1713.

[Defoe, Daniel.]

Characters Of The Court of Hannover; With A Word or Two of Some Body else, which No Body has yet Thought on. . . . London: Printed for J. Baker . . . 1714.

4°, text pp. 3–32.
(1) The Pretender (p. 10), (2) The court of Hanover (p. 11), (3) The Electress Dowager (p. 16), (4) The Elector George Lewis (p. 18), (5) The Electoral Prince George Augustus (p. 20), (6)

The Prince of Brunswick (p. 21).
BSC 2557.

There were at least two distinct editions in 1714. There may have been an earlier edition in 1702.

Guise, Henry II of Lorraine, Duke of.

The Duke of Lorraine's Letter To Her Majesty. Containing, A Description and Character Of The Pretender. To which is added, Some Reflections concerning his Birth and Pretences. London: Printed for and sold by J. Roberts . . . 1714.

4°, text pp. 1–31.
Begins: " 'Twas with Indignation I saw this Letter."

A very wandering, ineffective character.

La Bruyère, Jean de.

Works. 1714.*
Reprinted from 1713.

[Le Clerc, Jean.]

The Life and Character of John Locke. 1714.*
Reprinted from An Account of . . . John Locke, 1713.

[Manley, Mary de la Rivière.]

The Adventures of Rivella . . . With Secret Memoirs and Characters of several considerable Persons her Cotemporaries. London: Printed in the Year M.DCC.XIV.

4°, text pp. 1–120.
(1) Rivello (p. 13), (2) Hilaria (p. 34).
Attributed to Mrs. Manley by the CBEL. There were several other editions.

St. Evremond, Charles de Marguetel de Saint-Denis, Seigneur de.

Works. 1714.*
Reprinted from Miscellaneous Essays, 1692–94.

Smith, Edmund.

The Works of Edmund Smith. 1714.*
(1) Edmund Smith, by William Oldesworth.

[Steele, Sir Richard.]

The Lover. 1714.*
See 1715.

[Swift, Jonathan.]

Essays Divine, Moral, and Political . . . By the Author of the Tale of a Tub, sometime the Writer of the Examiner, and the Original Inventor of the Band-Box-Plot . . . London: Printed in the Year, 1714.

8°, text pp. 1–82.
(1) A critick (p. v), (2) An examiner (p. v), (3) A clergyman (p. vi).
Attributed to Swift by the CBEL.

Theophrastus.

The Moral Characters of Theophrastus. Translated from the Greek, By Eustace Budgell. . . . London: Printed for Jacob Tonson . . . 1714.

12°, text pp. 1–78.

(1–28) as (17–44) in La Bruyère's Characters, 1699.

[Ward, Edward.]

Adam and Eve Stript of their Furbelows: or, the Fashionable Virtues . . . In two parts. I. Of the Ladies. II. Of Gentlemen. With Familiar Descants upon each character. 1714.*

BSC 2562.

Reprinted from The Modern World Disrob'd, 1708.

[Ward, Edward.]

The Republican Procession; Or, The Tumultuous Cavalcade. A Merry Poem. Printed in the Year 1714.

4°, text pp. 3–44. In verse.

(1) An independant-brother (p. 19), (2) A lecturer (p. 20), (3) A Presbyterian (p. 22).

BSC 2560.

Attributed to Ward by the CBEL. Since the British Museum Catalogue describes its copy as 8°, there must have been two issues of this impression.

[Ward, Edward.]

The Republican Procession; Or, The Tumultuous Cavalcade. A Merry Poem. The Second Impression, with Additional Characters. Printed in the year MDCCXIV.

4°, text pp. 3–43.

(1–3) as in first impression of 1714, (4) A leather-selling roundhead (p. 23), (5) An independent wizard (p. 23), (6) A republican (p. 25), (7) A Whig (p. 25).

[Ward, Edward.]

The Whigs Unmask'd: Or, History of the Calf's-Head-Club Farther Unmask'd. The Ninth Edition. London, Printed by J. Morphew. 1714.*

Reprinted from 1713.

1715

Anonymous.

A Character of His Most Excellent Majesty, George Lewis, of Hanover, King of Great Britain, etc. 1715.*

The Character of Lewis XIV. in his Life. London, Printed by H. Meere. 1715.*

8°, text pp. 1–13.

The Description of a Presbyterian. 1715.*

Reprinted from 1710.

The Life and Reign of Lewis XIV, with his Character. London, Printed by H. Meere 1715.*

BSC 2565.

Probably related to The Life and History of Lewis XIV, 1709, or to The Character of Lewis XIV, 1715, or both.

The Monitor. 1715.*

8°.

See M. Smith, An Entire Set of the Monitors, 1715.

[Birkenhead, Sir John.]

The Assembly-Man.*

Reprinted from 1663.

Brown, Thomas.

The Works Of Mr. Thomas Brown . . . In Four Volumes . . . To which is prefix'd, A Character of Mr. Brown and his Writings, By James Drake, M.D. The fourth Edition, Corrected; with large Additions, and a Supplement. London: Printed for Samuel Briscoe. 1715[–19].

12°, 4 vols. in 2.

(1–7) as in 1707–11; (8) A low-church magistrate [i.e., a latitudinarian] (IV, 337).

[Burnet, Sir Thomas.]

A Character Of the Right Reverend Father in God, Gilbert Lord Bishop of Sarum . . . London: Printed for J. Roberts . . . 1715.

4°, text pp. 3–32.

Begins: "He was descended from the Honourable Family of the BURNETS of Leyes."

Attributed to Burnet by the Harvard Catalogue. There were three editions in this year.

[Burnet, Sir Thomas, and others.]

The Grumbler. By Squire Gizzard . . . Thursday, March. 3. 1715. . . . [colophon] London: Printed by W. Wilkins . . . and Sold by R. Burleigh. . . .

s.sh.fo, text pp. 1–2.

(1) Squire Gizzard's family (no. 2).

Attributed to Burnet by the CBEL.

Butler, Samuel.

Posthumous Works . . . by Mr. Samuel Butler . . . The Second Edition. London, Printed for Sam. Briscoe . . . 1715.

12°, 2 vols.

(1) A fanatick (Vol. I, p. 167, in verse), (2) The five sectaries, the Presbyterian, Independant, Anabaptist, Quaker, and Fifth Monarchy men (I, 223), (3) Charles I (I, 153), (4) The Assem-

bly-Man. Written by Mr. Sam. Butler, and Sir John Birkenhead, in the Year 1647 (II, 88), (5) A tub-preacher (II, 260).

The first edition was also in 1715, and one or more further editions appeared in the same year or soon after.

Hepburn, Robert.

A Discourse Concerning the Character Of A Man of Genius. By Mr. Hepburn. With A Poem On The Young-Company of Archers, By Mr. Boyd. . . . Edinbvrgh: Printed by J.W. for William Dickie . . . MDCCXV.

4°, text pp. 1–18.

Begins: "There is no character more generally and more vainly aspir'd to."

BSC 2564.

La Bruyère, Jean de.

Works. 1715.*

Reprinted from 1713.

Mackqueen, John.

British Valour Triumphing over French Courage: Under the Conduct of the Duke of Marlborovgh, Prince of the Empire. . . . To which is annexed A Discourse concerning casting our Care on God; concluding with a modest Character of his Grace. By John Mackqueen . . . London: Printed for J. Morphew . . . 1715.

8°, text pp. 1–280.

(1) The Duke of Marlborough (p. 184).

BSC 2566.

The BSC copy was the author's autograph presentation copy to the Earl of Dorset.

Mackqueen, John.

A Divine and Moral Essay on Courage . . . with Some Reflections on the Causes of British Valour, and more peculiar Remarks on the Victory at Ramillies . . . The Second Edition. London: Printed in the Year 1715.*

(1) A man of valour, apparently intended to suggest the Duke of Marlborough (p. 218).

Appended to Mackqueen's British Valour Triumphing over French Courage, 1715, with which its page numbering is continuous.

Mather, Cotton.

Benedictus. Good Men Described . . . with Some Character & History of . . . Mr. Thomas Bridge . . . By C. Mather . . . Boston: Printed by B. Green . . . 1715.

6°, text pp. 1–58.

Begins: "Behold, the Best thing."

A character of a good man.

Nelson, Robert.

The Works of the late Pious and Learned Robert Nelson, Esq; . . . With a Character of Mr. Nelson, By Dr. Marshall. London: Printed for G. Strahan, 1715.*

(1) Robert Nelson, by John Marshall.

[Peers, Richard.]

The Character of an Honest Dissenter, in Twelve Marks; Together with an Illustration of Each. Imprimatur, Ar. Charlett, 15 Jun. 1715. Oxford, Printed by Leon. Litchfield . . . sold by . . . Booksellers in London, 1715.*

BSC 2294.

Attributed to Peers by Halkett and Laing, and republished under his name.

Quevedo Y Villegas, Francisco Gomez de.

Divine Maxims of Government, without Whig or Tory; or, the true Character of a King, and of a Tyrant, or faithful ministers, and of a favorite Traitor. By D. Francisco de Quevedo Villegas, author of the "Visions of Hell," etc. London, J. Roberts. 1715.*

BSC 2567.

Smith, M.

An Entire Set of the Monitors, Intended for the Promoting of Religion and Virtue . . . in several Poems on Divine Subjects . . . by M. Smith . . . London: Printed for the author. [1715?]

8°, text pp. 1–93. In verse.

(1) The upright man (p. 15), (2) The reverse (p. 17), (3) The swearer (p. 19), (4) The gamester (p. 40), (5) An humble contented man (p. 56).

Dated [1715?] by the CBEL. There were earlier editions, under the present title and as The Monitor, in 1713, 1714, 1715.

[Steele, Sir Richard.]

The Lover. To which is added; The Reader; By the same Author. . . . London: Printed for J. Tonson . . . J. Brown . . . and O. Lloyd . . . MDCCXV.

12°, text pp. 1–297.

(1) Mr. Myrtle's assistants in this work (no. 1), (2) A lover vagabond (no. 3), (3) Three courtesans (no. 15), (4) Mr. Careless, of the Middle Temper (no. 20), (5) Will Wormwood's character illustrated by the discontented man of Theophrastus (no. 39), (6) A sloven as portrayed by Theophrastus and by La Bruyère (no. 39).

The dedication is signed Richard Steele. The first paper is headed The Lover, Written in Imitation of the Tatler. By Marmaduke Myrtle, Gent. No. 1. Thursday, February 25, 1714. First printed 1714. Several times reprinted.

[Ward, Edward.]

Female Policy Detected. 1715.*

See the undated edition.

1716

Anonymous.

The Character of a Protestant. 1716.*

A Discourse concerning the character of a gentleman. By a person of quality. W. Brown: Edinburgh, 1716.*
8°, text pp. 1–50.

Barber, John.

The Character Of The Reverend and Learned Dr. Robert South. Being, The Oration Spoken at his Funeral, on Monday July xvi. 1716. . . . By Mr. Barber. . . . London: Printed for E. Curll . . . and Sold by R. Burleigh . . . 1716.
4°, text pp. 1–17.
Begins: "Quod Populis Humanitatis & Literarum." [English translation, p. 9, begins: "That Solemnity, which was established of Old."]

[Darrell, William.]

The Gentleman Instructed, In the Conduct of a Virtuous and Happy Life . . . To which is added, A Word to the Ladies . . . The Sixth Edition. London, Printed by J. Heptinstall for E. Smith, and are to be sold by Rich. Wilkin . . . MDCCXVI.
4°, text pp. 1–584.
(1–2) as in 1707, (3) Eusebius (sig. a).

Field, Nathaniel.

Some Short Memorials Concerning the Life of that Reverend Divine Doctor Richard Field, Prebendarie of Windsor and Dean of Glocester. Written by his Son Nathaniel Field, Rector of Stourton in the Countie of Wilts. Published from the original by John Le Neve, Gent. London, Printed by N. Clark. 1716–7.*
According to Mr. Greenough's notes, there is a character on p. 21.

Hickeringill, Edmund.

The Works of Mr Edmund Hickeringill . . . collected into Three Volumes . . . London: Printed, and sold by John Baker . . . 1716.
8°, 3 vols.
(1) A sham-plotter or man-catcher (Vol. I, p. 212), (2) The ceremony-monger (II, 377), (3) The good old cause (II, 512).

[Lowman, Moses, and others.]

A Collection Of The Occasional Papers For The Year 1716. London, Printed for J. Knapton . . . J. Harrison . . . and A. Dodd . . . 1716.

4°, 2 vols., each number separately paged.
(1) A free and generous mind (Vol. I, no. 1), (2) A Protestant (I, 2), (3) A virtuous man (I, 5).
Attributed to Lowman by the CBEL.

[Ward, Edward.]

Female Policy Detected: or, The Arts of a Designing Woman Laid Open. By E.W. Author of the London-Spy, and Trip to Jamaica, Treating . . . III. A true Character of a Vertuous Woman; or, Wife indeed. To which is added, A Poetical Discription of a Widow, Wife, and Maid. London: B. Harris, 1716.*
See the undated edition.

[Ward, Edward.]

St. Paul's Church; or, the Protestant Ambulators. A Burlesque Poem. . . . London: Printed for John Morphew . . . 1716.
4°, text pp. 3–32. In verse.
Begins: "Amidst a City much decay'd."
Attributed to Ward by the CBEL.

1717

Anonymous.

The Agreeable Variety. In Two Parts. Containing, First, Discourses, Characters, and Poems, relating to the most useful Subjects; and extracted from many worthy Authors. Consisting, Secondly, Of Letters, Poems, &c. by several Private Persons, on divers Occasions. Never before Printed. London: Printed for the Author, and Sold by G. Strahan [and several others] . . . MDCCXVII.
8°, text pp. 1–338.
(1) A wise man, from the Tatler (p. 16), (2) Cowley, by Sprat (p. 60), (3) Laud, by Clarendon (p. 63), (4) Falkland, by Clarendon (p. 64), (5) Clergy in the reign of Charles I, by Clarendon (p. 65), (6) Sir P. Sidney, by Lloid (p. 66), (7) Gustavus Adolphus, from The Turkish Spy (p. 67), (8) Several characters from Plutarch (p. 68), (9) Prince George of Denmark, from The British Apollo (p. 185), (10) Lord Roscommon, by Dryden (p. 186), (11) Sprat, by Dryden (p. 186), (12) Seven characters from Mrs. Phillips's poems (p. 187), (13) Mr. ———, by Cowley, Mrs. Phillips, and Smith (p. 192).
BSC 2568.

A Character . . . Printed in the Year, 1717.
8°, text pp. 3–13. In verse.
Begins: "Sattyr, Audacious G----N's Wiles reherse."
The Harvard copy is bound with several related tracts, such as A Character Defended, A Letter to the Author of A Character, etc. It is a character of one Gibson, a preacher.

The Dissenters Cleared: being an Evening's Conference between Mr. Meanwell, a Lover of Peace, and Mr. Freeman, a Lover of Truth, with the Character of a Tory and a Tantivi-Man. Coventry. 1717.*

8°.

The Entertainer: Containing Remarks Upon Men, Manners, Religion and Policy . . . Together with . . . Characters . . . London, Printed by N. Mist.

6°, text pp. 1–307. Numbers 1–43 (Nov. 6, 1717 — Aug. 27, 1718).

(1) An enthusiast (no. 18), (2) A schismatick preacher (no. 19), (3) A noble benefactor (no. 35).

Essays Relating to the Conduct Of Life. Upon the Following Subjects . . . London: Printed, for E. Curll at the Dial and Bible against St. Dunstan's Church in Fleetstreet. 1717.*

12°, text pp. 1–84.

(1) The friend and pretended friend (p. 25, chap. vii), (2) The honest man (p. 30, chap. viii), (3) The man truly great (p. 84).

BSC 2570.

There was at least one other edition.

A Presbyterian getting on horse-back. London, 1717.*

[Bellegarde, Jean Baptiste Morvan de.]

Reflections Upon Ridicule . . . Wherein are Represented The different Manners and Characters of Persons of the present Age. In Two Volumes . . . The Third Edition. London: Printed for J. Nicholson . . . B. Tooke . . . and D. Midwinter . . . MDCCXVII.

12°, 2 vols.

(1–10) as in 1707.

Democri-Diogenes [pseud.].

Γιβσωνογραφια: Or, The Picture. By Democri-Diogenes. The Author of a Character — Hath Chastised you with Whips, but I will Chastise you with Scorpions. . . . London: Printed in the Year MDCCXVII.

4°, text pp. 1–6.

Begins: "G---n is a man (or rather a Monster)."

The object of the satire is perhaps Edmund Gibson, theological writer.

Halifax, George Savile, Marquis of.

Miscellanies By the most Noble George Lord Saville, Late Marquis and Earl of Halifax . . . The Third Edition. London: Printed for B. Tooke . . . MDCC.XVII.

12°, text pp. 3–312.

(1–2) as in 1700.

[Lewis, Thomas.]

The Scourge In Vindication Of The Church of England. . . . London, Printed in the Year, MDCCXVII.

12°, text pp. 1–368.

(1) The Presbyterian dissenter (no. 13), (2) The canting Presbyterian, or quack divine (no. 35).

Peers, Richard.

The Character Of An Honest Dissenter., In Twelve Marks: Together with An Illustration of Each. By Rich. Peers Vicar of Faringdon Berks. The Third Edition. . . . . Oxford, Printed for Stephen Fletcher. 1717.*

4°, text pp. 1–39.

Begins (the character): "The Honest Dissenter is sincerely desirous of Unity."

BSC 2572.

Reprinted from 1715.

[Theobald, Lewis.]

The Censor. . . . The Second Edition. London: Printed for Jonas Brown . . . 1717.

12°, 3 vols.

(1) A wise virgin (no. 4), (2) A shadow of a great man (no. 12), (3) A flatterer (no. 17), (4) An ill natured critic (no. 33), (5) A hypocrite in criticism (no. 33), (6) An absent man (no. 49), (7) Lelius, a sheepishly modest man (no. 52), (8) The unequal man (no. 81), (9) A politick knower and a politick affirmer (no. 94).

There were at least two editions. Attributed to Theobald by the CBEL.

1718

Anonymous.

The Doctor. No. 5. August, 1718.*

(1) The drunken devil, (2) The covetous devil, (3) The poor devil, (4) The lying devil.

The Honest Gentleman. London, for J. Peele. 1718–19.*

(1) The honest gentle-man (no. 1, Nov. 5, 1718), (2) Don Altiero, who is self-sufficient, and therefore always unequal, haughty, and disdainful (no. 19, March 11, 1718 [i.e., 1719?]), (3) Tony Trivial, Esq. who is looked upon as a man, sans consequence, and so has neither friends nor enemies (no. 19), (4) Simplus, who has good nature and nonsense (no. 19), (5) A husband who is a cipher (no. 19), (6) Mr. J. Peele, the author's publisher (no. 25, April 22, 1718 [i.e., 1719]).

The Picture Of A False Prophet; With Some Directions how to Know, and Avoid Him.

... London, Printed for John Morphew, 1718.*

Gildon, Charles.

The Complete Art of Poetry. In Six Parts. ... By Charles Gildon. ... London, Printed for Charles Rivington ... MDCCXVIII.

12°, 2 vols.

(1) Laudon, the ideal patron (vol. II, p. v), (2) Morisina, his wife, the ideal woman (II, vii), (3) Eusebia, who lives an exemplary life (II, vii), (4) Madame La Mode (II, vii), (5) Issachar La Mode, her husband, whose natural good taste is injured by his tendency to like whatever his wife likes (II, viii), (6) Tyro, a young poet (II, ix), (7) Manilia, who lacks reading but has sense and judgment (II, ix).

La Bruyère, Jean de.

Works. 1718.*

Reprinted from 1713.

[Marshall, Nathaniel.]

The Recompence of Virtue: or, the Just Man's Character ... a Sermon Preach'd at the Funeral of Mr. Richard Blundel, An Eminent Surgeon of this City. London, Printed by H.P. for William Taylor. 1718.*

Peers, Richard.

The Character of an Honest Dissenter. 1718.*

Reprinted from 1715.

[Penn, William.]

Fruits of Solitude. 1718.*

Reprinted from Some Fruits of Solitude, 1693.

[Philips, Ambrose.]

The Free-Thinker. ... London, Printed for W. Wilkins ... and Sold by W. Graves ... and J. Graves ... [1718].

s.sh.fo (each number).

(1) Thetfordius, a "Scholastic Juggler," contrasted with Euphronius, who reasons upon all subjects "with the same equitable Temper, as if his Thoughts were employed upon a Problem in Mathematicks" (no. 14, May 9), (2) Sophronia, "who does not aspire to masculine Virtues," yet is "above the capricious Terrours of Women" (no. 39, August 4), (3) The perts (no. 61, Oct. 20), (4) The peaceable enthusiast (no. 83, January 5, 1718/9).

Attributed to Philips by the CBEL.

[Sewell, George.]

The Resigners vindicated: or, the Defection re-consider'd ... By a Gentleman. ... The

Fourth Edition. London: Printed for R. Burleigh ... 1718.

4°, text pp. 3–34.

(1) The resigners (p. 31).

Theophrastus.

Characters. 1718.*

Reprinted from 1714.

[Ward, Edward.]

The London Spy. 1718.*

Reprinted from 1698.

1719

Brown, Thomas.

Amusements Serious and Comical. 1719–1721.*

Reprinted from 1700.

[Defoe, Daniel.]

The Anatomy of Exchange-Alley ... To which is added, Some Characters of the most Eminent Persons concern'd now, and for some Years past, in Carrying on this Pernicious Trade. By a Jobber. London: Printed for E. Smith ... 1719.

4°, text pp. 1–64.

(1) C---, a man of brass (p. 36), (2) S---, a man of cunning (p. 37), (3) T---, a gamester (p. 37).

The initials are expanded in the second edition in the Huntington Library to read Caswole, Sawbridge, and Turner. Attributed to Defoe by the CBEL. There were two editions in 1719. Reprinted 1849 as Chronicles and Characters of the Stock Exchange.

[Gordon, Thomas.]

The Character Of An Independent Whig. ... London: Printed for J. Roberts ... 1719.

4°, text pp. 1–31.

Begins: "Independency at Court is a Heresy in Politicks."

BSC 2573.

There was another edition of the same year. Attributed to Gordon by the Harvard Catalogue and also in Gordon's A Cordial for Low Spirits, 1763, in which it is reprinted.

[Kennett, White.]

A Complete History of England. ... Vol. III. ... The Second Edition. ... London: Printed for R. Bonwick [and others] ... 1719.

4°, text pp. 1–855.

(1–4) as in 1706.

[Lowman, Moses, and others.]

The Occasional Paper. The Second Edition. 1719.*

Reprinted from A Collection of the Occasional Papers, 1716.

Mather, Cotton.

Desiderius. Or, A Desirable Man Describ'd; In the Characters of One Worthy to be, A Man Greatly Beloved. And An Example of One, who Lived very much Desired . . . in some Commemoration of . . . Mr. James Keith, Late Minister of the Gospel in Bridgewater. . . . By Cotton Mather . . . Boston: Printed by S. Kneeland, 1719.

6°, text pp. 1–34.
Begins: "The Man to whom this comfortable Message was brought."

[Philips, Ambrose.]

The Free-Thinker. . . . [colophon] London, Printed for W. Wilkins . . . And Sold by J. Roberts . . . J. Graves . . . and T. Griffiths. . . .
s.sh.fo (each number). Printed on two sides.
(1) A coquette (no. 174, November 20).

Smith, Edmund.

The Works of Mr. Edmund Smith. 1719.*
Reprinted from 1714.

1720

Anonymous.

The Character of a Quaker. [Dublin? 1720?]*
s.sh.fo.
Begins: "A Quaker is the Spawn of Anarchy."

The Court of Honour. 1720.*
Reprinted from 1679.

Some Proposals To Benefit the Province. Boston: Printed for and sold by Benj. Eliot, 1720.
8°, text pp. 1–15.
(1) A publick spirit (p. 13), (2) A private spirit (p. 13).

Brown, Thomas.

The Works Of Mr. Thomas Brown, Serious and Comical, In Prose and Verse. In Four Volumes. The Fifth Edition, Corrected . . . With The Life and Character Of Mr. Brown . . . London: Printed for Sam Briscoe . . . and sold by R. Smith, A. Bell . . . 1720[–21].
12°, 5 vols. (Vol. V has title: The Fifth Volume Of The Works Of Mr. Thomas Brown . . . 1721).
(1–8) as in fourth edition of 1715[–19], (9) Mr. Brown, Written by . . . Joseph Addison (Vol. I, sig. *A4), (10) The Remains (V, 1), (11) A Legacy for the Ladies (V, 145), (12) A Puritan (V, 295, in verse), (13) The Characters of several ingenious designing gentlewomen, that put in to the Ladies Invention (V, 304).

[Darrell, William.]

The Gentleman Instructed. 1720.*
Reprinted from 1707.

[Dennis, John.]

The Characters and Conduct of Sir John Edgar Call'd by Himself Sole Monarch of the Stage in Drvry-Lane; And His Three Deputy-Governors. . . . London: Printed for M. Smith, in Cornhill. MDCCXX.
4°, text pp. 1–35.
Begins: "The World has a long Time."
BSC 2574.
This is a character of Sir Richard Steele. Attributed to Dennis by the Harvard Catalogue.

Gildon, Charles.

All for the better; or the World turn'd upside down, being the History of the Headlongs and the Long-heads, with several Characters of both. London. Printed and sold by John Applebee. 1720.*
8°.
BSC 2576.

[Gordon, Thomas.]

The Character Of An Independent Whig. . . . The Third Edition. . . . London: Printed for J. Roberts . . . 1720.
4°, text pp. 3–31 (wrongly printed 32).
Begins: "Independency at Court is a Heresy in Politicks."
There are two other editions of the same year, virtually identical except that one bears the phrase "The Fourth Edition" and the other "The Fifth Edition" on the title page. Reprinted from 1719.

[Gordon, Thomas.]

The Humorist: Being Essays Upon Several Subjects . . . By the Author of the Apology for Parson Alberoni . . . London, Printed for W. Boreham . . . 1720.
12°, text pp. 1–240.
(1) Mrs. Armful (p. 151), (2) Lady Pepper (p. 15), (3) Mrs. Bulkey (p. 21), (4) Lord Tittle (p. 32), (5) A pedant (p. 43), (6) Beau Grains (p. 44), (7) Mutatius (p. 54), (8) Tremulus (p. 57), (9) John Felix (p. 58), (10) Mrs. Fussock (p. 59), (11) Simon Wily (p. 96), (12) Lady Wince (p. 98), (13) Hannibal (p. 134), (14) Matilda (p. 155), (15) Dick Noodle (p. 155), (16) Beau Wittol (p. 156), (17) Miss Amble (p. 170), (18) Maria (p. 170), (19) Thomas Durfey (p. 189), (20) Nero (p. 189), (21) Col. Rugged (p. 192), (22) Lady Savoy (p. 196), (23) A gluttonous friar (p. 209), (24) Will Wasp (p. 218), (25) Beau Tinsel (p. 219), (26) John Brute (p.

220), (27) Poplicola (p. 229), (28) William Hackett (p. 235).

Attributed to Gordon by the CBEL.
A second volume appeared in 1725.

[Killigrew, Thomas.]

Miscellanea Aurea: or the Golden Medley. . . . London: Printed for A. Bettesworth . . . MDCCXX.

8°, text pp. 1–295. In verse.
(1) The fop (p. 130).
Faithorne's portrait of Killigrew, 1650, faces the title page.

[Lewis, Thomas.]

The Scourge: In Vindication of the Church of England. . . . By T.L. London: Printed in the Year M.DCC.XX.

8°, text pp. 1–384. The Scourge itself ends on p. 281. The remainder consists of other tracts.
(1–2) as in 1717.

Locke, John.

A Collection Of Several Pieces Of Mr. John Locke . . . Publish'd by the Author of the Life of . . . Mr. John Hales. . . . London: Printed by J. Bettenham for R. Francklin . . . M.-DCC.XX.

8°, text pp. 1–362.
(1) John Locke, by Peter Coste (p. iv).
Pforzheimer Catalogue No. 596, 597.

Mather, Cotton.

Detur Digniori. The Righteous Man Described and asserted as the Excellent Man. A Sermon upon the Death of the Rev. Mr. Joseph Gerrich. Boston. 1720.*

8°, text pp. 1–29.

[Mist, Nathaniel, Defoe, Daniel, and others.]

The Weekly Journal. Or Saturday's-Post . . . Saturday, March 19. 1720. . . . [colophon] London, Printed by N. Mist.

3°, text pp. 403–408 (no. 68 only).
(1) A female Quixote, in the form of a letter to Mr. Mist from Anna Donna Quixote.

Attributed to Mist and others by the CBEL. Each number, though without signature marks, consists of three leaves.

[Penn, William.]

Fruits of Solitude.*

Reprinted from Some Fruits of Solitude, 1693.
The date is uncertain.

[Steele, Sir Richard.]

The Theatre. By Sir John Edgar. . . . London: Printed for W. Chetwood . . . J. Roberts . . . and Charles Lillie.

s.sh.fo, unpaged, printed on two sides (each number).
(1) A wrong-head (no. 5, January 12–16).

[Swift, Jonathan.]

The Characters Of Two Independent Whigs, Viz. T,G--- of the North, And Squire T--- of the West. . . . London, Printed for John Morphew . . . 1720.

4°, text pp. 3–22.
Begins: "Independency is the thing in the World." BSC 2575.

Attributed to Swift in the Harvard Catalogue.
The two objects of the satire are Thomas Gordon and John Trenchard.

[Trenchard, John, and Gordon, Thomas.]

The Independent Whig. . . . Wednesday, January 20, 1720 [-January 4, 1720/1]. . . . [colophon] London: Printed for J. Roberts.

Each number s.sh.fo. 53 numbers.
(1) A domestic chaplain (no. 20), (2) Zeal (no. 23).
Attributed to Trenchard and Gordon by the CBEL.
Reprinted numerous times.

[Ward, Edward.]

The Delights of the Bottle: or, the Complete Vintner. With the Humours of Bubble Upstarts, Stingy Wranglers . . . And other Tavern Tormenters. . . . By the Author of the Cavalcade. . . . London: Printed by W. Downing . . . MDCCXX.

4°, text pp. 3–54. In verse.
(1) Bubble-upstarts (p. 45), (2) The stingy wrangler (p. 46), (3) Dinner-spungers (p. 47), (4) Jill Tiplers (p. 48), (5) Beef beggars (p. 49), (6) Cook teasers (p. 50), (7) Pan-soppers (p. 51), (8) Plate twirlers (p. 52), (9) Table whitlers (p. 52), (10) Drawer-biters (p. 53), (11) Spoon pinchers (p. 54).
Attributed to Ward by the CBEL. There were two editions in 1720.

[Ward, Edward.]

Female Policy Detected.*

See the undated edition. The date of the present edition is uncertain.

[Ward, Edward.]

The Poet's Ramble after Riches. A Poem. By the Author of the London Spy. Dublin: Printed, at the Rein Deer . . . by C. Hicks.

8° (no signature marks), text pp. 3–16. In verse.
(1) as in 1710.
Undated. Dated 1720 by the Yale University Library.

[Ward, Edward.]

The Second Part of the London Clubs . . . By the Author of the London Spy. . . . London,

Printed by J. Dutton . . . Also the First Part. [c. 1720].*

(1) Of the no nose club (p. 23), (2) The beau's club (p. 26), (3) The mollies' club (p. 28), (4) The quacks' club (p. 29).

Attributed to Ward by the CBEL, which dates it (c. 1720?). The first part, The History of the London Clubs, appeared in 1709.

1721

Anonymous.

The Character Of The Parliament. Commonly called the Rump, &c. Begun November 23. in the Year 1640. With a short Account of some of their Proceedings. . . . London: Printed; and Sold by the Booksellers of London and Westminster. MDCCXXI.

8°, text pp. 1-38.
Begins: "This famous *Parliament*, which sate so long, did so much Mischief."
BSC 2578.

BSC 2577 lists another issue of the same year, printed by J. Jones.

Buckinghamshire, John Sheffield, Duke of.

The Works of The Most Noble John Sheffield, Late Duke of Buckingham. . . . London: Printed for E. Curll . . . 1721.

4°, text pp. 1-151.
(1) Charles II (p. 1).

[Cotton, Charles.]

The Compleat Gamester: Or, Full and Easy Instructions For Playing at all Manner of usual, and most Genteel Games . . . To which is Added. The Gentleman's Diversion . . . London: Printed for J. Wilford . . . MDCC-XXI.

8°, in 2 parts, text pp. 1-104, 1-44.
(1-2) as in 1674.

[Foxton, Thomas.]

The Character Of A Fine Gentleman; With Reference to Religion, Learning, and the Conduct of Life. In which are added, Five Poems . . . All by Mr. Addison. . . . London, Printed for E. Curll . . . M.DCC.XXI.

4°, text pp. 1-77.
(1) Joseph Addison (p. 1).

Reprinted as Serino: Or the Character of a Fine Gentleman, [1721?], [1725?].

[Foxton, Thomas.]

Serino: Or, The Character Of A Fine Gentleman; With Reference to Religion, Learning, and the Conduct of Life. In which are included Six Poems by Mr. Addison . . . To which is prefixed An Account of the Life and

Writings of Joseph Addison, Esq; London; Sold by T. Tonson. . . .

12°, text pp. 1-134.
(1) as in The Character of a Fine Gentleman, 1721.

Reresby, Tamworth.

A Miscellany of Ingenious Thoughts and Reflections, In Verse and Prose; With some Useful Remarks. To which are added . . . Characters, Pleasant Narratives, Moral Observations, and Essays. By Tamworth Reresby, Gent. London, Printed by H. Meere . . . for the Author. MDCCXXI.

4°, text pp. 1-422.
(1) The C-- of S--d (p. 130), (2) Oliver Cromwell (p. 140), (3) Walstein (p. 142), (4) Tiberius (p. 143), (5) Marshal Ferte (p. 145), (6) Turenne (p. 146), (7) Cardinal Richelieu (p. 148), (8) Agricola (p. 150), (9) Marius (p. 152), (10) Lewis de Bourbon (p. 154), (11) Cardinal Mazarin (p. 191), (12) Agreeable Radius (p. 193), (13) Laud (p. 295), (14) Charles I (p. 336), (15) Louis XIV (p. 338), (16) Richelieu (p. 340), (17) The picture of man in miniature, from Shakespeare (p. 340), (18) The Romans (p. 372), (19) Cato (p. 388), (20) Mecænas (p. 392).
BSC 2579.

[Trenchard, John, and Gordon, Thomas.]

Cato's Letters.*

(1) A good and an evil magistrate, by Algernon Sidney (no. 37, for 1721).

Attributed to Trenchard and Gordon by the CBEL. First published, according to the CBEL, in The London Journal and The British Journal, 1720-27.

[Ward, Edward.]

The Delights of the Bottle. 1721.*
Reprinted from 1720.
There were two editions in this year.

1722

Anonymous.

The Art of Governing . . . The Second Edition. London . . . T. Warner . . . and A. Dodd . . . 1722.

4°, text pp. 1-58.
(1) A statesman, odious to the people (p. 20), (2) A good statesman, by Bacon (p. 21), (3) Parliament (p. 34).

Churchill's Annals . . . With His Character. . . . The Second Edition. London: Printed for John Clark . . . MDCCXXII.

4°, text pp. 1-48.
(1) John Churchill, Duke of Marlborough, by several writers (p. 24).
The first edition was 1714.

The Comical Pilgrim; Or, Travels Of A Cynick Philosopher, Thro' the most Wicked Parts of the World, Namely, England, Wales, Scotland, Ireland, and Holland. With His Merry Observations on the English Stage, Gaming-Houses, Poets, Beaux, Women, Courtiers, Politicians, and Plotters. Welsh Clergy, Gentry, and Customs. Scotch Manners, Religion, and Lawyers. Irish Ceremonies in their Marriages, Christenings, and Burials. And Dutch Government, Polity, and Trade. Being A Genrall Satyr on the Vices and Follies of the Age. London, Printed for S. Briscoe . . . 1722.

4°, text pp. 3–108.
(1) A modern beau (p. 8), (2) A Scotch Presbyterian (p. 59, in verse), (3) An Irish woman (p. 81, in verse), (4) The Dutch (p. 102).
There seem to have been two editions in 1722.

[Barrington, John Shute Barrington, first Viscount.]

A Letter to Protestant Dissenters concerning the Ensuing Election.*
(1) A Presbyterian.
Attributed to Barrington by Halkett and Laing, which dates it 1722.

Bona, Giovanni.
Manuductio ad Coelum. Seventh Edition. 1722.*
Murphy 146.
Reprinted from 1672.

Dart, John.
A Poem on Chaucer and his Writings. By Mr. Dart. . . . London: Printed, and Sold T. Paine . . . 1722.
fo, text pp. 1–8. In verse.
(1) Chaucer (p. 1).

[Defoe, Daniel.]
Applebee's Journal.*
(1) The great Duke of Marlborough (June 23, 1722), (2) An abandoned clergyman (Oct. 27, 1722), (3) A wicked landlord (Mar. 7, 1724), (4) An unmanageable wife (Dec. 5, 1724), (5) A jealous husband (Mar. 6, 1725), (6) A quarrelsome wife (Apr. 17, 1725), (7) One entitled to the name of scholar, but denied it because he knows but little Greek and Latin (Oct. 30, 1725), (8) A pedant (Nov. 6, 1725).

[Du Refuge, Eustache.]
Arcana Aulica, or Walsingham's Manual. 1722.*
12°, text pp. 9–328.
(1–4) as in 1652.

[Foulis, H.]
The Christians Character, or a Discourse perswading Mutual Love and Charity to one another. Edinburgh. Printed by William Adams Junior. 1722.*
4°, text pp. 1–35.
BSC 2580.

[Franklin, James (editor).]
The New-England Courant. Boston: Printed and Sold by J. Franklin . . . 1721–1723.
s.sh.fo (individual numbers).
(1) Benjamin Franklin, by himself (no. 37, April 9–16).

Gordon, Thomas.
The True Picture of a Modern Tory. 1722.*
Begins: "A Tory is a Monster with an English face."
This is virtually a reprint of Buckingham's Character of a Tory, 1681.

[Grey, Zachary.]
Presbyterian Prejudice Display'd. Or; An Answer to Mr. Benjamin Bennet's Memorial of the Reformation. By a Hearty well-wisher to the Established Church. London, Printed for T. Warner. 1722.*
(1) A Presbyterian (p. 6).
The character is quoted from A Letter to Protestant Dissenters concerning the Ensuing Election, 17--. Attributed to Grey by the CBEL.

[Philips, Ambrose.]
The Free-Thinker. Vol. I. From Lady-Day to Michaelmas, 1718. . . . London, Printed in the Year MDCCXXII[–III].
8°, 3 vols.
(1–4) as in 1718, (5) as (1) in 1719.

1723

Anonymous.
Button and Button-Hole, with a Character of the Drabs and the Change of Old-Hat. . . . A Moore, 1723.*
fo. In verse.
BSC 2581.

The Pettifoggers. A Satire. In Hudibrastick Verse. Displaying the various Frauds, Deceits, and Knavish Practices, of the Pettifogging Counsellors, Attorneys, Solicitors and Clerks. . . . With Characters of the Chief of them. . . . London: Printed for A. Dodd . . . MDCCXXIII.
4°, text pp. 3–30.
(1) A councillor at law (p. 8), (2) An attorney

(p. 13), (3) A solicitor (p. 15), (4) A pettifogger (p. 18), (5) Humeros, a councillor for the church (p. 25), (6) Councillor Catcall (p. 26), (7) Ralpho, a solicitor of Furnival's Inn (p. 27).

Atterbury, Francis, Bishop of Rochester.

Maxims, Reflections and Observations, Divine, Moral and Political. By the Right Reverend Dr. Francis Atterbury, Late Lord Bishop of Rochester. . . . London: Printed in the Year M.DCC.XXIII.

4°, text pp. 1–84.
(1) Queen Mary (p. 6), (2) The proud man (p. 78).

Buckinghamshire, John Sheffield, Duke of.

The Works of John Sheffield, Earl of Mulgrave, Marquis of Normandy, and Duke of Buckingham. . . . London: Printed by John Barber, Alderman of London, MDCCXXIII.

4°, text pp. 3–295.
(1) A tory, 1679 (p. 29), (2) Charles II (p. 57), (3) The Earl of Arlington (p. 65), (4) Julius Caesar (p. 195).

There were apparently two editions in 1723, varying considerably but both containing all four characters.

[Darrell, William.]

The Gentleman Instructed, in the Conduct Of a Virtuous and Happy Life. In Three Parts. . . . The Eighth Edition. London: Printed by W.B. for E. Smith, and are to be sold by Rich. Wilkin . . . M.DCC.XXIII.

8°, text pp. 1–584.
(1–3) as in 1716, (4) Beaus (p. 24), (5) Townsparks (pp. 474, 482), (6) A dun (p. 497).

[Franklin, James.]

The New-England Courant. [no. 111.] From Monday September 9. to Monday September 16. 1723. . . . [colophon] Boston: Printed and sold by Benjamin Franklin in Queen-Street. . . .

s.sh.fo. Printed on both sides.
(1) A gossip (in a letter signed Z.Y. and addressed to Doctor Janus).

Higgons, Bevil.

A Short View Of The English History: With Reflections . . . on the Reigns of the Kings, their Characters . . . By B. Higgons, Gent. London, Printed by Tho. Edlin. MDCC-XXIII.

8°, text pp. 1–435.
(1) Charles the First (p. 300), (2) Oliver Cromwell (p. 346), (3) Charles the Second (p. 366), (4) James the Second (p. 402).

Jesup, Mr.

The Lives of Picus and Pascal, Faithfully collected etc. To which is subjoined a Parallel Between those Two Christian Worthies. By Mr. Jesup. London: Printed by W. Burton, 1723.*

(1) Picus, Prince of Mirandula, (2) Pascal.

[Mather, Cotton.]

A Good Character. Or, A Walk with God characterized. With Some dues paid unto the Memory of Mr. Joseph Belcher. . . . By One of the Ministers in Boston. . . . Boston, N.E. Printed by B. Green. 1723.

4°, text pp. 1–24.
Begins: "Doubtless you will foresee."
A character of a sincere and just walker with God.

[Mist, Nathaniel, and others.]

The Weekly Journal or Saturday's-Post. . . . Saturday, October 12, 1723. . . . London: Printed by N. Mist, in Great-Carter-Lane.

fo, 6 pages (each number).
(1) Bromeo, a man of good sense but indolent, contrasted with Levis, active but unstable (no. 259, p. 1537).

[Puckle, James.]

The Club. Or, A Grey-Cap, For A Green-Head . . . The Fourth Edition, with Additions. London, Printed for Edward Symon . . . 1723.

12°, text pp. 1–179.
(1–14) as in 1713, (15) Swearer (p. 50), (16) Traveller (p. 53), (17) Usurer (p. 56).

The order has been somewhat changed, so that the new characters are nos. 12–14, and nos. 12–14 of the earlier editions become nos. 15–17 here.

[Sheridan, Thomas, and Swift, Jonathan.]

The Intelligencer. 1723.*
See 1729.

[Wharton, Philip Wharton, Duke of.]

The True Briton. Numb. LVIII. . . . Friday, December 20. 1723. . . . [colophon] Printed by T. Payne.

s.sh.fo, printed on both sides.
(1) An honest man, by C.D. (first page).
Attributed to Wharton by Halkett and Laing.

1724

Anonymous.

The Agreeable Variety. . . . The Second Edition. London; Printed for A. Bettesworth . . . M.DCC.XXIV.

8°, text pp. 1–338.
(1–12) as in 1717.

The Register of Folly; or Characters at the Hot Well, Bristol, in September, and at Bath, in October, 1723. London, Printed for James Lacy, 1724.*

(1) Mr. W. (p. 43), (2) L--y D---ss of K--t (p. 47).

BSC 2583.

Buckinghamshire, John Sheffield, Duke of.

Works. 1724.*

Reprinted from 1721.

Burnet, Gilbert.

Bishop Burnet's History Of His Own Time. . . . London, Printed for Thomas Ward . . . 1724[-34].

fo, 2 vols.

(1) Charles I (Vol. I, p. 47), (2) Charles II (I, 93, 611), (3) The Earl of Clarendon (I, 94), (4) The Earl of Shaftesbury (I, 96), (5) The Duke of Buckingham (I, 100), (6) The Duke of Lauderdale (I, 101), (7) The Marquis of Halifax (I, 267), (8) James II (II, 292), (9) William III (II, 304).

There are many other portrait-characters which, though lesser or shorter, might be included in the list.

Butler, William.

The Good Magistrate. A Sermon Preached . . . On Tuesday, September 29. 1724. . . . By William Butler . . . London: Printed for John Wyat . . . M DCC XXIV.

4°, text pp. 5-26.

Begins: "Nehemiah V. XIX./Think upon me, O my God."

[Gordon, Thomas.]

The Humorist: Being Essays Upon Several Subjects, Viz. News writers, Enthusiasm. The Spleen. . . . With a Dedication to the Man in the Moon. The Third Edition. . . . London: Printed for D. Browne . . . M.DCC.XXIV.

12°, text pp. 1-240.

(1-28) as in 1720.

Heywood, James.

Letters and Poems. 1724.*

See 1726.

Smith, M.

An Entire Set of the Monitors. 1724.*

Reprinted from 1715.

[Trenchard, John, and Gordon, Thomas.]

Cato's Letters. 1724.*

12°, 4 vols.

Reprinted from 1721.

1725

Anonymous.

Look Ere You Leap: or a History of the Lives and Intrigues of Lewd Women, with the arraignment of their several vices, to which is added the Character of a Good Woman. 1725.*

There were many later editions; the 11th appeared in 1741.

Seasonable Advice. With the Characters of the Late King Stanislaus, Augustus King of Poland, and his Son the Prince. London: Printed for A. Moore, near St. Paul's Church-Yard. 1725.*

[Cotton, Charles.]

The Compleat Gamester. 1725.*

Reprinted from 1674.

[Crossman, Samuel.]

The Young Man's Calling: or, the Whole Duty of Youth. The eighth Edition. London, for Thomas Crouch, 1725.*

(1-3) as in 1685.

[Foxton, Thomas.]

Serino, or the Character of a Fine Gentleman.*

Reprinted from 1721.

[Gordon, Thomas.]

The Humourist . . . Vol. II. London, Printed for T. Woodward . . . MDCCXXV.

12°, text pp. 1-267.

(1) Cardinal Beaufort (p. 122), (2) Humphrey, Duke of Gloucester (p. 122), (3) Giles Bookwit (p. 163), (4) The author's landlady (p. 175), (5) The French (p. 234), (6) The Hollanders (p. 234), (7) The Italians (p. 234), (8) The British nation (p. 235), (9) The people, or commons (p. 242), (10) Don Altiero (p. 260), (11) Tony Trivial (p. 263), (12) Simplus (p. 264), (13) A French couple (p. 265), (14) Emilia (p. 266), (15) Ennomius (p. 267).

Volume I first appeared in 1720.

[Grey, Zachary.]

A Looking-Glass for Schismaticks: or, The True Picture of Fanaticism. . . . By a Gentleman of the University of Cambridge. London: Printed for Tho. Warner . . . 1725.

4°, text pp. 1-116.

(1) Fanatics (p. v).

A very poor example of character.

Haywood, Eliza.

The Tea-Table: Or, a Conversation between some Polite Persons of both Sexes, at a Lady's Visiting Day. Wherein are Represented The Various Foibles, and Affectations, which form the Character of an Accomplish'd Beau, or Modern Fine Lady. Interspersed with several Entertaining and Instructive Stories. By Mrs. Eliza Haywood. . . . London, Printed: And Sold by J. Roberts . . . and the Booksellers of London and Westminster, 1725.

4°, in 2 parts, text pp. 1–51, 1–59.
(1) Amiana (Part I, p. 2).

A poor example of character. The whole book might be called a diffuse character of a fine lady, but little of the style of the true character is present.

[Manley, Mary de la Riviere.]

Bath-Intrigues: in four Letters to a Friend in London. . . . The Second Edition. London; Printed for J. Roberts . . . 1725.

4°, text pp. 1–51.
(1) Venario, a young man madly in love (p. 23).

Oldham, John (?)

A Character of the Reverend ----. [colophon] Dublin: Printed in the Year 1725.*

Text pp. 1–2.
Begins: "No wonder if I am at a Loss to describe him."

Theophrastus.

The Moral Characters of Theophrastus. Translated from The Greek, with Notes. To which is prefix'd A Critical Essay on Characteristic Writings. By Henry Gally . . . London: Printed for John Hooke . . . MDCCXXV.

8°, text pp. 1–290.
(1–28) as in 1714.

Young, Edward.

The Universal Passion. Satire I[–VII]. . . . London: Printed for J. Roberts . . . MDCC-XXV[–VIII].

fo, in 7 parts, each paged separately.
(1) My Lord (Satire I, p. 8), (2) Belus, a man of earth, who, on a South-sea tide (I, 9), (3) Pygmalion, in love with his antique statues (I, 10), (4) Court lords (I, 11), (5) Hippolytus, the country squire (I, 14), (6) Florio, a tulipomaniac (II, 4), (7) Codrus and Lorenzo, bibliomaniacs (II, 6), (8) Hilario, smitten with his own wit (II, 8), (9) Marcus, a malicious critic (II, 9), (10) Crassus, a formalist (II, 11), (11) Florello, a beau (II, 13), (12) Morose a sloven (II, 14), (13) Bad critics (III, 3), (14) Apicius and his fellow epicures (III, 5), (15) Vincenna, who pretends modesty (III, 8), (16) Chremes, who, though he can't conduct his own estate, devotes his service to the state and crown (IV, 2), (17) Gehenno, who deep in the secret of the universe, pities the dull rogue who saves his soul (IV, 3), (18) Narcissus, the graceful (IV, 4), (19)

Learned fools, Sloane and Ashmole (IV, 7), (20) Lico, shadow to their lordships (IV, 7), (21) The writing tribe (IV, 9), (22) A boastful soldier (IV, 13), (23) Britannia's daughters (VI, 2), (23) Various women (VII, 2).

Satires 1–4 are dated 1725, Satire 5, 1726, Satire 6, 1727, and Satire 7, 1728. They were later collected and published together a number of times.

1726

[Amhurst, Nicholas, and others.]

The Craftsman. 1726 ff.*

(1) A truly prime minister (no. 9), (2) An honest treasurer (no. 24), (3) A corrupt statesman (no. 46), (4) Col. Blunderbuss, a furious disputant (no. 48), (5) Mr. Lyn (no. 61), (6) An ambassador (no. 64), (7) A good senator (no. 76), (8) A bad senator (no. 76), (9) The haranguer (no. 89), (10) The true orator (no. 89), (11) A wicked potitician (no. 97), (12) A good minister (no. 154), (13) A modern European minister (no. 159), (14) A mock-minister (no. 238).

Attributed to Amhurst and others by the CBEL. There were several reprinted editions. Numbers 1 and 5 seem to refer to Sir Robert Walpole.

Baxter, Richard.

Reliquiæ Baxterianæ. 1726.*
Reprinted from 1696.

[Bond, William.]

The Spectator. Volume Ninth and Last. The Fifth Edition. London, Printed for W. Mears . . . 1726.

12°, text pp. 1–319.
(1) An accomplish'd lady (no. 638), (2) The fop, the beau, and the well-dress'd gentleman (no. 655), (3) Cynthia and Claudio (no. 656), (4) Alumnus (no. 663), (5) Will Voluble (no. 674), (6) Humphrey Cadence (no. 675).

There were several other editions, both later and earlier. Attributed to Bond by the CBEL.

Buckinghamshire, John Sheffield, Duke of.

The Works Of John Sheffield, Earl of Mulgrave, Marquis of Normanby, And Duke of Buckingham. . . . Printed for John Barber, Alderman of London. M.DCC.XXVI.

12°, 2 vols.
(1–4) as in 1721.

Carter, E.

The Artificer's Looking Glass. J. Willford. 1726.*
BSC 2585.

Cook, Thomas.

The Scandalous Chronicle, a Ballad of Characters. 1726.*

[Cotton, Charles.]

The Compleat Gamester. 1726.*

Reprinted from 1674.

Heywood, James.

Letters and Poems on Several Subjects . . . By Mr. Heywood. The Second Edition, with Additions. . . . London: Printed for W. Meadows . . . 1726.

6°, text pp. 1–249.

(1) Euphrenius (p. 43), (2) Philomusus (p. 43), (3) Cleanthes (p. 49), (4) Philalethes (p. 50), (5) Indocilis (p. 63), (6) Tom Airy (p. 83), (7) Philaretes (p. 91), (8) Mr. Barrow (p. 197), (9) Mr. Thompson (p. 197), (10) The celebrated beauties of Manchester: written in the year 1709 (p. 243).

First printed 1724.

Law, William.

A Practical Treatise Upon Christian Perfection. By William Law A.M. . . . London, Printed for William and John Innys . . . 1726.

8°, text pp. 1–546.

(1) Gustus, a grave, sober man (p. 236), (2) Titus, temperate but not a Christian, and Philo, a devotee of literature but not religious (p. 294), (3) Patronus, an architect, Eusebius, a grammarian, and Lycia, a gay woman (p. 295), (4) Matrona, who has no time for piety, Publius, a politician, Siccus, a builder (p. 296), (5) Silvius (p. 297), (6) Julia, a reader of foolish books (p. 352), (7) Trebonius (p. 433), (8) Julius, an insincere man (p. 434), (9) Clito, who prays without understanding (p. 443), (10) Credulo, who talks scandal (p. 446), (11) Clemens, Frevidus, Eugenia, of great piety (p. 474), (12) Urbanus, who is neither profane nor irreligious (p. 532).

1727

[Amhurst, Nicholas, and others.]

The Country Journal: Or, The Craftsman. By Caleb D'Anvers . . . Saturday, June 3. 1727. . . . [colophon] London: Printed for R. Francklin.

fo, 4 pages, unnumbered.

(1) Colonel Blunderbuss, a bullying talker (p. 1).

Attributed to Amhurst by the CBEL.

[Bellegarde, Jean Baptiste Morvan de.]

Reflections Upon Ridicule; Or, What it is that makes a Man ridiculous, and the Means to avoid it. Wherein are Represented The different Manners and Characters of Persons of the present Age. . . . The Fourth Edition. London: Printed for D. Midwinter . . . J.

Osborn and T. Longman . . . and B. Motte . . . MDCCXXVII.

12°, 2 vols.

(1–10) as in 1707.

Higgons, Bevil.

A Short View Of The English History . . . on the Reigns of the Kings; their Characters, and Manners . . . By B. Higgons, Gent. . . . Hagve: Printed by T. Johnston. MDCC-XXVII.

8°, text pp. 3–374.

(1–4) as in 1723.

Houghton, John.

A Collection For the Improvement of Husbandry and Trade . . . the Collector, John Houghton, F.R.S. Now Revised, Corrected . . . In Three Volumes. London: Printed for Woodman and Lyon . . . M,DCC,XXVII.

8°, 3 vols.

(1) as in 1695.

Pope, Alexander, Swift, Jonathan, and others.

Miscellanies in Prose and Verse. . . . London: Printed for Benjamin Motte . . . M.DCC.-XXVII.

8°, 4 vols.

(1) The Sentiments of a Church-of-England Man (Vol. I, p. 87), (2) John Bull (II, 10), (3) Nic. Frog (II, 11), (4) John Bull's mother (II, 76), (5) John Bull's sister (II, 81), (6) Umbra (III, 128), (7) Macer (III, 134), (8) Sylvia (III, 136).

The Preface is signed (p. 16): "Twickenham, May 27. 1727. Jonath. Swift, Alex. Pope." Vols. I, II, III are dated 1727. Vol. IV is dated 1732 and printed by Benj. Motte and Lawton Gilliver. The third volume is called on the title page the "last" and the fourth the "third," but actually these designations are reversed. Nos. 6–8 above are in verse.

[Ward, Edward.]

The Republican Procession, or, the Tumultuous Cavalcade; An Hudibrastick Poem. . . . London: Printed; and are to be Sold by the Booksellers of London and Westminster. MDCCXXVII.

4°, text pp. 3–48. In verse.

(1–7) as in second impression of 1714.

1728

[Baker, Henry, and others.]

The Universal Spectator and Weekly Journal.*

(1) A good writer (Oct. 12).

Attributed to Henry Baker and others by the CBEL.

[Choppin, Richard.]

A Just Character of the Revd. Mr. Boyce. Written by Mr. R--- C---. [Dublin? 1728?]*
s.sh.fo. In verse.
Begins: "A Goodly Teacher of the Holy Train."
The name of the author and the date and place of publication are taken from the British Museum Catalogue.

[Curll, Edmund?]

Characters Of The Times; Or, An Impartial Account of the Writings, Characters, Education, &c. of several Noblemen and Gentlemen libell'd in a Preface to a late Miscellany publish'd by P--pe and S--ft. . . . London, Printed, and Sold by A. Dodd [and others] . . . M.DCC.XXVIII.
4°, text pp. 9–46.
(1) George Dodington (p. 9), (2) Sir William Young (p. 10), (3) Lady Mary Wortley Montague (p. 12), (4) Thomas Burnet (p. 13), (5) James Moore (p. 15), (6) Ambrose Philips (p. 15), (7) Lewis Theobald (p. 16), (8) Anthony Hammond (p. 18), (9) Charles Johnson (p. 19), (10) Thomas Gordon (p. 20), (11) Leonard Welsted (p. 22), (12) Sir Richard Blackmore (p. 25), (13) Laurence Eusden (p. 26), (14) Lord Roscommon (p. 27), (15) Thomas Durfy (p. 27), (16) The Earl of Shaftesbury (p. 27), (17) Joseph Addison (p. 29), (18) Thomas Tickell (p. 30), (19) George Stepney (p. 32), (20) Rev. George Stanhope (p. 35), (21) Walter Cary (p. 36), (22) John Dennis (p. 39), (23) George Sewell (p. 40), (24) Sir John Vanbrugh (p. 41), (25) General Codrington (p. 42), (26) S--ft (p. 44), (27) P--pe (p. 45).
Anonymous in CBEL, but Huntington attributes to Edmund Curll.

Defoe, Daniel.

The Compleat English Gentleman.*
This is a manuscript. Printed in 1890.

[Du Refuge, Eustache.]

Arcana Aulica. 1728.*
Reprinted from 1652.

[Giffard, Martha Temple, Lady.]

The Life And Character Of Sir William Temple, Bart. Written by a particular Friend. Never before Published. . . . London: Printed for B. Motte . . . 1728.
fo, text pp. 1–22.
Begins: "SIR WILLIAM TEMPLE was descended."
First publication of the manuscript, written about 1690. The character proper begins on p. 19.

Houghton, John.

A Collection for the Improvement of Husbandry and Trade. 1728.*
Reprinted from 1695.

[Jones, Erasmus.]

A Trip Through London: Containing Observations on Men and Things . . . The Seventh Edition, Corrected. London: Printed, and Sold by J. Roberts [and others] . . . 1728.
4°, text pp. 1–62.
(1) A lady who labours to seem chaste (p. 56).
Attributed to Jones by Halkett and Laing. The earlier editions have not been traced. Some editions apparently include: (2) Ireland (p. 53), since Mr. Greenough's notes have such an entry. It does not, however, occur in the Harvard copy of the seventh edition.

[Mandeville, Bernard.]

The Fable of the Bees: or, Private Vices, Publick Benefits. . . . The Fifth Edition. . . . London: Printed for J. Tonson . . . MDCCXXVIII[–XXIX].
8°, two parts, text pp. 1–477, 1–432.
(1) A gentleman (part ii, p. 50).
There were numerous other editions of this book, both earlier and later.

St. Evremond, Charles de Marguetel de Saint-Denis, Seigneur de.

The Works Of Monsieur de St. Evremond, Made English from the French Original . . . The Second Edition . . . London: Printed for J. and J. Knapton [and many others] . . . M.DCC.XXVIII.
8°, 3 vols.
(1–19) as in 1692.

1729

Anonymous.

The American Weekly Mercury.*
(1) A charitable man (in the Busybody column for Feb. 11).

The Character of a Master of a Vessel. Printed in the year 1729.*
s.sh.fo. In verse.
Begins: "A Brawny Lump that scarce knows good from ill."

A Character Of John Sheffield Late Duke of Buckinghamshire; With An Account of the Pedigree Of The Sheffield-Family: To which is Annex'd, His Grace's Last Will and Testament, Written with His Own Hand. London, Printed for J. Stagg . . . M.DCC.XXIX.
4°, text pp. 1–48.
(1) The Duke of Buckingham (p. 1).
BSC 2587.

A Copy of the Paper drop'd in St. James's Park. Or, A Hue and Cry after a Coachman. London, Jan. 5, 1729. London: Printed for Tho. Davies Near St. Pauls.*

The "Coachman" may represent Sir Robert Walpole.

The Life and Character of James Butler, Late Duke, Marquis and Earl of Ormond . . . London: Printed for R. Walker . . . 1729.

4°, text pp. 9–35.
Begins: "If you would know the reason."

Not properly a character, but included here because of the title.

The New England Weekly Journal. 1729.*

(1) An unaffected gentleman (Nos. 124, 125, August 4–11), (2) The affected and ridiculous fop (no. 126, August 18).

[Amhurst, Nicholas, and others.]

The Country Journal: Or, The Craftsman. By Caleb D'Anvers . . . Saturday, June 14, 1729. . . . [colophon] London: Printed by R. Francklin.

fo, 4 pages, unnumbered.
(1) A good minister (p. 1).

Buckinghamshire, John Sheffield, Duke of.

A Short Character of Charles II. King of England. Written by John Duke of Buckingham. . . . London: Printed by and for R. Phillips . . . 1729.

4°, text pp. 3–30.
Begins: "I have pitch'd on this Character of King Charles."

A reprint of his Character of Charles II, 1696.

Buckinghamshire, John Sheffield, Duke of.

The Works Of John Sheffield . . . Duke of Buckingham. . . . The Second Edition Corrected. London, Printed for J.B. and sold by Aaron Ward [and five others] . . . M.DCC.-XXIX.

8°, 2 vols.
(1–4) as in 1723.

Butler, William.

The Character of a good Magistrate. A Sermon . . . By Will Butler. London, Printed by J. March . . . 1729.*

4°.
BSC 2586.
Reprinted from 1724.

Byles, Mather.

The Character of the Perfect and Vpright Man; his Peaceful End described; and Our Duty to Observe it laid down. In a Discourse On Psalm XXXVII. 37. By Mather Byles. . . .

Boston, Printed for S. Gerrish . . . MDCC-XXIX.

4°, text pp. 1–27.
Begins: "There is nothing more becoming rational creatures."

[Delaney, Patrick.]

The Tribune . . . Printed at Dublin: London Reprinted . . . MDCCXXIX.

4°, text pp. 1–84. 12 numbers.
(1) Sir Humphrey Thorowgood (p. 7), (2) His son Edward Thorowgood, M.D. (p. 9), (3) Dr. Hartshorn (p. 10), (4) Richard Marygold, Esq. (p. 11), (5) Thomas Verger (p. 13), (6) William Truman (p. 14).

Attributed to Delaney by the CBEL.

Law, William.

A Serious Call To A Devout and Holy Life. Adapted to the State and Condition of All Orders of Christians. By William Law. London: Printed for William Innys . . . MDC-CXXIX.

8°, text pp. 1–499.
(1) Flavia, the imprudent (chap. 7), (2) Miranda, the wise and pious (chap. 8), (3) Various humorous people (chap. 12), (4) Various good but not devout people (chap. 13), (5) Paternus, a well-educated man (chap. 18), (6) Eusebia, a well-educated daughter (chap. 19).

Midon, F., Jr.

The History Of The Rise and Fall Of Masaniallo, The Fisherman of Naples . . . By F. Midon, Junr. . . . London: Printed for C. Davis . . . and T. Green . . . M DCC.XXIX.

8°, text pp. 13–210.
(1) Masaniello (p. 13).
BSC 2605.

Poor example of character. Reprinted several times.

[Sheridan, Thomas, and Swift, Jonathan.]

The Intelligencer. . . . Printed at Dublin. London Reprinted, and sold by A. Moor. . . . MDCCXXIX.

8°, text pp. 1–217.
(1) Squire Wether, a brutal hypocrite (no. 2, p. 10), (2) Corusodes, who undeservedly succeeds in the church, and Eugenion, who undeservedly fails (no. 7, p. 57), (3) George [England], Patrick [Ireland], and Andrew [Scotland] (no. 16, p. 177).

The first numbers appeared in 1728; there was a reprint in 1730. Attributed to Sheridan and Swift by the CBEL.

Smith, Edmund.

The Works of Mr. Edmund Smith . . . To Which is prefix'd A Character of Mr. Smith,

By Mr. Oldisworth. Corrected and Inlarged by Dr. Adams, of Christ Church. The Fourth Edition. London: Printed for Bernard Lintot . . . M.DCC.XXIX.

12°, text pp. 1–103.
(1) as in 1714.

1730

Anonymous.

Claudian's Rufinus: Or, The Court-Favourite's Overthrow. Being a Curious and Correct Edition of One of the best Satyrical Poems, of One of the best Poets, on One of the Worst Statesmen that ever liv'd. . . . The Second Edition. London, Printed for E. Smith . . . M.DCC.XXX.

4°, text pp. 1–26.
(1) Rufinus, a wicked politician (p. vii), (2) Stilico (p. x), (3) Rufinus and Stilico (p. lx, in verse).

A Letter from Artemiza in the Town, to Chloë in the Country. By a Person of Honour.

fo, text pp. 1–4. In verse.
(1) The heir and hope of a great family in his degeneration (p. 4).
A border line example of character.

Brown, Thomas.

The Works Of Mr. Thomas Brown, Serious and Comical, in Prose and Verse. With his Remains, in Four Volumes Compleat. With The Life and Character Of Mr. Brown, And his Writings, By James Drake . . . The Seventh Edition carefully Corrected. . . . London: Printed by and for Edward Midwinter . . . 1730.

12°, 4 vols.
(1–8) as in fifth edition of 1720–21, (9) Amusements serious and comical (III, 1), (10) Letters serious and comical (III, 93), (11) Letters to gentlemen and ladies (III, 201), (12) A tavern (III, 244), (13) Doctors Commons (III, 249), (14) Four Quakers (III, 256).
BSC 2588.

Forman, Charles.

Protesilaus: Or, The Character Of An Evil Minister. Being A Paraphrase On Part of the Tenth Book of Telemachus. By Charles Forman, Esq; And Dedicated to the Right Honourable Sir R-- W--. . . . London: Printed for the Author and sold by the Booksellers of London and Westminster. 1730.

4°, text pp. 1–36.

Begins: "Mentor's Advice has all the good Effects."
BSC 2589.
A character of Sir Robert Walpole.

[Sheridan, Thomas, and Swift, Jonathan.]
The Intelligencer. 1730.*
Reprinted from 1729.

1731

Anonymous.

Chickens Feed Capons. 1731.*
8°.
There were at least four editions in 1731.

A Collection Of Loyal Songs Written against the Rump Parliament, Between the Years 1639 and 1661. Containing, A great Variety of Merry and Diverting Characters of the Chief Sectaries, who were the Principal Actors in that whole Scene of Affairs. . . . London: Printed for J. Stone . . . 1731.

12°, 2 vols.
(1) A roundhead, 1641 (Vol. I, p. 30).
A reprint of Brome's Rump, 1662.

The Flower-Piece: A Collection Of Miscellany Poems. By Several Hands. . . . London, Printed for J. Walthoe . . . M.DCC.XXXI.

4° and 8°, text pp. 13–251. In verse.
(1) The dangler (p. 93).

Read's Journal. 1731.*
(1) Sulpitius and Clarissa (March 27).

The Windsor Medley: Being A Choice Collection of several Curious Pieces in Prose and Verse. . . . London: Printed for A. Moore . . . 1731.

4°, text pp. 1–62.
(1) Characters of men and manners (p. 48).

Wits Cabinet: Or, A Companion for Young Men, and Ladies. . . . The Fifteenth Edition, much Enlarged. London: Printed for J. Clarke . . . And A. Wilde . . . 1731.

12°, text pp. 7–178 (pp. 97–106 skipped in the numbering, but the signature marks and the contents complete).
(1) The charmed lover (p. 134, in verse), (2) On beauty (p. 136, in verse), (3) The school of Bacchus; or, the art of drinking (p. 158).
Though the wording is different, it is probable that the contents are the same as in 1700.

[Baker, Henry.]

The Universal Spectator.*

(1) A character (January 2), (2) Various virtuosi (August 31).

[Neville, Henry.]

News from the New Exchange: Or, The Common-Wealth of Ladies: Drawn to the Life, in their several Characters and concernments. . . . London: Printed in the Year of Women without Grace, 1650. Reprinted; eke in the same Place, I'th Year of Women with some Grace, 1731. Whereunto (by way of Appendix) are subjoined The Loyal Satirist (Characterizing the Males of those Days, as the other does the Females) With an Apology for the Exchange Women. The Second Edition, with a Compleat Key. London: Printed by Tho. Edlin, for Captain Gulliver . . . and sold by the Booksellers of London and Westminster. 1731.*

BSC 2591.

Reprinted from 1650.

1732

Anonymous.

The Auditor. 1732.*

(1) Sir Charles Freeman, (2) Frank Easy, (3) An Italian who is "free from the deceitful Knavery of his Country-men," (4) Tom Cynick, whose "antiquated taste" nothing suits but Nature (no. 3).

The Character of a Prince. Written between the Years 80 and 90. 1732.*

Begins: "There are four Virtues properly called Regal."

A reprint of 1689 and (?) 1643. The present may be an incomplete reference to the same character as included in Morgan's Phoenix Britannicus, 1732.

The Character of the Times delineated in two Parts. London, Printed for J.Wilford. 1732.*

8°, text pp. 1–61.

BSC 2592.

The London Weekly Magazine. 1732.*

(1) A miser (May, p. 58).

The same character is found in The Weekly Register, May 6, 1732.

The New England Weekly Journal. 1732.*

(1) A miser (No. 289, October 2).

The Weekly Register; or Universal Journal. London, 1732.*

(1) A miser (no. 108).

The Weekly Rehearsal. 1732.*

(1) Various types of triflers or virtuosos (Jan. 17), (2) Tom Puzzle and Will Dry (Feb. 7).

[Arnall, William.]

The Free Briton.*

(1) The true patriot (no. 160).

Attributed to Arnall by the CBEL.

[Baker, Henry.]

The Universal Spectator.*

(1) Captain Frontley (No. 220).

Butler, Samuel.

Posthumous Works.*

Reprinted from 1715.

[Cave, Edward.]

The Gentleman's Magazine, Or Monthly Intelligencer. For the Year 1732. . . . Vol. II. . . . By Sylvanus Urban, Gent. London: Printed for D. Henry, and T. Cave . . . 8°.

(1) The female microcosm, to a lady who said man is a little world; the lady's answer (p. 907), (2) The country gentleman (p. 1074), (3) The miser (p. 1075).

The full title will not be repeated in subsequent entries. The editors, according to the CBEL, were: Edward Cave (1731–54), D. Henry and R. Cave (1754–66), D. Henry (1766–78), J. Nichols and D. Henry (1778–92), J. Nichols (1792–1826).

Clarke, John.

The Character of a good Magistrate. A Sermon Preached . . . on . . . the Guild-Day, on which the new-elected Mayor is sworn into his Office. London, for James and John Knapton. 1732.*

8°.

Collins, Arthur.

The Life Of that Great Statesman William Cecil, Lord Burghley . . . By Arthur Collins, Esq; London, Printed for Robert Gosling . . . MDCCXXXII.

4°, text pp. 1–118.

(1) William Cecil, Lord Burghley (p. 42), (2) The same, by Camden (p. 74).

[Defoe, Daniel.]

The Conference; or Greggs Ghost. 1732.*

Reprinted from 1711.

[Earle, John.]

Microcosmography: Or, A Piece of the World Discover'd. In Essays and Characters. . . . London: Printed by E. Say, Anno Domini M.DCC.XXXII.

8°, text pp. 1–176 (wrongly numbered 164, numbers 133–144 being used twice).
(1–78) as in 1633.
Murphy 42. BSC 2593.

Gwinnett, Richard.

The Honourable Lovers: Or, The Second and Last Volume Of Pylades and Corinna. . . . Letters . . . between Richard Gwinnett . . . and Mrs. Elizabeth Thomas. . . . London: Printed in the Year M.DCC.XXXII.
8°, text pp. 1–268.
(1) Sir William Temple (p. 11).

Morgan, J.

Phoenix Britannicus: Being a Miscellaneous Collection Of Scarce and Curious Tracts, Historical, Political, Biographical . . . Characteristical, &c. Prose and Verse. . . . Vol. I. . . . Collected by J. Morgan, Gent. London: Printed for the Compiler, and T. Edlin . . . and J. Wilford . . . M.DCC.XXXII.
4°, text pp. 1–562.
(1) King James, by Sir A.W., 1650 (p. 54), (2) A true English-man, by Pasquin, about 1679 (p. 80, in verse), (3) The honest Briton's character of himself (p. 94, in verse), (4) Oliver Cromwell, by Bevill Higgons (p. 187), (5) Valour anatomized in a fancy, by Sir Philip Sidney, 1581 and 1651 (p. 188), (6) A prince, written between 1680 and 1690 (p. 278), (7) An untrue bishop, 1641 (p. 280), (8) Roger the Canterburian, by G.T., 1642 (p. 285), (9) An Oxford incendiary, 1645 (p. 474), (10) The loyal non-conformist, by R.W., 1670 (p. 552).
Murphy 97, 99, 101, 108, 149, 152.

Prince, Thomas.

The Faithful Servant Approv'd at Death, and Entring into the Joy of His Lord. A Sermon . . . Occasion'd By the much Lamented Death of . . . Daniel Oliver, Esq; . . . By Thomas Prince, M.A. . . . Boston: Printed by S. Kneeland and T. Green . . . 1732.
4°, text pp. 1–35.
(1) Daniel Oliver (p. 3 and p. 26).

Wharton, Philip Wharton, Duke of.

The Life and Writings of Philip Late Duke of Wharton. In Two Volumes. Vol. II. London, Printed; And Sold by the Booksellers of London and Westminster. M.DCC.XXXII.
8°, text pp. 327–685 (continued from Vol. I, 1731).
(1) The true Briton (p. 500), (2) An honest man (p. 501).
Reprinted from Wharton's The True Briton, 1723.

1733

Anonymous.

The Character Of An Ill-Court-Favourite: Representing the Mischiefs That flow from Ministers of State. When they are More Great than Good . . . The Second Edition. London: Printed for J. Wilford . . . M,DCC,-XXXIII.
4°, text pp. 3–32.
Begins: "He that stands by and observes the supple Addresses."
A reprint of 1681.

The Rake of Taste, A Poem, Dedicated to Alexander Pope, Esq. . . . Dublin Printed: London Reprinted; and Sold by Mrs. Dodd . . . Mrs. Nutt . . . and by the Booksellers. . . .
fo, text pp. 1–14. In verse.
(1) A coquette (p. 4), (2) A spendthrift (p. 5), (3) Various gallants (p. 8).
Dated 1733 by the Yale University Library. Dated 1735 by the CBEL.

[Barrington, John Shute Barrington, first Viscount.]

A Letter to Protestant Dissenters.*
Reprinted from 1722.

[Cave, Edward.]

The Gentleman's Magazine. Vol. III. 1733.
(1) The flaps (p. 74), (2) The town lady's answer to — What tho' I am a Country Lass (p. 93), (3) Characters from the state-dunces: a poem, inscribe'd to Mr. Pope (p. 317), (4) From the women of taste, a poem (p. 372), (5) From the counterpart of the state-dunces (p. 372), (6) The beauties of Coventry Assembly (p. 656), (7) The glories of Bury (p. 657).

Chauncy, Charles.

Nathanael's Character display'd. A Sermon, Preached . . . after the Funeral of the Honourable Nathanael Byfield Esq; Late Judge of the Vice-Admiralty, And One of His Majesty's Council for this Province. . . . By Charles Chauncy. . . . Printed in the Year 1733.
4°, text pp. 1–35.
Begins: "If we take a view of those holy men."

Dedekind, Friedrich.

Grobianus; Or, The Compleat Booby. An Ironical Poem. . . . Done into English from the Original Latin of Fredirick Dedekindus, by Roger Bull. . . . London: Printed for T. Cooper . . . MDCCXXXIX.
8°, text pp. 1–276. In verse.
(1) Various types of dinner guests (p. 66).
The first edition (in Latin) was 1549.

[Halifax, Charles Montagu, Earl of.]

The Man Of Honour: A Poem . . . London: Printed for J. Wilford . . . MDCCXXXIII.

fo, text pp. 3–8. In verse.
Begins: "Not all the Threats or Favours of a Crown."
A reprint of [1688?].

Le Mercier, Andrew.

A Treatise against detraction . . . By the Reverend Mr. Andrew Le Mercier . . . Printed at Boston in New England . . . 1733.

8°, text pp. 1–303.
(1) Detraction (p. 99).
A border-line example of character.

Macky, John.

Memoirs of the Secret Services of John Macky, Esq; . . . including, also, The true Secret History of the Rise, Promotion, &c. of the English and Scots Nobility . . . and other Persons of Distinction, from the Revolution. In their respective Characters at large, drawn up by Mr. Macky . . . Published From His Original Manuscript; as attested by his son Spring Macky, Esq. London. Printed in the Year M.DCC.XXXIII.

4°, text pp. 9–143.
(Almost two hundred characters of public figures at the English court, too numerous to be listed here.)
Many of these characters appear to have been taken with little change from Burnet's History. See William A. Shaw, London Times Literary Supplement, June 14 and 21, 1928.

Pope, Alexander.*

An Epistle to the Right Honourable Richard Lord Visct. Cobham. By Mr. Pope. . . . London: Printed for Lawton Gilliver . . . 1733.

fo, text pp. 1–13. In verse.
Begins: "Yes, you despise the Man to books confin'd."
A character (though not very good) of various types of man.

[Puckle, James.]

The Club: Or, A Grey-Cap for a Green-Head. . . . In which is Interspers'd the following Characters. . . . The Fifth Edition. . . . London: Printed for John King . . . And Thomas King. . . .

12°, text pp. 1–179.
(1–14) as in 1713.
Dated 1733 by the Yale University Library.
Attributed to Puckle by the CBEL.

Swift, Jonathan.

The Life And Genuine Character Of Doctor Swift. Written by Himself. London: Printed for J. Roberts. . . . 1733.

fo, text pp. 9–19. In verse.
Begins: "Wise *Rochefoucault* a *Maxim* writ."
The dedication by L.M. to Alexander Pope, dated April 1, 1733, says that Swift showed copies of this poem to all visitors, and that a servant probably copied it, whence it reached a friend of L.M.'s in Dublin, who gave it to him. The first authorized edition, entitled "Verses on the Death of Dr. Swift. Written by Himself: Nov. 1731," appeared in 1739. The two versions, despite some passages in common, differ widely from each other. The CBEL gives three editions in 1733 and one in 1739; I have seen one 1733 edition and four of 1739.

[Trenchard, John, and Gordon, Thomas.]

Cato's Letters . . . In Four Volumes. . . . The Third Edition, carefully corrected. London: Printed for W. Wilkins, T. Woodward, J. Walthoe, and J. Peale. MDCCXXXIII.

12°, 4 vols.
(1) as in 1721.

Whitehead, Paul.

The State Dunces. Inscrib'd To Mr. Pope. . . . London, Printed for W. Dickenson . . . 1733.

fo, in 2 parts.
Contains a number of anonymous brief sketches which might possibly be called characters. Mr. Greenough considered them not true Theophrastan characters.
There were numerous editions.

1734

Anonymous.

Characteristicks — or a Specimen of the Worth and Integrity of some of the Most Favourite Authors. 1734.*

The Patriot. 1734.*
(1) The patriot, drawn by the minister, (2) The minister, drawn by the patriot.

The Weekly Amusement, or Universal Magazine.*
See 1735.

Alanson, Edward.

The Man of Integrity's Character, With the Advantageousness of it. On Job. XXVII, 5–6.*
Watt, Bibliotheca Britannica, 13i.

Brown, Thomas.

The Lover's Secretary: or, the Adventures of Lindamira. 1734.*
Reprinted from 1713.

[Cave, Edward.]

The Gentleman's Magazine. Vol. IV. 1734.
(1) A trimmer (p. 79), (2) On the folly of athe-

ism (p. 325), (3) Writ under a picture of Bp. Burnet in a gentleman's study (p. 621), (4) Dr. H--h, B--p of W--r (p. 673, in verse), (5) The gentleman address'd to John Joliffe, Esq; Commissioner of the Wine-Licence. By Richard Savage, Esq. (p. 694), (6) To the author of A Character (p. 694).

Chauncy, Charles.

The Character and Overthrow of Laish considered and applied. A Sermon . . . By Charles Chauncy. . . . Boston . . . 1734.

4°, text pp. 1–19.
Begins: "So many annual seasons."

[Forrester, James.]

The Polite Philosopher: Or, An Essay On That Art Which Makes a Man happy in Himself, and agreeable to Others. Edinburgh, Printed by Robert Freebairn. MDCCXXXIV.

4°, text pp. 3–55.
(1) Honorius, good but not beloved (p. 13), (2) Garcia, easy going (p. 14), (3) Draco, a military rake (p. 28), (4) Hecatilla, a female firebrand (p. 29).

Attributed to Forrester by the CBEL.

L'Estrange, Sir Roger.

Machiavel's Advice to his Son. 1734.*

Reprinted from 1681.

Roper, Joseph.

The Character of the Liberal Man, Set forth in a Sermon Preach'd before the Right Honourable The Lord-Mayor . . . On Wednesday in Easter-Week, April 17, 1734. By Joseph Roper . . . London, Printed for W. Innys and R. Manby . . . MDCCCXXXIV [sic, but actually 1734].

4°, text pp. 1–19.
(1) A liberal man (p. 4).

1735

Anonymous.

A Character of the Times Delineated. 1735.*

A reprint of 1732.

The History Of Intriguing . . . Together with Three Modern Characters . . . London: Printed for T. Boreman . . . M.DCC.XXXV.

8°, text pp. 1–62.
(1) The cunning wanton: or, intriguing lady (p. 41), (2) The fashionable bawd: or, the lady's confident (p. 49), (3) The great man's prostitute: or, the original of an actress taken into keeping (p. 55).

The Modern Fanaticks Characteriz'd. . . . London, for J. Cox, 1735.*

(1) An enthusiastic parson.
BSC 2595.

[A Trip through the Town. 1735.]

4°, text pp. 1–64.
(1) Maid servants (p. 15), (2) Rowellers (p. 36), (3) Women of virtue and reputation (p. 40), (4) Leonora (p. 41), (5) Prudentia (p. 42), (6) Lysetta (p. 43), (7) A girl who is too familiar with servants (p. 48).

The title page is missing.

The Weekly Amusement: or, the Universal Magazine. . . . Volume I. London: Printed for J. and T. Dormer . . . M.DCC.XXXV.

4°, text pp. 3–392.
(1) An extravagant heir, just come to an estate (p. 233, January 11, 1734), (2) The beau officer: or, the coward in commission (p. 259, January 18, 1734), (3) The formal precisian: or, the devout lady (p. 261, January 18, 1734), (4) The fashionable friend (p. 285, January 25, 1734), (5) The lady's confident (p. 288, January 25, 1734), (6) The censorious lady (p. 321, February 1, 1734).

[Baker, Henry.]

The Universal Spectator.*

(1) Agresthes (No. 356).

[Butler, Samuel.]

The Life and Character of Bishop Stillingfleet. 1735.*

Reprinted from Stillingfleet's Works, 1710.
Attributed to Butler by the CBEL.

[Cave, Edward.]

The Gentleman's Magazine. Vol. V. 1735.

(1) A new character among the infidels (p. 39), (2) The furniture of a woman's mind, by D--n Swift (p. 99), (3) The work-doctor's harangue (p. 214), (4) The quack doctor's speech (p. 324), (5) Modern politeness. Address'd to Mrs. M--ley (p. 678), (6) The picture of Lady Grace Lovely, and Beau Rakish (p. 672).

Du Bosc, Jacques.

The Compleat Woman. 1735.*

Reprinted from 1639.

[Hill, Aaron, and others.]

The Prompter. . . . To be Continued Tuesdays and Fridays. . . . [colophon] Printed for T. Cooper. . . .

s.sh.fo, printed on both sides (each number).
(1) The busy man and the man of business (no. 68, July 4, 1735).

Attributed to Hill and others by the CBEL.

[Lyttleton, George Lyttleton, Baron.]

Letters from a Persian in England to his Friend at Ispahan. . . . The Fourth Edition, Corrected. London: Printed for John Millan . . . MDCCXXXV.

12°, text pp. 1–254.
(1) A prelate (p. 177, letter 58).
This work was several times reprinted. In a note to the edition of 1776, the subject of this character is given as Dr. John Hough, Bishop of Worcester. Attributed to Lyttleton by the CBEL.

[Melmoth, William.]

Of Active and Retired Life, An Epistle. . . . London, Printed for T. Cooper . . . MDC-CXXXV.

fo, text pp. 3–16. In verse.
(1) Patrius (p. 7), (2) Rapax (p. 8), (3) Portio (p. 15), (4) Umbra (p. 15).

[Mist, Nathaniel, Defoe, Daniel, and others.]

Fog's Weekly Journal. . . . [colophon] London: Printed by J. Purser. . . .

4 pages, unnumbered (each issue).
(1) The statesman and the patriot (no. 322), (2) A patriot (no. 356).
No. 322 is dated January 4, 1735; no. 356, August 30, 1735.

Pope, Alexander.

Of the Characters of Women: An Epistle to a Lady. By Mr. Pope. London: Printed by J. Wright, for Lawton Gilliver . . . MDCC-XXXV.

fo, pp. 5–16. In verse.
Begins: "NOTHING so true as what you once let fall, *Most Women have no Characters at all*."
There was another slightly variant edition or issue in the same year, with slight differences in the title page and paged 5–15 instead of 5–16.

Russel, Richard, and Martyn, John.

The Grub-street Journal. . . . [colophon] London: Printed by J. Higgonson . . . and sold by J. Roberts . . . as also by Capt. Gulliver. . . .

fo, 4 pages unnumbered (each issue).
(1) A pretty fellow (no. 282 [wrongly numbered 285], May 22, 1735).
Attributed to Russel and Martyn by the CBEL.

1736

[Baker, Henry.]

The Universal Spectator.*
(1) A maid's husband (No. 423).

[Cave, Edward.]

The Gentleman's Magazine. Vol. VI. 1736.
(1) A good wife, as represented in the last chapter

of the Book of Proverbs (p. 349), (2) The choice of a batchelor's wife (p. 661), (3) Dr. H--gh, B-p of W-r (p. 673), (4) Mr. Jn Mills, a celebrated actor (p. 749).

Cummings, Archibald.

The Character of a righteous Ruler. A Sermon upon the Death of the Hon. Patrick Gordon, Esq; Lieutenant-Governor of the Province of Pennsylvania, &c. Philadelphia, 1736.*

[Forrester, James.]

The Polite Philosopher: Or, An Essay On That Art Which Makes a Man Happy in Himself, and Agreeable to Others. The Second Edition . . . London, Printed by J. Wilson: And Sold by E. Nutt . . . and A. Dodd . . . MDCCXXXVI.

4°, text pp. 1–54.
(1–4) as in 1734.
The Address to the Author on p. vi mentions Forrester by name.

Vaumoriers, Ortigue Pierre de.

The Art of Pleasing in Conversation. 1736.*
(1) The author (Vol. I, p. xi).

1737

Anonymous.

The Man of Honour. . . . To which is added The Curious Females, A Tale. London Printed: And sold by the Booksellers of London and Westminster. MDXXXVII [*sic*].

4°, text pp. 3–14. In verse.
(1) A man of honour (p. 13).
The character begins: "The Man of Honour, resolutely just." This poem is not to be confused with that by Charles Montagu, Earl of Halifax, with the same title.

Beach, Thomas.

Eugenio: Or, Virtuous and Happy Life. A Poem. Inscrib'd to Mr. Pope. Quicquid dignum Sapiente bonoque est. Hor. London: Printed for R. Dodsley, in Pall-mall. M.DCC.-XXXVII.

fo, text pp. 5–20.
(1) Life (p. 6), (2) Florio (p. 8), (3) Julio (p. 8), (4) Hyemio (p. 9), (5) Eugenio (p. 9).

[Bellegarde, Jean Baptiste Morvan de.]

Reflections Upon Ridicule.*
Reprinted from 1707.

[Cave, Edward.]

The Gentleman's Magazine. Vol. VII. 1737.
(1) The Scots. From Albania (p. 183), (2) The

virtuoso, by Akenside (p. 244), (3) Lord Talbot, from a poem to his memory, by Mr. Thomson (p. 372), (4) The wife (p. 373).

[Chesterfield, Philip Dormer Stanhope, fourth Earl of, and others.]

Common Sense.*

See 1738.

[Fenélon, François de Salignac de la Mothe-.]

The Characters And Properties Of True Charity Display'd. Translated from the Original French. London: Printed for C. Davis in Pater-noster Row. MDCCXXXVII.

8°, text pp. 1–256.
(1–16) characters of charity based on phrases from I Corinthians XIII.

A portrait of Fenelon as author faces the title page. Dedicated by the translator, J.B. de Freval, to Noel Antoine Pluche. Poor examples of character, though each is headed by a title in which the word is used. BSC 2597.

[Sedgewick, O.]

The World turn'd Inside-Out; Or, Humankind Unmask'd. . . . Vol. I. London . . . T. Woodman . . . and J. Chrichley . . . 1737.

12°, text pp. 1–302.
(1) An exchange broker (p. 28), (2) Of the bibliopol. character of many (p. 56), (3) The critick (p. 298).

A second volume, under the title of The Universal Masquerade: or, The World turn'd Inside-Out, appeared in 1742. It bore the name of the author, O. Sedgewick, Gent., on the title page. No characters have been noted in it.

South, Robert.

Sermons Preached Upon Several Occasions By Robert South, D.D. . . . London: Printed for H. Lintot . . . MDCCXXXVII[–XLIV].

8°, 10 vols.
(1) The False Methods of Governing and Establishing the Church of England, Exploded (Vol. V, p. 469), which in turn contains the conforming Christian (p. 511).

There were other editions of his sermons.

1738

Anonymous.

History of Intriguing, with three modern Characters, viz. the cunning Wanton, the fashionable Bawd, and the Great Man's Prostitute: or the original of an Actress taken into Keeping. The Second Edition. London: Printed for J. Welford. 1738.*

8°, text pp. 1–62.
BSC 2649.

Reprinted from 1735.

A Thee and Thou Almanack for 1738. . . . With the Character of a Wet Quaker. 1738.*

8°.
(1) A wet Quaker.

Mentioned in Joseph Smith, Bibliotheca Anti-Quakeriana, London, 1873, p. 5.

[Cave, Edward.]

The Gentleman's Magazine. Vol. VIII. 1738.
(1) A good prince (p. 38), (2) The country squire (p. 41), (3) The barber (p. 157), (4) The querist's reply (p. 485).

[Chesterfield, Philip Dormer Stanhope, fourth Earl of, and others.]

Common Sense; Or, The Englishman's Journal. . . . London: Printed, and sold by J. Purser . . . And G. Hawkins . . . MDCCXXXVIII.

6°, text pp. 1–387.
(1) A man of honour (p. 98), (2) Types of coxcomb (p. 217), (3) Types of woman (p. 224), (4) An underminer (p. 354).

The original numbers appeared from February 5, 1737, to January 8, 1738. Abstracts of these characters appeared in The London Magazine for April and September, 1737. Attributed to Chesterfield and others by the CBEL.

[Clarke, A.?]

An Essay Towards the Character. Of Her late Majesty Caroline, Queen Consort of Great Britain, &c. . . . London: Printed for J. & P. Knapton . . . 1738.

8°, text pp. 1–46.
Begins: "The following pages contain only."
BSC 2599.

Clarke, Samuel.

The Works of Samuel Clark . . . In Four Volumes . . . London . . . MDCCXXXVIII.

fo, 4 vols.
(1) A good man (Vol. I, p. 237), (2) Oppressive power in religion (I, 630).

[Constable, John.]

The Conversation of Gentlemen Considered. In most of the Ways, that make their mutual Company Agreeable, or Disagreeable. In Six Dialogues. . . . London, Printed by J. Hoyles: And Sold by the Booksellers of London and Westminster. MDCCXXXVIII.

6°, text pp. 1–272.
(1) Amathesius, a one-track mind (p. 14), (2) Alogius, a would-be scholar (p. 20), (3) Timander, a real scholar (p. 23), (4) Antimachus, a disputer (p. 33), (5) Asophius, a babbler of hard words (p. 38), (6) Morander, a would-be scholar (p. 47), (7) Macroleptus, a tiresome long-winded

speaker (p. 48), (8) Charisius, a man of excellent taste (p. 73), (9) Philotechnus, who is no undervaluer of domestic workmanship (p. 76), (10) Philoxenus, who undervalues everything but English (p. 76), (11) Laelius, an agreable but endless talker (p. 148), (12) Bradylogus, an unintelligible speaker (p. 148), (13) Pologlossus, a pedant (p. 155), (14) Phlyarius, another pedant (p. 157), (15) Thaumastus, a master of a wonderful servant (p. 161), (16) Dysarestus, dull and heavy (p. 175), (17) Logaster, a prater (p. 178), (18) Eutropius, a good keeper of secrets (p. 195), (19) Barius, who affects mysterious looks (p. 195), (20) Atelestus, who speaks first and thinks afterwards (p. 241), (21) Eranistius, a quarreler (p. 253).
Attributed to Constable by the Huntington Library.

Cornwallis, Sir Charles.
The Life And Character of Henry-Frederic, Prince of Wales. Written by Sir Charles Cornwallis. . . . London, Printed for J. Roberts . . . 1738.
4°, text pp. 1–60.
Contains characters of the Prince of Wales by (1) Sir Charles Cornwallis (p. 1), (2) Francis Osborne (p. 24), (3) A. Wilson (p. 30), (4) W.O. (p. 43), (5) Sir Anthony Weldon (p. 45), (6) Aulicus Coquinariae (p. 46), (7) James Maxwell (p. 57, in verse), (8) William, Earl of Stirling (p. 60, in verse).

[Darrell, William.]
[The Gentleman Instructed. 1738.]*
8°, text pp. 1–584.
(1–6) as in 1723.
The title page is missing in the Harvard copy, from which this note was taken.

[Grey, Zachary.]
An attempt towards the Character Of the Royal Martyr King Charles I. . . . Address'd to the Author of An Essay towards the Character of her late Majesty Caroline. . . . With an Appendix containing the Relation of his Baptism, the Order of the Regicides for his Funeral compared with the pompous one of Oliver Cromwell, and the Proclamation against Milton. London: Printed for J. Roberts. . . . MDCCXXXVIII.
4°, text pp. 1–70.
(1) Charles I (p. 1).
BSC 2598.
Attributed to Grey by the CBEL. The character consists of quotations from Clarendon and others.

1739
Anonymous.
The Country Correspondent. Being, A Letter

From A Country Gentleman to a Friend in Town. In Which is contained . . . An Essay towards the Character of 'Squire Flash . . . Number I. London: Printed for T. Cooper . . . 1739.
4°, text pp. 1–28.
(1) Squire Flash (p. 12).

An Essay Towards The Character of that Late Chimpanzee, who died Feb. 23, 1738–9. London: Printed for L. Gilliver. 1739.*

A Hue and Cry after Part of a Pack of Hounds, Which broke out of their Kennel in Westminster. To which is added, Modern Characters, By another Hand. London: Printed for F. Style . . . MDCCXXXIX.
4°, text pp. 1–28.
(1) Six principal opponents to the government (p. 13).
BSC 2600.

The Universal Spy: Or, The London Weekly Magazine . . . London: Printed by J. Nicholson, next the Rose in Fleet-Lane; and may be had of the News-Carriers.*
(1) The ladies of the age; or a legacy for the fair sex (no. 1; by Thomas Brown?), (2) A modest woman (no. 2; by Brown?). (3) Several ingenious designing gentlewomen, that put in to the ladies invention (no. 3; by Brown?), (4) A voyage to Jamaica, with a character of the country and its inhabitants (no. 4; by Edward Ward).

[Baker, Henry.]
The Universal Spectator.*
(1) A learned coxcomb (March), (2) Eubulus and Harry Modely (June 16).

Bellegarde, Jean Baptiste Morvan de.
Reflexions Upon Ridicule; Or, What it is that makes a Man ridiculous; and the Means to avoid it. Wherein are Represented The different Manners and Characters of Persons of the present Age. . . . The Fifth Edition. London: Printed for D. Midwinter, W. Innys and R. Manby . . . A. Ward . . . T. Longman . . . and C. Bathurst . . . MDCCXXXIX.
12°, two parts.
(1–10) as in 1707.
BSC 2601.

[Cave, Edward.]
The Gentleman's Magazine. Vol. IX. 1739.
(1) Characters: an epistle to Mr Pope and Mr Whitehead (p. 164), (2) Cloe: a character. By

Mr. Pope (p. 323), (3) The Methodists (p. 377), (4) The fanatic preacher, translated from Mr Bourn's Latin (p. 436).

[D'Urfey, Thomas.]

The Progress of Honesty: or, a View of the Court and City. London: Printed for J. Brett . . . and Sold by the Booksellers of London and Westminster. 1739.

fo, text pp. 3–18. In verse.
(1–7) as (1–7) in 1681.

The poem has been revised and shortened as compared with the edition of 1681, eliminating the last four characters of that year.

[Higgons, Bevil.]

Enthusiasm Display'd. 1739.*

(1) The general character of Oliver [Cromwell?], extracted from various authors, (2) His particular character, by Bevil Higgons.

Swift, Jonathan.

Verses on the Death of Dr. Swift. Written by Himself: Nov. 1731. London: Printed for C. Bathurst . . . MDCCXXXIX.

fo, text pp. 1–18. In verse.
Begins: "As *Rochefoucault* his Maxims drew."

For an earlier, probably unauthorized, version of this poem, see Swift's "The Life and Genuine Character Of Doctor Swift," 1733. There were at least four editions of the present poem in 1739. Three are nearly identical except that two are designated on the title pages: "The Second Edition" and "The Third Edition" respectively. The fourth is entitled: "Verses on the Death of Dr. S----, D.S.P.D. . . . Written by Himself, November 1731. London Printed: Dublin: Re-printed by George Faulkner, M,DCC,XXXIX." It is 4°, text pp. 5–44. The poem is a character of Swift as he imagines his friends might draw him after his death.

Wesley, John.

The Character of a Methodist. 1739.*
See 1763.

In his Works, London, 1872, XI, 370, Wesley says this was published late in 1739.

1740

Anonymous.

The Boston Weekly News-Letter. . . . [colophon] Boston: Printed by J. Draper . . . 1740.

fo, 2 or 4 unnumbered pages (each issue).
(1) The lady of one of the antient earls of Westmoreland, written by her husband (no. 1891, June 12–19, 1740, third page).

Taken from The Gentleman's Magazine, March, 1740, p. 109.

An Historical Account of the Lives of Dr. Martin Luther, and Mr. John Calvin . . . The Second Edition. London, Printed for T. Gardner . . . 1740.

4°, text pp. 1–127.
(1) Martin Luther (p. 47).

The Presbyterian on Horseback, with a Character of their Predecessors the Pharisees. Also a Character of a Presbyterian or Female Hypocrite, and a Receipt how to make a right Presbyterian in two Days. London: J. Perry.*
BSC 2604.

Buckinghamshire, John Sheffield, Duke of.

The Works of John Sheffield . . . Duke of Buckingham. In Two Volumes. . . The Third Edition, Corrected. London: Printed for T. Wooton [and five others] . . . M.-DCC.XL.

8°, 2 vols.
(1–4) as in 1723.

[Chesterfield, Philip Dormer Stanhope, fourth Earl of, and others.]

Common Sense. 1740.*

(1) A prince (February 2), (2) A country-town-clerk (March 15).

There are abstracts of both characters in The Scots Magazine of the corresponding dates.

[Earle, John.]

The World Display'd: Or, Several Essays; Consisting of the various Characters and Passions of its principal Inhabitants. . . . London: Printed for and Sold by C: Ward and R: Chandler . . . 1740.

6°, text pp. 1–164.
(1–78) as in his Microcosmography, 1633.
Murphy 43. BSC 2602.

Numbers 71–78 are wrongly numbered 72–79. There are some changes in order, in titles, and the like.

[Le Clerc, Jean.]

The Life and Character of John Locke. 1740.*
Reprinted from An Account of . . . John Locke, 1713.

1741

Anonymous.

The Boston Post-Boy. 1741.*

(1) A receipt, beginning: "Take the green leaven of Pretensions, Hypocrisy, and Ambition, of each three Handfuls" (August 17).

Look e're you leap; or, a History of the lives and intrigues of lewd women, with the arraignment of their several vices. To which is

added, The Character of a Good Woman. The
Eleventh Edition. London, 1741.*

12°, text pp. 1–114.

Reprinted from 1725.

[Cave, Edward.]

The Gentleman's Magazine. Vol. XI. 1741.

(1) The late P--t (p. 260), (2) A receipt to make
a patriot (p. 274, from the Daily Gazeteer, May
14), (3) A character. By Richard Savage, Esq.
(p. 494), (4) On the death of Sir John James,
Bart. (p. 550).

Franklin, Benjamin.

The General Magazine And Historical Chron-
icle, For all the British Plantations in America.
[To be Continued Monthly.] January, 1741.
. . . Vol. I. Philadelphia: Printed and Sold by
B. Franklin.*

6°, text pp. 1–426.

(1) An infallible receipt to make a new kind of
convert (p. 414).

Most sets are imperfect, lacking this character. The note is
made from the 1938 reprint in the Facsimile Text Society
Publications.

[Gordon, Thomas.]

The Humourist. 1741.*

Reprinted from 1720. The bibliography of this work is
confused.

Mather, Cotton.

[Ornaments For The Daughters Of Zion.
. . .] Written by Cotton Mather. . . . The
Third Edition. Boston: Re-printed & Sold by
S. Kneeland, and T. Green . . . 1741.

8°.

(1–5) as in 1694.

The Boston Public Library copy, which was used as the
basis for this entry, has lost the first part of its title page
and the latter portion of the text.

1742

Anonymous.

The Agreeable Variety. Third Edition.*
Reprinted from 1717.

A Curious Collection of Letters. 1742.*
See 1761.

Memoirs of the Life and Character of Mr. John
Locke. . . . London: Printed for F. Noble
. . . T. Wright . . . and J. Duncan . . .
MDCCXLII.

4°, text pp. 3–15.

(1) John Locke (p. 10).

[Cave, Edward.]

The Gentleman's Magazine. Vol. XII. 1742.

(1) Directions to a painter, how to draw Mr --'s
picture. By a young lady (p. 46), (2) Gripe, a
miser (p. 48), (3) The church. A religious satire
(p. 492).

Leechman, William.

The Temper . . . of a Minister.*
See 1744.

North, Roger.

The Life of the Right Honourable Francis
North . . . By the Honourable Roger North,
Esq; . . . London, Printed for John Whiston
. . . MDCCXLII.

4°, text pp. 7–333.

(1) Lord Keeper North as a young man (p. 28),
(2) Sir Matthew Hale (p. 61), (3) Lord Keeper
Bridgman (p. 88), (4) Sir William Scroggs (p.
151), (5) Sir George Jeffries (p. 219), (6) Sir
Edward Saunders (p. 223), (7) Sir Leoline Jenkins (p. 229), (8) Sidney Godolphin (p. 230),
(9) Sir John Hoskins (p. 284), (10) Sir Robert
Sawyer (p. 287), (11) William Longueville (p.
289), (12) Sir John King (p. 290), (13) Sir
Charles Porter (p. 290), (14) Summary character of Lord Keeper North (p. 332).

Thurloe, John.

A Collection of the State Papers of John Thur-
loe . . . By Thomas Birch . . . London:
Printed for the Executor of the late Mr.
Fletcher Gyles; Thomas Woodward . . . And
Charles Davis . . . MDCCXLII.

fo, 7 vols.

(1) Oliver Cromwell, by John Maidston (Vol. I,
p. 766).

The character is contained in a letter to John Winthrop
dated March 24, 1659.

Wesley, John.

The Character of a Methodist.*
See 1763.

1743

Anonymous.

The Boston Evening-Post. 1743.*

(1) The Spaniards, Hollanders, etc. (December
19).

This character is taken from the Gentleman's Magazine for
August, 1743.

The Boston Weekly Magazine. 1743.*

(1) A miser (March 2, p. 5).

This character is taken from the London Magazine, May,

1732, The Weekly Register, May 6, 1732, and The New England Weekly Journal, October 2, 1732.

The London magazine: and Monthly Chronologer. MDCCXLIII. . . London: printed for Tho. Astley . . .

4°, text pp. 1–659.
(1) The modern Simplicius (p. 140), (2) Sempronius (p. 140), (3) Atticus (p. 140).
Taken from Common Sense for March 5, 1743.

[The Patriot and the Minister Review'd By Way of Dialogue, etc. With their Characters at large, as mutually drawn by each other. London, Printed for S. Dial. 1743.]

4°, text pp. 9–48.
(1) The minister, drawn by the patriot (p. 40), (2) The patriot, drawn by the minister (p. 43).
The title page is missing in the Yale copy used for making this note. There was an earlier edition in 1734.

[Cave, Edward.]

The Gentleman's Magazine. Vol. XIII. 1743.
(1) An excellent actor (p. 253).

Chandler, Samuel.

A Defence of the Prime Ministry and Character of Joseph. . . . By Samuel Chandler. . . . London: Printed for J. Noon . . . MDCCXLIII.

8°, text pp. 257–610.
(1) The history and character of Joseph vindicated (p. 257).

[Chesterfield, Philip Dormer Stanhope, fourth Earl of, and others.]

Common Sense: Or, the Englishman's Journal . . . London: Printed by J. Purser . . . 1743.*
12°.
(1) The modern Simplicius, Sempronius, and Atticus (no. 316, March 5, 1743).

[Higgons, Bevil.]

Enthusiasm Display'd: Being a true Copy of a most Learned, Conscientious and Devout Exercise, or Sermon, held forth the Last Lord's Day of April 1649, at Sir P--- T---'s House in Lincolns-Inn-Fields . . . London, Printed by J. Tilly, 1743.*
Reprinted from 1739.

La Bruyère, Jean de.
Works. 1743.*
Reprinted from 1713.

[Silence, Timothy.]
The Foundling Hospital for wit. 1743.*
See 1746.

Theophrastus.
Moral Characters, translated from the Greek by E. Budgell. Printed in the year 1743.*
BSC 2606.
Reprinted from 1714.

[Ward, Edward.]
The Delights of the Bottle. 1743.*
Reprinted from 1720.

Wesley, John.
The Character Of A Methodist. The Third Edition. Bristol: Printed by Felix Farley, 1743.*
See 1763.

1744

Anonymous.
The American Magazine And Historical Chronicle. MDCCXLIII. MDCCXLIV. . . . Boston: Printed by Rogers and Fowle, and Sold by S. Eliot, and J. Blanchard . . . B. Franklin . . . J. Parker . . . J. Pomroy . . . C. Campbell . . . 1744.

4°, text pp. 1–704.
(1) A dialogue between a musician and a metaphysician (p. 65), (2) Eugenio, a weak man (p. 111), (3) In praise of buffoonery (p. 116), (4) A happy man (p. 215), (5) The art of storytelling (p. 469), (6) The difference between the busy man and the man of business (p. 545), (7) The characters of different nations (p. 580), (8) The different conduct of the man of genius, and the man of business accounted for (p. 647).
Several characters are reprinted from The Gentleman's Magazine, The London Magazine, and other sources.

An Epistle to the Fair-Sex On the Subject of Drinking. In which The Particular Consequences of this most Prevailing Custom are fully and fairly Exposed in the following Characters. . . . London: Printed and Published by T. Gardner . . . MDCCXLIV.

4°, text pp. 1–70.
(1) A young woman of quality (p. 11), (2) A gentleman's daughter (p. 12), (3) The daughter of a rich tradesman (p. 15), (4) The daughter of a middling tradesman (p. 16), (5) The daughter of a common tradesman (p. 18), (6) A housekeeper (p. 19), (7) A lady's-woman (p. 20), (8) A common servant (p. 21), (9) A married lady of quality (p. 25), (10) A gentleman's lady (p. 26), (11) The wife of a clergyman (p. 29), (12) The wife of an eminent tradesman (p. 30), (13) The wife of a middling tradesman (p. 32), (14) The wife of a common tradesman (p. 33), (15) The wife of a captain (p. 35), (16) A wife en-

gaged in separate business (p. 38), (17) A wife keeping a public house (p. 39), (18) Nurses of all kinds (p. 45), (19) A widow lady of quality (p. 48), (20) A widow left in narrow circumstances (p. 51), (21) A widow left to carry on business (p. 52), (22) The widow of a clergyman or an officer (p. 53).
BSC 2607.

The Harleian Miscellany ... London, Printed for T. Osborne ... MDCCXLIV [–VI].
4°, 8 vols.
(1) A trip to Dunkirk, by Swift (?), 1708 (Vol. I, p. 205, in verse), (2) A disbanded courtier, 1681 (I, 356), (3) An ill court favorite (II, 50), (4) The anatomy of a woman's tongue, 1638 (II, 167), (5) An honest and worthy Parliament-man (II, 336), (6) A sneaker, 1705 (II, 337), (7) Four for a penny, 1678 (IV, 141), (8) The petition of the widows, 1693 (IV, 381), (9) An humble remonstrance of the bachelors (IV, 479), (10) The leveller, 1659 (IV, 515), (11) The Earl of Strafford characterized, 1641 (V, 43), (12) The Assembly Man [by Birkenhead], written 1647, printed 1662/3 (V, 93), (13) An Oxford Incendiary, 1643 (V, 469), (14) Mr. John Milton's Character of the Long Parliament, 1681 (V, 540), (15) A nest of perfidious vipers, 1644 (V, 553), (16) Holland, 1665 (V, 575), (17) A modern account of Scotland, 1670 (VI, 121), (18) A coffee-house, 1673 (VI, 429), (19) Coffee-houses vindicated, 1675 (VI, 433), (20) The secret history of the Calves-Head Club, 1703 (VI, 552), (21) Scotland Characterized, 1701 (VII, 357), (22) A fanatic, 1675 (VII, 596), (23) The Marquis of Argyle's last will and testament (VIII, 26), (24) A certain great duchess deceased, from manuscript (VIII, 212), (25) London and the Countrey Carbonadoed, by Lupton (IX, 310).
Murphy, passim.

The Meddler. Dublin. 1744.*
(1) A smatterer (no. 4).
There are apparently also six characters in no. 2, but their subjects are not indicated in Mr. Greenough's notes.

Brown, Thomas.
Works. 1744.*
Reprinted from 1730.

Byles, Mather.
The Character of the perfect and upright Man; his peaceful End described ... in a Discourse on Psalm XXXVII.37. To which is added, An Exemplification of the Subject, In a short Account of the peaceful Death of Mrs. Anna Byles. By Mr. Byles. ... The Second Edition. ... Boston: Printed by B. Green and Comp. for D. Gookin ... 1744.

4°, text pp. 1–36.
Begins: "There is nothing more becoming rational creatures."

[Fielding, Henry.]
An Attempt Towards A Natural History Of The Hanover Rat. Dedicated to T***m. M******r, M.D. And S---y to the Royal Society. ... London: Printed for M. Cooper ... MDCCXLIV.
4°, text pp. 1–24.
Begins: "My ingenious friend Mr. Baker."
A character of the House of Hanover. Fielding's authorship is proved in the Yale University Gazette, October, 1935.

Fielding, Sarah.
The Adventures Of David Simple ... By a Lady. In Two Volumes ... The Second Edition. ... London: Printed for A. Millar ... MDCCXLIV.
12°, 2 vols.
(1) Certain "no-bodies" (Vol. I, p. 168).
The first edition also appeared in 1744. Reprinted several times.

Leechman, William.
The Temper, Character, And Duty Of A Minister of the Gospel. ... By William Leechman M.A. ... The Fourth Edition. Glasgow, Printed by Robert Foulis ... MDCCXLIV.
4°, text pp. 3–55.
Begins: "The wiser and more considerate part of mankind."
A sermon preached April 7, 1741. The first edition was about 1742.

[Morris, Corbyn.]
An Essay Towards Fixing the True Standards of Wit, Humour, Raillery, Satire, and Ridicule. To which is added, an Analysis Of the Characters of An Humourist, Sir John Falstaff, Sir Roger De Coverly, and Don Quixote. ... By the Author of a Letter from a By-Stander. ... London: Printed for J. Roberts ... and W. Bickerton ... MDCCXLIV.
4°, text pp. 1–75.
(1) A humourist (p. 15), (2) Sir John Falstaff (p. 25), (3) Sir Roger de Coverly (p. 31), (4) Abel Drugger (p. 35), (5) Don Quixote (p. 38).
The dedication is signed by Corbyn Morris.

[Ward, Edward?]
The Character of a Ship of War. 1744.*
Probably a reprint, under different title, of The Wooden World Dissected; or perhaps merely a variant title for that work.

[Ward, Edward.]

The Wooden World Dissected: in the Character of a Ship of War; as also, the Characters of all the Officers, from the Captain to the Common Sailor . . . By the Author of the London-Spy. London, Printed by M. Cooper, 1744.*

8°.

Reprinted from 1707.

There may have been another edition in the same year under the title of The Character of a Ship of War; but the latter may be simply an erroneous reference to the present issue.

1745

Anonymous.

The American Magazine And Historical Chronicle. Volume II. . . . Boston, New-England: Printed and Sold by Rogers and Fowle . . . 1745.

4°, text pp. 1–566.

(1) Of prating (p. 28), (2) A good bishop (p. 99), (3) Abuses of conversation (p. 121), (4) Great talkers exposed (p. 160), (5) A virtuous and contented wife (p. 169, in verse), (6) The happy man (p. 170, in verse), (7) Reflections in the manner of La Bruyere and Theophrastus (p. 204), (8) On the writing of satirical characters (p. 206), (9) Some odd characters expos'd (p. 209), (10) False politeness (p. 249), (11) Advantages of a private life (p. 250), (12) The fickle male humourist (p. 257), (13) The gentleman (p. 269), (14) Animadversions on the affectations of ill-suited characters among the female sex (p. 302), (15) The man of sense (p. 410, in verse), (16) A vapoury man (p. 501, in verse), (17) An account of a northern club (p. 528).

Several of these characters are reprinted from The London Magazine, The Gentleman's Magazine, and elsewhere.

Adams, John.

Poems on Several Occasions, Original and Translated. . . . By the late Reverend and Learned John Adams, M.A. . . . Boston . . . D. Gookin . . . 1745.*

(1) The cheerful man (p. 18), (2) The contented man (p. 20), (3) The parent (p. 28), (4) The lover (p. 29), (5) The constant friend (p. 32).

[Cave, Edward.]

The Gentleman's Magazine. Vol. XV. 1745.

(1) Aurelia, by George Ogle, Esq. (p. 48), (2) Emperor Charles VII (p. 84), (3) The choice, or the model of a wife (p. 327), (4) The Bristol charmers (p. 494).

Chauncy, Charles.

Cornelius's Character. A Sermon Preach'd

The Lord's-Day after the Funeral of Mr. Cornelius Thayer. . . . By Charles Chauncy. . . . Boston: Printed for D. Gookin . . . 1745.

4°, text pp. 5–38.

Begins: "'Tis an excellent Man we have here characterized."

[Fordyce, David.]

Dialogues Concerning Education. . . . London, Printed in the Year M.DCC.XLV.

8°, text pp. 1–435.

(1) Euphranor, the excellent master of the academy (p. 14), (2) The Club (p. 52), (3) Eugenio, a man of the world (p. 55), (4) Constant, a plain dealing patriot (p. 56), (5) Hiero, an excellent divine (p. 59), (6) A learned bookworm (p. 93), (7) Atticus, a benignant, retired country gentleman (p. 143), (8) Cleora, the beautiful and accomplished daughter of Atticus (p. 146).

Attributed to Fordyce in the CBEL.

[Harris, Thomas.]

Popery and Slavery Display'd. Containing The Character of Popery, and a Relation of Popish Cruelties . . . Addressed To all Protestant Subjects. The Third Edition. London: Printed for C. Corbett . . . T. Harris . . . and B. Dod . . . 1745.

4°, text pp. 1–76.

(1) Popery (p. 3).

BSC 2608.

The dedication is signed Tho. Harris. There was a fourth edition in the same year.

Walter, Nathanael.

The Character of a true Patriot. A Sermon Preach'd At The Thursday-Lecture in Boston, August 1. 1745. By Nathanael Walter, M.A. . . . Boston: Printed for D. Henchman . . . 1745.

4°, text pp. 5–20.

Begins: "The Excellency of the christian Religion."

Primarily a description of Moses.

1746

Anonymous.

The American Magazine And Historical Chronicle. Volume III. . . . Boston, New-England: Printed and Sold by Rogers and Fowle . . . 1746.

4°, text pp. 1–579.

(1) Of bodily wits (p. 68), (2) On flattery and morosity, containing characters of the Blunts (p. 169), (3) Of an unaffected behaviour (p. 367), (4) A man whose merit is less shining than solid

(p. 412), (5) A man whose virtue is free from affectation (p. 412), (6) Busybodies (p. 416).

Several of these characters are reprinted from other journals.

The Tricks of the Town Laid Open: or, A Companion for Country Gentlemen. Being the Substance of Seventeen Letters from a Gentleman at London to his Friend in the Country, to disswade him from coming to Town . . . London, 1746.*

A reissue of The Country Gentleman's Vade-Mecum, 1699.

[Cave, Edward.]

The Gentleman's Magazine. Vol. XVI. 1746.
(1) Extracts of a poem entitled The Modern Fine Lady by Mr. C. B--r (p. 321), (2) The smart. High taste in high life (p. 322), (3) The lounger (p. 322).

[Dodsley, Robert (editor).]

The Museum: or, the Literary and Historical Register. . . . London, Printed for R. Dodsley . . . M.DCC.XLVI.
4°, 3 vols.
(1) The Damascenes (Vol. I, p. 108), (2) One falsely deemed a wit (I, 136, in verse), (3) Lepidus (I, 148), (4) A certain lady (I, 251), (5) The natives of S. America (I, 343), (6) Pallavicini (I, 394), (7) Atticus (II, 41), (8) Rusticus (II, 262), (9) Philogynes (II, 262), (10) Miss ---- (III, 77), (11) Mrs. Lucy Littleton (III, 249), (12) The great king (III, 273).

[Jenyns, Soame.]

The Modern Fine Gentleman. . . . London: Printed for M. Cooper . . . M.DCC.XLVI.
4°, text pp. 3–8. In verse.
Begins: "Just broke from School, pert, impudent, and raw."

[Jenyns, Soame?]

The Modern Fine Lady. Or, A Counterpart to a Poem lately published, called, The Modern Fine Gentleman. . . . London: Printed for M. Cooper . . . 1746.
4°, text pp. 3–8. In verse.
Begins: "At Hackney, or at Chelsea bred."

The authorship is uncertain. This is a different poem from the same title of 1751, which the CBEL gives as the first edition. It is likely, therefore, that this one is not by Jenyns. But see the note to Timothy Silence's Foundling Hospital of Wit of this same year.

Pope, Alexander.

The Character of Katharine, Late Duchess of Buckinghamshire and Normanby. By the late Mr. Pope. London: Printed for M. Cooper . . . MDCC.XLVI.

4°, text pp. 3–7.
Begins: "She was the Daughter of James the Second."
BSC 2609.

A note at the end states: "The above Character was written by Mr. Pope some Years before Her Grace's Death."

Silence, Timothy.

The Foundling Hospital for Wit. Number III. . . . By Timothy Silence Esq; London: Printed for W. Webb . . . 1746.
4°, text pp. 1–61. 6 numbers. In verse.
(1) The modern fine lady (p. 46), (2) The modern fine lady (p. 49).

Both characters are said to be by Soame Jenyns. The six numbers are bound together, in the Harvard copy, with a common title page of 1763. Attributed by Halkett and Laing to Sir Charles Hanbury Williams. The bibliography of this title is very confusing. See CBEL, II, 210 ff. The first number appeared in 1743.

Walter, Nathaniel.

The Character Of A Christian Hero. A Sermon Preached before the ancient and honourable Artillery Company . . . June 2d. 1746. By the Reverend Nathaniel Walter, A.M. . . . Boston in New-England: Printed by J. Draper, for D. Henchman . . . M,DCC,XLVI.
4°, text pp. 5–22.
Begins: " 'Tis a remarkable Circumstance in sacred History."

Partly a character of the apostle Paul, the example of a Christian hero.

[Ward, Edward.]

A Compleat and Humorous Account of all the Remarkable Clubs. 1746.*

Reprinted from The History of the London Clubs, 1709.

Ward, Henry.

The Works of Henry Ward. Third Edition. 1746.*
(1) A Short Description of London (p. 118).

1747

Anonymous.

A Description of the young A--s Cavalcade, on circuit. Dublin, Printed in the Year, 1747.*
In verse.
(1) An attorney.

Helter Skelter, or the Hue and Cry after the Attornies going to ride the Circuit.*
(1) An attorney.

Not identical with A Description of the young A----s Cavalcade, Dublin, 1747, but frequently identical in phrasing.

The Retirement. An Ethic Poem. By a Gen-

tleman, late of Balliol College, Oxford. London: Printed for the Author, 1747.*
(1) A miser, (2) A happy life in the country.

The Tricks of the Town Laid open: or, a Companion for Country Gentlemen . . . second edition . . . London, 1747.*
Reprinted from 1746.

[Cave, Edward.]
The Gentleman's Magazine. Vol. XVII. 1747.
(1) The happy man (p. 94), (2) The dangler (p. 338).

Condy, Jeremiah.
The Godly and Faithful Man characterized: and his decease improved. A Sermon . . . On the Death of Mr. Benjamin Landon. . . . By Jeremiah Condy. . . . Boston, Printed for D. Gookin . . . 1747.
4°, text pp. 5–44.
Begins: "It is known to the greater part."

[Lancaster, Nathaniel.]
The Pretty Gentleman: or, Softness of Manners Vindicated From the false Ridicule exhibited under the Character of William Fribble, Esq; London: Printed for M. Cooper . . . 1747.
4°, text pp. 5–36.
(1) The pretty gentleman (p. 10).
Attributed to Lancaster by the CBEL.

Wesley, John.
The Character of a Methodist. 1747.*
See 1763.

1748

Anonymous.
The Boston Evening-Post. 1748.*
(1) A country justice called Clodpate. Written by Mr. Steers (February 8), (2) Sir Thomas De Veil (March 28).

A Collection Of . . . Tracts . . . Particularly That Of The Late Lord Sommers . . . London: Printed for F. Cogan . . . M.DCC.-XLVIII[–LII].
4°, four collections of four volumes each.
(1) A Hue and Cry after Dr. Swift (Collection I, Vol. i, p. 387), (2) Priestcraft in Perfection, by Anthony Collins (I, ii, 460), (3) The True Character of a Churchman (I, ii, 553), (4) A Character of King James, by Kennet (I, iv, 142), (5) A Character of King Charles, by Butler (I, iv, 210), (6) The Character of an Honest Man, 1683 (I,

iv, 277), (7) The Character of an Honest Lawyer, by H.C., 1676 (I, iv, 305), (8) The Character of the Wisest Men, 1696 (I, iv, 308), (9) The Character of a Tory (II, i, 282), (10) The Character of a True Protestant, 1682 (II, i, 393), (11) The Character of a Tacker, 1705 (II, iv, 395), (12) The True Character of a Churchman, by West (III, i, 408).
Murphy passim.

An Earnest Appeal To Passionate People: Wherein The Rise, Progress, and Consequences of that unhappy Disposition of Mind are fully displayed; and the Possibility of conquering that Temper, illustrated from several Characters in real Life. To which is added, An Essay on Envy, Malice, and Detraction. London, Printed for W. Owen, at Homer's-Head near Temple-Bar. 1748.*
8°, text pp. 1–63.
(1) A passionate man (p. 1), (2) Silvius, who, though amiable in early life, through pride became peevish and difficult (p. 34), (3) Horticulus, a tradesman, subject to momentary fits of passion (p. 40), (4) Furiosa (p. 43), (5) The benevolent man (p. 92).
BSC 2612.

The Independent Advertiser. Boston, May 16. 1748. Numb. 20. . . . [colophon] Boston, Printed and sold by Rogers and Fowle.
s.sh.fo, text pp. 1–2.
(1) A good magistrate, by Algernon Sidney (p. 1), (2) An evil magistrate, by Sidney (p. 1).

[Cave, Edward.]
The Gentleman's Magazine. Vol. XVIII. 1748.
(1) Mr. Thomson, in his poem of Indolence, there said to be written by a friend (p. 423).

[Coetlogon, Chevalier de?]
Diogenes at Court: or the Modern Cynic, discovering with the assistance of his Lantern, the Character of several Nations, and of most of the Princes, Heroes, and other great men of the Age. — By the Chevalier de Coetlogon. London: Printed by J. Jefferies at the Bible, Crown, and Star. 1748.*
8°, text pp. 1–62.
BSC 2611.

[Dodsley, Robert (editor).]
A Collection of Poems. In Three Volumes. By Several Hands. . . . London: Printed by J. Hughs, For R. Dodsley . . . M.DCC-XLVIII[–LVIII].

8°, 6 vols. In verse.

(1) Of Active and Retired Life, by William Melmoth (Vol. I, p. 209), (2) The modern fine gentleman (III, 165), (3) The modern fine lady (IV, 73), (4) The rake (IV, 325), (5) The indolent (VI, 294).

There were a good many later editions. The few which I have seen contain the same characters. Attributed to Dodsley as editor by the CBEL.

Higgons, Bevil.

A Short View of the English History. The Third Edition. London, 1748.*

Reprinted from 1723.

Richardson, Samuel.

Clarissa Harlowe. 1748.*

(1) Clarissa Harlowe, by Miss Howe (letter 150). There were many later editions.

[Smollett, Tobias George.]

The Adventures of Roderick Random. . . . In Two Volumes. . . . London: Printed for J. Osborne . . . MDCCXLVIII.

12°, 2 vols.

(1) An elderly female virtuoso (Vol. II, p. 15), (2) A Roman priest (II, 91), (3) A decayed general (II, 91), (4) Melinda, a coquette (II, 117).

There have been many later editions.

[Towgood, Michaijah.]

An Essay Towards Attaining A True Idea Of The Character and Reign of King Charles the First, And the Causes of the Civil War . . . London: Printed for John Noon . . . 1748.

8°, text pp. 1–158.

(1) Charles I, by the present author (p. 1), (2) Charles I, by Coke, Burnet, Neal, Whitelocke, and others (p. 145).
BSC 2610.

Attributed to Towgood by the Huntington Library. There were at least two later editions.

[Trenchard, John, and Gordon, Thomas.]

Cato's Letters. Fifth edition. 1748.*

Reprinted from 1721.

[Ward, Edward.]

Mars stript of his Armour, or the Army displayed in its true Colours. H. Serjeant. 1748.*
BSC 2613.

Reprinted from 1709.

1749

Anonymous.

The Boston Evening-Post. 1749.*

(1) A pedant, in "Advice to a young Clergyman"

(March 27), (2) A country squire as an example of a bigot (May 15).

[The Boston Weekly News-Letter. 1749.]

(1) Volpone. A modern character (Nov. 9, 1749, from the London Magazine for August, 1749), (2) Of ambition. Lord Bacon's character (Nov. 17, 1749, from the Westminster Journal for July 29, 1749).

The title page has not been verified.

The Character of a True Churchman. 1749.*

Reprinted from 1711.

The Independent Advertiser. Boston, March 27. 1749. Numb. 65. . . . [colophon] Boston, Printed and sold by Rogers and Fowle.

s.sh.fo, text pp. 1–2.

(1) Spaniards (p. 1), (2) The Dutch (p. 1), (3) The Italians (p. 1), (4) The French (p. 1).

These characters are reprinted from the Boston Evening Post, The London Magazine, the Gentleman's Magazine, or some similar source. Cf. The Post, Dec. 19, 1743.

A Tale of Two Tubs, or the B---rs in Querpo. Being a humorous and satirical description of some principal characters. London, 1749.*

8°. In verse.

(1) T. P. Holles, Duke of Newcastle, (2) John, 4th Duke of Bedford.

[Bolingbroke, Henry St. John, Viscount.]

Letters On The Spirit of Patriotism: On The Idea of a Patriot King: And On the State of Parties At the Accession of King George the First. London: Printed for A. Millar . . . MDCCXLIX.

8°, text pp. 9–251.

(1) A patriot king (p. 65).

Attributed to Bolingbroke by the CBEL. There were several later editions.

Dunton, John.

The New Practice of Piety. 1749.*

Reprinted from 1704.

Fielding, Henry.

The History of Tom Jones, A Foundling. In Six Volumes. By Henry Fielding . . . London: Printed for A. Millar . . . MDCCXLIX.

12°, 6 vols.

(1) Mr. Square the philosopher and Mr. Thwackum the divine (Book III, chap. 3), (2) Mrs. Western (VI, 2).

Reprinted many times.

[Fleming, Caleb.]

The Character of the Rev. Mr. Thomas Brad-

bury &c. &c. London. Printed for M. Cooper
. . . 1749.*
8°, text pp. 1–36.
BSC 2614.
Attributed to Fleming by Halkett and Laing.

Garrick, David.

Lethe, A Dramatic Satire. By David Garrick.
. . . London: Printed for and Sold by Paul
Waillant . . . MDCCXLIX.
4°, text pp. 1–43.
(1) A poet (p. 6), (2) An old man (p. 11), (3)
A fine gentleman (p. 14), (4) Mr. and Mrs.
Tatoo (p. 19), (5) A Frenchman (p. 23), (6)
Mrs. Rist (p. 27), (7) A drunken man and a tailor
(p. 33).

[Penn, William.]

Some Fruits of Solitude, in Reflections and
Maxims, relating to the Conduct of Human
Life. In Two Parts. The Eighth Edition.
Newport, Rhode Island: Printed by James
Franklin . . . 1749.
[Second title] More Fruits of Solitude . . .
Newport, Rhode Island: Printed by James
Franklin . . . 1749.
6°, in 2 parts, text pp. 1–158, 1–108.
(1–4) as in 1693, (5) The world's able man (Part
II, p. 7), (6) The vain man (II, 82), (7) The
right moralist (II, 106), (8) Of a good servant
(II, 144).

[Ward, Edward.]

The Wooden World Dissected. 1749.*
Reprinted from 1707.

1750

Anonymous.

The Boston Post-Boy. 1750.*
(1) An atheist (March 26, p. 1).

The Character of a Cavalier, with his Brother
Separatist, Both striving which shall bee most
active in dividing the two Nations, now so
happily, by the blessing of God, united.
Leedes.
Reprinted from 1647.

Characterism, Or, The Modern Age Display'd;
Being an Attempt to expose the Pretended
Virtues of Both Sexes: With a Poetical Essay
on each Character. In Two Parts. First, of
the Ladies, Second, of the Gentlemen. London: Printed by E. Owen.*
8°, text pp. 1–181.
(1) The hypocritical lady, (2) The female pedant,
(3) The censorious lady, (4) The intriguing lady,
(5) The toping lady, (6) The inquisitive lady,
(7) The jealous lady, or dis-satisfied wife, (8)
The gaming lady, (9) The lady's confident, (10)
From the spinning wheel to the coach, or the rich
hoyden, (11) The high birth, but no fortune, or
proud poverty, (12) Modern quality, or the fortune rais'd lady, (13) The great man's prostitute
or actress taken into keeping, (14) The sandy
hair'd lady or young wanton, (15) The bountiful
lady, (16) The modish gentleman or artful politician, (17) The corrupt statesman, or complete
courtier, (18) The ambitious clergyman, (19)
Captain Flash, or the coward in commission, (20)
The avaritious lawyer, (21) The city apprentice,
or mechanic turn'd gentleman, (22) The severe
magistrate, or proud man in authority, (23) The
extravagant heir, (24) The promising gentleman
or fashionable friend, (25) The dignify'd libertine, or marriage a-la-mode, (26) The temporising
priest or religious zealot, (27) Mr. Fribble, or the
self-admirer, (28) The false relation, or fashionable friendship, (29) The worthy patriot, or, the
true English nobleman.
BSC 2612 (dated 1748).
Part II begins with number 16.
The date is uncertain.

The Country Spy; or a Ramble thro' London.
Containing Many curious Remarks, diverting
Tales, and Merry Joaks. [ornament] London: Printed by R. Walker, for the Author;
and sold by the Booksellers in Town and
Country.*
8°.
(1) The true character of a Scotchman (chap.
2), (2) An Irishman (chap. 5), (3) A Sister of a
Ward in a hospital (chap. 9), (4) The true character of stockjobbers (chap. 13).
The date is not certain.

[Cave, Edward.]

The Gentleman's Magazine. Vol. XX. 1750.
(1) The art of coquetry. By Mrs. Charlotte Len-
nox (p. 518).

Halifax, George Savile, Marquis of.

A Character Of King Charles The Second:
And Political, Moral and Miscellaneous
Thoughts and Reflections. By George Savile,
Marquis of Halifax. London: Printed for J.
and R. Tonson and S. Draper . . . MDCCL.
8°, text pp. 1–183.
(1) Charles II (p. 1).
BSC 2610.

[Shaw, Peter?]

The Reflector: representing Human Affairs,
As they are . . . London: Printed for T.
Longman . . . MDCCL.

8°, text pp. 1–371.
(1) The stoical wise man (p. 110), (2) A wise man (p. 112), (3) A fool (p. 113), (4) A courtier (p. 219).

Attributed to Shaw doubtfully by the CBEL.

[Ward, Edward.]

Mars stript of his Armour, or the Army displayed in its true Colours. J. Collyer, 1750.*
BSC 2615.

Reprinted from 1709.

1751

[Coventry, Francis.]

The History of Pompey the Little: Or, The Life and Adventures of a Lap-Dog. London: Printed for M. Cooper . . . MDCCLI.

12°, text pp. 1–272.
(1) Hillario (p. 20), (2) Lady Tempest (p. 39), (3) Counsellor Tanturian (p. 107), (4) Theodosia (p. 143), (5) Aurora (p. 144), (6) Count Tag (p. 146), (7) An aged gallant (p. 149), (8) Sir Thomas Frippery (p. 174), (9) Jack Chase (p. 179), (10) A Master of Arts at a university (p. 240), (11) A Doctor of Divinity (p. 245).
BSC 2616.

Attributed to Coventry by the CBEL. There were many later editions.

[Gay, Ebenezer.]

The Character Of The Late Honorable Judge Dudley, As it was inserted in the Boston-News-Letter, February 7th, 1751.

4°, text pp. 1–4.
Begins: "Yesterday with great Decency and Respect."

Appended to Ebenezer Gay's Natural Religion, As Distinguish'd From Revealed, Boston, 1759.

Gordon, Thomas.

A Cordial for Low Spirits: Being a Collection of Valuable Tracts. . . . The Second Edition. 1751.*

12°, 3 vols.
(1) An independent Whig, 1719 (Vol. I, p. 189), (2) A modern Tory, 1722 (II, 257).

Vol. II is entitled Another Cordial for Low Spirits.

[Jenyns, Soame.]

The Modern Fine Lady. . . . London: Printed for R. Dodsley . . . 1751.

fo, text pp. 3–8. In verse.
Begins: "Skill'd in each Art."

A different poem from the same title of 1746.

[Johnson, Samuel.]

The Rambler . . . London: Printed for J. Payne . . . M.DCC.LI.

(1) The virtuoso (nos. 82,83), (2) The sceptic (no. 95), (3) The curious man (no. 103), (4) The fop (no. 109), (5) The fussy housekeeper (no. 112), (6) Mr. Busy, Mrs. Busy, Miss Busy (no. 138), (7) Squire Bluster (no. 142), (8) Detractors (no. 144).

These characters first appeared between Dec. 29, 1750, and Aug. 3, 1751. They have been reprinted a number of times.

La Bruyère, Jean de.

Works. 1751.*

Reprinted from 1713.

[Smart, Christopher.]

The Student, Or, The Oxford and Cambridge Monthly Miscellany. Vol. II. . . . Oxford, Printed for J. Newbery . . . MDCCLI.

4°, text pp. 1–400.
(1) An echo (p. 210), (2) Millario, a truly excellent and economical man (p. 370).

Theophrastus.

The Moral Characters Of Theophrastus, Translated from the Greek By Eustace Budgell Esquire. . . . Edinburgh, Printed for James Reid . . . MD.CC.LI.

4°, text pp. 1–32.
(1–28) as in 1714.

Trenchard, John, and Gordon, Thomas.

A Collection Of Tracts. By the Late John Trenchard, Esq; And Thomas Gordon, Esq. . . . London: Printed for F. Cogan . . . MDCCLI.

12°, 2 vols.
(1) An Independent Whig, by Thomas Gordon, 1720 (Vol. I, p. 311), (2) The True Picture of a Modern Tory, by Gordon, 1722 (II, 278).

[Ward, Edward.]

The Wooden World Dissected. The Fifth Edition. 1751.*

Reprinted from 1707.
Possibly an error for the edition of 1756, q.v.

Wesley, John.

The Character of a Methodist. 1751.*
See 1763.

1752

Anonymous.

The Character Of A True Christian: Drawn from the Doctrines Contained in the Holy Scriptures. Bristol: Printed by Felix Farley. And sold by E. Nowers . . . London. MDCCLII.*

Text pp. 1–23.

Begins: "He is one, who is not only called a Christian."

Apparently a later edition of The Character of a True Churchman, 1711.

Manners. Translated from the French. The Second Edition. . . . London: Printed for J. Payne and J. Bouquet . . . M.DCC.LII.*

Each chapter is said to contain a number of short characters.

Poetical Impertinence: Or, Advice Unasked. In Two Poems, The Good Wife: And The Good Husband. Containing Rules humbly proposed to those Ladies and Gentlemen, who are not intirely satisfied with the examples of the Polite Husbands and Wives of this present Age. London: Printed for W. Russel . . . 1752.

4°, text pp. 9–59. In verse.
(1) The man of pleasure (p. 11), (2) The tyrant (p. 12), (3) The fop (p. 12), (4) A worthy man (p. 14).

The Port Folio. 1752 ff.*

(1) A fearful man (Vol. I, p. 92), (2) A wise man (I, 283), (3) A bon vivant and a gamester (I, 378), (4) A sailor (II, 31), (5) A soldier (II, 31), (6) Irene and Clitus (II, 121), (7) The musician, (III, 85), (8) A physician (IV, 30).

Nos. 4 and 5 are by Overbury, no. 7 by Joseph Dennie, no. 8 by Lady Mary Wortley Montagu.

Buckinghamshire, John Sheffield, Duke of.

Works. 1752.*

Reprinted from 1740.

Campbell, George.

The Character of a Minister of the Gospel, as a Teacher, and Pattern; a Sermon on Matt. V. 13, 14. Aberdeen, Printed by James Chalmers, 1752.*

Watt 188q.

[Cave, Edward.]

The Gentleman's Magazine. Vol. XXII. 1752.

(1) A batchelor's address, or proposal to the maidens (p. 233).

Chandler, Samuel.

The Character and Reward of a Christian Bishop. A Sermon Occasioned by the Death of the late Reverend Mr. Moses Lowman. . . . By Samuel Chandler. . . . London: Printed for John Noon . . . 1752.

4°, text pp. 3–48.
Begins: "Fidelity in the various stations of life."

[D'Argens, John Baptist de Boyer, Marquis.]

The Chinese Spy. 1752.*

See 1765.

[Fordyce, David.]

Theodorus. 1752.*

See 1755.

La Bruyère, Jean de.

The Works Of Mons. De La Bruyere. A New Translation from the last Paris Edition. To which is added, The Manner of Living with Great Men: Written after the Manner of M. De La Bruyere. By N. Rowe, Esq; . . . London: Printed for D. Browne . . . J. Whiston and B. White . . . S. Baker . . . and L. Davis . . . MDCCLII.

12°, 2 vols.
(1–44) as in 1713.

1753

Anonymous.

The Dictionary of Love. In which is contained, The Explanation of most of the Terms used in that Language. London: Printed by R. Griffiths, 1753.

12°, text sigs. B-L5v.
(1) A beau (sig. B11), (2) A coquette (sig. C10v), (3) A coxcomb (sig. C11v), (4) A fop (sig. E6v), (5) A fribble (sig. E8v), (6) A gallant (sig. E10v), (7) Knights-errant (sig. G), (8) A prude (sig. H10), (9) Rakes (sig. I).

The Harleian Miscellany . . . The Second Edition. London. Printed for T. Osborne . . . MDCCLIII[-XLVI].

4°, 8 vols.
(1–25) as in 1744–46.

The Stage-Coach: Containing the Character of Mr. Manly, and the History of his Fellow-Travellers. . . . London: Printed for T. Osborne . . . 1753.

12°, 2 vols.
(1) Mr. Manly (Vol. I, p. 1).

Buckinghamshire, John Sheffield, Duke of.

The Works of John Sheffield, . . . Duke of Buckingham. In Two Volumes. . . . The Fourth Edition, corrected. London: Printed for D. Browne [and 5 others] . . . M.DCC.LIII.

8°, 2 vols.
(1–4) as in 1723.

There have been several later editions.

Fielding, Henry.
The Life of Mr. Jonathan Wild the Great.
1753.*
See 1754.

[Genard, François.]
The School of Man. Translated from the
French. To which is prefixed, A Key to the
Satyrical Characters. . . . London: Printed for
Lockyer Leavis . . . M.DCC.LIII.
12°, text pp. 1–384.
(Over 100 characters with Latin names, too nu-
merous to list here.)
BSC 2619.
The Huntington Library has The School of Women, 1753,
which may be an imitation or by the same author.

[Hall, Joseph.]
Virgidemiarum. 1753.*
Reprinted from 1598.

[Hawkesworth, Sir John.]
The Adventurer. Volume the First. . . . Lon-
don: Printed for J. Payne . . . MDCCLIII
[–IV].
3° (i.e., three sheets per issue), 2 vols.
(1) The adventurer (Vol. I, p. 1), (2) Charac-
ters illustrating unhappy marriage (I, 145), (3)
The gamester (I, 169), (4) Characters in prison
(I, 313), (5) Characters at Bath, by Philomedes
(Joseph Warton?) (II, 349).
Attributed to Hawkesworth by the CBEL.

[Hill, Sir John.]
The Inspector. . . . London: Printed for R.
Griffiths . . . MDCCLIII.
12°, 2 vols.
(1) Mr. Bend, whose politeness was that of a
dancing-master rather than a gentleman (no. 43),
(2) A Jemmy Fellow, without either courage or
manners (no. 47), (3) A buck (no. 56), (4) Sir
Civil Surly (no. 61), (5) Mr. Sudden, who is too
eager to please (no. 131), (6) Thersites, who
abused everybody, and everybody kicked Thersites
(no. 142).
Attributed to Hill by the CBEL.

Hill, Robert.
The Character of a Jew. [Chester?], 1753.*
Watt 497.

Howard, Leonard.
A Collection Of Letters. By L. Howard, D.D.
London: Printed for the Author, And sold
by E. Withers . . . MDCCLIII.
4°, 2 vols.
(1) Mr. Hastings (p. 152).
The paging is badly confused.

[Le Cointe?]
The Character of true Love. Translated from
the French Author's Manuscript by J. Peyton.
London: Printed for J. Bouquet. 1753.*
12°.
BSC 2617.

Maintenon, Françoise d'Aubigné, Marquise de.
The Letters of Madame De Maintenon; and
other Eminent Persons in the Age of Lewis
XIV. To which are added Some Characters.
Translated from the French. London: Printed
for J. Robinson, 1753.*
BSC 2618.
See 1759.

[Murphy, Arthur.]
The Gray's Inn Journal. By Charles Ranger,
Esq. . . . Nos. 1–52. Sept. 29, 1753–Sept. 21,
1754. London: Printed for W. Faden . . . and
J. Bouquet.
3°, text pp. 1–312.
(1) Jack Wildair, a modern philosopher and a
philosophic rake (no. 23, p. 135).
Previously published in The Craftsman. Attributed to
Murphy in the CBEL, and reprinted in his Works, 1786.

[Richard, William?]
Wallography. Dean Swift's Ghost. 1753.*
Text pp. 1–60.
Possibly a reprint of 1682, though the title sounds differ-
ent.

[Ward, Edward.]
The London Spy. 1753.*
Reprinted from 1698.

1754

Anonymous.
The New Universal Magazine . . . Published
monthly according to Act of Parliament. By
M. Cooper . . . London. 1754.
4°.
(1) Sir Isaac Newton (Vol. V, p. 144), (2) Sejanus, a prime minister and proselyte (V, 213),
(3) Sir Francis Bacon (V, 249).

Butler, Samuel.
Posthumous Works.*
Reprinted from 1715.

[Cave, Edward.]
The Gentleman's Magazine. Vol. XXIV. 1754.
(1) The parson (p. 39), (2) Proper ingredients to
make a modern beau (p. 90).

Fielding, Henry.

The Life Of Mr. Jonathan Wild The Great. A New Edition. . . . By Henry Fielding, Esq; London: Printed for A. Millar . . . MDCC-LIV.

12°, text pp. 1–263.
(1) Mr. Thomas Heartfree (p. 64, Book II, chap. I), (2) Jonathan Wild (255, IV, 15).
First published 1753. Reprinted many times.

Griffiths, Joshua.

The Christian Teacher characterized; an Ordination Sermon. 1754.*

Text pp. 1–443.

Maintenon, Françoise d'Aubigné, Marquise de.

Letters. 1754.*
See 1759.

[Shower, John.]

Some Account of the holy life and death of Mr. H. Gearing . . . With the trial and character of a real Christian. London, 1754.*
Reprinted from 1694.

Spence, Joseph.

An Account of the Life, Character, and Poems of Mr. Blacklock; Student of Philosophy, in the University of Edinburgh. By the Rev. Mr. Spence. . . . London: Printed for R. and J. Dodsley . . . MDCCLIV.

8°, text pp. 3–61.
(1) Thomas Blacklock (p. 9).

Swift, Jonathan.

Brotherly Love. A Sermon, Preached in St. Patrick's Church; On December 1st, 1717. By Dr. Jonathan Swift . . . Dublin: Printed by George Faulkner . . . MDCCLIV.

4°, text pp. 5–26.
(1) A man truly moderate (p. 21), (2) A moderate man, in the new meaning of the word (p. 22).
The sermon is dated at the end, Nov. 29, 1717. The CBEL records no printing before 1754.

[Trenchard, John, and Gordon, Thomas.]

Cato's Letters. 1754.*
12°, 4 vols.
Reprinted from 1721.

1755

Anonymous.

Detraction. An Essay in Two Parts. . . . London: Printed for J. Bouquet. 1755.*
8°.
(1) Mr. Tattle.

The Devil upon Crutches in England. 1755.*
See 1759.

The Friend. 1755.*
(1) Marcia (no. 4).

[Arnold, Cornelius.]

The Mirror. A Poetical Essay In the Manner of Spenser. . . . Anno M.DCC.LV.

4°, text pp. 5–19.
(1) The general (p. 5), (2) The magistrate (p. 6), (3) The miser (p. 7), (4) The epicure (p. 8), (5) The fine lady (p. 8), (6) The beau (p. 9), (7) The parson (p. 10), (8) The statesman (p. 11), (9) The actor (p. 12), (10) The physician (p. 13), (11) The fox-hunter (p. 14), (12) The prude (p. 15), (13) The lawyer (p. 16), (14) The dotard (p. 17), (15) The groupe (p. 18), (16) The lazar (p. 19).
The dedication to Garrick is signed C. Arnold.

Birch, Thomas.

Remarks on the Life of Archbishop Tillotson. Third Edition with Additions, London, Printed for W. Owen, 1755.*
(1) Archbishop Tillotson (p. 98).
According to the CBEL, Birch's life of Tillotson first appeared prefixed to Tillotson's Works in 1752; it was reprinted separately in 1752 and, in enlarged form, in 1753. But the author of Remarks on the Life is there given as George Smith; it appeared in 1753, 1754, and (enlarged) 1755.

[Colman, George, and others.]

The Connoisseur. By Mr. Town, Critic and Censor-General. . . . London: Printed for R. Baldwyn . . . MDCCLV [–VI].

fo, 2 vols.
(1) Demi-reps (no. 4), (2) Loving couples (no. 7), (3) Bookwits (no. 11), (4) Rustic politicians (no. 13), (5) An affected woman (no. 14), (6) Gamblers, and especially Montano (no. 15), (7) Virtuosi (no. 18), (8) A fashionable family (no. 22), (9) Rustic players (no. 23), (10) Vain people (no. 25), (11) Tom Dare-devil (no. 28), (12) A sharper (no. 40), (13) The English Club (no. 42), (14) A theater audience (no. 43), (15) Ladies of Great Britain (no. 44), (16) The Last Guinea Club (no. 50), (17) Mistresses and their keepers (no. 51), (18) A drunken lady (no. 53), (19) A frolick (no. 54), (20) Evites (no. 55), (21) Men who should be pressed into military service (no. 58), (22) Goody Cripple (no. 59), (23) Sectaries (no. 61), (24) Varieties of dog (no. 64, a fantasy), (25) The male beauty (no. 65), (26) A citizen's family at Vauxhall (no. 68).
Attributed to Colman by the CBEL.

Fordyce, David.

Theodorus: A Dialogue concerning the Art of

Preaching. By Mr. David Fordyce. . . . The Third Edition. . . . London: Printed for R. and J. Dodsley . . . M.DCC.LV.

12°, text pp. 3–298.

(1) Agoretes, a passionate lover of nature (p. 4), (2) Theodorus, a man of great simplicity of character (p. 57), (3) The good preacher (p. 197).

Hervey, James.

Theron and Aspasio: Or, A Series Of Dialogues And Letters, upon the Most Important and Interesting Subjects. In Three Volumes. By James Hervey. . . . London: Printed by Charles Rivington, For John and James Rivington . . . MDCCLV.

3 vols.

(1) Theron and Aspasio (Dialogue I).

Leechman, William.

The Temper, Character, and Duty of a Minister Of The Gospel. . . . By William Leechman . . . The Sixth Edition. Printed and sold by Robert and Andrew Foulis, at Glasgow: M.DCC.LV.

6°, text pp. 3–71.

Begins: "The wiser and more considerate part of mankind."

BSC 2620.

A reprint of 1744.

Shakespeare, the ghost of [pseudonym].

Memoirs of the Shakespeare's-Head Covent-Garden: In which are introduced Many entertaining Adventures, And several remarkable Characters. By the Ghost of Shakespeare. London, Printed for F. Noble, 1755.*

[Trenchard, John, and Gordon, Thomas.]

Cato's Letters: Or, Essays on Liberty . . . In Four Volumes. . . . The Sixth Editon, corrected . . . London: Printed for J. Walthoe [and several others] . . . M.DCC.LV.

12°, 4 vols.

(1) as in 1721.

Walker, Samuel.

The Christian. 1755.*

See 1759.

[Ward, Edward.]

Female Policy Detected. 1755.*

See the undated edition.

1756

[Baker, Henry.]

The Universal Spectator. Third Edition.*

(1) The author (Vol. I, p. 5), (2) Scholastic beaus

(II, 12), (3) Weathercock and Surly (II, 17), (4) Sir Peevy Captious (II, 94), (5) An excellent actor (II, 104), (6) An admirable preacher (II, 136), (7) A clergyman (II, 138), (8) Various ladies (II, 156), (9) An honest and a crafty merchant (II, 208), (10) A maid's husband (III, 110), (11) Harry Mutable (III, 136), (12) Hypocrites (III, 222), (13) A flatterer, from Terence (III, 270), (14) A learned coxcomb (IV, 12), (15) Scandal Club tormentors (IV, 36), (16) An excellent actor, from Overbury but applied to the late Benjamin Griffin (IV, 104), (17) General characteristics of women (IV, 156), (18) Sir Penurious Gripe (IV, 165), (19) Sir John Evergreen (IV, 255), (20) A character (no. 117, Jan. 2, 1731), (21) Captain Frontley (no. 220, 1732), (22) Agresthes (no. 356), (23) Eubulus and Harry Modely (June 16, 1739), (24) Various virtuosi (August 31, 1756).

Blacklock, Thomas.

Poems By Mr. Thomas Blacklock. To which is Prefix'd, An Account of the Life, Character, and Writings, of the Author, By the Reverend Mr. Spence, . . . The Third Edition. London: Printed for the Author, by R. and J. Dodsley, in Pallmall, M.DCC.LVI.

8°, text pp. 1–236.

(1) Thomas Blacklock, by Spence (p. viii).

Spence's character is not included in the first edition of the poems, 1746.

[Greville, Fulke.]

Maxims, Characters, And Reflections, Critical, Satyrical, and Moral. . . . London: Printed for J. and R. Tonson . . . MDCCLVI.

8°, text pp. 1–268.

(1) Chrysantes (p. 2), (2) Arcon (p. 5), (3) Meron (p. 8), (4) Polydore and Craterus (p. 11), (5) Praxiteles (p. 13), (6) Fogramo (p. 18), (7) Phorbas and Phormio (p. 24), (8) Eschylus (p. 31), (9) Dormion (p. 32), (10) Theocles and Cleon (p. 33), (11) Melissa (p. 44), (12) Camilla p. 47), (13) Flora (p. 50), (14) Pylades and Orestes (p. 53), (15) Fabricius (p. 79), (16) Sicinius (p. 98), (17) Corinna, Pharamond, and Fulvius (p. 114), (18) Torismond (p. 115), (19) Strabo (p. 118), (20) Brillus (p. 120), (21) Phocion (p. 122), (22) Adrastus (p. 124), (23) Furio (p. 128), (24) Peleus (p. 132), (25) Hermion (p. 137), (26) Aristarchus (p. 139), (27) Clitander (p. 148), (28) Misanthes (p. 152), (29) Helluo and Narcissus (p. 161), (30) Delicacy and captiousness (p. 163), (31) Minucius (p. 176), (32) Crito (p. 191), (33) Timoleon (p. 200), (34) Sophron (p. 215), (35) Avaro (p. 221), (36) Phryne (p. 222), (37) Hippias (p. 231), (38) Trasimond (p. 235), (39) Clara (p. 240),

(40) Silia (p. 242), (41) Cleontes (p. 253), (42) Pride (p. 256).
BSC 2621.
Attributed to Greville by the CBEL.

[Henry, D., and Cave, R.]
The Gentleman's Magazine. Vol. XXVI. 1756.
(1) Drunkenness. A satire (p. 36), (2) The cit's country box (p. 445).

Howard, Leonard.
A Collection of letters and State Papers. London, 1756.*
Reprinted from 1753.

[Murphy, Arthur.]
The Gray's Inn Journal. 1756.*
Reprinted from 1753.

Overbury, Sir. Thomas.
The Miscellaneous Works in Verse and Prose of Sir Thomas Overbury, Knt. with Memoirs of his Life. The Tenth Edition. . . . London: Printed for W. Owen . . . MDCCLVI.
12°, text pp. 1–252.
(1–80) as in ninth impression, 1616, but omitting Wotton's The Character of a Happy Life.
Murphy 25. BSC 2622.

Spence, Joseph.
An Account of . . . Mr. Blacklock. 1756.*
Reprinted from 1754.

[Ward, Edward.]
The History of the London Clubs. The Seventh Edition. 1756.*
Reprinted from 1709.

[Ward, Edward.]
The Wooden World Dissected: In The Character Of A Ship of War: As also, The Characters of all the Officers . . . By the Author of the London-Spy. The Fifth Edition. London, Printed for J. Wren . . . 1756.
4°, text pp. 1–76.
(1–14) as in 1707.

[Ward, Edward.]
The Wooden World Dissected: In the Character of A Ship of War: As Also, The Characters of all the Officers; from the Captain to the Common Sailor. . . . By the Author of the London Spy. The Seventh Edition. London; Printed in the Year 1756.*
(1–14) as in 1707.
The Dedication is signed Manly Plain-Dealer. The Address to the Reader is dated Portsmouth, Nov. 24, 1746.

1757

Anonymous.
Proposed for the Press . . . Curious and useful observations and directions especially concerning the education of young gentlemen . . . etc. Boston, new Printing Office opposite the Old Brick Meeting-House on Cornhill by Benjamin Mecom, 1757.*
(1) Fool (p. 16), (2) Gentleman (p. 10), (3) Wise man (p. 15).

[Brown, John.]
An Estimate of the Manners.*
See 1758.
Attributed to Brown by the CBEL.
There are said to have been five editions in 1757.

[Greville, Fulke.]
Maxims, Characters, and Reflections. Second Edition. 1757.*
Reprinted from 1756.

[Henry, D., and Cave, R.]
The Gentleman's Magazine. Vol. XXVII. 1757.
(1) The squire (p. 136), (2) The beau parson. Or, the male coquet (p. 565).

1758

Anonymous.
The Character of a Good Ruler. . . Being a discourse [on Matt. xx, 22,23] preached at a country parish-church in the diocese of Norwich. Ipswich. 1758.*
4°.

[Brown, John.]
An Estimate Of The Manners And Principles Of The Times. By the Author of Essays on the Characteristics, &c. . . . The Seventh Edition. . . . London, Printed for L. Davis and C. Reymers . . . . 1758.
4°, 2 vols.
(1) The French nation (Vol. I, p. 141), (2) A great minister (II, 252), (3) An impartial political writer (II, 260).
First published in 1757.

Byles, Mather.
A Sermon Preached at the Ordination of . . . Mr. Mather Byles [the younger?] . . . New London, 1758.*
Much of the sermon is thrown into the form of a character of a worthy minister.

[Forrester, James.]
The Polite Philosopher: or an Essay on that

Art, which Makes a Man happy in Himself, and agreeable to Others. . . . The Fifteenth Edition. London, Printed: New York, Reprinted, and Sold by J. Parker and W. Weyman . . . 1758.

4°, text pp. 1–44.

(1–4) as in 1734.

[Head, Richard.]

The English Rogue. 1758.*

Reprinted from 1665.

[Johnson, Samuel.]

The Idler.*

See 1761.

1759

Anonymous.

The Devil upon Crutches in England . . . By a Gentleman of Oxford. . . . The Fourth Edition. London, Printed for L. Pottinger . . . M.DCC.LIX.

12°, text pp. 1–190.

(1) A female gamester (p. 12), (2) A highwayman (p. 17), (3) Florio, a ruined man (p. 21), (4) Clandro, a gamester (p. 25), (5) A prelate and his chaplain (p. 31), (6) A miser (p. 34), (7) A gouty old gentleman (p. 36), (8) A whore (p. 46), (9) Several miserable prisoners in Newgate (p. 64), (10) Occupants of Bedlam (p. 71), (11) London rascals (p. 79), (12) Occupants of the Foundling Hospital (p. 116), (13) M. Ragout, a French cook (p. 132), (14) Vallius, a senator (p. 143), (15) Marcus, an author (p. 167).

Published earlier in 1755.

Butler, Samuel.

The Genuine Remains In Verse and Prose Of Mr. Samuel Butler, Author of Hudibras. Published from the Original Manuscripts. . . . In Two Volumes. . . . London: Printed for J. and R. Tonson, . . . MDCCLIX.

8°, 2 vols.

(1) A modern politician (Vol. II, p. 1), (2) A hypocritical nonconformist (II, 35), (3) A republican (II, 52), (4) A politician (II, 60), (5) A state-convert (II, 62), (6) A risker (II, 65), (7) A modern statesman (II, 69), (8) A duke of Bucks (II, 72), (9) A degenerate noble (II, 77), (10) A huffing-courtier (II, 80), (11) A court-beggar (II, 86), (12) A bumpkin, or country squire (II, 90), (13) An antiquary (II, 94), (14) A proud man (II, 98), (15) A fifth monarchy man (II, 101), (16) The henpeckt man (II, 104), (17) A small poet (II, 107), (18) A philosopher (II, 128), (19) A fantastic (II, 131), (20) A melancholy man (II, 134), (21) A haranguer (II, 137), (22) A Popish priest (II, 141), (23) A traveller (II, 144), (24) A Catholic (II, 147), (25) A curious man (II, 150), (26) A ranter (II, 153), (27) A corrupt judge (II, 155), (28) An amorist (II, 158), (29) An astrologer (II, 161), (30) A lawyer (II, 164), (31) A herald (II, 173), (32) A latitudinarian (II, 177), (33) A mathematician (II, 179), (34) An epigrammatist (II, 183), (35) A virtuoso (II, 185), (36) A justice of the peace (II, 190), (37) A fanatic (II, 194), (38) An intelligencer (II, 197), (39) A proselite (II, 200), (40) A clown (II, 203) (41) A quibbler (II, 206), (42) A wooer (II, 209), (43) An impudent man (II, 212), (44) An imitator (II, 216), (45) A time-server (II, 219), (46) A prater (II, 222), (47) An hermetic philosopher (II, 225), (48) An alderman (II, 253), (49) A disputant (II, 256), (50) A sot (II, 259), (51) An atheist (II, 261), (52) A juggler (II, 263), (53) A sceptic (II, 266), (54) A projector (II, 268), (55) A complimenter (II, 271), (56) A churchwarden (II, 273), (57) A romance-writer (II, 275), (58) A cheat (II, 278), (59) A libeller (II, 281), (60) A tedious man (II, 284), (61) A taylor (II, 287), (62) A factious member (II, 290), (63) A pretender (II, 293), (64) A newsmonger (II, 296), (65) An embassador (II, 298), (66) A playwriter (II, 301), (67) A mountebank (II, 304), (68) A modern critic (II, 307), (69) A wittal (II, 310), (70) A busy man (II, 313), (71) A litigious man (II, 315), (72) A pedant (II, 318), (73) A hunter (II, 321), (74) A humorist (II, 324), (75) A leader of a faction (II, 326), (76) A debauched man (II, 329), (77) A seditious man (II, 331), (78) An affected man (II, 334), (79) A medicine-taker (II, 336), (80) The rude man (II, 338), (81) A miser (II, 341), (82) A rabble (II, 345), (83) A shop-keeper (II, 348), (84) A Quaker (II, 351), (85) A swearer (II, 354), (86) A luxurious man (II, 357), (87) An ungrateful man (II, 360), (88) A knight of the post (II, 363), (89) An undeserving favourite (II, 366), (90) A cuckold (II, 372), (91) A malicious man (II, 375), (92) A squire of dames (II, 379), (93) A knave (II, 382), (94) An anabaptist (II, 385), (95) A vintner (II, 390), (96) A hypocrite (II, 393), (97) An opiniaster (II, 396), (98) A choleric man (II, 399), (99) A lover (II, 402), (100) A translator (II, 405), (101) A rebel (II, 408), (102) A city-wit (II, 411), (103) A superstitious man (II, 414), (104) A drole (II, 416), (105) An empiric (II, 419), (106) An obstinate man (II, 422), (107) A zealot (II, 425), (108) An overdoer (II, 427), (109) A jealous man (II, 430), (110) An insolent man (II, 432), (111) A rash man (II, 434), (112) A pimp (II, 437), (113) An affected or formal man (II, 441) (114) A flatterer (II, 443), (115) A prodigal (II, 446), (116) A pettifogger (II, 449), (117) A bankrupt (II, 452), (118) The inconstant (II, 455), (119) A

horse-courser (II, 458), (120) A glutton (II, 461), (121) A ribald (II, 463).

Maintenon, Françoise d'Aubigné, Marquise de.

Letters of Madame de Maintenon. Translated from the French. Volume the First. London: Printed for L. Davis and C. Reymers . . . M.DCC.LIX.

12°, text pp. 1–316. There are 2 vols, but all characters are in Vol. I.
(1) The Prince of Conde (p. 304), (2) Madame de la Valiere (p. 304), (3) M. de la Rochefoucault (p. 305), (4) Madame de Montespan (p. 306), (5) The Duke of Vendome (p. 306), (6) The Dauphin (p. 307), (7) Madame de Longueville (p. 307), (8) Marshal Turenne (p. 308), (9) Monsieur Colbert (p. 309), (10) The Marquiss de Louvois (p. 309), (11) The Prince of Conti (p. 310), (12) Marshal Luxembourg (p. 311), (13) The Duke of Orleans (p. 312), (14) Madame de Fiesque (p. 312), (15) M. de Berbezieux (p. 312), (16) Father de la Chaise (p. 313), (17) Madame de Fontanges (p. 313), (18) The Dauphiness (p. 314), (19) M. de Harlai, Archbishop of Paris (p. 314), (20) The Marquis de Seignelai (son of Colbert) (p. 315), (21) Louis XIV (p. 315), (22) Marshal Catinat (p. 316).

There were earlier editions in 1753 and 1754. According to an advertisement (Vol. I, p. 303), only Nos. 1, 7, 8, 9, 10, 13 are by Madame de Maintenon; the others are by another hand.

Walker, Samuel.

The Christian. Being a Course of Practical Sermons. . . . By Samuel Walker, A.B. Curate of Truro in Cornwal, and formerly of Exeter-College in Oxford. The Third Edition Corrected. . . . London, Printed for Edward Dilly. . . . 1759.

12°, text pp. 1–286.
(1) A careless sinner (p. 108), (2) A believer, a new creature (p. 111).

First published 1755. There were several other editions.

1760

Anonymous.

Wit and humour for town and country; being a new Collection of Repartees, Bon-Mots, Humourous Stories, and Characters, etc. To which are added — Six Humorous Characters by a celebrated Wit, &c. London: Printed for William Smith, at the Printing Office in Catharine Street.*

8°, text pp. 1–56.
BSC 2623.

Brown, Thomas.

Works. Ninth Edition. 1760.*

Reprinted from 1730.

Chandler, Samuel.

The Character of a great and good King Full of Days, Riches, and Honour. A Sermon Preached on Occasion of the Death of his late Majesty King George II . . . In The Old Jury, November the 9th. 1760. By S. Chandler . . . London, Printed for J. Noon . . . and A. Millar . . . 1760.

4°, text pp. 1–47.
Begins: "These words of the sacred historian."

[Henry, D., and Cave, R.]

The Gentleman's Magazine. Vol. XXX. 1760.
(1) A description of two celebrated riders of the modern Pegasus: from an ode to obscurity, lately published with an ode to oblivion (p. 291), (2) The picture of old age; paraphrased from the seven first verses of the 12th chapter of Ecclesiastes (p. 383), (3) The happy man (p. 536).

[Ridley, James.]

The Schemer. 1760.*

See 1763.

[Ward, Edward.]

The Wooden World Dissected, In The Characters Of I. A Ship of War . . . 1760.*

Reprinted from 1707.

1761

Anonymous.

A Character of the Rev. W. Law. London, 1761.*

s.sh.12°.
BSC 2624.

A Curious Collection of Letters . . . Chiefly Extracted From the Westminster Journal . . . London, Printed for and Sold by H. Serjeant . . . 1761.

12°, text pp. 1–322.
(1) The new-comers, including John the carter, Sandy Longbib, Daniel Raven, and Old Will (p. 214, from the Westminster Journal of September 25, 1742), (2) Will Trimmer and Bob Monopoly, late tally-man (p. 222, from the Westminster Journal of October 9, 1742).
BSC 2605.

There was an earlier edition in 1742.

Carsdale, K.

The Distinctive Character and Honour of the Righteous Man, Considered in Two Discourses. London, 1761.*

[Dodsley, Robert (editor).]

Fugitive Pieces, on Various Subjects. By several Authors. In Two Volumes. . . . London, Printed for R. and J. Dodsley . . . MDCC-LXI.

2 vols.

(1) The pretty gentleman, 1747 (Vol. I, p. 195), (2) The polite philosopher, or, an essay on that art which makes a man happy in himself, and agreeable to others . . . first printed in the year 1734 (I, 223).

[Hill, Sir Richard.]

An Address to Persons of Fashion, Containing some Particulars relating to Balls. . . . In which is introduced the Character of Lucinda. The third edition. . . . London, 1761.*

(1) Lucinda (Lecture vii).

Attributed to Hill by Halkett and Laing. See 1771.

1762

Anonymous.

The Political Controversy; or, Weekly magazine of ministerial and anti-ministerial essays; consisting of . . . The Trimmer. 1762.*

(1) A farmer, (2) A hop-planter.

[Goldsmith, Oliver.]

The Citizen of the World . . . London: Printed for J. Newbery. . . MDCCLXII.

12°, 2 vols.

(1) A woman's man (no. 9), (2) The man in black (no. 26), (3) Beau Tibbs, a trifler (nos. 54–55).

Attributed to Goldsmith by the CBEL. Often reprinted.

[Johnson, Samuel.]

The Idler. In Two Volumes . . . London, Printed for J. Newbery . . . MDCCLXI.

12°, 2 vols.

(1) Tom Tempest, a Jacobite, and Jack Sneaker, a Whig (no. 10), (2) Jack Whirler, a bustling man (no. 19), (3) Sober, busy at trifles (no. 31), (4) The bargain-hunter (no. 35), (5) Molly Quick's mistress, a dealer in riddles (no. 46), (6) A city wit (no. 47), (7) Tom Restless, an ambulatory student (no. 48), (8) Will Marvel, of the wonderful tales (no. 49), (9) Sophron, the prudent (no. 57), (10) Dick Minim, the critic (no. 60), (11) Tom Tranquil, the easy going (no. 73), (12) Tom Steady, the platitudinarian, Dick Snug, the sly wit, Will Startle, the emotional, Jack Solid, the dull pedant, and Dick Misty, a man of penetration (no. 78), (13) Dick Wormwood, a carper, Bob Sturdy, of unalterable opinion, Phil Gentle, the neutral, and Sim Scruple, always in doubt (no. 83), (14) Tom Double, Will Puzzle, proud of prophetic ability, and Ned Smuggle, the secretive (no. 92), (15) Sam Softly, a sugar baker (no.

93), (16) Hacho, king of Lapland (no. 96), (17) Miss Gentle, a good woman (no. 100).

First appeared 1758–1760. Several times reprinted.

Law, William.

The Works Of The Reverend William Law, A.M. In Nine Volumes. . . . London . . . J. Richardson . . . M,DCC,LXII.

4°, 9 vols.

(1) A Practical Treatise of Christian Perfection (Vol. III, p. 1), (2) A Serious Call to a Devout and Holy Life (IV, 1).

[Murphy, Arthur.]

The Auditor. 1762.*

(1) The favourite of the venal (no. 2), (2) The favourite of the mob (no. 2), (3) The favourite of the prince (no. 2), (4) A patriot prince (no. 5).

[Scott, Sarah.]

A Description of Millenium Hall, and the Country Adjacent: Together with the Characters of the Inhabitants . . . As May excite in the Reader proper Sentiments of Humanity . . . By a Gentleman on his Travels. London: Printed for J. Newbery, MDCCLXII.

12°, text pp. 1–262.

(1) Mr. Lamont (p. 3), (2) Mrs. Selvyn (p. 9), (3) Mrs. Marcel (p. 9), (4) Mrs. Trentham (p. 9), (5) Lady Mary Jones (p. 9), (6) Mrs. Morgan (p. 10), (7) Sir Charles Melvyn (p. 39), (8) Mr. d'Avora (p. 54), (9) Mrs. Susanna Morgan (p. 104), (10) Lady Lambton (p. 110), (11) Sir Edward Lambton (p. 111), (12) Lady Mary Jones (p. 156), (13) Lady Sheerness (p. 156), (14) Lady Brumpton (p. 180), (15) Miss Selvyn (p. 195), (16) Lady Emilia Reynolds (p. 201), (17) Mrs. Ilworth (p. 227), (18) Harriet Trentham (p. 228).

Attributed to Sarah Scott by the CBEL.

[Shaw, Peter.]

The Tablet, or Pictures of real Life. Representing Vices and Virtues . . . Fopperies, fooleries, etc. of the age . . . with the true characters of the wise and good; in select essays, serious and jocose upon the most interesting subjects. 1762 [or 1763].*

Attributed to Shaw by Halkett and Laing.

[Smollett, Tobias George.]

The Adventures of Sir Launcelot Greaves. By the Author of Roderick Random. In Two Volumes. . . . London: Printed for J. Coote . . . MDCCLXII.

12°, 2 vols.

(1) The characters (Vol. I, p. 1), (2) A modern

magistrate (I, 220), (3) Sir Sycamore (II, 29), (4) An affected widow (II, 183).

First printed in The British Magazine, 1760–61. Many times reprinted.

Yardley, Edward.

Philotheus: or the Character of a Reverend Learned and Pious Divine. In four Dialogues. London: Printed by J. and W. Oliver for B. Dod. 1762.*
BSC 2626.

1763

Anonymous.

The British Antidote to Caledonian Poison. The fifth edition. 1763–64.*
12°, 2 vols.
(1) The kingdom and people of Scotland.

The Character of a Disbanded Courtier. To-day is so like Yesterday, it cheats; We take the lying Sister for the same. Young's Night Thoughts. London: Printed for G. Burnett, at Bishop Burnett's Head, near Arundel-Street, in the Strand. 1763.*
8°, text pp. 1–12.
Begins: "He was born of a considerable family, heir to a fortune above contemptible."

A reprint of 1682.

Adams, John.

Recipe to make a patriot.*
Manuscript.
Begins: "Take of the several species of malevolence."

Entered in his diary under date of 1763. Printed in his Works, 1850.

[Bickerstaff, Isaac.]

Stephen's Green, a Rhapsody, exhibiting the characters of the Belles, Beaux, Bucks, Bloods, Fleshes, Fubbles, Jemmies, Jessamies, etc. of all ranks and professions that frequent the Beaux Walk. Dublin, 1763.*

Fitzosborne, Sir Thomas.

The Letters of Sir Thomas Fitzosborne, on Several Subjects . . . The Sixth Edition. London, Printed for R. and J. Dodsley . . . MDCCLXIII.
8°, text pp. 1–452.
(1) Varus, by William Melmoth (p. 23).

Gordon, Thomas.

A Cordial For Low Spirits . . . By Thomas Gordon . . . In Three Volumes. The Third

Impression . . . London: Printed for Messrs. Wilson and Fell . . . MDCCLXIII.
12°, 3 vols.
(1–2) as in 1751.

[Henry, D., and Cave, R.]

The Gentleman's Magazine. Vol. XXXIII. 1763.
(1) John Earl Grenville. By the Hon H.W. (p. 38), (2) The beauties of Epsom (p. 138).

[Ridley, James.]

The Schemer: Or, Universal Satirist. By That Great Philosopher Helter Van Scelter. . . . London . . . J. Wilkie . . . MDCCLXIII.
12°, text pp. 3–278.
(1) A minister of state, and several kinds of politicians (no. 6, p. 77).

Attributed to Ridley by the CBEL. This volume of periodical essays first appeared 1760–62; the essay noted above, no. 6, is dated July 29, 1760.

[Silence, Timothy.]

The Foundling Hospital for Wit . . . Containing All the Satires, Odes, Ballads, Epigrams, &c. that have been wrote since the Change of the Ministry, many of which have never before been printed. . . . London: Printed 1743. Reprinted for W. Webb . . . MDCCLXIII.
4°, 6 numbers. In verse.
(1–2) as in 1746.

Wesley, John.

The Character Of A Methodist. By John Wesley, M.A. . . . The Eighth Edition . . . Bristol: Printed by William Pine, 1763.
6°, text pp. 5–12.
Begins: "The distinguishing Marks of a METHODIST are not, His Opinions of any Sort.

Published earlier 1739, 1742, 1743, 1747, 1751.

1764

Anonymous.

The Visitor. By Several Hands. Published by William Dodd . . . Volume II. London: Printed for Edward and Charles Dilly . . . M.DCC.LXIV.
12°, text pp. 1–307.
(1) Tom Sweep-stakes (p. 28), (2) Jonas Crop-cram'd (p. 29), (3) Harry Guittar (p. 30), (4) Solomon Tomeswell (p. 31).

Border-line example of character.

Apthorp, East.

The Character and Example of a Christian Woman. A Discourse at Christ-Church, Cambridge, on the death of Mrs. Anne Wheelwright. By East Apthorp, M.A. Missionary at Cambridge. . . . Boston . . . Green and Russell. MDCCLXIV.

4°, text pp. 3–32.
Begins: "Part I. Conversant as I have been in the *howse of* mourning. . . ."

[Henry, D., and Cave, R.]

The Gentleman's Magazine. Vol. XXXIV. 1764.
(1) Characters in St. Giles's (p. 140), (2) King Henry VIII. From a poem called Priviledge. Just published (p. 189), (3) The happy man (p. 492).

[Moore, A.]

The Life and Character Of The Late Lord Chancellor Jeffreys. . . . London: Printed for J. Pottinger . . . MDCCLXIV.

4°, text pp. 9–54.
(1) Judge Jeffreys (p. 44).

Rogers, Samuel.

Poems on Various Occasions. Bath. 1764–82.*
2 vols.
(1) The glutton (Vol. I, p. 37, in verse), (2) The miser (II, 50), (3) Will Whimble, or the moder tigellinus (II, 116, in verse).

[Scott, Sarah.]

A Description of Millenium Hall, &c., with Characters of the Inhabitants. J. Newberry, 1764.*
BSC 2627.
Reprinted from 1762.

1765

[D'Argens, John Baptist de Boyer, Marquis.]

The Chinese Spy. . . . In Six Volumes. . . . London: Printed for S. Bladon . . . MDCCLXV.

6 vols.
(1) A Londoner of Lombard Street (Vol. IV, letter 30), (2) A Londoner of St. James's Square (IV, 30).
Attributed to D'Argens by Halkett and Laing. There was an earlier edition in 1752.

[Henry, D., and Cave, R.]

The Gentleman's Magazine. Vol. XXXV. 1765.
(1) A character (p. 186), (2) A happy life (p. 231), (3) The British epicure. Imitated from Horace (p. 433).

[Scott, Sarah.]

The Man of Real Sensibility: or The History

Of Sir George Ellison. Printed for Chapman Whitcomb. 1765.*
See 1774.

[Stevens, George Alexander.]

A Celebrated Lecture upon Heads. 1765.*
See 1766.

1766

[Henry, D., and Cave, R.]

The Gentleman's Magazine. Vol. XXXVI. 1766.
(1) The furniture of a beau's mind (p. 427).

[Stevens, George Alexander.]

The Celebrated Lecture on Heads . . . The Sixth Edition. . . . Printed for J. Pridden . . . 1766.

fo, text pp. 2–8.
(1) A quack doctor (p. 2), (2) A cuckold (p. 2), (3) A counsellor (p. 2), (4) Sir Languish Lisping (p. 3), (5) A horse-jockey (p. 3), (6) Generous, honest, clever fellows, a parcel of noughts (p. 3), (7) Laughing and crying philosophers (p. 5), (8) An old bachelor (p. 5), (9) Mama's darling, the tea-table critic (p. 6), (10) The city politician (p. 7), (11) A sharper (p. 7), (12) A wit, Tristram Shandy (p. 8).

First published in 1765. Reprinted 1766, 1770, 1772, 178–, 1784, 1785, 1787, 1788 (two editions), 1795, 1799, 1800, 1802, 1804, 1806, 1808, 1820, 1821, 1823. Some of these issues are spurious. According to the British Museum Catalogue, the first genuine edition is that of 1785. The contents vary widely.

1767

[Henry, D.]

The Gentleman's Magazine. Vol. XXXVII. 1767.
(1) Characters. A rhapsody (p. 470), (2) An Utopian character (p. 516).

[Hill, Sir Richard.]

An Address to Persons of Fashion. 1767.*
See 1771.

[Scott, Sarah.]

A Description of Millenium Hall. 1767.*
Reprinted from 1762.

1768

[Greville, Fulke.]

Maxims, Characters, And Reflections . . . The Third Edition . . . London: Printed for T. Cadwell . . . MDCCLXVIII.

8°, text pp. 1–223.
(1–42) as in 1756.

Mulso, Thomas.

Callistus; or, the Man Of Fashion, And Sophronius, or, the Country Gentleman. In Three Dialogues. By Thomas Mulso . . . London: Printed for Benjamin White . . . MDCCXLVIII.

8°, text pp. 1–213.

(1) Callistus (p. 1), (2) Sophronius (p. 2), (3) Urania (p. 73), (4) Eugenia (p. 111), (5) Melinda (p. 111).

The British Museum has a second edition of the same year.

1769

Anonymous.

The Boston Chronicle. 1769.*

(1) Members of the Medler Club (p. 285, Sept. 4–7).

The Oxford Magazine: or, University Museum. . . . London, Printed for the Authors . . . MDCCLXIX[–XXI].

4°, 7 vols. (through 1771).

(1) A good prince, by Constantine (Vol. II, p. 209), (2) An over-indulged son (VII, 96), (3) The miser (VII, 152, in verse), (4) The virtuous man (VII, 153, in verse), (5) A truly wise man, from the French of M. du Marsais (VII, 189), (6) Peregrine Puzzle, a singular man (VII, 274).

The Salem Gazette. 1769.*

(1) A French woman (May 16), (2) A great and good judge (August 1), (3) William Pitt the elder, by John Wilkes (October 3), (4) Captain James Griffin (December 5).

Dunkin, William.

Select Poetical Works of the late William Dunkin, D.D. In Two Volumes. . . . Dublin, Printed by W.G. Jones . . . MDCCLXIX.

2 vols. In verse.

(1) The happy man (Vol. I, 109), (2) The Bramin (II, 470), (3) A good parson, from Chaucer (II, 480).

Pennecuik, Alexander.

A Collection of Scots Poems on several occasions, By the late Mr Alexander Pennecuik, Gent. and Others. . . . Edinburgh: Printed for W. Coke . . . MDCCLXIX.

6°, text pp. 1–154.

(1) A prison (p. 37), (2) A gauger (p. 53), (3) A vintner (p. 56), (4) A whipman (p. 60), (5) The self-tormentor (p. 74).

1770

Anonymous.

Characterism, or the Modern Age Display'd . . . with a Poetical Essay on each Character. In Two Parts. [1770]*

Probably a reprint of 1750.

The Lady's Magazine; Or, Entertaining Companion For the Fair Sex . . . London: Printed for Robinson and Roberts . . . MDCCLXX.

4°, text pp. 5–552.

(1) Beau Trifle (Vol. I, p. 21), (2) Mrs. Bustle, a notable woman (I, 228).

[Felltham, Owen.]

A Brief Character of the Low Countries. 1770.*

Reprinted from 1660.

[Henry, D.]

The Gentleman's Magazine. Vol. XL. 1770.

(1) Female characters (p. 337), (2) The lownger (p. 535).

[Stevens, George Alexander.]

A Lecture upon Heads.*

See 1766.

[Thicknesse, Philip.]

Sketches and Characters of the most Eminent and most Singular Persons now living. By several Hands. Vol. I. Bristol, Printed for John Whebb, at No. 24, Pater-Noster Row, 1770.*

8°, text pp. 1–143.

BSC 2628.

Attributed to Thicknesse by Halkett and Laing.

1771

Anonymous.

The Lady's Magazine; Or, Entertaining Companion For the Fair Sex . . . London: Printed for John Wheble . . . MDCCLXXI.

4°, text pp. 1–286.

(1) R--t M--m, the portrait of virtue (Vol. II, p. 69), (2) Her present Majesty (II, 123), (3) Queen Elizabeth, by Goldsmith (II, 123), (4) The contrast: or, the characters of Lady Mary L--, and the Honourable Miss S--- (II, 162), (5) His present Majesty (II, 167), (6) William Henry D-- of G--, Henry Frederic D-- of C-- (II, 218), (7) The Duchess of Northumberland (II, 256).

[Henry, D.]

The Gentleman's Magazine. Vol. XLI. 1771.

(1) Il Bellicoso. By Mr. Mason (p. 183).

[Hill, Sir Richard.]

An Address to Persons of Fashion Relating to Balls: With a few occasional Hints concerning Play-Houses, Card-Tables, &c. . . . By the

Author of Pietas Oxoniensis. The Sixth Edition. Revised, Corrected, and very much Enlarged. Shrewsbury: Printed by J. Eddowes; And Sold by E. and C. Dilly, in the Poultry, London. MDCCLXXI.

6°, text pp. 1–176.

(1) as in 1761.

[Ward, Edward.]

The Wooden World. Dissected: In The Character Of A Ship Of War: As also, the Characters of all the Officers, From the Captain to the Common Sailor. . . . The Seventh Edition. London, Printed for the Booksellers of London, 1771.*

See 1707.

The Address to the Reader is dated Portsmouth, Nov. 24, 1770. There seems to have been some confusion between this edition and the "seventh" of 1756. Since neither one is now available, these contradictory entries are given for what they may be worth.

Wesley, John.

The Works Of The Rev. John Wesley, M.A. . . . Bristol: Printed by William Pine . . . MDCCLXXI.

12°, 32 vols.

(1) The almost Christian, 1741 (Vol. I, p. 32), (2) Flavia, by William Law, from A Serious Call to a Devout and Holy Life (V, 133), (3) Miranda, by Law (V, 140), (4) A Methodist (XV, 359).

There have been other editions of the Works.

1772

Anonymous.

The Contemplative Man, or the History of Cristopher Crab, Esq; of North-Wales. . . . Dublin: Printed for W. Sleator . . . M,DCC,-LXXII.

12°, 2 vols., paged continuously, text pp. 1–251.

(1) Mrs. Crab (p. 3), (2) Captain Gorget (p. 7), (3) Mr. Trundle (p. 18), (4) Mr. Heartwell (p. 130).

An Essay on Satirical Entertainments. To which is added, Stevens's new Lecture upon heads . . . with critical observations . . . London printed: Sold by J. Bell . . . M.DCC.-LXXII.

4°, text pp. 1–87.

(1) Stevens's A Lecture upon Heads. (See 1766.)

[Bonhote, Mrs. Elizabeth?]

The Rambles of Mr. Frankly. 1772.*

(1) The widowed wife (Vol. I, p. 15), (2) The merchant (I, 20), (3) The English nabob (I, 25),

(4) The indolent man (I, 33), (5) The West Indian (I, 34), (6) The physician (I, 55), (7) The miser (I, 69), (8) The officer (I, 92), (9) The master of the toy shop (I, 101), (10) Lord Frampton (II, 115), (11) Mr. and Mrs. Manly (II, 119), (12) Lady B-- (II, 122), (13) Mr. and Mrs. Moreton (II, 123).

Attributed to Mrs. Bonhote by the CBEL.

Evans, Nathaniel.

Poems on Several Occasions . . . By Nathaniel Evans . . . Philadelphia: Printed by John Dunlap . . . M.DCC.LXXII.

4°, text pp. 1–160.

(1) The blameless vestal, from Pope's Eloisa and Abelard (p. 149), (2) A parody on this, the country parson, by Laura Elizabeth Ferguson (p. 149).

[Stevens, George Alexander.]

A Lecture upon Heads. 1772.*

See 1766.

Whyte, Samuel.

The Shamrock. 1772.*

(1) Sylvia (p. 157, in verse).

1773

Anonymous.

The Friends. . . . In Two Volumes. . . . London: Printed for J. Bell . . . MDCCLXXIII.

12°, 2 vols.

(1) A Whig (Vol. II, p. 126).

The Happy Man. A True Gentleman. . . . [colophon] Boston: Printed and Sold by William M'Alpine. [1773?]

s.sh.fo.

(1) The happy man, (2) A true gentleman (the two in parallel columns).

The Register of Folly: or, Characters at Bath and at the Hot-Wells, Bristol. London, 1773.*

Reprinted from 1724.

The Salem Gazette. 1773.*

(1) The human species (March 30), (2) The miser (August 3), (3) The Earl of Chatham (November 2).

[Bonhote, Mrs. Elizabeth.]

The Rambles of Mr. Frankly. Published By His Sister. In Two Volumes. . . . Dublin . . . M.DCC.LXXIII.

12°, 2 vols.

(1–13) as in 1772.

[Dabott, Nathan?]

Freebetter's New-England Almanack, for 1773. New-London, Connecticut. 1773.*

(1) A good husband (inside back cover).

[Henry, D.]

The Gentleman's Magazine. Vol. XLIII. 1773.

(1) A happy life, by Sir Henry Wotton (p. 344).

Porteus, Beilby.

A Review Of The Life and Character Of Archbishop Secker. By Beilby Porteus, D.D. . . . New-York: Re-printed from the London Edition, by Hugh Gaine . . . MDCCLXXIII.

4°, text pp. i–lxviii.

(1) Archbishop Thomas Secker (p. liii).

[Trumbull, John.]

The Progress of Dulness, Part Second: Or An Essay On the Life and Character of Dick Hairbrain . . . Printed in the Year . . . M.DCC.-LXXIII.

4°, text pp. 11–27. In verse.

(1) A country clown, Dick's father (p. 11), (2) A coxcomb (p. 16), (3) Dick Hairbrain (p. 22 and *passim*).

There are also elements of character in Parts I (1772) and III (1773), but less well marked than the above.

1774

Anonymous.

Imitations of the Characters of Theophrastus. . . . London: Printed for S. Leacroft. 1774.*

The Royal American Magazine, or universal Repository of Instruction and Amusement. Boston, Greenleaf's Printing-Office.*

(1) A royal American patriot (p. 44), (2) A real character (p. 132), (3) Cowardice, from Theophrastus (p. 242).

Chesterfield, Philip Dormer Stanhope, fourth Earl of.

Letters Written By The Late Right Honourable Philip Dormer Stanhope, Earl Of Chesterfield, To His Son . . . Published by Mrs. Eugenia Stanhope . . . London: Printed for J. Dodsley . . . M.DCC.LXXIV.

4°, 2 vols.

(1) A respectable Hottentot (Vol. II, p. 105).

This character was said by Boswell to have been meant for Dr. Johnson. There have been many later editions.

[Duche, Jacob.]

Observations on a Variety of Subjects, Literary,

Moral, and Religious; In a Series of Original Letters . . . Written by a Gentleman of Foreign Extraction . . . Philadelphia: Printed by John Dunlap. M.DCC.LXXIV.

6°, text pp. 1–241.

(1) A truly meek man (letter 15).

[Henry, D.]

The Gentleman's Magazine. Vol. XLIV. 1774.

(1) Portrait of Mr. Garrick. From Dr. Goldsmith's poem stiled Retaliation, just published (p. 184), (2) Some lines, descriptive of five of the most beautiful ladies at the militia-ball, at Canterbury, May 27, 1774 (p. 279).

No. 2 is almost identical with The Beauties of Epsom, *ibid.*, XXX (1763), 138.

[Langhorne, John.]

The Country Justice. A Poem. By One Of His Majesty's Justices Of The Peace For The County Of Somerset. London: Printed for T. Becket . . . MDCCLXXIV [–VII].

fo, in 3 parts, paged 7–23, 9–27, 7–17.

(1) A country justice (Part I, p. 15).

[Scott, Sarah.]

The Man of Real Sensibility: Or The History Of Sir George Ellison. . . . Philadelphia: Printed by James Humphreys, Junr. . . . M DCC LXXIV.

6°, text pp. 3–84.

(1) A benevolent man (p. 34), (2) Sir George Ellison (p. 82).

First published 1765. There were numerous other editions. Attributed to Sarah Scott by the CBEL.

1775

Anonymous.

The Convivial Magazine and Polite Intelligencer; or, a real representation of the characters and sentiments of the times, etc. Volume I. London, 1775.*

8°.

[Penn, William.]

Fruits of Solitude. Eighth Edition. 1775.*

Reprinted from 1749.

1776

[Cogan, Thomas.]

John Buncle, Junior, Gentleman. London: Printed for J. Johnson . . . MDCCLXXVI-[–VIII].

2 vols.

(1) A fine lady (Vol. I, p. 185), (2) A good but

outspoken man (II, 246), (3) An impudent man (II, 258).

The Harvard Catalogue ascribes this work to Thomas Cogan.

Dawes, Manasseh.

Fugitive Essays in Prose and Verse, by Mr. M. Dawes. . . . London: Printed for the author . . . M.DCC.LXXVI.

4°, text pp. 1–214.
(1) A good man (p. 153).

[Head, Richard.]

The English Rogue; Or The Life Of Jeremy Sharp. . . . To which is added A Narrative Of Mary Toft; Of an extraordinary Delivery of Eighteen Rabbets, Performed by Mr. John Howard . . . MDCCXXVI. Published by Mr. St. Andre, Surgeon . . . The Eighth Edition in Three Volumes. . . . London:To be had at R. Hopwood's . . . and of all the Booksellers and News-Carriers in Town and Country. MDCCLXXVI.

6°, 3 vols.
(1–3) as in 1665.

The title of No. 3 has been changed to A Derby-captain.

[Henry, D.]

The Gentleman's Magazine. Vol. XLVI. 1776.
(1) The modern belle (p. 375).

[Mather, Allyn.]

The Character of a well accomplished Ruler describ'd. A Discourse delivered at the Freeman's Meeting in New-Haven, April 8, 1776. New-Haven, Printed by Thomas and Samuel Green.*

1777

Anonymous.

Bickerstaff's Boston Almanack, For The Year of our Redemption 1777. . . . Boston: Printed and sold by John Boyle . . . and Draper and Phillips.

4°, text sigs. A2–C4v.
(1) A patriot (sig. A2).

The Harvard copy has an interleaved manuscript diary. The character is said to be reprinted from the Middlesex North Briton.

Characters. Containing An Impartial Review of the Public Conduct and Abilities of the most eminent Personages in the Parliament of Great-Britain: considered as Statesmen, Senators, and Public Speakers. Revised and Corrected by the Author, since The Original Pub-

lication in the Gazetteer. London, Printed for J. Bew . . . M.DCC.LXXVII.

4°, text pp. 1–152.
(1) Lord Mansfield (p. 1), (2) Lord Camden (p. 6), (3) Attorney General Thurlow (p. 11), (4) Edmund Burke (p. 16), (5) Lord Lyttleton (p. 22), (6) The Earl of Chatham (p. 28), (7) Lord George Germain (p. 37), (8) Colonel Barré (p. 42), (9) Lord Hillsborough (p. 48), (10) The Duke of Grafton (p. 55), (11) Solicitor General Wedderburne (p. 67), (12) Charles Fox (p. 76), (13) Lord Suffolk (p. 84), (14) Lord Shelburne (p. 90), (15) Wellbore Ellis (p. 97), (16) Mr. Dunning (p. 105), (17) Lord Sandwich (p. 111), (18) The Duke of Richmond (p. 123), (19) Lord North (p. 134).

A Dictionary of Love, with notes, wherein is the description of a perfect beauty; the picture of a Fop, etc. London, J. Bew. 1777.*
12°.
Reprinted from 1753.

The Laughing Philosopher. Dublin, 1777.*
According to Mr. Greenough's notes there are characters in nos. 15, 16, 19.

Chesterfield, Philip Dormer Stanhope, fourth Earl of.

Characters Of Eminent Personages Of His Own Time, Written by the late Earl of Chesterfield; and Never Before Published. Printed for William Flexney, Holborn 1777.

4°, text pp. 9–54.
(1) George I (p. 9), (2) Queen Caroline (p. 12), (3) Sir Robert Walpole (p. 16), (4) Mr. Pulteney (p. 24), (5) Lord Hardwicke (p. 33), (6) Mr. Henry Fox (p. 38), (7) Mr. Pitt. (p. 43).
BSC 2628.

1778

Anonymous.

The Candid Philosopher: or, Free Thoughts on Men, Morals, and Manners. 1778.*
(1) A pedagogue (Vol. I, p. 103), (2) A busybody (II, 196), (3) An impudent man (II, 257).

The Devil's Wedding. A Poem. Exhibiting some of the most flagitious Characters of the Age. — London: Printed for J. Bladon. 1778.*
4°, text pp. 1–21.
BSC 2629.

Brooke, Henry.

A Collection Of The Pieces Formerly Published By Henry Brooke, Esq. To Which Are Added Several Plays And Poems, Now First

Printed. In Four Volumes. . . . London, Printed for the Author: And sold by Mr. White . . . Mr. Cadell . . . Messrs. Dilly . . . and Mr. Wallis . . . MDCCLXXXVIII.

8°, four volumes.

(1) Dr. Lucas, M.P. for Dublin (Vol. IV, p. 381).

Brown, Thomas.

Works. 1778–79.*

Reprinted from 1707.

Burney, Frances, later D'Arblay.

Evelina, Or, A Young Lady's Entrance Into The World. . . . London. Printed for T. Lowndes . . . M.DCC.LXXVIII.

12°, 3 vols.

(1) Mrs. Beaumont, court calendar bigot (Vol. III, p. 24).

There were many later editions.

[Chesterfield, Philip Dormer Stanhope, fourth Earl of, and others.]

Characters by Lord Chesterfield contrasted with Characters of the same Great Personages by other respectable Writers. Also Letters to Alderman George Faulkner, Dr. Madden, Mr. Lexton, Mr. Derrick, and the Earl of Arran. Intended as an Appendix to His Lordship's Miscellaneous Works. London: Printed for Edward and Charles Dilly . . . 1778.*

4°, in two parts, text pp. 1–65, 1–28.

(1) George I, (2) George I, by Tindal, (3) George II, (4) George II, by Smollett, (5) George II, by Dr. Chancellor, (6) Queen Caroline, (7) Lord Townshend, (8) Mr. Pope, (9) Pope, by Tyndale, (10) Pope, by Ruffhead, (11) Lord Bolingbroke, (12) Lord Bolingbroke, by Tindal, (13) Mr. Pulteney, (14) Sir Robert Walpole, (15) Walpole, by Smollett, (16) Walpole, by Tindal, (17) Lord Granville, (18) Mr. Pelham, (19) Pelham, by Tindal, (20) Richard Earl of Scarborough, (21) Lord Hardwicke, (22) Lord Hardwicke, from the Biographical Dictionary, (23) The Duke of Newcastle, (24) The Duke of Bedford, (25) Bedford, by Junius (?), (26) Mr. Fox, (27) Mr. Pitt, (28) Oratory, anon.

BSC 2630.

[Penn, William.]

Fruits of Solitude. Ninth Edition. 1778.*

Reprinted from 1749.

[Scott, Sarah.]

A Description of Millenium Hall, and the Country Adjacent: Together with the Characters Of The Inhabitants. . . . By A Gentleman On His Travels. The Fourth Edition.

London: Printed for T. Carnan . . . MDCC-LXXVIII.

12°, text pp. 1–262.

(1–18) as in 1762.

1779

Anonymous.

The Register of Folly. 1779.*

Reprinted from 1724.

Sketches from Nature in high Preservation, by the most honorable Masters, containing upwards of one hundred Portraits or Characters. 1779.*

BSC 2632.

[Mackenzie, Henry.]

The Mirror. . . . [colophon] Edinburgh: Published by William Creech.

Each number is fo, pp. 1–4. Dates of the characters listed below are from February 10, 1779 to May 6, 1780. Bound in one volume, the pages are 1–440.

(1) Pedants (no. 5), (2) Mr. Umphraville, a man of too aspiring mind (no. 6), (3) Mr. Fleetwood, a man of excessively delicate taste (no. 10), (4) An indolent man (no. 14, in first person), (5) A man of classical education contrasted with those educated according to the modern plan of education (no. 15), (6) On character-drawing (no. 31), (7) A man of fashion (no. 45), (8) Mr. Fleetwood, Mr. Morley, a self-styled critic of poor taste, Mr. Dacres, who realizes his taste is poor, Mr. Sidney, a man of admirable taste and goodness (no. 47), (9) Eubulus, a judge who deceives himself (no. 55), (10) Miss Hargrave, a self-sacrificing daughter (no. 63), (11) Sir Bobby Button, M.P. (no. 68), (12) One to whom trifles seem important (no. 93), (13) Maria, a coquette (no. 95), (14) A man of spirit (no. 102), (15) A country gentleman (no. 104).

Attributed to Mackenzie by Halkett and Laing. Reprinted several times.

[Nichols, J., and Henry, D.]

The Gentleman's Magazine. Vol. XLIX. 1779.

(1) The quack, a tale (p. 319), (2) A short character of Milton, extracted from Candour, a poem, printed in 1739 (p. 558).

1780

Beetham, Edward.

New Lectures on Heads, Describing The Characters, Passions, Morals, Fashions, Follies, Virtues, Vices, and Absurdities Incident to

Human Life . . . By E. Beetham . . . New-castle upon Tyne: Printed by T. Robson, and sold by the Author. . . .

4°, text pp. 9–48.

(1) Head of a Venus (p. 9), (2) Head of a pretended captain (p. 11), (3) Head of a horse jockey (p. 19), (4) Patience on a monument (p. 21), (5) A school-boy (p. 25), (6) Mistress A.B.C. (p. 26), (7) Bellower (p. 28), (8) Snuffler (p. 28), (9) Lispers (p. 28), (10) Stammerer (p. 29), (11) Ti-tam-ti-er (p. 29), (12) School-master (p. 30), (13) Jingler (p. 30), (14) Word clipper (p. 30), (15) Word grubber (p. 31), (16) The passions (p. 35), (17) Laughter (p. 35), (18) Jacky Wagtail (p. 38), (19) Tommy Trinket (p. 38), (20) Sir Fanciful Fringe (p. 38), (21) Lord Lofty (p. 38), (22) Orator, Welsh (p. 39), (23) Orator, Irish (p. 40), (24) Orator, Scotch (p. 41), (25) Orator, Macaroni (p. 41), (26) Westmoreland collier (p. 42), (27) Anecdote hunter (p. 43), (28) Captain of a collier (p. 44), (29) Sir Benj Bumper (p. 45), (30) His lady (p. 45), (31) Sir Gregory Greedy (p. 45).

Dated [1780?] in the British Museum Catalogue.

[Croft, Sir Herbert.]

The Abbey of Kilkhampton; Or, Monumental Records For The Year 1980. Faithfully transcribed From the Original Inscriptions. . . . Compiled with a View to ascertain, with Precision, the Manners which prevailed in Great Britain during the last Fifty Years of the Eighteenth Century. . . . London . . . G. Kearsly . . . M,DCC,LXXX.

fo, text pp. 1–131.

Contains a number of mock epitaphs and inscriptions, of which the following approach the form of characters: (1) Lord G-- G--d-n (p. 44); (2) Mr. W--y (p. 51), (3) F-- H--d, Earl of C----sle (p. 41); (4) Edw--d G-b-n (p. 32).

BSC 2632.

There were at least eight editions in 1780. Attributed to Croft by Halkett and Laing.

[Marshall, J.?]

The Masquerade: Containing . . . Characters . . . Calculated to Amuse and Instruct all the good Boys and Girls in the Kingdom . . . London, Printed and Sold at No. 4, Aldermary Church-Yard, Bow-Lane.*

Dated [1780?] by the British Museum Catalogue.

Minifie, M.

The Count de Poland, by Miss M. Minifie . . . Published for the Author . . . MDCCLXXX. 6°, 4 vols.

(1) A bachelor (Vol. IV, p. 128), (2) A married man (IV, 132).

[Stevens, George Alexander.]

A Lecture on Heads.*

See 1766.

1781

Anonymous.

Matrimony; or the Road to Hymen made plain, easy and delightful; containing a new Collection of familiar Letters, which have passed between Lovers in various Situations of Life, displaying humourous and entertaining Characters, with short Histories. 1781.*

The Salem Gazette. 1781.*

(1) The good wife (March 13), (2) A polite man (March 20), (3) Lady Craven (April 17).

[Forrester James.]

The Polite Philosopher. 1781.*

Reprinted from 1758.
The Huntington Library refers to this as the ninth edition.

[Nichols, J., and Henry, D.]

The Gentleman's Magazine. Vol. LI. 1781.

(1) A character (p. 188).

1782

Anonymous.

Bath Anecdotes and Characters. By the Genius Loci. London, 1782.*

The European Magazine, And London Review. . . . By the Philological Society of London. Vol. I. for 1782. . . . London. Printed for John Fielding . . . John Debrett . . . and John Sewell.

(1) The man of the town, No. I (p. 9), (2) Maria, by Y. (p. 13), (3) The country curate, No. I (p. 178), (4) The dabbler, No. I, by N. (p. 425).

The Salem Gazette. 1782.*

(1) A liar (February 21).

[Penn, William.]

More Fruits of Solitude.*

Reprinted from Fruits of Solitude, 1749.

1784

Anonymous.

The Character of Alfred the Great. 1784.*

The Critical Review. Vol. LVII. 1784.*

(1) Clytus, in Letters to Honoria and Marianne (p. 209).

The Female Monitor, or the young Maiden's best guide in the Art of Love, Courtship, and Marriage. 1784.*

12°.

Begins: "A good wife is a man's best moveable, who to her husband is more than a friend."

[Stevens, George Alexander.]

A Lecture upon Heads. 1784.*

See 1766.

1785

Anonymous.

Adventures of a Flea.*

(1) A young master who becomes a justice of the quorum (Vol. I, p. 119).

The Boston Magazine. Boston, Greenleaf and Freeman. 1785.*

(1) The envious man (p. 128, April).

The Lounger. A Periodical Paper, Published At Edinburgh In the Years 1785 and 1786. Edinburgh. Printed for William Creech.

fo, text pp. 1–404.

(1) Colonel Caustic, a severe critic of the present (nos. 4, 6, 14, 31, 32), (2) Sir Thomas Lounger of Loiterhall (no. 11), (3) The Phusalophagos, or toad-eater (no. 15), (4) A superannuated bachelor lounger (no. 26), (5) A country clergyman (no. 40), (6) Mr. Wilfull, an admirer of freedom (no. 65), (7) Mr. Bustle, who embodies useless activity (no. 78), (8) Dormer, a man of public spirit rather than private virtue (no. 88), (9) Mr. Edwards, a romantic husband (no. 92).

There were several later editions of this periodical.

[Cumberland, Richard.]

Character Of The Late Lord Viscount Sackville. . . . London: Printed for C. Dilly, . . . M.DCC.LXXXV.

4°, text pp. 1–24.

Begins: "Whoever stands forth as the advocate."

Signed at the end Richard Cumberland.

Hill, Mrs. Philippina (Burton).

Portraits, Characters, Pursuits and Amusements of the Present Fashionable World, interspersed with Poetic Flights of Fancy. By Mrs. P. Hill, . . Printed for Subscribers only.*

12°. Chiefly in verse.

Contains numerous brief portraits of the L--d Alg-r-n P-r-y type.

BSC 2631.

Dated [1785?] by the British Museum Catalogue.

Noyes, Robert.

Miscellanies in Verse and Prose; containing Characters, Essays, and Letters, on various Subjects. Scribimus indocti, &c. By Robert Noyes; author of a Poem entitled Distress. Canterbury, Printed for the Author.*

8°, text pp. 1–155.

BSC 2633.

Dated [1785] by the British Museum Catalogue.

[Stevens, George Alexander.]

A Lecture upon Heads, Written by G.A.S., with additions by Mr. Pilon, as delivered by Mr. Charles Lee Lewes . . . To which is added an Essay on Satire. G. Kearsley, London, 1785.*

See 1766.

The British Museum Catalogue calls this the first authentic edition.

1786

Anonymous.

The New Novelist's Magazine. . . . London, Printed for Harrison . . . 1786.

4°, text pp. 3–418.

(1) Eugenio, by Dr. Watts (Vol. I, p. 84).

The Salem Chronicle. 1786.*

(1) A merchant (May 4).

The Wisdom of Crop the Conjurer. Exemplified in Several Characters of Good and Bad Boys, with an Impartial Account of the Celebrated Tom Trot, who Rode before all the Boys in the Kingdom till he arrived at the Top of the Hill, called Learning. Written for the Imitation of those who love themselves. Worcester: I. Thomas. 1786.*

[Bowdler, Jane.]

Poems and Essays by A Lady Lately Deceased. . . . The Second Edition. . . . Bath: Printed by R. Cruttwill . . . MDCCLXXXVI.

8°, 2 vols.

(1) Laetitia (Vol. I, p. 121), (2) Curio (I, 199).

Attributed to Mrs. Bowdler by the Harvard Catalogue.

[Cumberland, Richard.]

The Observer: Being a Collection of Moral, Literary And Familiar Essays. . . . London: M.DCC.LXXXVI [–VIII].

8°, 4 vols.

(1) Lady Thimble, a female pedant (Vol. I, p. 27, no. 4), (2) Vanessa (I, 232, no. 25), (3) Leontine (I, 244, no. 26), (4) A contemptible, proud

man (IV, 35, no. 97), (5) Walter Wormwood (V, 41, no. 130), (6) A flatterer (V, 52, no. 131), (7) A flatterer (V, 64, no. 132), (8) Kit Cracker, a dealer in the marvellous (V, 86, no. 134).

The edition of 1798 bears Cumberland's name on the title page.

[Earle, John.]

Microcosmography ... London, Printed A.D. 1650. Salisbury, Reprinted and Sold by E. Easton, 1786. Sold also by G. and T. Wilkie, St. Paul's Church-Yard, London.*

12°.

(1–74) as in second edition of 1650.

Murphy 43. BSC 2634.

[Head, Richard.]

The Original English Rogue; Described in the Life of Meriton Latroon, A Witty Extravagant. In Two Parts. Comprehending the most eminent Cheats practised by both Sexes, in all Characters, Occuptions, Professions, Trades and Mysteries. ... Manchester: Printed by John Radford ... 1786.

8°, in 2 parts, text pp. 3–325, 1–179.

(1–3) as in 1665.

[Heathcote, Ralph.]

Sylva; or, The Wood: Being a Collection of Anecdotes, Dissertations, Characters . . . and Other Little Things. . . . By a Society of the Learned. London: Printed for T. Payne, and son . . . 1786.

8°, text pp. 1–315.

(1) Of fine gentlemen: with the character and description of an upstart (p. 26), (2) Upon justices of the peace (p. 55), (3) Of professional character (p. 148), (4) Of personal identity (p. 150), (5) Of coffee-house politicians (p. 186), (6) A vindication of Paracelsus (p. 197), (7) Of Madame de Maintenon (p. 230), (8) One trait of Oliver Cromwell (p. 276), (9) Another trait of Oliver Cromwell (p. 279), (10) Of great men, and of Dr. Samuel Johnson (p. 290), (11) Upon David Hume's moral character (p. 295).

Murphy, Arthur.

Works. 1786.*

See The Gray's Inn Journal, 1753.

[Nichols, J., and Henry, D.]

The Gentleman's Magazine. Vol. LVI. 1786.

(1) The country clergymen. In imitation of Dr. Goldsmith (p. 983).

Weatherwise, Abraham.

Weatherwise's Town and Country Almanack. For the Year of our Lord 1786. . . . By Abra-

ham Weatherwise, Philom. Printed and Sold by James D. Griffith.

6°, in 2 parts.

(1) A man of pleasure (Part I, sig. B5).

1787

Anonymous.

The American Museum. Volume I. . . . Philadelphia . . . 1787.*

See 1790.

Bentley, William.

Diary.*

Manuscript.

(1) A prudent man and an imprudent man (p. 139).

This entry occurs early in 1787. The manuscript was first published in 1905.

[Freneau, Philip?]

The Freeman's Journal. 1787.*

(1) The newsmonger, by Philip Freneau (February 21).

[Oulton, Walley C.]

The Busy Body. 1787.*

(1) A character (no. 11), (2) Sir George Generous, an original character (no. 12), (3) Two or three hints for making a fine gentleman (no. 14), (4) A character (no. 15).

Attributed to Oulton by the CBEL.

Pennecuik, Alexander.

A Collection of Scots Poems . . . By the late Mr Alexander Pennecuik, Gent. And Others. . . . Glasgow: Printed for Alex. Buchanan . . . MDCCLXXXVII.

4°, text pp. 1–64.

(1–5) as in 1769.

[Stevens, George Alexander.]

A Lecture upon Heads. 1787.*

See 1766.

1788

Anonymous.

The American Magazine For December 1787 [–November, 1788]. . . . New York . . . 1788.

4°, text pp. 3–882.

(1) Dr. Johnson, by himself (p. 630), (2) A well-bred man, by a lady (p. 812).

[Heathcote, Ralph.]

Sylva; or the Wood: being a collection of Anecdotes, Dissertations, Characters, &c. The Second edition corrected and enlarged. Lon-

don: Printed for T. Payne & Son . . . 1788.*
Reprinted from 1786.

[Oliphant, Robert, and others.]

The Trifler. No. I. A New Periodical Miscellany. By Timothy Touchstone . . . London. Printed For The Authors, And Sold by Messieurs Robinson . . . MDCCLXXXVIII [-IX].

8°, text pp. 1–554, 43 numbers.
(1) A modern senator (p. 206, in verse), (2) Amelia, a learned lady (p. 242), (3) Zaydor, an Eastern character (p. 338), (4) Dr. Cassock, a learned clergyman (p. 397), (5) Mr. Giddy, who is frail, inconsistent, and versatile (p. 399), (6) The justice, who is prejudiced (p. 400).
Attributed to Oliphant by the CBEL.

[Pratt, Samuel J.]

Curious Particulars and Genuine Anecdotes respecting the late Lord Chesterfield and David Hume, Esq. With . . . an Impartial Character of Lord Chesterfield. . . . By A Friend To Religious And Civil Liberty. London. Printed for G. Kearsley . . . 1788.

4°, text pp. 1–107.
(1) A parallel betwixt David Hume and Lord Chesterfield (p. 43), (2) Lord Chesterfield (pp. 51 and 57).
Attributed to Pratt by Halkett and Laing.

[Repton, Humphrey.]

Variety: A Collection Of Essays. Written In The Year 1787. . . . London: Printed For T. Cadell . . . MDCCLXXXVIII.

12°, text pp. 1–297.
(1) Two brothers, representing reason and passion (no. 4, p. 25), (2) Eucharis, or gratitude (no. 12, p. 96).
Attributed to Repton by the DNB and Halkett and Laing.

Stevens, George Alexander.

A Lecture On Heads, Written By George Alexander Stevens . . . London: Printed, By Assignment from Mr. Lewis, For G. Kearsley . . . M,DCC,LXXXVIII.

12°, text pp. 1–78.
(1) George Alexander Stevens (p. 2), (2) Sir Whiskey Whiffle (p. 4), (3) A jockey (p. 5), (4) A comical half-foolish face (p. 6), (5) Master Jacky, Mamma's darling (p. 7), (6) A lady in her fashionable uniform (p. 8), (7) A fool (p. 9), (8) A London blood (p. 10), (9) A connoisseur (p. 17), (10) A worldly wise man (p. 19), (11) A freeholder inoculated (p. 19), (12) A female moderator (p. 22), (13) A male moderator (p. 22), (14) Jones, the card-playing Jew (p. 25), (15) A self-interested man (p. 26), (16) An opera

dancer (p. 27), (17) An opera composer, or burletta projector (p. 28), (18) A nouveau riche lady (p. 30), (19) Cleopatra (p. 30), (20) An old maid (p. 31), (21) An old batchelor (p. 31), (22) Female orators (p. 33), (23) The groaners & the grinners (p. 34), (24) A servant-maid (p. 36), (25) A lady first amiable then disappointed (p. 39), (26) After-dinner wedlock tete a tete (p. 41), (27) Somebody & nobody & everybody & anybody (p. 46), (28) A busybody (p. 48), (29) Flattery (p. 49), (30) A Frenchman (p. 50), (31) A British tar (p. 51), (32) A Spaniard (p. 52), (33) A Dutchman (p. 53), (34) A British hero (p. 55), (35) A Londoner torn between state & kitchen (p. 60), (36) A proud man (p. 64), (37) Consequential people (p. 64), (38) A Methodist (p. 65).
The top of the title page carried the notice: A New Genuine Edition Corrected. Comparison with the edition of 1766 shows that the contents, though bearing some similarity, are almost entirely different. There was also another edition of 1788, published in Dublin.

Walker, Samuel.

The Christian's Mirror: Or, The Features of the Christian Delineated. As they are to be seen in his Daily Life and Conversation. London: Printed in the Year 1788.*

12°.
Extracted from Walker's The Christian.

1789

Anonymous.

The Character of a Pious King. 1789.*
A character of George III.

Gentleman and Ladies Town and Country Magazine. 1789–90.*
(1) A good senator (p. 186, May, 1789), (2) Friendship (p. 18), (3) General Lee [or Lie], (4) A notable woman.
No. 1 begins: "A Senator is a character of great dignity and power." No. 4 begins: "If a female lives to the age of thirty years unmarried."

Honoria Sommerville. 1789.*
(1) Mr. Fortescue, (2) Mrs. Fortescue.

The Massachusetts Magazine: or, Monthly Museum of Knowledge and rational Entertainment . . . Printed at Boston, By Isaiah Thomas and Ebenezer T. Andrews . . . MDCCLXXXIX.

4°, Vol. I for 1789.
(1) A good husband (p. 177), (2) The club (p. 219), (3) The difference between true and false politeness (p. 226), (4) A rural club (p. 260),

(5) The flatterer — a detestable character (p. 380).

The Stage-Coach. 1789.*
Reprinted from 1753.

Albion.

Four Pleasant Epistles, written for the Entertainment and Gratification of Four Unpleasant Characters, viz. A very Exalted Subject in his Majesty's Dominions; The most Unpatriotic Man alive!! The most Artful Man alive!! and Second Childhood. By Albion. London: Printed for W. Priest, Holborn; and sold by the booksellers . . . M.DCC.LXXXIX.*
4°, text pp. 1-39.
BSC 2636.

[Combe, William.]

A Letter from a Country Gentleman, to a Member of Parliament, on the Present State of Public Affairs: in which The Object of The Contending Parties, and the following Characters are particularly considered . . . London: Printed at the Logographic Press . . . MDCCLXXXIX.

8°, text pp. 1-75.
(1) The Duke of Portland (p. 20), (2) Mr. Fox (p. 21), (3) Lord North (p. 25), (4) The Duke of Norfolk (p. 26), (5) The House of Cavendish (p. 30), (6) The Name of Russel (p. 30), (7) The Duke of Northumberland (p. 32), (8) Edmund Burke (p. 34), (9) Lord Loughborough (p. 36), (10) Mr. Sheridan (p. 41), (11) Mr. Pitt (p. 58), (12) Lord Thurlow (p. 60), (13) The Prince of Wales (p. 62).
The Harvard Catalogue attributes this work to Combe.

D'Argenson, René Louis de Voyer de Paulmy, Marquis.

Essays, Civil, Moral, Literary, and Political. Written after the Manner of M. de Montaigne; interspersed with Characters, Portraits, &c. By the celebrated Marquis D'Argenson, many years Prime Minister of France &c. Translated from his valuable MSS. &c. Dublin, 1789.*

[Heathcote, Ralph.]

Sylva: Or The Wood. Being A Collection Of Anecdotes, Dissertations, Characters, Original Letters, Bon Mots, &c. By A Society Of The Learned. The Third Edition, Corrected And Enlarged. Dublin: Printed By P. Byrne . . . M,DCC,LXXXIX.
8°, text pp. 1-368.
(1-11) as in 1786.

[Nichols, J., and Henry, D.]

The Gentleman's Magazine. Vol. LIX. 1789.
(1) The college hero (p. 451).

1790

Anonymous.

The American Museum, Or, repository . . . The Third Edition . . . Philadelphia: Carey, Stewart, and Co. M.DCC.XC.
4°, text pp. 5-488.
(1) A whimsical man (p. 41), (2) A bachelor (p. 42), (3) A married man (p. 43), (4) The honest fellow (p. 43), (5) A jealous man (p. 137), (6) An unseasonable fellow (p. 137), (7) A knave (p. 138).

The Connecticut Magazine.*
See The New Haven Gazette, 1790.

Essay on the Origin, Character, and Views of the Protestant Dissenters. Oxford, 1790.*
BSC 2637.

The New Haven Gazette. 1790.*
(1) Benevolus or candor, by Timothy Dwight (The Friend, no. 6), (2) Gallio, or prejudice (*ibid.*).
These characters appeared also in The Connecticut Magazine.

The New York Magazine; or, Literary Repository. . . . New York . . . M,DCC,XC.
4°, text pp. 3-730.
(1) The Club (Vol. I, p. 318, for June, 1790), (2) A modern traveller (I, 424, for July, 1790).
The second character was reprinted in The New Haven Gazette for May 11, 1791, and in the American Mercury for November, 1791.

Homer, Jonathan.

The Character and Duties of a Christian Soldier . . . a Sermon Preached . . . June 7, 1790 . . . By Jonathan Homer . . . Printed in Boston, By Benjamin Russell, State-Street, 1790.
4°, text pp. 3-21.
Begins: "The people of *Israel* were so impressed."

[Penn, William.]

Fruits of a Father's Love. Tenth Edition. 1790.*
Reprinted from Fruits of Solitude, 1749.

[Wynne, Edward.]

Strictures On The Lives And Characters Of The Most Eminent Lawyers Of The Present

Day: Including . . . The Lord Chancellor And The Twelve Judges. . . . Dublin: Printed for E. Lynch [and 8 others] . . . M.DCC.XC.
8°, text pp. 1–136.
(1) Thurlow (p. 10), (2) William Earl Mansfield (p. 23), (3) The Earl of Camden (p. 40), (4) The Earl of Bathurst (p. 46), (5) Sir Richard Pepper Arden (p. 53), (6) Lord Kenyon (p. 58), (7) Sir Francis Butter (p. 63), (8) Sir Nash Grose (p. 68), (9) Sir William Henry Ashurst (p. 72), (10) Lord Loughborough (p. 79), (11) Sir Henry Gould (p. 84), (12) Sir John Heath (p. 89), (13) Sir John Wilson (p. 92), (14) Sir James Eyre (p. 97), (15) Sir Beaumont Hotham (p. 101), (16) Sir Richard Perryn (p. 104), (17) Sir Alexander Thompson (p. 110), (18) Sir Archibald Macdonald (p. 113), (19) Sir John Scott (p. 117), (20) Mr. Anstruther (p. 127), (21) An honest lawyer, by H.G. Χιλονομον, 1676 (p. 131).
BSC 2638.

1791

Anonymous.

The American Mercury. 1791.*
See The New York Magazine, 1790.

A Character of H.R.H. the Prince of Denmark. 1791.*
8°.
BSC 2639.

A Character of Rev. Robert Walker. 1791.*

Characters and Anecdotes collected in the reigns of William Rufus, Charles the Second, and King George the Third, by the celebrated Wandering Jew of Jerusalem. London, for J. Ridgeway, 1791.*
Contains characters from Earle and others.

Mirth in Perfection: Or, The Character of a Loving Wife Described. Showing how a Man undergoes a thousand times more Plagues and Torments, by a loving and kind Wife, than those that are married either to a Jealous Wife, a Wanton Wife, a Drunken Wife, or a Scolding Wife. By Mr. Telltruth, In A Letter To His Friend. . . . Glasgow, Printed In The Saltmarket. MDCCXCI.
4°, text pp. 2–6.
Begins: "The poor man is greatly to be pitied."

The New Haven Gazette. 1791.*
See The New York Magazine, 1790.

The New York Magazine, or Literary Repository. 1791.*
(1) Timothy Quillet, who does everything by rule (February, p. 2).

[Cumberland, Richard.]

The Observer. 1791.*
Reprinted from 1786–88.

Steele, Sir Richard.

The Theatre, By Sir Richard Steele. With The Anti-Theatre, &c. In Two Volumes. . . . MDCCXCI.

[second title] The Theatre, By Sir Richard Steele; To Which Are Added, The Anti-Theatre; The Character of Sir John Edgar . . . Illustrated With Literary And Historical Anecdotes By John Nichols. London: Printed by and for the Editor; And sold by G.G.J. and J. Robinson . . . J. Walter . . . and C. Dilly . . . MDCCXCI.
8°, 2 vols.
(1) A wrong-head (Vol. I, p. 36), (2) Sir Richard Steele, by Colley Cibber (II, 315), (3) Sir John Edgar (II, 339), (4) A deputy-governor (II, 359).

1792

[Nichols, J., and Henry, D.]

The Gentleman's Magazine. Vol. LXII. 1792.
(1) Bishop Hooper. By Bishop Ken (p. 596).

Penn, William.

Fruits Of Solitude, In Reflections And Maxims Relating To The Conduct Of Human Life. By William Penn. The Tenth Edition. Philadelphia: Printed By Benjamin Johnson. M.DCC.XCII.
6°, in 2 parts, text pp. 1–166, 3–86.
(1–8) as in 1749.
Includes More Fruits of Solitude (Part I, p. 106) and Fruits of a Father's Love (Part II).

1793

[Graves, Richard.]

The Reveries of Solitude: By the Editor of Columella . . . Bath, Printed by R. Cruttwell . . . MDCCXCIII.
8°, text pp. 1–207.
(1) Distrust (p. 86), (2) Unpleasant manners (p. 88).
Both of these characters are translations from Theophrastus. Attributed to Graves by the CBEL.

[Moser, Joseph?]

Lucifer and Mammon, an Historical Sketch

of the last and present Century; with Characters, Anecdotes, etc. 1793.*
Text pp. 1–296.

Penn, William.

Fruits of Solitude. 1793.*
Reprinted from 1749.

1794

Holcroft, Thomas.

The Adventures of Hugh Trevor. By Thomas Holcroft . . . The Second Edition . . . London: Printed for Shepperson and Reynolds . . . 1794[–97].
12°, 6 vols.
(1) People in the theatre (Vol. II, p. 118).
The first edition was in the same year. Reprinted several times.

Penn, William.

Fruits of Solitude. 1794.*
Reprinted from 1749.

[Pigott, Charles.]

The Whig Club, full of Characters, Male and Female. 1794.*

1795

Anonymous.

The Tablet. A Miscellaneous Paper, Devoted To The Belles Lettres . . . Vol. I, Tuesday, May 19, 1795. No. 1. . . . [colophon] From The Press Of William Spotswood . . . Boston.
fo, text pp. 1–52.
(1) Meander (p. 5), (2) Charles Camelion, the versatile man (p. 29).

D'Israeli, Isaac.

Essay on the Manners and Genius of the Literary Character. 1795.*

[Heywood, Thomas.]

A True Discourse. 1795.*
Reprinted from 1636.

Hill, Philippina (Burton).

Portraits, Characters, Pursuits, and Amusements. 1795.*
Reprinted from 1785.

[Nichols, J.]

The Gentleman's Magazine. Vol. LXV. 1795.
(1) Incidit in Scyllam, cupiens vitare Charybdim. Erasmi adagia (p. 327).
This is a character of a miser.

Stevens, George Alexander.

A Lecture upon Heads. 1795.*
See 1788.

[Ward, Edward.]

The Wooden World Dissected. 1795.*
Reprinted from 1707.

1796

Anonymous.

The Connecticut Gazette. New-London. Printed, And Published by Samuel Green. [July 28, 1796.]
fo, 2 leaves, unnumbered.
(1) The fop, by Castigator (last page).

A Good Wife, God's Gift; or a Character of a Wife Indeed! Also, A Poetical Description of the Chaste Virgin; of a Good Wife; and a Pious Widow, &c. Boston, Printed by J. White . . . 1796.
6°, text pp. 3–47. In verse.
(1) A chaste virgin (p. 31), (2) A good wife (p. 34), (3) A pious widow (p. 38).

The Theological Magazine, New York. 1796.*
(1) An adaptation of Chaucer's description of a good parson (Vol. I, p. 39, in verse).

Cole, William.

The Contradiction. By the Rev. William Cole . . . London: Printed for T. Cadell Jun. and W. Davis . . . 1796.
12°, text pp. 1–248.
(1) Dasher, a sporting parson (p. 180).

[de la Garde, Mary?]

Essays on Various Subjects: in which some characters of the present age are introduced. London: Printed by S. Low, 1796.*
(1) Orontes, an unjust man, (2) Theodosius, a benevolent man, (3) Belinda, a proud woman, (4) Aristus, whose dignity of mind enables him to resist the pride of the world, (5) Dorimond, an affected man, (6) Acastus, a man above affectation, (7) Clodi, a slave to fashion, by Mrs. Guppy, in verse, (8) Honorius, an egoist, (9) Eugenius, the opposite of the preceding.

Thomas, John.

The Sermons and Charges of the right reverend John Thomas, LL.D. . . . By G.A. Thomas. . . . To which is prefixed, A Sketch of the Life And Character Of the Author, By The Editor. . . . London: Printed by Bye and Law . . . 1796.

8°, 2 vols.

(1) John Thomas, by G.A. Thomas (Vol. I, pp. xxiv, cxxvii).

1797

Anonymous.

The American Universal Magazine. Vol. I. . . . Philadelphia. Printed for Richard Lee.

6°, text pp. 3–448.

(1) A good husband and a good wife (Vol. I, p. 283), (2) The modern fine lady and Prudentia (Sept. 4).

The title page is missing in the Rutgers copy, which was used for this entry. The above is the engraved title page. The second character is also missing from the Rutgers copy.

The Philanthrope: after the manner of A Periodical Paper. . . . London: Printed for T. Cadell Jun. and W. Davies. . . . MDCC-XCVII.

8°, text pp. 1–280.

(1) Placidio (no. 10, p. 68), (2) Leander (no. 13, p. 96), (3) Favonius, or indecision, and his obstinate neighbor, Sir Anster (no. 19, p. 144).

The Theological Magazine, New York. [1797.]*

According to Mr. Greenough's notes, there is a character at Vol. II, p. 38.

[Dibdin, Thomas F., Porter, Jane, Porter, Robert.]

The Quiz, By A Society Of Gentlemen. Vol. I. . . . London: Published by J. Parsons . . . And By T. Jones . . . [1797–98].

6°, text pp. 1–281.

(1) Sir Arthur Hildebrand and his family (no. 2, p. 8), (2) A man of ardent disposition and fervid imagination (no. 7, p. 43), (3) A man of reason (no. 7, p. 45), (4) Fidelius, a man of fortitude (no. 9, p. 59), (5) Ignorant people, averse to literature (no. 10, p. 68), (6) A friend (no. 22, p. 149), (7) Henry Weston, a tragic youth (no. 26, p. 179), (8) Rev. Dr. Wynne, a benevolent friend (no. 26, p. 181), (9) A dissipated man (no. 28, p. 191), (10) A man of fancied sorrows (no. 36, p. 257).

Attributed to Dibdin, Jane Porter, and Robert Porter in the CBEL.

Paine, Robert Treat.

The Ruling Passion . . . By Thomas Paine, A.M. . . . Boston: Printed by Manning & Loring, for the Author. 1797.

4°, text pp. 5–28.

(1) A pedant (p. 10), (2) A love-lorn maid (p. 11), (3) A miser (p. 16).

Porteus, Beilby.

A Review Of The Life And Character Of The Right Rev. Dr. Thomas Secker, Late Lord Archbishop Of Canterbury. By Beilby Porteus, D.D. . . . The Fifth Edition, Corrected. London: Printed for F. and C. Rivington . . . and B. and J. White . . . 1797.

8°, text pp. 1–118.

(1) as in 1773.

Theophrastus.

Characters. 1797.*

Reprinted from 1714.

1798

Anonymous.

Gretna Green, or Cupid's Introduction to the Temple of Hymen; describing many curious scenes, love anecdotes, and characters, in prose and verse; calculated for the entertainment of both sexes. By Cupid's Secretary, A.M. 1798.*

Cumberland, Richard.

The Observer . . . By Richard Cumberland, Esq. The Fifth Edition . . . In Six Volumes. . . . London: Printed for C. Dilly . . . 1798.

12°, 6 vols.

(1–8) as in 1786–88.

Langhorne, John.

The Poetical Works of J. Langhorne, D.D. . . . Cooke's Edition . . . London: Printed for C. Cooke.

8°, text pp. 27–210.

(1) The Country Justice (p. 83).

The engraved title page is dated 1798. There were one or two other editions of his poems.

1799

Stevens, George Alexander.

A Lecture upon Heads. 1799.*

See 1788.

1800

De Genlis, Mme.

La Bruyere the Less, or Characters and Manners of the Children of the Present Age. 1800.*

de la Garde, Mary.

Essays on Various Subjects: in which some Characters of the Present Age are introduced. The Second Edition. To which is added some Poetical Pieces by Mrs. Guppy. Bristol, Printed by R. Edwards, 1800.*

(1–9) as in 1796.

Kendall, Edward A.

The Stories of Senex; or, Little Histories of Little People. By E.A. Kendal . . . London: Printed for F. Newbery . . . 1800.

6°, text pp. 1–176.

(1) Arthur Heedless (p. 42).

Stevens, George Alexander.

A Lecture upon Heads.*

See 1788.

1801

[Williams, Thomas.]

The Evangelical Magazine. Vol. II.*

(1) The Sabbath (p. 40, in verse). (2) A just man (p. 258).

Attributed to Williams by the CBEL.

1802

Hervey, James.

Theron and Aspasia; or, A Series of Dialogues and Letters, upon the most important and interesting subjects. By James Hervey. . . . In Two Volumes. . . . Edinburgh: Printed by T. and J. Turnbull . . . 1802.

8°, 2 vols.

(1) as in 1755.

Lyman, William.

A Virtuous Woman . . . Considered in a Sermon, Delivered At Lyme, Jan. 6, 1802; at the Funeral of Mrs. Sarah Griswold. By William Lyman, A.M., Pastor of a Church in East-Haddam. New London: Printed by S. Green: 1802.

4°, text pp. 3–23.

(1) Mrs. Sarah Griswold (p. 3).

Stevens, George Alexander.

A Lecture upon Heads. 1802.*

See 1788.

Wesley, John.

The Character of a Methodist. 1802.*

Reprinted from 1763.

Wordsworth, William.

Lyrical Ballads . . . By W. Wordsworth. . . . Third Edition. London: Printed For T. N. Longman And O. Rees . . . By Biggs And Cottle . . . 1802.

8°, 2 vols. In verse.

(1) The poet (Vol. I, p. xxvii, in prose).

The character first appeared in this edition. Often reprinted.

1803

Anonymous.

Take your Choice: or the Difference between Virtue and Vice, shown in opposite Characters. London: Harris. 1803.*

[Colman, George, and others.]

The Connoisseur. By Mr. Town, Critic and Censor-General. . . . Philadelphia: Printed for Samuel F. Bradford . . . And John Conrad And Co. . . . 1803.

6°, 4 vols.

(1–26) as in 1755–56.

There was another edition of the same year printed at Newburyport.

Montagu, Lady Mary Wortley.

The Works of the right honorable lady Mary Wortley Montagu . . . In Five Volumes . . . London: Printed for Richard Phillips . . . 1803.

12°, 5 vols.

(1) A wise man, by Epictetus (Vol. I, p. 283).

There were a number of later editions.

[Williams, Thomas.]

The Evangelical Magazine, Vol. IV.*

(1) The virtuous woman described (p. 94).

1804

Edgeworth, Maria.

Idleness and Industry Exemplified, in the History of James Preston and Lazy Lawrence. 1804.*

There were several other editions.

Stevens, George Alexander.

A Lecture upon Heads. 1804.*

See 1788.

[Wilson, Charles Henry.]

The Polyanthea: or, A Collection of Interesting Fragments, in Prose and Verse: Consisting of Original Anecdotes, Biographical Sketches, Dialogues, Letters, Characters, &c. &c. London: Printed for J. Budd . . . 1804.

8°, 2 vols.

(1) National characters of the French, the Spanish, the Italians, and the Germans (Vol. I, p. 29), (2) John Dennis (I, 169), (3) General Greene (I, 177), (4) A common fiddler, by Earle (I, 203), (5) Bishop Maule (I, 255, in verse), (6) The French (I, 379), (7) Primate Stone (I, 381), (8) Catherine late empress of Russia (II, 11), (9) Walsingham (II, 15), (10) Rev. Mr. Ball (II, 48), (11) Thomas William Walker (II, 66), (12)

Samuel Clarke (II, 354), (13) The Duke of Ormond (II, 383), (14) Father Paul [Sarpi] (II,
400).

Attributed to Wilson by Halkett and Laing.

1805

Anonymous.

The Weekly Visitor or Ladies' Miscellany.*
(1) A bachelor (p. 229, April 20).

[Brydges, Sir Egerton.]

Censura Literaria. Containing Titles, Abstracts, And Opinions Of Old English Books.
. . . London: Printed by T. Bensley . . . for
Longman, Hurst, Rees, and Orme . . . 1805
[–09].

8°, 10 vols.
(1) Microcosmographie, by J. Earle, 1630 (Vol.
II, p. 145), (2) The Complete Gentleman, by H.
Peacham, 1622 (III, 97), (3) Characters and
Elegies, by Sir F. Wortley, 1646 (III, 213), (4)
Chrestoleros, by T. Bastard, 1598 (IV, 374), (5)
Characters upon Essays, by N. Breton, 1615 (V,
52), (6) The Schoolmaster, by R. Ascham, 1570
(V, 124), (7) The Wife, by Sir T. Overbury,
1614 (V, 363), (8) Picturae Loquentes, by W.
Saltonstall, 1631 (V, 372), (9) Bentivolio and
Urania, by N. Ingelo, 1669 (IX, 334), (10) The
Compter's Commonwealth, by W. Fennor, 1617
(X, 300).

Brydges' name appears on the title pages of later volumes.
The selections are all rather brief.

[Mangin, Edward?]

Light Reading at leisure hours; or, an attempt
to unite the proper objects of gaiety and taste,
in exploring the various sources of rational
pleasure, the fine arts, poetry, sculpture, painting, music, dancing, fashionable pastimes, lives,
memoirs, characters, anecdotes, etc. 1805.*

Text pp. 1–464.

Attributed to Mangin by Halkett and Laing.

[Rennell, T., Knight, H.G., and Canning, G.]

The Miniature, A Periodical Paper, By Solo-
mon Grildrig, of the College of Eton. . . .
Windsor: Printed and sold for the author by
C. Knight, 1805.

8°, text pp. 1–368.
(1) Metaphrastus, a pedant (no. 10, p. 111), (2)
Philomusus, a truly learned man (no. 10, p. 116),
(3) Atticus, Trebius, Rusticus, and Rapillus,
types of mistaken ambition (no. 13), (4) Papirius,
whose education comes from periodicals (no. 18,
p. 209).

Attributed as above by Halkett and Laing.

1806

Anonymous.

The Polyanthos. Volume I. . . . Boston: Published by J. T. Buckingham . . . 1806.

6°, text pp. 5–287.
(1) Learning, by Breton (p. 45), (2) Knowledge,
by Breton (p. 46).

Hutchinson, Lucy.

Memoirs of the Life Of Colonel Hutchinson,
Governor Of Nottingham Castle And Town.
. . . Written by His Widow Lucy, daughter
of Sir Allen Apsley. . . . Now first published
From The Original Manuscript By the Rev.
Julius Hutchinson. . . . London: Printed for
Longman, Hurst, Rees, and Orme . . . 1806.

4°, text pp. 1–446.
(1) Colonel Hutchinson (p. 6), (2) Colonel
Hutchinson (p. 445, in verse).

Stevens, George Alexander.

A Lecture upon Heads. 1806.*

See 1788.

[Williams, Thomas.]

The Evangelical Magazine. Vol. VII.*
(1) A Christian (p. 474), (2) Sabbath observances
(p. 316).

1807

Anonymous.

The Monthly Anthology and Boston Review.
Boston . . . Munroe & Frances . . . 1807. [Vol.
IV.]

4°, text pp. 1–686.
(1) Ned Worthy and Will Careless (p. 138).

[Hill, Sir Richard.]

An Address to Persons of Fashion. 1807.*

Reprinted from 1761.

[Ireland, William Henry.]

Stultifera Navis . . . The Modern Ship Of
Fools. . . . London: Printed for William Miller . . . 1807.

8°, text pp. 1–295. In verse.
(1) A wise man (p. 268).

There was another edition of the same year printed at
Philadelphia, Baltimore, etc. Attributed to Ireland by the
CBEL.

Penn, William.

Fruits Of Solitude, in Reflections & Maxims
relating to the Conduct Of Human Life. By
William Penn. The Eleventh Edition. . . .

New-Brunswick, N.J. Printed for Robert East-
burn, by William Elliot, 1807.

8°, text pp. 1–272.
(1–8) as in 1749, (9) The happy man (p. 263),
(10) The true gentleman (p. 267).
This volume includes More Fruits of Solitude, which here
forms Part II. There is no indication of authorship of the
new characters, which follow several other sections attributed to William Law and Matthew Hale.

[Ward, Edward.]
The Wooden World Dissected, In The Characters Of I. A Ship of War . . . Chatham,
1807.*
Reprinted from 1707.

1808

[The Lady's Weekly Miscellany. New York.
Vol. VII. 1808.]
8°, text pp. 1–416.
(1) A woman of fashion (p. 23), (2) The obstinate man (p. 28), (3) The excellent woman (p.
365).
The title page is missing from the Harvard copy, from
which this note was made.

[Colman, George, and others.]
The Connoisseur. 1808.*
Reprinted from 1755–56.

[Evans, Arthur B.]
The Cutter, in Five Lectures upon The Art
And Practice of Cutting . . . New-York: Published by D. Longworth . . . 1808.
6°, text pp. 3–84.
(1) A cutter (p. 40).
Attributed to Evans by Halkett and Laing.

Hall, Joseph.
The Works of Joseph Hall. Ed. J. Pratt. 1808.*
10 vols.
Murphy 13.
Reprinted from 1625.

Hutchinson, Lucy.
Memoirs of . . . Colonel Hutchinson. 1808.*
Reprinted from 1806.

North, Roger.
The Life of the Right Honourable Francis
North, Baron of Guilford, Lord Keeper of the
Great Seal . . . Wherein are inserted the
Characters of Sir Matthew Hale, Sir George
Jeffries, Sir Leoline Jenkins, Sidney Godol-
phin, and others the most Eminent Lawyers
and Statesmen of that Time. By the Hon.
Roger North. . . . Second Edition. . . . Lon-
don: Printed for W. Clarke . . . 1808.

8°, in 2 parts, text pp. 1–317, 1–347.
(1–14) as in 1742.

Oldys, William, and Park, Thomas.
The Harleian Miscellany . . . [edited by]
William Oldys, Esq. and Thomas Park . . .
London: Printed for John White . . . 1808
[–13].
4°, 10 vols.
(1–25) as in 1744–46, (26) England, 1659 (Vol.
X, p. 189).
Murphy 8.

[Pratt, Samuel J.]
The Cabinet of Poetry . . . In Six Volumes
. . . London: Printed for Richard Phillips . . .
1808.
6 vols.
(1) The modern fine gentleman, by Soame Jenyns
(Vol. VI, p. 214), (2) The modern fine lady, by
Jenyns (VI, 216).
Attributed to Pratt by the CBEL.

Stevens, George Alexander.
A Lecture upon Heads. 1808.*
See 1788.

1809

Anonymous.
The Character of Methodism, from the Publications of the Sectaries. 1809.*

A Friendly gift for servants and apprentices:
containing, Character of a good and faithful
Servant; Advice to Servants of every denomination; Letter from an Uncle to his Nephew,
on Taking him Apprentice; and Anecdotes of
good and faithful Servants. By the author of
"Lessons for Young Persons in Humble Life."
1809.*

Barrington, George.
The London Spy.*
See 1832.

Hall, John E.
The American Law Journal And Miscellaneous Repertory. . . . By John E. Hall, Esq. Of
Baltimore. Vol. II. . . . Published By P. H.
Nicklin And Co. Baltimore [and others] . . .
1809.
4°, text pp. 1–500.
(1) The Character of an Honest Lawyer [by
H.C.], 1676 (p. 169).

[Parr, Samuel.]
Characters of the late Charles James Fox, se-

lected, and in part written, By Philopatris Varvicensis. . . . London, Printed for J. Mawman . . . 1809.

4°, 2 vols.

Contains numerous characters of Fox extracted from newspapers, periodicals, etc.

BSC 2640.

Attributed to Parr by the CBEL.

Scott, Sir Walter.

A Collection Of . . . Tracts . . . Particularly That Of The Late Lord Somers. The Second Edition, Revised, Augmented, And Arranged, By Walter Scott, Esq. . . . London: Printed for T. Cadell . . . [and 6 others] . . . 1809 [–15]

4°, 13 vols.

(1–10) as (1–12) in anonymous edition of 1748–52, (but omitting 7 and 10, H.C.'s Character of an Honest Lawyer and The Character of a Protestant), (11) Fragmenta Regalia, by Naunton (Vol. I, p. 251), (12) Tom Tel-Troath (II, 469), (13) The Prince, by Raleigh (III, 281), (14) Fiue Hundred Points of Good Husbandrie, by Tusser (III, 403), (15) The Earl of Strafford Characterized, 1641 (IV, 230), (16) The Character of England, 1659 (VII, 176).

Murphy 8 and *passim*.

1810

Anonymous.

The Lady's Miscellany: or, The Weekly Visitor. Vol. XII.

8°, text pp. 1–416.

(1) A beau (p. 70), (2) A fine woman (p. 71).

On the Character and Influence of a Virtuous King. 1810.*

Boerner, Dr.

Compendium of Four Dispositions, translated by J. Wiesche. Lancaster, Jacson.*

BSC 2641.

Brydges, Sir Egerton, and Haslewood, Joseph.

The British Bibliographer. By Sir Egerton Brydges, K.J. . . . London: Printed for R. Triphook . . . by T. Bensley . . . 1810[–14].

8°, 4 vols.

(1) The Times Displayed, 1646, by S. Sheppard (Vol. I, p. 528), (2) Descriptions, by W. Fennor, 1616 (I, 546), (3) More Knaves Yet, by S. Rowlands, n.d. (I, 548), (4) The Fraternity of Vagabonds, by J. Awdeley, 1575 (II, 12), (5) The Knave of Clubs, by S. Rowlands, 1612 (II, 103), (6) The Knave of Hearts, by S. Rowlands, 1612

(II, 105), (7) Pasquils Passe, by N. Breton, 1600 (II, 232), (8) A Caveat, by T. Harman, 1567 (II, 515), (9) Sivqila, by T. Lupton, 1580 (IV, 148), (10) The Belman of London, by T. Dekker, 1608 (IV, 293).

Murphy 122.

Haslewood's name appears on the title pages of Vols. II, III, and IV. The selections are only partial and brief.

Chalmers, Alexander.

The Works of the English Poets . . . By Alexander Chalmers, F.S.A. In Twenty-One Volumes. . . . London: Printed for J. Johnson [and many others] . . . 1810.

8°, 21 vols.

(1) A character, by Henry Brooke (Vol. XVII, p. 428).

[Du Refuge, Eustache.]

Arcana Aulica. 1810.*

Reprinted from 1652.

1811

Anonymous.

La Belle Assemblée; or Bell's Court and Fashionable Magazine. London: Printed for J. Bell. 1811.*

(1) Various types of physician (N.S., Vol. II, p. 75).

Browne, Thomas.

Pinacotheca Classica; or, Classical Gallery of Characters, Ancient and Modern. 1811.*

[Earle, John.]

Microcosmography . . . A New Edition. To which are added, Notes And An Appendix. By Philip Bliss. . . . London, Printed for White and Cochrane . . . 1811.

8°, text pp. 1–210.

(1–78) as in 1732.

Murphy 43. BSC 2642, 2643, 2644.

The text is based on the edition of 1732, collated with that of 1628.

Foppling, Sir Frederic (pseud.).

Portraits of Fops, or, Illustrations of the Foppish Character in all its Curious Varieties; with Sketches of our principal Modern Fops . . . By Sir Frederic Foppling, F.F.F. . . . London: Printed for, and sold by, J. Johnston . . . 1811.

8°, text pp. 1–120.

(1) The city fop (p. 5), (2) The fashionable fop (p. 17), (3) The clerical fop (p. 28), (4) The medical fop (p. 37), (5) The legal fop (p. 47), (6) The military fop (p. 59), (7) The musical

fop (p. 71), (8) The driving fop (p. 83), (9) The literary fop (p. 95), (10) The political fop (p. 110).

[Scott, Sir Walter, editor.]

Secret History of the Court of James the First: containing . . . Sir Anthony Weldon's Court And Character of King James. . . . In Two Volumes. . . . Edinburgh: Printed by James Ballantyne and Co. . . . 1811.

8°, 2 vols.

(1) James I, by Weldon (Vol. II, p. 1), (2) A Perfect Description of the People And Country of Scotland, 1659, by Weldon (II, 75), (3) Aulicus Coquinariae, by Sir William Sanderson.

Ascribed to Scott by the CBEL.

1812

Habington, William.

Habington's Castara, with a Preface and Notes, By Charles A. Elton . . . Bristol. [1812.]

8°, text pp. 46–387.

(1–4) as in 1640.

Murphy 127.

[Paulding, James Kirke.]

The Diverting History of John Bull and Brother Jonathan. By Hector Bull — US. New-York: Published by Inskeep & Bradford; and Bradford & Inskeep, Philadelphia, 1812.

12°, text pp. 3–135.

(1) John Bull (p. 3), (2) Brother Jonathan (p. 7).

[Ward, Edward.]

Female Policy Detected. 1812.*

See the undated edition.

1813

Awdeley, John.

The Fraternitye of Vacabondes . . . Imprinted at London by Iohn Awdeley . . . 1575. . . . Westminster: Reprinted for Machell Stace, No. 12, Little Queen–Street, and R. Triphook, St. James's Street. 1813.*

(1–22) as in 1575.

[Earle, John.]

A Gallery of Portraits, Painted by an old and celebrated Master and Re-touched by an Irish Artist. . . . Dublin . . . 1813.*

8°.

Contains 32 portraits adapted from Earle's Microcosmographie.

Murphy 45.

[Paulding, James Kirke.]

The Diverting History of John Bull. 1813.*

Reprinted from 1812.

Peacham, Henry.

The Worth of a Penny, or, A Caution to keep Money. . . . By Henry Peacham. . . . Now newly reprinted according to Order, and made more publick than heretofore . . . London: Printed by S. Griffin, for William Lee . . . 1667. . . . [verso of title page] Leeds: reprinted by B. Dewhurst, for Robinson and Son. 1813.

4°, text pp. 1–71.

(1–2) as in 1641.

Penn, William.

Fruits of Solitude, in Reflections And Maxims . . . By William Penn . . . New-York . . . Samuel Wash . . . 1813.

6°, text pp. 1–129.

(1) The proud man (p. 6), (2) The covetous man (p. 20), (3) The wise man and politician (p. 86), (4) The wise man (p. 91), (5) The untrue servant (p. 113).

Warwick, Sir Philip.

Memoirs of the Reign of King Charles I. Edited by Dr. T. Smith. Edinburgh, 1813.*

Reprinted from 1701.

1814

Anonymous.

The Analectic Magazine . . . Volume III. Philadelphia: Published And Sold By Moses Thomas [and many others] . . . 1814.

4°, text pp. 1–528.

(1) The idea of a true patriot, by James K. Paulding (p. 137).

The only sign of authorship is the signature "P" at the end.

Edgeworth, Maria.

Patronage. By Maria Edgeworth. . . . In Four Volumes. Vol. I. . . . London, Printed for J. Johnson and Co. . . . 1814.

12°, 4 vols.

(1) French Clay and English Clay, two contrasted brothers (chap. 24).

This is the second edition. The first appeared in the same year. There were others later.

Harman, Thomas.

A Caveat or Warning for Common Cursetors, vulgarly called Vagabonds. By Thomas Harman. . . . London: Reprinted by T. Bensley . . . 1814.

4°, text pp. 11–72.
(1–24) as in 1567.
BSC 2645.

Peacham, Henry.

The Worth Of A Penny; Or, A Caution to keep Money. . . . By Henry Peacham . . . London, Printed by S. Griffin, for William Lee . . . 1664 [1814].

8°, text pp. 1–40.
(1–2) as in 1664.
A reproduction of the edition of 1664.

Rowlands, Samuel.

The Letting of Humours Blood In The Head Vaine, &c. By S. Rowlands. Edinburgh: Reprinted by James Ballantyne and Co. For William Blackwood . . . 1814.

8°, text sigs. A4–D6v.
(1–26) as in 1600.
Edited by Sir Walter Scott.

1815

Brydges, Sir Egerton.

Archaica. Containing A Reprint of Scarce Old English Prose Tracts. With Prefaces . . . In Two Volumes. By Sir E. Brydges . . . London . . . 1815.

4°, 2 vols.
(1) Characters upon Essays, by Nicholas Breton, 1615 (Vol. I, Part 5), (2) The Good and the Badde, 1616, by Nicholas Breton (I, 5), (3) Essays upon the Five Senses, by Richard Brathwaite, 1625 (II, 6).
Murphy 8, 26, 27.

Brydges, Sir Egerton.

Censura Literaria. . . . By Sir Egerton Brydges. . . . Second Edition. . . . London: Printed for Longman, Hurst, Rees, Orme, and Brown . . . 1815.

8°, 10 volumes.
(1–10) as in 1805–09.
Murphy 8.

Rowlands, Samuel.

The Letting of Humours Blood In The Head Vaine, &c. By S. Rowlands. Edinburgh: Reprinted by James Ballantyne and Co. for William Laing, And William Blackwood. 1815.

8°, text sigs. A4–D6v.
(1–26) as in 1600.

[Williams, Thomas.]

The Evangelical Magazine. Vol. VIII.*
(1) The upholding laws about the Sabbath (p. 80).

1816

Hedgehood, Humphrey.

The Busy Body, or Men and Manners. Edited by Humphrey Hedgehood. 1816.*
8°, 2 vols.
(1) The fashionable belle, (2) The fashionable fop, (3) The Methodist's special retainer, (4) Foppish attitudes, (5) The life of Cobbett.

Hunt, Leigh.

The Examiner. 1816.*
(1) An old lady (September 30), (2) A maidservant (October 20).

Milton, John.

Milton's 'Second Defence Of The People Of England; In Answer To An Infamous Work, Entitled 'The Cry of the Royal Blood to Heaven against the English Parricides.'
8°, text pp. 9–199.
(1) Alexander More (p. 28), (2) John Bradshaw (p. 135), (3) Oliver Cromwell (p. 172), (4) Thomas, Baron Fairfax (p. 176).

The original Latin edition appeared in 1654; the above is the first English translation, done by Francis Wrangham. The date is from D. H. Stevens's Reference Guide to Milton. There have been other later editions.

1817

Anonymous.

The Management Of The Tongue, Under The Following Very Important And Useful Heads . . . Translated From The French. Third Edition. Boston: Published By Isaiah Thomas, Jun. M. & W. H. Mann, Printers. 1817.

6°, text pp. 21–252.
(1–27) as in 1706.

[Lodge, Thomas.]

A fig for Momus . . . By T.L. of Lincolnes Inne . . . 1595 . . . Reprinted, At the Auchinleck Press, By Alexander Boswell. MDCCC-XVII.

4°, text sigs. A4–H2v.
(1) as in 1595.

[Paulding, James Kirke.]

Letters from the South . . . By the author of John Bull and Brother Jonathan, &c. &c. . . . In two volumes. Vol. II. New York . . . James Estburn & Co. . . . 1817.

6°, text pp. 3–260.
(1) Brother Jonathan (p. 69).

1818

Anonymous.

The Pocket Magazine Of Classic and Polite

Literature. With Engravings, Illustrative of Lord Byron's Works. . . . London: Printed And Published By John Arliss . . . M.DCCC.-XVIII.

6°, 5 vols.

(1) A popular preacher (Vol. I, p. 17).

Dunton, John.

The Life and Errors of John Dunton, Citizen of London; with the Lives and characters of more than a thousand Contemporary Divines. . . . Printed by and for J. Nichols. . . . London. 1818.

8°, 2 vols.

(1 . . .) as in 1705.

Lamb, Charles.

The Works Of Charles Lamb. In Two Volumes. . . . London: Printed for C. and J. Ollier . . . 1818.

8°, 2 vols.

(1) Recollections of Christ's Hospital (Vol. I, p. 265), (2) On the genius and character of Hogarth (II, 88), (3) The Londoner (II, 139), (4) On burial societies; and the character of an undertaker (II, 143), (5) On the inconveniences resulting from being hanged (II, 166), (6) On the melancholy of tailors (II, 184), (7) Hospita on the immoderate indulgence of the pleasures of the palate (II, 193), (8) Edax on appetite (II, 199).

Penn, William.

Fruits of Solitude. 1818.*

Reprinted from 1749.

Simpleton, Samuel.

The Idiot, Or, Invisible Rambler. By Samuel Simpleton. Vol. I. Boston, Saturday January 24, 1818. No. 3.

fo, 2 leaves unpaged.

(1) A sloven (last page).

1819

Anonymous.

The Biographical Magazine; Containing Portraits Of Eminent And Ingenious Persons Of Every Age And Nation, With Their Lives And Characters. . . . London: Printed for Effingham Wilson . . . and Sherwood, Neely, & Jones . . . MDCCCXIX.

8°, 2 vols., without paging or signature marks.

(1) Sir Ralph Abercrombie, (2) Joseph Addison, (3) Michael Angelo, (4) Lord George Anson, (5) Lord Francis Bacon, (6) Sir William Blackstone, (7) Lord Bolingbroke, (8) George Buchanan,

(9) Count de Buffon, (10) Edmund Burke, (11) Robert Burns, (12) The Earl of Bute, (13) Miguel Cervantes, (14) The Earl of Chatham, (15) Geoffrey Chaucer, (16) John Churchill, Duke of Marlborough, (17) William Congreve, (18) Captain James Cook, (19) William Cowper, (20) Archbishop Cranmer, (21) Oliver Cromwell, (22) Richard Cumberland, (23) John Philpot Curran, (24) Dr. Erasmus Darwin, (25) John Lovis De Lolme, (26) John Dryden, (27) The Earl of Essex, (28) Prince Eugene, (29) John Evelyn, (30) Archbishop Fenelon, (31) Henry Fielding, (32) The Right Honourable Charles James Fox, (33) George Fox, (34) Dr. Benjamin Franklin, (35) Frederick the Great, King of Prussia, (36) David Garrick, (37) John Gay, (38) Edward Gibbon, (39) Dr. Oliver Goldsmith, (40) Thomas Gray, (41) Sir Thomas Gresham, (42) Sir Matthew Hale, (43) John Hampden, (44) George Frederic Handel, (45) Dr. William Harvey, (46) Dr. Hawkesworth, (47) William Hogarth, (48) John Howard, (49) David Hume, (50) Dr. Samuel Johnson, (51) Sir William Jones, (52) Ben Jonson, (53) John Caspar Lavater, (54) Dr. John Coakley Lettson, (55) Charles von Linnaeus, (56) John Locke, (57) John Milton, (58) Sir Thomas More, (59) George Morland, (60) Sir John Moore, (61) Lord Nelson, (62) Sir Isaac Newton, (63) Lord North, (64) Thomas Otway, (65) William Paley, (66) Thomas Parnell, (67) William Penn, (68) The Right Honourable William Pitt, (69) Alexander Pope, (70) Beilby Porteus, Bishop of London, (71) Racine, (72) Sir Walter Raleigh, (73) Raphael, (74) Sir Joshua Reynolds, (75) Samuel Richardson, (76) Dr. William Robertson, (77) Rousseau, (78) Archbishop Secker, (79) Edward Seymour, Duke of Somerset, (80) William Shakespeare, (81) Richard Brinsley Sheridan, (82) Tobias George Smollett, (83) Edmund Spenser, (84) Sir Richard Steele, (85) Lawrence Sterne, (86) Dr. Jonathan Swift, (87) James Thompson, (88) Sir James Thornhill, (89) Archbishop Tillotson, (90) Voltaire, (91) General Washington, (92) Richard Watson, Bishop of Landaff, (93) Samuel Whitbread, (94) Arthur Wolfe, Lord Kilwarden, (95) Cardinal Wolsey, (96) Sir Christopher Wren, (97) Mark Akenside, (98) John Armstrong, (99) Dr. Beattie, (100) Francis Beaumont, (101) William Beckford, (102) Joseph Blachet, (103) Dr. Hugh Blair, (104) Blucher, (105) Nicholas Boileau, (106) Charles Bonnet, (107) Bossuet, (108) Lord Camden, (109) Lord Arthur Capel, (110) William Caxton, (111) William Cecil, (112) Lord Charlmont, (113) Thomas Chatterton, (114) Lord Clarendon, (115) Sir Edward Coke, (116) Christopher Columbus, (117) Peter Corneille, (118) Abraham Cowley, (119) Thomas Cromwell, Earl of Essex, (120) William Curtis, (121) Sir Kenelm Digby, (122) Philip Dod-

dridge, (123) Sir Francis Drake, (124) Lord Ellenborough, (125) Thomas Lord Fairfax, (126) Lord Falkland, (127) La Fontaine, (128) Froissart, (129) Solomon Gesner, (130) Dr. Gill, (131) The Marquis of Granby, (132) Bacon Haller, (133) Warren Hastings, (134) Dr. Matthew Henry, (135) Lord Herbert of Cherbury, (136) Hans Holbein, (137) Charles Howard, Earl of Nottingham, (138) Thomas Howard, 3rd Duke of Norfolk, (139) Lord Howe, (140) John Hunter, (141) Bishop Hurd, (142) Henry Ireton, (143) Inigo Jones, (144) Lord Kaimes, (145) Dr. King, (146) Sir Godfrey Kneller, (147) John Knox, (148) Augustus von Kotzebue, (149) John Lambert, (150) Bishop Latimer, (151) Archbishop Laud, (152) Martin Luther, (153) Lord Lyttleton, (154) William Mason, (155) Philip Melancthon, (156) Sir Hugh Middleton, (157) The Marquis of Montrose, (158) The Earl of Morton, (159) Arthur Murphy, (160) John Opie, (161) Dr. Pearce, (162) Thomas Pennant, (163) Professor Playfair, (164) Dr. Priestley, (165) Matthew Prior, (166) John Ray, (167) Van Rhin Rembrandt, (168) Sir Samuel Romilly, (169) Rubens, (170) Lord William Russel, (171) Lucius Annaeus Seneca, (172) Michael Servetus, (173) Sir Philip Sidney, (174) Philip Dormer Stanhope, Earl of Chesterfield, (175) Lord Thurlow, (176) Horne Tooke, (177) Joseph Tournefort, (178) Dr. Vincent, (179) Edmund Waller, (180) Horatio Walpole, (181) Sir Robert Walpole, (182) Isaac Walton, (183) Bishop Warburton, (184) Thomas Warton, (185) Dr. Watts, (186) William Waynfleet, (187) Henry Kirke White, (188) William Wickham, (189) John Wilkes, (190) Archbishop Williams, (191) Dr. Walcott, (192) Dr. Young.

Nos. 1–96 are in Volume I, the rest in Volume II.

Branch, William.

Life, A Poem In Three Books; Descriptive of the various characters . . . passions . . . good and evil . . . and of the perfect man. . . . By William Branch, Junior. . . . Richmond . . . 1819.

6°, text pp. 2–218.

(1) A dunce (p. 83), (2) A genius (p. 91), (3) An industrious boy (p. 97), (4) A mere learner of words (p. 102), (5) A learner of things (p. 108), (6) A child of fancy (p. 120), (7) A son of reason, a philosopher (p. 124), (8) A criterion (p. 132), (9) A griping miser (p. 150), (10) A miser's bantling (p. 154), (11) A man inspired by self-love (p. 155), (12) A general lover (p. 157), (13) A flatterer (p. 160), (14) A wife of noble virtues (p. 167), (15) Avaro, a profane lover (p. 172), (15) A man disappointed, a "senseless empiric," a "dishonest monger of the laws" (p. 187), (16) A mere husband — what he should be (p. 193), (17) A good man (p. 209).

[Irving, Washington.]

The Sketch book Of Geoffrey Crayon, Gent. . . . New York: Printed by C.S. Van Winkle. 1819[–20].

4°, 2 vols, in 7 parts, text pp. 5–335 (parts 1–4), 5–108, 5–120, 5–123.

(1) A coachman (no. 5, p. 19, in The Stage Coach), (2) Squire Bracebridge, an old English country gentleman (no. 5, p. 31, in Christmas Eve), (3) John Bull (no. 6, p. 5, in John Bull).

Frequently reprinted.

[McDonough, Felix.]

The Hermit In London; Or, Sketches Of English Manners. London, Printed for Henry Colburn. 1819–20.

12°, 5 vols.

(1) A patron (Vol. I, p. 27), (2) The new member of Parliament (I, 129), (3) The female charioteer (I, 171), (4) A stranger (I, 183), (5) Female gamblers (I, 195), (6) Fortune hunters (II. 25), (7) The pedant (II, 191), (8) Learned women and accomplished women (III, 57), (9) Female politicians (III, 217), (10) Les Chevaliers d'Industrie (III, 259).

North, Roger.

The Lives of . . . Francis North . . . 1819.*

Reprinted from 1808.

Porson, Professor [Richard?].

Eloisa in Deshabille: A Satirical Poem. By the Late Professor Porson. To which are added: The Modern Fine Gentleman; Modern Fine Lady; Curtain Lectures; and The Squire and the Parson. . . . London, 1819.*

(1) The modern fine gentleman, by Soame Jenyns, (2) The modern fine lady, by Soame Jenyns.

1820

[Hunt, Leigh.]

The Indicator. Vol. I and II. . . . London: Printed for Joseph Appleyard . . . 1820.

2 vols.

(1) The old gentleman (Vol. I, p. 129), (2) Seamen on shore (I, 177), (3) The maid servant (II, 54), (4) The old lady (II, 62).

Numbers 3 and 4 are reprinted from The Examiner, 1816.

[McDonough, Felix.]

The Hermit in London; Or, Sketches of English Manners. . . . Philadelphia: Published by M. Carey & Son . . . 1820.

6°, 2 vols.

(1–10) as in 1819–20.

[McDonough, Felix.]

The Hermit in the Country; or, Sketches of English Manners . . . New-York . . . L. and F. Lockwood. 1820.

6°, 2 vols.

(1) The widow (Vol. I, p. 101), (2) A good fellow (II, 77), (3) A valuable character, Mrs. Mildmay (II, 209), (4) A rusticated Londoner, Jack Townly (II, 283).

Stevens, George Alexander.

A Lecture upon Heads.*

See 1788.

1821

[McDonough, Felix.]

The Hermit in London. 1821.*

Reprinted from 1819–20.

Mackenzie, Sir George.

A Moral Paradox: Maintaining, That it is much easier to be Vertuous then Vitious. London, 1821.*

Reprinted from Moral Gallantry, 1667.

Mynshul, Geffray.

Essayes and Characters of a Prison and Prisoners. By Geffray Mynshul. Edinburgh: Reprinted for W. and C. Tait, By James Ballantyne & Co. MDCCCXXI.

8°, text pp. 11–91.

(1–8) as in 1618.

Murphy 33. BSC 2647.

Philanthropos.

The Character of a Peer. London, 1821.*

Philanthropos.

The Character of a Priest. London, 1821.*

Philanthropos.

The Character Of A Soldier; By Philanthropos. London: Printed And Published By R. Carlile . . . 1821.

4°, text pp. 3–8.

Begins: "Nothing prevails more abundantly than hypocrisy."

BSC 2646.

Philanthropos.

The Character of the Jew Books; being, a defence of the natural innocence of man, against kings and priests, or tyrants and impostors. London, 1821.*

Stevens, George Alexander.

A Lecture upon Heads. 1821.*

See 1788.

Warwick, Arthur.

Spare Minutes; Or, Resolved Meditations And Premeditated Resolutions. Written By Arthur Warwick. . . . The Sixth Edition. London: Printed By G. M. for Walter Hammond, and are to be sold by Michael Sparke . . . 1637. . . . [colophon] Maurice, Printer, Fenchurch Street.

8°, text pp. 1–120.

(1) The good man and the hypocrite (p. 18), (2) A bad great one (p. 34).

The first edition was 1634. Reprinted several times. The present is a nineteenth-century reproduction of the edition of 1637. The date is uncertain.

1822

Butler, Samuel.

Genuine Remains.*

Reprinted from 1759.

Egerton, D. T.

Fashionable Bores.*

Hutchinson, Lucy.

Memoirs of . . . Colonel Hutchinson . . . by His Widow Lucy . . . Fourth Edition. London, Printed for Longman, Hurst, Rees, Orme, and Brown . . . 1822.

4°, 2 vols.

(1–2) as in 1806.

[Irving, Washington.]

Bracebridge Hall, Or The Humourists. A Medley, By Geoffrey Crayon, Gent. . . . New-York: Printed by C.S. Van Winkle . . . 1822.

2 vols.

(1) The busy man (no. 3), (2) An old soldier (no. 8).

There have been numerous later editions.

[Philalethes.]

A Character of the late Rev. John Wesley, M.A. Otley, Printed By and For W. Walker. 1822.*

(1) John Wesley (p. 6).

Philanthropos.

The Character of the Jew Books. Second Edition. London, 1822.*

Reprinted from 1821.

1823

Anonymous.

The Ladies' Monthly Museum; or, Polite Repository of Amusement and Instruction . . . Vol. XVII. . . . London . . . Dean and Munday . . . 1823.

6°, text pp. 1–352.
(1) The suspicious man (p. 92), (2) The purse-proud man (p. 150), (3) The hypocrite (p. 269). All three characters are signed Verax.

Deacon, W. F.

The Inn-Keeper's Album, Arranged for Publication by W.F. Deacon.... London: Thomas McLean, Haymarket. 1823.
8°, text pp. 1–429.
(1) The old lady (p. 1), (2) The coachman (p. 40), (3) The commonplace man (p. 72), (4) The schoolmaster (p. 129), (5) The village girl (p. 198).

[Lamb, Charles.]

Elia. Essays Which Have Appeared Under That Signature In The London Magazine. London: Printed for Taylor and Hessey ... 1823.
8°, text pp. 1–341.
(1) The South-Sea House (p. 1), (2) Oxford in the vacation (p. 15), (3) Christ's Hospital five and thirty years ago (p. 27), (4) The two races of men (p. 51), (5) New Year's Eve (p. 61), (6) Mrs. Battle's Opinions on Whist (p. 73), (7) A chapter on ears (p. 86), (8) All Fools' Day (p. 95), (9) A Quakers' meeting (p. 102), (10) The old and new schoolmaster (p. 111), (11) Valentine's Day (p. 127), (12) Imperfect sympathies (p. 133), (13) Witches, and other night-fears (p. 148), (14) My relations (p. 160), (15) Mackery End, in Hertfordshire (p. 172), (16) Modern gallantry (p. 181), (17) The old benchers of the Middle Temple (p. 189), (18) Grace before meat (p. 209), (19) My first play (p. 221), (20) Dream-children; a reverie (p. 230), (21) Distant correspondents (p. 238), (22) The praise of chimney-sweepers (p. 249), (23) A complaint of the decay of beggars in the metropolis (p. 262), (24) A dissertation upon roast pig (p. 276), (25) A bachelor's complaint of the behaviour of married people (p. 289), (26) On some of the old actors (p. 302), (27) On the artificial comedy of the last century (p. 323), (28) On the acting of Munden (p. 338).

For previous separate appearances of these essays, which are not recorded in this bibliography, the reader is referred to the notes to Lamb's Works, ed. E. V. Lucas. Often reprinted.

Locke, John.

The Works of John Locke ... In Ten Volumes ... London: Printed for Thomas Tegg ... W. Sharpe and son ... 1823.
8°, 10 vols.
(1) Dr. Edward Pocock, from a letter of July 23, 1703 (Vol. X, p. 299).
There have been several other editions.

[McDonough, Felix.]

The Hermit in the Country. 1823.*
Reprinted from 1820.

[Maugham, Robert?]

Outlines Of Character: Consisting Of The Great Character, — The English Character, — Characteristic Classes in Relation To Happiness, — The Gentleman, — External Indications Of Character, — Craniology, — The Poet, — The Orator, — Literary Characters, — The Periodical Critic, — The Man Of Genius. By A Member Of The Philomathic Institution. ... London: Printed For Longman, Hurst, Rees, Orme, And Brown ... 1823.
8°, text pp. 3–306.
(1) The gentleman (p. 77), (2) A reviewer (p. 241), (3) The talented (p. 267), (4) The learned (p. 268), (5) The fine genius (p. 271), (6) The sublime genius (p. 273).

Stevens, George Alexander.

A Lecture upon Heads. 1823.*
See 1788.

[Westmacott, Charles Molloy.]

The English Spy, or Characteristic Sketches and Scenes of the present Age. 1823.*
See 1825–26.

1824

Buchan, Peter.

Scriptural & Philosophical Arguments; or, Cogent Proofs from Reason & Revelation that Brutes have Souls; and that, their Souls Are Immortal: With A Dedicatory Epistle to Mr. Charles Forbes Buchan, wherein is given the character of a just and an unjust lawyer; a quack doctor and real doctor of medicine; a heterodox and an orthodox preacher, &c. By Peter Buchan. ... Peterhead: Printed for and by P. Buchan ... 1824.
6°, text pp. 13–120.
(1) A pettifogging lawyer (p. xvi), (2) A quack doctor (p. xvii), (3) A heterodox preacher (p. xviii), (4) A just lawyer (p. xix), (5) A good doctor (p. xx), (6) An orthodox preacher (p. xxii).

Egerton, D. T.

Fashionable Bores or Coolers in High Life. By Peter Quiz. London, 1824.*
Reprinted from 1822.

[McDonough, Felix.]

The Hermit in Edinburgh; or, Sketches Of Manners and Real Characters And Scenes in the Drama of Life. . . . London: Printed for Sherwood, Jones, & Co. . . . 1824.

12°, 3 vols.

(1) Lord Flimsy (Vol. II, p. 121), (2) Lady Mordante, a malevolent woman (II, 133), (3) The retired officer (III, 159).

[McDonough, Felix.]

The Hermit in London. 1824.*

Reprinted from 1819-20.

Mitford, Mary Russell.

Our Village: Sketches Of Rural Character And Scenery. By Mary Russell Mitford. London: B. And W.B. Whittaker. 1824.

8°, text pp. 1–292.

(1) The talking lady (p. 107), (2) The talking gentleman (p. 213).

Reprinted several times. Possibly other characters, missing from the copy examined, could be included. Possibilities are: (3) Tom Hopkins, (4) The touchy lady, (5) The inquisitive gentleman.

Theophrastus.

Characters. 1824.*

Reprinted from 1714.

1825

Anonymous.

Characters and Opinions; or, The Blue Book. London: Printed for Saunders and Otley, 1825.*

(1) The melancholy man, by Maria (p. 260).

[Westmacott, Charles Molloy.]

The English Spy: An Original Work, Characteristic, Satirical, And Humorous. Comprising Scenes And Sketches In Every Rank Of Society, Being Portraits Of The Illustrious, Eminent, Eccentric, and Notorious. Drawn From The Life By Bernard Blackmantle. The Illustrations Designed By Robert Cruikshank. . . . London: Published by Sherwood, Jones, and Co. 1825[–26].

8°, 2 vols.

(1) Bernard Blackmantle, by Horatio Heartley (Vol. I, p. 29), (2) The Hon. Lilyman Lionize (I, 37), (3) Tom Echo (I, 39), (4) Horace Eglantine (I, 40), (5) Dick Gradus (I, 42), (6) A fashionable opera-goer (I, 225), (7) Old Crony, the dinner man (I, 243).

1826

[Barker, Matthew H.?]

The Log Book; Or, Nautical Miscellany. London: Published By J. & W. Robins.

8°, text pp. 1–508.

(1) The Greenwich pensioner (p. 49).

Attributed to Barker by the Harvard Library catalogue, from which the tentative date is also taken.

[Colman, George, and others.]

The Connoisseur. 1826.*

Reprinted from 1755-56.

North, Roger.

The Lives of the right hon. Francis North . . . The Hon. Sir Dudley North . . . and the Hon. and Rev. Dr. John North . . . By The Hon. Roger North. . . . London: Henry Colburn . . . 1826.

8°, 3 vols.

(1–14) as in 1808.

Theophrastus.

Characters. 1826.*

Reprinted from 1714.

1827

Butler, Samuel.

Genuine Remains.*

Reprinted from 1759.

[Scargill, William Pitt.]

Blue-Stocking Hall. 1827.*

See 1829.

1828

Anonymous.

Timothy Grub: his Life and Opinions and Wild Thoughts Tamed. London, 1828.*

2 vols.

(1) Mr. Wick, (2) Captain Freelove, (3) Sir Tallyho, (4) Mrs. Freemantle, (5) Mrs. Trouble.

Baxter, Richard.

Works.*

Reprinted from 1707.

Henderson, C.

Sketches of Character, drawn on stone by M. Bauci. London, 1828.*

Hunt, Leigh.

The Companion. By Leigh Hunt . . . London: Printed for Hunt and Clarke . . . 1828.

4°, text pp. 1–432.

(1) Watchmen (p. 43).

Attributed to Hunt by the CBEL.

[Smeeton, George.]

Doings in London Southwark: G. Smeeton.*
8°.
(1) A sailor, by Overbury (p. 318), (2) A stock-jobber (p. 371).
The British Museum Catalogue, which ascribes this title to Smeeton, dates it 1828 without question.

Theophrastus.

Characters. 1828.*
Reprinted from 1714.

[Ward, Edward.]

Female Policy Detected. 1828.*
See the undated edition.

[Webbe, Cornelius.]

The Posthumous Papers, Facetious and Fanciful, of A Person Lately About town. . . . New York: Printed By J. & J. Harper . . . 1828.
6°, text pp. 9–243.
(1) The humorous man (p. 36), (2) The awkward man (p. 53), (3) The eccentric poet (p. 214).

1829

[Scargill, William Pitt.]

Blue-Stocking Hall. . . . Second Edition. In Three Volumes. . . . London: Henry Colburn . . . 1829.
12°, 3 vols.
(1) Mrs. Fitzroy (Vol. II, p. 93).
The first edition appeared in 1827. Attributed to Scargill by the CBEL.

1830

Baxter, Richard.

The Practical Works Of The Rev. Richard Baxter: With A Life Of The Author . . . By the Rev. William Orme. . . . In Twenty-Three Volumes. London: James Duncan . . . MDCCCXXX.
8°, 23 vols.
(1–8) as in 1707.

Grahame, Simion.

The Anatomie Of Humors . . . By Simion Grahame . . . Edinburgh . . . M.DCCC.XXX.
4°, text sigs. B–R2v.
(1–24) as in 1609.
Edited by R. Jameson, who dedicated it to the Bannatyne Club.

[Lytton, Edward George Earle Lytton Bulwer-Lytton, Baron.]

Paul Clifford. By The Author Of "Pelham," "The Disowned," And "Devereux." . . . In

Two Volumes. . . . New York: Printed by J. & J. Harper . . . Sold by Collins & Hannay [and numerous others] . . . 1830.
12°, 2 vols, text pp. 1–215, 3–216.
(1) Paul Clifford (Vol. I, p. 17), (2) Bachelor Bill (I, 27).

1831

[Mudford, William]

The Premier. In Three Volumes. . . . London: Henry Colburn and Richard Bentley . . . 1831.
12°, 3 vols.
(1) Various gentlemen (Vol. I, p. 134).
Attributed to Mudford by the CBEL.

Theophrastus.

Characters. 1831.*
Reprinted from 1714.

1832

Barrington, George.

The London Spy; or the frauds Of London Detected . . . By G. Barrington. . . . Boston 1832.
12°, text pp. 11–216.
(1) Bawds (p. 11), (2) Bullies (p. 15), (3) Duffers (p. 20), (4) Fortune tellers and conjurors (p. 23), (5) Footpads (p. 28), (6) Gamblers (p. 30), (7) Gossips (p. 43), (8) Hangers-on (p. 52), (9) Highwaymen (p. 54), (10) Housebreakers (p. 58), (11) Intelligences (p. 59), (12) Jilts (p. 61), (13) Insolvents (p. 64), (14) Kidnappers (p. 68), (15) Lottery office keepers (p. 71), (16) Mock auctioneers (p. 73), (17) Money droppers (p. 75), (18) Ring droppers (p. 79), (19) Pimps (p. 81), (20) Procurers and procuresses (p. 87), (21) Pretended friends (p. 92), (22) Pickpockets (p. 96), (23) Quacks (p. 99), (24) Receivers of stolen goods (p. 102), (25) Spungers (p. 104), (26) Sharpers (p. 108), (27) Swindlers (p. 114), (28) Setters (p. 124), (29) Smugglers (p. 125), (30) Shoplifters (p. 129), (31) Trappers (p. 135), (32) Whores (p. 138), (33) Waylayers (p. 147), (34) Wagon-hunters (p. 153), (35) A patient in a hospital (p. 162), (36) A young spark (p. 167), (37) A usurer (p. 170), (38) A confined debtor (p. 174), (39) River pirates (p. 192), (40) Light horsemen (p. 196), (41) Heavy horsemen (p. 196), (42) Mud larks (p. 197), (43) Rat catchers (p. 198), (44) Game lightermen (p. 199), (45) Scuffle hunters (p. 200), (46) Resurrection men (p. 202).
There was an earlier edition in 1809. I am not sure whether The Frauds and Cheats of London Detected, 1802, and Barrington's New London Spy for 1805 or the Frauds of London Detected [1805?] are earlier versions of the same work, since I have not had access to them.

Hood, Thomas.

The Comic Annual. By Thomas Hood . . .
London: Charles Tilt . . . M.DCCC.XXXII.
8°, text pp. 1–174.
(1) A Lord Mayor (p. 31, in verse), (2) The
illuminati (p. 62), (3) A horse-dealer (p. 132).

[Kennedy, J.P.]

Swallow Barn. . . . In Two Volumes. . . .
Philadelphia . . . 1832.
6°, 2 vols.
(1) A country gentleman (chap. 2), (2) Family
portraits (chap. 3).

1833

[Halifax, George Savile, Marquis of.]

The Character of a Trimmer. 1833.*
Reprinted from 1688.

[Lamb, Charles.]

The Last Essays of Elia. Being A Sequel To
Essays Published Under That Name. London:
Edward Moxon . . . 1833.
12°, text pp. 1–283.
(1) Preface — by a friend of the late Elia (p. v),
(2) Blakesmoor in H--shire (p. 1), (3) Poor relations (p. 10), (4) Stage illusions (p. 22), (5) To
the shade of Elliston (p. 29), (6) Ellistoniana
(p. 34), (7) Detached thoughts on books and
reading (p. 44), (8) The old Margate hoy (p.
56), (9) The convalescent (p. 70), (10) Sanity of
true genius (p. 78), (11) Captain Jackson (p. 84),
(12) The superannuated man (p. 92), (13) The
genteel style in writing (p. 105), (14) Barbara
S-- (p. 114), (15) The tombs in the Abbey (p.
124), (16) Amicus redivivus (p. 129), (17) Some
sonnets of Sir Philip Sidney (p. 138), (18) Newspapers thirty-five years ago (p. 153), (19) Barren-
ness of the imaginative faculty in the productions
of modern art (p. 166), (20) Rejoicings upon the
New Year's coming of age (p. 187), (21) The
wedding (p. 197), (22) The child angel — a
dream (p. 208), (23) A death-bed (p. 213), (24)
Old china (p. 216), (25) Popular fallacies (p.
227).
Often reprinted.

Shirley, James.

The Dramatic Works And Poems of James
Shirley . . . collected . . . by . . . William
Gifford, Esq. and . . . Alexander Dyce. In
Six Volumes. . . . London: John Murray . . .
MDCCCXXXIII.
8°, 6 vols.
(1) The Witty Fair One (Vol. I, p. 273).

1834

Anonymous.

The Young Gentleman's Book; Containing A
Series Of Choice Readings . . . Together
With Retrospective Essays, Conversations, Literary Reminiscences, etc. Third Edition. London: Printed For Baldwin and Cradock . . .
M.DCCC.XXXIV.
6°, text pp. 1–468.
(1) A benevolent man (p. 255).
There were several editions in 1834.

Hunt, Leigh.

The Indicator and the Companion. . . . By
Leigh Hunt. In Two Volumes. . . . London:
Published for Henry Colburn . . . 1834.
2 vols.
(1–4) as in 1820.

Reldpen, Peregrine.

Our Town; or, Rough Sketches of Character,
Manners. 1834.*

1835

Hunt, Leigh.

Leigh Hunt's London Journal and The Printing Machine. . . . Vol. II . . . London: Charles
Knight . . . 1835.
4°, text pp. 1–460.
(1) The waiter (p. 177), (2) The butcher (p.
185).

Martin, Thomas.

The Character of Lord Bacon: His Life and
Works. London. Printed by A. Maxwell Law
Bookseller. 1835.*
(1) Bacon (p. 98).
BSC 2648.
Mr. Greenough's notes indicate another character at p. 309.

[Paulding, James Kirke.]

Letters from the South. 1835.*
Reprinted from 1817.

1836

Theophrastus.

Characters. [Translated by Isaac Taylor.]
1836.*
Reprinted from 1714.

1837

Beaconsfield, Benjamin Disraeli, first Earl of.

Political Writings. By Benjamin Disraeli.
New York. Macmillan. 1914.*
(1) Whigs and Whiggism (p. 400).

[Caswall, Edward.]

Sketches Of Young Ladies: In Which These Interesting Members Of The Animal Kingdom Are Classified, According To Their Several Instincts, Habits, And General Characteristics. By "Quiz." London: Chapman and Hall. . . . MDCCCXXXVII.

8°, text pp. 1–80.

(1) The young lady who sings (p. 1), (2) The busy young lady (p. 5), (3) The romantic young lady (p. 8), (4) The evangelical young lady (p. 12), (5) The matter-of-fact young lady (p. 16), (6) The plain young lady (p. 19), (7) The literary young lady (p. 21), (8) The manly young lady (p. 26), (9) The young lady who is engaged (p. 31), (10) The stupid young lady (p. 37), (11) The interesting young lady (p. 40), (12) The petting young lady (p. 42), (13) The natural historian young lady (p. 44), (14) The indirect young lady (p. 48), (15) The hyperbolical young lady (p. 50), (16) The whimsical young lady (p. 52), (17) The abstemious young lady (p. 56), (18) The sincere young lady (p. 60), (19) The affirmative young lady (p. 61), (20) The clever young lady (p. 63), (21) The mysterious young lady (p. 66), (22) The extremely natural young lady (p. 70), (23) The lazy young lady (p. 72), (24) The young lady from school (p. 75).

Attributed to Caswall by the CBEL.

Hall, Joseph.

The Works of Joseph Hall. Edited by P. Hall. Oxford: Talboy. 1837–39.*

12 vols.
Murphy 13.
Reprinted from 1625.

1838

Baxter, Richard.

The Practical Works Of Richard Baxter . . . In Four Volumes . . . London: George Virtue . . . MDCCCXXXVIII.

8°, 4 vols.
(1–8) as in 1707.

[Caswall, Edward.]

Sketches of Young Ladies: In which these interesting Members of the animal Kingdom are classified, according to their several instincts, habits, and general characteristics. By "Quiz." With six illustrations by "Phiz." Seventh Edition. London: Chapman and Hall . . . MDCCCXXXVIII.

8°, text pp. 1–80.
(1–24) as in 1837.

[Dickens, Charles?]

Characteristic Sketches of Young Gentlemen, By "Quiz," Junior . . . London, Published for the author, by William Kidd. . . .

4°, text pp. 7–68.

(1) The young gentleman from school (p. 7), (2) The young gentleman in his teens (p. 13), (3) The improving young gentleman (p. 18), (4) The ladies' young gentleman (p. 25), (5) The musical young gentleman (p. 30), (6) The spoonified young gentleman (p. 35), (7) The dandified young gentleman (p. 40), (8) The literary young gentleman (p. 45), (9) The aristocratic young gentleman (p. 53), (10) The married young gentleman (p. 60).

Attributed to Dickens by the CBEL, though elsewhere to Edward Caswall.

[Dickens, Charles.]

Sketches Of Young Gentlemen. Dedicated to the Young Ladies. . . . London: Chapman And Hall . . . MDCCCXXXVIII.

8°, text pp. 1–76.

(1) The bashful young gentleman (p. 1), (2) The out-and-out young gentleman (p. 8), (3) The very friendly young gentleman (p. 14), (4) The military young gentleman (p. 20), (5) The political young gentleman (p. 28), (6) The domestic young gentleman (p. 33), (7) The censorious young gentleman (p. 39), (8) The funny young gentleman (p. 44), (9) The theatrical young gentleman (p. 49), (10) The poetical young gentleman (p. 55), (11) The throwing-off young gentleman (p. 60), (12) The young-ladies' young gentleman (p. 66).

BSC 2650.

Attributed to Dickens by the CBEL. A distinct work from his Characteristic Sketches of Young Gentlemen of the same year.

Gresley, William.

Portrait of an English-Churchman . . . London, 1838.*

There were several later editions.

Hutchinson, Lucy.

Memoirs of . . . Colonel Hutchinson. 1838.*

Reprinted from 1806.

Jerrold, Douglas.

Men of Character. 1838.*

See 1851.

Meadows, Joseph Kenny, [Jerrold, Douglas, and others].

Heads of the People; or, Portraits of the English; Drawn by Kenny Meadows. With original essays by distinguished writers. London: Willoughby & Co.

4°, 2 vols.

(1) The dress-maker (Vol. I, p. 1), (2) The diner-out (I, 9), (3) The stock-broker (I, 17), (4) The lawyer's clerk (I, 25), (5) The "lion" of a party (I, 33), (6) The medical student (I, 41), (7) The maid of all-work (I, 49), (8) The fashionable physician (I, 57), (9) The spoilt child (I, 65), (10) The old lord (I, 73), (11) The parish beadle (I, 81), (12) The draper's assistant (I, 89), (13) The monthly nurse (I, 97), (14) The auctioneer (I, 105), (15) The tavern head (I, 113), (16) The old housekeeper (I, 169), (17) The teetotaler (I, 177), (18) The factory child (I, 185), (19) The omnibus conductor (I, 193), (20) The common informer (I, 201), (21) The family governess (I, 209), (22) The midshipman (I, 217), (23) The pew-opener (I, 224), (24) The chimney sweep (I, 233), (25) The undertaker (I, 241), (26) The postman (I, 249), (27) The English peasant (I, 257), (28) The commercial traveller (I, 265), (29) The street-conjuror (I, 273), (30) The young lord (I, 281), (31) The balladsinger (I, 289), (32) The Irish peasant (I, 298), (33) Captain Rook and Mr. Pigeon (I, 305), (34) The cockney (I, 321), (35) The theatrical manager (I, 328), (36) The retired tradesman (I, 337), (37) The English pauper (I, 345), (38) The cabinet minister (I, 353), (39) The hangman (I, 361), (4) The exciseman (I, 369), (41) The farmer's daughter (I, 377), (42) The apothecary (I, 385), (43) The printer's devil (I, 393), (44) The chaperon and the debutante (II, 1), (45) The money-lender (II, 14), (46) The old squire (II, 25), (47) The ballet mistress (II, 33), (48) The mute (II, 38), (49) The Whig (II, 49), (50) The farmer (II, 57), (51) The country schoolmaster (II, 65), (52) The fashionable authoress (II, 73), (53) The basket woman (II, 85), (54) The lodging-house keeper (II, 95), (55) The bricklayer's labourer (II, 101), (56) The debtor and creditor (II, 109), (57) The young squire (II, 121), (58) The bum-boat woman (II, 129), (59) The poor curate (II, 137), (60) The quack doctor (II, 145), (61) The pawnbroker (II, 153), (62) The artists (II, 161), (63) The solicitor (II, 177), (64) The dowager (II, 184), (65) The Tory (II, 193), (66) The collegian (II, 189), (67) The capitalist (II, 208), (68) The waiter (II, 216), (69) The coachman and the guard (II, 225), (70) The policeman (II, 249), (71) The parish clerk (II, 257), (72) The Spitalfields weaver (II, 265), (73) The sporting gentleman (II, 273), (74) The barrister (II, 285), (75) The judge (II, 294), (76) The bishop (II, 304), (77) The jockey (II, 313), (78) The British soldier (II, 324), (79) The Chelsea pensioner (II, 333), (80) The British sailor (II, 341), (81) The Greenwich pensioner (II, 348), (82) The radical M.P. (II, 354), (83) Corporation heads (II, 361).

Mr. Greenough's notes attributed nos. 33, 52, 62 to William Makepeace Thackeray. The date of issue seems to be 1838–40.

1839

Hobbes, Thomas.

The English Works of Thomas Hobbes . . . Edited by Sir William Molesworth . . . London: John Bohn . . . MDCCCXXXIX- [–XLV].

11 vols.

(1) The Whole Art of Rhetoric (Vol. VI, p. 466).

1840

Fuller, Thomas.

The Holy State And The Profane State By Thos Fuller D D London William Pickering 1840.

8°, text pp. 1–400.

(1–51) as in 1642.

Murphy 58.

Meadows, Joseph Kenny, [Jerrold, Douglas, and others].

Heads of the People . . . Drawn By Kenny Meadows. . . . London: Robert Tyas . . . MDCCCXL[–XLI].

4°, 2 vols.

(1–83) as in [1838–40.]

Middleton, Richard.

Epigrams and Satyres. 1840.*

Reprinted from 1608.

[Rowlands, Samuel.]

The Knave of Harts. Haile Fellow, well met. . . . London. Printed for Iohn Bache . . . 1613. . . . [colophon] Reprinted at the Beldornie Press, by George Butler, for Edwd. V. Utterson, in the year MDCCCXL.

4°, text pp. 1–46.

(1–18) as in 1612.

1841

Anonymous.

The Percy Society. Early English Poetry, Ballads, and Popular Literature of the Middle Ages. . . . London: Printed for the Percy Society, By C. Richards . . . MDCCCXLI [ff.].

8°, 18 vols.

(1) Newes from Hell, by Thomas Dekker (1842), (2) Follies Anatomy, by Henry Hutton (Vol. VI, 1842), (3) The Man in the Moone, by W.M. (Vol. XXIX, 1849).

Murphy 8, 121.

Adams, Thomas.
Works.*
Reprinted from 1629.

Fuller, Thomas.
The Holy State and the Profane State. 1841.*
Reprinted from 1840.

Jordan, G. W.
Chaucer's Persone of a Town altered. 1841.*
BSC 2652.

[Rowlands, Samuel.]
Look To It: For, Ile Stabbe Ye. Imprinted at
London, by E. Alde, for W. Ferbrand, and
George Loftes. . . . [colophon] Reprinted at
the Beldornie Press, by J.N. Lydall, for Edwd.
V. Utterson, in the year MDCCCXLI.
4°, text pp. 3–47.
(1–33) as in 1604.

[Rowlands, Samuel.]
More Knaues Yet? The Knaues Of Spades
And Diamonds. London: Printed for Iohn
Tap . . . [colophon] Reprinted at the Bel-
dornie Press, by G.E. Palmer, for Edwd. V.
Utterson, in the year MDCCCXLI.
4°, text sigs. A4–F4v.
(1–4) as in 1613.

[Rowlands, Samuel.]
The Night-Raven. By S.R. . . . London.
Printed by G: Eld for Iohn Deane and
Thomas Baily. 1620. . . . [colophon] Reprinted at the Beldornie Press, by G.E. Palmer,
for Edwd. V. Utterson, in the year MDCCC-
XLI.
4°, text pp. 1–34.
(1) as in 1620.

[Sanderson, Sir William.]
Aulicus Coquinariæ. 1841.*
Reprinted from 1650.

1842

Bastard, Thomas.
Chrestoleros.*
Reprinted from 1598.

Crossman, Samuel.
The Young Man's Monitor. . . . By Samuel
Crossman. . . . London: The Religious Tract
Society. [1842.]
6°, text pp. 1–148.
(1–3) as in The Young Man's Calling, 1685.

Nash, Thomas.
Pierce Penniless's Supplication To The Devil.
By Thomas Nash. From The First Edition of
1592. . . . By J. Payne Collier, Esq., F.S.A.
London: Reprinted For The Shakespeare Society. 1842.
8°, text pp. 5–93.
(1–10) as in 1592.

O'Brien, Edward.
The Lawyer, His Character. 1842.*
See 1843.

1843

Herbert, George.
A Priest to the Temple. 1843.*
Reprinted from Herbert's Remains, 1652.

O'Brien, Edward.
The Lawyer, His Character And Rule Of Holy
Life: After the Manner of George Herbert's
Country Parson. By Edward O'Brien. . . .
Philadelphia: Carey and Hart. 1843.
8°, text pp. 5–96.
(1) The good lawyer (p. 23).

Scrope, William.
Days and Nights of Salmon Fishing in The
Tweed. . . . By William Scrope . . . London:
John Murray . . . 1843.
8°, text pp. 1–255.
(1) Mr. Pooley (p. 2), (2) Mr. Poplin (p. 4), (3)
An artist-angler (p. 5).

[Wilson, John, "Christopher North."]
The Noctes Ambrosianæ Of "Blackwood."
Complete In Four Volumes. . . . Philadelphia: Carey And Hart. 1843.
8°, 4 vols.
(1) Contributors (Vol. I, p. 470), (2) Popular
preachers (I, 501), (3) Clever young men (II,
23), (4) Literary men (II, 229).
First published in Blackwood's Magazine 1822–25. There
were numerous reprints. Poor examples of character.

1844

Beecher, Henry Ward.
Lectures to Young Men on Various Important
Subjects. 1844.*
See 1846.

**Meadows, Joseph Kenny, [Jerrold, Douglas, and
others].**
Heads of the People. Philadelphia. 1844.*
(1–7) as (5, 30, 33, 41, 52, 57, 73) in [1838–40].

1845

Baxter, Richard.

Practical Works. 1845.*

Reprinted from 1707.

1846

Beecher, Henry Ward.

Lectures To Young Men On Various Important Subjects. By Henry Ward Beecher ... Seventh Thousand. Salem: Published by John P. Jewett & Co Cincinnati: Wm. H. Moore & Co. 1846.

6°, text pp. 15–251.

(1) The wit (p. 107), (2) The humorist (p. 111), (3) The cynic (p. 115), (4) The libertine (p. 119), (5) The politician (p. 124), (6) The demagogue (p. 125), (7) The party man (p. 127).

First published 1844. Often reprinted.

Blanchard, Samuel Laman.

Sketches From Life; By The Late Laman Blanchard: With a Memoir of the Author, By Sir Edward Bulwer Lytton, Bart. . . . In Three Volumes. . . . London: Henry Colburn, Publisher . . . 1846.

12°, 3 vols.

(1) The guest that won't go (Vol. II, p. 231), (2) The picture-hunter (II, 292), (3) Persons who don't know what to do (III, 77), (4) The theatrical lessee (III, 139), (5) The oldest inhabitant (III, 142), (6) The editor (III, 144), (7) The police magistrate (III, 147), (8) The borrower (III, 149), (9) The man who belongs to no party (III, 154), (10) The anti-punster (III, 157), (11) The penny-a-liner (III, 160).

Hutchinson, Lucy.

Memoirs of the Life of Colonel Hutchinson . . . London: Henry G. Bohn. . . . 1846.

8°, text pp. 1–518.

(1–2) as in 1806.

Meadows, Joseph Kenny, [Jerrold, Douglas, and others].

Heads of the People. 1846.*

Reprinted from 1838–40.

North, Roger.

The Lives of . . . Francis North. 1846.*

Reprinted from 1808.

Parker, Martin.

Harry White his humour so neare as may be set forth By M.P. . . . Printed at London for Thomas Lambert . . . [Oxford, 1846].

4°, text pp. 5–12.

Begins: "Very good, sir; but why Harry White's humour?"

Smith, Albert.

The Physiology of Evening Parties. 1846.*

(1) The uninteresting young lady (chap. 10), (2) The old young lady (chap. 10), (3) The young lady just out (chap. 10), (4) The loquacious young lady (chap. 10), (5) The belle of the evening (chap. 11), (6) The professed flirt (chap. 11), (7) The wallflower (chap. 12).

1847

Reach, Angus B.

The Natural History of "Bores." By Angus B. Reach. Illustrated by H. G. Hine. London: D. Bogue . . . MDCCCXLVII.*

[Reach, Angus B.?]

The Natural History of Humbugs. By Angus B. Reach. Illustrated by A. Henning. London: D. Bogue . . . MDCCCXLVII.

8°, text pp. 9–126.

(1) Some too common humbugs (p. 17), (2) More about keeping up big appearances (p. 26), (3) On a philanthropic humbug (p. 34), (4) On humbugs connected with rank, and its worshippers (p. 45), (5) A slight sketch of two neglected geniuses, Mr. Blank, dramatist, and Mr. Pumpitup, tragedian (p. 53), (6) Various kinds of humbugs: bragging, meek, well-to-do, professional (p. 73), (7) On some travelled and travelling humbugs (p. 86), (8) On certain humbugs . . . in convivial circles, speech-making humbugs, professional diner-out (p. 99), (9) A small pantheon of minor humbugs, of general invitations, extra tidy folk, ascetics (p. 112).

Smith, Albert.

The Natural History of 'Stuck-Up' People. By Albert Smith. . . . London: D. Bogue . . . MDCCCXLVII.

8°, text pp. 9–112.

(1) The 'stuck-up' Spangle Lacquer family (p. 9), (2) The Misses Lacquer (p. 33), (3) The Champignon Stiffbacks, high rural gentility (p. 91).

Smith, Albert.

The Natural History of the Ballet-Girl. By Albert Smith. . . . London: D. Bogue . . . MDCCCXLVII.

8°, text pp. 9–103.

(1) The ballet-girl (p. 84).

There was also another edition in 1847.

Smith, Albert.

The Natural History of the Gent. By Albert Smith. London: David Bogue . . . MDCCC-XLVII.

8°, text pp. 1–104.

(1) Various gents (p. 2), (2) The gent at the theatre (p. 24), (3) The gent at a tavern (p. 29), (4) The gent in the open air (p. 33), (5) The gent at the races (p. 43), (6) The gent in society (p. 50), (7) The gent on the river (p. 57), (8) The gent at the casinos (p. 64), (9) The gent at the sea-side (p. 74), (10) Other gents (p. 88).

There were at least five editions in this year, of which the above is the fifth.

1848

Anonymous.

Cambridge University Magazine.*

(1) Freshmen, (2) Other people.

Hutchinson, Lucy.

Memoirs of . . . Colonel Hutchinson . . . written by His Widow Lucy . . . Seventh Edition . . . London: Henry G. Bohn . . . 1848.

8°, text pp. 1–518.

(1–2) as in 1806.

Mayhew, Horace.

Model Men, Modelled by Horace Mayhew, Sculptured by H.G. Hine. New York: Harper & Brothers. Publishers.

8°, text pp. 13–114.

(1) The model husband (p. 1), (2) The model bachelor (p. 16), (3) The model son (p. 20), (4) The model policeman (p. 22), (5) The model waiter (p. 50), (6) The model magistrate (p. 37), (7) The model labourer (p. 40), (8) The model agitator (p. 45), (9) The model tailor (p. 51), (10) The model M.P. (p. 56), (11) The model debtor (p. 59), (12) The model friend (p. 64), (13) The model fast man (p. 66), (14) Model clerks (p. 74), (15) The model gentleman (p. 84), (16) The model Irish speaker (p. 88), (17) The model banker (p. 92), (18) The model sponge (p. 94), (19) The model lodger (p. 97), (20) The model beadle (p. 101), (21) The model omnibus conductor (p. 108), (22) The model pet parson (p. 112), (23) The model actor (p. 113).

The British Museum Catalogue dates 1848 without question. There may have been two or more editions.

Mayhew, Horace.

Model Women and Children Modelled by Horace Mayhew Sculptured by H. G. Hine. Harper & Brothers.

8°, text pp. 10–114.

(1) The model sister (p. 10), (2) The model wife (p. 14), (3) The model mother-in-law (p. 19), (4) The model mother (p. 25), (5) The model spoilt boy (p. 30), (6) The model baby (p. 34), (7) The model monthly nurse (p. 39), (8) The model governess (p. 49), (9) The model daughter (p. 53), (10) The model lodging-house keeper (p. 59), (11) The model tiger (i.e., boy behind a coach) (p. 64), (12) The model fast lady (p. 69), (13) The model actress (p. 79), (14) The model lodging house (p. 85), (15) The model genius (p. 89), (16) The model widow (p. 93), (17) The model young lady (p. 97), (18) The model maid-of-all-work (p. 105), (19) The model milliner (p. 107).

The British Museum Catalogue dates 1848 without question. There may have been two or more editions.

[Reach, Angus B.?]

The Natural History Of Tuft-Hunters And Toadies. . . . London: D. Bogue . . . MDCCC-XLVIII.

8°, text pp. 13–121.

(1) Of tuft-hunters in general (p. 13), (2) Of tuft-hunting families (p. 24), (3) Of an university tuft-hunter (p. 35), (4) Of profesisonal tuft-hunters (p. 42), (5) Of tuft-hunting authors (p. 49), (6) Of some habits of tuft-hunters (p. 57), (7) Of "imaginary" tuft-hunters (p. 65), (8) Of tuft-hunting mammas (p. 73), (9) Of tuft-hunting tradesmen (p. 86), (10) Of tuft-hunters, historically considered (p. 91), (11) Of tuft-hunters at the present day (p. 104), (12) Of the means requisite for the extinction of tuft-hunters (p. 112).

Attributed to Theodore A. Buckley by the Harvard and British Museum Catalogues, but to Angus B. Reach by the CBEL.

Smith, Albert.

The Natural History of the Idler Upon town. By Albert Smith. Illustrated by A. Henning. London: D. Bogue . . . MDCCCXLVIII.

8°, text pp. 1–120.

(1) The West-End lounger (p. 11), (2) Exhibition loungers (p. 36), (3) Mooner (p. 46), (4) Park idler (p. 81), (5) Theatrical idler (p. 87), (6) Street boy (p. 111).

Thackeray, William Makepeace.

The Book of Snobs. By W. M. Thackeray . . . London: Punch Office . . . MDCCCXLVIII.

8°, text pp. 1–180.

(1) Snob-royal (p. 9), (2) Some respectable snobs (p. 24), (3) Great city snobs (p. 32), (4) Military snobs (p. 36), (5) Clerical snobs (p. 43), (6) University snobs (p. 53), (7) Literary snobs (p. 60), (8) Irish snobs (p. 63), (9) Party-giving snobs (p. 66), (10) Dining-out snobs (p. 70), (11) Dinner-going snobs (p. 73), (12) Continental snobs (p. 77), (13) English snobs on the con-

tinent (p. 85), (14) Country snobs (p. 89), (15) Club snobs (p. 142).

Reprinted several times.

[Winstanley, William.]

Poor Robin's True Character Of A Scold. Totham: Printed by Charles Clark (an Amateur) at his Private Press. 1848.*

Printed on recto pages only. Black letter.
(1) as in 1678.
Murphy 87. BSC 2653.

1849

Blanchard, Samuel Laman.

Sketches from Life. 1849.*

Reprinted from 1846.

[Defoe, Daniel.]

Chronicles and Characters of the Stock Exchange. 1849.*

Reprinted from The Anatomy of Exchange Alley, 1719.

Smith, Albert.

Gavarni in London: Sketches of Life and Character, with Illustrative Essays By Popular Writers. Edited by Albert Smith. London: David Bogue . . . MDCCCXLIX.

4°, text pp. 1–115.
(1) The street beggar, by Angus B. Reach (p. 7), (2) Carmen and coal-heavers, by Thomas Miller (p. 37), (3) The Lounger in Regent Street, by Angus B. Reach (p. 70), (4) The barmaid, by J. Stirling Coyne (p. 87).

Another edition appeared in 1859 with the title Sketches of London Life and Character.

Smith, Albert.

The Natural History of Evening Parties. 1849.*

Reprinted from his Physiology of Evening Parties, 1846.

1850

Adams, John.

The Works Of John Adams . . . With A Life Of The Author . . . By His Grandson Charles Francis Adams. . . . Boston: Charles C. Little And James Brown. 1850.

6°, 10 vols.
(1) Recipe to make a patriot (Vol. II, p. 143).
An entry in his diary under date of 1763.

[Lewis, John Delaware.]

Sketches of Cantabs. By John Smith. . . . Second Edition. London: George Earle . . . 1850.

8°, text pp. 1–244.
(1) The reading Cantab (p. 1), (2) The fast Cantab (p. 11), (3) The boating Cantab (p. 24), (4) The unionic Cantab (p. 38), (5) The Cantab fond of London life (p. 56), (6) The aristocratic Cantab (p. 77), (7) The Cantab who is in love (p. 91), (8) The married Cantab (p. 117), (9) The ultra-evangelical Cantab (p. 127), (10) The sporting Cantab (p. 150), (11) A word to the public school Cantab (p. 182), (12) The model Cantab — description of the author (p. 190).

[Mitchell, Donald Grant.]

The Lorgnette: or, Studies of the Town. By An Opera Goer. New York: Henry Kernot. . . . MDCCCL.

6°, text pp. 1–294.
(1) The fashionable man (no. 2), (2) The fashionable lady (no. 9), (3) The Bostonian (no. 10), (4) Belles (no. 14), (5) The Wall Street brokers (no. 17), (6) Watering place people (no. 18), (7) The cockney in the country (no. 19), (8) The young man about town (no. 22).

1851

Jerrold, Douglas.

Men of Character. By Douglas Jerrold. London: Bradbury and Evans . . . 1851.

8°, text pp. 1–340.
(1) Job Pippins, the man who couldn't help it (p. 1), (2) Jack Runnymede, the man of many thanks (p. 56), (3) Adam Buff, the man without a shirt (p. 119), (4) Matthew Clear, the man who saw his way (p. 134), (5) John Applejohn, the man who meant well (p. 153), (6) Barnaby Palms, the man who felt his way (p. 283), (7) Christopher Snub, the man who was born to be hanged (p. 305), (8) Creso Quattrine, the man who died rich (p. 328).

Printed earlier in 1838.

1852

Anonymous.

The Character of a True Churchman. 1852.*
Reprinted from 1711.

[Mitchell, Donald Grant.]

The Lorgnette. 1852.*
Reprinted from 1850.

Newman, John Henry, Cardinal.

Discourses on the Scope and Nature of University Education. 1852.*

See The Idea of a University, 1910.

1853

Moore, Thomas.

The Poetical Works of Thomas Moore . . . In Ten Volumes. . . . New York: D. Appleton And Co. . . . 1853.

8°, 10 vols.

(1) A mongrel statesman, half Whig and half Tory (Vol. IX, p. 207).

This piece is dated 1834. The Poetical Works went through numerous editions.

1854

Baxter, Richard.

Practical Works. 1854.*

Reprinted from 1707.

Halliwell, James O.

The Literature of the Sixteenth and Seventeenth Centuries . . . Edited by James Orchard Halliwell . . . London: For Private Circulation Only. M.dccc.liv.

4°.

(1) Harry White his humour, by Martin Parker (p. 3).

Scrope, William.

Days and Nights of Salmon Fishing. 1854.*

Reprinted from 1843.

1855

Blanchard, Samuel Laman.

Corporation Characters: forming a select Portrait Gallery of Civic Celebrities. Illustrated with twelve heads taken off by Kenny Meadows, with an essay under each head by the late Laman Blanchard. London: Willoughby and Company. 1855.*

(1) The lord-mayor, (2) The lady mayoress, (3) The sword-bearer, (4) The chamberlain, (5) The alderman, (6) The common-council-man, (7) The sheriff, (8) The city pleader, (9) The city marshal, (10) The chaplain, (11) The city remembrancer, (12) The recorder.

1856

Ellis, Clement.

Character of the True Gentleman. By Clement Ellis. . . . Edinburgh . . . MDCCCLVI.*

(1–17) as (13–29) in The Gentile Sinner, 1660.

Murphy 142.

Overbury, Sir Thomas.

The Miscellaneous Works In Prose And Verse Of Sir Thomas Overbury, Knt. Now First Collected. Edited with notes, and a biographical account of the author, By Edward F. Rimbault. . . . London: John Russell Smith . . . 1856.

8°, text pp. 1–278.

(1–80) as in 1756, (81) Observations upon the XVII Provinces (p. 221).

Murphy 25.

Published in the Library of Old Authors.

Rous, John.

Diary Of John Rous, Incumbent Of Santon Downham, Suffolk, From 1625 to 1642. Edited By Mary Anne Everett Green . . . Printed For The Camden Society. M.DCCC.LVI.

8°, text pp. 1–131.

(1) as in 1635.

1857

Halliwell, James O.

Books of Characters, illustrating the Habits and Manners of Englishmen from the Reign of James I, to the Restoration: selected by James O. Halliwell . . . London: Printed by J.E. Adlard . . . MDCCCLVII.

4°, text pp. 1–332.

(1) The wandering Jew telling fortunes to Englishmen, 1649 (p. 1), (2) The man in the moon, 1609 (p. 73), (3) Essayes and characters, by Stephens, 1615 (p. 131), (4) London and the country carbonadoed and quartered, by Lupton, 1632 (p. 257), (5) Selections from Fantasticks, by Breton, 1626 (p. 321).

BSC 2654.

1859

Anonymous.

The Tinker of Turvey, or, Canterbury Tales . . . Edited by James O. Halliwell . . . London: Printed by Thomas Richards . . . 1859.

4°, text pp. 9–109.

(1–14) as in 1630.

Brathwaite, Richard.

The Whimzies . . . Edited by James O. Halliwell . . . London: Printed by Thomas Richards . . . 1859.

4°, text pp. 13–148.

(1–28) as in 1631.

Murphy 48.

Nichols, John Gough.

Narratives Of The Days Of The Reformation . . . Edited By John Gough Nichols, F.S.A.

Printed for the Camden Society. M.DCCC.-LIX.

4°, text pp. 1–351.

(1) A Declaration concerning . . . Thomas Cranmer, by Ralph Morice (p. 238).

The original manuscript was composed about 1563–76.

Ossoli, Margaret Fuller.

Life Without And Life Within. . . . By Margaret Fuller Ossoli . . . Edited By Her Brother Arthur B. Fuller. . . . Boston: Brown, Taggard And Chase . . . [verso of title page] Entered . . . 1859.

6°, text pp. 13–424.

(1) The rich man. An ideal sketch (p. 287), (2) The poor man. An ideal sketch (p. 297).

Smith, Albert.

Sketches of London Life and Character. 1859.*

Reprinted from Gavarni in London, 1849.

1860

Anonymous.

The Character of a Cavalier. [c. 1860?]*

BSC 2303.

A nineteenth-century manuscript copy of 1644.

The Character of a Jesuit. [c. 1860?]*

BSC 2303.

A nineteenth-century manuscript copy of 1712.

The Character of a Phanatique. [c. 1860?]*

BSC 2303.

A nineteenth-century manuscript copy of 1660.

The Character of a Roundhead. [c. 1860?]*

BSC 2303.

A nineteenth-century manuscript copy of 1645.

A Character of a Turn-Coat. [c. 1860?]*

BSC 2303.

A nineteenth-century manuscript copy of 1707.

The Character of Sir. G. Treby. [c. 1860?]*

BSC 2303.

A nineteenth-century manuscript copy of 1707.

Blanchard, E. L.

A Handy Book On Dinners. Dinners and Diners at home and abroad. By E.L. Blanchard. . . . London: W.R.H. Adamson. . . . 1860.

8°, text pp. 1–115.

(1) The diner that dines with Duke Humphrey (p. 5), (2) The diner-out (p. 13), (3) The philanthropic diner (p. 22), (4) Divers diners.

Breton, Nicholas.

The Will of Wit, otherwise called, Wit's Will, or Will's Wit. By Nicholas Breton; now first reprinted from the rare edition of 1599. Edited by James O. Halliwell, Esq., F.R.S. London: Printed by Thomas Richards . . . 1860.

4°, text pp. 9–89.

(1–8) as in 1597.

[Du Gard, Thomas.]

Confused Characters of Conceited Coxcombs, or, A Dish Of Traitorous Tyrants; reprinted from The Original Edition of A.D. 1661. Edited by James O. Halliwell, Esq., F.R.S. London: Printed By Thomas Richards . . . 1860.

4°, text pp. 19–96.

(1–23) as in 1661.

Murphy 73.

Ossoli, Margaret Fuller.

Life Without And Life Within; Or, Reviews, Narratives, Essays, and Poems, By Margaret Fuller Ossoli . . . Edited By Her Brother, Arthur B. Fuller. Boston: Brown, Taggard And Chase. New York: Sheldon & Co. Philadelphia: J.B. Lippincott & Co. London: Sampson Low, Son & Co. 1860.

6°, text pp. 13–424.

(1–2) as in 1859.

Wilkins, William Walker.

Political Ballads Of The Seventeenth And Eighteenth Centuries Annotated By W. Walker Wilkins . . . In Two Vols. . . . London Longman, Green, Longman, and Roberts MDCCCLX.

8°, 2 vols.

(1) The Puritan, 1648, by Cleveland or Butler (Vol. I, p. 71), (2) The Geneva Ballad, 1678, by Butler (I, 202), (3) The Trimmer, 1690 (II, 96).

1861

Adams, Thomas.

Works.*

Reprinted from 1629.

1862

Anonymous.

The Cobler of Canterburie. Edited by Frederic Ouvry, Tr.S.A. London: Printed by J.E. Taylor . . . 1862.

4°, text pp. 1–83.

(1–5) as in 1590.

1863

Hall, Joseph.

The Works Of The Right Reverend Joseph Hall, D.D. . . . By Philip Wynter, D.D. . . . Oxford: At The University Press. MDCCC.-LXIII.

8°, 10 vols.

(1–4) as in 1625, (5) The Character of Man (Vol. V, p. 446), (6) Virgidemiarum Libri Sex (IX, 563).

Murphy 13.

Penn, William.

Fruits of Solitude. 1863.*

Reprinted from 1749.

Younge, Richard.

The Blemish of Government. 1863.*

Reprinted from 1658.

1864

Norris, Thaddeus.

The American Angler's Book . . . By Thad. Norris. Philadelphia: Published by E.H. Butler & Co. . . . 1864.

8°, text pp. 27–600.

(1) The snob angler (p. 30), (2) The spick-and-span angler (p. 30), (3) The literary angler (p. 30), (4) The pretentious angler (p. 31), (5) The shad-roe fisherman (p. 31), (6) The English Admiral, an angler (p. 33), (7) The true angler (p. 33).

1865

Anonymous.

A Book of Characters: Selected from . . . Overbury, Earle, And Butler. Edinburgh. William P. Nimmo. 1865.*

8°.

(1–189) characters from Overbury, Earle, and Butler.

Murphy 26.

Norris, Thaddeus.

The American Angler's Book. 1865.*

Reprinted from 1864.

Palmer, Herbert.

Lord Bacon Not The Author of "The Christian Paradoxes:" Being A Reprint Of "Memorials of Godliness and Christianity," by Herbert Palmer, B.D. With Introduction, Memoir, And Notes. By the Rev. Alexander B. Grosart . . . Printed For Private Circulation. 1865.

8°, text pp. 1–126.

(1–2) as in Memorials, 1657.

[Stephen, Sir Leslie.]

Sketches from Cambridge, by A Don. London and Cambridge: Macmillan and Co. 1865.

8°, text pp. 1–144.

(1) The rowing man (p. 11), (2) Athletic sports (p. 21), (3) Mathematics (p. 31), (4) Reading men (p. 44), (5) The Union (p. 58), (6) Dons (p. 83), (7) College tutors (p. 108), (8) Heads of houses (p. 121).

Trollope, Anthony.

Hunting Sketches. 1865.*

(1) The man who hunts and doesn't like it, (2) The lady who hunts and does like it, (3) The lady who rides to hounds, (4) The hunting farmer, (5) The man who hunts and never jumps, (6) The hunting parson, (7) The master of hounds, (8) How to ride to hounds.

First published in the Pall Mall Gazette. Reprinted at least twice.

1866

Trollope, Anthony.

Clergymen Of The Church Of England. By Anthony Trollope. . . . London: Chapman And Hall . . . 1866.

8°, text pp. 1–130.

(1) The modern English archbishop (p. 1), (2) English bishops, old and new (p. 16), (3) The normal dean of the present day (p. 31), (4) The archdeacon (p. 42), (5) The parson of the parish (p. 54), (6) The town incumbent (p. 66), (7) The college fellow who has taken orders (p. 78), (8) The curate in a populous parish (p. 92), (9) The Irish beneficed clergyman (p. 105), (10) The clergyman who subscribes for Colenso (p. 119).

Originally published in the Pall Mall Gazette.

Trollope, Anthony.

Travelling Sketches. 1866.*

(1) The man who travels alone, (2) The unprotected female tourist, (3) The united Englishmen who travel for fun, (4) The art tourist, (5) The tourist in search of knowledge, (6) The Alpine Club man, (7) Tourists who don't like their travels.

First published in the Pall Mall Gazette.

1867

Dunton, John.

John Dunton's Letters From New-England. . . . Boston: Printed for the [Prince] Society . . . 1867.

4°, text pp. 7–307.

(1) A happy life (p. 6, in verse), (2) A damsel

(p. 98), (3) A wife (p. 102), (4) A widow (p. 106).

On Dunton's debts to older character-writers, see Chester N. Greenough, John Dunton's Letters from New England, Publications of the Colonial Society of Massachusetts, XIV (1912), 213.

Earle, John.

Microcosmography . . . By John Earle . . . [edited] By Philip Bliss . . . First American Edition. Edited By L. L. Williams. . . . Albany: Joel Munsell. MDCCCLXVII.

4°, text pp. 1–156.
(1–78) as in 1633.

Paulding, William I.

Literary Life of James K. Paulding. Compiled by his son, William I. Paulding. . . . New York: Charles Scribner and Company. 1867.

8°, text pp. 15–389.
(1) Brother Jonathan (p. 90), (2) An eccentric sage (p. 132), (3) Franklin (p. 155), (4) Randolph of Roanoke (p. 238), (5) Washington (p. 258), (6) John Forsyth (p. 276), (7) Andrew Jackson (p. 287), (8) The American people (p. 338), (9) Paulding (p. 381).

1868

Ashbee, Edmund William.

Occasional Fac-simile Reprints Of Rare And Curious Tracts Of The 16th And 17th Centuries. Produced Under The Superintendence Of Edmund Wm. Ashbee. . . . London: Printed For 100 Subscribers Only.

4° (?), two volumes, unpaged.
(1) Heads of All Fashions, by John Taylor (Vol. II, no. 24).
Dated 1868–72 by the CBEL.

[Earle, John.]

Micro-Cosmographie . . . Edited by Edward Arber. . . . London: Alex. Murray & Son. . . . 1868.

8°, text pp. 21–104.
(1–78) as in 1633.
Murphy 43.

Furnivall, F. J. (editor).

The Babees Book . . . Edited By Frederick J. Furnivall . . . London: Published For The Early English Text Society, By N. Trübner & Co. . . . MDCCCLXVIII.

8°, text pp. 1–405.
(1) The Schoole of Vertue, by F. Seager (p. 337).

1869

Anonymous.

The Mirror of Character. . . . Edinburgh . . . 1869.*
(1–189) as in A Book of Characters, 1865.
Murphy 26, 45.

Alsop, George.

A Character of the Province of Maryland.*
Reprinted from 1666.

Awdeley, John.

The Fraternitye of Vacabondes By John Awdeley. . . . From the Edition of 1575. . . . A Caveat or Warening for Common Cursetors. . . . By Thomas Harman Esquiere. From The 3rd Edition Of 1567. . . . Edited By Edward Viles & F.J. Furnivall. London: Published For The Early English Text Society. By N. Trübner & Co. . . . MDCCCLXIX.

8°, text pp. 1–103.
(1) The Fraternitye of Vacabondes, by Awdeley (p. 1), (2) A Caueat or Warening, by Harman (p. 17), (3) [The Parte added to Harman's Caueat to make] the Groundworke of Connycatching. . . done by a Justice of the Peace (p. 97).

Defoe, Daniel.

Daniel Defoe: His Life, And Recently Discovered Writings: Extending From 1716 To 1729. By William Lee. . . . In Three Volumes. . . . London: John Camden Hotten, Piccadilly. 1869.

8°, 3 vols.
(1) A female Quixote, from Mist's Journal, 1720 (Vol. II, 212), (2) The great Duke of Marlborough, from Applebee's Journal, 1722 (III, 19), (3) An abandoned clergyman, from the same (III, 62), (4) A wicked landlord, from the same, 1724 (III, 239), (5) An unaccountable sort of fellow, that is willing to marry, if he could get an agreeable woman, who would consent without ceremony, from Mist's Journal (III, 258), (6) A Dundreary, from the same, 1724 (III, 258), (7) An unmanageable wife, from Applebee's Journal, 1724 (III, 338), (8) A jealous husband, from the same, 1725 (III, 361), (9) A quarrelsome wife, from the same (III, 376), (10) One entitled to the name of scholar, but denied it because he knows but little Greek and Latin, from the same (III, 435), (11) A pedant, from the same (III, 437), (12) A good writer, from the Universal Spectator and Weekly Journal, 1728 (III, 465).

[Earle, John.]

Microcosmography. 1869.*

[Howell, James.]

Instructions for Foreign Travel. 1869.*

Reprinted from 1642.

Spenser Society.

[Publications of the Spenser Society, 1869 ff.]
Complete or selected works of (1) John Taylor
(parts 2, 3, 4, 7, 14, 19, 21, 25), (2) George
Wither (9–13, 16, 18, 22, 24, 26–34, 36, 37, 41),
(3) Mancinus (38), (4) Barclay (39), (5) Willobie his Avisa (42), (6) Bastard (47).

1870

Habington, William.

English Reprints. William Habington. Castara. . . . Edited . . . by Edward Arber. . . .
London: 5 Queen Square . . 1870.

8°, text pp. 17–144.

(1–4) as in 1640.

Murphy 127.

Nash, Thomas.

Pierce Penniless's Supplication to the Devil.
Edited by J. Payne Collier. 1870.*

Reprinted from 1592.

Theophrastus.

Characters. 1870.*

Reprinted from 1714.

1871

Andrews, John.

The Anatomie Of Basenesse (1615) By John
Andrews: Edited . . . By The Rev. Alexander B. Grosart . . . Printed For Private Circulation. 1871.

8°, text pp. 19–60.

(1–4) as in 1615.

[Corbet, Richard?]

The Times Whistle: or A Newe Daunce of
Seven Satires. . . . Edited . . . by J.M. Cow-
per. . . . London; Published For The Early
English Text Society, By N. Trübner & Co.
. . . MDCCCLXXI.

8°, text pp. 1–152.

(1–10) as in 1614.

Harman, Thomas.

A Caveat or Warning for Common Cursetors.
1871.*

Probably identical with the first entry under Hindley below.

Hindley, Charles.

The Old Book Collector's Miscellany. . . .

Edited by Charles Hindley . . . London:
Reeves and Turner 1871[–73].

3 vols.

(1) A Caveat, by Harman, 1573 (Vol. I), (2) The
Honest Briton's Character of Himself, 1680 (I),
(3) A Town-Gallant, 1675 (II), (4) A Town-
Miss, 1680 (III).

Murphy 85.

Hindley, Charles.

The Old Book Collector's Miscellany. . . .
Edited by Charles Hindley . . . London:
Reeves and Turner 1871[–72].

2 vols. Second edition.

(1–3) as (1–3) in first edition, 1871–73, (4) The
Gull's Hornbook, by Dekker, 1609 (Vol. II), (5)
A Kicksey-Winsey, by Taylor, 1619 (II), (6)
Poor Robin's true Character of a Scold, 1678 (II).

Vol. I is identical with the first edition, but Vol. II is different.

[Taylor, John.]

Heads of all Fashions. 1871.*

Reprinted from 1642.

1872

Anonymous.

The Character of a Town Gallant. 1872.*

Reprinted from 1675.

Hake, Edward.

News out of Powles Churchyarde. Written In
English Satyrs. By Edward Hake . . . Accu-
rately Reprinted From The Excessively Rare
Edition Of 1579 . . . By Charles Edmonds
. . . London: Henry Sotheran, Baer and Co.
1872.

8°, text sigs. A–H8.

(1–13) as in 1579.

Smith, Albert.

The Natural History of Evening Parties.
1872.*

Reprinted from The Physiology of Evening Parties, 1846.

Smith, Albert.

The Natural History of Stuck-Up People.
1872.*

Reprinted from 1847.

Smith, Albert.

The Natural History of the Ballet Girl. 1872.*

Reprinted from 1847.

Smith, Albert.

The Natural History of the Gent. 1872.*

Reprinted from 1847.

Smith, Albert.

The Natural History of the Idler Upon Town. 1872.*

Reprinted from 1848.

1873

Newman, John Henry, Cardinal.

The Idea of a University, 1873.*

See 1910.

1874

[Head, Richard.]

The English Rogue. 1874.*

Murphy 144.

Reprinted from 1665.

Ossoli, Margaret Fuller.

Life Without And Life Within. . . . By Margaret Fuller Ossoli. Boston, Roberts Brothers. 1874.*

Reprinted from 1859.

Hannay, Patrick.

A Happy Husband. 1875.*

Reprinted from 1619.

1875

Penn, William.

Fruits of Solitude.*

Reprinted from 1749.

1876

Davies, Sir John.

The Complete Poems Of Sir John Davies. Edited, With Memorial-Introduction and Notes, By The Rev. Alexander B. Grosart. . . . In Two Volumes. . . . London: Chatto and Windus, Piccadilly. 1876.

8°, 2 vols.

(1–20) as in Ovid, All Ovids Elegies, *c.* 1595.

Thynne, Francis.

Emblemes and Epigrames. . . . Edited By F.J. Furnivall . . . London: Published For The Early English Text Society . . . MDCCC-LXXVI.

8°, text pp. 5–96.

(1) Flatterers (p. 39), (2) A godly mann (p. 87).

Attributed to Thynne by Furnivall and by the CBEL. This was the first publication of the manuscript, written probably about 1600.

1877

Arber, Edward.

An English Garner; Ingatherings from our History And Literature By Edward Arber . . . London and Birmingham, 1877[–96].

8°, 8 vols.

(1) The Interpreter, by Scott (Vol. VI, p. 231), (2) The Worth of a Penny, by Peacham (VI, 245).

Murphy 126.

1878

[Brathwaite, Richard.]

A Strappado for the Devil. 1878.*

Reprinted from 1615.

Daniel, George.

The Poems of George Daniel, Esq . . . from the Original MSS. in the British Museum: hitherto unprinted. Edited . . . by the Rev. Alexander Grosart . . . In Four Volumes . . . Printed for Private Circulation Only. 1878.

4 vols.

(1) Woman charactred (Vol. I, p. 46), (2) The wise man (III, 82; chap. 39 of Ecclesiasticus).

Davies, John, of Hereford.

The Complete Works Of John Davies of Hereford . . . Edited . . . By the Rev. Alexander B. Grosart . . . In Two Volumes . . . Printed For Private Circulation. 1878.

4°, 2 vols. Each title has separate pagination and signatures.

(1) A Select Second Husband (Vol. II), (2) The Scourge of Folly (II), (3) The Muses Sacrifice (II).

[Guilpin, Edward.]

Skialetheia, edited by A.B. Grosart. 1878.*

Reprinted from 1598.

1879

Breton, Nicholas.

The Works in Verse And Prose of Nicholas Breton . . . Edited . . . by The Reverend Alexander B. Grosart . . . In Two Volumes . . . Printed For Private Circulation. 1879.

4°, 2 vols. Each item separately paged.

(1) A True Description of Unthankfulness (Vol. I), (2) Characters upon Essays, 1615 (II), (3) The Good and the Badde, 1616 (II), (4) Fantasticks, 1626 (II), (5) The Wil of Wit (II), (6) Queen Elizabeth (II).

Murphy 27 and 34.

Eliot, George (Mary Ann Evans, later Cross).

Impressions of Theophrastus Such By George Eliot William Blackwood and Sons Edinburgh and London MDCCCLXXIX.

8°, text pp. 3–357.

(1) The author, Theophrastus Such (chap. 1), (2) The author's father (chap. 2), (3) Merman, a would-be scholar (chap. 3), (4) Lentulus, a man surprised at his originality (chap. 4), (5) Hinze, a too deferential man (chap. 5), (6) Touchwood, a man of bad temper (chap. 6), (7) Spike, a political molecule (chap. 7), (8) Mordax, the watch-dog of knowledge (chap. 8), (9) Mixtus, a half-breed (chap. 9), (10) Ganymede, an old-young coxcomb (chap. 12), (11) Pepin, the too-ready writer (chap. 14), (12) Vorticella, a small author (chap. 15), (13) Sir Gavial Mantrap, a moral swindler (chap. 16), (14) Trost, an optimist (chap. 17), (15) Jews (chap. 18).

This has been reprinted.

1880

Alsop, George.

A Character of the Province of Maryland.*

Reprinted from 1666.

Awdeley, John.

The Fraternity of Vagabonds.*

Reprinted from 1575.

Bastard, Thomas.

Chrestoleros.*

Reprinted from 1598.

Rowlands, Samuel.

The Complete Works Of Samuel Rowlands 1598–1628 Now First Collected . . . Printed For The Hunterian Club MDCCCLXXX.

4°, 3 vols.

(1) Diogenes Lanthorne (Vol. I), (2) The Letting of Hvmovrs Blood (I), (3) Looke to it (I), (4) The Knave of Clubbes (II), (5) More Knaues Yet? (II), (6) The Night-Raven (II), (7) A Paire of Spy-Knaves (II), (8) The Knave of Harts (II).

It is impossible to give references except by volume, since each title is separately paged.

1881

Breton, Nicholas.

Choice, Chance, and Change. Edited by A. B. Grosart. 1881.*

Reprinted from 1606.

Greene, Robert.

The Huth Library. The Life and Complete Works In Prose And Verse Of Robert Greene,

M.A. . . . In Twelve Volumes. . . . Edited . . . By The Rev. Alexander B. Grosart, LL.D. (Edin.) F.S.A. . . . Printed For Private Circulation Only. 1881–83.

4°, 12 vols.

(1) The Spanish Masqverado (Vol. V, p. 235), (2) Greene's Vision.

Lang, Andrew.

The Library. 1881.*

(1) The robustious Philistine (chap. 2).

1883

Lodge, Thomas.

The Complete Works Of Thomas Lodge . . . Now First Collected . . . Printed For The Hunterian Club MDCCCLXXXIII.

4°, 4 vols.

(1) A Fig for Momus (Vol. III, no. 2), (2) Wits miserie (IV, 1).

Lupton, Donald.

London and the Country Carbonadoed, etc. Aungervyle Society Reprints. . . . Edinburgh. 1883.

8°, text pp. 59–94 (nos. 15 and 16 of second series).

(1–36) as in 1632.

Murphy 52.

1884

Dekker, Thomas.

The Non-Dramatic Works Of Thomas Dekker. In Four Volumes. . . . Edited . . . By the Rev. Alexander B. Grosart . . . Printed For Private Circulation Only. 1884[–86].

4°, 5 vols.

(1) The Seaven Deadly Sinnes of London (Vol. II, p. 1), (2) Newes from Hell (II, 83), (3) The Double PP (II, 155), (4) Iests to make you merrie (II, 267), (5) The Belman of London (III, 61), (6) Lanthorne and Candle Light (III, 171), (7) Strange Horse-Race (III, 305), (8) Worke for Armourours (IV, 85).

Fuller, Thomas.

The Holy and Profane States. . . . London: W. Swan Sonnenschein & Co.*

(1–42) as in 1642 (omitting nos. 19, 20, 27, 29, 32, 33, 37, 38, 39).

Murphy 58.

Harvey, Gabriel.

The Works of Gabriel Harvey, D.C.L. In Three Volumes. . . . Edited . . . by the rev.

Alexander B. Grosart . . . Printed For Private Circulation Only. 1884.

8°, 3 vols.

(1) Pierce's Supererogation (Vol. II, p. 294).

1885

Hutchinson, Lucy.

Memoirs of . . . Colonel Hutchinson . . . By his Widow Lucy . . . Revised . . . By C. H. Firth . . . In Two Volumes . . . London John C. Nimmo . . . 1885.

2 vols.

(1–2) as in 1806.

La Bruyère, Jean de.

Works. 1885.*

Reprinted from 1713.

[Lancaster, Nathaniel.]

The Pretty Gentleman. 1885.*

Reprinted from 1747.

Scrope, William.

Days and Nights of Salmon Fishing. 1885.*

Reprinted from 1843.

1886

Anonymous.

The Clarendon Historical Society's Reprints. Series II. 1884–6. Edinburgh.

4°, text pp. 3–362.

(1) The Character of a Modern Whig, 1681 (p. 355, no. 11).

Murphy 115.

The Impostor Painted In His Own Colours; Or, The base Birth and Parentage Of The Chevalier De St George, Alias The Pretender, Now truly brought to Light . . . London: Printed by J. Read . . . [Edinburgh, 1886].

4°, text pp. 6–16.

(1) as in the undated edition.

This is No. 9 of the reprints in the series, Ten Scarce Books in English Literature. It bears the caption at the top of the title page, Historical Reprints. — IX.

Penn, William.

Fruits of Solitude. 1886.*

Reprinted from 1749.

Vines, Richard.

The Hearse of the Renowned . . . Earle of Essex. 1886.*

Reprinted from 1646.

1887

Anonymous.

An Epistle to a Professor, on the Characters of Dons: in imitation of Pope's Second Epistle on the Characters of Women. By an Oxford Undergraduate. Oxford: Thomas Shrimpton & Son.*

(1) A don, (2 ff) Individual dons.

The Bodleian copy was received in 1887.

1888

Bastard, Thomas.

Chrestoleros.*

Reprinted from 1598.

[Defoe, Daniel.]

An Essay upon Projects. 1888.*

Reprinted from 1697.

Horne, Herbert P., and others.

The Best Plays Of The Old Dramatists. Nero & Other Plays Edited . . . By Herbert P. Horne, Havelock Ellis, Arthur Symons, And A. Wilson Verity . . . London: Vizetelly & Co. . . . 1888.

8°, text pp. 11–488.

(1) The Parliament of Bees, by John Day (p. 209).

Shirley, James.

James Shirley With An Introduction By Edmund Gosse . . . London T. Fisher Unwin Ltd New York Charles Scribner's Sons. [1888].

8°, text pp. 1–466.

(1) The Witty Fair One (p. 1).

A title in the Mermaid Series.

Temple, Dorothy, Lady.

Letters From Dorothy Osborne To Sir William Temple 1652–54 Edited By Edward Abbott Parry . . . Printed for Dodd, Mead, & Company . . . MDCCCLXXXVIII.

8°, text pp. 1–332.

(1) What her husband must and must not be (no. 36, 1653).

There were several editions of this year.

1890

Defoe, Daniel.

The Compleat English Gentleman By Daniel Defoe Edited for the First Time from the Author's Autograph Manuscript in the British

Museum . . . By Karl D. Bülbring. . . . London: Published by David Nutt. MDCCCXC.

8°, text pp. 11–278.

(1) A mere scholar (p. 201), (2) A good father (p. 240).

The original manuscript, written about 1728, is in the British Museum.

La Bruyère, Jean de.

The Morals And Manners Of The Seventeenth Century, Being The Characters Of La Bruyère. Translated by Helen Stott. Chicago A.C. McClurg & Co. 1890.

8°, text pp. 1–307.

(1–16) as (1–16) in his Characters, 1699.

The names of the characters differ somewhat from previous editions.

North, Roger.

The Lives of . . . Francis North . . . Edited by Augustus Jessopp, D.D. In three volumes. London: George Bell . . . 1890.

8°, 3 vols.

(1–14) as in 1742.

1891

Morley, Henry.

Character Writings of the Seventeenth Century Edited By Henry Morley . . . London George Routledge and Sons . . . 1891.

4°, text pp. 15–445.

Selections from: (1) Theophrastus (p. 15), (2) Harman (p. 17), (3) Jonson (p. 20), (4) Overbury (p. 28), (5) Hall (p. 104), (6) Earle (p. 154), (7) Breton (p. 238), (8) Minshull (p. 282), (9) Parrot (p. 283), (10) R.M.'s Micrologia (p. 285), (11) [Breton's] Whimzies (p. 286), (12) Milton (p. 291), (13) Saltonstall (p. 294), (14) Lupton (p. 295), (15) Ford (p. 296), (16) Cleveland (p. 298), (17) Flecknoe (p. 313), (18) Butler(p. 316), (19) Wordsworth (p. 443).

Murphy 8, 26, 27, 44.

1893

Fuller, Thomas.

The Marvellous Wisdom And Quaint Conceits Of Thomas Fuller, D.D., Being "The Holy State" Somewhat Abridged . . . By Adelaide L.J. Gosset. . . . London. Pickering and Chatto . . . Anno. Dom. MDCCCXCIII.

8°, text pp. 1–150.

(1–29) as (1–7, 11–17, 19, 21–26, 28, 32–36, 38, 40) in The Holy State, 1642.

Murphy 58.

1894

Drummond, William.

The Poems Of William Drummond Of Hawthornden Edited By Wm. C. Ward . . . London: George Routledge & Sons, Limited New York: E.P. Dutton & Co. [The Muses' Library. 1894.]

8°, 2 vols.

(1–2) as in 1711.

There have been several other editions of Drummond's Poems.

1895

Bradford, Gamaliel.

Types of American Character By Gamaliel Bradford, Jr. New York Macmillan and Company and London 1895.

8°, text pp. 1–210.

(1) The American pessimist (p. 1), (2) The American idealist (p. 22), (3) The American Epicurean (p. 53), (4) The American philanthropist (p. 87), (5) The American man of letters (p. 118), (6) The American out of doors (p. 163), (7) The scholar (p. 185).

1896

[Ward, Edward.]

The History Of The London Clubs. Or, The Citizens' Pastime. . . . By the Author of the London Spy . . . London, Printed by J. Dutten . . . 1709.

8° (?), text pp. 7–31.

(1–6) as in 1709, (7–10) as (1–4) in The Second Part of the London Clubs, [1720?].

The reprint uses for its title a reproduction of the title page of 1709.

Dated c. 1896 by the CBEL.

1897

Earle, John.

Earle's Microcosmography Edited With Introduction And Notes By Alfred S. West. . . . Cambridge: At The University Press. 1897.

8°, text pp. 1–160.

(1–77) as in 1629.

Murphy 44.

Earle, John.

Microcosmography. . . . A Reprint of Dr. Bliss's Edition of 1811. With a Preface and Supplementary Appendix By S.T. Irwin. Bristol: Published by W. Crofton Hemmons.

London: Simpkin, Marshall, Hamilton, Kent & Co. Ltd. 1897.*
See 1633.
8°.
Murphy 44.

Penton, Stephen.

The Guardian's Instruction or the Gentleman's Romance . . . By Stephen Penton Reprinted . . . by Herbert H. Sturmer London F.E. Robinson . . . 1897.
8°, text pp. 1–82.
(1–4) as in 1688.

Swift, Jonathan.

The Prose Works of Jonathan Swift, D.D. Edited by Temple Scott . . . London George Bell and Sons. [1897–1908.]
8°, 12 vols.
(1) The Sentiments of a Church of England Man (Vol. III, p. 51), (2) Brotherly Love (IV, 138), (3) A Short Character of His Ex. T.E. of W[harton]. (XII, 123).
There have been other editions of Swift's works.

1898

Bona, Giovanni.

Manuductio ad Coelum. 1898.*
Murphy 146.
Miss Murphy calls this an adaptation.

Herbert, George.

George Herbert's Country Parson Edited by H.C. Beeching, M.A. . . . Oxford B. H. Blackwell . . . London T. Fisher Unwin . . . MDCCCXCVIII.
8°, text pp. 1–175.
(1) A Priest to the Temple.
Murphy 135.

1899

[Earle, John.]

Micro-cosmography. . . . Published by J.M. Dent & Sons.
8°, text pp. 5–149.
(1–78) as in 1633, (79–106) as in Healey's Theophrastus, 1616.
Murphy 44.
The Temple edition, edited by W. H. D. Rouse.

Theophrastus.

Characters. 1899.*
Reprinted from 1714. Probably a reference to the second part of the preceding entry.

1900

Bona, Giovanni.

Manuductio ad Coelum. 1900.*
Murphy 146.
Reprinted or adapted from 1672.

Puckle, James.

The Club: or, A Grey Cap for a Green Head. . . . By James Puckle N.P. With . . . an Introduction by Austin Dobson London: Printed at the Chiswick Press . . . MDCCCC.
8°, text pp. 9–214.
(1–17) as in 1723.

1901

Penn, William.

Fruits of Solitude. 1901.*
Reprinted from 1749.

1902

Alsop, George.

A Character of the Province of Maryland.*
Reprinted from 1666.

Burnet, Gilbert.

A Supplement To Bishop Burnet's History Of My Own Time Derived From Sources . . . All Hitherto Unpublished. Edited by H.C. Foxcroft . . . Oxford . . . M.DCCCC.II.
8°, text pp. 1–541.
(1–9) as in 1724.

Freneau, Philip.

The Poems Of Philip Freneau . . . Edited . . . By Fred Lewis Pattee . . . Princeton N.J. The University Library 1902[–07].
8°, 3 vols.
(1) The Newsmonger (Vol. II, p. 263).
First printed in The Freeman's Journal, 1787.

Theophrastus.

Characters. 1902.*
Reprinted from 1714.

1903

Arber, Edward.

An English Garner . . . Westminster. 1903–04.
8°, 12 vols.
(1–2) as in 1877–96.
Murphy 126.

Bona, Giovanni.

A Guide to Eternity.*

Murphy 146.

An adaptation of Manuductio ad Coelum, 1672.

Cleveland, John.

The Poems of John Cleveland. Annotated . . .
by John M. Berdan . . . The Grafton Press
New York [copyright 1903].

Text pp. 7–198.
(1) The Hue and Cry after Sir John Presbyter (p.
154), (2) A protector (p. 185).

Earle, John.

Micro-cosmographie. . . . By John Earle. . . .
At the University Press, Cambridge . . .
MDCCCCIII.

8°, text pp. 1–128.
(1–78) as in 1633.
Murphy 44.

Lamb, Charles.

The Works Of Charles And Mary Lamb
Edited By E.V. Lucas. . . . New York: G.P.
Putnam's Sons London: Methuen & Co.
1903[–05].

8°, 7 vols.
(1–28) as in Elia, 1823, (29–53) as (1–25) in
The Last Essays of Elia, 1833, (54–61) as (1–8) in
Works, 1818, (62) On the custom of hissing at the
theatres (Vol. I, p. 87), (63) The good clerk (I,
127), (64) Memoir of Robert Lloyd (I, 132),
(65) Confessions of a drunkard (I, 133), (66)
The gentle giantess (I, 211), (67) Many friends
(I, 270), (68) Readers against the grain (I, 272),
(69) Mortifications of an author (I, 274), (70)
Tom Pry (I, 276), (71) Tom Pry's wife (I, 277),
(72) Egomet (I, 279), (73) The last peach — a
bank clerk fearful of becoming a thief (I, 283),
(74) Remarkable correspondent (I, 297), (75)
Captain Starkey (I, 299), (76) Twelfth of August (I, 302), (77) The ass (I, 303), (78) In re
squirrels (I, 306), (79) An appearance of the season — The parish beadle (I, 307), (80) The
months (I, 308), (81) Reminiscences of Sir Jeffrey
Dimstan (I, 312), (82) An autobiographical
sketch (I, 320).

The Works of 1818 are not reprinted as such but are dis-
tributed among the miscellaneous writings. Lamb's Works
have been published in many editions. Only the present,
which is the most complete, is included here. For first appearances of individual essays in periodicals the reader is
referred to Lucas's notes.

Pope, Alexander.

The Complete Poetical Works Of Alexander
Pope Cambridge Edition . . . Boston And
New York Houghton Mifflin Company
[1903].

(1) Macer, 1727 (p. 102), (2) Umbra, 1727 (p.
119), (3) Epistle I, to Sir Richard Temple, Lord
Cobham, Of the knowledge and characters of
men, 1733 (p. 157), (4) Epistle II, to a lady. Of
the characters of women, 1735 (p. 161).

Nos. 1 and 2 were first published in Miscellanies, 1727.
Nos. 3 and 4 form parts 1 and 2 of the Moral Essays.
Macer is a character of Ambrose Phillips, Umbra of Walter
Carey. There have been many editions of these poems.

1904

Ascham, Roger.

English Works . . . Edited By William Aldis
Wright, M.A. Cambridge: at the University
Press 1904.

8°, text pp. 1–304.
(1) The Scholemaster, 1570 (p. 171).

[Earle, John.]

Microcosmographie Faithfully Reprinted
From The Edition Of 1633 Methuen & Co.
London 1904.

12°, text sigs. B–N12v.
(1–78) as in 1633.
Murphy 44.

Horne, Herbert P., and others.

The Mermaid Series Nero & Other Plays
Edited . . . By Herbert P. Horne, Havelock
Ellis, Arthur Symons, And A. Wilson Verity
. . . London T. Fisher Unwin Ltd New York
Charles Scribner's Sons.

8°, text pp. 11–488.
(1) as in The Best Plays, by the same editors,
1888.

Nash, Thomas.

The Works of Thomas Nashe Edited From
The Original By Ronald B. McKerrow . . .
A.H. Bullen . . . London. MCMIV.

8°, 5 vols.
(1) Pierce Penniless his Supplication (Vol. I, p.
137), (2) The Unfortunate Traveller (II, 187).

Theophrastus.

Characters. 1904.*

Reprinted from 1714.

1905

Bentley, William.

The Diary of William Bentley, D.D. . . .
Salem, Mass. The Essex Institute. 1905[–14]
8°, 2 vols.
(1) as in 1787.

Dekker, Thomas.

The Belman of London, edited by O. Smeaton. The Temple Classics. 1905.*
Reprinted from 1608.

Herbert, George.

The English Works Of George Herbert Edited By George Herbert Palmer . . . Boston and New York Houghton Mifflin And Company MDCCCCV.
8°, 6 vols.
(1) A Priest to the Temple (Vol. II, p. 15). Murphy 135.

Penn, William.

Fruits of Solitude. 1905.*
Reprinted from 1749.

Saintsbury, George.

Minor Poets Of The Caroline Period . . . Edited By George Saintsbury, M.A. Oxford At The Clarendon Press 1905[–21].
8°, 3 vols.
(1) Lyric Poems, by Philip Ayres (Vol. II, p. 263).

[Ward, Edward.]

A Trip to New England. 1905.*
Reprinted from 1699.

1906

Erasmus, Desiderius.

Opvs Epistolarvm Des. Erasmi Roterodami . . . Avctvm per P.S. Allen . . . Oxonii . . . MCMVI[——].
Numerous volumes, still incomplete.
(1) John Colet, 1499 (Vol. I, p. 268), (2) Sir Thomas More, 1519 (IV, 12).

Hutchinson, Lucy.

Memoirs of . . . Colonel Hutchinson . . . 1906.*
Reprinted from 1806.

Russell, George W. E.

Social Silhouettes. By George W. E. Russell. . . . London Smith, Elder & Co. . . . 1906.
8°, text pp. 1–328.
(1) The schoolboy (p. 1), (2) The schoolmaster (p. 13), (3) The Oxford don (p. 24), (4) The Oxford undergraduate (p. 30), (5) The B.A. (p. 37), (6) The candidate for orders (p. 43), (7) The curate (p. 49), (8) The country parson (p. 56), (9) The town parson (p. 62), (10) The bishop (p. 68), (11) The painful preacher (p. 74), (12) The popular preacher (p. 80), (13) The

journalist (p. 89), (14) The faddist (p. 94), (15) The soldier (p. 102), (16) The doctor (p. 108), (17) The eldest son (p. 114), (18) The candidate for Parliament (p. 120), (19) The happy candidate (p. 129), (20) The middle-aged M.P. (p. 138), (21) The Labour-Member (p. 144), (22) The Whig (p. 150), (23) The party hack (p. 157), (24) The official M.P. (p. 164), (25) The author (p. 170), (26) The authoress (p. 177), (27) The busy idler (p. 184), (28) The clubman (p. 191), (29) The diner-out (p. 198), (30) The dinner-giver (p. 204), (31) The invalid (p. 211), (32) The squire (p. 218), (33) The plutocrat (p. 224), (34) The election-agent (p. 231), (35) The carpet-bagger (p. 238), (36) The disinherited knight (p. 245), (37) The victor (p. 252), (38) The quidnunc (p. 260), (39) The collector (p. 267), (40) The city man (p. 275), (41) The philanthropist (p. 283), (42) The professional philanthropist (p. 290), (43) The toady (p. 298), (44) The buck (p. 305), (45) The worlding (p. 312), (46) L'envoi (p. 321).
There was another edition in the same year, printed in London and New York.

1907

Herbert, George.

The English Works Of George Herbert Newly Arranged And Annotated . . . By George Herbert Palmer . . . Boston And New York Houghton Mifflin And Company MDCCCC-VII.
8°, 3 vols.
(1) as in 1905.

[Westmacott, Charles Molloy.]

The English Spy. 1907.*
Reprinted from 1825–26.

1908

Butler, Samuel.

Samuel Butler Characters And Passages From Note-Books Edited By A.R. Waller, M.A. . . . Cambridge: at the University Press 1908.
8°, text pp. 1–480.
(1–121) as in Genuine Remains, 1759, (122–187) as (1–66) in MS Characters, n.d.

Duncon, John.

'Lady Lettice Vi-Countess Falkland' By John Duncon Edited . . . by M.F. Howard. . . . London John Murray . . . 1908.
4°, text pp. 33–106.
(1) The Viscountess Falkland, by Jasper Mayne (p. 13, in verse).

Hutchinson, Lucy.

Memoirs of Colonel Hutchinson [by] Lucy Hutchinson London: J.M. Dent [Everyman's Library] 1908.

2 vols.

(1–2) as in 1806.

Sheridan, Richard Brinsley.

The Plays Of Richard Brinsley Sheridan Macmillan And Co. . . . London 1908.

8°, text pp. 1–455.

(1) A portrait addressed to Mrs. Crewe (p. 193).

This character precedes The School for Scandal, of which there have been many editions since its first appearance in 1780. The character does not appear in the first edition.

1909

Anonymous.

Life . . . [Vol. LIII.] Published at the Life Office, New York. [1909.]

Text pp. 5–894.

(1) The female gadder (June 3, p. 767).

Theophrastus.

Characters. 1909.*

Reprinted from 1714.

1910

Newman, John Henry, Cardinal.

The Idea Of A University Defined And Illustrated. . . . By John Henry Cardinal Newman New Impression . . . Longmans, Green, And Co. . . . London New York Bombay And Calcutta 1910.

8°, text pp. 1–521.

(1) A gentleman (p. 208).

First published as The Idea of a University, 1873, but under the title of Discourses on the Scope and Nature of University Education, 1852. Many other editions.

1912

Halifax, George Savile, Marquis of.

The Complete Works Of George Savile First Marquess Of Halifax Edited with an Introduction By Walter Raleigh Oxford At The Clarendon Press 1912.

8°, text pp. 1–256.

(1) The Lady's New Years Gift, 1688 (p. 1), (2) The Character of a Trimmer, 1688 (p. 47), (3) A Character of King Charles II, 1750 (p. 187).

1913

Hutchinson, Lucy.

Memoirs of . . . Colonel Hutchinson. Everyman's Library. 1913.*

Reprinted from 1806.

1915

Galsworthy, John.

The Little Man and Other Satires. By John Galsworthy New York Charles Scribner's Sons 1915.

Text pp. 3–279.

(1) The writer (p. 89), (2) The critic (p. 103), (3) The plain man (p. 114), (14) The superlative (p. 125), (5) The preceptor (p. 134), (6) The artist (p. 143), (7) The housewife (p. 152), (8) The latest thing (p. 164 — referring to a woman), (9) The perfect one (p. 172), (10) The competitor (p. 181).

1917

Hanscom, Elizabeth Deering.

The Heart Of The Puritan Selections From Letters And Journals Edited By Elizabeth Deering Hanscom . . . New York The Macmillan Company 1917.

8°, text pp. 1–277.

(1) A Boston old maid, by John Dunton, 1686 (p. 261).

1918

Smith, David Nichol.

Characters from the Histories & Memoirs of the Seventeenth Century With an Essay on the Character . . . By David Nichol Smith Oxford At The Clarendon Press MDCCCC-XVIII.

8°, text pp. 1–322.

(1) James I, by Arthur Wilson (p. 1), (2) James I, by Sir Anthony Weldon (p. 3), (3) The Duke of Buckingham, by Edward Hyde, Earl of Clarendon (p. 9), (4) Sir Thomas Coventry, by Clarendon (p. 17), (5) Sir Richard Weston, by Clarendon (p. 21), (6) The Earl of Arundel, by Clarendon (p. 29), (7) The Earl of Pembroke, by Clarendon (p. 32), (8) Sir Francis Bacon, by Ben Jonson (p. 35), (9) Sir Francis Bacon, by Arthur Wilson (p. 36), (10) Sir Francis Bacon, by Thomas Fuller (p. 38), (11) Sir Francis Bacon, by William Rawley (p. 39), (12) Ben Jonson, by Clarendon (p. 42), (13) Ben Jonson, by James Howell (p. 43), (14) Henry Hastings, by Anthony Ashley, Earl of Shaftesbury (p. 44), (15) Charles I, by Clarendon (p. 48), (16) Charles I, by Sir Philip Warwick (p. 53), (17) The Earl of Strafford, by Clarendon (p. 61), (18) The Earl of Strafford, by Warwick (p. 64), (19) The Earl of Northampton, by Clarendon (p. 67), (20) The Earl of Carnarvon, by Clarendon (p. 69), (21) Lord Falkland, by Clarendon (p. 71), (22) Lord Falkland, by Clarendon (p. 86), (23) Sidney

Godolphin, by Clarendon (p. 95), (24) William Laud, by Clarendon (p. 97), (25) William Laud, by Fuller (p. 102), (26) William Laud, by Warwick (p. 106), (27) William Juxon, by Warwick (p. 111), (28) The Marquis of Hertford, by Clarendon (p. 114), (29) The Marquis of Newcastle, by Clarendon (p. 116), (30) Lord Digby, by Clarendon (p. 120), (31) Lord Capel, by Clarendon (p. 123), (32) Royalist generals: Patrick Ruthven, Earl of Brentford; Prince Rupert; George, Lord Goring; Henry Wilmot, Earl of Rochester; by Clarendon (p. 127), (33) John Hampden, by Clarendon (p. 127), (34) John Pym, by Clarendon (p. 132), (35) Oliver Cromwell, by Clarendon (p. 136), (36) Oliver Cromwell, by Clarendon (p. 139), (37) Oliver Cromwell, by Warwick (p. 140), (38) Oliver Cromwell, by John Maidston (p. 142), (39) Oliver Cromwell, by Richard Baxter (p. 143), (40) Sir Thomas Fairfax, by Baxter (p. 149), (41) Sir Henry Vane, the younger, by Clarendon (p. 150), (42) Sir Henry Vane, by Clarendon (p. 152), (43) Colonel John Hutchinson, by Lucy Hutchinson (p. 154), (44) The Earl of Essex, by Clarendon (p. 157), (45) The Earl of Salisbury, by Clarendon (p. 159), (46) The Earl of Warwick, by Clarendon (p. 160), (47) The Earl of Manchester, by Clarendon (p. 162), (48) Lord Say, by Clarendon (p. 165), (49) John Selden, by Clarendon (p. 167), (50) John Earle, by Clarendon (p. 168), (51) John Hales, by Clarendon (p. 170), (52) William Chillingworth, by Clarendon (p. 174), (53) Edmund Waller, by Clarendon (p. 178), (54) Thomas Hobbes, by Clarendon (p. 181), (55) Thomas Hobbes, by John Aubrey (p. 182), (56) Thomas Fuller, anon. (p. 186), (57) John Milton, by Aubrey (p. 192), (58) John Milton, by Edward Phillips (p. 194), (59) John Milton, by Jonathan Richardson (p. 194), (60) Abraham Cowley, by himself (p. 197), (61) Abraham Cowley, by Thomas Sprat (p. 202), (62) Charles II, by The Earl of Halifax (p. 205), (63) Charles II, by Thomas Burnet (p. 218), (64) Charles II, by Burnet (p. 220), (65) The Earl of Clarendon, by Burnet (p. 224), (66) The Earl of Lauderdale, by Clarendon (p. 225), (67) The Earl of Lauderdale, by Burnet (p. 227), (68) The Earl of Shaftesbury, by Burnet (p. 230), (69) The Earl of Shaftesbury, by John Dryden (p. 232), (70) The Duke of Buckingham, by Burnet (p. 235), (71) The Duke of Buckingham, by Dryden (p. 236), (72) The Marquis of Halifax, by Burnet (p. 238), (73) Sir Edmund Saunders, by Roger North (p. 240), (74) Two groups of divines: Benjamin Whitchcot, Ralph Cudworth, John Wilkins, Henry More, John Worthington; John Tillotson, Edward Stillingfleet, Simon Patrick, Wililam Lloyd, Thomas Tenison, by Burnet (p. 244), (75) James II, by Burnet (p. 253), (76) James II, by Burnet (p. 257).

1921

Thorn-Drury, George.

A Little Ark Containing Sundry Pieces Of Seventeenth-Century Verse Collected And Edited By G. Thorn-Drury . . . P.J. & A.E. Dobell . . . 1921.

8°, text pp. 1–57.

(1) A Valiant Martyr and other Poems, by Robert Davenport (p. 9).

Here first printed from the original manuscript.

1922

[Forrester, James.]

The Polite Philosopher. 1922.*

Reprinted from 1734.

1923

Donne, John.

Paradoxes and Problemes by John Donne with two Characters and an Essay of Valour. . . . Soho. The Nonesuch Press . . . 1923.

6°, text pp. 1–80.

(1–3) as in 1652.

Murphy 135.

1924

Aldington, Richard.

A Book Of 'Characters' from Theophrastus; Joseph Hall, Sir Thomas Overbury, Nicolas Breton, John Earle, Thomas Fuller, And Other English Authors; Jean De La Bruyère, Vauvenargues, And Other French Authors Compiled and Translated by Richard Aldington With an Introduction and Notes London George Routledge & Sons Ltd. New York: E. P. Dutton & Co. [1924.]

8°, text pp. 1–559.

Contains characters by [or from, if anonymous]: (1–30) Theophrastus, (31–56) Hall, (57–137) Overbury, (138–167) Breton, (168–244) Earle, (245–254) Fuller, (255–307) Butler, (308–329) Jonson, (330) W.M., (331–333) Stephens, (334) Minshull, (335) Parrot, (336) R.M., (337) Whimzies, (338) Saltonstall, (339–343) Lupton, (344) A Strange Metamorphosis, (345–346) Habington, (347) St. Hilary's Tears, (348) The Character of an Oxford Incendiary, (349–350) Lord North, (351) Wortley, (352) Birkenhead, (353) Forde, (354) Cleveland, (355–356) The Wandering Jew, (357–358) Donne, (359–360) Margaret Duchess of Newcastle, (361) Characters; or Wit and the World, (362) The Character of a Coffee-House, 1665 (363–368) Flecknoe, (369) The Character of a Coffee-House, 1673, (370) The Character of a Quack Astrologer, (371) The Character of a Town Miss, (372) The Character of a Town Gallant, (373) The Character of an Informer, (374) The Character of a Tavern, (375) The Character of a Fanatic, (376) The Character of a Quack Doctor, (377) Four for a Penny, (378) The Duke of Buckinghamshire, (379) Denham, (380) The Character of a Sham Plotter, (381) The Character of a Disabled Courtier, (382) Milton, (383) The Character of London Village, (384) Oldham, (385) Twelve Ingenious Characters, (386) A London Pamphlet, (387) The Lively Character of a Contented Cuckold, (388) Scotland Characterised, (389) A Female Hypocrite, (390) Mee, (391–397) The Tatler, (398–412) The Spectator, (413) The Guardian, (414) The Compleat Gamester, (415–417) Johnson, (418–420) The Connoisseur, (421) The World, (422–423) The Connoisseur, (424–425) The World, (426–428) The Connoisseur, (429–431) The Mirror, (432) The Lounger, (433–436) The Observer, (437) The Looker-On, (438–522) La Bruyère, (523–542) Vauvenargues, (543) Boyer, (544–545) Cyrano de Bergerac, (546) Le Gouz, (547–548) Britten, (549) Goussault, (550) The Countess de Genlis.

Nash, Thomas.

Pierce Penilesse His Svpplication to the Diuell. . . . Written by Tho. Nash, Gent. . . . London, printed by Abell Ieffes, for I.B. 1592.

[Second title:] The Bodley Head Quartos Edited by G.B. Harrison Thomas Nashe Pierce Penilesse . . . Published by John Lane . . . and by E.P. Dutton & Company, New York.

8°, text pp. 1–137.
(1–10) as in 1592.

Ward, Edward.

The London-Spy Compleat, In Eighteen Parts, by Ned Ward With an Introduction by Ralph Straus London, Published and Sold by The Casanova Society . . . MCMXXIV.

8°, text pp. 1–444.
(1–26) as in 1698.

1925

Murphy, Gwendolen.

A Cabinet Of Characters Chosen And Edited By Gwendolen Murphy . . . 1925 London: Humphrey Milford Oxford University Press.

8°, text pp. 1–431.
Characters by [or from, if anonymous]: (1–2) Theophrastus, (3–4) Pope Innocent III, (5–6) Chaucer, (7) Brant, (8) Guevara, (9) Davies, (10) Griffin, (11–12) Marston, (13–14) Rowlands, (15) Fitzgeffrey, (16–17) Nashe, (18–20)

Dekker, (21–25) Mynshul, (26) Burton, (27) Andrews, (28–33) Adams, (34–36) Fuller, (37) Fulwell, (38–40) Jonson, (41–43) The Returne from Pernassus, (44–48) Hall, (49–71) Overbury, (72–74) Stephens, (75–93) Breton, (94–95) Wither, (96–120) Earle, (121–122) R. M., (123–125) Brathwaite, (126–127) Lenton, (128–135) Saltonstall, (136–138) Lupton, (139–140) A Strange Metamorphosis, (141) Crashaw, (142) Lord North, (143–146) Ford, (147–149) A Fresh Whip, (150–157) Flecknoe, (158) Cleveland, (159) A Phanatique, (160) Margaret Duchess of Newcastle, (161–162) Head, (163–174) Butler, (175–176) Coffee-house pamphlets, (177) An Honest Loyal Merchant, (178) H.C., (179) A Nice, Affected Beau, (180–183) A Lady, (184–186) Money Does Master All Things, (187–188) La Bruyère, (189) Pope, (190–197) Steele and Addison and others, (198–199) Law, (200–203) Johnson, (204–208) The World, (209) Cumberland, (210) Wordsworth, (211) Coleridge, (212–213) Lamb, (214) Jerrold, (215) Thackeray, (216–219) Blanchard, (220) Russell, (221) Galsworthy.

Many of these authors and titles are not included in Miss Murphy's Bibliography, and some are omitted from the present list.

1927

Anonymous.

Tricks Of The Town. Being Reprints of Three Eighteenth Century Tracts, With An Introduction By Ralph Straus . . . Chapman, Hall London MCMXXVII.

8°, text pp. 7–256.
(1) The Tricks of the Town laid open, 1746 (p. 1), (2) A Trip through the Town, 1735 (p. 113).

Brown, Thomas.

Amusements Serious And Comical And Other Works By Tom Brown Edited . . . by Arthur L. Hayward London George Routledge & Sons, Ltd. 1927.

8°, text pp. 1–471.
(1–17) as in 1702, (18) A tavern (p. 83), (19) Doctors' Commons (p. 87), (20) The Quakers' meetings (p. 93), (21) Letters from the dead to the living (p. 211).

Halifax, George Savile, Marquis of.

The Lady's New-Years-Gift or Advice to a Daughter by the late Lord Marquis of Halifax . . . Kensington: Printed and sold by Philip Sainsbury . . . 1927.

4°, text pp. 7–68.
(1–4) as in 1688.

Shadwell, Thomas.

The Complete Works Of Thomas Shadwell Edited by Montague Summers . . . The Fortune Press . . . London 1927.

8°, 5 vols.
(1) The Virtuoso (Vol. III, p. 95), (2) A True Widow (III, 277).

Trollope, Anthony.

London Tradesmen — Anthony Trollope — Foreword By Michael Sadleir . . . London Elkin Mathews & Marrot Ltd. New York Charles Scribner's Sons MDCCCCXXVII.

6°, text pp. 1–97.
(1) The tailor (p. 1), (2) The chemist (p. 12), (3) The butcher (p. 23), (4) The plumber (p. 32), (5) The horsedealer (p. 40), (6) The publican (p. 48), (7) The fishmonger (p. 56), (8) The greengrocer (p. 65), (9) The wine merchant (p. 73), (10) The coal merchant (p. 81), (11) The haberdasher (p. 89).

Originally published in the Pall Mall Gazette, 1880.

Ward, Edward.

The London Spy . . . By Ned Ward Edited With Notes By Arthur L. Hayward . . . Cassell and Company, Ltd London, Toronto, Melbourne and Sydney . . . [verso of title page] First Published 1927.

8°, text pp. 1–301.
(1–26) as in 1698.

The text of this edition is considerably expurgated and altered, but the characters remain substantially the same.

1928

Earle, John.

Micro-cosmographie . . . By John Earle. Edited By Gwendolen Murphy Printed and Published At The Golden Cockerel Press MCMXXVIII.

8°, text pp. 5–73.
(1–78) as in 1633.

Head, Richard, and Kirkman, Francis.

The English Rogue . . . By Richard Head & Francis Kirkman . . . London George Routledge & Sons, Ltd. 1928.

8°, text pp. 1–660.
(1–3) as in 1665.

Temple, Dorothy, Lady.

The Letters of Dorothy Osborne to William Temple Edited . . . by G.C. Moore Smith Oxford At the Clarendon Press MCMXXVIII.

8°, text pp. 3–206.
(1) as in 1888 (here numbered 44).

1929

La Bruyère, Jean de.

The Characters of Jean de la Bruyère. Translated by Henri van Laun. . . . Publishers Brentano's New York 1929.

8°, text pp. 7–494.
(1–16) as in The Morals and Manners, 1890.

Theophrastus.

Characters. 1929.*
Reprinted from 1714.

Ward, Edward.

The Wooden World. By Edward Ward First published 1707 Reprinted from the Edition of 1751 With a Foreword by Geoffrey Callender The Society For Nautical Research Occasional Publications No. II 1929.

6°, text pp. 11–99.
(1–14) as in 1707.

1930

Anonymous.

Characters and Observations An 18th Century Manuscript. London, John Murray . . . 1930.

8°, text pp. 1–296.
(1) Harpagon, a rich miser (p. 128), (2) Timon, a justice of the peace (p. 134), (3) Sophrona, a stingy woman (p. 140).

A number of other observations might almost be called characters.

[Cotton, Charles.]

The compleat gamester: or, Instructions How to play at Billiards, Trucks, Bowls, and Chess. 1930.*

8°, text pp. 1–269.
(1–2) as in 1674.

Temple, Sir William.

The Early Essays And Romances Of Sir William Temple Bt. With The Life And Character of Sir William Temple by his sister Lady Giffard Edited from the Original MSS. by G.C. Moore Smith . . . Oxford At the Clarendon Press MCMXXX.

4°, text pp. 1–215.
(1) Sir William Temple, by Martha Temple, Lady Giffard (p. 27).

1931

Dixon, W. Macneile.

The Englishman By W. Macneile Dixon. . . . London . . . 1931.

8°, text pp. 9–224.
(1) The Englishman (p. 83).

Glanvill, Joseph.

The Vanity Of Dogmatizing Reproduced from the Edition of 1661 With A Bibliographical Note By Moody E. Prior . . . Published For The Facsimile Text Society By Columbia University Press New York M.CM.XXXI.

8°, text pp. 1–250.
(1) as in 1661.

Willis, Leota Snider.

Francis Lenton, Queen's Poet — Leota Snider Willis A Thesis . . . Philadelphia 1931.

Text pp. 7–98.
(1) Characterismi, by Francis Lenton, 1631 (p. 60).

1932

Anonymous.

The Young Gentleman's Book. 1932.*
Reprinted from 1834.

1933

Breton, Nicholas.

Brittons Bowre Of Delights 1591 Edited By Hyder Edward Rollins . . . Cambridge Harvard University Press 1933.

8° (?), text pp. 1–116.
(1-2) as in 1591.

[Earle, John.]

Microcosmography. 1933.*
Reprinted from 1899.

Osborne, Harold.

A Mirror of Charactery. A Selection of Characters as depicted by English Writers From Chaucer to the present day. Ed. by Harold Osborne. London University Tutorial Press . . . 1933.

8°, text pp. 1–259.
Contains characters from: (1) Chaucer (p. 1), (2) Awdeley (p. 5), (3) Harman (p. 8), (4) Hall (p. 9), (5) Overbury (p. 19), (6) John Stephens (p. 37), (7) Breton (p. 44), (8) Mynshal (p. 57), (9) Parrot (p. 61), (10) Jonson (p. 63), (11) Earle (p. 68), (12) R.N. (p. 81), (13) Alexandrinus (p. 82), (14) Milton (p. 102), (15) Fuller (p. 103), (16) Saltonstall (p. 107), (17) Lupton (p. 122), (18) Brathwait (p. 131), (19) Anonymous (p. 135), (20) Wortley (p. 143), (21) Cleveland (p. 147), (22) Ford (p. 153), (23) Flecknoe (p. 156), (24) K.W. (p. 165), (25) Butler (p. 172), (26) Bunyan (p. 180), (27) Steele (p. 183), (28) Addison (p. 190), (29) Chesterfield (p. 196), (30) Johnson (p. 200), (31) Goldsmith (p. 205), (32) Lamb (p. 221), (33) Leigh Hunt (p. 225), (34) De Quincey (p. 239), (35) Dickens (p. 244), (36) Newman (p. 252), (37) Lowell (p. 255), (38) Henry James (p. 257).

Ward, Edward, and others.

Five Travel Scripts Commonly Attributed To Edward Ward Reproduced from the Earliest Editions Extant With A Bibliographical Note By Howard William Troyer [ornament] Published For The Facsimile Text Society By Columbia University Press New York: M.CM.XXXIII.

8°, text forty unnumbered leaves.
(1) A Trip to Jamaica, by [Edward Ward], 1700, (2) A Trip to New-England, by [Edward Ward], 1699, (3) A Trip to Ireland, 1699, (4) A Trip to Holland, 1699, (5) A Trip to North-Wales, 1701.

1934

[Earle, John.]

Micro-cosmography. . . . MCMXXXIV. Published by J.M. Dent & Sons.

8°, text pp. 5–149.
(1–106) as in 1899.

[Halifax, George Savile, Marquis of.]

The Lady's New-Years-Gift. 1934.*
Reprinted from 1688.

1936

Donne, John.

Ivvenilia Or Certaine Paradoxes And Problems By John Donne Reproduced from the First Edition With A Bibliographical Note By R.E. Bennett. . . . Published For The Facsimile Text Society By Columbia University Press New York: M.CM.XXXVI.

4°, text sigs, A3–H4v.
(1) as in 1633.

Hutchinson, Lucy.

Memoirs of . . . Colonel Hutchinson. Everyman's Library. 1936.*
Reprinted from 1806.

Overbury, Sir Thomas.

The Overburian Characters To which is added A Wife By Sir Thomas Overbury Edited by W. J. Paylor. . . . Oxford Basil Blackwell 1936.

8°, text pp. 1–108.
(1–82) as in Sir Thomas Overbury His Wife, 1622.

1937

Stephen, Sir Leslie.

Sketches from Cambridge. 1937.*

Reprinted from 1865.

1938

Defoe, Daniel.

Defoe's Review Reproduced from the Original Editions, with an Introduction and Bibliographical Notes by Arthur Wellesley Secord . . . Published for the Facsimile Text Society By Columbia University Press New York: MCMXXXVIII.

22 vols.

(1) as in 1708.

Franklin, Benjamin.

The General Magazine And Historical Chronicle . . . Published by Benjamin Franklin Reproduced from the Original Edition Philadelphia, 1741 With A Bibliographical Note By Lyon N. Richardson . . . Published For The Facsimile Text Society By Columbia University Press New York: M.CM.XXXVIII.

6°, text pp. 1–426.

(1) as in 1741.

1941

Chapman, George.

The Poems of George Chapman Edited by Phyllis Brooks Bartlett . . . 1941.

(1–4) as in Petrarchs Seven Penitentiall Psalms, 1612.

There have been other editions of Chapman's works.

TITLES OF UNCERTAIN DATE

Anonymous.

The Character and History of Will Trimmer.*

The Character of a Freshman.*
Bodleian Library manuscript.

The Character of a Projector.* Manuscript.

Begins: "A Projector is the onely corne cutter of the age."
Bodleian Library Douce MS. 286.

Described as written in the first quarter of the seventeenth century. Perhaps by Thomas Heywood; see, for instance, his Machiavel, 1641.

The Character of a Welshman.*

Characters and Observations.*

See 1930.
A 19th century manuscript, location unknown.

A Collection of Modern Statues and Characters.*

A Comprehensive, tho Compendious Character of the late Royal Martyr King Charles I. of ever-blessed Memory. Delineated by One of the Most Eminent Divines of the Church of England.*

The dame of honour; or, hospitality.

s.sh.fo. In verse.
Begins: "Since all the World's turn'd upside down."
The Boston Public Library dates this London, 18—? Mr.

Greenough's notes give a title: London, Printed for J. Hodges, but in the present copy there is no indication of printer or place of publication.

A Definition in Rhyme of the foure Sorts of Melancholy Men.*

British Museum Add. MS. 22587 (13), f. 21.

A Faithful Servants Properties . . . Printed for the Proprietor, & Sold by B. Dickinson . . .*

In verse, 22 lines.
Ends: "Then let the Whifflers of these Times all know,
    How Servants were esteem'd an Age ago."

The Imposter . . . or, The base Birth and Parentage of the . . . Pretender, Now truly brought to Light . . . London, Printed by J. Read.*

(1) The [Old] Pretender (p. 14).

The Lying-Whig Drawn in his own Colours. . . To the Tune of Packingtons Pound. this may be Printed R.L.S. . . . [colophon torn off.]

s.sh.fo.
Begins: "How wretched is *England* above any Nation."

[Manuscript.]*

(1) Characters of nations and towns, 1625.
Phillipps MS. 9569 (not traced).

[Manuscript.]*
(1) A prison (f. 45v).
Trinity College, Cambridge, MS. R.3.19.
Written in manuscript at the end of a copy of George Ashby's Lament, 1463.

[Manuscript.]*
(1) The Queen of Great Britain.
Bibliothèque Nationale, Paris, MS. 57.

[Manuscript.]*
(1) The kings of England.
Bodleian Library MS. 9772.

[Manuscript.]*
(1) An elder brother (fol. 1), (2) A wise courtier (f. 2), (3) A mere courtier (f. 2v), (4) A young courtier (f. 3), (5) A meere travailer (f. 3v), (6) A wittall (f. 4), (7) A whore (f. 4), (8) A bawde (f. 4v), (9) A lye (f. 5), (10) A good black-man (f. 5v), (11) A dunce (f. 5v), (12) A fine man in debt (f. 6), (13) A cheating-gamester (f. 6), (14) A tauerne (f. 6v), (15) A character-maker (f. 6v), (16) An informer (f. 7), (17) A sayler (f. 7v), (18) A lowse (f. 7v), (19) A yeoman of ye guard (f. 8), (20) A wayting woman (f. 10), (21) A herrauld (f. 10), (22) A mother of ye maides (f. 10v), (23) A decayed painted lady (f. 11), (24) The second part of a wayting woman (f. 11v), (25) A maide (f. 11v).
A manuscript belonging to James M. Osborn of New Haven.

[Manuscript characters.]*
(1) A humourous, preposterous woman (p. 95), (2) A good woman (p. 96), (3) An essay of a king (p. 177).
Bodleian Library Ashmole MS. 826.

[Manuscript characters.]*
(1) A king, (2) A bishop, (3) An ambassador.
Bodleian Library Ashmole MS. 1382.

[Manuscript characters.]*
(1) A Puritan, (2) A church papist, (3) A covetous man, (4) A courtier, (5) A virgin, (6) A widow, (7) An honest and modest woman.
British Museum Harl. MS. 1221.

[Manuscript Commonplace Book.]*
(1) A satyrick character of scandelous stayle virgins (p. 201), (2) One that writes characters (p. 246), (3) A covetous man (p. 247), (4) A proud man (p. 248), (5) An idle person (p. 249), (6) A constant woman, (7) A common huntsman.
Bodleian Library Ashmole MS. A. 301.
There seems to be some confusion as to contents and pages. The date is sometime during the seventeenth century.

A Murmurer Described.*
A copy of [1660?].
Trinity College, Cambridge, MS 1495.[5].
Dates from the eighteenth or nineteenth century.

A Receipt, How to Make a True Methodist.*
Begins: "Take of the herbs."
Probably another edition of Wonder upon Wonder, n.d., or a variant reference to the same work.

Two Female Characters Contrasted: of a sister; of a wife.*
Manuscript.
(1) Of a humorsome woman, by her brother, (2) Of a woman of incomparably sweet disposition.
Bodleian Library Ashmole MS. 826 (96).

The Whole Life, Birth and Character Of his most Serene Highness George Lewis Elector of Hanover. Printed for Rich. Pool near the Royal-Exchange.*

Wonder upon Wonder: Or, A Receipt to make a True Methodist.
s.sh.fo.
Begins: "Take of the Herbs of Hypochrysy."
Another edition of A Receipt, How to Make a True Methodist, n.d. There is no imprint or colophon.

Bacon, Sir Francis.
In felicem memoriam Elizabethae Reginae.*
(1) Queen Elizabeth (f. 79).
British Museum Harl. MS. 6769.

[Bellasys, Margaret, supposed author.]
Characterismes of Vices.
Manuscript, fo, text pp. 1–310.
(1) Flatterer (p. 1), (2) Covetous (p. 4), (3) Prodigal (p. 8), (4) Lustful (p. 11), (5) Brainesicke (p. 14), (6) Proud (p. 18), (7) Ambitious (p. 22), (8) Timorous suspitious (p. 26), (9) Angry man (p. 31), (10) Inconstant (p. 34), (11) Envious (p. 40), (12) Idle (p. 43), (13) Usurer (p. 47), (14) Hypocrite (p. 51), (15) Profane (p. 56), (16) Vaine-glorious (p. 59), (17) Secure (p. 63), (18) Weary well-doer (p. 67), (19) Busie-bodie (p. 70).
British Museum Add. MS. 10309.
On the last page is the signature of Margaret Bellasys. Lambert Ennis shows in PMLA LVI (1941), 141 ff. that these characters are taken almost word for word from Adams's Diseases of the Soul, q.v.

Breton, Nicholas.
The Character of Queen Elizabeth.*
Begins: "In the yere of oᵣ Lord 1534."
British Museum Harl. MS. 6207, f. 22.
The reference is taken from Breton's Works, 1879, ed.

A.B. Grosart, in which this piece is printed. The manuscript is in Breton's own hand.

Butler, Samuel.
Characters.*

(1) An antisocordist, (2) A banker, (3) A bowler, (4) A brisk man — pert, (5) A broker, (6) A buffoon, (7) A catchpole, (8) A clap'd man, (9) A coffee man, (10) A coiner, (11) A conjurer, (12) A constable, (13) A court-wit, (14) A coward, (15) A credulous man, (16) A cruel man, (17) A cully, (18) A cutpurse, (19) A dancing-master, (20) A detractor, (21) A dueller, (22) A dunce, (23) An envious man, (24) A fencer, (25) A fidler, (26) A fool, (27) A forger, (28) A gamester, (29) An hector, (30) An highwayman, (31) An host, (32) An ignorant man, (33) An impertinent, (34) An impostor, (35) An incendiary, (36) An informer, (37) A jailor, (38) A juror, (39) A lampooner, (40) A liar, (41) A merchant, (42) The modish man, (43) A musitian, (44) The negligent, (45) An officer, (46) An oppressor, (47) A parasite, (48) The perfidious man, (49) A plagiary, (50) A player, (51) A proud lady, (52) A publican, (53) A quareller, (54) A rook, (55) A sailor, (56) A scold, (57) A scrivener, (58) The self conceited or singular, (59) A sharke, (60) A silenc'd Presbyterian, (61) A soldier, (62) A stationer, (63) A tennis-player, (64) An usurer, (65) The vainglorious man, (66) The voluptuous.
British Museum Add. MS. 32625-6.

In default of being able to consult the original manuscript, the editor has taken the above information from its first appearance in print in A. R. Waller's edition of Butler's Characters, Cambridge, 1908.

[Butler, Samuel.]
The Geneva Ballad.*
See 1674.

[Earle, John.]
[Characters.]*
Contains 13 characters.
Murphy 46.
British Museum Stowe MS. 962.

[Earle, John.]
[Characters.]*
(1) A gallant, (2) A weak man, (3) A sceptick in religion.
Murphy 46.
The Bright manuscript, location now unknown.

Fulwell, Ulpian.
Tom Tosspot.*
Begins: "From morning to night I sit tossing the black bob."

Glanvill, Joseph.
Bensalem; being a Description of a Catholick & Free Spirit, Both in Religion and Learning, in a Continuation of the story of Lord Bacon's New Atlantis.*

Manuscript, fo, text pp. 1-63.
(1) Chudorvet, (2) Votheci, (3) Pratci, (4) Retus, (5) J[i]cambo, (6) Cardo, (7) Ottamur, (8) Sithim, (9) Meor, (10) Ilegon, (11) Tonsillo, (12) Stenfegill.

Manuscript belonging to the University of Chicago. These characters are thinly veiled descriptions of certain clergymen of the latter seventeenth century, some of which may be identified as follows: (1) Cudworth, (2) Whichcot, (3) Patrick, (4) Ruste, (5) Jacombe, (8) Smith, (9) More, (10) Ingelo, (11) Tillotson, (12) Stillingfleet.

[Grey, Zachary.]
An Attempt towards the Character of the Royal Martyr King Charles I.*
Manuscript.
See 1738.

Hildesley, Mark.
Religio Jurisprudentis: Or, The Lawyer's Advice to his Son.*
Murphy 151.
British Museum Harleian MS. 4726.
See 1685.

Honeycombe, Polly.
Modern Characters illustrated by Histories.*

Honeycombe, Polly.
Sedan, in which many new and entertaining Characters are introduced.*

Oberndoerffer, Johann.
The Anatomyes of the True Physition.*
Manuscript, 4 leaves.
British Museum Sloane MS. 121, ff. 62-65.
See 1602.

Ogilby, John.
The Character of a Trooper.*

Parlett, Sir Edmond.
The General Character of Woman.*
Bodleian Library Rawlinson MS. Misc. 164.
Mr. Greenough thought this not a character.

[Scott, Thomas.]
The Interpreter.*
A manuscript in the Sutro Library, San Francisco, California.
See 1622.

[Settle, Elkanah.]

The Character of a Popish Successour.*

A manuscript in the Boston Public Library.

See 1681.

Smith, Albert.

The Natural History of the Ballet Girl.*

See 1847.

[Southwell, Sir Robert?]

Verse and prose written by Sir Robert Southwell when an undergraduate at Queen's College, Oxford.*

(1) A drunkard (p. 41).

Bodleian Library MS. Eng. poet. f. 6.

[Ward, Edward.]

Female Policy Detected: Or, The Arts of a Designing Woman Laid Open Treating . . . III. A True Character of a Vertuous Woman: or, Wife indeed. With a Poetical Description of a Maid, Wife, and Widow By E. VV. Author of the London-Spy, and Trip to Jamaica. . . . London: Printed for John Willis and Joseph Boddington.

12°, text pp. 1–140, plus 6 additional leaves.

(1) An ambitious hypocritical woman (p. 51), (2) A froward widow (p. 66), (3) A good vvife (p. 104), (4) A good vvife . . . or . . . a wife indeed (p. 136, in verse).

Attributed to Ward by the CBEL, but noting that he later denied authorship.

[Ward, Edward.]

Mars stript of his Armour.*

See 1709.

[Ward, Edward.]

The Reformer. Exposing the Vices of the Age in several Characters. viz. 1. The Vitious Courtier . . . 13. A Jacobite. To which is added, The Rambling Rake; or, London Libertines . . . Together with Three Nights Adventures: . . . Also A Step to the Bath . . . And a Character of the Place. The Fourth Edition. London Printed and Sold by J. How. . . .*

(1–12) as in 1700, (13) The Jacobite, (14) The rambling rake, (15) Bath.

Woodward, G. M.

County Characters. London, R. Ackerman.*

[Younge, Richard.]

The Seduced Soul reduced, and rescued from the Subtilty, and Slavery of Satan, that bloody devouring Dragon, and vowed Enemy of all Mankind . . . These being small pieces, are sold onely by James Crump, in Little Bartholmews, welyard; And by Henry Cripps, in Popes-head Alley.*

(1) The state of a Christian, (2) The drunkard (p. 11).

APPENDIX OF TITLES CONSIDERED BUT REJECTED

Professor Greenough's files contained many additional titles of works which he thought of as possibilities for this bibliography. Some of them he eventually saw and discarded as being not properly characters, or inadmissible for some other reason, such as being in a foreign language. Others which he did not see I have looked at and discarded as having no proper place in the list. Still others neither of us has seen, but the information about them is so slight that it seems unwise to include them. Yet it seems better to give the titles here briefly rather than to omit them without mention. It may be that some items, especially among those which neither of us saw, will prove later to have a rightful claim to a place in the bibliography. About others, as always about border-line cases in any question, there may be a difference of opinion. In the hope that they may be useful to the reader they are therefore included in this place.

The arrangement is alphabetical. An asterisk (*) before a title indicates that it was consulted but rejected by Professor Greenough; a dagger (†) means that I saw it and rejected it. When both occur together, the title was seen by us both, and both of us discarded it. A title not preceded by either mark has not been seen by either of us. All titles in the appendix are included in the indexes like those in the main bibliography.

† A., O. [Oliver Almond?], The Vncasing of Heresies, 1623.

† Abbot, George, A Briefe description of the whole worlde, 1599.

† Abbot, Robert, The Trve, Ancient Roman Catholike, 1611.

† The Anatomy of an Arbitrary Prince, 1689.

† The Anatomie of Sinne, 1603.

Answer a Foole, 1664.

† An Answer to . . . the Character of a Popish Successor, 1681.

† The Anti-Politician, 1734.

† [Asgill, John], Mr. Asg..l's Congratulatory Letter To The L..d B....p of S...m, 1713.

Averell, William, A Dyall for dainty darlings, 1584.

† Aylesbury, Thomas, Paganisme and Papisme parallel'd, 1624.

† Aylett, Robert, A Wife, Not Ready Made, but Bespoken, 1653.

† Bacon, Sir Francis, Apophthegmes New and Old, 1625, 1626.

*† Bacon, Sir Francis, An Essay of a King, 1642.

† Barton, John, The Art of Rhetorick, 1634.

The Batchelor, 1766–67.

† Baxter, Richard, Directions for Weak Distempered Christians, 1669.

† Bell, Thomas, The Anatomie of Popish tyrannie, 1603.

A Belman for England, 1586.

† Blount, Thomas, Glossographia, 1656.

†Bona, John, Manuductio ad Coelum, 1681. [A spurious edition?]

* Bourn, Benjamin, Sure Guide to Hell, 1750, 1752, 1755, 1787.

† Bowle, John, A Sermon preached at Flitton . . . at the Funerall of . . . Henrie Earle of Kent, 1615.

*† Brathwaite, Richard, The Golden Fleece, 1611.

† [Brathwaite, Richard], The History of Moderation, 1669.

†Brathwaite, Richard, A Spiritval Spicerie, 1638.

† Brathwaite, Richard, The Trimmer, or the Life and Death of Moderation, 1684.

†Breton, Nicholas, The Arbor of Amorous Deuices, 1594.

† Breton, Nicholas, Conceited Letters, 1632.

[Breton, Nicholas?], The Chesse Play, 1593.

† [Breton, Nicholas], Crossing of Proverbs, 1616.

† Breton, Nicholas, The Figure of Foure, 1597, 1607, 1626, 1631, 1653.

† Breton, Nicholas, A Floorish vpon Fancie, 1577.

† Breton, Nicholas, Honest Counsaile, 1605.

† Breton, Nicholas, I Pray Yov Be Not Angry, 1632.

† Breton, Nicholas, Melancholike Humours, 1600.

† Breton, Nicholas, The second part of Pasquils Mad-cap, 1600.

*† A Briefe Discourse Vpon Tyrants, 1642.

The British Censor, 1712.

† Buckingham, George Villiers, Duke of, Advice to a Painter, 1673, 1681.

† [Burnet, Sir Thomas], Some New Proofs . . . James the Third, 1745.

† Busche, Alexander van den, The Orator, 1596.

*† C., L., The Good Wive's Vindication, 1678.

† C., T., The Schismaticke Sifted through a Sive, 1646.

† Carleton, George, Heroici Characteres, 1603.

† Carter, Richard, The Schismatick Stigmatized, 1641.

† Casa, Giovanni della, Galateo, 1576.

† Caussin, N., The Unfortunate Politique, 1638.

Certain True Marks whereby to knowe a Papist, 1581.

† [Chamberlain, Robert], Jocabella, 1640.

† [Chamberlain, Robert], A New Booke of Mistakes, 1637.

† Chamberlain, Robert, Nocturnall Lucubrations, 1638.

† Chamberlain, Robert, The Swaggering Damsell, 1640.

† [Chambre, Ma. de la], The Art to know Men, 1664.

The Church Rambler, 1723.

The Cloak in its Colours, 1679.

† Closse, George, The Parricide Papist, 1606.

The Coffee-Man's Granado discharged upon the Maiden's Complaint against Coffee, 1663.

The Cognizance of a New [or True] Christian, 1597.

† A Comparison of the English and Spanish Nations, 1589.

† Cooke, Edward, The Perspective Glass of War, 1628.

· † Copley, Anthony, Wits Fittes and Fancies, 1614.

The Counterfeet Court Lady, n.d.

The Country Parson's Honest Advice, [1700?].

† Cowper, William, The Anatomie of a Christian Man, 1611, 1613.

Crane, Thomas, Job's Assurance of the Resurrection, 1690.

† Cuffe, Henry, The Differences of the Ages of Mans Life, 1607.

Cyprian, Saint, A Looking Glasse for England, 1590.

† Davies, John, of Hereford, Microcosmos, 1603.

† Davies, Sir William, An Anatomy of Atheisme, 1693–94.

† The Definition of a Parliament, 1642.

† [Defoe, Daniel], A Second Volume of the Writings of the Author of the True-Born Englishman, 1705.

† [Defoe, Daniel?], The White-Staff's Speech to the Lords, 1714.

† Dodd, William, The Beauties of History, 1795, 1800.

† Doddridge, Sir John, A Compleat Parson, 1630.

† [Doyle, John], Political Sketches, 1829–33.

† Draxe, Thomas, Calliepeia, 1631.

Drops of Myrrh, [1654?].

*† Ducci, Lorenzo, Ars Avlica, 1607.

† Du Moulin, Lewis, Morum Exemplar seu Characteres, 1654,1662.

† Du Moulin, Lewis, Theophrasti Characteres Ethici, 1669.

Durant, John, The Spiritual Seaman, 1654.

Dwight, Timothy, The Smooth Divine, 1788.

† Dymocke, James, Le Vice Ridicule, 1671.

The Ear-Wig, 1781.

† Eikon Basilike Deutera, The Pourtraiture of his Sacred Majesty King Charles II, 1694.

Elslyot, Thomas, The True Mariner, 1652.

† Elyot, Sir Thomas, The Boke named the Governour, 1546.

England's Merry Jester, 1693.

† England's Remembrancer, [1757?].

Epictetvs his Manuall, 1610. (See Healey, 1616, in main list.)

† Erasmus, Desiderius, Enchiridion Militis, 1534.

† Erasmus, Desiderius, Letter to Sixtinus, 1499.

† Erasmus, Desiderius, Letter to Ulrich von Hutten, 1519.

Essays Theological and Moral, n.d.

The Estate of Swearing and Swearers, 1578.

† Faret, Nicholas, The Honest Man, 1632.

† [Farnaby, Thomas], Index Poeticus, 1634.

† Farnaby, Thomas, Phrases Oratoriae et Poeticae, 1631, 1638.

*† Farnworth, Richard, A Character whereby the false Christs, 1654.

† Featley, Daniel, The Dippers Dipt, 1645.

† Fénelon, François de Salignac de La Mothe-, Characters and Criticisms, 1714.

[Fenn, Lady Eleanor], The Juvenile Tatler, [1789?].

[Fenn, Lady Eleanor?], Sketches of little Boys, [1840?].

[Fenn, Lady Eleanor?], Sketches of little Girls, [1840?].

*† Fenner, Dudley, The Artes of Logike and Rethorike, 1584.

*† Fennor, William, The Souls Looking-glasse, 1640.

*† Flavell, John, The Character of a Complete Evangelical Pastor, 1731.

*† Fuller, Thomas, Good Thoughts in Bad Times, 1645.

† Furetière, Antoine, Le roman bourgeois, 1712.

Gauden, John, Eikon e Piste; or the faithfull pourtraicture of a loyal subject, 1649.

† [Gay, John], Wine, 1709.

† The General Review, or Impartial Register, 1752.

† Glanvill, Joseph, Essays on several important Subjects, 1676.

† Glanvill, Joseph, Ne Plus Ultra, 1668.

A Glasse for vayne glorious women, 1594.

Gooch, Thomas, A Sermon preach'd . . . the death of . . . Henry late Lord Bishop of London, 1713.

Good Manners for Schools, 1700.

* Gordon, Thomas, A Medicine for the Times, 1641.

† Grahame, Simion, The Passionate Sparke, 1604.

† [Grimefield, John?], The Sage Senator Delineated, 1660.

† The Grub-Street Journal, 1730.

† Guevara, Antonio de, The Diall of Princes, 1557, 1582, 1592.

Gulliver, John, Travels, translated from the French, 1731.

*† Hall, John, Horae Vacivae, 1646.

† Hampton, William, A Map of Judgement, 1667.

† Hanapus, Nicolaus, The ensamples of Vertue, 1561.

† Hardy, Nathaniel, The Pious Votary and Prudent Traveller, 1658.

Harris, John, The Puritanes Impuritie, 1641.

The Harvard Advocate, 1905.

† Harvey, Christopher, The Synagogue, 1640.

† Harvey, Gabriel, G. Harvei Rhetor, 1577.

† Hearne, Thomas, Impartial Memorials, 1736.

† Heinsius, Daniel, Aristotelis Ethicorum Nicomachiorum Paraphrasis, 1607.

*† Heywood, Thomas, The General History of Women, 1657.

*† Heywood, Thomas, Philocothonista, 1635.

† The History of Ingratitude, 1712.

* Holyband, Claude, Campo di fior, 1583.

† Homes, Nathaniel, Daemonologie, or the Character of the Crying Evils of the Present Times, 1650.

The Honest London Spy, [1779?].

† Honesty the Best Policy, 1752.

Howell, James, A Brood of Cormorants, n.d.

The Humble Remonstrance of Bachelors in Answer to the Petition, &c. for Husbands, 1693.

Jesuita Seductor Sueco, 1604.

† Johnson, Ralph, The Scholar's Guide from the Accidence, 1665, 1699.

† [Johnstone, Mrs. Christian Isabel], The Saxon and the Gael, 1814.

† Jones, Captain Thomas, Plain English, 1646.

† Kettlewell, John, The Religious Loyalists, 1686.

† The Knave Uncloak'd, 1679.

* La Mesnardière, Jules de, La Poétique, 1640.

*† La Primaudaye, Pierre de, The French Academie, 1586.

[Lawrence, George, and Love, Christopher?], The Debauched Cavalier, 1642.

† [Ledyard, T.?], The German Spy, 1740.

*† Leighton, Sir William, Vertue Triumphant, 1603.

*† L'Estrange, Sir Roger, The Reformed Catholique, 1679.

† A Letter from a Whig Gentleman, 1712.

*† A Letter to the People, 1712.

The Life and Adventures of a Female Soldier, 1775.

The Life of . . . Dr. Cranmer, 1751.

† A Lively Pourtraict of our New-Cavaliers, 1661.

The London Puppies' Memorial, 1710.

A Looking-Glass for a Tory, 1682.

The Loyal London Prentice, 1681.

*† The Loyal Protestant, 1681.

† [Lupton, Donald], Emblems of Rarities, 1636.

† [Lupton, Thomas], The Second Part . . . of . . . Too Good to be True, 1581.

M., C., The second part of . . . the Nature of a Woman, 1596.

Mackqueen, John, The Good Patriot set forth, 1694.

Malvezzi, Marchese Virgilio, The Pourtract of the Politicke Christian Favourite, 1647.

† [Markham, Gervase], The Gentlemans Academie, 1595.

† Mason, Robert, Reasons Academie, 1605.

Mayhew, Augustus Septimus, Change for a Shilling, n.d.

*† Melampus, The Contemplation of Mankind, 1571.

The Men's Answer to the Women's Petition against Coffee, 1674.

The Mercenary Souldier, 1646.

* Miniature Pictures, 1781.

† The Mirrour of Complements, 1635.

The Modern Christian, 1737.

Montalvan, Francisco Baltheo de, Cupid Stripped, 1703.

Moral Reflections and Pleasant Remarks, 1707.

* Morellus, Theodoricus, and Ross, Alexander, Enchiridion Duplex, 1651.

*† N., C., Jesuita Vapulans, n.d.

The Nativity of Sir John Presbyter, 1645.

The Nature of a Woman, 1595.

† Nelson, Robert, Instructions for the Conduct of Young Gentlemen, 1718.

A New Ballad with the definition of the word Tory, 1682.

The New Projector, n.d.

The New Westminster Wedding, 1693.

Nicholls, William, The Duty of Inferiours towards their Superiours, 1701.

*† [Norden, John], The Mirror of Honor, 1597.

[Norden, John?], The Mirror of the Multitude, 1586.

Oberndoerffer, Johann, De Veri et Falsi Medici Agnitione, 1600.

* Observations on Bothmar's Memorial, 1712.

An Occasional Dialogue at a Coffee-House, 1667.

*† [Ormerod, Oliver?], The Picture of a Papist, 1605, 1606.

*† Ormerod, Oliver, The Picture of a Puritane, 1605.

† Osborne, Francis, Advice to a Son, 1658.

† P., J., Advice to a Painter, 1688.

† P., K., The Scholar's Instructor, [1700?].

*† [Parker, Henry?], The Atheisticall Polititian, 1642.

† Pasqualis, Carolus, Virtutes et Vitia, 1615.

† Peacham, Henry, The Garden of Eloquence, 1577.

† Pelegromius, Simon, Synonymorum Sylva, 1585.

† [Penn, William?], Vlmorum Acherons, 1682.

† [Perkins, William], A Reformed Catholike, 1598.

† Person, David, Varieties, 1635.

The Petition of the Widows, 1690, 1693.

Philips, Erasmus, The Country Gentleman, 1726.

† [Phiston, William], The Welspring of Wittie Conceites, 1584.

Pierse, Charles, Vertues Anatomie, 1618.

[Plume?], John Hacket, 1672.

Plummer, Timothy, The Favourite, 1622.

*† Poetical Recreations, n.d., 1688.

*† The Portraicture of Roger L'Estrange, 1681.

*† The Protestation Protested, 1641.

The Quaker Champion, 1727.

† [Quarles, Francis], The Loyall Convert, 1643, 1644.

*† Ratcliffe, Aegremont, A Politike Discourse, 1569, 1578.

[Rede, L.S.a T., or L'Estrange, Sir Roger?], The Barrister at Law, 1793.

*† The Reformed Catholicqve, 1621.

† Richardson, Charles, A Workeman, that Needeth not to be Ashamed, 1616.

Riveley, B., A Sermon Preach'd . . . at the Funeral of . . . Edward, Lord Bishop of Norwich, 1677.

*† Roberts, William, The Looker-On, 1793.

Robertson, Bartholomew, The Anatomie of a Distressed Soule, 1619.

Robson, Simon, A New Yeares Gift, 1582, 1597.

*† Rogers, Nehemiah, The Good Samaritan, 1640.

*† Rogers, Nehemiah, The Penitent Citizen, 1640.

S., J., A Brief Anatomie of Women, 1653.

*† Saltonstall, Wye, Englands Complaint, 1640.

*† Scott, Sarah, The History of Sir George Ellison, 1766.

† Scott, Thomas, Christs Politician, 1616.

* Scott, Thomas, Vox Populi, 1620.

[Seabury, Samuel?], The Republican Dissected, [1775?].

† A Sectary Dissected, 1647.

*† Semper Idem, 1661.

† Settle, Elkanah, A Vindication of the Character of a Popish Successour, 1681.

The Ship of Careless Conversation, 1580.

† Shirley, James, The Gentleman of Venice, 1655.

A Short Dialogue concerning the Arraignment of certain Caterpillars, 1593.

Sidney, Sir Philip, Valour Anatomized in a Fancy, 1581.

† [Smollett, Tobias], The Adventures of Ferdinand Count Fathom, 1753.

Le Spectateur François, 1728, 1791.

Spencer, Benjamin, Christophilos, 1642.

*† A Spirituall Journey of a Young Man, 1659.

† [Spooner, Lawrence], Poetical Recreations, 1705.

The State Proteus, 1690.

† Stockwood, John, Progymnasma Scholasticum, 1597.

Sweeper, Walter, A brief Treatise declaring the true Christian Nobleman, 1622.

Symptoms of Growth, and Decay to Godliness, 1672.

A Synopsis, or Contract View, of the Life of John Armand, 1643.

†T., C., Lavgh and lie downe, 1605.

Tate, Faithful, The Uncharitable Informer Charitably Informed, 1660.

† Tatham, John, The Rump, 1660, 1661.

† Taylor, Jeremy, Eniantos, A Course of Sermons, 1668.

Taylor, R., Pulpit Popery, 1688.

Thoughts or Comparisons imagined on seeing a King, n.d.

The Times New Churchman, 1635.

*† To Poet Bavius, 1688.

A Total Rout, 1653.

† Trenchfield, Caleb, A Cap of Gray Hairs, 1671, 1678, 1688.

*† Trescot, Thomas, The Zealous Magistrate, 1642.

A Trimmer's Confession of Faith, 1694.

*† The Trimming Court-Divine, 1690.

A True-blue Priest, 1683.

The True-born English-Woman, 1703, 1705.

The True-Born Scot, 1744.

The True Catholick and Catholick Church, 1660.

*† A True Character of Worster's Late Hurley-Burley, 1642.

Twenty-one Questions seriously propounded to . . . Quakers, 1701–02.

Twenty Orders of Knaves, 1586.

† [Tymme, Thomas], A Silver Watch-bell, 1608, 1634, etc.

Underwood, Robert, A New Anatomie, 1605.

† Vaughan, Robert, The Povrtraitvres at large of Nine Moderne Worthies, 1622.

† Venning, Ralph, Venning's Remains, 1675.

Villars, Abbé de Montfaucon de, The Count de Gabalis, 1680, 1692.

Walker, John, The English Pharise, 1616.

† Ward, Edward, A Frolick to Horn Fair, 1700.

Ward, Edward, The London Terraefilius, 1707.

† Ward, Edward, The Metamorphosed Beau, 1700.

† [Ward, Edward], The Secret History of the Calves-Head Club, 1703. [No characters till later editions.]

† Ward, Edward, A Step to Stir-Bitch Fair, 1700.

Waring, Henry, The Court Convert, 1698.

The Westminster Doctor, [1675?].

White, Charles, Almack's Revisited, 1828.

*† Widdowes, Giles, The Schysmatical Puritan, 1630.

[Wilcox, Thomas?], A Glasse for Gamesters, 1580, 1581.

† Willard, Samuel, The Man of War, 1699.

† Williams, Daniel, A Sermon Preach'd before the Societies for Reformation of Manners, in Dublin, 1700.

[Wither, George], The Modern Statesman, 1653. (More likely by George Walker.)

† Woodcock, Francis, Lex Talionis, 1645.

Woodward, G.M., The Characteristic Mirror, [1780?].

Woodward, G.M., Chesterfield Travestied, 1808.

Woodward, G. M., Eccentric Excursions, 1796.

The Worthy Knight, 1606.

Wright, Thomas, The Passions of the Minde, 1601.

Younge, Richard, The Natural Man Anatomized, 1652.

INDEXES

INDEXES

According to Professor Greenough's plan three indexes are here provided: (1) authors, (2) titles, and (3) subjects. Entries in all three are given in modern spelling, regardless of how they appear in the text.

1. The *author index* includes authors (whether correctly or incorrectly ascribed), editors, and pseudonyms.

2. In the *title index* books are filed under the first word of the title not an article. Other editions with different titles appear under the revised forms, so that to find all editions of a work the reader needs to look under all titles. But the author index will of course help him, and usually the first occurrence in the text gives cross-references to later editions. Again, if two or more authors publish books by the same title, both appear without distinction in the same entry in the index. An exception has been made for "Poems" and "Works," for which the editor has regularly added the author's name in the index.

3. In the *index of subjects* or of individual characters entries are placed under their basic or most important word unless it is "man," "woman," or "person." Thus "happy life" is indexed as "life, happy"; "happy man" as "happy man"; the Duke of Somerset as "Somerset, Duke of," whether he is referred to in the text by this title or by his family name or by some other title. Full personal names are given in the index when ascertainable. Mr. Greenough originally intended fairly complete cross-references, but the pressure of time and other duties and the enormous mass of material have forced the abandonment of this ideal. But otherwise, it is hoped, the indexes are complete.

I. INDEX OF AUTHORS

166, 170, 174, 178, 182, 183, 193, 196, 200, 204, 217, 225, 267

Browne, Humphrey, 53

Browne, Simon, 166

Browne, Sir Thomas, 159

Browne, Thomas, 237

Brugis, Thomas, 50

Brydges, Sir Egerton, 235, 237, 239

Bryskett, Lodowick, 15

Buchan, Peter, 243

Buckingham, George Villiers, Duke of, 186, 276

Buckinghamshire, John Sheffield, Duke of, 112, 116, 119, 126, 129, 131, 140, 185, 187, 188, 189, 192, 201, 211, 267

Buckley, Theodore A., 251

Budgell, Eustace, 178, 203

Bülbring, Karl D., 261

Bull, Hector, 238

Bull, Roger, 195

Bulteel, John, 104

Bulwer, John, 65, 70, 72

Bulwer Lytton: see Lytton

Bunyan, John, 269

Burgess, Daniel, 134, 142

Burghley, William Cecil, Baron, 172

Burnet, Gilbert, 122, 126, 135, 138, 160, 166, 188, 196, 208, 262, 266

Burnet, Sir Thomas, 171, 172, 174, 177, 178, 276

Burney, Frances, later D'Arblay, 225

Burton, Robert, 267

Busche, Alexander van den, 276

Butler, Samuel, 96, 97, 105, 112, 116, 122, 131, 159, 170, 178, 179, 194, 197, 207, 212, 216, 242, 244, 254, 255, 261, 264, 266, 267, 269, 272

Butler, William, 188, 192

Byles, Mather, 192, 204, 215

Byron, George Gordon, Lord, 240

C., A., 53, 116

C., H., 109, 127, 128, 137, 152, 207, 236, 237, 267

C., L., 276

C., O., 92

C., R., 10, 11, 14, 28

C., S., 103, 111

C., T., 63, 276

Callender, Geoffrey, 268

Camden, William, 194

Campbell, George, 211

Canning, G., 235

Care, Henry, 114, 116

Carew, Richard, 10

Carleton, George, 276

Carsdale, K., 217

Carter, E., 189

Carter, Richard, 276

Cartwright, William, 67

Casa, Giovanni della, 26, 27, 91, 94, 99, 103, 114, 128, 276

Castaniza, Jean, 69

Castigator, 232

Caswall, Edward, 247

Catlin, Zachary, 11

Caton, William, 84

Caussin, Nicolas, 276

Cave, Edward, 194, 195, 196, 197, 198, 199, 200, 202, 203, 205, 206, 207, 209, 211, 212

Cave, Richard, 215, 217, 219, 220

Chalmers, Alexander, 237

Chamberlain, Robert, 276

Chancellor, Dr., 225

Chandler, Samuel, 203, 211, 217

Chandos, Grey Brydges, Fifth Baron, 31

Chapman, George, 20, 270

Charleton, Walter, 87, 98, 107, 135

Chaucer, Geoffrey, 221, 232, 267, 269

Chauncy, Charles, 195, 197, 205

Cheeke, Henry, 6, 7

Cheeke, Sir John, 50

Chelidonius, Tigurinus, 4

Cherbury, Edward Herbert, First Baron Herbert of, 64, 102

Chesterfield, Philip Dormer Stanhope, fourth Earl of, 199, 201, 203, 223, 224, 225, 269

Chevreau, Urbain, 109

Cheynell, Francis, 59

Chillester, James, 4

Choppin, Richard, 191

Chudleigh, Lady Mary, 155

Cibber, Colley, 140, 231

Clarendon, Edward Hyde, first Earl of, 160, 171, 176, 180, 200, 265, 266

Clarke, A., 199

Clarke, John, 194

Clarke, Samuel, 199

Claudian, 164, 166

Cleland, James, 16, 20

Cleveland, John, 57, 61, 62, 63, 64, 65, 66, 67, 71, 72, 75, 76, 81, 85, 86, 87, 89, 90, 94, 98, 111, 123, 128, 145, 254, 261, 263, 266, 267, 269

Clifford, Martin, 117

Closse, George, 276

Coetlogon, Chevalier de, 207

Cogan, Thomas, 223, 224

Coke, Col. Edward (?), 208

Cole, William, 232

Coleridge, Samuel Taylor, 267

Collier, J. Payne, 249, 257

Collier, Jeremy, 138, 142, 143, 155

Collins, Anthony, 207

Collins, Arthur, 194

Collop, John, 75

Colman, George, 213, 234, 236, 244

Combe, William, 230

Condy, Jeremiah, 207

Congreve, William, 149

Constable, John, 199, 200

Constantine, 221

Cook, John, 62, 63, 69

Cook, Thomas, 189

Cooke, Edward, 36, 276

Cooke, John, 22, 33, 37

Cooke, William, 57

Copley, Anthony, 276

Copp, Abiezar, 116

Coppinger, Matthew, 122

Corbet, Richard, 23, 257

Cornwallis, Sir Charles, 200

Cornwallis, Sir William, 27, 29

Coryat, Thomas, 19

Coste, Peter, 184

Cotton, Charles, 105, 109, 116, 129, 140, 166, 169, 185, 188, 190, 268

Coventry, Francis, 210

Coventry, Sir William, 130, 143

Cowley, Abraham, 56, 66, 91, 98, 114, 116, 122, 180, 266 (see also entries under C., A.)

Cowper, J. M., 257

Cowper, William, 276

Coyne, J. Stirling, 252

Crackenthorpe, Mrs., 166

Crane, Thomas, 276

Crashaw, Richard, 267

Crayon, Geoffrey: see Irving, Washington

Croft, Sir Herbert, 226

Crooke, Samuel, 75, 78

Crosse, Henry, 14, 15

Crossman, Samuel, 92, 126, 139, 188, 249

Crouch, John, 94

Crowley, Robert, 3

Crowne, John, 126

Crowther, 69

Cuffe, Henry, 276

Culpeper, Sir Thomas the younger, 73, 74

Cumberland, Richard, 227, 228, 231, 233, 267

Cummings, Archibald, 198

Curll, Edmund, 191

Cyprian, Saint, 276

D., A. S. V. D. M., 164

D., C., 187

Dabott, Nathan, 223

Daniel, George, 47, 258

D'Anvers, Caleb, 190, 192

Darbishire, Helen, 147

Dare, Josiah, 103, 143, 169

D'Argens, John Baptist de Boyer, Marquis, 211, 220

D'Argenson, René Louis de Voyer de Paulmy, Marquis, 230

Darrell, William, 156, 162, 166, 180, 183, 187, 200

Dart, John, 186

Davenant, Charles, 151, 152, 162, 166, 174

Davenant, Sir William, 68, 76

Davenport, Robert, 56, 266

Davies, John, of Hereford, 19, 20, 27, 258, 276

Davies, John, of Kidwelly, 105, 117

Davies, Sir John, 10, 11, 65, 258, 267

Davies, Sir William, 276

Dawes, Manasseh, 224

Day, John, 50, 260

II. INDEX OF TITLES

III. INDEX OF SUBJECTS

shrew, 31
Shute, Josiah, 55, 87
Siccus, 190
Sicinius, 214
Sidney, Mr., 225
Sidney, Sir Philip, 9, 51, 138, 180, 241
Sidney, some sonnets of Sir Philip, 246
Sidonius, 83
sievers, 141
Sigillo, 157
Sigismond, Emperor, 44
silence, 75
silent man, 160
Silia, 215
Silius Italic, 83
Silkworm, 78
Silla, 10
Silvius, 190, 207
simplicity of character, man of great, 214
Simplicius, modern, 203
Simplus, 181, 188
Simula, Mistress, 23
sin, 27, 88
sincere man, 88, 137
sincerity, 128
Singer, Madame, 169
singing men in cathedral churches, common, 37
singular, 272
singular man, 221
singularity, 27
sinner (s), 76, 86, 88
sinner, careless, 217
sinner, gentile, 114, 133
sinner, holy, 47
sinner, liberty of conscience, 162
sinner, old, 74
sinner, repentant, 27, 35
sir, grave formal, 94
Sirmond, James, 157
sister, 271
sister, holy, 55, 122, 170
sister, John Bull's, 190
sister, model, 251
sister of a ward, 209
Sithim, 272
six of the clock, 35
skeptic, 210, 216
skeptic in religion, 37, 155, 164, 272
skipper, true-born Dutch, 158
skippers, 141
Skippon, Philip, 80
slander, 112, 146
slanderer, 18, 112
slanderer, malicious, 29
slasher, 148
slave, woman's, 34
slight man, 20
Sloane, Sir Hans, 189
sloth, 16, 18, 113
slothful, 17, 18
slothful man, 90
sloven, 11, 146, 179, 189, 240

slovenly man, 43
slovenry, 20
sluggish person, 86
slut, foul idle, 15
smart, 206
smatterer, 204
smith, 39
Smith, Edmund, 177, 183, 192, 272
Smith, Henry, 77
Smith, Miles, 89
Smithfield, 41
smoker, 13
Smollett, Tobias George, 240
smoothness, 20
Smuggle, Ned, 218
smugglers, 245
Smut, 176
snail, 43
snake, 43
snakes, curled winding, 57
sneaker, 158
Sneaker, Jack, 218
Sneakup, Mr., 70
Sneakup, Mrs., 70
snob royal, 251
snobs, clerical, 251
snobs, club, 252
snobs, continental, 251
snobs, country, 252
snobs, dining-out, 251
snobs, dinner-going, 251
snobs, great city, 251
snobs, Irish, 251
snobs, literary, 251
snobs, military, 251
snobs on the continent, English, 251
snobs, party-giving, 251
snobs, respectable, 251
snobs, university, 251
Snub, Christopher, 252
snuffler, 226
Snug, Dick, 218
Sober, 218
sober man, 190
society, 146
society, civil and loving, 126
Socinianism, 145, 146
Socrates, 44, 82
Softly, Sam, 218
Soissons, House of, 97
soldier (s), 12, 16, 20, 23, 27, 59, 77, 93, 131, 211, 242, 264, 272
soldier, boastful, 12, 189
soldier, British, 248
soldier, Christian, 230
soldier(s), common, 8, 18, 51
soldier, counterfeit, 16, 28
soldier, debauched, 83
soldier, dissembling, 14
soldier, foot, 144
soldier, good, 53, 101
soldier, Low Country common, 41
soldier of fortune, 62
soldier, old, 242
soldier, perfect, 54
soldier, true, 15

soldier, true English, 112
soldier, untrained, 27, 34, 56
soldier, Williamite, 133
soldier, worthy, 27, 34, 56, 113
soldier, zealous, 59
soldiers, apprentice, 19
soldiers, land, 141
Soleisel, James de, 157
solicitor, 77, 106, 171, 187, 248
solicitor of Furnival's Inn, 187
Solid, Jack, 218
solitary, 12
solitary man, 128
Solomon, 9
Solon, 44
Solon, just, 125
somebody, 229
Somers, John, Baron, 157, 161
Somerset, Charles Seymour, Duke of, 161
Somerset, Edward Seymour, Duke of, 240
Somerset, William Seymour, Marquis of Hertford and Duke of, 57, 176, 266
son, eldest, 264
son, lord's younger, 54
son, model, 251
son of reason, 241
son, over-indulged, 221
son, prodigal, 150
Sooterkin, of melancholy spleen, 161
soph. from the universities, young pert, 100
Sophia, Princess, 153
Sophocles, 82, 138
Sophron, 214, 218
Sophrona, 268
Sophronia, 182
Sophronius, 167, 221
Sophrosynians, 86
soppers, pan-, 184
sordid rich man, 38
Sordido, 23
sorrow, 27, 75
sorrows, man of fancied, 233
sot, 145, 148, 216
Soto, 13
Soubise, Prince of, 152, 165
soul, grateful, 108
soul, magnanimous, 108
soul, perfect, 108
South, Robert, 180
South-Sea House, 243
Southampton, Thomas Wriothesley, Earl of, 176
sovereign, 146
sovereignty, 88
Spain, 40, 48, 84, 98, 99, 149, 150, 151
Spain, officers of, 8
Spain, signior of, 12
Spaniard(s), 53, 54, 84, 202, 208, 229
Spaniard, pride of, 9
Spaniards, contrariety to the French, 50
Spanish, 126, 234